TIMELINE : 1850-1900

Freud's *Interpretation of Dreams* Thorndike's puzzle box research	**1900**	Wilde's *Importance of Being Earnest*
Dewey on the reflex arc/Witmer's clinic founded		
	1895	Roentgen discovers X-rays
Hall starts APA/Titchener arrives at Cornell		Chicago Exposition (World's Fair) Immigration center opens at Ellis Island
James' *Principles of Psychology*	**1890**	
		London murders by "Jack the Ripper" Rimsky-Korsakov symphony, *Sheherazade*
Hall starts *American Journal of Psychology*		Stevenson's *Dr. Jekyll and Mr. Hyde*
Ebbinghaus' *On Memory* Galton's Anthropometric Lab opens in London First psychology research lab in U.S., Johns Hopkins	**1885**	Brooklyn Bridge opens
Breuer begins treating Anna O. Wundt's lab at Leipzig	**1880**	Game of Bingo created
		Gilbert and Sullivan's *H.M.S. Pinafore*
		Bell invents telephone
Wundt's *Principles of Physiological Psychology*	**1875**	Twain's *Adventures of Tom Sawyer*
		First color photographs
Darwin's *Expressions of the Emotions*		Carroll's *Through the Looking Glass*
Mill's *The Subjection of Women*	**1870**	Clipper ship Cutty Sark launched Cro-Magnon skeleton found in France
		Nobel invents dynamite
James accompanies Aggassiz to the Amazon	**1865**	
		Lincoln's Gettysburg Address
Broca's autopsy on "Tan"		U.S. Civil War begins
Fechner's *Elements of Psychophysics* Darwin's *Origin of Species*	**1860**	First British Open golf championship
		Burton and Speke explore the Nile
Spencer's *Principles of Psychology* Helmholtz on the speed of neural impulse	**1855**	Florence Nightingale nurses in Crimea
		Stowe's *Uncle Tom's Cabin* Melville's *Moby Dick*
Fechner's psychophysics insight	**1850**	

A HISTORY OF MODERN PSYCHOLOGY

C. James Goodwin

WHEELING JESUIT UNIVERSITY

John Wiley & Sons, Inc.

New York • Chichester • Weinheim • Brisbane • Singapore • Toronto

ACQUISITIONS EDITOR   Ellen Schatz
MARKETING MANAGER   Bonnie Cabot
PRODUCTION EDITOR   Deborah Herbert
DESIGNER   Michael Jung
ART DIRECTION   Dawn L. Stanley
PHOTO EDITOR   Lisa Gee
ILLUSTRATION EDITOR   Anna Melhorn
COVER ART   Michael Jung
COVER   Ceiling of the Hall of the Labyrinth, Palazzo Ducale, Mantua, Italy
                             (Scala/Art Resource, NY).

This book was set in 10/12 Meridien by LCI Design and printed and bound by Quebecor-Fairfield. The cover was printed by Phoenix Color Corporation.

This book is printed on acid-free paper.

The paper in this book was manufactured by a mill whose forest management programs include sustained yield harvesting of its timberlands. Sustained yield harvesting principles ensure that the numbers of trees cut each year does not exceed the amount of new growth.

Library of Congress Cataloging in Publication Data
Goodwin, C. James
    History of modern psychology/C. James Goodwin
        p.   cm.
    Includes bibliographical references and index.
    ISBN 0-471-12805-8 (pbk.: alk. paper)
    1. Psychology—History—20th century.   2. Psychology—
History—19th century.   I. Title.
    BF105.G66   1999
    150′.9′04—dc21   98-5650
                                                      CIP

Printed in the United States of America

10 9 8 7 6 5 4 3 2 1

To Susan

▶ PREFACE

TO THE INSTRUCTOR

As you already know if you have taught the history and systems course, it can be a hard sell to students. They often come into the course with firm and long-standing negative preconceptions about studying history and prepared to agree that history is "just one d——d thing after another," as someone once said. And when they discover the last name of psychology's premier historian, E. G. Boring, they may nod their heads knowingly. This of course is unfortunate, because I can think of no more fascinating subject than the history of psychology. It is replete with extraordinary persons and events, and it yields insights into the basic questions still being asked in psychology today.

No one can be an informed psychologist without some knowledge of the discipline's history. Our task as instructors is to show students how valuable a knowledge of psychology's history can be, help them connect psychology's present with its rich past, and get them to understand how exciting the journey from past to present has been. I hope that my textbook will aid in this process.

The book is titled a history of *modern* psychology, reflecting the decision about where to begin the course that faces everyone who teaches it. Psychology has deep roots in Western philosophical thought; hence, a full understanding of important and recurring themes requires an understanding of this heritage. Texts, however, differ in the depth of coverage given to our philosophical ancestors, tending to fall into two groups. Some books invest considerable effort in exploring philosophical issues and provide in-depth coverage dating back to the ancient Greeks. This certainly is a legitimate strategy (indeed, a philosopher colleague of mine thinks that nothing much of importance has happened since Plato and Aristotle), but not the one I have chosen to follow. Instead, my text belongs in the second grouping—that is, although not by any means ignoring philosophical roots, it devotes less space to them and more space to the recent history of psychology, especially that of the past 150 years. Like other "modern" histories, its treatment of philosophy will begin in the general vicinity of Descartes and the British empiricists.

The decision about a starting point is partly pragmatic—it has been my experience as a teacher of this course, which has to fit typically into a 15-week semester, that extensive treatment of philosophical thought between the time of the Greeks and Descartes makes it impossible to get very far into the twentieth century ("It's December and we've just started Watson!"). I always remind myself that the course is not just a history or a philosophy course, but part of the psychology curriculum, and that if I want students to make meaningful connections between my course and their other psychology classes, it is necessary to get to the nineteenth and twentieth centuries as quickly as possible. The history course must teach students about the ideas and research of pioneer psychologists, especially those who worked within the past 100 years or so. Students have heard about some of these people in other courses (e.g., Hall in adolescent psychology, Watson in the learning course, Freud in personality, Binet in tests and measurements); the history course serves to build on that rudimentary knowledge and interconnect it.

A unique feature of this text is the *Original Source Excerpt*. I believe that students in the history and systems course should not just read accounts *about* psychology's pioneers; they should also be reading what the pioneers themselves wrote. The usual strategy for reaching this goal is to use a textbook and supplement it by putting copies of original source materials on reserve in the library or by using a supplementary book of readings. One problem with this approach is that even good students often find the readings difficult because authors in different historical eras have a variety of styles, use terms and phrasing no longer used, take certain contemporary but now forgotten theories and research for granted, and in general write for their peers rather than for today's students. Students often have a difficult time connecting readings with the narrative in their textbook and reading these original works critically; consequently, much valuable class time can be spent explaining what was meant by certain phrases, how an argument in a reading might be directed at some unnamed critic, and so on. I have tried to address the problem by including Original Source Excerpts in each chapter (except the opening and closing ones). These are reprintings of substantial portions of famous books or papers, interwoven with some of my own narrative. Hence, the student has the opportunity to read writings of such luminaries as William James, John Watson, and B. F. Skinner, while the interspersed narrative helps to explain what the material means and to fit it into the context of the rest of the chapter. In a limited sense, then, the book has a set of readings built into it.

The book includes several other pedagogical tools. Chapters begin with a Preview, which sets the stage for what is to come, and end with a detailed Summary of the chapter's contents and a brief annotated list of articles and/or books in a For Further Reading section. Each chapter begins with a carefully selected quote that is also worked into the narrative at some point in the chapter. For each chapter I have also identified a year that corresponds to some especially important event in psychology's history, and have included a Key Date Box that highlights other events occurring outside of psychology during that year. To further enable the student to make some links between psychology and the rest of the world, several timelines are included on front and back end papers of the book.

TO THE STUDENT

One of the primary themes of this book is that knowing the present requires knowing the past. You know something about psychology's present state by virtue of the other psychology courses you have taken, but you are probably not aware of the many interconnections that exist between the different areas of psychology you have encountered. One goal of a history course is to make those connections. For example, although I am sure that you know something about the nature-nurture issue, you probably are not knowledgeable about how our current understanding of it has been affected by the consequences of Darwinian theory, by the search for tests of mental ability, and by the behavior of rats in mazes. Presumably, this last sentence will have deeper meaning for you after you have finished the course than it does now.

You are about to meet some fascinating individuals who helped shape the psychology that you have been studying in other courses. While we tend to think of historical figures as being somehow above the rest of us, I have tried to show that these individuals were real human beings, often struggling with the kinds of problems that affect the rest of us. In the pages that follow, you will be meeting some people whose efforts led to some extraordinary accomplishments, but who also dealt with some of the same issues that are of concern to you. For example...

- Are you tired of school and ready to get out into the "real" world?
    Read about René Descartes (Chapter 2)

- Are you fed up with the way things are, wish you could change them, and willing to take on authority?
    Learn about John B. Watson (Chapter 10)
    or B. F. Skinner (Chapter 11)

- Are you faced with major decisions about your future and worried about taking a big risk?
    Refer to the discussion about E. B. Titchener (Chapter 7)
    or Wolfgang Köhler (Chapter 9)

- Are you fascinated by research and enjoy collecting and analyzing data?
    See Hermann Ebbinghaus (Chapter 4)
    or Ivan Pavlov (Chapter 10)

- Do you have a strong desire to help others?
    Read about Dorothea Dix (Chapter 12)
    or Carl Rogers (Chapter 12)

- Do you have a strong desire to achieve but face a stacked deck because of racism or sexism?
    See Francis Sumner (Chapter 14)
    or Mary Calkins (Chapter 6)

- Are you a slow starter, not doing well in school, and wondering if you have a future?
    Study the description of the life of Charles Darwin (Chapter 5)
    or Donald Hebb (Chapter 14)

- Are you concerned that health problems or a handicap will make it difficult for you to reach your goals?
    Read about Lewis Terman (Chapter 8)
    or Clark Hull (Chapter 11)

I hope that you will enjoy reading this book, that you will learn something about psychology's present by learning about its past, and that you will gain some insight into human behavior (including your own) in the process. At the end of the course, I hope that you will want to continue to learn more about psychology's fascinating history.

ACKNOWLEDGMENTS

The helpful reviews and recommendations of the following colleagues are gratefully acknowledged: Gerald Clack, Loyola University; Stephen Coleman, Cleveland State University; James Council, North Dakota State University; Charles Early, Roanoke College; David Edwards, Iowa State University; Mark Garrison, Kentucky State University; Kathleen Jones, Virginia Tech; Mike Knight, University of Central Oklahoma; Richard Metzger, University of Tennessee; Robert Presbie, SUNY New Paltz; Maxine Warnath, Western Oregon State College; Michael D. Zeiler, Emory University.

C.J.G.

▶ CONTENTS

Chapter 5 Darwin's Century: Evolutionary Thinking *118*

Chapter 6 American Pioneers *149*

Chapter 7   Structuralism and Functionalism   *182*

Chapter 8   Applying the New Psychology   *217*

Chapter 13 The Postwar Emergency of Cognitive Psychology   397

Chapter 14 Linking Psychology's Past and Present   425

▶ SUMMARIES OF IMPORTANT FEATURES

Original Source Exceprts Summary

Chapter 2   Descartes on Mind-Body
Interactionism

Chapter 3   Broca Discovers the Speech
Center

Chapter 4   Ebbinghaus on Memory and
Forgetting

Chapter 5   Galton on Measurement,
Imagery, and Association

Chapter 6   William James on Emotion

Chapter 7   Titchener's Structuralism

Chapter 8   Münsterberg and Employee
Selection

Chapter 9   Köhler on Insight in Apes

Chapter 10   Watson and Rayner's Little
Albert Study

Chapter 11   Creating the Skinner Box

Chapter 12   Freud's Lectures on
Psychoanalysis at Clark
University

Chapter 13   Neisser on Cognitive Psychology

Key Date Boxes—Date Summary

Chapter 1   1892 (APA founded)

Chapter 2   1843 (Mill's *Logic*)

Chapter 3   1861 (Broca's "Tan")

Chapter 4   1879 (Wundt's lab)

Chapter 5   1859 (Darwin's *Origin*)

Chapter 6   1890 (James's *Principles*)

Chapter 7   1906 (Angell's APA address)

Chapter 8   1917 (Army testing program)

Chapter 9   1929 (International Yale
conference)

Chapter 10   1913 (Watson's manifesto)

Chapter 11   1932 (Tolman's book)

Chapter 12   1900 (Freud's dream book)

Chapter 13   1960 (Miller, Galanter, &
Pribram—Plans)

INTRODUCING PSYCHOLOGY'S HISTORY

▼

To neglect history does not mean to escape from its influence.

Robert I. Watson, 1960

▼

Preview

This chapter opens by describing the evolution of psychology's interest in its past and the reasons why it is important to know and appreciate history. A contrast will be drawn between traditional histories of psychology, which emphasize the contributions of distinguished psychologists, the outcomes of famous experiments, and the debates among adherents of different "schools" of psychology, and a newer approach, which tries to situate events and people in the broader historical context. This chapter also considers the methods used by historians to conduct research in history and the problems they face when constructing a historical narrative from the accumulated data.

PSYCHOLOGY AND ITS HISTORY

One hundred is a nice round number and a one-hundredth anniversary is ample cause for celebration. In recent years, psychologists have celebrated often. The festivities began back in 1979, with the centennial of the founding of Wilhelm Wundt's laboratory at Leipzig, Germany. More recently, in 1992, the American Psychological Association (APA) created a yearlong series of events to commemorate the centennial of its founding in G. Stanley Hall's study at Clark University on July 8, 1892. During the centennial year, historical articles appeared in all of the APA's journals and a special issue of *American Psychologist* focused on history; several books dealing with APA's history were commissioned (e.g., Evans, Sexton, & Cadwallader, 1992); regional conventions had historical themes; and the annual convention in Washington featured events ranging from the usual symposia and invited addresses on history to a fancy dress ball at Union Station featuring period (i.e., 1892) costumes and a huge APA birthday cake.

Interest in psychology's history has not been limited to centennial celebrations, of course. Histories of psychology were written soon after psychology itself appeared on the academic scene (e.g., Baldwin, 1913), and at least two of psychology's most famous books, E. G. Boring's *A History of Experimental Psychology* (1929; 1950) and Edna Heidbreder's *Seven Psychologies* (1933), are histories. It wasn't until the 1960s, however, that significant interest in the history of psychology as a specialized area of research began. During that decade, a number of individuals with training as psychologists and a keen interest in history banded together and did the sorts of things that mark the creation of a new specialized discipline—they formed organizations, they created a journal, and they established bases for the production of research.

Many people were involved, but the major impetus came from a clinical psychologist with a passion for history, Robert I. Watson (1909–1980). He began with a call to arms, an *American Psychologist* article entitled "The History of Psychology: A Neglected Area" (Watson, 1960). He then mobilized a group of like-minded psychologists within APA into a History of Psychology Group, the eventual outcome being the creation of a new APA division (#26) in 1965 (Hilgard, 1982). Naturally, Watson was first president of the division. Also in 1965, (a) John Popplestone and Marian White McPherson (two more clinicians in love with history) established the archives of the History of American Psychology at the University of Akron, with Watson named to chair the Archive's Board of Advisors, and (b) the first issue of the *Journal of the History of the Behavioral Sciences* was published, edited by Watson. A few years later, as part of a reorganization of their graduate programs, the University of New Hampshire created the first doctoral program in the history of psychology. Guess who was named its first director? Finally, also under the leadership of Watson, Joseph Brozek, and Barbara Ross, the National Science Foundation sponsored a six-week summer institute on the campus of UNH in 1968 which spawned Watson's final creation, the Cheiron Society, an "International Society for the History of Behavioral and Social Sciences" (Brozek, Watson, & Ross, 1970). Within a decade, then, Watson was the prime mover in developing the history of psychology as a research specialty.

Over the past 30 years, interest in psychology's history has grown steadily. For example, membership in APA's division 26 in 1995 stood at more than 1000, compared with the 234 who joined as charter members in 1965. The story is the same for Cheiron. Psychologists also recognize the importance of the history course to the psychology curriculum. At the most recent conference on the undergraduate curriculum, held at St. Mary's College in Maryland in 1991, one of the group's recommendations was for the psychology curriculum to include a senior capstone course that integrated student experi-

This year marked the founding of the American Psychological Association. These events also occurred:

**Key Date
1892**

- The first automatic telephone switchboard was introduced
- Diesel patented his internal combustion engine
- "Gentleman Jim" Corbett defeated John L. Sullivan to win the heavyweight boxing title
- Tchaikovsky completed his *Nutcracker* ballet
- Toulouse-Lautrec painted *At the Moulin Rouge*
- Grover Cleveland was elected President of the United States
- These people were born:

  Francisco Franco, Spanish dictator

  Pearl S. Buck, American Nobel Prize-winning novelist

  J. R. R. Tolkien, British philologist and author
- These people died:

  Walt Whitman, American poet

  Alfred Lord Tennyson, British poet

ences in other courses; the history and systems course was mentioned as an ideal example of such a capstone (Lloyd & Brewer, 1992).

Despite the consensus among psychologists that studying the discipline's history is important, students majoring in psychology are often surprised to discover that a course in the history of psychology is offered in and perhaps required by their department. They check with their chemistry-major friends and find nothing comparable in that department. They examine the college catalog and discover that the closest course is one in the History of Science, but it's taught by the *history* department, not one of the science departments. What's going on? Why is there a history of psychology course taught by a psychologist, but not a history of chemistry course taught by a chemist?

The rationale for a history of *psychology* course is important and will be considered shortly. First, however, let us examine the more general question of why it is important to study the history of *anything*. Is it true that "history is more or less bunk," as Henry Ford put it, or is it more likely, in the words of Abraham Lincoln, that "we cannot escape history" (both quotes from Simonton, 1994, p. 3) and that to "neglect history does not mean to escape from its influence," as Robert Watson (1960) declared in his call for psychologists to become more involved in the history of their discipline (p. 255).

WHY STUDY HISTORY?

Every history course you have ever taken has preached to you that a knowledge of history helps us to avoid the mistakes of the past and provides us with a guide to the future. There is certainly some truth to those old and well-worn platitudes, but a more important reason to study history is that it is impossible to understand the present time without knowing something about the past. Historian David McCullough (1992) expressed this idea eloquently in a commence-ment address when he drew an analogy between knowing history and knowing some-one we love:

> Imagine a man who professes over and over his unending love for a woman but who knows nothing of where she was born or who her parents were or where she went to school or what her life had been like until *he* came along—and furthermore, doesn't care to learn. What would you think of such a person? Yet we appear to have an unending supply of patriots who know nothing of the history of this coun-try, nor are they interested. (p. 222, italics in the original)

Think of any current event and you will rec-ognize that it is impossible to really understand that event without knowing some of the histo-ry leading to it. For example, consider some recent history within psychology. I am sure that you have heard about the APA, the American Psychological Association. You probably also know about or at least have heard of the APS—the American Psychological Society. You might even know that the APS is a fairly recent crea-ture, having been formed in 1988. Perhaps you also recognize that the APS seems more focused on scientific research than the APA, although maybe you are not quite sure about that. A knowledge of history would help you here. Specifically, your understanding of why the APS exists and what its purpose is would be vastly enhanced if you knew of the long-stand-ing tensions between research psychologists and psychologists whose prime interest is in the professional practice of psychology. The prob-lem traces to the very beginnings of the APA in the late nineteenth century and contributed to the formation of a separate group of "Experimentalists" in 1904 (the story of this group is elaborated in Chapter 7). Also, when the APA was reorganized after World War II, the divisional structure that exists today was designed in part to reconcile the conflicting

goals of scientists and practitioners. Without knowing something of this history, you could never have a clear understanding of the APS, why it exists today, or why there is lingering tension between APS leaders and the APA gov-erning structure.

Another aspect of the importance of the past for understanding the present is that a knowl-edge of history helps us put present events in a better perspective. In the same commencement address quoted from earlier, David McCullough related the story of an encounter in Washington with an apparently well-educated friend who had just visited the Vietnam Memorial and, like everyone who visits, was visibly moved by it. She asked if McCullough had visited the site and he said that he had; his first visit was late on a day spent at the nearby Civil War battlefield of Antietam. She could not recall ever hearing of this battle, which included a day during which more American lives were lost than on any other day in history. McCullough pointed out that the Vietnam Memorial holds the names of about 57,000 Americans killed during 11 years, but at Antietam on September 17, 1862, there were 23,000 casualties—on one day. Knowing about Antietam in no way lessens the tragedy of the Vietnam War, and certainly every American should visit the wall, but an important perspec-tive is gained by knowing about the battlefield just up the road. Knowledge of this kind adds an appreciation of the sacrifices of those from other times and in general yields an understanding of the idea that war and senseless death are not uniquely associated with just one period of recent history.

There is another way in which a knowledge of history lends perspective to the present-day. We sometimes believe that our current times are, as Dickens wrote, "the worst of times." We complain about the evils and seemingly insur-mountable problems that accompany life near the end of the twentieth century. We long for the "good old days," a simpler time when nobody locked their doors and a good house could be ordered from a Sears kit. We think that there really used to be places like Disney World's Main Street, USA. But a knowledge of history points up the narrowness of such thinking. Noted historian and former Librarian of Congress Daniel Boorstin, in an essay entitled "The Prison of the Present" (1971), describes this fallacy:

> We sputter against the Polluted Environment—as if it had come with the age of the automobile. We compare our air not with the odor of horse dung and the plague of flies and the smells of garbage and human excrement which filled the cities of the past, but with the honeysuckle perfumes of some nonexistent City Beautiful. We forget that even if the water in many cities today is not spring-pure…, still for most of history the water of the cities (and of the countryside) was undrinkable. We reproach ourselves for the ills of disease and malnutrition, and forget that until recently, enteritis and measles and whooping cough, diphtheria and typhoid, were killing diseases of childhood,…[and] polio was a summer monster. (pp. 47–48)

Knowing history won't give us easy answers to all our current problems, but it certainly can immunize us against the belief that these problems are many times worse than they used to be. In fact, knowing the past can provide a comforting connection with it, and being aware of how others have wrestled with similar problems can provide us with some present-day guidance.

Besides making it possible for us to understand the present better, studying history provides other benefits. For example, it forces an attitude adjustment: it keeps us humble. Sometimes an ignorance of the past can lead us to believe that the present is the culmination of centuries of progress and that modern-day accomplishments and thinking are more sophisticated and far surpass those of a crude and uninformed past. A knowledge of history, however, forces an understanding that each age has its own marvelous accomplishments and its own creative geniuses. Modern-day neuroscientists seem to make fascinating discoveries every day, but the importance of their discoveries and the quality of their scientific thinking does not outdo the elegance of Pierre Flourens's nineteenth-century investigations of the brain, which effectively disproved phrenology (see Chapter 3).

Finally, studying history ultimately means searching for answers to one of life's most fundamental yet perplexing questions: What does it mean to be human? For instance, to study the history of World War II is to delve into the basic nature of prejudice, aggression, and violence. To study the American Revolution is to examine the human desire for freedom and self-determination. To study the history of Renaissance art is to study the human passion for aesthetic pleasure. And to the extent that history involves people acting in various contexts, studying history means studying human behavior. For this reason, psychologists should be inherently attracted to the subject.

WHY STUDY PSYCHOLOGY'S HISTORY?

The preceding rationale for studying history is by itself a sufficient justification for studying the history of psychology, but there are additional reasons why psychologists should be interested in their ancestry. First, compared with other sciences, psychology is in its infancy. One hundred years may be a ripe old age for a human, but it is quite young for an academic discipline. Much of the content of the other psychology courses you have taken traces back through at least half of those years, and many of the so-called classic studies that you learned about (e.g., Pavlov's conditioning studies) formed a major part of the first half of those years. Hence, modern psychology is closely tied to its past; being a literate psychologist necessarily requires knowing some history.

A second and related reason for an interest in psychology's history among psychologists is that the field is still grappling with many of the same topics that occupied it a century ago. Thus, an important issue today is the heritability of traits ranging from intelligence to shyness to schizophrenia. This nature-nurture issue, first popularized more than 100 years ago by Sir Francis Galton (see Chapter 5) and pondered by humans for centuries, reverberates through the history of psychology. Seeing the parallels between the arguments made now about the relative influence of heredity and environment, and comparing them with those made in earlier times, allows the psychologist a more informed understanding of the issue. Understanding something about the origins and early development of the IQ concept gives the modern psychologist a greater depth of understanding of the problems surrounding it.

Earlier, a question was raised about the presence of a history of psychology course and the absence of a history of chemistry course. While an understanding of current research and related issues is essential in psychology, the situation is somewhat different in chemistry. Although the history of alchemy makes for a fascinating story and can teach us a great deal about how science works, it doesn't inform today's students about the chemical properties of lead or of gold. Chemists, who tend to think (naively, as it happens) of their science as steadily progressing from the errors of the past to the truth of the present, aren't normally interested in cluttering their students' minds with "old" ideas. There is some truth to this model of science as advancing through history (nobody tries to reach the alchemist's goal of turning lead into gold anymore), but it is nonetheless unfortunate that many scientists don't see the value of studying the history of their discipline. At the very least, it would round out their education and teach them something about how scientific thinking has evolved. Indeed, there ought to be a history of chemistry course for chemistry students to take.

A third reason for the existence of the history of psychology course is that it provides a unifying force for what has become a diverse and highly specialized field. Despite its youth, psychology in the late twentieth century is notable for its lack of unity. Indeed, some observers (e.g., Koch, 1992) believe that a single field of psychology no longer exists, that a neuroscientist investigating the functioning of endorphins has virtually nothing in common with the industrial psychologist studying the effectiveness of various management styles. Yet all psychologists do have something in common—history. For the student who has taken a seemingly disconnected variety of courses ranging from developmental to abnormal to social psychology, the history course can serve as a synthesizing experience. By the time you reach the final chapter of this text, where the issue of psychology's increased diversity and specialization will again be addressed, you will have learned enough to begin to understand the interconnectedness of the different areas of psychology.

Fourth, an understanding of psychology's history makes one a more critical thinker. Aware of the history of various treatments for psychological disorders, the discerning psychologist is better able to evaluate claims for a "revolutionary breakthrough" in psychotherapy. A close examination of this allegedly unique therapy might reveal similarities to earlier approaches. The historically literate psychologist will also be aware that on many other occasions, initial excitement over a flashy new therapy is tempered by a later failure to find any evidence that it works. Furthermore, knowing about the developmental course of various historical pseudoscientific approaches to psychotherapy, and understanding their common features, enables the psychologist to spot the presence of a new one.

Finally, the history of psychology course may be a history course but it is also a psychology course. Thus, one of its goals is to continue educating us about human behavior. Studying historical individuals as they helped develop the science of psychology can only increase our understanding of what makes people behave the way they do. For instance, our understanding of scientific creativity can be enhanced by studying the lives and works of historically creative individuals (Hermann Ebbinghaus is a good example; his work is featured as part of Chapter 4). Some insight into the psychology of controversy and the rigid, dogmatic adherence to one's beliefs can be gained by studying the behavior of scientists engaged in bitter debate with their peers (e.g., the Baldwin-Titchener controversy, described in Chapter 7). In general, if all human behavior reflects a complex interplay between individual attributes and the environment, then studying the lives of historical characters being shaped by and in turn shaping their environments can only increase our understanding of the forces that affect human behavior.

KEY ISSUES IN HISTORY

A common misconception of history is that historians simply "find out what happened" and then write it down in chronological order. As you will learn in the next two sections of this chapter, the process is infinitely more complicated. When they are engaged in their craft, historians have to confront and take a stand on several important issues.

OLD VERSUS NEW HISTORY

In 1980, the APA created the G. Stanley Hall Lecture Series. These invited addresses by prominent psychologists are designed to aid undergraduate instruction by informing teachers of the latest developments in the various subfields of psychology. In 1988, Laurel Furumoto, a psychologist/historian from Wellesley College, delivered the first of these lectures which was devoted to the teaching of psychology's history. The focus of her talk was on a distinction between what she referred to as "old" and "new" history.

The old history of psychology, according to Furumoto (1989), refers to an approach emphasizing the accomplishments of "great" philosophers and psychologists and concentrates on celebrating "classic studies" and "breakthrough discoveries." Within psychology, the preservation and retelling of these "great events" helped psychology secure an identity as a scientific discipline. The milestones, whether accurately described or not, are passed down from history text to history text as their authors rely heavily on secondary sources (e.g., earlier history texts). Furthermore, previous insights or achievements are valued only if they somehow "anticipated" some modern idea or research outcome. Old research that is of no current value is considered erroneous and is to be discarded. Thus, from the standpoint of old history, the purpose of the history of psychology is to emphasize and even to glorify present-day psychology, and to show how it emerged triumphant from the murky depths of its past.

According to Furumoto, old history tends to be presentist, internal, and personalistic. New history, on the other hand, is more historicist, external, and naturalistic. Let's examine these concepts in more detail.

Presentism Versus Historicism

Earlier, I argued that a major reason for studying history is to better understand what is happening in the present. This is indeed a valid argument. On the other hand, to interpret the past *only* in terms of the present is to be guilty of what George Stocking (1965) called presentism. In an editorial published in the opening volume of the *Journal of the History of the Behavioral Sciences*, Stocking contrasted the **presentist** with a **historicist** orientation. As Stocking put it, the presentist attempts "to understand the past for the sake of the present" (p. 211), whereas the historicist desires "to understand the past for the sake of the past" (p. 211). That is, the presentist interprets historical events only with reference to modern knowledge and values, whereas the historicist tries to understand the same event in terms of the knowledge and values in existence at the time of the event. Because the historicist tries to place historical events within the overall context of their times, this approach is sometimes called a *contextual* approach to history.

To some extent, presentist thinking is impossible to avoid. Our current thinking has been shaped by our experiences, and it is difficult to negate those experiences. To illustrate, think of situations where you had to make the same basic decision at two different times. For example, suppose you just bought a computer to replace the one you acquired five years ago. In the present moment, you might say to yourself, "How could I have been so shortsighted back then, buying a hard drive that *only* had 20MB?" To say that is to forget the original context in which that first computer was bought, a time when a 20MB drive seemed as appropriately sized as a 2GB drive might seem now. Thus, it is easy to criticize the past when relying on the values or knowledge of the present. It is also easy to think that because you have gone from a 20MB to a 2GB hard drive, that you have somehow progressed as a decision maker. The larger hard drive might indeed make your life easier (i.e., there has been some progress), but it doesn't mean that you are any better as a decision maker now than you were five years ago. The old decision seems stupid now, but that's only because of what we now know; back then, it was precisely as reasonable a choice as the one made in the present. To understand the old decision requires us to avoid seeing it in the light of what we know now.

To demonstrate the point made above with reference to a more complex historical event than computer buying, consider some aspects of the history of intelligence testing. As you will learn in Chapter 8, in the years just prior to World War I, an American intelligence tester named Henry Goddard was invited to Ellis Island in New York to help in the screening of immigrants. Immigrants deemed "unfit" for some reason were returned to their country of origin. Goddard firmly believed that intelligence was an inherited trait and that it could be measured with a brand new tool—something created in France and just beginning to be called an IQ test. Goddard used a version of an IQ test that he had translated from the French version to identify "mentally defective" immigrants. He even convinced authorities that he could pick out defective immigrants simply by looking at them. His work resulted in the questionable deportation of untold numbers of people and his conclusion that large percentages of "foreigners" were "morons" (a term he invented) contributed to the atmosphere that led Congress to pass restrictive immigration quotas in the 1920s. From today's standpoint, on the basis of an additional 75 years or so of research, we know about the problems with IQ testing and we find it difficult to believe that someone as intelligent as Goddard could have behaved with such obvious bias. But to truly understand his behavior, it is necessary to study it from the vantage point of the historical context in which it occurred instead of that of the present time. This means being knowledgeable about such things as (a) the powerful influence of Darwinian thinking on psychological testers of that day, which led easily to a belief that intelligence was a trait that had been naturally selected and enabled a physically weak species (humans) to adapt to their environment during the "struggle for existence" and was therefore inherited; (b) the nation's fears of being overrun with immigrants (large-scale immigration was a new phenomenon at that time); and (c) the assumption, not yet brought into question by such things as atomic bombs and aerosol cans, that any new technology (e.g., IQ tests) with the "scientific" seal of approval had to be good. The list could be continued but the point is clear. Goddard's work cannot be fairly evaluated by modern standards; it can only be understood in the context of its times. On the other hand, his work *does* have relevance for the present. Knowing about it can (a) help us better understand modern concerns about immigration; (b) inform us of the subtle influence of racism and other forms of bigotry, even in intelligent people; and (c) make us properly cautious about the alleged wonders of new technologies that arrive in our own day.

The Goddard episode illustrates how difficult it is for us to avoid a presentist orientation. After all, we are the products of our own personal histories, and it is perhaps impossible to ask us to think like a person who never experienced MTV, computers, World War II, or the fall of the Berlin Wall. Nonetheless, for the historian and the reader of history it is important to at least be aware of the dangers of a strictly presentist view of history, and to constantly seek to understand historical episodes on their own terms.

Internal Versus External History

Histories of psychology are often written by psychologists who wish to trace the development of theories of behavior that have been held by various psychologists, based on research completed by psychologists. This kind of approach is referred to as an **internal history**; what is written about occurs entirely within ("internal to") the discipline of psychology. Such an approach has the value of providing detailed descriptions of the evolution of theory and research, but it ignores those influences outside of psychology that nonetheless have influenced the discipline. An **external history** focuses on those influences.

Internal histories are often referred to as histories of ideas. They are written by people trained in the specific discipline being analyzed, and they tend to be written by people with little or no expertise in history per se; they are *inward-looking*, focusing on the development of ideas to the exclusion of the larger world. On the other hand, external histories take the broader view: They examine societal, economic, institutional and extra-disciplinary influences. An exclusively internal history is narrow and loses the richness of historical context, whereas an excessively external history fails to

convey an adequate understanding of the ideas and contributions of a discipline's key figures. A balance is needed.

The interplay between internal and external history is demonstrated nicely in the history of comparative psychology, the laboratory study of animal behavior that sheds light on similarities and differences in the behavior of various species. It developed in the second half of the nineteenth century, primarily out of interest in demonstrating the continuity between species implied by Darwinian evolution. One interest of early comparative psychologists was in determining the extent to which other species showed evidence of consciousness. From the standpoint of internal history, students learn that comparative psychologists helped make the transition from psychology as the study of consciousness to psychology as the study of behavior. Why? Because studying animal behavior, even if the interest is in understanding "animal consciousness," requires developing procedures (e.g., maze learning) that involve the objective measurement of observable behaviors. John B. Watson, usually considered the founder of behaviorism as a school of thought (see Chapter 10), cut his research teeth in the world of comparative psychology. Thus, there appears to be a logical progression from (a) being required to use behavioral methods if one is interested in studying animals, to (b) seeing that these methods could be applied to the study of humans as well. In Watson's research, for example, there is a gradual shift from the study of animal behavior to the study of human behavior. In addition, other comparative psychologists of the time, especially Robert Yerkes, made a similar transformation from the study of animals to the study of humans.

There is a degree of truth to this internal history of comparative psychology. Watson himself argued that his system of behaviorism first evolved out of his animal work. Nonetheless, a full understanding of the impact of comparative psychology requires knowing about some of the external factors that led researchers to shift from studying animals to studying humans. For example, consider the institutional context. In the early years of the twentieth century, experimental psychology was relatively new and psychologists normally resided within departments of philosophy. In the fight for an adequate slice of the budget pie, psychologists found it necessary to justify the costs of their laboratories. Senior members of the department, usually philosophers, could be difficult to convince. One approach was to demonstrate the usefulness of psychological knowledge in solving practical problems. For instance, sometimes it was argued that the fruits of psychological research would improve education. This problem of demonstrating utility was difficult enough for researchers studying humans in their laboratories; it was infinitely more arduous for comparative psychologists. Their arguments for the value of their research were even more difficult to sustain. In addition, they had a problem unique to their research interests—their laboratories were an assault on the olfactory senses. A combination of smell and no air-conditioning relegated many laboratories to obscure corners of campuses (O'Donnell, 1985). For many, then, the desire to improve their institutional status was a major driving force in their change from animal to human psychology.

The experience of Robert Yerkes illustrates the problem for animal researchers. A brilliant comparative psychologist at Harvard University at the turn of the century, he found himself initially encouraged to pursue his animal work, primarily for political reasons. Harvard wished to maintain its exalted position in the academic world, and that meant competing successfully with young upstarts like Clark University, 30 miles to the west in Worcester. Clark had established an active program in comparative psychology; Harvard would not be outdone, and Yerkes would carry the torch. But he quickly discovered that his work was not valued very highly in a department that featured three of America's most famous philosophers: Josiah Royce, Charles S. Peirce, and William James. He was not promoted, he had difficulty securing laboratory space, and as the years passed, he was subtly told that his animal work was irrelevant. To be promoted, he would have to do more "on the human side." This he did, first by producing an undergraduate textbook that emphasized human experimental psychology and introspective methods, and later by embracing psychology's love affair with intelligence testing (O'Donnell, 1985). Thus, understanding the shift that some psychologists made from studying animals to studying humans requires knowing more than just the ideas that are internal to a discipline.

Personalistic Versus Naturalistic History

In addition to the presentist/historicist and internal/external distinction, one additional contrast needs to be drawn before returning to Furumoto's old versus new history. That distinction is between a personalistic history, one that sees the actions of individual historical characters as primary, and a naturalistic history, one that emphasizes the overall intellectual and cultural climate of a particular historical era—what the German philosopher Hegel called the **zeitgeist**.

According to a **personalistic** history, or what used to be called the "Great Man" theory, the important events in history result from the heroic (or evil) actions of individuals and without those individuals, history would be vastly different. This approach is often associated with the nineteenth-century historian and essayist Thomas Carlyle, whose "On Heroes, Hero Worship and the Heroic in History," written in 1840, is best remembered for this line: "The history of what man has accomplished in this world is at bottom the history of the great men who have worked here" (cited in Boring, 1963a, p. 6). According to this view, people like Newton, Darwin, and Freud changed the course of the history of science. Without them, the history would have been completely differ-

eponyms

ent. From this standpoint, the preferred method of writing history is biography, and as a consequence of this approach, what are sometimes called **eponyms** (Boring, 1963a) are created. That is, historical periods are identified with reference to the individuals whose actions are believed to be critical in shaping events. Thus, we read of Newtonian physics, Darwinian biology, and Freudian psychology.

The personalistic approach has intuitive appeal. Although psychology's most famous historian, Edwin G. Boring (see the Close-Up in this chapter), favored a naturalistic model of history, arguing that "[h]istory is continuous and sleek," he recognized that great people "are the handles that you put on its smooth sides"

(Boring, 1963b, p. 130). Boring argued that the persistence of a personalistic approach to history results from several factors, including a human need for heroes and the need of hardworking scientists for personal recognition (Who wants to eliminate the Nobel Prizes for science?). More important, if history is continuous and sleek, then it is also immensely complex. In seeking to understand it, we try to reduce the complexity to understandable dimensions. More generally, a universal cognitive process, essential for achieving understanding, is to organize information into categories. Our recall of concepts like *Freudian unconscious* and *Pavlovian conditioning* is easier when the eponyms serve as retrieval cues.

► CLOSE-UP:

Edwin G. Boring (1886–1968)

It is unfortunate that psychology's most famous historian has a name that students often associate with the general topic of history. In fact, E. G. Boring's writings are lively and elegant. In recent years, his version of psychology's history has been found to be flawed, but just as Newton said that he was able to see farther than others because he stood on the shoulders of giants (e.g., Galileo) who came before him, so it is also true that historians of psychology owe a great debt to Boring's pioneering historical work.

While an engineering student at Cornell University, Boring first encountered psychology in the fall of 1905 by taking an elective course in elementary psychology, taught by the great E. B. Titchener. He described the lectures as "magic, so potent that even my roommates demanded, each lecture day, to be told what had been said" (Boring, 1961, p. 18). Yet he was not converted at that point and continued his engineering studies, earning a master's degree in 1908. After two marginally successful years as an engineer for a steel company and as a high school teacher, he returned to Cornell and earned a Ph.D. from Titchener in 1914. While at Cornell his research interests included (a) human maze learning, during which he met, fell in love with, and eventually married one of his subjects, fellow doctoral student Lucy May (who died in 1996 at the age of 109); (b) nerve regeneration, studied firsthand and rather dramatically by severing a nerve in his arm and charting its recovery; (c) the learning processes of schizophrenics; and (d) his dissertation topic, visceral sensitivity. Boring studied this by learning to swallow a stomach tube to varying depths, then pouring different substances into the tube and noting the (often unpleasant) sensory effects (Jaynes, 1969).

After finishing his degree at Cornell and staying on briefly as an instructor, Boring served in World War I in the Army IQ testing program, taught briefly at Clark University, then chose Harvard over Stanford in 1922. He remained there for the rest of his career. At Harvard, Boring spent the next decade building up the laboratory and trying to convince the authorities that psychology should be a separate department, not a part of the

Figure 1.1   Teaching to the masses: E.G. Boring on educational TV, from Boring (1961).

philosophy department. This did not occur until 1934. It was during the 1920s that he wrote his famous *A History of Experimental Psychology* (1929), partly to further his political fight with the philosophers and administrators at Harvard, and partly to bolster basic research in experimental psychology at a time when the majority of American psychologists seemed to be interested in applied psychology.

In his years at Clark and Harvard, Boring's work habits, in imitation of Titchener, were legendary. In his words,

> ...my friends, my children, and my students know how I have talked about the eighty-hour week in the fifty-week year (the 4000-hour working year) and I have scorned those forty-hour academicians who take long summers off from work. I have no hobbies, except for a shop in my cellar. My vacations were never successful until I got a little study with a typewriter in it and could answer eight letters a day and write up the waiting papers. (Boring, 1961, p. 14)

Also in the tradition of Titchener, Boring taught the introductory course in psychology, believing that a student's first encounter with psychology should be from the master. He even became a pioneer in the video-course: 38 half-hour programs on Boston's educational TV channel WGBH in 1960 featured Boring demonstrating various phenomena, but mainly sitting "on the corner of a table and talk[ing] in a friendly, enthusiastic, paternal manner to the red lights on whatever camera was on the air" (Boring, 1961, p. 77; see Figure 1.1).

We've seen that the APA's Division 26, established in 1965, elected Robert Watson as its first president. According to Hilgard, this occurred after Boring refused to run for the office but agreed to be named "honorary president." Boring's increasing deafness kept him away from the division's inaugural meeting during the APA's 1966 convention, but he sent a written introduction to Watson's presidential address, describing himself as the "ghost of History Past, when the interest in the history of psychology had not yet become as vigorous as it is now" (Hilgard, 1982, p. 310). Clearly the current vigorousness of today's interest in psychology's history owes much to Boring's example.

multiple

The alternative to a personalistic history is a **naturalistic** one, an approach emphasizing the forces of history that act on individuals. The Russian novelist Leo Tolstoy was a famous advocate of this determinist approach. One of his goals in writing the massive *War and Peace* was to demonstrate that history is moved by forces beyond the control of individuals. For Tolstoy, so-called "Great Men" like Napoleon were in reality mere agents of historical causes larger than themselves. In Book IX in *War and Peace* he refers to kings and generals as history's slaves: "Every act of theirs, which appears to them an act of their own will, is in an historical sense involuntary and is related to the whole course of history and predestined from eternity" (Tolstoy, 1942, p. 671).

Among psychologists, Boring has most vigorously promoted a naturalistic view of history. Especially in his later years, he championed the zeitgeist concept, both in the second edition of his famous *A History of Experimental Psychology* (1950) and in numerous essays. For Boring, understanding history meant understanding the historical forces that influenced the men and women living in a particular era. While not denying Darwin's genius, for example, Boring would argue that the concept of evolution was common in the nineteenth century and extended beyond just biology (to geology, for instance). Without Darwin, someone else would have produced a theory of biological evolution. Indeed, Darwin's theory was for a brief time called the Darwin-Wallace theory of evolution, in recognition of Alfred Russell Wallace, a contemporary of Darwin's who independently developed virtually the identical theory (see Chapter 5). A great scientist can and does influence events, but simply focusing on the person leaves unanswered the question of how that individual was affected by his or her contemporary environment.

In support of the zeitgeist concept, Boring pointed to two kinds of historical events. In the first, called a **multiple** by historian Robert Merton (1961), two or more individuals independently make the same discovery at about the same time. Darwin and Wallace codiscovering natural selection at a time when evolutionary thinking was "in the air" is an example. Darwin's grandfather, Erasmus Darwin, illustrates the second type of event, a discovery or a theory that is said to be "ahead of its time." Like his more famous grandson, Erasmus developed a theory of evolution, but did so in the eighteenth century, when belief in the immutability of species (i.e., each species is created in its finished form by God and it doesn't change over time) was stronger than in the nineteenth century.

Relying on the zeitgeist as a way of *explaining* history can be problematic, however. For example, the uncritical observer might be tempted to reify (i.e., give a concrete and detached existence to an abstraction) the concept and consider it to be a controlling force that is independent of the historical persons who in fact give it meaning. That is, in answer to the question, "Why did event X occur instead of event Y at time Z?", one might be tempted to answer, "Because of the zeitgeist." But such an answer hardly explains the events in question. The concept of the zeitgeist invites one to examine the attitudes, values, and theories in existence at the time of some event to be explained, but it cannot exist by itself as some mysterious directing agent. As historian Dorothy Ross (1969) pointed out with reference to the history of educational psychology,

> It has been stated, for example, that neither James, Dewey, Hall, Thorndike, Cattell, Galton, nor Darwin were necessary to the rapid development of educational psychology in America, for that was the trend of the 'Zeitgeist.' But certainly we only know what the Zeitgeist in fact *was* by the way in which James, Hall, Cattell, Darwin and others behaved. If they had not thought and acted the way they did, neither would the 'Zeitgeist' they are said to embody. (p. 257, italics in the original)

Thus, a balanced view of history recognizes the complex interrelationships between people and events. The historical characters you are about to encounter were all products of the world in which they lived, but they also made decisions that helped form and transform the historical context that surrounded them. Wallace might have been inspired to write a paper proposing a theory of evolution that matched the essence of Darwin's, but it is no accident that recent years have seen at least three major biographies of Darwin and none of Wallace. It was Darwin who invested the years of research examining the intricacies of numerous species, and it was Darwin who followed up his initial writings with the monumental texts (*Origin of Species*; *Descent of Man*) that brought evolution into its fullest development.

This Book's Point of View

This section of the chapter began with a reference to Laurel Furumoto's distinction between old and new history; presentist, internal, and personalistic approaches typically go together and comprise what she refers to as the old history of psychology. It is a history that interprets events only from the standpoint of the present, concentrates on the development of ideas within a specific discipline, and views progress as reflecting the sequential accomplishments of important people. The new history of psychology, on the other hand, combines historicist, external, and naturalistic approaches. It tries to examine historical events on their own terms, with reference to the times in which they occurred, looks for the influence of extradisciplinary contextual forces, and looks beyond great men and women to examine the factors that produced their ideas. Furumoto also points out that new history relies more on archival data and primary source materials than on secondary textbooks, and it is more critically analytical than ceremonial and celebratory.

For historians of psychology conducting research, Furumoto's description of the new history of psychology provides a clear set of guidelines about how to proceed. The best historical research being published today is historicist,

external, and naturalistic. For the author of a textbook and the teacher of the history course, however, the prescriptions about how to proceed are not as clear. As Dewsbury (1990) points out in a review of several history of psychology texts, it is important to distinguish between "scholarly research directed at colleagues and...textbooks directed at introductory students" (p. 372). For the latter, the ideals of the new history need to be weighed against a need to inform students about content that is relevant to the psychology curriculum. This book presents a history of psychology that leans toward the values espoused by Furumoto, but it is important to remember that the course for which this text is designed is not just a history course, but is also a psychology course. Thus, while it is important to understand Pavlov's work within the historical climate of the early twentieth century in Russia, it is also important to understand the various classical conditioning phenomena that he investigated and how his work related to American behaviorism and conditioning research in more recent times. While it is important to understand the influence of the institutional context on the fate of comparative psychologists like Yerkes, it is also important for the psychology student to know about the animal research that Yerkes was able to complete. And although a purely personalistic history can degenerate into cute anecdotes and can overlook the complexities of historical events, it is also true that persons are interesting to study, and biographical information can increase the psychology student's understanding of human behavior.

In summary, this book will take a point of view that combines (a) presentist and historicist views, (b) internal and external histories, and (c) personalistic and naturalistic models. If each of the dichotomies can be conceived of as existing on a continuum, then this book will take the following stance:

presentist   ....•... historicist

internal   ....•......... external

personalistic ....•......... naturalistic

The only strong tendency will be to avoid presentist interpretations. On the other two dimensions, the book will blend (a) the various ideas, research, and theories that constitute psychology's history with the historical context in which they developed, and (b) accounts of the persons who produced the history of psychology and the important features of the times in which they lived.

HISTORIOGRAPHY: DOING AND WRITING HISTORY

The simplest definition of **historiography** derives from the origins of the word itself: it is to write history. But the term goes far beyond the writing of historical narrative. It also refers to theoretical issues like the ones just described and to the methods that historians use when doing historical research.

Although the primary purpose of this book is to inform you about the history of psychology, a secondary goal is to give you some insight into the professional behavior of historians. That is, we will examine the kinds of data of interest to historians and the problems confronting historians as they do their work.

SOURCES OF HISTORICAL DATA

Traditionally, historians of psychology have often relied on secondary sources to write their histories, especially their textbook histories. By definition, a secondary source is one that has already been published in some form. These sources typically include books and articles published in journals, magazines, and newspapers. As Furumoto's new history of psychology replaces the old history, however, researchers are relying more on primary sources of information, usually found in archives. An **archive** is normally an area within a university library that holds unpublished information. This information ranges from university records to the letters and papers donated by individuals connected in

Figure 1.2   Marian White McPherson and John Popplestone of the Archives of the History of American Psychology, University of Akron, from Cohen (1991).

some way with the university. In addition to these separate university archives, historians of psychology often find primary source material at the Library of Congress archives in Washington, D.C., the British Museum Library in London, England, and the Archives of the History of American Psychology (AHAP) at the University of Akron, Akron, Ohio.

As mentioned previously, AHAP's 1965 founding by Popplestone and McPherson (Figure 1.2) was one of a series of events sparked by the efforts of Robert I. Watson to generate interest in psychology's history. The archives holds the papers of more than 550 psychologists (e.g., Abraham Maslow) and organizations (e.g., APA's history division, #26), more than 700 pieces of original laboratory apparatus, several thousand psychological tests, and about

3000 photographs. By one estimate, stacking the archive's materials vertically would produce the equivalent of two Washington Monuments (Cohen, 1991)!

What can you expect to find in an archive? Just about anything. Looking into the records of a professional organization, for instance, you would probably find lists of officers and correspondence between them, minutes of meetings, early drafts of position papers, and the like. When examining the papers of an individual psychologist, you might find (a) correspondence between that person and other psychologists, (b) personal diaries and/or calendars, (c) course lecture notes and course schedules, (d) laboratory protocols, drawings of apparatus, data summaries, and other laboratory-related information, (e) early draft manuscripts of writings that eventually became secondary sources, (f) photographs of people, places, and research equipment, and (g) minutes of professional meetings attended by the psychologist. There will also be some surprises. For instance, AHAP holds the papers of the experimental psychologist Raymond Dodge. They include the usual materials, but they also contain several folders full of annotated wine bottle labels. In each case the label was carefully removed from the bottle, glued onto plain white paper, and accompanied by a review of the wine by Dodge. A more startling example was recently reported in *Civilization*, a magazine published by the Library of Congress. A researcher was studying a nineteenth-century Viennese physician (Carl Koller) who was experimenting with the use of cocaine as an anesthetic in eye surgery. One of the folders contained a small pharmacist's packet containing, you guessed it, white powder. Federal authorities were called in to remove the drug, but the envelope remains in the archive collection, labeled as follows: "Remainder of the 1st dose of cocaine, which I used in my first cocaine experiments in August 1884. Dr. Koller" ("A Stash in the Stacks," 1996, p. 15).

How does a researcher interested in psychology's history know which archives to contact or visit when starting a project? Because their holdings are so extensive, AHAP is a good place to start. Even if the archives is not the primary repository for the papers of the person being studied, AHAP might hold some correspondence from that person in the papers they do have. Another good starting place is the university where the person in question worked. Third, bibliographic sources exist. The best known is *A Guide to Manuscript Collections in the History of Psychology and Selected Areas* (Sokal & Rafail, 1982). Suppose you are interested in the work of IQ researcher Henry Goddard, for instance. The guide briefly describes the contents of the Goddard papers, which happen to be held at AHAP. It also informs you of additional Goddard materials in the papers of Edgar Doll and Emily Stogdill at AHAP, and in the papers of developmental psychologist Arnold Gesell in the Library of Congress.

Historians also rely on their general knowledge to aid in their search. For example, some years ago I became interested in Edmund Clark Sanford (1859–1924), the first director of the psychology laboratory at Clark University (Goodwin, 1987). Naturally, Clark was the starting point for the search, and through contact with the archivist there and two visits, I accumulated some information, but not a great deal. Sanford didn't seem to save very much, or if he did, the information didn't find its way to Clark. Some of the university records were helpful, however, in determining such things as laboratory purchases, and the papers of psychologist/university president G. Stanley Hall yielded some addition data, including one exciting discovery— a series of photographs taken in the laboratory in 1892, several of which are to be found in later chapters of this book. Many of them showed (or simulated, most likely) experiments in progress, thus providing a glimpse of what it was like to be doing research in psychology then. By searching through secondary sources, I knew about other psychologists who were contemporaries of Sanford and I knew from his obituaries that Sanford was very close to E. B. Titchener of

Cornell and Mary Calkins of Wellesley (Sanford died in 1924 on his way to give a talk at Wellesley). A visit to Wellesley and two visits to Cornell yielded more information. The Titchener papers were especially helpful—Titchener seemed to keep just about everything. I also wrote to about two dozen other archives that I guessed might be holding papers of Sanford's other professional peers, and hence some Sanford correspondence. Copies of a few pieces trickled in. At the same time, I was reading everything that Sanford published (not much, actually) and everything else that could shed some light on him and the world he inhabited.

PROBLEMS WITH THE WRITING OF HISTORY

From an archives visit to a published paper or book is a long, often tedious, occasionally exhilarating, but never easy journey. Along the way, the historian must confront two major difficulties. First, there are problems associated with the collection of data. The historian must evaluate the validity of data and select a subset of these data for inclusion in the historical narrative. The second problem concerns writing history. Historians are human, so their interpretations of the data will reflect their beliefs, their theories about the nature of history, and potentially, their unexamined biases.

Data Selection Problems

Historians usually collect more information than will ever make its way into the historical narrative they write. Hence, they must make judgments about the adequacy and relevance of the data at hand and they must select a sample of the data while discarding the remainder. Sometimes, despite the large amount of data that might be collected at an archives, important pieces might be missing, further complicating the historian's life. For example, Titchener

and Sanford wrote to each other frequently, but only Titchener saved his correspondence. The Titchener papers contain several hundred letters from Sanford to Titchener, but the Sanford papers include none from Titchener. In trying to piece together the Sanford-Titchener relationship, the historian gets only half the story.[1] Another example concerns Walter Miles, an experimental psychologist from Stanford, who once wrote an article on the early development of mazes (Miles, 1930) that included excerpts of letters he received from some of the early pioneers (e.g., Willard Small, who completed the first maze learning study with rats at Clark University). The Miles papers, in residence at AHAP, do not contain any of the correspondence related to the maze history paper, however. This is surprising, considering the size of the Miles collection. It fills 128 boxes and the inventory *alone* runs to a numbing 756 pages (Goodwin, 1993).

Sometimes information that could aid a historian can be lost through what insurance adjusters would call an act of God. For example, after painstakingly tracking down descendants of Mary Whiton Calkins, the APA's first woman president, Laurel Furumoto discovered that many of Calkins's papers had been entrusted to her younger brother. Unfortunately, he put them in his cellar where they were destroyed by flooding that accompanied a devastating New England hurricane in 1938 (Furumoto, 1991).

Data might also be missing on purpose. In the last year of his life, John Watson, behaviorism's founder, burned all of his remaining notes, correspondence, and rough manuscripts. According to Watson's biographer, when "his secretary protested the loss to posterity and to history, Watson only replied: 'When you're dead, you're all dead'" (Buckley, 1989, p. 182). Similarly, on two separate occasions Sigmund Freud also destroyed his papers, partly to make it difficult for

---

[1] More than half, actually. After about 1910, Titchener often made and kept carbon copies of the letters he sent.

others to trace the sources of his ideas (Chapter 12 details one of these episodes—see page 368).

In addition to missing data, some information might be restricted by the donor and inaccessible to the historian. Even someone with the status of E. G. Boring could be denied. In a letter to John Popplestone of AHAP, Boring wrote that even as a known historian and a faculty member at Harvard, he had been denied access to some papers at the Harvard archives. In his words,

> I trust the general atmosphere of the Archivists at Harvard. This is because I have been denied access to some things that are none of my business, graciously denied it because I am a Harvard professor. But, nevertheless, shut off from certain files of William James. (Popplestone, 1975, p. 21)

Beyond dealing with missing or incomplete information, the historian must make judgments about the adequacy of the available data. We know that eyewitness descriptions of everyday events can be quite wrong, that two witnesses can differ dramatically in their accounts. If eyewitness unreliability can be demonstrated easily in late twentieth-century psychology laboratories, then it is safe to say that the same lack of reliability exists for eyewitness accounts of historical events. Thus, while a firsthand account of a psychologist who went to APA's first annual meeting might yield important data, it is also likely to produce errors, especially if the account is written some time after the event. In general, any autobiographical description is subject to memory lapses.

Information found in someone's correspondence or diary can also be of questionable value. Was the letter writer providing insight into the personality of a colleague or merely passing on cruel and unsubstantiated gossip? When the diarist described the meeting as meaningless and a waste of time, would that same conclusion be drawn by others at the same meeting? Can letters and diaries be slanted by the writer's knowledge that historians might someday read his or her words? To what extent do the contents of letters and diaries reflect the personal prejudices of the writer? I think you can see the difficulty here.

Those who create the records that eventually occupy archives are human and therefore susceptible to the subtleties of human belief, preconception, and bias. Those who explore the archives and write the history are also human and subject to the same frailties. By virtue of their training, historians are certainly more disciplined than laypeople; nonetheless, when making decisions about what information to select for historical analyses and narratives, the historian is not a machine. E. G. Boring expressed the problem eloquently in the preface to his 1942 text on the history of research in sensation and perception.

> Indeed, so much a matter of selection is the preparation of an historical text, that I am sobered by the responsibility. The [history of psychology] text of 1929 has existed long enough for me to see how *the mood that determined the choice of an afternoon's exposition can fix the 'truth' of a certain matter upon graduate students for years to come*. With industry and patience one may avoid the falsification of facts, but those virtues are not enough to make one wise in choosing what to ignore. For that one also needs the wisdom and the integrity of objectivity, and who knows for sure whether he commands such? (Boring 1942, p. viii, italics added)

As you will learn shortly, this passage from Boring is ironic. One of the themes of modern historiography within psychology is that Boring seriously distorted psychology's history and that his writings reflect a strong bias for a specific brand of psychology. It also appears that he was motivated at least partly by the political and institutional context that he occupied.

Interpretation Problems

Decisions about selection and about writing the historical narrative both involve interpreting the information at hand. Those interpretations are influenced by the individual characteristics of the historian *and* by the features of the historical context in which the historian is writing. That is, historians will be influenced by their preconceptions, by the amount of knowledge they already have, as well as by the theories they hold about the nature of history (e.g., personalistic versus naturalistic). In addition, even without their being aware of it, historians can be influenced in many ways by elements of the environment in which their histories are being written. For example, you will discover in Chapter 4 that the work of Wilhelm Wundt has been reevaluated recently (e.g., Blumenthal, 1975), and many of his ideas have been found to be similar to those of modern cognitive psychologists. This similarity, of course, could not have been noticed prior to the advent of modern cognitive psychology—Blumenthal was writing at the height of the so-called *cognitive revolution* in psychology. Thus, historical characters are not the only ones influenced by the historical context in which they live; historians are affected as well.

The history written by E. G. Boring is a case in point. You know from this chapter's Close-Up, that Boring was a devoted student of E. B. Titchener's, and in the 1920s he was a vigorous advocate for the development of a separate psychology department at Harvard that would emphasize "pure" laboratory research rather than application. Both of those facts played a role in the way he wrote history. First, his training as an experimental psychologist in Titchener's laboratory at Cornell surely affected his overall conception of psychology. More specifically, it influenced what Boring thought about Wilhelm Wundt, in whose laboratory Titchener earned a Ph.D. in 1892. In general, Boring believed that Titchener's brand of experimental psychology, called structuralism, was virtually identical to Wundt's psychology, and that Titchener had merely imported it to America. In fact, Wundt's system was quite different from Titchener's system (the details of Wundt's and Titchener's systems will become clear in Chapters 4 and 7,

respectively), but because of Titchener's influence on Boring, combined with the fact that Titchener translated much of Wundt's work and that Boring was not conversant with some of Wundt's nonexperimental writings, the distinctions were lost. Thus, when writing his history, Boring's description of Wundt was filtered through Titchener's version and was consequently flawed. Because most psychologists trained in the period 1950 to 1980 learned their history by reading Boring's *A History of Experimental Psychology* (1929; 1950), the mythological identification of Wundt's and Titchener's systems became conventional wisdom.

A second distortion in Boring's history relates to his emphasis on basic *experimental* psychology to the exclusion of applied psychology. As O'Donnell (1979) has shown, Boring was disturbed by the growing status of applied psychology, especially mental testing. Believing basic laboratory research to be in jeopardy, he took several steps to restore its status. One was writing the first edition of his *A History of Experimental Psychology* (1929), which largely ignored the work of a substantial number of psychologists who were busily applying psychological principles to education, mental health, and the workplace. The reader of the 1929 history could be excused for believing that applied psychology barely existed.

A common misconception of history goes like this: The events occurred in the past; now that they have been described in a historical narrative, that's the end of it. As the E. G. Boring evidence shows, however, historical analyses are in continual need of revision in the light of new information and new ways of examining old information. In recent years, for instance, scholars (e.g., Leahey, 1981) have taken a fresh look at (a) the relationship between Wundt's and Titchener's ideas, and (b) the role of application in the development of psychology in America. As a result, newer histories describe the Wundt-Titchener differences more accurately and document the pervasive influence of applied psychology.

Comparing different editions of a history text can illustrate this reexamination process. For example, one popular undergraduate history text, clearly influenced by Boring in its early editions, also shows the impact of the recent scholarship on Wundt in its later editions. In the book's third edition (Schultz, 1981), Wundt is described in a chapter that has "structuralism" in its title. The following chapter, on Titchener, refers to Wundtian psychology being "transplanted" to America by Titchener and includes sentences like this: "A knowledge of Wundt's psychology provides a reasonably accurate picture of Titchener's system" (p. 87). Six years later, in the fourth edition, "structuralism" no longer appears in the title of the Wundt chapter, there is an explicit description of the problems with Boring's historical account, and the Titchener chapter opens by saying that the systems of Wundt and Titchener were "radically different," and that Titchener "altered Wundt's system dramatically while claiming to be a loyal follower" (Schultz & Schultz, 1987, p. 85).

The important lesson for the reader of history is to be alert to the dangers of assuming that if something is printed in black and white, it somehow must be true. Rather, it is important to read histories, including this one, with a healthy dose of skeptical awareness that other information might have been selected for inclusion in the narrative and that other ways of interpreting the historical record exist. This raises an interesting question: Can history uncover the truth?

APPROACHING HISTORICAL TRUTH

From the foregoing discussion, you might be tempted to accept a version of historical relativism in which five different historians make five different claims for truth and there is no reasonable way to decide among them. Relativism among historians is a *postmodern* outgrowth of a reaction against traditional his-

tory, which held that the job of the historian is to search out the facts of "what really happened" and place them into a chronological narrative with enough style to attract readers. The outcome was a tendency to write history from the standpoint of "what really happened" to those who happened to be in positions of power and influence, while ignoring the rich variety of alternative perspectives. Thus, a traditional history of the American West, taught to American schoolchildren and grounded in a belief in the idea of manifest destiny, glorified the rugged pioneer who persevered in the face of daunting obstacles, including wild men who liked to shoot arrows. It is clear, though, that the very same history could be written from the standpoint of the Native American who valiantly defended the homeland against the invasion of wild men who liked to shoot guns.

The postmodern critique of the narrowness and arbitrariness of traditional history has had the meritorious effect of enriching our knowledge of it. Thus, we have come to recognize that history extends beyond the lives, deeds, and misdeeds of the stereotypical dead, white, European male; it must be more inclusive. On the other hand, an unfortunate consequence of this critique has been a relativism that, taken to extreme (an absolute relativism?), can lead to absurd claims like the one made recently that the Jewish Holocaust in World War II never really happened but was merely "constructed" out of a few isolated events (said to have explanations other than genocide) by historians sympathetic to the Jewish movement who wished to encourage the creation of the nation of Israel following the war. Those arguing for the "myth" of the Holocaust claim that their version is as valid as any other. Yet this example makes it clear that some versions of history are indeed better (i.e., closer to truth) than others. How does one decide?

To reach the truth through historical analysis requires an objectivity that recognizes the limits of one historian's views but also has faith in the notion that meaningful historical narrative and analysis can emerge from the combined efforts of many scholars, according to historians Joyce Appleby, Lynn Hunt, and Margaret Jacob. In *Telling the Truth About History* (1994), they argue for a historiography in which truth about history emerges from a Darwinian-like struggle between competing ideas held by historians, that "knowledge-seeking involves a lively, contentious struggle among diverse groups of truth-seekers" (p. 254). Some measure of truth, then, evolves out of this struggle. Thus, just as individual variation within a species provides the basis for natural selection to operate, so do different versions of historical episodes exist, subject to competing critical analyses that determine which version adapts best to the scholarly environment. This does not mean that the goal is a single version of truth that is then immune to change. Rather, historical truth continues to evolve as new information is discovered and brought to light and as old information is subjected to new interpretations. Also, evolving historical truth includes a variety of perspectives. Multiple eyewitnesses to an event might give different versions of it, but all agree that the event did indeed occur. From their combined information, a complex truth might emerge that would improve on a single description from one perspective. If one historian of the Civil War period "sees an event from a slave's point of view, that rendering does not obliterate the perspective of the slaveholder; it only complicates the task of interpretation" (p. 256).

Just as theories in science are temporary working truths that guide future research, their futures depending on the open and honest inquiry of scientists, so may historical truths be considered tentative yet valuable guides for further research by intellectually honest historians with open access to historical materials. And just as some theories in science are more durable than others, so are some historical truths: "all knowledge can be provisional, in theory, without eliminating the possibility of some truths prevailing for centuries, perhaps forever" (Appleby, Hunt, & Jacob, 1994, p. 284).

Presumably, on the basis of the hard work of many historians of psychology, some degree of truth about the discipline's history has emerged over the past 100 years, and I will try my best to describe it to you in the following chapters. Many disagreements among historians of psychology exist, but Appleby, Hunt, and Jacob would consider that to be a good thing, the basis for future historical truths to develop during psychology's next 100 years. Placing the word "A" in the title of this book, rather than "The," recognizes the fact that other histories exist now and more will exist in the future. Nonetheless, I believe that what you are about to read contains some truth about the discipline you have chosen to study. To the extent that some of the truth might be tentative, I hope it will motivate you to continue learning about psychology's history long after you have finished with this particular version of it.

SUMMARY

Psychology and Its History

- Recently, psychologists have celebrated several centennials, including the anniversary of the founding of Wilhelm Wundt's laboratory at Leipzig, Germany, in 1879, and the creation of the American Psychological Association in 1892.

- Interest in the history of psychology has grown steadily since the mid-1960s, primarily through the initiatives of Robert Watson. He helped establish professional organizations for historians of psychology (Division 26 of the APA, Cheiron), a journal (*Journal of the History of the Behavioral Sciences*), an archives at the University of Akron (Archives of the History of American Psychology), and a graduate program in the history of psychology at the University of New Hampshire.

Why Study History?

- Knowing history helps us to avoid mistakes of the past and to predict the future, but its more important value is that it helps us understand the present day. Knowing history puts current events into a better perspective.

- Knowing history can immunize us against the belief that our current time has insurmountable problems, compared to the "good old days." Every age has its own set of problems. Knowing history also reduces the tendency to think that modern-day accomplishments represent a culmination of the "progress" we have made from the inferior accomplishments of the past.

Why Study Psychology's History?

- Because psychology is a relatively young science, much of its history is recent and of relevance for understanding psychological concepts and theories. Also, many of the issues of concern to psychologists 100 years ago (e.g., nature-nurture) are still important.

- The history of psychology course provides a synthesizing experience tying together the loose threads that comprise the modern diversity of psychology.

- Knowing of historical examples of (a) supposed breakthroughs in psychological research or practice, or (b) new theories that were shown to be pseudoscientific, the student of history is better able to critically evaluate modern claims.

- Because the history of psychology course informs the student about historically important people behaving within their historical context, the course provides a further understanding of human behavior.

Key Issues in History

- The traditional approach to the history of psychology has been presentist, internal, and personalistic. Recently, historians have tended to be more historicist, external, and naturalistic.

- The presentist evaluates the past in terms of present values, studying the past for the sake of the present. The historicist tries to avoid imposing modern values on the past, studying the past for the sake of the past.

- An internal history of psychology is a history of the ideas, research, and theories that have existed within the discipline of psychology. An external history emphasizes the historical context—institutional, economic, social, political—and how it influenced the history of psychology.

- A personalistic approach to history glorifies the major historical figures and argues that history moves through the action of heroic individuals. A naturalistic approach emphasizes the zeitgeist, the mood or spirit of the times, as the prime moving force in history. The existence of multiples is consistent with a naturalistic view.

Historiography: Doing History

- Historiography refers to the process of doing research in history and writing historical narratives.

- Historical research often takes place in archives, which hold unpublished information such as diaries, notes, original manuscripts, and correspondence. The major archives for historians is the Archives of the History of American Psychology, located at the University of Akron.

- Archival collections can be extensive, but they can also be incomplete, with important information missing for various reasons. The information that is available is subject to numerous sources of error (e.g., the biases of the diary writer).

- Historians are faced with two major problems: the selection of information for their historical narratives and interpretation of the information at hand. These decisions can reflect bias on the part of the historian, and they can reflect the historical context within which the historian is writing. Nonetheless, most historians believe that some degree of truth can be reached through the open exchange of information and by examining historical events through a variety of perspectives.

FOR FURTHER READING

Appleby, J., Hunt, L., & Jacob, M. (1994). *Telling the truth about history.* New York: W. W. Norton.

Traces the rise of "intellectual absolutisms," such as the Enlightenment ideal of science and history as a purely objective chronicling of the facts, and their replacement with a postmodern relativism that questions the possibility of history ever achieving truth; proposes a "pragmatic" approach to history that steers a middle course.

Boring, E. G. (1963a). Eponym as placebo. In Robert I. Watson & Donald T. Campbell (Eds.), *History, psychology, and science: Selected papers by Edwin G. Boring, Harvard University* (pp. 5–25). New York: John Wiley & Sons.

A good example of Boring's erudition and his championing of the zeitgeist concept; argues that the effect of a "great man" theory is to create "eponyms" that give us an over-simplified and distorted view of history; the article is also the source of the chapter-opening quote in Chapter 14.

Furumoto, L. (1989). The new history of psychology. In I. S. Cohen (Ed.), *The G. Stanley Hall lecture series* (Vol. 9, pp. 9–34). Washington, DC: American Psychological Association.

An excellent introduction to historiographic issues, written for teachers, but of interest to students as well; includes an example of old and new history by comparing early and more recent articles written by Furumoto about Mary Whiton Calkins, APA's first woman president.

O'Donnell, J. M. (1979). The crisis of experimentalism in the 1920s: E. G. Boring and his uses of history. *American Psychologist, 34,* 289–295.

The best brief description of how Boring's concerns over applied psychology contributed to his efforts to reestablish the primacy of basic research through his behind-the-scenes APA activities and by constructing a history that emphasized experimental psychology.

2

THE PHILOSOPHICAL CONTEXT

▼

Psychology has a long past, yet its real history is short.

Hermann Ebbinghaus, 1908

▼

Preview

This chapter introduces you to the major philosophical issues and concepts that have been and continue to be important for psychologists. A working knowledge of these ideas, along with an understanding of how they were dealt with by key philosophers, provides a necessary foundation for comprehending modern psychology. Although philosophers grapple with a wide range of problems, those especially relevant for psychology concern (a) whether mental and physical events are essentially the same or different and if the latter, how the two kinds of events relate to each other; (b) whether our knowledge of the world is derived primarily from our unique ability to reason or results from the cumulative effects of our sensory experiences; (c) the extent to which our heredity and our environment shape the way we are; (d) whether the things we think, feel, and do result from our own free choices or are the result of deterministic laws of nature; and (e) whether or not complex phenomena can be best understood by breaking them into their component parts. These issues will be explored through an examination of the ideas of several well-known philosophers, with special attention given to René Descartes, history's most famous rationalist and the father of modern philosophy, John Locke, the founder of British Empiricism, and John Stuart Mill, the nineteenth-century British empiricist/associationist. The Original Source Excerpt is from Descartes' writings on the mind-body problem.

A LONG PAST

Most psychology students know Hermann Ebbinghaus as the inventor of the "nonsense syllable" and as the first person to study human memory experimentally (see Chapter 4). One cannot get through the memory chapter of an introductory psychology text, even today, without encountering the famous Ebbinghaus curve of forgetting, which seems to explain why students never seem to remember much the day after an exam. Among historians of psychology, Ebbinghaus is also known for the opening sentence of a brief introductory textbook that he wrote in 1908. It is the "long past, short history" quote that opened this chapter.

By referring to psychology's "long past," Ebbinghaus was reminding readers that the basic questions about human nature and the causes of human behavior are not new. Rather, they have been asked in some form or another since humans first started asking questions. More specifically, Ebbinghaus was pointing out that psychologists must recognize their deep roots in philosophy; psychology's history cannot be understood adequately without knowing something of philosophy's history. All of the important issues of concern to modern psychologists have been addressed by philosophers.

Does this mean that a psychologist is just a philosopher with a good thesaurus? No. In the last half of the nineteenth century, a number of converging forces produced an attempt to study human behavior and mental processes through the application of scientific methods rather than through philosophical analysis and speculation—by working in the laboratory rather than in the armchair. Thus, what came to be called the "New Psychology" began to emerge as a separate discipline about 150 years ago, which led Ebbinghaus, about 90 years ago, to proclaim that psychology's history as a natural science had been quite brief.

A thorough analysis of the long past referred to by Ebbinghaus requires much more space than this chapter can offer. It would take us through ancient Greece, deep into the writings of Plato and Aristotle and others, through the great medieval church philosophers such as Thomas Aquinas, who united Christian faith with Aristotelian logic, and into the Renaissance. Instead, while we will reach into the Renaissance for some historical context, we will begin with the seventeenth century and the multitalented René Descartes, sometimes considered the father of modern philosophy, mathematics, physiology, and psychology.

DESCARTES AND THE BEGINNINGS OF MODERN PHILOSOPHY AND SCIENCE

Descartes appeared on the scene at the tail end of the Renaissance, thus benefitting from the changes that occurred during that dramatic historical era. The Renaissance lasted for approximately 200 years, during the fifteenth and sixteenth centuries. It derives its name from the rediscovery of ancient Greek and Roman texts, especially those of Plato and Aristotle, which had been lost to the Western world for hundreds of years. The period was marked by tremendous advances in the arts, starting in northern Italy, but quickly spreading throughout Europe. It was the time of Leonardo Da Vinci (1452–1519), the prototypical "Renaissance Man," whose genius encompassed both art and science. His *Last Supper* and *Mona Lisa* are among the world's best known paintings, and his scientific interests encompassed geology, astronomy, botany, anatomy, and the applied sciences of aeronautics, engineering, and weaponry. Another giant of the Renaissance was Michelangelo Buonarotti (1475–1564), who created artistic treasures ranging from a portrayal of the book of Genesis on the ceiling of the Sistine Chapel in the Vatican to the massive 17-foot-tall sculpture of David, now found in Michelangelo's home city of Florence.

In addition to rediscovering ancient texts and revolutionizing the arts, the Renaissance produced some notable advances in technology and science. In the 1450s, for instance, Johannes Gutenberg (c. 1394–1468) created a new form of the printing press, which enabled books to be created in larger numbers than ever thought possible, and at prices that brought literature, philosophy, and the Bible to more people than ever before. Also during this time, clockmakers improved upon simple medieval instruments to produce the elaborate mechanical displays mounted on the cathedrals and public buildings of Europe. On the hour at the Wells Cathedral in England, for instance, viewers would be treated to a performance that included lifelike figures of armored knights in combat, one of whom would unhorse the other as another uniformed character struck the hour with a hammer (Boorstin, 1983). Knowledge about the inner workings of the human body was advanced significantly in 1543, when the Belgian physician Andreas Vesalius established his reputation as the founder of modern anatomical studies with his *Fabric of the Human Body*, which featured incredibly detailed illustrations (Klein, 1970). In astronomy in the mid-1500s, the Polish amateur astronomer Nicolas Copernicus challenged the traditional **geocentric** view of the universe, which held that the earth ("geo") was at the center of the universe, and replaced it with a **heliocentric** theory, which argued that sun ("helio") was at the center and the earth moved around it just like the other planets. Well aware of the religious controversy sure to result from the idea that "God's planet" was not in the center of the cosmos after all, Copernicus delayed publication until just before his death in 1543. The appearance of classic scientific works by Vesalius and Copernicus in the same year led one historian of science to declare 1543 as the year when modern science was born (Singer, 1957).

The Copernican model of the universe, which appeared near the end of the Renaissance, is the clearest example of one of its gradually evolving themes—a questioning of authority, especially the authority of the Church and the Church's official philosopher, Aristotle. The ancient geocentric model placed God's greatest creation, man, at the focal point of the universe. Copernicus questioned this notion. An even greater challenge soon arrived in the person of the renowned Italian scientist, Galileo Galilei (1564–1642), who supported Copernican theory with empirical observations aided by a telescope that he invented in 1609. Galileo's observations of things never seen before, such as the moons of Jupiter, further eroded traditional authority. How could Aristotle's view of the universe be correct when he was not capable of seeing what now could be seen? Galileo would eventually be forced by Church authorities to recant his claim of a heliocentric universe, but he did so with his fingers crossed. By the end of the seventeenth century, the geocentric model was, as they say, history.

Another threat to the established order occurred in England, during the time of Galileo, in the person of Sir Francis Bacon (1561–1626). Bacon was a strong advocate of an **inductive** approach to science. That is, he argued that the scientist must observe nature systematically and carefully as it presents itself, rather than follow the conclusions derived from a deductive analysis of Aristotle and other authorities. From many observations of individual cases, general statements about nature could be made. Bacon also believed that science should play an active role in controlling nature directly; indeed, for Bacon, a true understanding of nature only follows from the ability to create and recreate its effects at will (Smith, 1992). This, of course, is a plea for direct experimentation to supplement careful observation. Bacon's insistence on acquiring knowledge through experience makes him an ancestor of British empiricism; his emphasis on induction and the control of nature made him a hero in the eyes of the twentieth-century behaviorist B. F. Skinner (Chapter 11), who adopted a Baconian value system.

DESCARTES AND THE RATIONALIST ARGUMENT

In the year that Galileo invented his telescope, René Descartes (1596–1650), a 13-year-old son of a prosperous French lawyer, was already in his third year of study at the College de la Flèche, which had recently opened and was being run by Jesuits, known for their skills as educators.[1] The education that Descartes received was in the **scholastic** tradition, which combined the received wisdom of Church authority with the careful use of reason. In particular, it relied on rational argument derived from the works of Aristotle to support the precepts of the Church. Descartes quickly established himself as a star pupil, so good that he was granted special privileges. He was given a rare private room and he was exempted from regular class attendance and routine assignments. The Jesuits also allowed him to stay in bed as long as he wished in the morning in order to conserve his apparently fragile health. Out of this Descartes developed a lifelong habit; his best ideas came while lying in bed while reflecting on whatever problem happened to be at hand.

Descartes left the college in 1614 at the age of 18, not entirely satisfied with his Jesuit education. Like modern-day students surprised to learn that their formal education fails to give them clear answers to life's significant questions, he was dismayed to discover of philosophy that "it has been studied for many centuries by the most outstanding minds without having produced anything which is not in dispute" (Descartes, 1637/1960, p. 8). Consequently, he resolved to find things out for himself. Reflecting a sentiment familiar to all college students, he was ready to abandon the classroom and get out into the real world, "resolved to seek no other knowledge than that which I might find within myself, or perhaps in the great book of nature" (p. 8).

Because Descartes tried to keep his personal life private, the next few years are not well documented, but it appears that he spent some time sampling all that Paris had to offer (Vrooman, 1970). In 1619 he experienced what can only be called a conversion experience, in which a series of dreams effectively told him to get serious about making a meaningful contribution to knowledge. He spent the next 10 ten years living in and around Paris, learning as much as he could about as many different topics as possible, especially the sciences, firmly believing that he could produce a "unity of knowledge" that was to be grounded in mathematics. Although it seems rather absurd in today's age of information overload to think that someone could aspire to unify all knowledge into a single system, such was not the case in the seventeenth century. A weakening of authority, combined with an increasing faith in science, created an optimism that everything about the world could be known, perhaps in one's lifetime.

Descartes' time, the early seventeenth century, is known as an era of revolutionary developments in science. It was the time of Bacon, Galileo, and in the latter half of the century, the incomparable Sir Isaac Newton. It featured Galileo's telescope and the microscope of the Dutch lensmaker Antoni van Leeuwenhoek, tools which made it possible to observe things never seen before both in the heavens and in a drop of water (Boorstin, 1983). In medicine, for example, systematic observation by the British physician William Harvey refuted a widely-held belief that the heart creates blood to be consumed by other parts of the body, and demonstrated (in 1628) instead that it acts as a

---

[1] Descartes' birthdate was March 31, 1596, a fact known only because it appeared below a portrait published after his death. During his lifetime, Descartes was very secretive about his private life, refusing to disclose his birthday out of fear that it would lead to speculation by astrologers (Vrooman, 1970).

mechanical pump that recirculates blood throughout the body.

During the early 1620s, Descartes resembled a scientist more than a philosopher, studying physics, optics, geometry, and physiology. For example, he combined his interests in optics and physiology by extracting the eye of an ox and examining the properties of the lens, thereby discovering the fact that retinal images are inverted (Vrooman, 1970). By 1633 he had written *The World*, designed to summarize his life's work to that point, demonstrating how the various disciplines could be united through the careful use of reason and based on a foundation of mathematics. The book attempted to describe the origins and the structure of the known universe, and it included topics such as geology, astronomy, and human physiology. The section on astronomy, centering on a strong defense of the Copernican/Galilean heliocentric model of the universe, was a problem, however. Descartes was ready to publish *The World* when he learned that Galileo's work had been condemned by the Church. Fearing a similar fate, and desiring to avoid notoriety and remain in the good graces of the Catholic Church, Descartes suppressed publication and the book did not appear until after he died. Portions of it, however, appeared in various forms in several treatises that Descartes published during his lifetime, including his *Discourse on Method*, to which we now turn.

THE CARTESIAN SYSTEM: RATIONALISM, NATIVISM, AND MECHANISTIC INTERACTIONISM

Although skeptical of the merits of the scholasticism he encountered as a student, Descartes was always grateful to the Jesuits for teaching him to be precise and logical in his thinking. His belief that truth could emerge from the careful use of reason became his modus operandi and marks him as a **rationalist**. In his *Discourse on Method* (1637/1960), he explained how he would accept as truth only that which could

not be doubted. Thus, he rejected the evidence of the senses as being absolutely truthful, because the senses can deceive; he also questioned the plausible arguments of other philosophers, because equally plausible counterarguments existed. Yet he found that the one thing that he was unable to doubt was the fact of his doubting. As he put it in one of philosophy's most famous passages,

> I noticed that while I thus wished to think everything false, it was necessarily true that I who thought so was something. Since this truth, '*I think, therefore I am*' was so firm and so assured that all the most extravagant suppositions of the sceptics were unable to shake it, I judged that I could safely accept it as the first principle of the philosophy I was seeking. (Descartes, 1637/1960, p. 24, italics added)

For Descartes, then, the way to truth was through the human capacity to reason. In his *Discourse on Method*, he described the four basic rules he used to arrive at the truth of some matter. First, he would accept nothing as true unless "it presented itself so clearly and distinctly to my mind that there was no reason to doubt it" (Descartes, 1637/1960, p. 15). Second, he would take problems and analyze them, reducing them to their fundamental elements. Third, he would systematically work from the simplest of these elements to the more complex, and fourth, he would carefully review his conclusions to be certain of omitting nothing. Now to our twentieth-century way of thinking, these rules of method may not appear to be extraordinary. Descartes seems to be saying not much more than to think clearly, logically, and without bias, to reduce problems to subproblems, to work systematically from the simple to the complex, and to check your work. Yet to conclude that these rules are ordinary is to fall prey to the kind of presentist thinking discussed in Chapter 1. In the context of Descartes' times, when the power of authority was weakening but still considerable, his rules of method were truly revolutionary. In effect, he was casting off authority completely. The only way to get to the certainty of truth is to *arrive at it oneself*, relying on the clear use of one's own reasoning powers. An indication of how unsettling this notion was to the authorities is the fact that after Descartes' death, the Catholic Church placed his writings on their "Index," a list of books to be avoided by right-thinking Catholics (Vrooman, 1970).

An implication of Cartesian rationalism was that the ability to reason is inborn or innate and that certain types of knowledge did not rely directly on sense experience, but derived from our native ability to reason. For example, although we come to know the properties of wax (e.g., heat melts it) on the basis of our experience with it, there are certain things about wax that we come to understand simply as a result of a logical analysis, using our native reasoning powers. Thus, Descartes would say that we can conclude, without doubt, that wax has the inherent property of "extension"—it exists in space and even though it may change form (e.g., through melting), it can never disappear. Because we can use our native reason to arrive at a knowledge of the concept of extension, Descartes considered this particular attribute to be an example of an **innate idea**. Similarly, he believed that we have other innate ideas that we can derive through the use of our reasoning ability. These included the ideas of God, the self, and some basic mathematical truths. On the other hand, many of our concepts result from our experiences in the world. These Descartes called **derived ideas**. Knowing that a wax candle of a certain size will burn for about 10 hours would be an example of such an idea. Descartes' position on innate ideas means that he can be considered a **nativist** as well as a rationalist. His innate versus derived ideas distinction foreshadows one of psychology's recurring issues, the relationship between nature and nurture.

Descartes was also history's best-known **dualist**, arguing for a clear separation between mind (or "soul") and body. They can be distinguished, according to Descartes, by the above-mentioned property of extension and by the additional property of movement—bodies take up space and move through it. Mind, on the other hand, possesses neither extension nor movement. The centerpiece of the unextended mind is the human ability to reason, while the body is in essence a machine. One implication of this dualism has come to be called the **Cartesian dichotomy**, which divides humans and animals. Descartes argued that animals were simple machines, incapable of reason and language, and therefore lacking a mind. Humans, on the other hand, combined a mechanical body with a mind that could reason. Thus, animals consist only of bodies, whereas humans combine both bodies and minds. In addition to the labels rationalist and nativist, then, Descartes can also be considered a **mechanist**, for his belief that the body operates like a complicated machine. He was also an **interactionist**, believing that the mind could have a direct influence on the body (a decision to improve our health causes us to exercise) and the body could have a direct influence on the mind (a pulled hamstring causes us to redesign our exercise plan).

Descartes' use of the machine metaphor when describing the properties of bodies was no accident. We have seen that in the Renaissance, clock-building technology had advanced to the point where mechanical yet lifelike figures would put on an hourly show on the cathedrals and public buildings of Europe. Similarly, the wealthy of Europe created gardens that included elaborate mechanical fountains and statues that moved through the action of water-driven hydraulic systems. The unwary visitor to one of these seventeenth-century Disney Worlds might step on a hidden plate, thereby activating a system that would result in a statue of Neptune rising from the water in an adjacent pond. A less whimsical example of the mechanistic zeitgeist that infused Descartes' times was Harvey's demonstration of the heart as a mechanical pump.

▶ ORIGINAL SOURCE EXCERPT

Descartes on Mind-Body Interactionism

In the year before his death, Descartes published *Passions of the Soul* (1649/1969), which established his status as a pioneer psychologist and physiologist. A portion of it is excerpted here. Primarily a treatise on human emotions, it included an attempt to explain what we now call the reflex, and it provided a physiological model for Descartes' position on the mind-body question. Descartes opened the book with a characteristic attack on the traditional, authority-based approach to the study of the emotions, arguing in his opening sentence that "[t]here is nothing in which the defective nature of the sciences which we have received from the ancients appears more clearly than in what they have written on the passions" (Descartes, 1649/1969, p. 331). He then introduced his mind/body distinction and began a discussion of the "bodily machine" which included a direct reference to Harvey, a description of the antagonistic action of the muscles, and an opening discussion of the nervous system:

> In order to render this more intelligible, I shall here explain in a few words the whole method in which the bodily machine is composed. There is no one who does not already know that there are in us a heart, a brain, a stomach, muscles, nerves, arteries, veins, and such things.... Those who have acquired even the minimum of medical knowledge further know how the heart is composed.... Likewise all those whom the authority of the ancients has not entirely blinded, and who have chosen to open their eyes for the purpose of investigating the opinion of Harvey regarding the circulation of blood, do not doubt that all the veins and arteries of the body are like streams by which the blood ceaselessly flows with great swiftness.... We further know that all the movements of the members [e.g., arms and legs] depend on the muscles, and that these muscles are so mutually related one to another that when the one is contracted it draws toward itself the part of the body to which it is attached, which causes the opposite muscle to become elongated.... We know finally that all these movements of the muscles, as also all the senses, depend on the nerves, which resemble...little tubes, which all proceed from the brain, and thus contain like it a certain very subtle air or wind which is called the animal spirits. (pp. 333–334)

The **animal spirits** referred to by Descartes, a notion that traces to the ancient Greeks, were said to be derived from the "heat" of the blood and were the driving forces behind all movement. Descartes believed these spirits were tiny particles in constant motion and were found in the brain, the nerves, and the muscles.

> ...for what I here name spirits are nothing but material bodies and their one peculiarity is that they are bodies of extreme minuteness and that they move very quickly like the particles of the flame which issues from a

torch. Thus it is that they never remain at rest in any spot, and just as some of them enter into the cavities of the brain, others issue forth by the pores which are in [the brain], which pores conduct them into the nerves, and from there into the muscles, by means of which they move the body in all the different ways in which it can be moved....

For the sole cause of all the movements of the members is that certain muscles contract, and that those opposite to them elongate...and the sole cause of one muscle contracting rather than that set against it, is that there comes from the brain some additional amount of animal spirits, however little it may be, to it rather than to the other. Not that the spirits which proceed immediately from the brain suffice in themselves to move the muscles, but they determine the other spirits which are already in these two muscles, all to issue very quickly from the one of them and to pass into the other. (p. 336)

Muscle movement results from the action of animal spirits, but what determines which muscles will move? Two things, according to Descartes. First, the mind can initiate the movement of animal spirits in the brain by activating the nerves controlling certain muscles rather than others. That is, the mind can influence the body (more on this shortly). Second, certain muscles can move automatically in response to the results of certain sensory events. That is, *reflexes* occur.

Descartes explained the relationship between sensation and reflex action by proposing the existence of thin wirelike "filaments" that existed within the nerves and extended to the brain. On the basis of his animal dissections and without the benefit of Leeuwenhoek's microscope, yet to be invented, Descartes believed the nerves to be hollow tubes (thus allowing for animal spirits to move through them) containing these thin filaments. Whenever our senses are stimulated, according to Descartes, these filaments move, causing certain "pores" in the brain to be opened. This in turn results in the flow of animal spirits that produces the reflex movement, as when we accidentally burn ourselves. Figure 2.1 shows a famous sketch by Descartes of this involuntary (i.e, reflexive) withdrawal of one's foot from a fire, taken from an earlier work called *Treatise on Man*, published in 1637. The fire touches the foot, causing a tug on the filaments within the nerve there. These filaments extend all the way to the brain where animal spirits are released into the nerve "tube." The spirits in turn are carried "partly to the muscles which pull back the foot from the fire, partly to those which turn the eyes and the head in order to regard it, and partly to those which serve to advance the hands and to bend the whole body in order to shield itself" (Descartes, 1637, quoted in Fearing, 1930, p. 24).

Figure 2.1   Descartes' illustration of reflex action, from Fearing (1930).

In *Passions of the Soul*, Descartes extended the reflex concept to include all of our automatic functioning (e.g., breathing, digesting) and drew an analogy to the mechanics of a clock:

> In this way all the movement which we make without our will contribut-
> ing thereto (as frequently happens when we breathe, walk, eat, and in fact
> perform all those actions which are common to us and to the brutes), only
> depend on the conformation of our members, and on the course which
> the spirits, excited by the heat of the heart, follow naturally in the brain,
> nerves, and muscles, just as the movements of a watch are produced sim-
> ply by the strength of the springs and the form of the wheels. (pp.
> 339–340)

In addition to resulting in reflex action, sensations can also give rise to the
movement of animal spirits in the brain that lead to deliberate decisions to act
and the mind by itself can initiate action. That is, the mind can intervene
between sensory stimulus and motor response. How to explain the nature of
this interaction between mind and body was a problem, however. It is one
thing to say that the mind can directly affect bodily movement and vice versa,
but it is quite another thing to demonstrate just how this occurs. After careful
analysis, Descartes

> …clearly ascertained that the part of the body in which the soul exercises
> its functions immediately is in nowise the heart, nor the whole of the
> brain, but merely the most inward of all its parts, to wit, a certain very
> small gland which is situated in the middle of its substance and so sus-
> pended above the duct whereby the animal spirits in its anterior cavities
> have communication with those in the posterior, that the slightest move-
> ments which take place in it may alter very greatly the course of these
> spirits; and reciprocally that the smallest changes which occur in the
> course of the spirits may do much to change the movements of this gland.
> (pp. 345–346)

The structure in question is the **pineal gland**, and it was selected by
Descartes as the locus for mind-body interaction because it was strategically
located in a place where all the animal spirits would flow and it was found only
in humans, or so he erroneously thought. Also, it appeared to be the only structure in the brain that was not duplicated on both the left and right side.
Because the mind (or soul) was considered to be unitary, Descartes reasoned, it
must exert its effect through a structure that was also a single unit:

> The reason which persuades me that the soul cannot have any other seat
> in all the body than this gland wherein to exercise its functions immedi-
> ately, is that I reflect that the other parts of our brain are all of them dou-
> ble, just as we have two eyes, two hands, two ears, and finally all the
> organs of our outside senses are double; and inasmuch as we have but one
> solitary and simple thought of one particular thing at one and the same
> moment, it must necessarily be the case that there must somewhere be a
> place where the two images which come to us by the two eyes, where the
> two other impressions which proceed from a single object by means of the
> double organs of the other senses, can unite before arriving at the soul, in
> order that they may not represent to it two objects instead of one. (p. 346)

Descartes was not saying that the mind was *in* the pineal gland, only that the gland serves as the place where mind and body influence each other. Thus, sensations produce a stretching of the small filaments that open pores in the brain, thereby moving the animal spirits. These movements are felt by the pineal gland and somehow result in the mental event of a "sensation." The animal spirits also continue their movement back down the nerve fibers into the muscles, producing movement. Movement can also be created by the direct action of the will. The decision to move causes the pineal gland to move, which in turn produces the movements of the spirits that eventually move the muscles.

Descartes used his model of the nervous system to explain other mental and emotional processes. For instance, he proposed that memory was the result of animal spirits moving more easily along pathways that have been made more accessible by experience:

> Thus when the soul desires to recollect something, this desire causes the [pineal] gland, by inclining successively to different sides, to thrust the spirits towards different parts of the brain until they come across that part where the traces left there by the object which we wish to recollect are found; for these traces are none other than the fact that the pores of the brain, by which the spirits have formerly followed their course because of the presence of this object, have by that means acquired a greater facility than the others in being once more opened by the animal spirits which come towards them in the same way. Thus the spirits in coming in contact with these pores, enter into them more easily than into the others, by which means they excite a special movement in the gland which represents the same object to the soul, and causes it to know that it is this which it desired to remember. (p. 350)

Of course, despite his noble effort, Descartes had the nervous system all wrong. The nervous system does not operate as he proposed and the pineal gland, which remains little understood today, is not a mind-body Grand Central Station. Also, critics quickly pointed out that his proposal of the pineal gland as the point of mind-body interaction really did not explain anything, but merely pushed the problem back by one step. If it is unclear how the unextended mind can influence and be influenced by an extended body in general, it is just as unclear how the unextended mind can influence, and be influenced by, the movements of a small, extended piece of the brain (Cottingham, 1986). For psychology, the significance of Descartes' work is not that he made a serious yet fatally flawed effort to solve the mind-body problem, but that in so doing, he created the concept of reflex action, with its explicit distinction between sensory stimulus and motor response, and he tried to explain psychological concepts (e.g., memory) by using a physiological model. He was the first physiological psychologist.

Shortly after publishing *The Passions of the Soul* in 1649, Descartes was persuaded by Queen Christina of Sweden to move to Stockholm in order to tutor her. Hardly the stereotype of female royalty, "she lacked virtually every feminine charm" (Vrooman, 1970, p.

212). Yet she had a keen mind, was fluent in five languages, and was determined to make Stockholm a center of learning in Europe. To that end she created a world-class library and began inviting scholars to her court, Descartes being among the first to be asked. He accepted with some misgivings and soon found himself conversing with and tutoring Christina for five hours a day, three days a week, beginning at 5 A.M., during a winter that was severe even by Swedish standards. For someone accustomed to lounging in bed until late morning while reflecting on the great issues of the day, the schedule was a killer. Sure enough, Descartes contracted pneumonia on February 1, 1650, and died 10 days later, just shy of his fifty-fourth birthday.

THE BRITISH EMPIRICIST ARGUMENT AND THE ASSOCIATIONISTS

Philosophy on the European continent has often been rationalist in spirit, especially after Descartes. In England, however, a different tradition arose at about the same time that Descartes' influence was spreading. This British tradition is strongly **empiricist**, based on the idea that our knowledge of the world is constructed from our experiences in it. Because this knowledge is woven together by the associations between our ideas, British empiricism is closely tied to the doctrines of **associationism**. Much of the history of British philosophy, from the seventeenth century on, has been concerned with the question of how experience creates knowledge and how the rules of association work to organize that knowledge.

British empiricism has its roots in the inductive scientific thinking of Sir Francis Bacon and the social theories of Thomas Hobbes, a contemporary of Bacon and Descartes. We may conveniently begin with John Locke, however, usually considered the founder of this movement. We will then examine the work of other leading British empiricists and associationists, ending with the dominant British philosopher of the nineteenth century, John Stuart Mill.

JOHN LOCKE (1632–1704): THE ORIGINS OF BRITISH EMPIRICISM

John Locke was a reasonable man who lived during unreasonable times. He spent most of his adult life in the rational academic environment of Oxford as a lecturer and tutor, but he interspersed the contemplative life of a philosopher with a political and diplomatic career. Also, he was trained in medicine, but he was primarily interested in the scientific aspects of it and he seldom practiced as a physician. In his lifetime, he witnessed (a) the English Civil War, which ousted the British monarchy in favor of a civilian Parliament; (b) the execution of one king and the overthrow of another (he might have been present at the former and had a hand in the latter); (c) several changes in England's official religion, each accompanied by varying degrees of persecution of those professing the "wrong" faith; (d) a fire that destroyed two-thirds of London (he could see the smoke from Oxford); and (e) a political alliance that led him to flee England for a time and settle in the safety of Holland (Jeffreys, 1967). Out of these experiences, he developed a liberal political philosophy based on tolerance of dissent and the right of the people to determine how they would lead both their worldly and their more spiritual lives, and in particular, how they would be governed. In his best-known political work, *Two Treatises on Government* (1690/1960), he elaborated the Hobbesian idea of a **social contract** between government and the people. The government would agree to govern wisely and protect the rights, welfare, and common good of its citizens; the citizens in turn would agree to support the government and participate in it. Citizens failing to do so could expect the government to act against them (e.g., throw them in jail for not paying taxes). On the other hand, governments failing their end of the bargain could expect to be overthrown by the people and replaced by a more just government. This concept should sound familiar. Thomas Jefferson modeled the Declaration of Independence on Locke's ideas.

Locke is important to psychology as a consequence of the concepts expressed in two of his books, *An Essay Concerning Human Understanding* (1690/1963) and *Some Thoughts Concerning Education* (1693/1963). The former explains Locke's views on how knowledge is acquired, how we as humans come to understand our world. The latter is based on a series of letters to a friend and shows how empiricist thinking can be applied to all aspects of a child's education.

Locke on Human Understanding

Like Descartes, Locke was much enamored of the science that was such a prominent feature of the seventeenth century. While a student at Oxford, he was drawn to the ideas of Sir Francis Bacon and he firmly rejected the same scholasticism that Descartes rejected. While studying medicine, Locke befriended other scientists, including Robert Boyle (1627–1692), one of modern chemistry's pioneers and a founder of the British Royal Society, established in 1662 to further the interests of science (Boorstin, 1983). Locke was also a contemporary of Sir Isaac Newton, whose *Principia Mathematica* was published just three years before Locke's *Essay*. What Bacon, Boyle, Newton, and others were doing for the physical sciences, transforming it from the Aristotelian-based "natural philosophy" into an experimental, empirically based group of disciplines, Locke was determined to do for **epistemology**, the study of human knowledge and its acquisition.

As Locke noted in the book's opening "epistle to the reader," the ideas in his *Essay* derived from discussions with friends at Oxford and evolved into a series of notes, "written by incoherent parcels; and, after long intervals of neglect, resumed again, as my humor or occasions permitted" (Locke, 1690/1963, p. xlvii). Twenty years after the originating discussions,

it finally emerged in 1690 as *An Essay Concerning Human Understanding*.

Before describing how our ideas originate, Locke considered and rejected the existence of innate ideas. He was not entirely on the nurture side of the nature-nurture issue, however. He granted that we have innate "faculties" such as the ability to think, but he did not accept Descartes' contention that ideas derived from logical thinking (e.g., extension) could be considered innate ideas. He began by arguing that there is no need to propose innate ideas, because it can be shown that ideas originate from other sources, requiring only the use of our basic mental abilities ("faculties"). For instance, while our reasoning ability enables us to conclude that all physical objects have the property of extension, the conclusion is based on the fact that we have experienced lots of extended objects during our lifetimes. In the absence of such experiences, Locke believed that we would not arrive at the conclusion about extension being a property of all matter; indeed, it would not even occur to us to think about it.

Another argument for innate ideas was the belief that some ideas were universal, found in all people. If all cultures include the concept of the Deity, for example, it could be said that the concept of God does not require any specific experiences, but is innate. Locke would not buy it. Although he did not use this specific example, Locke's reply would be that a universal belief in God does not necessarily mean the idea is innate. Instead, it could be that because all people die (i.e., a common experience), they all worry about death and whether there is an afterlife, and proposing the idea of a supreme being is a natural consequence of this line of thought.

A final argument for innate ideas is that some ideas seem to appear so early in life that they must be innate. Locke rejected this argument also, pointing out that even before children can use language, they are profiting from experience, by learning to recognize the difference between bitter and sweet for instance. Furthermore, in a tone similar to that taken later by American behaviorists in the twentieth century, Locke pointed out that we often overlook the fact that a child can have quite a few important experiences early in life. Thus, a two-year-old talking about God does not allow us to conclude that God is an innate idea. That child has probably been exposed to quite a bit of religion in two years.

Having rejected the concept of innate ideas, Locke turned to the question of how our minds develop ideas. In one of philosophy's most quoted passages, Locke declared that *all* of our knowledge about the world derives from our experiences in it:

> ...Let us then suppose the mind to be, as we say, white paper, void of all characters, without any ideas; how comes it to be furnished? Whence comes it by that vast store, which the busy and boundless fancy of man has painted on it with an almost endless variety? Whence has it all the materials of reason and knowledge? *To this I answer, in one word, from experience*; in that, all our knowledge is founded, and from that it ultimately derives itself. (Locke, 1690/1963, pp. 82–83, italics added)

The mind at birth, then, is an empty sheet of paper (Locke was renaming an old Aristotelean metaphor of the mind as a blank slate or wax tablet), ready to be written upon by the experiences of one's lifetime. Furthermore, the ideas that result from our experience and compose the mind have two and only two sources, according to Locke. He believed that every idea we have, without exception, originated from the two processes of sensation and reflection. As he described it:

> First, our senses...convey into the mind several distinct perceptions of things...: and thus we come by those ideas we have, of yellow, white, heat, cold, soft, hard, bitter, sweet, and all those which we call sensible

qualities.... This great source of most of the ideas we have, depending wholly upon our senses, and derived by them to the understanding, I call SENSATION.

> ...Secondly, the other fountain, from which experience furnisheth the understanding with ideas, is the perception of the operations of our own mind within us, as it is employed about the ideas it has got; [these] operations...are perception, thinking, doubting, believing, reasoning, knowing, willing, and all the different actings of our own minds; ...I call this REFLECTION, the ideas it affords being such only as the mind gets by reflecting on its own operations within itself. (Locke, 1690/1963, pp. 83–84)

Sensation, then, refers to all of the information taken in by our senses from the environment, and reflection refers to the mental activities involved in processing information from both the senses and from memory. Thus, our concept of green derives from all of our experiences with green objects and our further reflections about "greenness." The reflection process also can produce new ideas not encountered initially by our senses. For instance, even without encountering the Dr. Seuss story directly through sensation, we can conceive of "green eggs and ham" by combining, through the reflective processes of memory and imagination, our ideas of green, eggs, and ham.

In another part of the *Essay*, Locke made a distinction between simple and complex ideas. **Simple ideas** resulted from experiencing basic sensory qualities such as yellow, white, heat, and so on, and from making simple reflections such as "pleasant." A **complex idea** includes several other ideas, which can be a combination of simple and other complex ideas. The complex idea of a cold drink on a very hot day, for example, is composed of a number of simple ideas relating to color, temperature, shape, pleasantness, taste, and the additional complex idea of the good life. Complex ideas are compounds and can be ultimately reduced to simple ones, much as chemical compounds are composed of simple elements. This idea of the mind being an elaborate construction incorporating layers of ideas of varying complexity was a common feature of all British empiricist thinking, and reflects the influence of the other sciences, especially physics and chemistry. Just as water can be reduced to its elements and light can be broken down into the colors of the spectrum, so the mind could be analyzed into its fundamental units. The idea that complexity in nature can be understood by reducing objects to their most basic elements is sometimes referred to as **atomism**, and it is an assumption underlying many of the early systems of psychology, including Titchener's structuralism (Chapter 7) and Watson's behaviorism (Chapter 10).

In the fourth edition of his *Essay*, Locke addressed the question of how simple ideas form compound ones, and in the process introduced the concept of **association** into the discussion. Just as gravity was the central concept of Newtonian physics, holding together the elements of the universe, so would association be the glue that held together one's experiences in life. But while Locke discussed the concept of association to some extent, it was for the other British philosophers we will meet shortly to develop it more fully. As will become evident, British empiricism and associationism went hand in hand.

A final distinction worth noting is between what Locke referred to as the primary and secondary qualities of matter. This was a distinction well-known in the seventeenth century, first popularized by Galileo. **Primary qualities** were said to exist as an inherent property of an object. Extension, shape, and motion are examples. These were the features believed by Descartes to be innate ideas. To Locke, there was nothing innate about them; the concepts might indeed result from the mind's reflection, but the data for that reflection came from one's sensory experiences with a range of objects. **Secondary qualities**, on the other hand, are

not inherent attributes of objects, but depend on perception. The color, smell, warmth, and taste of objects are examples. Thus, the redness of an object exists not in the object itself but in the perceptual experience of the observer. As it gets darker, the tomato in the garden does not change its shape, but its color changes, gradually fading from red to near-black. In the next chapter, you will see how the concept of secondary qualities was a cornerstone of a famous nineteenth-century model of the nervous system, which proposed that the senses differed in terms of "specific energies." The primary/secondary distinction also raised questions that led naturally to a direct examination of how sensory systems actually work to create our "understandings." If "red" is not in the object but in the brain, how does it get there?

Locke's empiricist philosophy had several interesting implications. First, if our knowledge of the world is based on our experiences, and sensation is a major source of that experience, then defective senses should produce a distorted view of the world. This issue was posed to Locke in the form of a letter from William Molyneux, a friend in Dublin. Molyneux asked what would happen if a man blind from birth, whose experience of objects like cubes and spheres would be limited to the sense of touch, would recognize the objects if his sight was suddenly restored. Molyneux answered his own question in the negative, and Locke agreed. Once sight had been restored, the man would have to learn to distinguish cube from sphere all over again, by relating the information from the visual and the tactile senses. As early as the eighteenth century, congenital cataracts were being removed surgically, thus providing a direct test and strong support for this empiricist claim (Morgan, 1977).

Another implication of Locke's theory connects his psychology with his political theory and illustrates how the turbulent times in which he lived helped shape his ideas. If human understanding results from experience, then people living in different environments will necessarily have different sets of experiences. The result will be differences between people that range from food preferences to beliefs about the best way to live one's life to one's personal religious preferences. Locke did not believe in a total relativism—not all belief systems are of equal value, both intellectually and morally. But his commitment to the importance of the environment in shaping the mind, and the resulting differences between people, was tied closely to his political liberalism and in particular to his belief that individual differences, even differences in religious beliefs, should be tolerated. Having lived through several periods of extreme religious intolerance, Locke was aware of its destructive influence.

Locke on Education

A final implication of Locke's empiricist thinking concerned how to raise and educate children. If the mind is shaped by its experiences, then a deliberate program of education based on empiricist principles could be expected to produce the ideal person. Locke's contribution to the issue was *Some Thoughts Concerning Education* (1693/1963), a brief volume based on letters written to a friend who was seeking advice about the education of his son. Locke's advice was wide-ranging, and included the following:

1. Trained in medicine, Locke was a strong believer in the importance of physical health, and he began the book by advocating that a sound mind requires a sound body. His specific suggestions reflected his own strict Puritan upbringing, which fostered simplicity, individual initiative and effort, and the belief that good outcomes require some degree of suffering. Children should have hard rather than soft beds, for example; the former toughens the person, whereas "being buried every night in feathers, melts and dissolves the body, is often the cause of weakness, and the forerunner of an early grave" (Locke, 1693/1963, p. 22). Using an inoculation logic, he also suggested that children could develop resistance to dis-

ease by having their feet washed in cold water every day and by wearing leaky shoes.

2. Training must begin early, because young children are more malleable, and if they don't develop good habits early in life, they will develop bad ones. Locke believed that one of the greatest mistakes made by parents was that their child's "mind [had] not been made obedient to discipline, and pliant to reason, when at first it was most tender, most easy to be bowed" (Locke, 1693/1963, p. 27). Good habits also require practice. Children learn such habits by doing things repeatedly, not by learning rules, "which will be always slipping out of their memories" (p. 46).

3. Locke argued against the use of punishment, especially as children get older. The child who is beaten for not doing lessons soon comes to dislike learning (and tutors) completely. Furthermore, while punishment might reduce unruly behavior in a child, severe and repeated punishment carries the danger of "breaking the mind, and then, in place of a disorderly young fellow, you have a low-spirited moped creature" (Locke, 1693/1963, p. 38).

4. Concrete rewards are to be avoided also. Giving a child sweets for good performance produces a child only interested in obtaining sweets. On the other hand, Locke recommended the use of rewards and punishments in the form of parental approval and disapproval. "If you can once get into children a love of credit, and an apprehension of shame and disgrace, you have put into them the true principle, which will constantly work, and incline them to the right" (Locke, 1693/1963, p. 41).

Locke's views on education, and his empiricist philosophy in general, show a strong affinity with twentieth-century behaviorism, as will be clear when you read Chapters 10 and 11. Although Locke was concerned with mental life and the behaviorists focused on overt action, strong resemblances exist. Like the modern behaviorists, Locke believed that mental complexity could be understood by analysis into component parts, that the environment directly shaped the mind and behavior, and that you can tell a great deal about a person if you know something of the person's experiences in life. Empiricism and behaviorism also share an emphasis on the importance of association, but as mentioned earlier, it was for empiricists subsequent to Locke to develop associationist doctrine to its fullest. It is to Locke's intellectual descendants that we now turn.

GEORGE BERKELEY (1685–1753): EMPIRICISM APPLIED TO VISION

As the seventeenth century drew to a close, it was clear to the intelligentsia that the century had been marked by a steady decline in the authority of the Church and scholasticism, accompanied by, and to a large extent precipitated by, enormous advances in science. From Bacon to Galileo to Harvey to Boyle to Newton, a zeitgeist evolved that envisioned the universe as a large machine, composed of material parts, and operating according to laws that could only be discovered by combining scientific methods with mathematical rigor. Although it was not until the nineteenth century that the "ism" called **materialism** would reach its full development, its roots were in the seventeenth century. Materialists are monists on the mind-body question, believing that the only reality is a physical reality, and that every event in the universe, including what we think of as mental events, involve measurable, material objects in motion in physical space. Materialism includes the above-mentioned atomism, the idea that complex entities can be understood by reducing them to their component parts. Materialism also poses a threat to the concept of free will by implying **determinism**, the belief that all events have prior causes. If we are not free to choose, then perhaps we cannot be held responsible for our actions.

Such a materialistic worldview does not necessarily rule out religion (Newton thought of

God as a great clockmaker who created the rules, set the universe in motion, and tinkered every once in a while to keep things working smoothly), but it threatens the concepts of free will and moral responsibility, and so it was seen by some as a danger. One thinker who was especially concerned about the materialistic implications of seventeenth-century science was George Berkeley, a bishop of the Anglican Church in Ireland.

Berkeley (pronounced "Bark'-lee") was a child prodigy who entered college at age 15 and completed his most important philosophical work before his thirtieth birthday. He was born in Ireland, educated at Dublin's Trinity College, and made a deacon in the Anglican Church in 1709 at age 24. He held several professorships and would eventually (1734) be named Bishop of Cloyne in Ireland. In his middle years, he became fascinated with the missionary possibilities in the New World. He believed that America was the great hope for civilization and reflected it in his poem entitled "Destiny of America," which contains the often-quoted line "Westward the course of empire takes its way." He lived for a time in Newport, Rhode Island, and tried unsuccessfully to establish a university in Bermuda. The city of Berkeley, California, about as westward as one can get in America, is named for him.

Berkeley is important for psychology because of two books that he published when he was in his mid-twenties: *An Essay Towards a New Theory of Vision* (1709) and *Treatise Concerning the Principles of Human Knowledge* (1710). Both are strongly empiricist and focus on an analysis of sensory processes. Legend has it that Berkeley's interest in sensation had its roots in a hanging that he witnessed while a student. Curious about the sensations accompanying being hung, he arranged to have *himself* hung from the rafters in the company of friends who were instructed to cut him down after a few minutes! Evidently, Berkeley lost consciousness and almost died from the incident, which contributed to his reputation for being a bit eccentric (Klein, 1970).[2]

Berkeley's work on vision was the first systematic example of how empiricist thinking could be applied to the study of perception. It was timely, written when advances in optics were producing new and improved telescopes, microscopes, and eyeglasses, while at the same time knowledge of the visual system was primitive. In his book, Berkeley tried to show that our perceptions of the distance, size, and locations of objects are judgments that depend entirely on *experience*. When judging distance, for example, Berkeley made use of what your general psychology book referred to as monocular (only one eye needed) cues:

> [T]he estimate we make of the distance of objects considerably remote is rather an act of judgment grounded on experience than of sens[ation]. For example, when I perceive a great number of intermediate objects, such as houses, fields, rivers, and the like, which I have experienced to take up considerable space, I thence form a judgment or conclusion that the object that I see beyond them is at a great distance. Again, when an object appears faint and small, which at a near distance I have experienced to make a vigorous and large appearance, I instantly conclude it to be far off. (Berkeley, 1709/1948, p. 171)

Berkeley also examined the question of judging depth for objects that are relatively close, and provided a clear description of phenomena today referred to as convergence, a binocular (two eyes needed) cue, and accommodation. In **convergence**, when objects move closer to us or farther away, "we alter the disposition of our eyes, by lessening or widening the interval between the pupils" (Berkeley, 1709/1948, p. 174). These eye movements are

the result of muscle movements which in turn create sensations that we come to associate with various distances. Similarly, objects are perceived clearly through **accommodation**, in which changes in the shape of the lens serve to keep objects focused on the retina. Closer objects produce a greater bulging of the lens than objects farther away. Again, these changes are accompanied by muscle action and sensations to be associated with different distances.

The basic principles of optics had been known for some time, and it had been common knowledge since Descartes that the retinal image was inverted, as shown in Figure 2.2, taken from Berkeley's book. The question was how we manage to see an upright world. Berkeley rejected as oversimplified the notion that our brain simply makes a correction and proposed instead that once again, the key lies in our experience with the world. Specifically, we learn to relate what we see with what we experience using our other senses, especially touch and the senses related to physical movement. We develop concepts of up and down through our sense of touch, according to Berkeley, by learning that "up" is farther away from the earth than "down." When we touch the top and the bottom of the cross in Figure 2.2, we learn to make the connection between the lower portion of the retinal image and the top of the cross and we come to "see" the top of the cross as being farther away from the earth (i.e., higher) than the bottom of the cross. Again, all depends on experience.

An important theme of Berkeley's theory of vision, clear from the opening sentence of the monocular cues quote, is that we do not see objects directly; rather we make judgments about them based on visual information *and* our experiences. The theme was carried into his other major work, *Treatise Concerning the Principles of Human Knowledge* (1710/1957), and

---

[2] The reputation was enhanced when Berkeley died. He believed that noticeable decay was the only sure sign of death, so he gave instructions that he not be buried until his body became offensive to the senses.

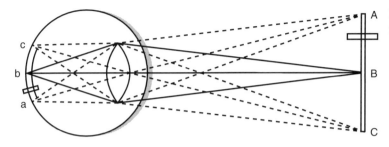

Figure 2.2 The inverted retinal image, from Berkeley (1709/1948).

provided the basis for Berkeley's attack on materialism. Just as we do not see "distance" directly, so it is the case that we do not see "material objects" directly. In both cases, they are "judged" on the basis of perception. Thus, we cannot be entirely certain of the reality of material objects; the only certainty is that we are perceiving. This position of Berkeley's is known as **subjective idealism** (sometimes "immaterialism"). It is in the empiricist tradition because experience is the source of all knowledge, but it destroys the distinction that Locke made between primary and secondary qualities of matter. For Berkeley, everything was a secondary quality. Just as color depends on the perceiving person, so does extension. The only thing that has reality for us is our own perception.

Does this mean that we can never be sure about the reality of the world? Does a tree falling in the forest only exist if we hear it? No. Reality truly exists, according to Berkeley, because objects, including the tree in the forest, are *always* perceived by God, who Berkeley referred to as the "Permanent Perceiver." We can be sure of the permanence of reality, but only through our faith in God. In this way, Berkeley sought to attack what he saw as a Godless materialism. Instead, faith in God becomes essential to our understanding of the world.

Berkeley was not successful in countering the trend toward materialism, as will be clear in the next chapter, and despite the complexity of his work on vision, he did not do experiments and thus cannot be considered an early experimental psychologist. By emphasizing the importance of perception in one's understanding of reality, however, and by directly attacking the question of how visual perception actually works, he furthered the cause of British empiricism, while at the same time turning the issue of *how knowledge is acquired* from a purely philosophical question to a more psychological one. As historian of psychology Daniel Robinson put it, Berkeley "rendered epistemology a branch of psychology, and the two have never been divorced since" (1981, p. 228). Once the problem of human knowledge became a psychological one, people began asking different questions. Rather than asking a philosophical question like "How much can be known about the nature of reality?" thinkers now began asking questions like "Just exactly how does visual perception work to enhance what we know?" This shift would eventually bring about a scientific psychology.

BRITISH ASSOCIATIONISM

Like John Locke, Berkeley had little to say about how our sensory experiences and our reflections combine to produce the more complicated forms of our knowledge. That is, while both addressed the issue of association of ideas, neither carefully examined the phenomenon. Association would soon occupy center stage for British philosophers, however, and be seen as a force controlling the events of mental life. **Associationism** is the doctrine that the mind can be understood as a complex set of ideas, related to each other by the force of the associations between them. Things become associated in our minds by virtue of our experiences in the world; thus, associationism is grounded in empiricism. The British philosophers David Hume and David Hartley both made important contributions to the understanding of how association operated.

David Hume (1711–1776): The Rules of Association

Hume was born near Edinburgh, Scotland, around the time Berkeley was publishing the two books mentioned previously. He entered the University of Edinburgh at age 12, fell in love with literature and philosophy, but left after three years without finishing a degree. He tried the study of law, hated it, then decided on a business career and hated it as well. Determined to become a scholar, he retreated to the French countryside[3] for three years and wrote his first book, *A Treatise of Human Nature* (1739–1740/1969). Thus, like Berkeley, Hume published a major treatise while still in his twenties. Unfortunately, the book did not sell well, disappointing the ambitious Hume, who later said of the book: "It fell deadborn from the press, without reaching such distinction, as even to excite a murmur from the zealots" (quoted in Klein, 1970, p. 552). He later wrote shortened versions of the *Treatise* under different titles, but as a writer he was best known not for his philosophical works, but for a massive, five-volume history of England. Still highly regarded, it went beyond the usual military and political history and incorporated social and literary history into the narrative.

Never modest, Hume believed that his *Treatise* would do for philosophy what Newton had accomplished for physics. Indeed, the subtitle of the treatise is "Being an Attempt to Introduce the Experimental Method of Reasoning into Moral Subjects." By "experimental method," Hume did not mean the use of experiments as we understand the term today, but the careful and systematic observation of

human thinking and behavior, mainly his own, accompanied by a logical analysis of the process in order to uncover basic laws of the mind.

In good British empiricist tradition, Hume built his system on the basic premise that all of our understanding is rooted in experience. To dissect human experience, Hume first tried to discover the mind's basic elements, analogous to the physicist's atoms. Upon reflection, Hume believed these elements were two in number: impressions and ideas. **Impressions** are basic sensations, the raw data of experience. We feel pleasure, we see red, we taste sweetness, and so on. **Ideas**, on the other hand, are "faint copies" of impressions. That is, while similar to impressions, and deriving from them, ideas are not as vivid. To support his contention that ideas derived from impressions, Hume noted that it is possible to reduce all of our ideas to impressions, even complex ideas that have never been experienced directly. Thus, even if we have never found a real four-leaf clover, we can have a complex idea of it by combining simple ideas (e.g., "four" and "clover" and "green") that can indeed be traced to impressions.

Note that Hume's analysis of impressions and ideas is mainstream British empiricism. If all ideas are faint copies of impressions, then all ideas derive from the impressions we experience in life. Hence, there are no innate ideas. Also, Hume included the Lockean distinction between simple and complex ideas. But how do impressions connect with ideas and how are complex ideas formed? How does one idea lead to another? In a word, from the process of association, the analysis of which Hume considered perhaps his major achievement.

Hume proposed three laws of association: resemblance, contiguity, and cause/effect. Sometimes an object reminds us of another because it is similar to or has a **resemblance** to it. Thus, a photo of the Yosemite's Half Dome resembles the actual piece of granite, and brings to mind memories (ideas), perhaps of a visit to

---

[3] He chose the quiet town of La Flèche, known for the Jesuit school that trained Descartes.

Yosemite Valley. **Contiguity** means experiencing things together. Thus, because the purist eats lobster only in Maine, thinking of lobster brings to mind the Maine coast. Hume's third law of association concerned the relationship between **cause and effect**. If one event follows another with some regularity, we will develop an association between the two. Hume's example was a healed wound. The original wound "caused" us to experience pain; thus, when we now examine the old wound, we are reminded of the pain and the circumstances that produced it. But what determines causes and effects? Hume's answer made him a controversial figure in his day, but might have been his most important contribution to modern psychology.

Hume believed that we can never be absolutely certain about the causes of events. Rather, all we can know is that events occur together with some predictable regularity. To conclude that A causes B, he argued, it is necessary to know that (a) when A occurs, B occurs regularly, (b) A occurs before B does, and (c) B does not occur unless A does. Invoking empiricist thinking and aware of the basic problem of induction, Hume pointed out that we only know about these regularities because of our experience. Furthermore, because our experiences are limited, we can never be certain about the causes of events. Hume's conclusion that absolute certainty was unattainable labeled him a "skeptic," and brought him into conflict with sources of authority such as the church, which naturally took offense at the implication that the existence of God could be questioned.

It is important to note, however, that Hume did not deny the existence of reality, God, or the possibility of there being absolute causes of events. His point was that we could never arrive at them with certainty. From the practical standpoint of day-to-day living, what is important, Hume believed, is to be able to accumulate enough experience to make the best possible predictions. If events occur together reliably in the past, we have every reason to expect that they will co-occur in the future. Thus, Hume

was not denying causality; he was merely shifting it from a search for absolute causes to a search for greater-than-chance regularities. Modern psychologists searching for the "causes" of behavior are essentially following Hume's lead in this regard. They recognize that multiple factors contribute to all behaviors; the best one can hope for is to identify the factors that predict behaviors with probabilities greater than chance.

David Hartley (1705–1757): A Physiological Associationism

Hume certainly paid heed to the process of association, but the topic commanded an even greater share of David Hartley's attention. He broke little new ground and is not known as an original thinker, but his *Observations on Man, His Frame, His Duty, and His Expectations* (1749/1971) summarized the essentials of British empiricist thought with great clarity and added a forceful description of how association could be the guiding principle for a theory of how the human mind was structured and how it operated. Because the book also attempted to describe the neurological correlates of mental activity, it also marks an important step in the development of physiological psychology. Published exactly 100 years after Descartes' *Passions of the Soul*, Hartley's *Observations* is a worthy successor.

Hartley was born in the north of England (in Yorkshire), educated at Cambridge, and headed for a career in imitation of his minister father when doctrinal problems intervened. He discovered that he was unable to believe in the idea of eternal damnation, one of the so-called Thirty-Nine articles of faith that had to be accepted by ministers of the Anglican Church. His next choice was medicine and he eventually earned his living as a successful practitioner. In his spare time, he founded British Associationism.

Hartley was a contemporary of Hume, but not influenced by him. He began preliminary drafts of his *Observations* in the early 1630s, prior to Hume's 1639 *Treatise*, and he seemed to be unaware of Hume's work (not surprising, considering the latter book's poor sales). Three years before producing the final *Observations*, Hartley published a version of the book as an appendix to a medical book on kidney and bladder stones. The appendix was written in Latin, under the tentative-sounding title of *Conjecturae*; apparently, Hartley wished to preview his ideas to a restricted group of scholars before going public with it (Webb, 1988).

Hartley made it clear in the book's opening sentence that he was a dualist on the mind-body question: "Man consists of two parts, body and mind" (Hartley, 1749/1971, p. i). Unlike Descartes' interactionism, however, Hartley took more of a parallelist stance. That is, he considered mental and physical (physiological) events separately, even structuring the book as a series of propositions that alternated between the mind and the body. The widely-quoted propositions X and XI outline the core of his associationism, first on the mental side, then on the physical. Proposition 10 reads, in part:

> Any Sensations A, B, C, &c. by being associated with one another a sufficient Number of Times, get such Power over the corresponding Ideas a, b, c, &c. that any one of the Sensations A, when impressed alone, shall be able to excite in the Mind b, c, &c. the ideas of the rest.
>
> Sensations may be said to be associated together, when their Impressions are either made precisely at the same Instant of Time, or in the contiguous successive Instants. We may therefore distinguish Association into two sorts, the synchronous, and the successive. (Hartley, 1749/1971, p. 65)

For Hartley, then, the main law of association is **contiguity**, the experiencing of events together. If we repeatedly see Adam (A), Brent (B), and Charlie (C) together, with each sensory experience producing the corresponding ideas of them (a, b, and c), then in the future if we see Adam (A), the ideas of Brent (b) and Charlie (c)

will occur to us. The chances of this happening relate to how often we have seen the three of them together. Thus, the strength of association relies on **repetition**. Furthermore, contiguity occurs either for events experienced simultaneously or in quick succession. Although Hartley used the terms synchronous and successive, these concepts are commonly referred to as **spatial contiguity** and **temporal contiguity**, respectively. Thinking of your house might lead you to think of your dog sitting by the front door (spatial), while your dog's drooling might be the result of it associating your smiling face with the immediate presentation of food (temporal).[4]

There is no need to quote Hartley's Proposition 11 because it is identical to Proposition 10, except that the word "Vibrations" substitutes for "Sensations" and the phrase "miniature Vibrations" replaces "Ideas." This was Hartley's version of nervous system activity, taken from Sir Isaac Newton, who suggested that all matter could be conceptualized as vibrating particles in space. Hartley had the advantage over Descartes in knowing that the nerves were not hollow; hence, there was no space for animal spirits to be flowing back and forth. Rather, nerves were tightly packed fibers and he believed they conveyed sensory information by vibrating. In the brain, smaller nerves produced even smaller vibrations, which Hartley called "miniature vibrations" or miniatures. These correspond to ideas. Like Hume, who referred to ideas as "faint copies" of impressions, Hartley thought of ideas (miniature vibrations) as less "vigorous" than sensations (vibrations).

Hartley's model of the mind was a kind of building-block structure in which complex ideas were constructed from the individual component parts. He used the complex idea of a horse as an example, writing that "we could have no proper idea of the Horse, unless the particular Ideas of the Head, Neck, Body, Legs, and Tail, peculiar to this Animal, stuck to each other in the Fancy

---

[4] As you can guess from the latter example, contiguity was an important concept for the Russian physiologist, Ivan Pavlov, whom you will encounter in Chapter 10.

[i.e., occurred to us], from frequent joint Impression" (Hartley, 1749/1971, p. 71). These subparts can also be divisible into even simpler ideas (e.g., legs include hoofs, etc.). If we experience all these atomistic elements frequently enough, then seeing a part of a horse (e.g., a hoof) will make us think of the horse as a whole.

Hartley's analysis brings the issue of atomism versus "holism" into focus. Most of the British philosophers took an atomistic approach, with Hartley perhaps being the most explicit of the philosophers considered thus far. One problem with this approach is that it requires a knowledge of parts before one can know the whole. That is, complex ideas are built up from simpler ones. In his horse example, Hartley wrote of the parts "coalescing" into the whole animal. The whole is equal to the sum of its parts. **Holism**, on the other hand, argues for the primacy of the whole over its constituent elements, that the parts have no meaning without first knowing the whole. The psychologist G. F. Stout once used the example of a pyramid constructed of oval stones as an example (Klein, 1970). Each element of the pyramid may be perfectly round, but the whole figure has an overall triangular shape not found in any of its parts. The holistic approach would eventually find a voice within psychology through the work of the Gestalt psychologists (Chapter 9).

Hartley was clearly in the atomist camp and he had a direct influence on James Mill (1773–1836), another in the long line of British empiricists and associationists. The influence is clear from this often-quoted example provided by Mill in his *Analysis of the Phenomena of the Human Mind* (1829/1948):

> Brick is one complex idea, mortar is another complex idea; these ideas, with ideas of position and quantity, compose my idea of a wall. My idea of a plank is a complex idea, my idea of a rafter is a complex idea, my idea of a nail is a complex idea.
>
> These, united with the same ideas of position and quantity, compose my duplex idea of a floor. In the same manner, my complex idea of glass, wood, and others, compose my duplex idea of a window; and these duplex ideas, united together, compose my idea of a house.... How many complex, or duplex ideas, are all united in the idea of furniture? How many more in the idea of merchandise? How many more in the idea called Every Thing? (p. 154)

Mill was an important character in British philosophy, and like Hume was also well-known as a historian; his *History of British India*, written in 1817, helped him to become financially secure. James Mill was not as important as his son, however, an outcome that Mill, Senior, deliberately set out to produce by systematically applying empiricist and associationist doctrine to the early education of Mill, Junior. Read the Close-up for more on the deliberate shaping of a philosopher.

▶ CLOSE-UP

Raising a Philosopher

James Mill was not content simply to write about the importance of experience for developing the mind. When his son was born, he was determined to put empiricism into action by filling the empty white paper of his son's mind with as much information as possible. John Stuart Mill experienced (endured might be a better term) an unusual childhood and described it later in a brief yet remarkable autobiography (Mill, 1873/1989).

Mill, Junior, never went to school with other children, but by his twelfth birthday, he could match the intellectual accomplishments of any university graduate. Under his father's stern tutelage, he started learning Greek vocabulary at age three, Latin at age eight, and by the time he was 10 he had read most of the classic Greek and Roman texts, ranging from Aesop's *Fables* to Plato's *Dialogues* to the Greek histories of Herodotus (the "father" of history) to Aristotle's *Rhetoric*. He also devoured art and literature and mastered algebra and geometry. For fun he read books like *Robinson Crusoe*, the *Arabian Nights*, and Shakespeare's history plays. The latter might have reflected a minor rebellion against his father, who "never was a great admirer of Shakespeare, the English idolatry of whom he used to attack with some severity" (Mill, 1873/1989, p. 35).

Young Mill spent the better part of each day in his lessons. His father tutored him directly, but he was also expected to learn a great deal on his own. A typical routine was for Mill to read a portion of some book, take notes, then report on it to his father the following day, during prebreakfast walks through the countryside. Mill later wrote that "my earliest recollections of green fields and wild flowers [were] mingled [with] the account I gave him daily of what I had read the day before" (p. 29). During the walks, his father would also lecture to him on "civilization, government, morality, [and] mental cultivation, which he required me afterwards to restate to him in my own words" (p. 30). The education continued even when Mill, Senior, was doing his own work. Mill admired his father's ability to write while being constantly interrupted by the small boy at the other end of the table. The image painted by Mill is unintentionally humorous:

> What he was himself willing to undergo for the sake of my instruction, may be judged from the fact, that I went through the whole process of preparing my Greek lessons in the same room and at the same table at which he was writing: and as in those days Greek and English Lexicons were not [available], I was forced to have recourse to him for the meaning of every word which I did not know. This incessant interruption he, one of the most impatient of men, submitted to, and wrote under that interruption several volumes of his *History* [of India] and all else that he had to write during those years. (p. 28)

John Stuart Mill is often cited as an example of a brilliant child prodigy, one whose innate intellectual gifts enabled him to learn so much so soon. There is probably some truth in this, but Mill never believed it for a minute. Because he was not allowed to play with other children as he was growing up, he had no point of comparison except for his father. In fact, throughout his childhood he was under the impression, as he put it, that "I was rather backward in my studies, since I always found myself so, in comparison with what my father expected from me" (Mill, 1873/1989, p. 46). When he eventually realized how far advanced he was, he showed the empiricist spirit by crediting it to his experiences rather than to any innate ability. Indeed, he believed his "natural gifts [to be] rather below than above par" (p. 44) and that his advantages over others resulted from their inferior educations. In his self-effacing words, his accomplishments "could not be ascribed to any merit in me, but to the very unusual advantage which had fallen to my lot, of having a father who was able to teach me" (pp. 46–47).

JOHN STUART MILL (1806–1873): ON THE VERGE OF PSYCHOLOGICAL SCIENCE

Mill's adult life was no less extraordinary than his childhood. Following in his father's foot-steps, he supported himself through what amounted to foreign service work with the British East India Company, starting as a clerk at age 17 and gradually rising through the ranks to an executive position; royalties from the sales of his books eventually assured him a comfortable living. In his later years, he was elected to Parliament's House of Commons and served there for three years. Very little else about his life was conventional. Raised by his father to be a "reasoning machine," he became a committed activist for political and social reform by age 15, but then suffered a severe "mental crisis" at age 20. While in a generally "dull state of nerves," he asked himself,

> "Suppose that all your objects in life were realized; that all the changes in institutions and opinions which you are looking forward to, could be completely effected at this very instant: would this be a great joy and happiness to you?" And an irrepressible self-consciousness distinctly answered, "No!" At this my heart sank within me: the whole foundation on which my life was constructed fell down.... I seemed to have nothing to live for. (Mill, 1873/1989, p. 112)

After several lethargic years, Mill emerged from this depression, partly as a result of discovering Wordsworth. The beauty of the Lake poet's words awakened an emotional life in Mill for the first time, showing him there was more to life than cold rationality. His feelings were further developed when he met and fell madly in love with Harriet Taylor, a remarkable woman who combined great beauty with a keen intellect. Unfortunately for Mill, Taylor was married, happily it appears. Despite the impediment, a relationship between the two developed, with Mill even living with the Taylors for a brief time and tagging along on vacations. The alliance was evidently platonic, but it created a minor scandal nonetheless. They finally married in 1851, two years after John Taylor's death. Harriet contributed significantly to Mill's work while she lived, especially his most important political work, *On Liberty*, published in 1858. After she died unexpectedly in 1858, her daughter carried on the intellectual partnership with Mill. Helen Taylor contributed to Mill's classic feminist essay, *The Subjection of Women* (1869), which argued force-

fully and well ahead of its time for equal treatment for women, including the vote. Helen was more of an activist than her mother, helping to create Britain's first women's suffrage organization and recruiting such well-known women as Florence Nightingale into the group (see Figure 2.3).

Mill's politics derived from and contributed to his psychology. As an empiricist, he believed that all knowledge came through experience and that under the proper circumstances, anyone could become knowledgeable. Thus, he favored government support for universal education and was appalled at the traditional English system that favored the landed gentry, an elite minority. At the same time, he was opposed to allowing everyone the vote. Rather, he endorsed a type of meritocracy, in which the vote would be given only to those men and women who had reached a certain level of edu-

Figure 2.3 John Stuart Mill and stepdaughter Helen Taylor, from Mazlish (1975).

cation. In short, he aimed for a society that endeavored to fill everyone's blank slates to the maximum.

Mill's Psychology

Mill's views on psychology can be found scattered in several places, including his *System of Logic* (1843/1987), which will be examined shortly, in the extensive notes that he wrote for a republication of his father's *Analysis*, published in 1869, and in his *Examination of Sir William Hamilton's Philosophy* (1865). His attack on Hamilton is another illustration of the strong connection between Mill's reforming zeal and his psychological views, and places him squarely on the nurture side of the nature-nurture issue. Mill identified Hamilton's rationalism with a belief in innate ideas and argued that the result produced an antireform philosophy. As he put it,

> I have long felt that the prevailing tendency to regard all the marked distinctions of human character as innate, and in the main indelible, and to ignore the irresistible proofs that by far the greater part of those differences, whether between individuals, races, or sexes, are…produced by differences in circumstances, is one of the chief hindrances to the rational treatment of great social questions and one of the greatest stumbling blocks to human improvement. (Mill, 1873/1989, p. 203)

Mill subscribed to the basic tenets of British empiricism/associationism, but he extended the ideas of his father and others (especially Hartley) by using a chemical rather than a mechanical metaphor in his description of how complex ideas are built from simple ones. The earlier quote from James Mill ("Brick is one complex idea, mortar is another complex idea," etc.) portrays the mind as passively accumulating experiences in which the elements combine mechanically to form larger wholes. John Stuart Mill, however, believed the mind to be a more active force in synthesizing our experi-

ences; he argued the holistic position that complex ideas are more than a passive combination of elements:

> When many impressions or ideas are operating in the mind together, there sometimes takes place a process of a similar kind to chemical combination. When impressions have been so often experienced in conjunction that each of them calls up readily and instantaneously the ideas of the whole group, those ideas sometimes melt and coalesce into one another, and appear not several ideas, but one…. [So] it appears to me that the Complex Idea, formed by blending together of several simpler ones, should, when it really appears simple (that is, when the separate elements are not consciously distinguishable in it), be said to *result from*, or be *generated by*, the simple ideas, not to *consist* of them. (Mill, 1843/1987, p. 39–40, italics in the original)

A wall, then, derives from the simple ideas of our experiences, but goes beyond the basic combination of brick and mortar and has properties all its own, just as water has its own properties even though it results from the simple elements of hydrogen and oxygen. To use the phrase later popularized by Gestaltists, the whole is greater than the sum of its parts.

Mill's Logic

In 1843, Mill published *A System of Logic, Ratiocinative and Inductive, Being a Connected View of the Principles of Evidence, and the Methods of Scientific Investigation*. It included some of his arguments about association and mental chemistry, but more important, it outlined a series of methods for trying to determine causality in science. He called them the methods of Agreement, Difference, and Concomitant Variation. Descriptions of these methods remain popular today—in my collection of some two dozen modern research methods texts, Mill is mentioned in the majority of them and his methods are described in some detail in half a dozen.

> ### Key Date
> ### 1843
>
> This year marked the publication of John Stuart Mill's *Logic*, which included the foundational rules for conducting empirical research.
>
> These events also occurred:
>
> - English physicist J. P. Joule determined the amount of work needed to produce a unit of heat
> - The SS *Great Britain*, first propeller-driven ship to cross the Atlantic, was launched
> - Congress granted S. F. B. Morse $30,000 to build first telegraph line (Washington-Baltimore)
> - Charles Dickens published *Martin Chuzzlewit* and *A Christmas Carol*
> - William Wordsworth was appointed English poet laureate
> - Daniel Webster retired as U.S. Secretary of State
> - These people were born:
>   William McKinley, U.S. President
>   Henry James, novelist and brother of psychologist William James
> - These people died:
>   John Trumbull, American painter
>   Noah Webster, American lexicographer

In the **Method of Agreement**, one looks for a common element in several instances of an event. For example, suppose a researcher suspects that a particular gene causes depression. Let X symbolize the proposed cause (the gene) and Y symbolize the effect (depression). To use the method of agreement, the researcher studies a sample of depressed people and looks to see if they all have gene X. If they do, then it can be said that X is *sufficient* for Y to occur: "if X, then Y." Does this mean that X caused Y? Not necessarily, and the example illustrates the problem with induction. Every depressed person in the sample might have X, but it is possible that some yet undiscovered person is depressed but does not have gene X. Also, the coexistence of X and Y does not by itself mean that they are connected. It could be coincidental that the depressed people in the sample all have gene X. The method of agreement can both support some hypothesis and call it into question, but it cannot establish cause by itself.

Neither can the **Method of Difference**, in which one looks for evidence that the absence of an effect is always accompanied by the absence of a proposed cause: "if not X, then not Y." To stay with the depression example, this would mean examining nondepressed people and looking for gene X, hoping *not* to find it. If this occurs, then one can say that gene X is *necessary* in order for depression to occur, because without X (the gene), nobody is Y (depressed). Again, there are problems. A sample of nondepressed people, none of whom have the gene, does not prove the case; there still could be some nondepressed people out there with gene X.

Combined, the methods of agreement and difference have the potential for identifying cause, within the limits of induction (i.e., you will never study every case). Thus, if it could be determined that *every* person with gene X is also depressed, and that *every* person without gene X is not depressed, then it could be concluded that gene X is both sufficient and necessary for depression to occur (i.e., the gene causes depression).

The logic of the methods of agreement and difference underlie the use of the modern-day experimental method in psychology, with the method of agreement corresponding to an experimental group and the method of difference corresponding to a control group (Rosnow & Rosenthal, 1993). Thus, a hypothetical experiment on the effect of gene (X) on depression (Y) would involve identifying two equal groups and implanting the gene in the experimental group but not in the control group. If everyone in the experimental group comes down with depression (if X, then Y), *and* if nobody in the control group gets depressed (if not X, then not Y), then you have evidence that X causes Y (again, within the limits of the sample for your study). Of course, you would have a hard time finding volunteers for this study, an ethical limitation that Mill that recognized and, along with a concern about precision of measurement and control, made him skeptical of psychology becoming rigorously experimental:

> ...Are the laws of the formation of character [i.e., personality] susceptible of a satisfactory investigation by the method of experimentation? Evidently not, because, even if we suppose unlimited power of varying the experiment (which is abstractly possible, but no one but [a] despot has that power...), a still more essential condition is wanting—the power of performing any of the experiments with scientific accuracy. (Mill, 1843/1987, pp. 50–51)

Mill's third method, that of **Concomitant Variation**, is reminiscent of Hume and underlies today's correlational method. Using this approach, one looks to see if changes in X are associated with predictable changes in Y. The method is especially useful when either X or Y

(or both) will be found in every person to some degree. For example, everyone gets at least some exercise and everyone is more or less healthy. Using the method of concomitant variation, a researcher could see if those who exercise a great deal are healthier than those who exercise infrequently.

Unlike any of the philosophers considered thus far, John Stuart Mill did not attempt to write anything like an essay on human understanding (Locke), a treatise on human knowledge (Berkeley) or human nature (Hume), a series of observations on man (Hartley) or an analysis of the mind (his father). That is, none of his books can be pointed to and labeled as "J. S. Mill's psychology." Because he saw himself above all as a political and economic philosopher, this is not too surprising. Yet Mill is as important for modern psychology as any of those philosophers who did write a "psychology." He brought British associationism to its zenith and he provided an analysis of scientific thinking that guides psychological research to this day. He was a key transition figure in the shift from the philosophy of the mind to the science of the mind.

RATIONALIST RESPONSES TO EMPIRICISM

Except for the section on Descartes, this chapter has focused on British empiricist and associationist philosophy. This makes sense: American psychologists today, especially those who lean toward some version of behaviorism, view John Locke and his intellectual descendants as kindred spirits. But other strong voices were heard during the times that have been described above, and those voices also resonate with aspects of modern psychology. Two German philosophers make a notable contrast to British empiricism/associationism. Gottfried Leibnitz was a contemporary of Locke and responded to Locke's *Essay Concerning Human Understanding* with his own *New Essays on*

Human Understanding, published posthumously in 1765. Immanuel Kant (1724–1804) lived during the same time as Hume and Hartley and wrote in response to them (especially Hume).

GOTTFRIED WILHELM LEIBNITZ (1646–1716)

Leibnitz had a remarkably wide range of interests, from politics to mathematics to engineering to alchemy to philosophy. As a mathematician, he is best known as the coinventor (with Newton) of calculus. His importance for psychology rests with his reply to Locke, his approach to the mind-body problem, and his "monadology." He was a great admirer of Locke, agreeing that experience is essential to the formation of knowledge. However, he disagreed with Locke's "mind = white paper" metaphor, proposing instead that the mind be seen as analogous to veined marble (Leibnitz, 1765/1982). The sculptor can take a block of marble and shape it in many different ways, but the way the marble is veined limits the number of shapes that are possible. The veins in essence represent the innate properties of the marble, to be revealed by the artist's skill. Similarly, according to Leibnitz, the mind has innate properties that help determine and shape the effects of experience. The innate properties, such as reason, enable the individual to arrive at what Leibnitz called "necessary truths," truths that are proven with reason and logic and not by direct experience. The fundamental principles of mathematics (e.g., three sides of a triangle will always add up to 180°) are examples of necessary truths. In response to the empiricist claim that there was nothing in the intellect that was not first in the senses, Leibnitz replied, "except the intellect itself." Like Descartes, Leibnitz agreed that animals lacked the innate properties found in humans, and thus could be considered pure "empirics."

On the mind-body question, Leibnitz could not accept the Cartesian notion of direct and mutual influence, because it led inevitably to a search for the manner of interaction and resulted in what Leibnitz considered to be a fruitless hunt for things like pineal glands. Instead, he proposed that mind and body work in parallel to each other, kept in synchrony by the hand of God. He illustrated his **parallelism** with a metaphor of two clocks that are constructed to be in perfect harmony. Like mind and body, they operate independently of each other, but in agreement. By implication, parallelism legitimizes the separate study of mental and physical events, thus providing a philosophical basis for "the eventual emergence of psychology as a separate science as distinct from physiology as a separate science" (Klein, 1970, p. 353).

The elements of both physical and mental reality were called **monads** by Leibnitz. These were infinite in number and more like energy forces than individual material atoms. They were said to be arranged in a hierarchy, from rational to sentient to simple. Rational monads, according to Leibnitz, form the essence of the human mind, sentient monads are found in all living beings that were not human, and simple monads make up physical reality. Rational monads account for consciousness, but Leibnitz believed that awareness was not an all-or-nothing affair. Rather, he proposed a continuum of awareness, thus laying a foundation for two important developments in psychology. First, the continuum implies a level of unawareness, an idea similar to the concept of the unconscious, which was later to become the centerpiece of Freud's theories. Leibnitz distinguished between what he called apperception, perception, and petites perceptions. **Apperception**, a term he coined, was the highest level of awareness, in which we focus our full attention on some information and apprehend it fully. Perception is an awareness of something, but it is not as sharp as in apperception. **Petites perceptions** were below the level of awareness, but ultimately essential for enabling higher levels of perception to occur. To illustrate the latter, Leibnitz used the example of an ocean wave or a waterfall. Petite perceptions are created by individual drops of water, which we never hear. Yet all of the drops, taken together, are necessary in order for us to perceive or apperceive the larger reality of the ocean wave.

The second implication of the proposal about different levels of awareness is that there must exist points on the continuum of consciousness where one goes from unawareness to awareness; these points can be called **thresholds** and as we will learn in the next chapter, identifying and measuring thresholds became an important feature of the earliest experiments in psychology.

IMMANUEL KANT (1724–1804)

In his role as a diplomat, Leibnitz traveled throughout Europe. In contrast, Immanuel Kant evidently never ventured more than 40 miles from his home in the eastern German city of Königsberg. He was born there, went to school there, and eventually taught at the university there. Despite the apparent provincialism, Kant was a towering intellect in eighteenth-century German philosophy, doing for the rationalist view what Leibnitz had done in the seventeenth century. Kant is best known to psychologists for three books published in his later years, *Critique of Pure Reason* (1781/1965), *Critique of Practical Reason* (1788/1959), and *Critique of Judgment* (1790/1952).

Kant agreed with the empiricists that our knowledge is built from experience, but like Leibnitz, he argued that the more important question was how the process occurs. That is, he wondered how experience itself was possible, and he concluded that it required the existence of some a priori (prior to experience) knowledge that helps shape the experiences we have. For instance, Kant pointed out that whenever we experience events in the world, we organize them with reference to space and time. Thus, we water the garden, which occupies space, and which takes X amount of time to complete. Our understanding of the concept "water the garden" is not possible without the a priori knowledge of space and time. The concepts of space

and time, then, we know "intuitively," according to Kant; we don't have to "learn" about the concepts. To contrast Hume's view that we can never be certain of causality, Kant argued that the mind inevitably thinks in terms of cause and effect—everyone's experience of the world is that it operates according to causal laws (milk poured on earth always goes down). Like space and time, cause and effect were considered by Kant to be innate properties of the mind.

A final point about Kant is that he argued that psychology could never become a science like the physical sciences. He pointed out that compared with physical objects, mental phenomena could not be observed directly, nor could they be defined or measured with the precision of mathematics. As we shall learn, when German psychologists such as Wilhelm Wundt declared psychology a science in the nineteenth century, they had to specifically disavow their countryman's contentions about the feasibility of the endeavor.

IN PERSPECTIVE

This chapter only scratches the surface of psychology's "long past." Nonetheless, you should emerge from your reading of this material with a basic understanding of some of the philosophical underpinnings of modern psychology. Furthermore, you should be starting to develop a sense of the continuity of ideas in our discipline's history. Psychology did not just pop out of the ground in the late nineteenth century. Rather, psychology's founders were wrestling with the same issues that concerned the people highlighted in this chapter. They chose to attack the questions from a slightly different angle than the philosophers, that of direct experimentation, but they were trying to answer the same questions: How do we accumulate our knowledge of the world? How is the mind organized? How do the senses work? Is any of our knowledge built in to the system (i.e., innate)? The founders of nineteenth-century psychology also had an ever-increasing knowledge of how the brain and the rest of the nervous system worked and they were beginning to develop objective methods for studying the mind. These developments in physiology and methods you are about to encounter in Chapter 3.

Before closing this chapter, however, there is an important point to be made about presentism. From the standpoint of the late twentieth century, knowing that psychology has evolved into a successful scientific discipline, it is easy to look back at the early philosophers and wonder why they failed to take what appears to be an easy step—the one from careful observations and a close logical analysis of some mental phenomenon to the experimental investigation of it. That is, when we first read of people like Descartes and Locke and Mill, we tend to see them as gradually approaching but not quite reaching the "holy grail" of scientific psychology. It is a serious mistake, however, to think of these individuals as somehow falling short. In fact, they were clearly the best and the brightest of their day, going far beyond their peers in the brilliance of their insights. The proper way to view the philosophers in this chapter is to think of them as people living in the context of their times and grappling as best they could with the issues of their day. That these philosophers wrestled with the same questions that exist today is not an indication of steady progress upward from then to now, but of the universality of the issues. It is futile to criticize them for not seeing what others saw later on—after all, to borrow from Isaac Newton's famous quote, the others were standing on their shoulders.

SUMMARY

A Long Past

- The Ebbinghaus statement that psychology has a long past but a short history is a reminder that the issues of concern to psychologists have been addressed by serious thinkers for thousands of years, even though psychology as a self-defined discipline is just over 100 years old. The "new psychology" that emerged in the late nineteenth century differed from philosophy in that the questions about human behavior and mental life were taken into the laboratory for the first time.

Descartes and the Beginnings of Modern Philosophy and Science

- Descartes lived during the end of the Renaissance and during years of great advances in science and technology. It was a time when the authority of the Church and of Aristotle came to be questioned, by Galileo's replacement of a geocentric model of the universe with a heliocentric model, for example. Descartes' life also overlapped that of Sir Francis Bacon, who argued for an inductive approach to science.

- Descartes was a rationalist, believing that the way to true knowledge was through the systematic use of his reasoning abilities. Because he believed that some truths were universal and could be arrived at through reason and without the necessity of sensory experience, he was also a nativist. In addition, he was a dualist and an interactionist, believing that mind and body were distinct essences, but that they had direct influence on each other.

- To explain mind-body interactionism, Descartes developed a model of nervous system activity and was the first person to describe reflex action. His model of bodily action was a mechanistic one—the body was like a machine. According to the Cartesian dichotomy, animals are pure machines, but humans have a rational mind (soul) to complement their machinelike bodies.

The British Empiricist Argument and the Associationists

- The founder of British empiricism was John Locke, who rejected the nativist belief in innate ideas and argued that the mind was like a blank piece of paper, to be written on by our experiences. Ideas that result from our experiences have two sources: sensation and reflection. Locke used an atomistic model, assuming that complex ideas were built from the basic elements of simple ideas. Primary qualities (e.g., extension) exist independently of the perceiver, but secondary qualities (e.g., the perception of color) depend on perception. Locke's beliefs led him to recommend that parents take an active role in educating their children.

- George Berkeley wrote a detailed analysis of visual perception based on empiricist arguments, in the process describing visual phenomena such as convergence, accommodation, and the effects of the inverted retinal image. He rejected Locke's primary/secondary qualities distinction, and to counter materialism, he proposed (subjective idealism) that we cannot be sure of the reality of objects except through our belief in God, the Permanent Perceiver.

- David Hume was an empiricist/associationist known for his distinction between impressions, which result from sensation, and ideas, which he said were faint copies of impressions. He also identified the rules of association as resemblance, contiguity, and cause/effect. He believed that we cannot know true causality, only that certain events occur together regularly.

- David Hartley is considered the founder of associationism because of his systematic attempt to summarize all that was known about it and his argument that the essence of association was contiguity (both spatial and temporal) and repetition. He developed a model of nervous system action based on the Newtonian concept of vibrations, and his position on the mind-body issue was that of parallelism.

- John Stuart Mill, a child prodigy, was the leading British philosopher of the nineteenth century. Compared with others (including his father, the empiricist philosopher James Mill) who described the mind in mechanical, building-block terms, J. S. Mill used a more holistic chemical metaphor: complex ideas are greater than the sum of simple ideas. Mill analyzed the logic of science, and described three methods for trying to arrive at scientific truth: the method of agreement, the method of difference, which underlie today's experimental method, and the method of concomitant variation, similar to the modern correlational method.

Rationalist Responses to Empiricism

- Gottfried Leibnitz challenged Locke's white paper analogy and said the mind was more like veined marble, with the veins being analogous to the innate ideas and abilities that shape our experiences. He also challenged Descartes' interactionism, arguing for a parallelism and using the metaphor of two synchronous clocks to make his point. His monadology provided a basis for the concepts of the unconscious and sensory thresholds.

- Immanuel Kant recognized the importance of our experiences for developing our understanding of the world, but argued that experience itself was not possible without a basis in some a priori knowledge to provide the framework for our experiences. Kant believed that psychology could not achieve the status of a science.

FURTHER READING

VROOMAN, J. R. (1970). *René Descartes: A biography.* New York: G. P. Putnam's Sons.

A relatively brief and very readable biography of Descartes, especially descriptive of the times in which Descartes lived; provides a good summary of Descartes' ideas, and how he developed them from his varied experiences.

BOORSTIN, D. J. (1983). *The discoverers.* New York: Vintage Books.

Includes substantial treatment of many of the scientists briefly mentioned in this chapter, including Vesalius, *Galileo, Bacon, Boyle, Newton, and Harvey, written in a style that makes Boorstin one of the more popular modern historians.*

MILL, J. S. (1989). *Autobiography.* London: Penguin Books. (Original work published 1873)

Fascinating account of Mill's childhood and relationship with his father, his mental crisis and how he overcame it, his relationship with Harriet Taylor, and the development of his ideas; can be occasionally confusing without some knowledge of British political history during Mill's time.

3

THE NEUROPHYSIOLOGICAL CONTEXT

▼
_____

The entire doctrine of [phrenology] is contained in two fundamental propositions, of which the first is, that understanding resides exclusively in the brain, and the second, that each particular faculty of the understanding is provided in the brain with an organ proper to itself.

Now, of these two propositions, there is certainly nothing new in the first one, and perhaps nothing true in the second one.

Pierre Flourens, 1846

▼
_____

Preview

Partitioning the philosophical antecedents to psychology and the neurophysiological background into two chapters implies the presence of two nonoverlapping paths that eventually merged to form the new psychology of the late nineteenth century. There is a grain of truth to this—the British empiricists did not spend their time cutting into spinal cords or stimulating nerves connected to frogs legs, and the scientists to be encountered in this chapter did not write long philosophical treatises on "human understanding." But the distinction between philosophical and physiological antecedents to psychology is somewhat artificial, brought about by the decisions made when structuring a textbook. In fact, developments in philosophy and in the natural sciences proceeded apace, especially in the eighteenth and nineteenth centuries. The physiologists and other natural scientists were deeply concerned with philosophical issues, especially the epistemological questions about human understanding and the problem of the relationship between mental and physical reality (the mind-body problem). In turn, philosophers were well aware of, and in some instances contributed to, developments in physiology (e.g., Berkeley's work on vision), and they proposed theories that led naturally to physiological research.

This chapter will focus on nineteenth- and early twentieth-century studies of the nature and functioning of the nervous system. In particular, we will examine research that explored (a) the physiology of basic sensory-motor processes and reflexes, (b) the issue of whether specific functions could be "localized" in different areas of the brain, and (c) the nature of the basic unit of the nervous system, the neuron. The chapter closes with a description of Karl Lashley's research on the role of the cortex in learning. Lashley was the twentieth century's first prominent physiological psychologist. The Original Source Excerpt is from Broca's famous case history of "Tan." This case helped establish the clinical method of determining brain function.

HEROIC SCIENCE IN THE AGE OF ENLIGHTENMENT

As discussed in the last chapter, the years marking the end of the Renaissance were characterized by a gradual change from a reliance on authority as the source of truth to a reliance on scientific methodology and human reasoning powers. Bacon, Galileo, Harvey, and Descartes exemplified this shift in the beginning of the seventeenth century. Sir Isaac Newton solidified the change in the second half of the century. With the publication of his *Principia Mathematica* in 1687, serious thinkers began to take for granted the idea that objective truth could be gained through the methods of science and the unbiased use of reason. Because science and reason came to be seen as the only sure way to shed light on the darkness of ignorance, this period became known as the **Enlightenment** (Appleby, Hunt, & Jacob, 1994). Scientists like Newton became heroic figures, searching impersonally for objective truth about the universe by applying scientific methodology to its study. Newton's influence on the philosophers was mentioned in the last chapter—Newton's analysis of light into basic components and his theory of gravitation influenced the British empiricists, who tried to produce a similar analysis of the mind and thought of association as a force analogous to gravity.

Enlightenment thinking even spread into the political arena. America's founding fathers were passionate and knowledgeable about science, and Benjamin Franklin made substantial contributions to the theory of electricity, including the invention of the lightning rod. The Constitution itself borrowed from the Newtonian concept of equilibrium when developing the concept of a balance of powers among the executive, legislative, and judicial elements of government (Cohen, 1995).

The Enlightenment reached its height of influence in the second half of the eighteenth century, but its ideals remained strong throughout the nineteenth century, and well into the twentieth. By the early nineteenth century, the faith in science seemed to be paying dividends in the form of the kinds of technological innovations that eventually produced the Industrial Revolution. Thus, science seemed to lead inevitably to progress and scientists were viewed as being totally objective, simply looking for the truth without imposing their values in any way, and improving society through the inventions that derived from their science. It wasn't until such technological innovations as the poison gas that "efficiently" reduced the populations of concentration camps and the atom bomb that serious questions began to be raised about whether science could possibly be totally objective and value-free and whether scientific discoveries necessarily meant progress. Nonetheless, during the period when the idea of a scientific approach to psychology began to take shape in the minds of such philosophers as the British empiricists, the model of scientist as hero held sway. If scientific thinking and human reason could enlighten the world about physics and chemistry, why not biology? If biology, why not psychology?

In the middle of the nineteenth century, scientific psychology evolved out of the philosophical questions examined in Chapter 2 and research on the nervous system to be described in this chapter. Physiologists trying to "shed light" on how the senses and the nervous system actually worked developed methods and made discoveries that were directly relevant to the epistemological questions about the nature and origins of human knowledge being raised by philosophers such as John Stuart Mill. This dynamic convergence of philosophy and physiological science created an atmosphere out of which a "scientific" psychology was perhaps inevitable.

SENSORY PHYSIOLOGY

From the time of Descartes, scientists had been intrigued by the nature of nervous system activity. Most of the advances resulted from the medical community trying to deal with the problem of brain and nervous system damage, which was quite common in the context of two European wars in the middle of the eighteenth century and both the American and French revolutions during the second half of that century. At a time long before the development of antiseptic surgical procedures and antibiotic drugs, the vast majority of those suffering head wounds died from infection. Many of those who lived, however, became case studies that increased our knowledge of the brain and nervous system.

One issue of interest was whether the brain was the center of consciousness and the controller of voluntary action. Decapitated soldiers who nonetheless showed arm and leg movements raised questions about how soon consciousness left the body after death and where consciousness was localized. The problem was directly investigated with reference to executions that used the invention of noted French physician Joseph Ignace Guillotin. The device, which now bears his name, was said to be a marvelous improvement over large hairy men

with axes, who sometimes required several tries before completing their gruesome task of separating head from body. Although the guillotine was clean and quick and therefore considered humane, bodies continued to twitch for a brief time after execution. Eye movements and quivering facial muscles could also be seen. Did some level of awareness remain after a beheading? If so, then perhaps the instrument was not so humane after all. The problem was investigated in the early nineteenth century by Theodor Bischoff, who arranged to conduct tests on the decapitated head of a criminal immediately after execution. If consciousness remained, Bischoff reasoned, then the head should react predictably to having fingers thrust toward its eyes, having smelling salts placed under its nose, and having the word "Pardon!" spoken in its ear. Bischoff tried all of these tests, but the unfortunate head showed no reaction (Fearing, 1930). He concluded that consciousness ended with the moment of execution, thereby reinforcing the theory that consciousness resides in the brain, while at the same time reassuring investors in guillotines. The muscle twitches that occurred after death were therefore involuntary actions unrelated to consciousness. The question of why they occurred at all still remained, however, resulting in intensive research into the nature of basic reflex action and the role of the spinal cord in these movements.

REFLEX ACTION

Prior to the nineteenth century, the most significant contribution to the study of reflexes was made by Robert Whytt (1714–1766) (pronounced "White") of Edinburgh, Scotland. The leading neurologist of his day, Whytt is known primarily by historians of psychology for his research into the physiology of the involuntary reflex, but he is also justly famous in the history of pediatric medicine for being the first person to adequately describe tuberculous meningitis (Radbill, 1972). With regard to reflexes, in

1751 Whytt published *The Vital and Other Involuntary Motions of Animals*,[1] the outcome of years of research on the role of the spinal cord in mediating reflex action. It was the first extensive treatment of reflexes to be based on experimental research (Fearing, 1930). Studying decapitated animals (mainly frogs) Whytt was able to show that leg muscles responded in predictable ways to physical stimulation. Pinching the leg of a headless frog produced a reliable muscle contraction. On the other hand, if the frog was deprived of its spinal cord, these "involuntary motions" failed to occur. Hence, Whytt demonstrated that the spinal cord played a vital role in reflexive behavior.

Whytt distinguished between voluntary and involuntary actions, the former under the control of the will, with the action originating in and requiring an intact brain, and the latter controlled through the spinal cord. In between voluntary and involuntary control, and serving to link them, was habit formation. Thus, actions that begin as voluntary, and under the deliberate control of the will, become similar to reflexes when they have been sufficiently practiced. As Whytt put it,

> We not only acquire, through custom and habit, a faculty of performing certain motions with greater ease than we are wont to do them, but also, in proportion as this facility is increased, we become less sensible of any share or concern the mind has in them. (cited in Fearing, 1930, p. 79)

Whytt also pointed out that a consequence of the formation of habits was that the mere idea of a stimulus was sometimes sufficient to bring about a response. In a passage that will make you think of Ivan Pavlov (Chapter 10), Whytt illustrated the point with two everyday examples of what would eventually come to be called conditioned reflexes: "Thus the sight, or even the recalled idea of grateful food, causes an uncommon flow of spittle into the mouth of a hungry person; and the seeing of a lemon cut produces the same effect in many people" (cited in Fearing, 1930, p. 80).

The existence of the kinds of reflexes documented by Whytt demands that a distinction be made between the sensory and motor components of a reaction, which in turn implies that some nerves may be for the purpose of conveying sensory information and others designed to pass messages along to the muscles, telling them to move. This distinction between sensory and motor nerves became established through the work of two scientists working at about the same time in different countries.

THE BELL-MAGENDIE LAW

As you recall from Chapter 1, a "multiple" refers to a case in which two or more people make the same discovery during the same historical era, but do so independently of each other. E. G. Boring (1950) used the concept to support his idea that the zeitgeist helped to determine the activities and ways of thinking of scientists during a particular historical era. The Bell-Magendie law is sometimes used as an example of a multiple—two scientists, working in different laboratories (different countries in this case) at about the same time and neither aware of the other's research, arrive at the same results. The situation was not quite that simple in the case of Bell and Magendie, however, and during the years following their codiscovery, there was a nasty fight over priority. The judgment of history is that Magendie should have been credited with the discovery;

---

[1] Whytt was a contemporary of David Hartley and published his book just two years after Hartley's *Observations of Man* appeared. You will recall that Hartley went beyond a philosophical treatment and attempted to explain the nervous system by appealing to "vibrations." Whytt does not seem to have been directly influenced by Hartley, but the fact that both men were concerned with the nervous system indicates the importance of the topic to intellectuals of the day.

his research was more systematic and he published it in the public forum of a journal. Bell's research, while occurring a few years earlier than Magendie's, was not conclusive and he published it in a private pamphlet with limited distribution. That Bell's name became paired with Magendie's is more of a tribute to the public clamoring of the politically influential Bell and his equally vociferous friends than to the quality of his research.

François Magendie (1783–1855) grew up during the turbulent years of the French Revolution, the son of a surgeon who was a politically active "Republican" in the efforts to overthrow the French monarchy. Lacking much in the way of formal education, François used his father's influence to become an apprentice at a Paris hospital, where, at the tender age of 16, he was entrusted with the task of doing anatomical dissections (Grmek, 1972). After becoming a medical student and completing a degree in 1808, he quickly earned a reputation as a gifted scientist who distrusted theorizing in favor of inductively collecting "facts." This Baconian attitude he once described in this way: "I compare myself to a ragpicker: with my spiked stick in my hand and my basket on my back, I traverse the field of science and gather what I find" (cited in Grmek, 1972, p. 7).

In 1822, Magendie published a three-page article that summarized the results of a study on the posterior and anterior roots of the spinal cord. From his earlier dissections he knew that nerve fibers exited the spinal cord in pairs before joining together, with one type of fiber, the posterior root, closer to the surface of the skin, and the other (anterior root) closer to the interior of the body. Different structures suggest different functions, and Magendie's research aimed at identifying these functions.

Using a six-week old dog as the subject, Magendie exposed its spinal cord and cut the posterior fibers (i.e., those closer to the surface) while leaving the spinal cord intact. He sutured up the wound and observed the animal after it recovered. As he described it,

...I did not know what would result from this operation.... At first I believed the limb corresponding to the cut nerves to be completely paralyzed; it was insensitive to pricking and the hardest pressures and, further, it seemed immobile; but soon, to my very great surprise, I clearly saw it move, although sensibility remained completely absent. (Magendie, 1822/1965, p. 20)

Hence, the posterior roots controlled sensation. When destroyed, the animal could still move the limb, but had no sensation in it. Next, Magendie severed the anterior root in another animal, a task that required all of his considerable surgical skills. Because the anterior root lies below the posterior one, it is difficult to get to the former without damaging the latter. Nonetheless, Magendie worked out a successful procedure and managed to sever an anterior root cleanly (Bell, on the other hand, was never able to accomplish this). The results were clear: "there could be no doubt whatsoever; the limb was completely immobile and flaccid, although it retained an unequivocal sensibility" (Magendie, 1822/1965, p. 20). In summary, then, Magendie's finding, now known as the **Bell-Magendie law**, was that the posterior roots of the spinal cord controlled sensation, while anterior roots controlled motor responses. This was a major discovery, for it provided anatomical foundation for further study of the two sides of the reflex: sensation and movement. Furthermore, the distinction implied that nerves send messages in a single direction and there were different sensory and motor tracts within the spinal cord and perhaps different sensory and motor regions within the brain.

As for Sir Charles Bell (1774–1842), his *Idea of a New Anatomy of the Brain: Submitted for the Observation of His Friends* had been written 11 years prior to the publication of Magendie's work, but it had been sent privately to no more than 100 colleagues. Bell was a prominent English anatomist with influential friends, however, and together they launched a campaign against Magendie when the latter's work was published, accusing the Frenchman of everything from unnecessary replication of Bell's original finding to animal cruelty. Bell went as far as to alter the wording of some of his earlier work and republish it to make it appear that he had anticipated Magendie by a decade (Gallistel, 1981). Yet Magendie was unaware of Bell's work with "stunned rabbits," which was not nearly as decisive as Magendie's research. Bell had severed the more accessible posterior root and observed a paralysis of a muscle in the rabbit's back; he then found that touching the anterior root with his knife produced a convulsion in that same muscle.

Magendie, personally affronted by the attacks from across the English Channel, recognized the value of Bell's research once he learned of it, but refused to concede priority for discovering the critical distinction between sensory and motor functions. In particular, while acknowledging Bell's priority concerning the strategy of segregating the spinal roots and the discovery that the anterior root influenced "muscular contractility" more than the posterior root did, Magendie vigorously asserted that "as for having established that these roots have distinct properties, distinct functions, that the anterior ones control movement, and posterior ones sensation, *this discovery belongs to me*" (cited in Grmek, 1972, italics added).

THE SPECIFIC ENERGIES OF NERVES

Another feature of Bell's 1811 pamphlet was his argument that different sensory nerves have different "qualities." Thus, "an impression made on two different nerves of sense, though with the same instrument, will produce two distinct sensations" (Bell, 1811/1965, p. 24). As an example, Bell pointed to the "papillae" on the tongue, some of which convey the sense of

taste, others the sense of touch. When touching these latter papillae with a sharp steel pin, the resulting sensation is one of "sharpness." When touching one of the taste papillae with the same pin, however, the resulting sensation is one of a "metallic taste." Similarly, if two different types of stimuli affect a single type of nerve, then the sensation experienced will be determined by the type of sensory nerve stimulated. Thus, light waves stimulate the optic nerve to produce a visual sensation, but pressing on the side of the eyeball also results in the sensation of a flash of light and, according to Bell, cataract patients often reported seeing a "spark of fire" when the surgeon's needle pierced their eye.

This idea of Bell's eventually developed into the **doctrine of the specific energies of nerves**, and although Bell's 1811 paper once again had chronological priority, credit went elsewhere, this time to the leading German physiologist of the first half of the nineteenth century, Johannes Müller (1801–1858). Müller, whose frenetic pace of work alternated with several long periods of severe depression,[2] was the first person ever named a professor of "physiology" at the University of Berlin, Germany's premier university. Müller elaborated on the specific energies doctrine and developed it more fully than Bell. In addition to making the point about different sensory qualities, Müller argued that in perception, we are not directly aware of the external world; rather we are only aware of the action of our nervous system, which conveys information of the world to us. Thus, our knowledge of the world is filtered through the physiology of the nervous system.

The doctrine of specific energies of nerves eventually became associated more with Müller than with Bell, mainly because Müller named it as such and presented it as a series of

---

[2] Müller believed that his status had declined after his famous *Handbook* was published and by the mid-1850s, he was convinced that his years as a productive scientist were over. This plunged him into his final depression, and few of his friends believed that his death in 1858 was anything but a deliberate overdose of morphine (Steudel, 1972).

10 related principles in his massive (eight books totaling more than 1600 pages) *Handbook of Human Physiology*, which first appeared in 1840. This was the authoritative physiology text of the mid-nineteenth century, and its stature guaranteed that Müller's name, not Bell's, would become attached to the doctrine (Boring, 1950).

HELMHOLTZ: THE PHYSIOLOGIST'S PHYSIOLOGIST

If Müller was the leading German physiologist of the first half of the nineteenth century, the honor for the second half goes to one of his followers, Hermann von Helmholtz (1821–1894). Shortly after he died, Helmholtz was eulogized by Carl Stumpf, another well-known German physiologist, as the person most responsible for building the "bridge between physiology and psychology that thousands of workers today go back and forth upon" (cited in Turner, 1972). Helmholtz became *the* nineteenth-century authority on the sensory systems for vision and audition, developing theories still considered to be at least partly correct. He also provided a simple demonstration of nerve impulse speed that paved the way for one of psychology's most enduring methods, reaction time. And despite accomplishing more than any other nineteenth-century physiologist, his true love actually was physics, to which he also made original contributions!

Helmholtz was born in 1821 into a family of modest means (his father was a teacher) in Potsdam, Germany. He quickly emerged as an academic star at the local gymnasium (high school), where he developed his lifelong love for physics, but financial straits prevented him from attending a University. The government was offering full scholarships for students to attend the medical school in Berlin, however, and Helmholtz jumped at the opportunity, even though it meant committing himself to eight years of service in the army's medical corps (after completing five years of schooling).

He left for Berlin in 1838, where he completed the five-year program in four years. While enrolled at the medical institute, he also studied informally at the University of Berlin with the great Johannes Müller. Helmholtz quickly moved into Müller's inner circle and developed lifelong friendships with three other students destined to become leaders in the world of German science: Ernst Brücke, Emil du Bois Reymond, and Karl Ludwig.

Although he was the leading physiologist of his day, Müller was already being challenged by his students in the 1840s, especially on the issue of **vitalism** versus **materialism**. Müller believed that in addition to the physical and chemical components that made up physiological systems, there also existed a "vital force," or a life force that could not be reduced further. It was an idea with deep roots and obvious theological connotations. Opposed to vitalism was a position that also had a long history but was becoming especially prominent in the nineteenth century—materialism (see Chapter 2, pp. 39–41). According to this view, the vital force was a myth: physical matter was the only reality and all living organisms could be reduced to physical, mechanical, and chemical processes that would eventually be understood by applying scientific methods. The movement was naturally congenial to the advances in science that occurred during this time. Müller's students, joined by Helmholtz, were committed materialists with all the enthusiasm and confidence of youth (all were under 30), and all made important contributions to physiology that supported the materialist position.

After finishing his medical degree in 1842, Helmholtz began his stint as an army surgeon, while at the same time maintaining his Berlin connections. It was during this time that he made the first of his lasting contributions, one that simultaneously reflected his love of physics and his desire to support a materialist physiology. It was a paper on the mathematical basis for a law of **conservation of energy**, first read to a scientific society in Berlin in 1847, then

published privately after being rejected for publication by a leading journal (Warren, 1984).
Helmholtz is today considered one of the originators of this important principle in physics,
which states that the total energy within a system remains constant, even if changes occur
within the system. For Helmholtz, the principle
was an important weapon in the fight against
vitalism. Thus, he argued that body heat and
muscle force could be explained by chemical
energy accumulated during the oxidation
process that accompanied digestion—there was
no need to propose a special life force that
could create its own energy. He supported his
argument by showing that muscle contractions
generated measurable amounts of heat (Turner,
1972).

Measuring the Speed of Neural Impulses

After being released early from his army commitment, Helmholtz was hired by the University
of Königsberg in 1849, where he stayed for six
years.[3] It was during this time that he completed a series of studies that had important implications for the study of the reflex and that laid the
groundwork for the reaction time methodology
that would become a key feature of every laboratory of experimental psychology.

When Helmholtz began studying the problem of nerve impulse speed in the early 1850s,
it was already known that the impulse had
electrical properties. A theory of electricity had
arisen in the eighteenth century, and several
scientists, including Helmholtz's materialist
friend du Bois Reymond, had demonstrated
that nerves could conduct electricity in order to
make muscles twitch. Authorities such as
Müller believed that the nerve impulse might
be instantaneous or at the very least that it
occurred too rapidly to be measured, but a
study by du Bois Reymond in 1850 suggested

that the impulse was propagated along the
nerve by an electrochemical process that would
be slower than a pure electrical transmission. If
so, then perhaps impulse speed could be measured. Helmholtz succeeded in doing so by isolating a motor nerve and a connected muscle
from the leg of a frog. He then stimulated the
nerve electrically at several different distances
from the muscle and recorded the time from
stimulus to response. Knowing distance and
time, the calculation of rate was easy (rate =
distance/time). It averaged about 90 feet per
second (or just over 60 miles per hour), quite
sluggish compared with estimates that placed it
near the speed of light. Helmholtz also estimated impulse speed in sensory nerves by showing
that human subjects took longer to respond to
stimulation of their toe than their thigh.

For Helmholtz, the implications of the
research were obvious. Here was more evidence that vitalism was wrong and materialism
was right. Vitalists argued that the conscious
decision to move an arm and the arm's movement were simultaneous, but Helmholtz had
shown that the event took a measurable
amount of time, a conclusion consistent with
the idea that nervous action involved the
movement of physical, material entities. For
Helmholtz, this conclusion was enough: he was
not interested in any further applications of the
concept of reaction time. It would be for others
to develop the idea into a technique for measuring the time of various mental activities.
That story will be told in the next chapter.

Helmholtz on Vision and Audition

During the Königsberg years, Helmholtz also
began investigating the physiology of vision
and audition and invented a tool that made
him famous among eye doctors: the **ophthalmoscope**, a device for directly examining the

---

[3] Having well-connected friends never hurts. The position at Königsberg opened when Brücke,
one of Helmholtz's Berlin friends, left a position there to take one at Vienna (where his prize student would be Sigmund Freud). The Königsberg job was first offered to du Bois Reymond, who
turned it down but apparently recommended Helmholtz, who accepted (Turner, 1972).

retina. His research on vision culminated in a massive three-volume *Handbook of Physiological Optics*, published over an 11-year period, from 1856 to 1867. During this same time he moved twice, first to Bonn and then to Heidelberg, where he spent 13 of the most productive years of his life (1858–1871).

Helmholtz is perhaps best remembered for elaborating a theory of color vision first proposed by the English scientist Thomas Young at the beginning of the nineteenth century. Sometimes considered another example of a multiple, it has come to be called either the Young-Helmholtz theory or as Helmholtz called it, the **trichromatic theory**. It is based on the facts of color-matching experiments. If you shine a red spotlight against a wall and then shine a green light so that it overlaps the red, the colors in the area of overlap will "mix" and be seen as a new color, yellow. Both Young and Helmholtz demonstrated that by mixing various combinations of three colors together, red, green, and blue, the resulting color could be made to match any other single color. On this basis, they concluded that the eye must contain three different kinds of color receptors, one for each of these so-called primary colors, red, green, and blue (or violet). Incoming light of a particular wavelength was said to stimulate these receptors to different degrees, resulting in the perception of a certain color. In Helmholtz's words,

> ...Suppose that the colors of the spectrum are plotted horizontally in Fig. [3.1] in their natural sequence, from red to violet, the three curves may be taken to indicate something like the degree of excitation of the three kinds of fibers, No. 1 for the red-sensitive fibres, No. 2 for the green-sensitive fibres, and No. 3 for the violet-sensitive fibres.
>
> Pure *red* light stimulates the red-sensitive fibres strongly and the two other kinds of fibres feebly; giving the sensation red.
>
> Pure *yellow* light stimulates the red-sensitive and green-sensitive fibres moderately and the violet-sensitive fibres feebly; giving the sensation yellow.
>
> Pure *green* light stimulates the green-sensitive fibres strongly and the two other kinds much more feebly; giving the sensation green.
>
> ...When all the fibres are stimulated about equally, the sensation is that of *white* or pale hues. (Helmholtz, 1860/1965, p. 42)

Although Helmholtz's Figure 3.1 was hypothetical, it is quite similar to modern-day data plotted in what are called spectral sensitivity curves. Thus the trichromatic theory has held up over the years, at least in part. It failed to account for certain color phenomena that were better explained by other theories, however, most notably Ewald Hering's **opponent process theory**. Hering proposed that color-sensitive cells were designed to respond to opposing pairs of colors (i.e., red-green, yellow-blue, black-white). When seeing red, for instance, Hering proposed a chemical breakdown in the receptor for red-green, what he called a "catabolic" process. Seeing green resulted in an "anabolic" or building-up process. If both red and green were mixed together, Hering believed the two processes would cancel each other, resulting in the perception of a neutral gray color. One of the trichromatic theory's problems was its prediction that someone with

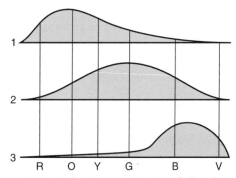

Figure 3.1   Relative sensitivity of the three color receptors proposed by Helmholtz, from his *Handbook of Physiological Optics*.

severe red-green color blindness would not be able to see yellow properly either. Yellow, according to Helmholtz, relies on the stimulation of properly functioning red and green fibers, both of which would be defective for someone with red-green color blindness. Such persons do see yellow, however. Also, the phenomenon of color afterimages seemed to fit Hering's model better than the Helmholtz model. After staring at a red square for a minute or so, then shifting one's gaze to a white surface, an afterimage in the form of a green square appears briefly. Yellow and blue complement each other in a similar manner. Today, theories of color vision include elements of both theories. The Young-Helmholtz version applies well at the retinal level—there do seem to be three different kinds of cones, each maximally responsive to the three colors of trichromatic theory, red, green, and blue. As for the Hering theory, his notions of anabolic and catabolic processes within individual receptors have not held up, but there do seem to be opposing pairs of cells located in numerous sections of the visual pathway. For example, in the lateral geniculate nucleus, about midway between the retina and the visual cortex, there are cells that fire rapidly whenever red is presented to the retina, but are inhibited from firing when green is shown. In addition to these R+G- cells, the nucleus also holds a collection of R-G+, B+Y-, and B-Y+ cells (Goldstein, 1996).

Color vision was only a small portion of Helmholtz's work on the visual sense. His love of physics, for example, led him to examine the basic question of optics: How does light become focused on the retina? Thus, he provided a systematic analysis of how light rays are bent, both by the cornea and through the process of **accommodation**, in which the lens changes shape in order to alter the focus of objects at different distances. He also examined the perception of depth through the operation of **binocular vision**, and in the spirit of Bishop Berkeley, took a strong empiricist stance on the question of how we come to perceive objects in space.

Helmholtz would be justly famous even if he restricted his expertise to vision. In 1863, between the publication of volumes II and III of his *Optics*, however, he also published what quickly became the authoritative text on the sense of hearing, *The Theory of the Sensation of Tone as a Physiological Basis for the Theory of Music.* It is still in use today. In it Helmholtz presented his famous **resonance theory** of hearing, which proposed that different frequencies of sound were detected by receptors located in different places along the basilar membrane of the cochlea.

It is worth noting that both the trichromatic theory of color vision and the resonance theory of hearing were elaborations of Müller's doctrine of the specific energies of nerves. Whereas Müller proposed a single specific energy for each of the five basic senses, Helmholtz's theories amounted to proposing more than one specific energy for *each* sense: three for color vision and many for hearing.

Helmholtz and the Problem of Perception

As a physicist, Helmholtz was accustomed to look for precision in nature. Hence, he was perplexed by what could be called the **problem of perception**. On the one hand, it appears that the human sensory systems for seeing and for hearing are remarkably capable. On the other hand, the structures designed to deliver these senses seem to be terribly flawed. In vision, for example, Helmholtz noted that aberrations in the cornea often distorted light waves, that the fluids within the eye distorted the perceptions of shape, motion, and color, and worst of all, when light reached the retina, it had to pass through several layers of blood vessels and nerve fibers before reaching the receptors. Helmholtz once said that "…if an optician wanted to sell me an instrument which had all these defects, I should think myself quite justified in blaming his carelessness in the strongest terms, and giving him back his instrument" (cited in Warren, 1984, p. 257). Similar problems occurred with hearing.

Given such design flaws, Helmholtz asked, what accounts for the quality of our perception? The answer, he believed, could be found in the doctrine of the specific energies of nerves and in traditional empiricist philosophy. Thus, because our nervous system mediates between reality and the mind, we are only indirectly aware of the external world. As a result, the role of experience must be central to perception, he argued. The raw information processed by the sensory systems is meaningless in itself, then, but takes on meaning only when a particular combination of sensory events becomes associated with specific consequences. Consider, for example, the perception of objects located at different distances. According to Helmholtz, we make what he called an **unconscious inference** about distance, based on our past experiences of various cues that are associated with distance. As a person gets closer to us, for example, the retinal image enlarges, but we perceive the person getting closer, not bigger. Helmholtz would say that because we know through experience that people don't grow or shrink as they approach or recede, we conclude logically (i.e., unconsciously infer) that the person must be getting closer. All of this occurs quickly and without our awareness, hence the term "unconscious" inference.

Despite being sickly as a youth, Helmholtz was strong and energetic in his later years. His favorite hobby was mountain climbing, for example, and he could often be found hiking through the Alps (Wade, 1994). The experience gave him a metaphor that summed up his approach to science. The elegance of his final theorizing contrasted with the messy and unpredictable day-to-day process of doing research. To explain how he proceeded, he compared himself to

> …an Alpine climber who, not knowing the way, ascends slowly and with toil, and is often compelled to retrace his steps because his progress is stopped; sometimes by reasoning, and sometimes by accident, he hits upon traces of a fresh path, which again leads him a little further; and finally, when he has reached the goal, he finds to his annoyance a royal road on which he might have ridden up if he had been clever enough to find the right starting-point at the outset. In my memoirs I have, of course, not given the reader an account of my wanderings, but I have described the beaten path on which he can now reach the summit without trouble. (cited in Warren, 1984, p. 256)

In 1871, at age 50, Helmholtz left Heidelberg for Berlin when he was offered a prestigious professorship in physics. Thus, in the last stage of his career he returned to his first love, physics. He traveled widely, even visiting the United States in 1893 to represent German science at the World's Fair in Chicago. On the return voyage he suffered a severe concussion and prolonged double vision from a fall down a flight of stairs. He died of a cerebral hemorrhage the following year.

LOCALIZATION OF BRAIN FUNCTION

In addition to the advances in knowledge about sensory physiology, nineteenth-century scientists also explored the nature of the brain, and argued over the problem of localization. Even a superficial visual inspection of the brain reveals some obvious structural differences. There are clearly two hemispheres, the cortex subdivides further into a number of ridges (convolutions), the cerebellum is separate from the cerebrum, and the lower brain areas, an extension of the spinal cord, have their own distinct shapes and features. It is only natural to suppose that there are functional differences corresponding to these structures, and this raises the question of **localization of function**. To what extent do the different locations in the brain correspond to different physiological and psychological attributes? That is, just how precise can localization be delineated? The answers range from very much to very little to it depends on the area of the brain being studied.

THE PHRENOLOGY OF GALL AND SPURZHEIM

The phrenologists proposed the first major theory of localization and their answer to the question just raised was "very much." According to advocates of **phrenology**, human "faculties" could be identified and located in precisely defined areas of the brain. Phrenology began as a legitimate scientific attempt to study brain function, but it gradually degenerated into the nineteenth century's best example of pseudoscience. When portrayed in today's introductory psychology texts, it is usually caricatured as a bizarre scientific dead end in which charlatans read character by looking at the bumps on someone's head. Actually, the story is considerably more complicated and much that is characteristic of American psychology has its roots in the phrenological movement.

The origins of phrenology may be traced to the respected but eccentric Viennese physician and comparative anatomist Franz Josef Gall (1758–1828). Gall was born in Tiefenbronn, Germany, into an intensely devout Catholic family—his parents assumed that he would one day become a priest. Instead, his theory about the brain came to be considered antireligious, his books were banned by the Church, the best that could be said about his personal life was that it was morally unconventional, and upon his death in 1828 he was denied a religious burial (Young, 1972). Gall decided on a career in medicine early in life, and he earned an M.D. in Vienna in 1785. There he developed a successful practice and became a skilled anatomist, although he was criticized for charging admission to those who wished to observe him in surgery and his theory about brain function became controversial. After his public lectures and surgical demonstrations were banned for allegedly promoting immorality and atheism, he took the show on the road and lectured throughout Europe before settling in Paris in 1807, where he remained until his death.

Gall secured a place in the history of medicine with his careful anatomical work. He identified the fibers connecting the two hemispheres and confirmed earlier speculation that some fibers crossed from one side of the brain to the opposite side of the spinal cord. Thus, Gall confirmed the concept of **contralateral function**, the notion that each side of the brain controls the opposite side of the body. Gall also compared the brain structures of different species and made a convincing argument that the mental abilities of different species correlated with the size and complexity of the brain, especially the cortex. He was also the first to argue that the brain's convolutions formed the same pattern within a given species; hence, the surface of the brain was not a random jumble of ridges and valleys but had a reliable structure. His anatomical research was impeccable—the great French physiologist Pierre Flourens, phrenology's harshest critic (below), nonetheless reported that when he saw Gall dissect a brain, it was like seeing the organ for the first time. Unlike most anatomists, including Flourens, who dissected brains by slicing off segments from the top down, Gall worked from the brain stem up, removing structures one by one and thereby tracing the interconnections between structures with a precision that was impossible when starting at the top (Temkin, 1947).

Despite these notable accomplishments, Gall is best known for originating phrenology, or what he called "cranioscopy." The theory is historically significant as the first serious theory of the localization of brain function, and Gall is justly credited with being among the first to argue that the brain was the organ of both the intellectual and the emotional components of the mind. Unfortunately, though, Gall identified the wrong functions and put them in the wrong places in the brain. In addition, his logic and his methods were flawed.

Gall began developing his ideas about localization very early in his life—as a youth, he thought he detected a relationship between the shape of a person's head and certain behavioral characteristics of that person. He noticed, for example, that schoolmates with protruding eyes seemed to have better memories than he did. This early experience began a lifelong pursuit of anecdotal evidence to support his theories. Thus, he claimed that the impulse to steal resulted from an overdevelopment of the faculty of "Property" (later called "Acquisitiveness"), located in the temporal lobe of the cortex about an inch above and in front of the ear. According to Gall,

> ...[w]hen these cerebral parts are very much developed, they produce a prominence on the head and skull.... I have constantly found this prominence, in all inveterate thieves confined in prison, in all idiots with an irresistible propensity to steal, and in all those who, otherwise well endowed with intellect, take an inconceivable pleasure in stealing, and even feel incapable of resisting the passion which forces them to theft. (Gall, 1825/1965, p. 218)

Gall's beliefs eventually developed into the theory that his followers came to call phrenology, a term that derives from the Greek words for the study of ("-ology") the mind ("phrenos"). The term was coined by Joseph Spurzheim (1776–1832), who collaborated with Gall for a time, but later broke with him. Spurzheim is the person most responsible for popularizing the theory, both in Europe and in America. As described in his *Outlines of Phrenology* (1832/1978) and elsewhere, phrenology's main principles reduced to five:

a. The brain is the organ of the mind.

b. The mind is composed of a large number (about three dozen) of abilities or attributes called "faculties"; some of these faculties are intellectual (cognitive) and some are affective (emotional).

c. Each faculty is associated with a specific brain location.

d. For a given faculty, some people have more than others, and those with more of a particular faculty will have more brain tissue in the corresponding location than those with less of that same faculty.

e. Because the skull corresponds roughly to the shape of the brain, the strength of various faculties can be inferred from the shape of the skull.

This last point came to be known as the "doctrine of the skull" and for the phrenologists it was the key to measurement. If the size and shape of various brain locations reflected the strength of faculties and if brain shape affected skull shape, then measuring the skull would yield a measurement of faculties. In short, everything of importance about people could be known by examining the shapes of their skulls. Figure 3.2 shows a typical phrenological skull with its faculties labeled.

In the first two decades of the nineteenth century, cranioscopy/phrenology was a legitimate

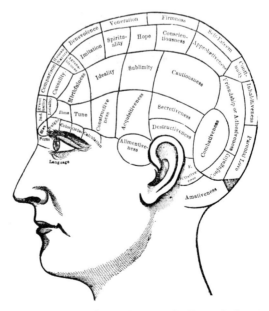

Figure 3.2   A phrenological skull, with faculties identified.

attempt to identify the localized functions of the brain. By the time Spurzheim produced his *Outlines of Phrenology*, in the year he died while on an American lecture tour (1832), thousands of skulls had been examined with an eye toward correlating skull shape with character. The *Outlines* includes detailed delineations of the faculties, with each description identifying the faculty's location in the brain and describing some of the supporting evidence for the faculty. On close examination, however, it is clear that there were serious weaknesses with the evidence. As indicated above in connection with the faculty of Property (Acquisitiveness), the phrenologists relied heavily on **anecdotal evidence**. That is, they looked for specific case examples to support their theory. This approach is not necessarily flawed—gathering lots of data and then looking for generalizations is a standard inductive strategy. The problem, however, is that the phrenologists were not interested in examples that did not support their case. Thus, their theory failed an important criterion of an authentic scientific theory: it must be stated precisely enough to be capable of disproof. But the phrenologists would not do this. A thief with a small area of Acquisitiveness would either be ignored, described as a potential thief ("he will start stealing any day now") or explained away by referring to combinations of other faculties that would be said to offset the lack of Acquisitiveness. For instance, the thief might be described as having large faculties of Imitation and Self-Esteem, causing him to maintain his self-image by copying his pickpocket older brother, despite his lack of "natural" Acquisitiveness. Perhaps the ultimate example of phrenological refusal to consider disproof was a comment attributed to a phrenologist upon learning that Descartes' skull was rather small in the areas related to some of the intellectual faculties. The phrenologist concluded that perhaps Descartes wasn't so smart after all (Fancher, 1990)!

This failure of phrenology as a theory did not seem to bother the phrenologists, but it was quickly recognized as a fatal flaw by other scientists, and phrenology was relegated to the status of pseudoscience by the mid-1830s. Unfortunately, it shared an important feature with other pseudosciences (e.g., biorhythms in the late twentieth century)—the general public loved it. Phrenology became enormously popular throughout the rest of the nineteenth century. Gall and Spurzheim spread the faith throughout Europe and Spurzheim and others exported it to the United States.

It was in America that phrenology reached its zenith of popularity. The version that was imported by Spurzheim and spread by him and others fit in perfectly with the American culture of the "common man," especially during the middle and last half of the nineteenth century (Bakan, 1966). Although Gall believed the size of a person's faculties was an indication of native traits, Spurzheim argued that faculties could be affected by nurture. To Spurzheim, the brain was analogous to a muscle—its faculties could be exercised and strengthened through education and self-help. Thus, phrenology provided a seemingly scientific basis for the traditional American belief that anyone, regardless of heritage, could "pull oneself up by one's bootstraps" and accomplish virtually anything in life (e.g., go from a log cabin to the White House). The hopeful notion that children's brains and therefore their futures could be shaped by controlling their environments and improving their educations resonated with Americans. That same optimism would make behaviorism just as fashionable with the public in the 1920s. Phrenology also was consistent with the American idea that everyone is a unique person, possessing his or her own special talents. In phrenological terms, this translated into everyone having his or her own distinctive configuration of faculties, to be measured with proper phrenological tools. Thus, phrenology was an important early example of a major theme of research in psychology that continues today: the search for ways to identify and gauge individual differences (Bakan, 1966). And if individual differences could be identified and measured, then a person's strengths and weaknesses could be known and he or she could be counseled about careers, mate selection, and so on. A final reason for phrenology's appeal, then, was in its promise to deliver practical applications to improve daily living.

Phrenology's popularity with the masses was enhanced through the energetic marketing efforts of the New York firm of Fowler and Wells. Despite the fact that the scientific and more educated community rejected phrenolo-gy rather quickly, the public never seemed to tire of it. After all, it appeared to provide simple answers to life's difficult problems. Fowler and Wells published thousands of "improve-your-life-through phrenology" pamphlets, a phrenological journal, and paraphernalia ranging from busts with the faculties clearly marked on them to charts to simple tools for measuring head shapes. As you can see from the Close-up, phrenology held the American public's interest into the early years of the twentieth century.

▶ CLOSE-UP

The Marketing of Phrenology

When Orson Fowler was a student at Amherst College in the early 1830s, he made pocket money by examining the heads of classmates for two cents per head (Joynt, 1973). Upon graduation, he joined with his brother Lorenzo and sister Charlotte in forming a museum of phrenology in New York City that featured a large collection of skulls, casts of heads, and other phrenological tools of the trade. Admission was free, but once the museum-goers were in the door, the Fowlers tempted them with a phrenologi-cal assessment that cost from one to three dollars. When Charlotte married a medical student named Samuel Welles, the firm of Fowler and Wells was born. Located at 753 Broadway, with branches in Boston and Philadelphia, it dominated the phrenology business from its inception in 1844 to the turn of the twentieth century.

Fowler and Wells, Inc., published a seemingly endless list of pamphlets designed to bring phrenological insights into every home. They also began the popular *Phrenological Journal*, trained and "certified" phrenologists, and during an era when the public lecture was a primary means of communication, maintained a list of accomplished public speak-ers ready to spread the phrenological faith. To give you some idea of the range of topics addressed by the firm, consider the following titles of pamphlets and books that could be ordered from Fowler and Wells, as advertised in the October 1881, issue of the *Phrenological Journal*:

> *The Indications of Character*, as manifested in the general shape of the head and the form of the face. Illustrated. 15 cents.
> *Wedlock*; or, The Right Relations of the Sexes. A Scientific Treatise disclosing the Laws of Conjugal Selection, Pre-natal Influences, and showing Who Ought and Who Ought Not to Marry. $1.50; in fancy guilt, $2.00.
> *Amativeness*; or, Evils and Remedies of Excessive and Perverted Sexuality; including Warning and Advice to the Married and Single. 25 cents.
> *Choice of Pursuits*; or, What to do and Why. Describing Seventy-five Trades and Professions, and the Temperaments and Talents required for each. 508 pp. $1.75.

As for the journal itself, each issue contained brief phrenological sketches of well-known individuals, articles on other hot topics of the day (e.g., hypnotism, spiritualism) and short pieces covering just about anything (e.g., "Why Bees Work in Darkness"; "The Morality of Brakemen"). Although nothing quite like the *Phrenological Journal* exists today, the annual *Old Farmer's Almanac*, with its down-east commonsense wisdom, bears some similarity.

A typical phrenological article in the journal featured some well-known person and showed how a phrenological assessment could "explain" that person's character and behavior. For example, the September 1873, issue included a piece about a notorious triple murderer. Here's how he was described by a phrenologist who interviewed him:

> I found his head to be 22 inches in circumference, 13.5 inches from Individuality to the occipital spine, and 14 inches from Destructiveness to Destructiveness, over the top of the head at Firmness. The animal portion of the brain predomi- nates over all others. Destructiveness is the largest organ in his brain, the head swelling out enormously over the ears. The organ of Conscientiousness is, I think, the smallest I ever saw.... All the spiritual organs are small and inactive, while Cautiousness and Secretiveness are both below the average.

The firm of Fowler and Wells had a long run, but interest in phrenology finally began to wane near the end of the nineteenth century, as the general public became more informed about the workings of the brain and as other approaches to measurement (e.g., IQ testing) began to be popularized. In 1911, the *Phrenological Journal* published its last issue.

FLOURENS AND THE METHOD OF ABLATION

Phrenology might have seemed like good science to Main Street America, but the real scientists were not fooled. As mentioned earlier, the scien- tific community rejected the Gall/Spurzheim the- ory well before the middle of the nineteenth cen- tury. Phrenology's worst enemy was the distin- guished French physiologist and surgeon Pierre Flourens (1794–1867), who deliberately set out to show that the phrenologists were wrong. He reduced phrenology to two main points: the mind is centered in the brain, and the mind is composed of numerous faculties, each located in specific places in the brain. In his sharply worded *Examination of Phrenology*, first published in 1843, he sarcastically observed that "of these two propositions, there is certainly nothing new in the first one, and perhaps nothing true in the sec- ond one" (Flourens, 1846/1978, p. 18).

To falsify the phrenologists' claims, Flourens took an experimental approach to the problem of localization, using the method of **ablation**. Although he did not create the procedure, he raised it to such a level of refinement that it is now associated with his name. Rather than wait for natural experiments to occur, in the form of accidental brain damage, Flourens removed specific sections of the brain and observed the effects ("ablation" derives from the Latin words for "carry away" or "remove"). If the result of an ablation is an inability to see, then presumably the area of the removed por- tion has something to do with vision. Clearly, the method required animals as research sub- jects, and Flourens experimented on numerous species, ranging from dogs to pigeons.

Flourens's attack on phrenology took the form of showing that specific areas of the brain that were alleged to serve function X in fact served function Y, and that the cerebral cortex operates as an integrated whole, rather than as a large collection of faculties located in specific places. One focus of his research was the cere- bellum. To the phrenologists, this portion of the brain controlled sexual behavior and was the center of the faculty of "amativeness." Flourens had little trouble disproving this and demon- strating instead that the cerebellum is the center of motor coordination. Thus, pigeons deprived of the organ were unable to coordinate wing movements in order to fly, and dogs were unable to walk properly and would be observed staggering, falling down, and bumping into objects they could normally avoid. Also, the degree of abnormality in movement was directly proportional to the amount of cerebellum ablated.

As a result of removing varying amounts of the cerebral cortex, Flourens found a similar relationship between the amount removed and the seriousness of the ensuing problem. He could find no indication of distinct functions residing in specific areas of the cortex, however, so he concluded that it operated as a whole and served the general functions of perception, intelligence, and will. Thus, pigeons without a cortex or with most of it removed did seem to be able to perceive the world around them, but showed no indication of an ability to learn from their experiences, and did not seem to be able to do anything except to vegetate. The difference between a pigeon without a cerebellum and one without a cortex was that the first bird would attempt to fly but could not, while it would never occur to the second bird that flying was an option in life.

The general principles that the cortex acts as a whole and that the amount of disability is proportional to the extent of ablation were verified and extended by the discoveries of the great American physiological psychologist Karl Lashley, who referred to them as the principles of equipotentiality and mass action, respectively. (Lashley's work will be considered briefly at the end of the chapter.) Yet while Flourens was able to use these principles to attack phrenology in such a way that it never recovered, at least in the eyes of scientists, he overstated his case. He argued against any degree of localization in the cortex, a position soon to be shown inadequate by other brain scientists using methods other than ablation.

THE CLINICAL METHOD

The results of ablation studies are not always easy to interpret, mainly because destroying one portion of a brain also influences connections to that portion, producing outcomes that are not always predictable or consistent. Also, ablation studies are sometimes impossible to do, as in the case of human subjects. It is one thing to systematically ablate portions of a person's brain for certain beneficial medical reasons (e.g., severing the corpus callosum to treat epilepsy), but destroying human brain tissue simply for the purpose of observing what happens is obviously indefensible.[4] An alternative way to study human brain function is called the **clinical method**. This involves either (a) studying the behavioral and mental consequences of brain injury, events such as strokes, or illness, or (b) identifying people with some behavioral or mental disorder and examining their brains after death. The person generally credited with developing the clinical method is Paul Broca, whom we will meet shortly, but there are numerous examples of famous clinical cases in the mid-nineteenth century. One of the best-known concerned a well-respected Vermont railroad worker, Phineas Gage.

The Remarkable Phineas Gage

While blasting rock in preparation for a new railway line near Cavendish, Vermont, in 1848, Gage survived an accident that seemed certain

---

[4] This rather obvious ethical point was lost on Dr. Roberts Bartholow of Cincinnati in 1874, who inserted electrodes into the cortex of an unwitting immigrant domestic worker (i.e., powerless) who had come to him for treatment of an ulcerous scalp wound that had exposed a portion of her brain. Mild stimulation produced some muscular contractions, but when the curious Bartholow inserted the electrodes deeper and increased the strength of the current, the unfortunate woman went into severe convulsions and soon died (Hothersall, 1995).

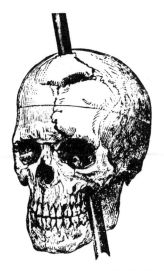

Figure 3.3   Sketch of Gage's skull, showing position of tamping iron, from the original medical report by Harlow (1869).

was never able to work productively again and his personality changed dramatically. From a dependable, conscientious, respected community leader (he was foreman of the railroad crew), Gage degenerated into an obstinate, profane, irresponsible embarrassment to the community (MacMillan, 1986).

One of Gage's doctors, John Harlow, was amenable to phrenology and saw the case as providing support for the phrenologist's belief in cerebral localization. Harlow kept meticulous notes on the case and published accounts of it in 1848 and 1868, describing this case of frontal lobe damage as one in which

> …[t]he equilibrium or balance…between his intellectual faculties and animal propensities seems to have been destroyed. He is fitful, irreverent, indulging at times in the grossest profanity (which was not previously his custom), manifesting but little deference for his fellows, impatient of restraint or advice when it conflicts with his desires, at times pertinaciously obstinate, yet capricious and vacillating, devising many plans of future operation, which are no sooner arranged than they are abandoned…. Previous to his injury, although untrained in the schools, he possessed a well-balanced mind, and was looked upon by those who knew him as a shrewd, smart businessman, very energetic and persistent in executing all his plans of operation. In this regard his mind was radically changed, so decidedly that his friends and acquaintances said he was "no longer Gage." (Harlow, 1868, cited in MacMillan, 1986, pp. 13–14)

to be fatal. After pouring some gunpowder and a fuse into a hole drilled into rock that was about to be blasted away, Gage used a "tamping iron" to compress the powder. Momentarily distracted, he scraped the edge of the rock hard enough to create a spark that ignited the gunpowder. This converted the tamping iron into a missile which flew into the air and landed 30 meters away. Unfortunately for Gage, his head was in the flight path. The missile entered just below his left eye and exited from the top left of his forehead, taking a healthy portion of his left frontal cortex with it (see Figure 3.3). Miraculously, Gage only lost consciousness for a brief time, and once he arrived back in town, was able to walk (assisted) to a doctor's office. There he sat and conversed with friends (!) until the doctor arrived, about 30 minutes after the accident. Within two months he was sufficiently recovered to live independently,[5] but he

Thus, while Gage survived the injury, he was radically altered by it—the brain damage resulted in irreversible changes to his personality and behavior. Within 12 years (at age 37) he

---

[5] That he survived at a time prior to the use of antibiotics to treat infection was nothing short of amazing, but his recovery was probably aided by fact that the entry wound provided a natural drainage area that prevented him from developing the kind of abscess that would almost certainly be fatal (MacMillan, 1986).

died, after experiencing a number of increasingly severe convulsions. The tamping iron and Gage's skull can be seen today at Harvard's Warren Anatomical Medical Museum.

▶ ORIGINAL SOURCE EXCERPT:

Broca Discovers the Speech Center

In the Gage case, it was possible for Harlow to trace events from the initial brain injury to the resulting psychological outcome. Another type of clinical case occurs when a patient manifests some specific mental or behavioral problem, but it cannot be correlated with brain damage until after death. Such was the situation facing the French neurologist Paul Broca (1824–1880) in April of 1861, when confronted with a very unusual patient, known to history as "Tan," for reasons that will soon be apparent. This patient had been in the Bicêtre hospital in Paris for 21 years, and had been incapacitated and in bed for the seven years prior to 1861, when a severe case of gangrene brought him to Broca's attention. What follows is an excerpt from Broca's description of this remarkable case (Broca, 1861/1965), which eventually resulted in Broca's name being forever associated with a specific location on the cortex.

> On 11 April 1861 there was brought to the surgery…a man named Leborgne, fifty-one years old, suffering from a diffused gangrenous cellulitis of his whole right side, extending from the foot to the buttocks. When questioned the next day as to the origin of his disease, he replied only with the monosyllable *tan*, repeated twice in succession and accompanied by a gesture of his left hand. I tried to find out more about the antecedents of this man,…and here is the result of this inquiry.
>
> Since youth he had been subject to epileptic attacks, yet he was able to become a maker of lasts,[6] a trade at which he worked until he was thirty years old. It was then that he lost his ability to speak and that is why he was admitted to the hospice at Bicêtre.…
>
> …He was then quite healthy and intelligent and differed from a normal person only in his loss of articulate language. He came and went at the hospice, where he was known by the name of "Tan." He understood all that was said to him. His hearing was actually very good, but whenever one questioned him he always answered, "Tan, tan," accompanying his utterance with varied gestures by which he succeeded in expressing most of his ideas. If one did not understand his gestures, he was apt to get irate and added to his vocabulary a gross oath ["Sacré nom de Dieu!"].…
>
> Ten years after he lost his speech a new symptom appeared. The muscles of his right arm began to get weak, and in the end they became completely paralyzed. Tan continued to walk without difficulty, but the paralysis gradually extended to his right leg; after having dragged the leg for some time, he resigned himself to staying in bed. About four years had elapsed from the beginning of the paralysis of the arm to the time when

---

[6] A "last" is a wooden block in the shape of a foot, used in the making or repairing of shoes.

> paralysis of the leg was sufficiently advanced to make standing absolutely impossible. Before he was brought to the infirmary, Tan had been in bed for almost seven years. (pp. 224–225, italics in the original)

During the seven years in bed, Tan was more or less forgotten, and little information was available about him, except that his vision began to deteriorate. Because he remained continent, his linen was not changed regularly; thus, the gangrene that brought him to Broca's attention was not discovered until it had advanced considerably, infecting the whole leg. Broca reported that he hesitated examining Tan, because his general state "was so grave that it would have been cruel" (p. 225). Nonetheless, Broca proceeded, both with a physical exam that confirmed the paralysis of the right arm and leg, and with an examination of Tan's mental capacities:

> The state of Tan's intelligence could not be exactly determined. Certainly he understood all that was said to him, but, since he could express his ideas or desires only by movements of his left hand, this moribund patient could not make himself understood as well as he understood others. His numerical responses, made by opening or closing his fingers, were best. Several times I asked him for how many days had he been ill. Sometimes he answered five, sometimes six days. How many years had he been at Bicêtre? He opened his hand four times and then added one finger. That made 21 years, the correct answer. The next day I repeated the question and received the same answer, but, when I tried to come back to the question a third time, Tan realized that I wanted to make an exercise out of the questioning. He became irate and uttered the oath, which only this one time did I hear from him.... He could understand even quite complicated ideas. For instance, I asked him about the order in which his paralyses had developed. First he made a short horizontal gesture with his left index finger, meaning that he had understood; then he showed successively his tongue, his right arm, and his right leg. That was perfectly correct, for quite naturally he attributed his loss of language to paralysis of his tongue. (p. 226)

Broca guessed that Tan had a cerebral lesion that for the first 10 years of the illness remained confined to a fairly limited area in the left side of the brain, but then had spread. He did not have long to wait in order to confirm the diagnosis:

> The patient died on 17 April [1861]. The autopsy was performed as soon as possible—that is, after 24 hours. The weather was warm but the cadaver showed no signs of putrefaction. The brain was shown a few hours later to the Société d'Anthropologie and was then put immediately into alcohol. It was so altered that great care was necessary to preserve it. It was only after two months and several changes of the fluid that it began to harden. Today it is in perfect condition and has been deposited in the Musée Depuytren. (p. 227)

Remarkably, Tan's brain still resides in the Musée Depuytren, with the damage to the left frontal cortex clearly visible. As Broca summed up the case,

Anatomical inspection shows us that the lesion was still progressing when the patient died. The lesion was therefore progressive, but it progressed very slowly, taking twenty-one years to destroy a quite limited part of the brain. Thus it is reasonable to believe that at the beginning there was a considerable time during which degeneration did not go past the limits of the organ where it started. We have seen that the original focus of the disease was situated in the frontal lobe and very likely in its third frontal convolution. Thus we are compelled to say, from the point of view of pathological anatomy, that there were two periods, one in which only one frontal convolution, probably the third one, was attacked, and another period in which the disease gradually spread toward other convolutions, to the insula, or to the extraventicular nucleus of the corpus striatum.

When we now examine the succession of symptoms, we also find two periods, the first of which lasted ten years, during which the faculty of speech was destroyed while all other functions of the brain remained intact, and a second period of eleven years, during which paralysis of movement...successively involved the arm and the leg of the right side....

It follows that the first period of ten years, clinically characterized only by the symptom of aphemia, must correspond to the period during which the lesion was still limited to the frontal lobe. (pp. 228–229)

Broca's term for Tan's disorder was soon replaced with "aphasia" when it was pointed out that the Greek origin of "aphemia" refers to reputation or fame, while the root translation of "aphasia" is "without speech" (Ryalls, 1984). The disorder is now referred to as expressive or **motor aphasia**, and it is characterized by an inability to articulate ideas verbally, even though the vocal apparatus is intact and general intelligence is normal. Over the next few years, Broca encountered several other aphasic patients like Tan, found the same general pattern of left frontal lobe damage, and concluded that the ability to produce speech was localized in the left frontal lobe. In his honor, the area is now known as Broca's area.

Broca's research challenged Flourens's conclusions about the degree of localization to be found in the cortex. Additional evidence for localized language function came from clinical studies by the German neurologist Carl Wernicke (1848–1905). He studied a group of 10 patients who could produce articulate speech, but the speech tended to be nonsensical; they also had difficulty comprehending the speech of others. He named the disorder **sensory aphasia**, to distinguish it from motor aphasia, and discovered consistent brain damage to an area of the left temporal lobe of the brain, several centimeters behind Broca's area.

MAPPING THE BRAIN: ELECTRICAL STIMULATION

We have seen that in the nineteenth century, discoveries about the nature of electricity were being applied to research on sensory physiology, and the idea was evolving that neural activity was electrochemical. In that context, two young German physiologists, both lecturers at the University of Berlin, asked whether the surface of the cortex would respond to mild electrical current. Although listed as second author in their famous paper, the primary investigator was lifelong brain researcher Edward Hitzig

**Key Date
1861**

This year marked the year that Paul Broca discovered and studied the aphasic patient "Tan" and discovered the location of the brain's speech center.

These events also occurred:

- Louis Pasteur proposed a germ theory of fermentation
- Daily weather forecasts began in Britain
- The skeleton of a link between reptile and bird (archaeopteryx) was discovered in Germany
- The United States introduced the passport system
- Russia emancipated its serfs
- The U.S. Civil War began with Confederate victories at Fort Sumter and Bull Run
- These people were born:
  Alfred North Whitehead, English mathematician and philosopher
  Nellie Melba, Australia operatic soprano
- These people died:
  Elizabeth Barrett Browning, English poet
  Frederick Wilhelm IV of Prussia

(1838–1907); he was assisted by Eduard Fritsch (1838–1927), who soon left physiology for the study of anthropology. Hitzig had observed muscle movements when the exposed brain of a wounded soldier had been mechanically stimulated, but it was generally believed that touching the surface of the brain did not produce reliable effects. Using dogs as their subjects, Hitzig and Fritsch exposed the cortex and probed different surfaces. The stimulus was an electric current of "an intensity that just barely evoked a sensation of feeling on the tongue" (Fritsch & Hitzig, 1870/1965, p. 230). It was delivered across two thin platinum wires that could be placed anywhere from 2 to 3 mm apart. Despite the relative crudeness of their procedures—the experiments were done in Fritsch's home—they contributed evidence of localization by identifying several motor centers in the front half of the brain. Stimulation of the areas marked in Figure 3.4 produced consistent movements in the right side of the dog's body, as follows:

Area 1:	neck
Areas 2 and 3:	anterior leg (extension and flexion, respectively)
Area 4:	posterior leg
Area 5:	face

The Fritsch and Hitzig research motivated a number of physiologists, who proceeded to map out motor areas in other species and with more precision. This activity became known as the "new" phrenology or "scientific phrenology": localization was the goal, but now the brain's functions would be identified scientifically, rather than through the selected anecdotes of Gall and Spurzheim. Just a few years after Fritsch and Hitzig published their work, for example, the Scottish neurologist David Ferrier (1843–1928) wrote *Functions of the Brain* (1876), which included the map of a monkey's brain shown in Figure 3.5. Comparing this with Figure 3.4 makes it clear how rapidly brain sci-

Figure 3.4   Motor centers of a dog's brain, identified via electrical stimulation by Fritsch and Hitzig (1870/1965).

EARLY TWENTIETH-CENTURY STUDIES OF THE NERVOUS SYSTEM AND BEHAVIOR

As the nineteenth century drew to a close, knowledge of the nervous system in general and of the brain in particular was increasing at a rapid pace. In addition to research on sensory physiology and the localization of brain function, however, another line of research developed toward the end of the century and spilled over into the twentieth. This concerned the nature of the basic unit of the nervous system itself, the neuron. This is a long and complicated history in itself, but a few of the highlights can be sketched here.

NEURON THEORY

The discovery of the neuron as the basic element of the nervous system did not occur until the second half of the nineteenth century, when several important developments occurred in histology (the study of the microscopic structure of plant and animal tissue). Microscopes became more powerful, for instance, and techniques for hardening the brain were perfected. Before it was discovered that the brain could be solidified by soaking it in alcohol, precise dissection was impossible. Once it was known how to harden

ence was advancing. Ferrier also extended the localization search beyond motor functions, identifying several sensory areas. Using both electrical stimulation and ablation, Ferrier was able to identify the occipital lobe as the primary sensory area for vision, and a portion of the temporal lobe as the center for hearing. It began to look like sensory nerves differed more in terms of their destinations in the cortex than in terms of "specific energies."

Figure 3.5   David Ferrier's map of the cortex of a monkey (from Boring, 1950).

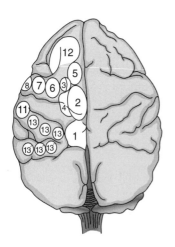

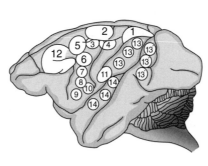

the brain, however, its nerve pathways could be traced with some precision for the first time. For example, in 1857, Gratiolet was able to trace the optic nerve from the retina all the way to the back of the brain, where it radiated like a fan into the occipital cortex (Diamond, 1985).

It was also discovered that the brain could be immersed in paraffin, hardened, then cut into very thin slices, a procedure called sectioning. Furthermore, if these sections were stained with various dyes, identifiable structures could be observed in a microscope because the dyes would collect within these structures. When the Italian Camillo Golgi (1844–1926) began using what he called his "black stain," for instance, the result was the first picture of an intact nerve cell, complete with elaborately branching dendrites, intact cell body, and main axon. Golgi's discovery earned him a share of the 1906 Nobel Prize for medicine. He believed the nervous system to be composed of these neurons, but he also contended that the cells were physically connected to each other, a position that brought him into conflict with the other winner of the 1906 Nobel Prize for medicine.

Santiago Ramón y Cajal (1852–1934) was a gifted Spanish neuroanatomist with a love of art, whose research laid the foundation for the modern theory of the neuron (Taylor, 1972). Ramón y Cajal's artistic side can be seen in his eloquent description of the neuron as the "aristocrat among the structures of the body, with its giant arms stretched out like the tentacles of an octopus to the provinces on the frontier of the outside world" (cited in Restak, 1984). Like Golgi, Ramón y Cajal believed the neuron to be the nervous system's basic unit. In contrast with Golgi, however, he argued that each neuron was a separate unit that was not physically connected with other units but merely in contact with them. Ironically, when he first proposed his neuron theory in 1889, he used Golgi's own staining techniques to make his case. Thus, the two winners of the 1906 Nobel Prize for medicine were strongly opposed over the nature of their discovery, the neuron. To complicate matters further, Golgi the Italian and Ramón y Cajal the Spaniard were both fiercely patriotic and convinced of the inferiority of each other's research. The 1906 Nobel Prize ceremony must have been interesting.

SIR CHARLES SHERRINGTON: THE SYNAPSE

Direct photographic evidence supporting Ramón y Cajal's neuron theory and refuting Golgi's would have to await the discovery of the electron microscope, but empirical evidence supporting the existence of gaps between neurons was provided by a British contemporary of both men, Sir Charles Sherrington (1857–1952).[7] It was Sherrington who coined the term **synapse** (from the Greek word meaning "to join together") for this proposed space between neurons. He did not observe its existence directly; rather he deduced it from a brilliant series of studies on spinal reflexes. The research was presented as part of a prestigious series of lectures at Yale University in 1904, then published as *The Integrative Action of the Nervous System* in 1906, the same year that Golgi and Ramón y Cajal shared the Nobel Prize. Sherrington would eventually win a Nobel Prize of his own in 1932 (Swazey, 1972).

In the tradition of Robert Whytt, but with the advantages of improved technology, Sherrington examined reflex action in "spinal

---

[7] Obituary accounts of Sherrington describe him as a genial and mild-mannered man. He was said to be "[g]entle in criticism, whole hearted in admiration and appreciation of the work of others, embod[ying] the intellectual and physical serenity which appears so characteristic of the Victorian era" (Denny-Brown, 1952, p. 477). Yet this "serenity" did not keep him from his favorite sport during his youth—while a lecturer in physiology at St. Thomas's Hospital in London, he spent his Sunday mornings parachute jumping from the hospital's tower (Swazey, 1972).

dogs," dogs with spinal cords surgically severed from their brains. As all dog owners know, stimulating a dog's side in the area of the rib cage will cause the dog's hind leg to produce a rapid and repetitive scratching reflex. The fact that Sherrington found these reflexes in spinal dogs replicated Whytt's basic finding about the role of the spinal cord in reflex action. Furthermore, the reflex was even more pronounced in spinal dogs than in intact dogs, which led Sherrington to conclude that the cortex has an inhibitory effect on reflex action.

Sherrington made several observations in his spinal dogs that led him to believe that synapses must exist. First, the reaction time of the reflexes he observed was much slower than predicted from what was known of the speed of neural transmission. Thus, something must have been slowing down the impulse. A second line of evidence came from the phenomena of temporal and spatial summation. Sherrington discovered that a single stimulation at a certain point on the skin might fail to elicit a scratch reflex, but if the point was stimulated many times in succession (at a rate of about 18 per second), the reflex occurred (Sherrington, 1906). This is **temporal summation**—stimuli separated in time combine to produce a response. **Spatial summation** occurred when two or more adjacent points on the skin were stimulated at the same time. Again, responses only occurred to the combined stimulation. Sherrington concluded that summation must occur at the points where the endpoints of neurons met each other, the synapse. Each subthreshold stimulus caused some unspecified action at the end of neuron A that was by itself insufficient to fire neuron B, but the combined action of information coming many times from A (temporal) or from other locations (spatial) triggered the firing of B. That is, Sherrington anticipated the later discovery of neurotransmitters, chemicals that we now know cross the synapse to promote (or inhibit) neuron firing. After Golgi, Ramón y Cajal, and Sherrington, then, the neuron was established as the funda-mental unit of the nervous system, interrelated with other neurons through synaptic activity.

KARL LASHLEY: LEARNING AND THE CORTEX

A brief consideration of the life and work of Karl Spencer Lashley (1890–1958) is a fitting way to end this chapter. Like the nineteenth-century physiologists, neurologists, and physicists encountered thus far, his training was not in psychology. Unlike anyone else in the chapter, however, he eventually came to think of himself primarily as a psychologist. Thus, Lashley provides a transition between the physiologists of the nineteenth century and the physiological psychologists of the twentieth. You will encounter him again in Chapter 10, as a research colleague of behaviorism's founder, John B. Watson, and again in Chapter 13, where his paper on "serial order" attacked simplistic S-R models of behavior and helped set the stage for the shift from behaviorism to cognitive psychology, and yet again in Chapter 14, as the mentor of Donald Hebb, a contender with Lashley for the title of the most important physiological psychologist of the twentieth century.

Karl Lashley was born in rural West Virginia and earned a bachelor's degree in zoology from West Virginia University and a master's degree in bacteriology from the University of Pittsburgh, before enrolling in a doctoral program in zoology at Johns Hopkins University in 1911. There he completed the Ph.D. under the tutelage of noted zoologist H. S. Jennings. More important for psychology's history, Lashley also came under the influence of the behaviorist Watson and S. I. Franz, a psychologist at a psychiatric hospital (St. Elizabeth's) in Washington, D.C., who was interested in the effects of brain damage on behavior. With Watson, Lashley conducted field studies of animal behavior, laboratory experiments on the sensory abilities of various species, and research on the conditioning of salivary and motor responses, adapting the procedures of two Russian physiologists who were just beginning to be known to Americans: Vladimir Bekhterev and Ivan Pavlov. The conditioning research is especially noteworthy because it marked the point at which Lashley decided that his future would be not just in biology but in the intersection between biology and psychology (Bruce, 1986). This decision was cemented when he completed postdoctoral research on the effects of brain injury on behavior with Franz. By 1920, he knew he would be an experimental psychologist specializing in how learning and memory affect the brain.

Lashley's distinguished academic career included stops at the Universities of Minnesota and Chicago, and at Harvard University. In 1942, he became director of the Yerkes Laboratory of Primate Biology in Florida, where his research on animal behavior bridged the laboratory-based comparative psychology favored by American scientists and the field-based, naturalistic approach of European ethologists (Bruce, 1991). He died of heart failure in 1958, while on holiday in France. Among psychologists, Lashley is best known for the research he completed in the 1920s while at Chicago, a series of experiments that was characterized at the time of his death as being "without equal in recent experimental psychology" (Hebb, 1959).

Equipotentiality and Mass Action

The year 1929 was an important one for Lashley. His peers elected him president of the American Psychological Association, recognizing the value of the research he had been engaged in during the decade of the 1920s. That research was summarized in *Brain Mechanisms and Intelligence*, which also appeared in 1929. Lashley defined the term intelligence in an animal learning context, using it to cover the behavior of rats learning to negotiate mazes and solve simple discrimination and puzzle box

problems. He readily admitted that his choice of tests could be criticized: "They all deal with some aspect of the learning process, [but their] relation to the problem of intelligence is not yet clearly established" (Lashley, 1929, p. 14). Nonetheless, he argued that simple mechanical or reflexive explanations of learning, such as the ones proposed by Watson and Pavlov, were inadequate to capture the complexity of how animals went about solving the kinds of problems that enabled them to survive in their environments. Thus, he considered the tasks presented to his rats to be sufficiently intricate to bear at least some relation to the intelligent, adaptive behavior found in the animals' real-world environments.

Lashley's procedures were in the tradition of the great French physiologist Flourens—he observed the effects of brain ablations on behavior, systematically destroying different amounts of cortex and observing the effects on learning and retention. One of his procedures was maze learning and Figure 3.6 shows three of the four mazes he used. Maze I was a simple T-maze in which the animal had to make a single left-right choice. Maze II had three possible dead-ends, while Maze III had eight.[8] During training, each brain-damaged rat negotiated one of the mazes five times per day and learning was defined as 10 consecutive errorless runs through the maze. The relationship between the extent of cortical damage and performance for each of these mazes can be seen in Lashley's graph, Figure 3.7. For simple mazes such as Maze I, performance was quite good even after large amounts of cortical destruction. With maze II, the performance deteriorated slightly, but was still only marginally affected by the brain lesions. It is only with a more difficult problem, Maze III, that the rat's performance was dramatically affected by the extent of the damage. As the percent of destruction

---

[8] Maze IV had the same design as Maze III, but with the pattern reversed. In addition, while Mazes I–III were alley mazes (i.e., they had walls), Maze IV was an elevated maze, which required the rat to run on the edges of boards (only 3/16 of an inch wide) that were placed vertically on a table.

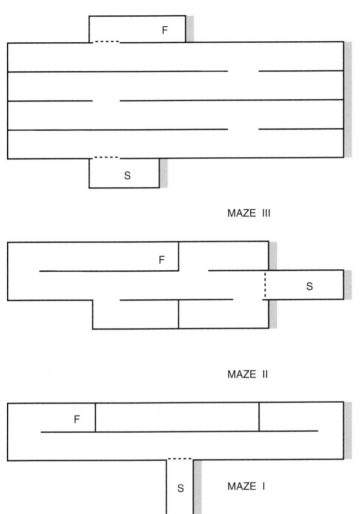

Figure 3.6   Mazes used by Lashley (1929) in his studies of equipotentiality and mass action (S = start box; F = food).

MAZE III

MAZE II

MAZE I

increased, performance declined precipitously. Hence, Lashley was reporting what amounted to an interaction between maze complexity and the degree of cortical lesioning. In simple tasks, the extent of destruction had little effect, while on difficult tasks, performance was directly related to the amount of destruction.

On the basis of the maze studies and similar experiments with his other procedures, Lashley reached two general conclusions very similar to the ones arrived at by Flourens nearly a century earlier. First was the principle that Lashley called **equipotentiality**, a term

...used to designate the apparent capacity of any intact part of a functional area to carry out, with or without reduction in efficiency, the functions which are lost by destruction of the whole. This capacity varies from one area to another and with the character of the functions involved. It probably holds only for the association areas and for functions more complex than simple sensitivity or motor coordination. (Lashley, 1929, p. 25)

Equipotentiality was a strong argument against cerebral localization of function, at least

Figure 3.7   The effects of maze difficulty and degree of cortical destruction on maze learning, from Lashley (1929).

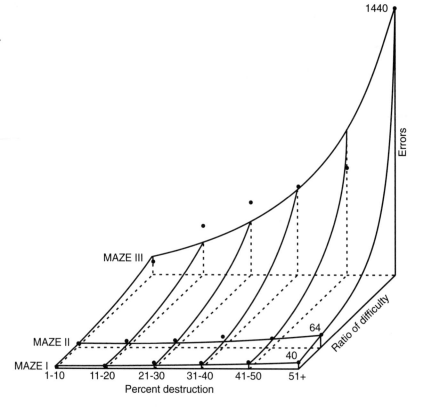

within the broad area of learning and in those cortical areas not known to govern specific sensory-motor functions. It was supplemented, however, by the law of **mass action**:

> [E]quipotentiality is not absolute but is subject to a law of mass action whereby the efficiency of performance of an entire complex function may be reduced in proportion to the extent of brain injury within an area whose parts are not more specialized for one component of the function than for another. (Lashley, 1929, p. 25)

Thus, the process of learning does not seem to be localized in any specific area of the cortex, but learning efficiency is proportional to the amount of cortical destruction.

These principles of equipotentiality and mass action were Lashley's key findings, but he was

also interested in the general process of maze learning. He was well aware of the maze research of his former colleague John Watson, for example, and disagreed with Watson's belief that maze learning involved the kinesthetic sense and the conditioning of a chain of specific motor responses (see Chapter 10). Lashley argued that Watson's model could not account for the strange behavior of those animals with lesions affecting their motor movements. They could still make it through the maze, even if their motor movements were considerably altered:

> One drags himself through with his forepaws; another falls at every step but gets through by a series of lunges; a third rolls over completely in making each turn, yet manages to avoid rolling into a cul-de-sac and makes an errorless run.... If the

customary sequence of movements employed in reaching the food is rendered impossible, another set, not previously used in the habit, and constituting an entirely different pattern, may be directly and efficiently substituted without any random activity. (Lashley, 1929, p. 136)

Lashley's conclusions about how the rat learned the maze were similar to those soon to be drawn by the neobehaviorist Edward Tolman (Chapter 11), who argued that rats developed an overall "cognitive map" of the maze and were thus aware of the general direction of the goal. When describing such maps, Tolman (1948, p. 203) referred specifically to Lashley's work for support. Although Lashley did not use the term "map," he clearly had the concept of directionality in mind when planning the following variation with Maze III. Removing the mesh cover normally on top of the maze, a few of his rats (5 out of 20 tested)

climbed on top of the maze and went straight across the top of it to the point where the goal was located. Lashley noted that "the behavior of the 5 that followed the direct course to the food suggested that they were perfectly oriented with respect to its direction, although they had never before reached it save by the indirect path of the maze" (Lashley, 1929, p. 137).

Lashley's research on the relationship between brain and behavior was a natural culmination of the developments in nervous system physiology that occurred in the nineteenth century and a link to the physiological psychology of the twentieth century. We are now a bit ahead of the story, however, and must return to the nineteenth century to examine how psychology emerged as a "new science" in Germany (Chapter 4) and how it was influenced by the theory of evolution, the nineteenth century's most important intellectual event (Chapter 5).

SUMMARY

Heroic Science in the Age of Enlightenment

- The Enlightenment was a period during the eighteenth and nineteenth centuries when great faith existed in the ability of science and human reason to produce true knowledge about the world. Scientists were heroes, considered to be objective and value free, with Newton being the prime exemplar. Science was thought to lead inevitably to progress through technological innovation. In this context, the belief that psychology could become scientific began to take hold.

Sensory Physiology

- From the time of Descartes, scientists have been interested in the nature of the simple reflex. In the eighteenth century, Whytt completed the first systematic studies, showing conclusively that the spinal cord was necessary in order for reflexes to occur. Anticipating the concept of conditioning, Whytt also pointed out that the stimulus-response connections could develop through habit.

- When Magendie severed the posterior root of a dog's spinal cord, the affected area could move but was insensitive to stimulation. When the anterior root was severed, no movement occurred. Magendie concluded that the posterior root controlled sensation, while the anterior root controlled motor movements. Bell made similar observations, and the distinction is now known as the Bell-Magendie Law.

- According to Müller's doctrine of the specific energies of nerves, (a) we are directly aware of our nervous systems, not the world, and (b) each of the five basic sensory systems has nerve fibers designed for that specific sense.

- Helmholtz was opposed to vitalism and fought it through his doctrine of conservation of energy and by measuring the finite speed of the neural impulse. He was without peer as an expert on visual and auditory perception, known for the trichromatic theory of color vision, the resonance theory of audition, and his empiricist approach to perception, which emphasized unconscious inference.

Localization of Brain Function

- Phrenology, developed by Gall and promoted by Spurzheim, was the first serious theory of localization of brain function. Phrenologists believed that different parts of the brain served different faculties, that the portion of brain allocated to a faculty was proportional to the strength of the faculty, and that faculties and their strengths could be determined by measuring the skull.

- Because it relied too heavily on anecdotal evidence and faulty logic, phrenology lost scientific credibility quickly. It remained popular with the general public, however, being consistent with the American ideals of individuality and self-improvement.

- By developing the method of ablation, Flourens was able to falsify phrenological doctrine, while at the same time showing that the cortex operates as an integrated system.

- Evidence for localization came from clinical studies, in which those suffering from various forms of brain disease or damage were studied. The case of Phineas Gage illustrated the effects of severe frontal lobe damage on judgment and personality. Broca's study of "Tan," who suffered from motor aphasia, showed that the ability to produce articulate speech depended on a fairly circumscribed area of the left cortex.

- By developing the procedure of electrically stimulating the surface of the cortex, Fritsch and Hitzig in Germany and Ferrier in Great Britain began to map the functions of the surface of the brain with a "scientific phrenology."

Early Twentieth-Century Studies of the Nervous System and Behavior

- The identification of neurons as the basic units of the nervous system was made by Golgi, who thought they were physically connected to each other, and Ramón y Cajal, who thought they were physically separate from each other.

- Ramón y Cajal's theory was verified by Sherrington, who is credited with discovering the synapse and demonstrating its existence in his research on reflexes and through the phenomena of temporal and spatial summation.

- Lashley's research on the brain and learning showed that maze learning was not localized in any particular area of the cortex. Rather, the cortex operated as a system and was characterized by equipotentiality and mass action.

FOR FURTHER READING

BAKAN, D. (1966). The influence of phrenology on American psychology. *Journal of the History of the Behavioral Sciences, 2,* 200–220.

A close analysis of the development of phrenology, its rejection by the scientific community, and its popularity with the American public; shows how phrenology fit in with the temperament of progressivism and was an early example of the approach to psychology that emphasizes individual differences.

BRUCE, D. B. (1986). Lashley's shift from bacteriology to neuropsychology, 1910–1917, and the influence of Jennings, Watson, and Franz. *Journal of the History of the Behavioral Sciences, 22,* 27–44.

A description of Lashley's formative years and how his eventual self-identification as a physiological psychologist was affected by his doctoral studies with Jennings, his collaboration with Watson, and his postdoctoral work with Franz.

FEARING, F. (1930). *Reflex action: A study in the history of physiological psychology.* New York: Hafner Publishing Company.

Not exactly a page-turner, but an excellent reference source for information on how the reflex has been studied from the Greeks until the date of publication; good example of an internal history, emphasizing research outcomes that gradually expanded knowledge about reflex action.

MACMILLAN, M. B. (1986). A wonderful journey through skull and brain: The travels of Mr. Gage's tamping iron. *Brain and Cognition, 5,* 67–107.

Despite the odd title, a scholarly and detailed account of the case of Phineas Gage, including a description of his medical treatment by Harlow, and an analysis of how the case bears on the localization issue.

4

WUNDT AND GERMAN PSYCHOLOGY

The book which I here present to the public is an attempt to mark out a new domain of science.

Wilhelm Wundt, 1874

▼
___

Preview

Chapters 2 and 3 describe the context out of which modern psychology emerged in the nineteenth century. Philosophers, interested in the same fundamental questions about the human mind and behavior that occupy psychologists today, began to speculate about the need to examine these issues scientifically. At least one nineteenth-century British philosopher, John Stuart Mill, explicitly called for a scientific psychology. Meanwhile, physiologists and physicians in Europe made great strides in furthering our understanding of the physiology of the nervous system and, in particular, of the brain. This chapter examines how this experimental physiology combined with philosophical inquiry to create a new experimental psychology in Germany in the late nineteenth century. The chapter opens with a brief discussion of some aspects of German education that made it attractive to American students, then continues with a look at how Gustav Fechner's psychophysics provided a standardized set of methods for studying the mind. The creation of the New Psychology and its first laboratory by Leipzig's Wilhelm Wundt forms the focus of the middle of the chapter. The chapter ends with consideration of three other important German psychologists, Hermann Ebbinghaus, G. E. Müller, and Oswald Külpe. The Original Source Excerpt is from Ebbinghaus's famous book about his experiments on memory.

AN EDUCATION IN GERMANY

American students have always looked to European universities as a way to further their educations. Even today, a semester abroad is a valued experience. In the nineteenth century, Germany was an especially attractive location for young scholars; it has been estimated that in the 100-year span beginning in 1820, at least 9000 American students enrolled in one German university or another (Sahakian, 1975), usually to study medicine or one of the sciences. By the end of the century, they were going there to study psychology.

One reason for the popularity of German universities was mere quantity. Between the time of the 1815 Congress of Vienna and the unification of Germany under Bismarck in 1871, Germany did not exist as a "country," but was a loosely organized federation of 38 autonomous "principalities" (e.g., Bavaria, Hanover, Saxony) (Palmer, 1964). Each ministate wanted to keep up with its neighbors, of course, and one means of accomplishing this goal was to have its own university. Hence, universities proliferated throughout the federation of principalities, although many of them were little more than a building with some classrooms and a few professors. Several gained international stature, however, and drew students from all over Europe as well as from America.

Circumstances in nineteenth-century Germany were especially conducive to the development of a new and more scientific approach to psychology. Beginning in the middle of the century, and originating at the University of Berlin, German universities developed a distinctive philosophy of education known as *Wissenschaft*. It was an approach that emphasized scholarly research combined with teaching and academic freedom for professors to pursue their research interests without fear of censure. Students were free to wander from one university to another, and earning a degree resulted more from the passing of special exams and the defense of a research thesis than from the completion of a specific curriculum.

For the professors who would create a new scientific psychology, many of whom you will meet in this chapter, the timing was perfect. The success of the physiologists (Chapter 3) reinforced the *Wissenschaft* emphasis on a research-based atmosphere and contributed directly to the growth of the new experimental approach to psychology in Germany, especially at Leipzig. As Blumenthal has pointed out, the methods being developed by the physiologists, "involving measurement, replicability, public data, and controlled tests" (1980, p. 29), which were being applied to the study of the nervous system, might just as well be applied to other aspects of human behavior. Gradually the term "physiological" in German came to mean "experimental." When Wilhelm Wundt referred to the new psychology as a "physiological psychology," he meant it in this broader sense of psychology being a discipline based on scientific methodology.

For the American student of the 1880s who desired to learn about this new field of study firsthand, several choices were available (e.g., Gottingen, Heidelberg, Berlin: see map in Figure 4.1), but Wundt's laboratory was the best equipped and had the strongest reputation, so traveling to Leipzig became the most fashionable option. During Wundt's tenure, approximately three dozen Americans completed doctorates under his supervision and a number of others at least sampled the Leipzig environment (Benjamin, Durkin, Link, Vestal, & Accord, 1992). Before considering Wundt and his influence on the development of American psychology, however, some important preliminaries are in order.

ON THE THRESHOLD OF EXPERIMENTAL PSYCHOLOGY: PSYCHOPHYSICS

A strong case can be made that scientific research on psychological topics began as a natural extension of the physiological research being done in the nineteenth century. Later in this chapter you

Figure 4.1   Map of Germany, showing locations of the universities relevant for psychology's history.

will encounter one example of this in the connection between Helmholtz's physiological studies of nerve impulse speed and the psychological method of reaction time. In this section, we examine an association between physiological research on sensory processes and the development of **psychophysics**, the study of the relationship between the perception of a stimulus event ("psycho") and the physical dimensions of the stimulus being perceived ("physics"). Psychophysics originated in the sensory research of Ernst Weber and became clearly defined with the enigmatic Gustav Fechner.

ERNST WEBER (1795–1878)

Weber spent most of his academic career at the University of Leipzig, first as a student and then as a professor of anatomy and physiology from

1818 until his retirement in 1871. In the 1820s physiologists were beginning to learn a great deal about visual and auditory sensation, but little was known of the other senses. Weber set out to correct the imbalance by becoming the leading authority on the tactile senses (Dorn, 1972). He made two major contributions: mapping the relative sensitivity of various locations on the skin, and demonstrating a mathematical relationship between the psychological and the physical that would later be known as Weber's Law.

Two-Point Thresholds

To examine tactile sensitivity, Weber used a technique in which he touched the skin with a simple device resembling a two-point compass. The distance between the points could be varied, and the blindfolded observer's task was to judge whether one or two points were being felt. For any specific area of the skin, there exists a **two-point threshold**—the point where the perception changes from "one" point to "two." For skin areas of great sensitivity, the thumb for instance, Weber found the threshold to be quite small. That is, the points didn't have to be very far apart before being noticed as two distinct points rather than one. On the other hand, for areas of less sensitivity, the upper arm for instance, the points would have to be placed farther apart before they were perceived as being two separate ones. Figure 4.2 shows a series of two-point thresholds from shoulder to fingertip, taken from a later (1870) study by Vierordt (cited in Boring, 1942, p. 478).

Weber believed that the different two-point thresholds resulted from differences in the sizes of what he called "sensory circles," shown as hexagons on Weber's sketch in Figure 4.3 (Weber, 1852, shown in Boring, 1942, p. 476). These were areas of the skin that were sensed by the branching fibers of a single sensory nerve. If two points of a compass would both touch the skin within a single sensory circle, the perception would be of a single point, Weber thought. When the two points touched two different cir-

Figure 4.2   Two-point thresholds for various locations between shoulder and fingertip, from Boring (1942).

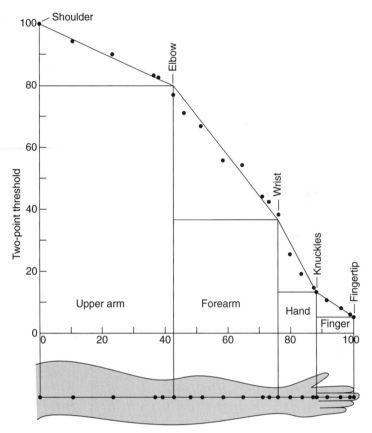

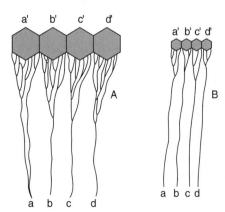

Figure 4.3   Weber's conception of sensory circles, from Boring (1942).

cles, two points would be felt. Skin areas of greater sensitivity had smaller circles. Thus, the set of four sensory circles on the left in Figure 4.3 might be from an area near the shoulder, while the circles on the right might be closer to the fingertip. The sense of touch turns out to be more complicated than this, but Weber's model had the beneficial effect of generating considerable research on just how the tactile senses worked. Also, although he did not think of the research in these terms, Weber was measuring mental events (perceptions).

Weber's Law

Weber's second contribution derived from his interest in the "muscle sense," what we would today call kinesthesis. He wanted to know how important this sense was for making judgments about the comparative weights of objects (Heidbreder, 1933). Picture two tasks. In the first, your hand is resting on a table and first one then another weighted cylinder is placed in your palm. Your task is to judge which cylinder is heavier. In the second task, the two cylinders are on the table and this time you lift each one before making the same judgment. In performing such an experiment, Weber found that he and other observers could make finer discriminations when they lifted the weights, which brings the muscle sense into play. More important for the history of psychology, Weber also discovered that the ability to discriminate between two weights did not depend on the absolute difference between them in weight, but on a more complicated relationship. This relationship later became known as Weber's law.

In the weight-lifting experiments, Weber was dealing with thresholds again. For example, if observers cannot distinguish between 30 and 31 grams, and between 30 and 32 grams (they judge them to be the same weight), but *can* distinguish between 30 and 33 grams, then clearly some kind of threshold has been passed at 33 grams. Weber referred to the discrimination between 30 and 33 grams as a "just noticeable difference" or **jnd**. What he discovered was that the jnd depended not on the absolute size of the difference between the weights, but on the relationship between this jnd and the smaller of the two weights (called the "standard stimulus," or *S*). As the standard stimulus became heavier, a greater difference between the weights was necessary before the difference was noticed. That is, **Weber's law** was this: *jnd/S = k*. So observers would notice a difference between 30 and 33 grams, but not between 60 and 63 grams. If the standard stimulus is 60 grams instead of 30, no difference can be detected until the second weight is at least 66 grams (3/30 = 6/60). Similarly, if S = 90 grams, the jnd will be 9 grams. Hence, the jnd was proportional to the size of S.

The importance of Weber's law is threefold. First, as with the two-point threshold research, Weber was subjecting mental events to measurement and mathematical formulation. This would eventually make psychophysics an essential element of Wilhelm Wundt's "New Psychology," which would claim to be a science. Science demands objective measurement and threshold research seemed to fit the bill nicely. Second, Weber showed that there is not a one-to-one relationship between changes in the physical world and the psychological experience of those changes. Increasing a weight by 3 grams does not always produce the same sensation. Sometimes differences will be perceived (if S = 30), sometimes not (if S = 60). Consequently, understanding how the mind organizes its experiences requires knowing more than just the physical dimensions of the stimuli to which we are exposed; it also requires an attempt to determine how the mind perceives those physical stimuli. Third, Weber's law showed that mental and physical events could be related mathematically. That insight would be developed more fully by another Leipzig scientist.

GUSTAV FECHNER (1801–1889)

Weber's goal as a physiologist was to understand the nature of the tactile and muscle senses and to do so he used methods that would eventually be known as psychophysical. His younger Leipzig colleague Gustav Fechner had an even more ambitious goal, however. Fechner was obsessed with the idea of resolving the ageless mind-body problem in a way that would defeat materialism, and he thought that psychophysics was the way to do it. Fechner can be considered the first genuine experimental psychologist, even though he was trained as a physician, made his reputation as a physicist, and when he was in the midst of his pioneering research in psychophysics, thought of himself as a philosopher.

Fechner was born in a Lutheran parsonage in southern Germany in 1801; he was a precocious child, familiar with Latin by age five. At age 16 he entered the University of Leipzig to study medicine, and his education included a dose of physiology with Weber. The M.D. was earned in 1822, but Fechner never practiced medicine. During the 1820s, his interests focused on math and physics, and during this time he lectured in these areas (without pay) and earned a living by translating physics and chemistry texts from French to German. He also made original research contributions in the new physics of electricity during this time.[1] His research was notable enough to earn him a position at Leipzig as professor of physics in 1834, the same year that Weber published his research on the sensation of touch.

Fechner's interests in science broadened in the 1830s to include the study of visual afterimages, the kind that occur after a bright light is flashed on and off. He discovered a relationship between the brightness of the light and the strength of the afterimage, which led him to consider the quality of afterimages resulting from a quick glance at the brightest of all lights: the sun. Quick glances become longer glances and even though Fechner wore filters to reduce the effects of staring at the sun, he severely damaged his eyesight. The problem was serious enough to force him to resign his professorship in 1839 and accept a disability pension from the university.

Long before the afterimage episode, Fechner suffered from headaches and an occasional inability to control his thoughts, but the blindness triggered a descent into neurosis that lasted several years (Balance & Bringmann, 1987). Fechner became an invalid, forced to spend long periods of time in total darkness and plagued by

a variety of anxiety, depressive, and somatic symptoms. In his words,

> My situation…became even more depressing. Since I was accustomed to using my mind and had few skills in dealing with others merely on a social basis and was not good at anything other than working with pen and textbook, I suffered soon the tortures of deadly boredom…. (cited in Balance & Bringmann, 1987, p. 39)

Fechner's ascent to normality began in 1842 and was complete by the mid-1840s. It was accomplished largely through his own efforts at regaining control over his life, but was facilitated by a steady improvement in his vision. After recovering, he turned his attention to philosophical matters and in 1851 he was reappointed to the Leipzig faculty. It was during this period that he became immersed in the question of the relationship of mind to body and consumed with the idea of defeating materialism. As you recall from the last chapter, materialism, the belief that all events have causes that can be traced to physical and chemical changes, was favored by most of the younger physiologists of the day (e.g., Helmholtz).

Fechner referred to materialism as the *Nachtansicht*, or "Night View," and he hoped to replace it with a contrasting *Tagesansicht*, or "Day View." This Day View derived from an idealism movement then popular in German philosophy which held that the universe as a whole had a form of consciousness to it that went beyond the individual consciousnesses of the organisms within it. Upon death, one's personal consciousness merged with this cosmic

---

[1] Fechner's research on electricity reveals an interesting connection with his father, a Lutheran minister whose faith extended into the realm of science. The elder Fechner was aware of the famous electricity experiments of Benjamin Franklin, and of Franklin's invention of the lightning rod in 1787. Knowing that church steeples were a favorite target of lightning bolts, he prudently installed one of Franklin's devices on his church steeple. Members of the church felt that their pastor was not showing much faith in God's ability to protect the church, but Pastor Fechner commented that the laws of physics also had to be considered (Boring, 1950). Pastor Fechner died when his son was only five, but young Gustav apparently inherited his father's love of and respect for science.

consciousness. For Fechner, this meant that while mind and body could be considered two aspects of the same fundamental reality, the mind was the primary and dominant feature of that reality. It was in searching for a way to conceptualize the exact mind-body relationship that he created psychophysics. He later claimed that he achieved the insight suddenly, upon waking on the morning of October 22, 1850.[2] It occurred to him that mind and body could be united harmoniously and with mathematical precision by measuring psychological sensations and the physical stimuli that produced the sensations. The insight triggered a decade of intense work, resulting in the publication in 1860 of the *Elements of Psychophysics*, often considered the first book of experimental psychology.

FECHNER'S *ELEMENTS OF PSYCHOPHYSICS*

Fechner was aware of Weber's research on thresholds, but it was only after his great insight of 1850 that he realized its significance. The breakthrough for Fechner was the conviction that sensations could be subjected to exact measurement by assuming that jnd's were subjectively equal in magnitude. Thus, weights of 30 and 33 grams are just noticeably different, as are weights of 60 and 66 grams. The differences in weight between the two pairs of stimuli are 3 and 6 grams, respectively. Psychologically, however, the difference between 30 and 33 feels the same as (i.e., is subjectively equal to) the difference between 60 and 66, according to Fechner. This assumption of subjective equality led Fechner to reformulate Weber's law as

$$S = k \log R$$

where S is the sensation, the perceived size of some stimulus in jnd units, k is a constant, and R is the physical measurement of the stimulus.

By assuming that jnd's could be the unit of psychological measurement, Fechner was able to conceive of a scale that began at the point where sensation was first noticed. This point he called the **absolute threshold**. As stimulus intensity increases above this threshold, the person eventually experiences a just noticeable difference, then another, and so on. These jnd's above the absolute threshold are **difference thresholds**. Consider the familiar example of a light with a dimmer switch. With the light completely off, there is of course no stimulation and no sensation of light. As the dimmer switch is slowly turned, there will continue to be zero sensation for a brief time, but soon we just barely notice the first glimmerings of light. This is the absolute threshold. If the dimmer switch continues to be turned, a point is reached where the light is now just noticeably brighter than a second ago. This is a difference threshold.

Fechner's assumption of equal jnd's was challenged almost immediately, and his mathematical relationship was shown to be true only under limited circumstances. No matter. The enduring legacy of his *Elements of Psychophysics* was his systematization of the methods used to establish thresholds, which are still in use, both in the laboratory and in such applications as vision and hearing tests. These are known today as the methods of limits, constant stimuli, and adjustment.[3] Consider them in the context of a hearing test designed to establish absolute thresholds. In the **method of limits**, a stimulus is presented that is well above threshold, then gradually reduced in intensity until the subject reports that it can no longer be heard.

---

[2] If you want to impress your professor, send him or her a "Happy Fechner Day" card on October 22. To this day, experimental psychologists, especially those who study sensation and perception, take some time out on that day to raise a glass in honor of Fechner's insight.

[3] Fechner referred to them as the methods of just noticeable differences, right and wrong cases, and average error, respectively.

Now Methods Fechner
LIMITS ← just notable differences
Constant Stim ← right + wrong cases

Adjustment ← Average Error

This is called a descending trial, and it is followed by an ascending trial, in which the stimulus is first presented below threshold, then increased until the subject hears it for the first time. Descending and ascending trials are alternated a number of times, and the threshold is calculated as an average of all the trials. In the **method of constant stimuli**, sounds of varying intensities are presented in a random order and the subject's task is to indicate whether or not they are heard. This method solves a problem with the method of limits, which is a tendency to anticipate the place where the threshold lies. In the **method of adjustment**, the subject directly varies the intensity of the stimulus until it seems to be at threshold. While these examples involve absolute thresholds, all three methods can also be used in experiments on difference thresholds. Of the three techniques, a study using the method of adjustment takes the least amount of time, but is the least accurate; the method of constant stimuli is the most accurate, but takes the longest time (Goldstein, 1996). In an actual hearing test, the method of limits with descending trials is normally used, with "catch trials" inserted to prevent subjects from raising their hands ("I hear it") when there is in fact no stimulus presented.

Boring (1963b) has referred to Fechner as the "inadvertent founder of psychophysics." He believed that Fechner's main purpose was philosophical: to establish his Day View while defeating materialism (the Night View). Unfortunately for Fechner, that goal was not reached and the philosophical implications of his work were largely ignored. Fortunately for psychology, Fechner's efforts resulted in the creation of a program of research and a set of methods that enabled others to see what Fechner did not: that psychological phenomena could be subjected to scientific methodology. By inadvertently creating psychophysics in 1860, Fechner paved the way for another German physiologist, Wilhelm Wundt, to proclaim a "New Psychology" a few years later.

WUNDT ESTABLISHES A NEW PSYCHOLOGY AT LEIPZIG

The quote that opens this chapter comes from the preface of the epoch-making two-volume *Principles of Physiological Psychology*, published in 1873–1874 by the German most often described as the "founder" of experimental psychology, Wilhelm Wundt. To claim, as Wundt did, that one is making an "attempt to mark out a new domain of science" is the kind of statement that separates founders from their contemporaries. Clearly, Fechner's work on psychophysics entitles him to a claim as the first experimental psychologist. We've seen, however, that Fechner had other, more philosophical, purposes. Thus, as Boring (1950) has pointed out, founders are promoters; they might not be the first to accomplish something, but they are the first to proclaim loudly that their accomplishment breaks dramatically new ground. They might make some important scientific contribution, but their talent lies in their ability to propagandize. Wundt had that talent.

WILHELM WUNDT (1832–1920): CREATING A NEW SCIENCE

Experimental psychology's founder had a childhood of modest accomplishment. Excessive daydreaming and marginal performance characterized his early school years, and it wasn't until his late teens that he became interested in the direction of his education. Despite a dismal academic record, family connections enabled him to begin medical studies at the University of Tübingen at the age of 19; after a year he switched to Heidelberg, where he finally began to show promise. By 1855, he had earned an M.D. (summa cum laude) from the University of Heidelberg and had finished first on a state board certifying exam (Bringmann, Balance, & Evans, 1975).

The Heidelberg years also saw the blossoming of Wundt's interests in science. The famous chemist Robert Bunsen (yes, he invented the Bunsen burner) made a lasting impression: When Wundt eventually became a professor himself, he copied Bunsen's technique of illustrating points in class through the frequent use of visual displays and demonstrations. Bunsen also inspired Wundt's first independent research project, an examination of the effects of restricting salt input on the chemical composition of his urine. During these years, Wundt also completed some more sophisticated research, including a study of the roles played by several cranial nerves in breathing. This required an ablation method using live dogs and rabbits, a procedure that Wundt found troubling. He was bolstered by the support of his mother, who assisted in the surgery, which was completed in Wundt's home rather than at the university (Bringmann, Balance, & Evans, 1975). Wundt also conducted an experiment on the touch sensitivity of hysteric patients, using Weber's two-point threshold technique; this study served as his M.D. dissertation research.

Following completion of the M.D. in November of 1855, Wundt practiced medicine for a brief six months as a clinical assistant at Heidelberg's university hospital, but he was already beginning to think that a life of research was more appealing than a life of writing prescriptions and setting bones. He spent a semester in Berlin studying experimental physiology with the great Johannes Müller (Chapter 3), then resolved to become a professor of physiology upon his return to Heidelberg. He was given a position of *Privatdozent* in February of 1857, which in the German system meant that he was entitled to offer courses, but that his entire salary depended on student fees. Wundt's first course attracted only four students and near the completion of the course he

fell seriously ill, probably with tuberculosis (Bringmann, Bringmann, & Balance, 1980). After a yearlong recovery, he applied for an opening as the assistant in the laboratory of the esteemed Hermann Helmholtz (Chapter 3), who had just begun his tenure at Heidelberg. Wundt got the job, a major boost for his career.

Wundt toiled as Helmholtz's assistant for six years, from 1858 to 1864, but he did much more with his time than just run the laboratory. He continued to offer courses as *Privatdozent* and he began publishing at a rate that is astounding by any standard.[4] In addition to technical papers and two brief texts based on his lectures, Wundt published two important books that marked him as a emerging experimental psychologist. *Contributions to a Theory of Sensory Perception* appeared in 1862, followed a year later by *Lectures on Human and Animal Psychology*. The first book is noteworthy because it marks the first time that Wundt called for an explicitly experimental approach to basic psychological questions. Thus, he was thinking about the possibility that psychology could be a science long before his famous pronouncement of 1873–1874. The second book repeated the call and described some of the early research in psychophysics and reaction time.

Wundt left Helmholtz's laboratory in 1864 but remained at Heidelberg for another decade. He set up his own private laboratory and earned a livable wage through teaching fees and book royalties. In 1871 his efforts were finally rewarded by the university, which appointed him to the rank of Extraordinary Professor (similar to the associate professor level in American universities). This meant that for the first time in his life, Wundt had full faculty status and a salary that was not tied to student enrollment. Nearing the age of 40, he was finally secure enough to marry his fiancée of many years. During this time he

1862
1863

---

[4] By one estimate, Wundt published 53,735 pages during his professional years, an average of 2.2 pages per day (Boring, 1950, p. 345)!

wrote the work best-known to psychologists, his two-volume *Principles of Physiological Psychology* (1873–1874/1910), which included the chapter's opening quote in its Preface. The book, which eventually went through six editions, earned him a professorship in "inductive philosophy" at the University of Zurich (academic year 1874–1875). After just a year in Switzerland, Wundt was offered a similar position at the more prestigious University of Leipzig, Germany's largest university at the time, and he accepted immediately. There he remained until his retirement in 1917. He died three years later.

We tend to associate Wundt only with Leipzig, but it is important to realize that when he arrived there in 1875, he was already in his mid-forties and had been an active scientist at Heidelberg for 17 years. He had already written three important books and numerous papers, more than most professors produce in a lifetime. Furthermore, he had announced that at least some aspects of psychology could be experimental, and he had set out a plan for establishing what quickly came to be called the New Psychology. Thus, he had accomplished what would be a life's work for many. Yet Wundt still had more than *40* highly productive years left in him during his time at Leipzig.

During his years at Heidelberg, Wundt had accumulated a private collection of laboratory apparatus, both for his own research and for demonstrating various phenomena during his lectures (in the spirit of his old chemistry professor, Robert Bunsen). Upon arrival at Leipzig, he requested space to store the equipment. Although traditional accounts have it that the university gave him some space upon his arrival in 1875 and that the room eventually became his famous laboratory, careful archival research (Bringmann, Bringmann, & Ungerer, 1980) has shown that Leipzig delayed the assignment for a year, despite Wundt's repeated requests. Nonetheless, that the university granted the request at all is noteworthy, because space was quite limited at the time.

This modest beginning, a room with approximately 400 square feet, eventually became experimental psychology's first laboratory and the model for dozens of imitators. Wundt used the lab for demonstrational purposes initially, but by 1879 he and his students were conducting original research in what he now called the *Psychologisches Institut*. The Institute quickly became a magnet, attracting curious students from all over Europe and from America. Additional rooms were added over the years, and in 1897 a new and more elaborate laboratory was built to Wundt's specifications. It was destroyed by an Allied bombing raid in 1943. An inside look at the workings of Wundt's laboratory, a glimpse of which can be seen in Figure 4.4, will follow shortly; first, however, it is necessary to examine Wundt's vision for his New Psychology.

WUNDT'S CONCEPTION OF THE NEW PSYCHOLOGY

The "new domain of science" that Wundt attempted to "mark out" in his *Principles of Physiological Psychology* was a vision first outlined 12 years earlier in his 1862 book on perception (*Contributions to a Theory of Sensory Perception*). It called for the scientific examination of human conscious experience, using methods borrowed from experimental physiology and supplemented by new strategies. It included two major programs: the examination of "immediate" conscious experience using the experimental methods of the laboratory and the study of higher mental processes, using nonlaboratory methods.

Studying Immediate Conscious Experience

To understand the contrast that Wundt drew between immediate experience and "mediate" experience, consider a simple example. If you look out the window at a thermometer and it reads 15°F, you are not experiencing the phenomenon of temperature directly. Rather, temperature is being *mediated* by a scientific instru-

This year marks the date normally associated with the establishment of Wundt's laboratory of experimental psychology in Leipzig.

These events also occurred:

- The first electric tram was exhibited at the Berlin Trade Exhibition
- London established its first telephone exchange
- Ferdinand de Lesseps formed the Panama Canal Company
- The American novelist Henry James, brother of psychologist William James, published *Daisy Miller*
- Anti-Jesuit laws were introduced in France
- Mary Baker Eddy became pastor of the Church of Christ, Scientist, in Boston
- These people were born:

    Joseph Stalin, Soviet dictator

    Albert Einstein, German physicist
- This person died:

    Charles de Coster, Belgian author

**Key Date
1879**

ment. On the other hand, if you then step outside without a coat, you have a direct experience of coldness. It is an immediate conscious experience. That is, there is no thermometer standing between you and the weather; you are encountering it firsthand. For Wundt, it was this immediate conscious experience that was to be the subject matter of his laboratory psychology.

Wundt recognized the problem with studying immediate consciousness. To examine mediate experience objectively is simple. Because the temperature reading is a public event, two or more observers can agree on it

Figure 4.4   An aging Wilhelm Wundt (center) in his laboratory at Leipzig.

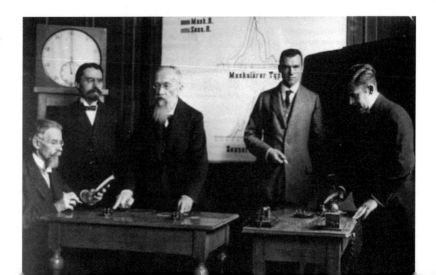

and it is a fairly straightforward matter to apply scientific methods. Various aspects of the environment can be manipulated systematically, and the resulting effects on temperature can be assessed with some precision. Describing immediate experience is more difficult, however. How can you be sure that your experience of coldness compares with mine? Here Wundt made a critical distinction between *self observation* and *internal perception*. The distinction has been blurred over the years, according to Danziger (1980), with both terms being called **introspection**. Self-observation is the traditional philosophical attempt to analyze life's experiences through introspective reflection. This was unsystematic and because such observations by definition take place some time after the experienced event has occurred, they rely too heavily on faulty memory. Wundt rejected self-observation as nothing better than philosophical speculation. **Internal perception**, on the other hand, was like self-observation, but a much narrower process of responding immediately to precisely controlled stimuli. The problem of memory was reduced by the immediacy of the response and by using observers (Wundt and his students) trained to respond automatically and without bias. Such precision came with a price, however. Internal perception could only yield valid scientific data if its results could be replicated. For Wundt, this meant that laboratory research had to be limited to a narrow range of experiences. In practice, this amounted to basic sensory/perceptual ones. Such experiences could be controlled by means of sophisticated apparatus used to present stimuli to observers, who in turn would give simple responses to these stimuli. In Wundt's lab, these types of introspective responses were "largely limited to judgments of size, intensity, and duration of physical stimuli, supplemented at times by judgments of their simultaneity and succession" (Danziger, 1980, p. 247). These, of course, are the kinds of judgments made in psychophysics experiments, which comprised a significant portion of the research in Wundt's

laboratory. As we will learn, Wundt's conception of introspection as internal perception differed sharply from the "systematic experimental introspection" used by two of his better known students, Oswald Külpe (below) and Edward B. Titchener (Chapter 7).

Studying Higher Mental Processes

Although Wundt believed that laboratory investigation was necessarily limited to the immediate conscious experience of basic mental processes, he also had a broader aim for his psychology. He wished to examine higher mental processes such as learning, thinking, language, and the effects of culture, but he believed that because these processes were so intertwined with an individual's personal history, cultural history, and the social environment, they could not be controlled sufficiently to be examined in the laboratory. Instead, they could only be studied through inductive observational techniques, cross-cultural comparisons, historical analysis, and case study.

These higher mental processes were a lifelong interest of Wundt's, first outlined in detail in his second major book (*Lectures on Human and Animal Psychology*, 1863). They fully occupied the last two decades of his life and during this time, he enhanced his reputation as a prodigious writer by publishing the massive 10-volume *Völkerpsychologie* ("volker" translates roughly as "cultural," "ethnic," or "communal"). The books include detailed analyses of language and culture, and encompass topics that would today be considered under the headings of psycholinguistics, the psychology of religion and myth, social psychology, forensic psychology, and anthropology. Of the 10 volumes, there were three on myth and religion, two on language, two on society, and one each on culture and history, law, and art (Blumenthal, 1975)

Wundt, like other thinkers of his time, believed that an implication of evolutionary theory was that cultures could be arranged on a continuum, from "primitive" (e.g., Australian aboriginal) to "advanced" (German, presumably). By studying the social customs, myths, religions, and languages of cultures differing in their level of sophistication, Wundt thought that an understanding of the evolution of human mental processes could be attained (Farr, 1983). He was especially interested in language, and his descriptions give him a legitimate claim to the title of founder of modern psycholinguistics. Much of what he wrote about language was ignored at the time, only to be rediscovered in the 1950s and 1960s, when psycholinguistics became a key element in the rise of cognitive psychology (Blumenthal, 1975). For example, Wundt distinguished between the idea that was to be conveyed by a sentence, the actual structure of the sentence itself, and the manner in which the listener took the sentence structure and inferred the speaker's meaning from it. The relationship between the idea to be conveyed and the sentence structure is similar to the distinction later made by Chomsky between the deep and surface structures of a grammar, and Wundt's belief that the listener would not recall the actual sentence but the meaning of it is similar to later research on memory for the "gist" of communicated messages.

INSIDE WUNDT'S LABORATORY

Once Wundt's students began producing original research at Leipzig, the need for a way to publicize the work became apparent. Wundt solved the problem in 1881 by creating the journal *Philosophische Studien* (*Philosophical Studies*). It was the first journal designed to report the results of experimental research in psychology and Wundt served as editor for its first two decades (1881–1903). The journal became a mouthpiece for the work done by Wundt and his students, so a look at its contents reveals the kind of research done at Leipzig during the last two decades of the nineteenth century. According to Boring (1950), who examined the 100 or so experimental

studies published in the journal during this time, at least half of the research was in the area of sensation and perception. Of the remaining half, reaction time studies were the most popular, followed by studies on attention, feeling, and association.

Sensation and Perception

Most of the basic information about sensory systems encountered in today's courses in sensation/perception was known by the turn of the century and some of the research was carried out in Wundt's laboratory. As mentioned earlier, most of these "internal perception" studies were psychophysical in nature, examining such topics as the abilities to distinguish colors presented to different areas of the retina and tones presented in various combinations of pitch and loudness. In perception, Wundtians studied such topics as positive and negative afterimages, visual contrast, illusions, and the perception of size, depth, and motion (Boring, 1950).

Mental Chronometry

When Helmholtz measured the duration of a nerve impulse and found it to be more leisurely than expected (Chapter 3), he provided the impetus to a method that came to be known as **mental chronometry** in Wundt's lab. Today we call it reaction time. Wundt was aware of this research long before he arrived in Leipzig. He became Helmholtz's assistant at Heidelberg shortly after the nerve impulse studies had been carried out and he became very interested in the problem of measuring mental speed in the 1860s. The problem had also been around for a number of years in the form of a practical difficulty faced by astronomers. The creation of tables for calculating longitude required knowing the precise positions of various stars and planets at specific times of a lunar cycle (Sobel, 1995). Identifying these positions involved a complicated procedure which measured the time taken for a planet to make a "transit" from one side of the crosshair of a telescope lens to the other. Humans were making the judgments of course, and even though they were trained astronomers, their judgments of transit times tended to be different because of small differences in their reaction times. To solve the problem, an attempt was made to calibrate one astronomer against another by determining each one's **personal equation**. Thus, if astronomer A was regularly 0.12 second slower than astronomer B, their transit times could be made comparable through a personal equation: $A = B + 0.12$ second.

The individual who developed the reaction time procedure as it came to be used by the Wundtians was F. C. Donders (1818–1889), a Dutch physiologist. Donders reasoned that if nerve impulses take a measurable amount of time and if mental activity is composed of nerve impulses, then various mental events potentially could be determined with some precision. Assuming that mental events could be combined in an additive fashion, Donders developed the **subtractive method** in the late 1860s. First, he would measure the time taken for a simple reaction: holding down a telegraph key, then releasing it as soon as possible after perceiving a light, for example. The procedure would then be "complicated" by adding other mental tasks. For instance, the observer might be asked to respond only if a red light came on; if the light was another color, no response was to be made. This "discrimination reaction time" (DRT) was composed of everything involved in simple reaction time (SRT), *plus* the mental event of discriminating between the colors. Thus:

$$DRT = SRT + \text{discrimination time}$$

$$\text{discrimination time} = DRT - SRT$$

Similarly, "choice reaction time" (CRT) involved releasing one key if the light was one color and another key if the light was a second color. In addition to simple reaction time and the time taken to discriminate between the two colors, the observer also had to choose which key to release. Thus:

$$CRT = SRT + \text{discrimination time} + \text{choice time}$$

$$\text{choice time} = CRT - (SRT + \text{discrimination time})$$

$$\text{choice time} = CRT - DRT$$

For reasons that are apparent, this procedure was also called the **complication experiment**; studies using it flourished in Wundt's laboratory, especially in the 1880s. The procedure was eventually discarded, however, when it became clear that the additive assumptions underlying the method were overly simplistic. In the above procedures, for instance, certain more complicated reactions should always be longer than less complicated ones, but in actual experiments this outcome did not always occur. Wundt's student Oswald Külpe, to be discussed in more detail below, pointed out that altering the procedure by adding discrimination and/or choice does not simply add elements; rather, it changed the entire experimental situation.

James McKeen Cattell (Chapter 8), perhaps the best known of the American students who studied with Wundt, was an enthusiastic advocate of the reaction time method (Garrett, 1951). He began his research while a student at Johns Hopkins in Baltimore, then continued it after arriving in Leipzig in 1883. An examination of one of his studies (Cattell, 1885/1948) nicely illustrates the logic of the reaction time method and the close attention to detail needed to carry out such research. In the article, Cattell described some research on simple, discrimination, and choice reaction times that were completed with his German colleague Gustav Berger. The research formed the basis for Berger's doctoral dissertation for Wundt on the effects of stimulus intensity on reaction time (Sokal, 1981).

In the first experiment, Cattell and Berger gave simple reaction times to lights that varied in intensity. The experimental setup probably looked something like the one in Figure 4.5 (photo taken at Clark University in 1892). As Cattell described it, "[t]he observer sat in the dark, and looked through a telescopic tube at

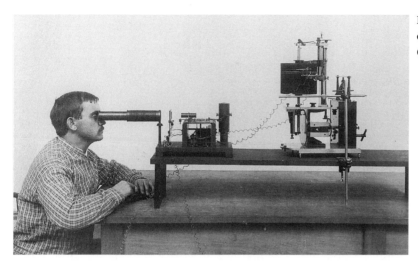

Figure 4.5 Reaction time experiment in progress at Clark University, 1892.

the point where the light was to appear" (1885/1948, p. 323). Cattell and Berger each made 150 reactions for each of eight intensity levels, finding that reaction time generally decreased as the light brightened. They also found individual differences—Cattell was consistently faster. *No – slower.*

In a similar manner, Cattell and Berger varied the intensity of an electrical shock to the left forearm, to examine its effect on the reaction time of the right hand. Again, reaction time quickened with increased intensity, although at the highest intensity "the reaction was probably retarded, because the shock was painful" (p. 325). In his data summaries, Cattell described both the mean score and a measure of variability (the average deviation, an early forerunner of today's standard deviation). Also, note that there are just two observers in the study, Berger and Cattell. This was a common situation in early experimental psychology: Very few participants, each person contributing a great deal of data, and no clear distinction between what we would today call the *experimenter* and the *subject*. Furthermore, data from several participants would not be averaged together. Rather, all data from each subject would be reported, with additional subjects serving the purpose of replication.

After reporting the simple reaction times, Cattell described the logic of the complication experiment and, using three of the eight light intensities, reported results for simple RT ("reaction time"), discrimination RT ("reaction with perception time"), and choice RT ("reaction with perception and will time"). Thus, "perception time" means discrimination time and "will time" means choice time. Here is his description of the complication rationale and the data:

> The time is longer when it is necessary to distinguish the colours before the reaction is made. We can determine this time, if instead of always reacting as quickly as possible, we react if it is red, but not at all if it is blue. We thus add to the simple reaction time. We can further let the subject lift his right hand if the light is red, his left hand if it is blue; we then have, besides the time necessary for the simple reaction and for distinguishing the colour, the time it takes to make a choice between two motions. The results of experiments made with three intensities of light (V, III, and I) are given in the table.[See Table 4.1] (Cattell, 1885/1948, p. 325)

As you can see, Cattell used the Donders system to arrive at his "perception" (i.e., discrimi-

Table 4.1

	B[erger]			C[attell]		
	V	*III*	*I*	*V*	*III*	*I*
Reaction Time	189	218	273	189	209	303
Reaction with Perception Time	238	293	373	274	328	417
Reaction with Perception and Will Time	287	320	393	356	388	495
Perception Time	49	75	100	85	119	114
Will Time	49	27	20	82	60	78

nation) and "will" (i.e., choice) times. For example, with Cattell as the observer and the stimulus intensity at V:

discrimination time = DRT - SRT
= 274 - 189
= 85 (i.e., 0.85 sec)

choice time = CRT - (SRT +
discrimination time)
= 356 - (189 + 85)
= 82 (i.e., 0.82 sec)

Like Külpe, Cattell eventually became a critic of the complication experiment while continuing to see the usefulness of the reaction time method to test various hypotheses about mental processing. That is, he eventually rejected the additive model while retaining the idea that reaction time could be used to compare mental activities that differed in complexity. This led him to study individual differences in reaction time and such phenomena as recognition times for different letters of the alphabet and reaction times for verbal associations (e.g., Cattell, 1886). Cattell also left a detailed account of day-to-day life in Wundt's laboratory, some of which is described in the Close-Up for this chapter.

▶ CLOSE-UP

An American in Leipzig

The most prominent of the three dozen or so American students who completed doctorates with Wundt was James McKeen Cattell (1860–1944). In 1886, he became the first American to earn a Leipzig Ph.D. in experimental psychology under Wundt's supervision (Benjamin, Durkin, Link, Vestal, & Accord, 1992). While at Leipzig, Cattell kept a detailed journal and corresponded frequently with his parents in America. These materials have been collected, organized, and annotated with great care by historian of science Michael Sokal, and published as *An Education in Psychology: James McKeen Cattell's Journal and Letters from Germany and England, 1880–1888* (1981). The book is a rich source of information about life in the early years of Wundt's laboratory at Leipzig.

Cattell first went to Leipzig as part of a European tour in 1881–1882. He then spent the 1882–1883 academic year at Johns Hopkins University in Baltimore, studying in the lab created by G. Stanley Hall (Chapter 6). He returned to Leipzig in the fall of 1883 and emerged with his doctorate three years later. Here are some of the observations he made about working in Wundt's laboratory, all taken from Sokal (1981).

Most of Cattell's research concerned the problem of reaction time. In a letter to his parents in 1884, he briefly described this research. Like others immersed in basic research that might seem trivial to outsiders, Cattell apparently felt a bit defensive and believed it necessary to convince his parents that his work was valuable:

Letter to Parents, 8 October 1884

In [my research] I determine the time required by simple mental processes—how long it takes us to see, hear or feel something—to understand, to will, to think. You may not consider this so very interesting or important. But if we wish to describe the world—which is the end of science—surely an accurate knowledge of our mind is more important than anything else.... [I]f one thinks that knowledge for its own sake is worth the pursuit, then surely a knowledge of mind is best of all. Not only is the mind of man of infinitely more worth and importance than anything else, but on its nature the whole world depends.

As to my special work—it is surely...in itself interesting to know how fast a man thinks—for on this, not on the number of years he lives depends the length of his life (p. 125)

Cattell's parents were apparently concerned that their son might overwork himself during his time at Leipzig. To reassure them, Cattell described a typical research day with his colleague, Gustav Berger. Only a portion of it required the kind of focused attention that would be fatiguing, Cattell reported:

Letter to Parents, 26 November 1884

Berger began work with me again this morning. I do not think I shall hurt myself in working, if I keep taking...constant exercise. It is undoubtedly true that making experiments on one's self is trying, but I do not do this continuously. If I spend six hours a day at this work, perhaps two must be given to looking after apparatus, preparing things &c. This is very easy work indeed. Then in two of the other four hours the other man is the subject and my work is not especially difficult. So you see I only spend two hours in work that strains. It were a pity if at twenty–five I could not stand that. (p. 141)

Cattell's observation about the two hours set aside for the apparatus illustrates the difficulty of developing a new science. Most of the apparatus had to be either adopted from the physics or physiology lab or invented on the spot. Apparatus problems were a constant irritant, as Cattell made clear in this letter:

Letter to Parents, 5 January 1885

Berger turned up early this morning and we started work. By way of variety not one but both of the electric batteries were out of order. You have no idea how much one must fuss over apparatus. The trouble is not that one must know physics, but that he must be an original investigator in physics. For example Prof. Wundt thought that when a magnet was made by passing a current around a piece of soft iron, it was made instantaneously. I find with the current he used it takes over a tenth of a second. All the times he measured were that much too long. Now the time required for magnetism to be developed in soft iron has nothing on earth to do with psychology, yet if I had not spent a great deal of time on this subject all my work would have been wrong.

Then it is hard to get apparatus made properly.... All this, the getting the apparatus and running it, is very aggravating when one is in a hurry. (pp. 151–152)

Throughout his career, Cattell never hesitated to speak his mind and was not known either for modesty or tolerance. In the following comment, made near the end of his time at Leipzig, he made it clear what he thought of Wundt's laboratory.

Letter to Parents, 22 January 1885

I worked in Wundt's laboratory this afternoon probably for the last time.... Wundt's laboratory has a reputation greater than it deserves—the work done is decidedly amateurish. Work has only been done in two departments—the relation of the internal stimulus to the sensation [i.e., psychophysics], and the time of mental process [i.e., reaction time]. The latter is my subject—I started working on it at Baltimore [at Johns Hopkins] before I had read a word written by Wundt—what I did there was decidedly original. I'm quite sure my work is worth more than all done by Wundt & his pupils in this department, and as I have said it is one of the two departments on which they have worked. Mind I do not consider my work of any special importance—I only consider Wundt's of still less. (p. 156)

REWRITING HISTORY: THE NEW AND IMPROVED WILHELM WUNDT

In Chapter 1, you learned that histories are continually being rewritten in light of new information, new ways of interpreting information, and so on. Wundt's psychology is a perfect illustration. If you had taken a history of psychology course about 30 years ago, you would have learned this about Wundt:

- He founded the first "school" of psychology, called structuralism.

- The main goal of Wundt's school was to analyze the contents of the mind into its basic structural components or elements, using introspection of mental contents as the chief method.

- He was not really interested in cultural psychology; the 10-volume *Völkerpsychologie* was just a secondary hobby for an old man.

- Wundt's intellectual son was E. B. Titchener, who carried out Wundt's program and spread the Wundtian gospel of structuralism in America.

- His model of the mind was similar to that of the British empiricists; that is, he did not believe in the concept of the mind as an active agent, but as the result of passive associative experiences.

Today, the only time you read descriptions like this one will be in chapter sections pointing out that each of these points is either a serious distortion or just wrong. In the 1970s, historians began taking a closer look at Wundt (e.g., Blumenthal, 1975; Danziger, 1980; Leahey, 1979) and discovered that the traditional accounts were problematic. Since that time, histories have begun to include more accurate descriptions of Wundt's life and work. Three questions arise: How did the distortions occur, why were they discovered only recently, and what did Wundt really say?

The Source of the Problem

Part of the difficulty derives from the fact that Wundt wrote more in his lifetime than most people can read in theirs. Also, much of his work has not been translated from German. Hence, there is a tendency for non-German speakers to rely on what others have written about Wundt, rather than on what Wundt said himself. Most psychologists learned their history from E. G. Boring, Boring learned most of his from Titchener, and therein lies the root of the problem. As you will learn in Chapter 7, Titchener studied with Wundt for two years and earned a Leipzig Ph.D. in 1892. He then spent his academic career at Cornell, where he spread the gospel of structuralism—his school, not Wundt's. Titchener also translated several of Wundt's books and wrote a long obituary shortly after Wundt's death (Titchener, 1921). In essence, Titchener took a portion of Wundt's work and exaggerated its importance, while downplaying or ignoring other parts of Wundt's work. The distortions were reflected in the way he taught about Wundt and in his translations of Wundt's writings. There is no evidence of a deliberate attempt to distort. Titchener was simply emphasizing what was most congenial to his own way of thinking. For example, Titchener's lack of interest in nonexperimental psychology led him to shrug off Wundt's interest in cultural psychology, making the remarkable comment in his obituary that Wundt's 20-years-in-the-making, 10-volume *Volkerpsychologie* was little more than "a grateful occupation for his old age" (Titchener, 1921, p. 175) and that "the dominant idea of Wundt's life...is the idea of an experimental psychology" (p. 175).

Boring was Titchener's best-known student and psychology's most venerable historian (see Chapter 1's Close-Up). His *A History of Experimental Psychology*, written in 1929 and revised in 1950, was the book that informed several generations of psychologists and provided the model for other history texts, until recently. It was dedicated to Titchener and the chapter on Wundt contains many of the distortions perpetuated by Titchener. The *Volkerpsychologie*, for instance, is barely mentioned.

The Rediscovery of Wundt

There are two reasons why Wundt's ideas began to be reexamined in the 1970s. First, as you recall from Chapter 1, it was during the late 1960s and early 1970s that the history of psychology as a discipline gathered new momentum, under the leadership of people like Robert Watson. To some extent, new scholarship directed at Wundt's history reflects the increased interest in psychology's history. The second reason is more subtle and provides another reason why history is continually being rewritten. As you will learn in Chapter 13, during the decade of the 1960s, cognitive psychology happened. That is, psychologists became increasingly interested in the experimental study of mental processes, a topic that languished in America between 1930 and 1960, due to the influence of behaviorism. Some scholars versed in the new cognitive research, most notably Arthur Blumenthal and Thomas Leahey, saw connections between the cognitive psychology of the 1960s and Wundtian psychology. Indeed, some of the cognitive research methods essentially duplicated research completed at Leipzig, even though the modern researchers seemed unaware of it. Blumenthal and Leahey began examining Wundt's work in light of the new cognitive psychology, producing papers that showed the connections between the two (Blumenthal, 1975; Leahey, 1979). The broader lesson is that while not necessarily being presentist, histories can be strongly influenced by the historical context within which they are written. One effect of modern cognitive psychology was to view Wundt in a new light. In the days of behaviorism's dominance, such a reexamination of Wundt would not have occurred.

The Real Wundt

The traditional but erroneous view of Wundt is that he was a structuralist. Now there is no question that one of Wundt's goals for his laboratory work was to identify the elements of immediate conscious experience. After all, he was originally trained in medicine and physiology and had a natural penchant for classification. Thus, his experimental papers include descriptions of the basic elements of conscious-ness, which he decided were sensations and feelings. Furthermore, each of these elements could be further categorized along certain dimensions. Sensations, for instance, were classified according to such dimensions as quality (e.g., different colors), intensity, and duration.

Analysis and classification, however, were only minor aspects of Wundt's system, and he was relatively uninterested in them. Rather, he was more concerned with the manner in which the mind actively organizes its experiences through an act of will. He labeled his system **voluntarism** to reflect the active nature of the mind. A central concept of his voluntaristic system was the phenomenon of **apperception**, a term borrowed from the German philosopher Leibnitz (Chapter 2). To apperceive some event is to perceive it with full clarity and have it in the focus of one's attention. As you are reading this page, for example, your full attention and focus (let's hope) is on this sentence and its meaning. It is being apperceived. Other information is in the periphery of your attention; Wundt would say that it is being apprehended, but not apperceived. Thus at any given time, there is information that is in the focus of attention, and other information in the margins. The former is said to be apperceived, the latter apprehended. Furthermore, apperception is a process that actively and vigorously organizes information into meaningful wholes. When we see the word "dog," we do not perceive three separate letters; we perceive a single concept that has meaning for us. Our visual sense might be initially processing meaningless lines and symbols, but our mind creates a meaningful whole. Wundt referred to the apperceptive process as a "creative synthesis."

Wundt's concept of apperception is a far cry from a more passive associationism. Yet Wundt did recognize that some elements of conscious experience do combine as passive associations. As the British associationists said, if you see John and Mary together often enough, you will

soon come to think of one when you see the other. This happens automatically because of a passively formed association. On the other hand, apperception is occurring if, when you see John and Mary, you bring them into the focus of your attention and perceive them as a special couple, or perhaps as two people who seem completely ill-suited for one another. That is, you are going beyond the information given and perceiving them clearly and distinctly.

The association/apperception difference was the key component of an important theory proposed by one of Wundt's more famous students, the psychiatrist Emil Kraepelin (1856–1926). Kraepelin devised a classification scheme for mental illness not unlike today's and his theory of schizophrenia is similar to modern attentional theories of the disorder. He argued that the thought processes of schizophrenics lack the normal apperceptive ability and their attentional capacity is severely limited. While normal people can focus their attention and direct their mental activity along meaningful paths (i.e., they can apperceive), schizophrenics cannot. Hence, their mental activity resembles random associations. This accounts for one of the common symptoms of schizophrenia: the meaningless strings of phrases ("word salad") often emitted by those suffering from the disorder.

THE WUNDTIAN LEGACY

Because it was his intention to create a new way of conceptualizing psychology, Wundt is justifiably considered the first true psychologist of the modern era. Although it is difficult to identify a single Wundtian among the early American psychologists, he had a strong influence on the origins of American psychology. The Americans who studied with Wundt may not have returned as disciples, and Blumenthal (1980) has suggested that most came back with little more than a floor plan and an equipment list. Nonetheless, they emerged from Leipzig convinced that something new and exciting was in the air and they wanted to be a part of it. American psychology quickly established its own distinctive and non-Wundtian shape, but much of the motivation for it derived from Wundt's example.

THE NEW PSYCHOLOGY SPREADS

It should not be surprising to learn that Wundt did not hold a monopoly on the New Psychology. As you recall from the opening of the chapter, the *Wissenschaft* environment created an atmosphere conducive to the creation of an empirically-based examination of psychological phenomena. Sure enough, several German contemporaries of Wundt were actively engaged in exploring this new approach to understanding the human mind. We will examine three of them: Hermann Ebbinghaus, G. E. Müller, and Oswald Külpe.

HERMANN EBBINGHAUS (1850–1909): THE EXPERIMENTAL STUDY OF MEMORY

One indirect effect of Fechner's *Elements of Psychophysics* is that it helped launch the experimental study of human memory. This occurred sometime in the mid-1870s when a young German philosopher named Hermann Ebbinghaus stumbled on an English translation of Fechner's book while browsing in a used bookstore in Paris. Fechner's demonstration that the mind could be subjected to scientific methods inspired Ebbinghaus, who was wrestling with the philosophical problem of the association of ideas at the time.

Not much is known about the formative years of Hermann Ebbinghaus. After finishing a gymnasium education, he studied at several universities and fought briefly for the German side in the Franco-Prussian War in the early 1870s. His academic interests shifted from history to philology (the historical study of language) to philosophy, and he eventually earned a doctorate in the latter from the University of Bonn in 1873. His dissertation topic was an analysis of "Hartmann's Philosophy of the Unconscious." During the mid-1870s he traveled in England and in France, discovered Fechner's *Elements* along the way, and evidently began to think about how to study the formation of associations.

As a philosopher, Ebbinghaus was thoroughly familiar with the British empiricist/associationists and their analysis of association processes. As you recall from Chapter 2, they considered association to be analogous to gravity as a force that attracted and bound together ideas. The British philosophers all considered association to be an essential component of the mind's organizational structure, but they argued over the basic laws of association (e.g., is contiguity sufficient to explain associations or are other principles necessary?). For Ebbinghaus, Fechner's scientific approach to the mind apparently triggered a creative leap. If sensations could be measured, why not other mental processes? Why not association? Sometime during the late 1870s, Ebbinghaus became resolved to study the formation and retention of associations scientifically. By the middle of the next decade, he had produced *Memory: A Contribution to Experimental Psychology* (1885/1964). This brief book (123 pages in a 1964 reprinting) inaugurated a research tradition that continues today and includes results that are still described in textbooks of general psychology. As Ernest Hilgard pointed out in an introduction to the 1964 reprinting, "[f]or the experimental study of learning and memory there is one source that is pre-eminent over all others: this small monograph by Ebbinghaus" (Hilgard, 1964, p. vii). Let us consider this remarkable achievement in more detail, through the following excerpt (page numbers from the 1964 reprinting of a 1913 English translation).

►ORIGINAL SOURCE EXCERPT

Ebbinghaus on memory and forgetting

Ebbinghaus opened his book by considering the various forms of memory and the difficulty of studying the process experimentally. He pointed out that what little was known about memory was known through common sense and from anecdotes about "extreme and especially striking cases" (p. 4). As for more fundamental questions about the exact relationships between our experiences and our memories, however, "[t]hese and similar questions no one can answer" (p. 5).

For Ebbinghaus, the only way to understand memory was through the "method of natural science" (p. 7). In his opening description of this method, Ebbinghaus did not use the exact terms you might have learned in a research methods course, but you will recognize the following as a description of the essential components of the experimental method: manipulating an independent variable, holding extraneous factors constant, then measuring the outcome, the dependent variable:

> We all know of what this method consists: an attempt is made to keep constant the mass of conditions which have proven themselves causally connected with a certain result; one of these conditions is isolated from the rest and varied in a way that can be numerically described; then the accompanying change on the side of the effect is ascertained by measurement or computation. (p. 7)

Ebbinghaus recognized that keeping the "mass of conditions" under control was no easy task. In one of psychological science's more notable acts of creativity, he hit upon the idea of using materials that did not meaningfully relate to each other and were not especially meaningful in themselves. That is, he created **nonsense syllables**, three-letter units comprised of two consonants with a vowel in the middle:

> Out of the simple consonants of the alphabet and our eleven vowels and diphthongs all possible syllables of a certain sort were constructed, a vowel sound being placed between two consonants.
>
> These syllables, about 2,300 in number, were mixed together and then drawn out by chance and used to construct series of different lengths, several of which each time formed the material for a test.
>
> ...The syllables used each time were carefully laid aside till the whole number had been used, then they were mixed together and used again.
>
> The aim of the tests carried on with these syllable series was, by means of repeated audible perusal of the separate series, to so impress them that immediately afterwards they could voluntarily just be reproduced. This aim was considered attained when, the initial syllable being given, a series could be recited at the first attempt, without hesitation, at a certain rate, and with the consciousness of being correct. (pp. 22–23)

Ebbinghaus realized that memorizing meaningful materials like poems or prose would be a problem; these materials would already carry with them innumerable meaningful associations that would affect how quickly they could be learned:

> The nonsense material, just described, offers many advantages, in part because of this very lack of meaning. First of all, it is relatively simple and relatively homogeneous. In the case of the material nearest at hand, namely poetry or prose, the content is now narrative in style, now descriptive, or now reflective; it contains now a phrase that is pathetic, now one that is humorous; its metaphors are sometimes beautiful, sometimes harsh; its rhythm is sometimes smooth and sometimes rough. There is thus brought into play a multiplicity of influences which change without regularity and are therefore disturbing. Such are associations which dart here and there, different degrees of interest, lines of verse recalled because of their striking quality or their beauty, and the like. All this is avoided with our syllables. Among many thousand combinations there occur scarcely a few dozen that have a meaning and among these there are again only a few whose meaning was realized while they were being memorized. (p. 23)

Thus, Ebbinghaus recognized that some of the syllables would have meaning, but he was not overly concerned about it. Also, it is important to keep in mind that his main interest was in how associations *between* syllables were formed, not the relative meaningfulness of individual syllables. Individual syllables might have some meaning, but the chances were quite remote that two successive syllables would be meaningfully related to each other. Gundlach (1986) has pointed out that one of Ebbinghaus's phrases was translated as a "series of nonsense syllables"[5] when a better translation might have been "meaningless series of syllables." That Ebbinghaus chose **serial learning** as his task is a further indication of his intent to analyze the buildup of associations between elements of a fixed sequence. Serial learning, in which correct recall includes accurately reproducing a set of stimuli in the exact order of their presentation, is well suited for examining associations between a "meaningless series of syllables."

How Ebbinghaus actually hit upon the idea to use nonsense syllables is not clear, but Hilgard's (1964) analysis makes the most sense. Familiar with the mechanistic and atomistic assumptions of British empiricism/associationism, Ebbinghaus would have looked for the simplest possible unit that would still yield a large number of stimuli. Individual letters or numbers were too few, words too meaningful. Syllables of words comprise the simplest pronounceable unit in the language, so they would be a logical choice. The fact that Ebbinghaus called his stimuli nonsense "syllables" suggests that he was deliberately thinking of this reduction to a small functional unit.

---

[5] The phrase appears at the bottom of page 23, in the context of a comparison with memorizing poetry.

Once he had created the materials, Ebbinghaus turned to other control problems and set up a standardized set of procedures:

The following rules were made for the process of memorizing.

1. The separate series were always read through completely from beginning to end; they were not learned in separate parts which were then joined together; neither were especially difficult parts detached and repeated more frequently. There was a perfectly free interchange between the reading and the occasionally necessary tests of the capacity to reproduce by heart. For the latter there was an important rule to the effect that upon hesitation the rest of the series was to be read through to the end before beginning it again.

2. The reading and the recitation of the series took place at a constant rate, that of 150 strokes per minute. A clockwork metronome placed at some distance was at first used to regulate the rate; but very soon the ticking of a watch was substituted, that being much simpler and less disturbing to the attention....

3. During the process of learning, the purpose of reaching the desired goal as soon as possible was kept in mind as much as was feasible. Thus, to the limited degree to which conscious resolve is of influence here, the attempt was made to keep the attention concentrated on the tiresome task and its purpose. It goes without saying that care was taken to keep away all outer disturbances in order to make possible the attainment of this aim. The smaller distractions caused by carrying on the test in various surroundings were also avoided as far as that could be done.

4. There was no attempt to connect the nonsense syllables by the invention of special associations of the mnemotechnik type; learning was carried on solely by the influence of the mere repetitions upon the natural memory. As I do not possess the least practical knowledge of the mnemotechnical devices, the fulfillment of this condition offered no difficulty to me. (pp. 24–25)

This last point reveals an important feature of the study—Ebbinghaus was the *only* subject. He completed the research during two yearlong periods: 1879–1880 and 1883–1884, with the second set of experiments serving primarily to replicate those of the first. Also, in order to become proficient at the task, he spent an unspecified "long time" (p. 33) practicing before he began the 1879–1880 studies. Thus, for more than two years, he devoted a significant portion of his time to memorizing lists of nonsense syllables (about an hour or two per day), by his own admission a "tiresome task." On just one set of experiments, the ones that produced his famous forgetting curve (below), Ebbinghaus memorized just over 1300 different lists. One attribute said to characterize famous scientists is a total immersion in their research. Ebbinghaus was certainly a case in point.

Ebbinghaus described the results of his research in several different chapters. First, he examined how quickly a series of syllables could be learned as a function of the number of syllables per list. *Quickly* meant the number of repetitions needed before the list could be produced without errors. He reported the results in a table (p. 47):

| | Number of repetitions | |
Number of syllables in a series	necessary for first errorless reproduction (exclusive of it)	Probable Error
7	1	
12	16.6	+/- 1.1
16	30.0	+/- 0.4
24	44.0	+/- 1.7
36	55.0	+/- 2.8

There are two things to note here. First, although it might not be surprising that it takes more repetitions to learn longer lists, this marks the first time that anyone had documented, with precision, the exact relationship between the length of material to be learned and the amount of effort required to learn it. Second, very little effort was needed when the list had just seven syllables.

> The question can be asked: What number of syllables can be correctly recited after only one reading? For me the number is usually seven. Indeed I have often succeeded in reproducing eight syllables, but this has happened only at the beginning of the tests and in a decided minority of the cases. In the case of six syllables on the other hand a mistake almost never occurs. (p. 47)

This result has recurred frequently in experimental psychology's history, and George Miller's (1956) systematic investigation of this "magic number seven" became a landmark paper in the rise of cognitive psychology (see Chapter 13). You probably recall learning about the number "7 plus or minus 2" in your general psychology course in the memory chapter under the heading "capacity of short-term memory."

After showing that it takes more repetitions to learn longer lists, Ebbinghaus wondered whether increasing the number of *original* repetitions would strengthen memory. Thus, he repeated lists of 16 syllables 8, 16, 24, 32, 42, 53, or 64 times, and discovered that the ease of relearning the list 24 hours later was directly proportional to the number of original repetitions. He apparently considered extending the number of repetitions beyond 64 , but thought better of it:

> An increase of the readings used for the first learning beyond 64 repetitions proved impracticable.... For with this number each test requires about 3/4 of an hour, and toward the end of this time exhaustion, headache, and other symptoms were often felt which would have complicated the conditions of the test if the number of repetitions had been increased. (p. 55)

Some aspects of the research were too intense even for the redoubtable Ebbinghaus.

The most famous of the studies completed by Ebbinghaus concerned the rate of forgetting for information that had already been learned. Here, Ebbinghaus relied on an ingenious measure of recall that he called the **savings method**, which enabled him to measure memory after the passage of time, even if nothing could be recalled after the interval. He described the logic of it early in the book:

> A poem is learned by heart and then not again repeated. We will suppose that after a half year it has been forgotten: no effort at recollection is able to call it back into consciousness. At best only isolated fragments return. Suppose that the poem is again learned by heart. It then becomes evident that, although to all appearances totally forgotten, it still in a certain sense exists and in a way to be effective. The second learning requires noticeably less time or a noticeably smaller number of repetitions than the first. (p. 8)

To examine the effects of time on memory, Ebbinghaus memorized lists of syllables, tried to relearn them after the passage of a fixed amount of time, and applied his savings method to assess the outcome.

> The investigations in question fell in the year 1879–1880 and comprised 163 double tests. Each double test consisted in learning eight series of 13 syllables each...and then in relearning them after a definite time. The learning was continued until two errorless recitations of the series in question were possible. The relearning was carried to the same point; it occurred at one of the following seven times—namely, after about one third of an hour, after one hour, after 9 hours, one day, two days, six days, or 31 days. (pp. 65–66)

Ebbinghaus recorded the total time for the original learning of the eight lists, which was typically about 20 minutes, and the time for relearning. Original learning minus relearning yielded a measure of savings, which was converted to a percentage by dividing by the time of original learning. Thus, if original learning took 20 minutes and relearning took 5 minutes, 15 minutes or 75% (15/20 $\times$ 100) of the original learning time was saved.

Ebbinghaus reported the results for each of the 163 separate experiments (i.e., "double tests") that he completed over the different retention intervals, then summarized the results as follows (p. 76):

After X hours	So much of the series learned was retained that in relearning a saving of Q% of the time of original learning was made	The amount forgotten was thus equivalent to v% of the original in terms of time of learning
X =	Q =	v =
0.33	58.2	41.8
1.	44.2	55.8
8.8	35.8	64.2
24.	33.7	66.3
48.	27.8	72.2
6 x 24	25.4	74.6
31 x 24	21.1	78.9 (p. 76)

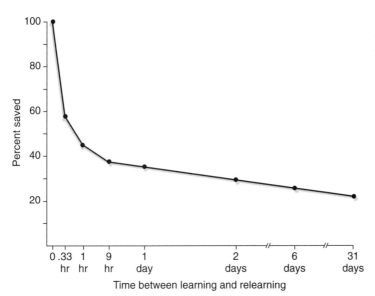

Figure 4.6   The Ebbinghaus forgetting curve, constructed from data in the excerpt.

The information found in this table has made its way into almost every introductory psychology textbook of the twentieth century. It is normally shown as a graph like the one in Figure 4.6, but Ebbinghaus did not include a graph in his book. Either way, the results are clear—forgetting was very rapid at first, then slowed in its rate. Thus, after just 20 minutes (0.33 hour), Ebbinghaus's memory held only about 60% of the learned material; 40% had been lost. After an hour, 55% was lost, and after just a day, about two-thirds was lost.

The forgetting curve is Ebbinghaus's most recalled result, but he also studied other memory phenomena. For example, he provided an early example of the advantages of distributed over massed practice by showing that:

> For the relearning of a 12-syllable series at a definite time, accordingly, 38 repetitions, distributed in a certain way over the three preceding days, had just as favorable an effect as 68 repetitions made on the day just previous.... It makes the assumption probable that *with any considerable number of repetitions* a suitable distribution of them over a space of time is decidedly more advantageous than the massing of them at a single time. (p. 89, italics in the original)

A final example of the Ebbinghaus research program is his investigation of **remote associations**. When the sequence of syllables A, B, and C, is to be learned in order, direct associations are formed between A and B and between B and C, but are they also formed (remotely) between A and C? If so, then the association concept extends beyond the idea of two immediately contiguous events. Ebbinghaus devised a clever procedure to test for these potential remote associations. He first learned a list of 16 syllables in the usual serial order:

LIST A. 1 2 3 4 5 6 7 8 9 10 11 12 13 14 15 16

Next he would relearn the list in an order that skipped a syllable:

LIST B. 1 3 5 7 9 11 13 15 2 4 6 8 10 12 14 16

Similarly, for other lists he would relearn a list that skipped two syllables:

LIST C. 1 4 7 10 13 16 2 5 8 11 14 3 6 9 12 15

If remote associations had been forming during the original learning of syllables 1 through 16 (list A), then the relearning of lists B and C would be faster than learning a new list of 16 syllables, and this is exactly what Ebbinghaus found. Furthermore, there was a direct relationship between the ease of relearning and the degree of remoteness of the associations. As Ebbinghaus put it,

> ...the associative threads, which hold together a remembered series, are spun not merely between each member and its immediate successor, but beyond intervening members to every member which stands to it in any close temporal relation. The strength of the threads varies with the distance of the members, but even the weaker of them must be considered as relatively of considerable significance. (p. 94)

In Chapter 13, you will learn about the development of modern cognitive psychology. One of its recent trends is a tendency to criticize the narrowness and artificiality of the "Ebbinghaus tradition." For modern cognitive psychologists, the memorizer is actively processing information, not passively strengthening associations through mindless repetition. Also, there is more emphasis today on **ecological memory**: memory for more realistic everyday events rather than for abstract lists. One prominent contemporary researcher lamented the "terrible struggle our field has had just to overcome the nonsense syllable" (Kintsch, 1985, p. 461). The criticism has some merit, but for the historian it has a distinctly presentist tone. Considering the Ebbinghaus memory research in the context of its time, a more apt evaluation of its importance comes from a retrospective review of *On Memory* by Roediger, written 100 years after its original publication:

> In sum, the corpus of Ebbinghaus's experimental results is large. Considering that he only began his research in the same year that Wundt founded his psychology lab

and that he performed all experiments on himself and still produced such regular and compelling results, his achievement is nearly incredible. (Roediger, 1985, p. 522)

Other Contributions by Ebbinghaus

The memory research was Ebbinghaus's greatest accomplishment, but not his only one. He was also a pioneer in the field of mental testing, inventing a sentence completion test in 1895 that was similar in spirit to the intelligence test soon to be developed in France by Binet (see Chapter 8). Ebbinghaus held academic positions in the German universities at Berlin and Breslau, creating the psychology laboratories at each university, and at Halle, where he rebuilt an existing but inadequate lab. In 1890, he started the *Zeitschrift für Psychologie und Physiologie der Sunnesorgane* (*Journal of Psychology and Physiology of the Sense Organs*). While Wundt's *Philosophische Studien* was primarily a means for publishing the work completed in his Leipzig laboratory, Ebbinghaus's *Zeitschrift* filled its pages with research from laboratories throughout Germany. The journal's catholicity of interests and the prestige of its contributing authors (e.g.,

Helmholtz, G. E. Müller) led one historian to describe it as "the most important psychological organ in Germany" (Shakow, 1930, p. 509). Ebbinghaus also wrote two popular introductory psychology texts, including a brief version (just before his sudden death from pneumonia in 1909) that included the famous opening sentence, quoted at the start of this book's Chapter 2: "Psychology has a long past, yet its real history is short" (Ebbinghaus, 1908, p. 3).

G. E. MÜLLER (1850–1934): THE EXPERIMENTALIST PROTOTYPE

Although Wundt is rightly given credit as experimental psychology's founder, the psychology of the laboratory occupied only a small portion of his interest. This is a theme that will be repeated: Many of the early pioneers of laboratory psychology actually spent little time in the laboratory. An exception is G. E. Müller,[6] an experimenter's experimenter, who devoted 40 years of his professional life to the psychology laboratory at the University of Gottingen. From 1881 to his retirement in 1921, Müller's laboratory rivaled the other German facilities in terms of the quality of research produced. Studies completed in Müller's lab were known for their precision, experimental control, and meticulous attention to detail. That Müller is not well known today is primarily because little of his work was translated into English. Also, none of his research broke radically new ground; rather, it systematically replicated and extended the research of others. Thus, he made important contributions in extending Fechner's work in psychophysics,[7] Hering's work on color vision, and Ebbinghaus's work on memory. In

this last area, Müller was a worthy successor to the venerable Ebbinghaus.

During the decade of the 1890s, Müller and his students replicated many of the Ebbinghaus findings, added several refinements, and reached different conclusions about the formation of associations. Whereas Ebbinghaus concluded that associations were formed automatically and mechanically as a result of stimulus factors such as the number of repetitions and list length, and that the memorizer played a relatively *passive* role in the process, Müller believed that the individual forming the associations played a more *active* role. The conclusion resulted from a procedural modification—Müller added introspection to the process, and his observers reported that they engaged in a number of active strategies to learn the nonsense syllables. For example, they found themselves grouping nonsense syllables in clusters, organizing them by different degrees of meaning, and in general doing much more than just associating them by contiguity. This outcome foreshadows the modern view of memory, which assumes that the learner is actively involved in the memorizing process.

Müller and his students also made some discoveries that went beyond what Ebbinghaus had found. For example, with Alfons Pilzecker he discovered that if a second list is learned between the learning of list 1 and the subsequent attempt to relearn list 1, the second list interferes with the relearning. They named the phenomenon **retroactive inhibition**, thus initiating a long line of research that eventually produced the interference theory of forgetting. With another student, Adolph Jost, Müller discovered that if two associations have equal strength, further practice will strengthen the

---

[6] No relation to Johannes Müller, the famous physiologist you met in Chapter 3. The name Müller is a very common one in Germany, a bit like their version of "Smith."

[7] According to Boring (1950), E. B. Titchener held up publication of the second volume of his famous laboratory manual (Chapter 7) until Müller had published a handbook of psychophysics in 1903. Titchener had to rewrite the psychophysics portions of his manual after Müller's book appeared, and the second volume of the lab manual was not published until 1905, four years after volume 1.

older of the associations more than the recent one. This phenomenon, later called **Jost's law**, was based on rather meager evidence, but was considered important as part of the explanation for the advantage of distributed practice over massed practice, another phenomenon studied in Müller's lab (Woodworth, 1938).

Another contribution of Müller to the experimental study of memory was the invention of the **memory drum**, which automated the presentation of stimulus materials. Müller and his assistant Friedrich Schumann cleverly altered a kymograph, a rotating drum normally used to record data (as shown in the reaction time photo of Figure 4.5). Stimuli were mounted on the drum which revolved at a fixed speed, thereby displaying stimuli for measured amounts of time (Popplestone, 1987). Memory drums were standard laboratory equipment until recently, when computer presentation of stimuli became more efficient.

One final point is that although the University of Gottingen did not award degrees to women, Müller welcomed several notable American women psychologists into his laboratory, including Christine Ladd-Franklin of Columbia (Chapter 6), Lillien Martin of Stanford, and Eleanor Gamble of Wellesley.

OSWALD KÜLPE (1862–1915): THE WÜRZBURG SCHOOL

After flirting with history and philosophy, Oswald Külpe became interested in psychology after taking a course from Wundt in the early 1880s. He then went to Berlin to study history and to Gottingen, where a year and a half in G. E. Müller's lab convinced him that psychology was to be his career. He eventually returned to Leipzig and earned a doctorate under Wundt's supervision in 1887, then remained with his mentor for another seven years, earning a living as a *Privatdozent* and as Wundt's assistant in the laboratory (he succeeded Cattell). It was during this time that he developed a lifelong friendship with E. B. Titchener (Chapter 7), who was at

Leipzig during this time. In 1894, Külpe was called to Würzburg, where he created a laboratory sometimes considered second only to Wundt's and certainly a match for Müller's at Gottingen. It was at Würzburg that Külpe created a brand of experimental psychology distinctive enough to earn the label "Würzburg school." It investigated topics and produced outcomes that put Külpe at odds with both his mentor Wundt and his friend Titchener.

Wundt had declared higher mental processes (e.g., memory, thinking) off limits for laboratory research. He believed them to be too complex and too heavily influenced by one's language and culture to be controlled adequately. Instead, such topics needed to be investigated with non-laboratory methods, while the lab was to be restricted to such topics as sensation/perception and mental chronometry. Yet Ebbinghaus and Müller had managed to control conditions reasonably well in their studies of memory. It was up to Külpe, however, to challenge his former mentor directly by studying thought processes in the lab and by significantly elaborating upon the introspective procedure.

Külpe published little experimental research under his own name, but he exercised close but congenial supervision over his students. According to one of his American students, Robert Ogden, Külpe

> …was intimately engaged in all that went on in his laboratory. It was a matter of principle to him to act as observer in the experimental work of his students. In the instance of my own study…he came almost daily to the laboratory for what must have been weary hours of committing nonsense syllables to memory. His influence upon his students was never dominating. Instead, they were engaged together in a joint enterprise of scientific discovery. (Ogden, 1951, p. 9)

In order to study thought processes in the laboratory, Külpe found it necessary to expand the Wundtian concept of introspection. Recall that Wundt distinguished between "self-observation," in which someone experiences some event, then from memory describes the mental processes that occurred during the event, and "inner perception," a more controlled introspective procedure in which simple stimuli are presented many times (i.e., replicated) and responses are given immediately after stimulus presentation. For Wundt, only the latter procedure was appropriate in the laboratory. In Külpe's laboratory, however, introspection was more like Wundt's concept of self-observation. It came to be called **systematic experimental introspection**. Observers would experience more complicated events than in Wundt's laboratory, then give a full description of the mental processes involved. This created a potential memory problem, because as Woodworth (1938) later pointed out, the mental experience of a 10-second event might take 10 minutes to describe. To deal with the fact that giving an introspective account of a complicated event might be distorted by memory, Külpe and his students developed a procedure called **fractionation**, a separation of the task into its components, each of which could be introspected. For example, in a study on word association by Watt (i.e., given a stimulus word, say the first word that comes to mind), the task was fractionated into "the preparation for the experiment, the appearance of the stimulus-word, the search for the reaction-word (if such search occurred), and finally the cropping up of the reaction-word" (Watt, 1904, cited in Sahakian, 1975, p. 162).

Külpe believed he was improving the introspective procedure, enabling it to be applied to higher mental processes, but Wundt rejected the Würzburg technique, calling it nothing but the unsystematic self observation he had rejected years earlier. Thus, because he believed them to be built on unsound methods, Wundt dismissed the results of the Würzburg research. What were those results?

Mental Sets and Imageless Thoughts

The Würzburg research on thinking produced several surprising results. For example, in a study by Narziss Ach, observers were shown pairs of numbers after first being instructed that they would be performing some specific operation (e.g., add them, subtract them). Ach measured reaction time and also asked for detailed introspections. What he found was that reaction time was the same, regardless of the type of operation asked of subjects, and that observers reported no conscious awareness of the instructions themselves, once the task had begun. In other words, after receiving the instructions, their mind was "prepared" to function in a specific way (e.g., adding), so that once the number pair was presented, the addition occurred automatically and without further thought. Thus, the instructions created what the Würzburgers called a determining tendency or **mental set**. This concept would eventually become important for the German gestalt psychologists (Chapter 9). The absence of a difference in reaction time was also significant, because Külpe used it to question the validity of the subtractive assumption underlying the mental chronography experiments that were such an important part of the Leipzig laboratory. Because instructions create a mental set, he argued, discrimination reaction time cannot be equal to simple reaction time plus the mental event of discrimination. Rather, DRT results from a different kind of "set" than SRT.

A second important finding of the Würzburg lab, and a controversial one, concerned the phenomenon of **imageless thought**. According to Titchener (and Wundt), a close analysis of thought processes reveals that the essential element in all thinking is an image of some form. In a psychophysics weight-lifting experiment, for example, the standard description was that the observer would lift one weight and form a kinesthetic image of it, then lift the second weight and compare the sensation of it with the image of the first one in order to decide if the weights were the same or different. The judgment process was composed of sensory and image components from the two weights. In a weight-lifting study by Karl Marbe, however, no sensations or images occurred at the moment of judgment. Observers reported sensations and images while lifting the weights, but the judgment seemed to occur automatically and without images. That is, the judgment was an imageless thought. Furthermore, Marbe's observers reported other mental processes occurring just before the judgment and these didn't seem reducible to sensations and images either. These processes included things like hesitation, doubt, and vacillation; collectively they were referred to as **conscious attitudes**.

The potential existence of imageless thoughts, mental sets, and conscious attitudes posed an especially serious threat to Külpe's colleague E. B. Titchener, who believed that all mental content under analysis would be found to contain the basic elements of conscious experience. If some thoughts occur without images, however, then not all thinking can be reduced to the elements. This imageless thought controversy was never resolved; its most notable side effect, however, was to raise questions about the validity of introspection as a method and to help pave the way for a radical new movement in psychology that you will learn about in Chapters 10 and 11: behaviorism.

SUMMARY

An Education in Germany

- In the nineteenth century a large number of American students studied the sciences in Europe, especially in Germany. In the latter half of the century, many students went to Germany, in particular to Leipzig, to study a new approach to psychology that was developing there.

- The German educational system promoted a philosophy of *Wissenschaft*, which emphasized academic freedom and research. This created an environment conducive to new ideas, including the idea of a new psychology.

On the Threshold of Experimental Psychology: Psychophysics

- Psychophysics is the study of the relationship between physical stimuli and the psychological reaction to them. The first research in this tradition was completed by Ernst Weber, who investigated the relative sensitivity of various areas on the surface of the body using the two-point threshold. In experiments in which observers made comparisons between two weights, Weber discovered that the ability to distinguish between them depended on the relative rather than the absolute differences in their weights (Weber's Law).

- Gustav Fechner elaborated Weber's research and his *Elements of Psychophysics* is considered experimental psychology's first text. Although more interested in using his research to defeat materialism, Fechner is known for developing several important psychophysics methods in use today (limits, constant stimuli, adjustment) and for the precision of his work in measuring absolute and difference thresholds.

Wundt Establishes a New Psychology at Leipzig

- Wundt is generally known as the founder of experimental psychology. He explicitly set out to create a new psychology that emphasized the experimental methods borrowed from physiology, and he created the first laboratory of experimental psychology and the first journal devoted to describing the results of psychological research.

- Wundt's new science involved studying immediate conscious experience under controlled laboratory conditions. Because they could not be subjected to experimental control and replication, higher mental processes (e.g., language) had to be studied through nonlaboratory methods (e.g., observation).

- In Wundt's laboratory, most of the research concerned basic sensory and perceptual processes. The lab also produced a large number of "mental chronometry" studies, which attempted to measure the amount of time taken for various mental activities. James McKeen Cattell, an American student, and Wundt's first official lab assistant, completed a number of these studies, which utilized a subtraction procedure developed by F. C. Donders.

- Recent historical scholarship has uncovered serious distortions in the traditional accounts of Wundt's theories. Rather than being a structuralist, seeking to reduce consciousness to its basic elements, Wundt was more interested in the mind's ability to actively organize information. One of his main interests was the process of apperception, an active, meaningful, and attentive perception of some event. He called his system voluntarism to reflect the active nature of mental processing.

The New Psychology Spreads

- One of the most important programs of research carried out in psychology's history involved the study of memory by Hermann Ebbinghaus. To investigate the development of new associations between unassociated stimuli, he invented nonsense syllables. Ebbinghaus measured retention in terms of the amount of effort "saved" in relearning. His famous forgetting curve showed that forgetting occurs at a very rapid rate shortly after initial learning, then tapers off. He also documented the benefits of distributed practice and the effects of remote associations.

- G. E. Müller and his students significantly extended contemporary research on color vision, the psychophysics research of Fechner, and the memory research of Ebbinghaus. By adding introspection to the nonsense syllable experiments, he argued that memory was an active process, not the passive buildup of associative strength. He was the first to identify retroactive inhibition (i.e., forgetting results from interference from events occurring between initial learning and recall), and he invented the memory drum.

- Oswald Külpe and his students created the Würzburg school of psychology, which defied Wundt by studying thinking under laboratory conditions and liberalizing the method of introspection. In their research they found evidence for mental sets, imageless thought, and conscious attitudes.

FOR FURTHER READING

BLUMENTHAL, A. L. (1975). A reappraisal of Wilhelm Wundt. *American Psychologist, 30,* 1081–1086.

Probably the most frequently cited of the articles appearing in the 1970s that pointed out the errors in the traditional accounts of Wundt; draws comparisons between Wundt's research and theorizing and modern concepts from cognitive psychology.

EBBINGHAUS, H. (1964). *Memory: A contribution to experimental psychology* (H. A. Ruger & C. A. Bussenius, Trans.). New York: Dover. (Original work published 1885)

A very readable, and brief (123 pages), account of the famous experiments by Ebbinghaus; the Dover republication includes a helpful foreward by Ernest Hilgard; a good retrospective review of the book can be found in Roediger (1985).

SOKAL, M. M. (Ed.). (1981). *An education in psychology: James McKeen Cattell's journal and letters from Germany and England, 1880–1888.* Cambridge, MA: MIT Press.

A fascinating and highly detailed account of Cattell's years with Wundt at Leipzig, Hall at Johns Hopkins, and Galton in England. The entries are from letters written by Cattell, usually to his parents, and a diary/journal; the annotations by Sokal are highly detailed and as informative as Cattell's firsthand accounts.

BRINGMANN, W. G., & TWENEY, R. D. (Eds.).(1980). *Wundt studies: A centennial collection.* Toronto: C. J. Hogrefe, Inc.

A collection of 21 articles about Wundt's life and work, ranging from biographical treatment to interpretation; main sections are the Heidelberg years, the Leipzig period, and impact and assessment.

5

DARWIN'S CENTURY:
EVOLUTIONARY THINKING

This preservation of favorable individual differences and variations, and the destruction of those which are injurious, I have called Natural Selection.

Charles Darwin, 1859

▼
___

Preview

Chapter 4 documented the rise of scientific psychology in Germany in the nineteenth century. Preceding chapters examined the explosive growth of knowledge about the brain and nervous system in that same century, and the maturation of British empiricist and associationist thought during that time. As remarkable as these nineteenth-century developments were, they were overshadowed by the impact of one man's theory about the evolution of life itself. Charles Darwin is rightly claimed by biologists as their most eminent historical figure, but his ideas also shaped the direction of psychology's history. This chapter examines Darwin's life and the development of his theory, then considers the impact of his ideas on psychology. His argument for continuity between species challenged the Cartesian distinction between humans and animals and led to comparative psychology, the study of animal behavior. And his emphasis on the variability found within species led to the study of individual differences, most clearly manifested in the work of his cousin, Sir Francis Galton. This chapter's Original Source Excerpt is from Galton's research on a variety of topics relevant to psychology. In later chapters we will describe how Darwinian thinking resonated with the functionalist movement that has always been central to American psychology.

THE SPECIES PROBLEM

From the time that Newtonian physics burst on the scene in the late seventeenth century, intellectuals became increasingly convinced that the *scientific approach* was the way to all truth, that it would shed light on our ignorance of the laws of nature, and that it would lead to the inevitable improvement of life through technological advancement. Thus, as we discussed in Chapter 3, the eighteenth century became known as the era of Enlightenment, in which science became religion and scientists seemed heroic.

One manifestation of Enlightenment science was a questioning of the literal truth of the Bible's version of the origin of the earth's plants and animals. Global exploration was uncovering new species of plants and animals by the thousands. How did the earth come to be populated by such diversity? Why did some species seem to disappear, their existence known only from fossils? And for those accepting the literal truth of the Bible, how did all these species fit on the Ark? Collectively, these questions became known as the **species problem**, sometimes referred to as the "mystery of mysteries."

The problem created great stress within the academic community in Great Britain, where the intellectual elite were also leaders of the Anglican Church, the Church of England. One solution was to turn the problem into an argument for the supreme power of the deity. This **argument from design** is normally associated with the Reverend William Paley's 1802 *Natural Theology*, but it is also recognizable as one of the proofs for the existence of God suggested by the great medieval philosopher Thomas Aquinas (Scott-Kakures, Castagnetto, Benson, Taschek, & Hurley, 1993). The argument held that the very existence of precision and complexity in nature required a supreme being to create and to manage it. Paley drew an analogy between the complex design of a watch, which necessitates a watchmaker to make it, and that of the infinitely more compli-

cated human eye, which requires an "eyemaker" who is by definition infinitely superior to the humans using those eyes (Ruse, 1979). The argument from design enabled a minister/scientist to study the workings of nature while maintaining a belief in the Supreme Designer. There was no need to speculate about how species might develop; it was simpler to assume that God in His infinite wisdom had created each species and designed each to fit into its place in the world. Hence, the orderliness to be found in nature derived from explicit design, which in turn came from a mind greater than all of nature, and that mind belonged to God.

Despite the power of the theological version of the argument from design, numerous evolutionary ideas developed in the eighteenth and early nineteenth centuries. Two pre-Darwinian examples are worthy of note. First, Darwin was not even the first person in his family to propose an evolutionary solution to the species problem. A century earlier, his eccentric grandfather, Erasmus Darwin (1731–1802), a physician, had firmly rejected the biblical account of creation and proposed that all organic life evolved from a single living filament. Over time, new species developed from old ones, with later species being more "advanced" than earlier ones. The human species represented the culmination of evolution, but there was no reason to assume that humans would not continue to improve. In 1794, he produced *Zoonomia*, a rambling account of the medical knowledge of his era, spiced with his speculations on the origins and evolution of life.

The best-known pre-Darwinian theory of evolution belonged not to Darwin's grandfather, however, but to a leading French naturalist, Jean Baptiste de Lamarck (1744–1829). Like Erasmus Darwin, Lamarck believed that all the species on earth could be lined up with reference to their complexity, an idea sometimes referred to as the *chain of being* (Ruse, 1979). Furthermore, each species is constantly evolving into a species that is more complex, he believed, and new life at the bottom of the scale is continually being created from inorganic life. Thus, at any one point in time, a variety of species exists that can be classified in terms of how much they have evolved from the first spark of life. Lamarck also believed that an important mechanism of evolution was the idea that changes occurring during the lifetime of an organism could be passed on to offspring. For instance, if during the course of its life an animal developed the ability to use simple tools, that new ability would be inherited by the next generation. This concept became known as the **inheritance of acquired characteristics**. It was taken seriously throughout most of the nineteenth century before being discarded, and it was included as part of Darwin's original theory. But we are getting ahead of the story.

CHARLES DARWIN (1809–1882) AND THE THEORY OF EVOLUTION

There was little in the early life of Charles Robert Darwin to predict the greatness that would eventually come—he appeared to be just another aimless and spoiled child of wealthy parents. He was born and raised in the rural west of England, in Shrewsbury. His father, Robert, was a successful and affluent country doctor and his mother, Susannah Wedgwood, was heir to a fortune from the family that created the renowned Wedgwood china. Like most successful and ambitious men, Robert Darwin expected great things of his son, and was frustrated by the boy's indifferent performance in school and his apparent lack of purpose. By early adolescence, Darwin's wayward behavior drove his father to distraction. "You care for nothing but shooting, dogs, and rat-catching, and you will be a disgrace to yourself and all your family," he exclaimed (quoted in Desmond & Moore, 1991, p. 20), in a scene easily imagined by parents of adolescents.

THE SHAPING OF A NATURALIST

Determined that his son would follow in his footsteps, Robert Darwin sent Charles to study medicine at Edinburgh, Scotland, one of Europe's best medical schools, and more prestigious at that time than either Oxford or Cambridge. The experiment failed, however. Darwin's academic performance did not improve and he was nauseated by the clinical procedures of the day. Anesthesia did not exist then, nor was the importance of a sterile environment widely recognized. Thus, surgery was a gruesome experience in which the main goal was to relieve the screaming patient by completing the procedure as soon as possible. For young Charles, medicine would not do. He left Edinburgh in 1827.

The next stop was Christ's College, Cambridge University, where Darwin studied for the clergy. The Cambridge that he encountered in the period 1828 to 1831 was not the fine academic university that we think of today. Rather, it was an institution under the firm control of the Church of England (the Anglican Church); its professors were Anglican priests who normally expected little scholarship on the part of their students, and its students (all male) tended to live up to those expectations.[1] Most students were there to prepare for the clergy, but they were primarily concerned with learning how to become proper gentlemen. Studying to be a clergyman in the Anglican Church was a common vocation for sons of wealthy Britishers, an activity described as a "safety net to stop second sons [from] becoming wastrels" (Desmond & Moore, 1991, p. 47). Honors programs for serious students did exist in the classics and in mathematics, but at a time when England was the most powerful nation on earth and was leading the Industrial

---

[1] The same could be said at this time of England's other famous university, Oxford.

Revolution, the university was strangely deficient in the study of science and technology (Ruse, 1979). Darwin never became a priest of the Anglican Church, of course. Nonetheless, he entertained the notion for several years, even after he had found his true vocation.[2]

Although he was not destined for the clergy, the Cambridge experience proved to be crucial for Darwin. He found his calling there. Young people who grow up in rural areas often seem to develop a love for the natural world, and Darwin was no exception. He might have been a mediocre student and an incipient failure in his father's eyes, but he also had the insatiable curiosity that marks the scientist. From his earliest youth, he recalled being a collector of natural objects ranging from rocks to beetles to butterflies. The habit continued during his time at Edinburgh, where he often escaped the horrors of his clinical studies by walking the beaches of the North Sea, accumulating various items washed up on shore. It was at Cambridge, however, that Darwin realized for the first time that his love of the natural world could become a life's work.

Darwin's model and mentor was the Reverend John Henslow (1796–1871), a professor of botany at Cambridge. In the minister/scientist Henslow, Darwin saw his future: he could become a respectable Anglican clergyman, use his wealth to acquire a quiet rural parish, then devote most of his time to science. Darwin sat in on Henslow's classes and his fervor quickly caught the botanist's attention. Before long, Henslow began including Darwin in weekly meetings in his home, at which a small group of like-minded enthusiasts, including some of Cambridge's leading scientists, debated the scientific issues of the day (including evolution). Between 1828 and 1831, Darwin continued to be an average student in

his formal preparation for the ministry, but he was in regular contact with some of the leading scientific minds of the day, and he was making a favorable impression on them (Ruse, 1979).

One of those scientific minds belonged to a noted geologist, the Reverend Adam Sedgwick (1785–1873). Sedgwick became a second mentor to Darwin, teaching him the basic tools of the geologic trade and sharpening his ability to make precise observations by taking him on a long geological field trip through the mountains of Wales in the summer of 1831. Darwin eventually rejected Sedgwick's views about the earth's formation, but he profited immensely from the experience. Darwin began thinking of himself as a geologist.

After returning from the walk through northern Wales, opportunity knocked at Darwin's door. A voyage to South America was being planned, and the captain, 26-year-old Robert FitzRoy, was advertising for an on-board dinner companion, a "gentleman" whose intelligent conversation could relieve the long hours of boredom at sea. It would also help if this person had some training in science, for there would be many opportunities for collecting specimens of South America's fauna and flora. Henslow was asked to recommend someone, and Darwin was his choice. After refusing permission initially, mainly on the grounds that it seemed yet another example of his son's desultory meandering through life, Darwin's father eventually approved of the scheme, and Darwin began the voyage of a lifetime aboard the HMS *Beagle*. It lasted five years and took him around the globe. In his autobiography, Darwin had this to say about the trip:

> The voyage of the *Beagle* has been by far the most important event in my life, and has determined my whole career.... I have

---

[2] In his autobiography, Darwin reported that later in his life, a German phrenological society requested a photograph of his head. He complied, the photo was carefully examined, and a member of the society proclaimed that Charles had "the bump of reverence developed enough for ten priests" (Darwin, 1892/1958, p. 18).

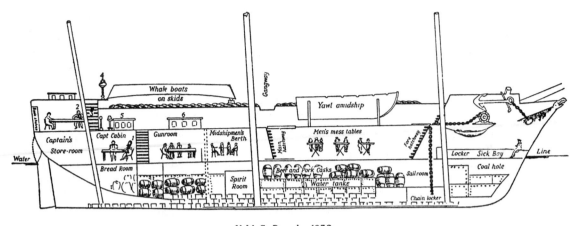

H. M. S. Beagle 1832

1 Mr. Darwin's seat in Captain's Cabin   2 Mr Darwin's seat in Poop Cabin   3 Mr. Darwin's drawers in Poop Cabin
4 Azimuth Compass   5 Captain's skylight   6 Gunroom skylight

Figure 5.1   Cross section of the HMS *Beagle.*

always felt that I owe to the voyage the first real training or education of my mind; I was led to attend closely to several branches of natural history, and thus my powers of observation were improved.... (Darwin, 1892/1958, p. 28)

THE VOYAGE OF THE *BEAGLE*

Darwin's home away from home for five years was a small (90 feet long and 24 feet wide) three-masted brig that carried just over 70 officers, marines, geographer/surveyors, and crew. Darwin shared a small cabin at the rear of the ship with two of the survey officers, sleeping in a hammock with his face two feet from the underside of the main deck, and contending with the surveyors for work space on the small charting table during the day (Thomson, 1975). Some idea of the cramped living arrangements can be seen in Figure 5.1, a cross section of the ship.

The primary purpose of the *Beagle*'s voyage was to survey the southern coasts of South America, especially its port areas, thus allowing the powerful British merchant fleet to retain its edge in the competition for trade with developing South American countries; the ship would also circumnavigate the earth, using its 24 chronometers to check the precise longitude of various locations on the globe (Desmond & Moore, 1991). Once the *Beagle* reached South America, much of its time was spent going back and forth from one coastal region to another.[3] This enabled Darwin to spend months at a time ashore, exploring the continent, observing nature, and collecting. Long periods away from the ship were beneficial for another reason— Darwin suffered from a violent seasickness that lasted for the entire trip. When aboard ship, he was ill every day.

Darwin the Geologist

At the outset of the voyage, Darwin's prime interest was geology. The field trip with Sedgwick was still fresh in his mind, and just off the press and among his possessions was the first volume of a book destined to have the

---

[3] The *Beagle* spent 57 months at sea. Forty-two of those months were spent in South American waters, 27 on the east coast and 15 on the west coast (Browne, 1995).

same effect on geology that his own book would have on biology. Its simple title, *Principles of Geology*, belied its revolutionary nature. Its Scottish author, Charles Lyell (1797–1875), took issue with the prevailing theory of geological change, called **catastrophism**. Much like the argument from design, catastrophism was an attempt to maintain the supremacy of God and the Bible while accounting for what scientists were discovering about nature. Catastrophists, who counted Darwin's geologist/mentor Sedgwick among their number, argued that geological change occurred abruptly and dramatically as the result of major catastrophic events under the control and direct command of God. The flood in the Book of Genesis was the most obvious example. Lyell, on the other hand, argued that geological change occurred more slowly and involved forces that are constantly at work. These forces included such things as volcanic action, earthquakes, erosion, and the cumulative effects of weather. This view came to called **uniformitarianism**, because of the assumption that uniform laws of nature operated to produce gradual geologic change. The Swiss Alps were not thrust up overnight in some cataclysmic upheaval; they only arose gradually, over vast amounts of time, Lyell believed.[4]

Lyell's revolutionary ideas about the origins and development of the earth's structures were never far from Darwin's thoughts. At the ship's very first landfall, in the volcanic Cape Verde islands (off the west coast of Africa), he came across some evidence to support Lyell's uniformitarian views. About 30 feet above sea level, the rocks contained a layer of compressed seashells and coral. The Atlantic could not have dropped that much during the island's lifetime,

so the sea bed must have risen, presumably because of volcanic activity. The geologic event seemed to be gradual rather than catastrophic, because Darwin observed that the shell/coral layer varied in height, suggesting the slow-moving effects of subsidence; the layer also included intact fossils. Darwin began to think the *Beagle* voyage might make his reputation as a Lyellian geologist. Indeed, while we now think of the trip as the event that gave Darwin the raw material for his theory of evolution of species, he also made important contributions to geology. For instance, he uncovered additional support for Lyell by finding fossilized seashells at numerous elevations in the Andes Mountains, thereby supporting the Lyellian notion that the Andes had been raised gradually from the sea. He also experienced, firsthand, the landscape-altering effects of an earthquake in Chile, and during the Pacific portion of the trip, he was able to demonstrate that coral reefs were built on the rims of slowly sinking volcanos. Finally, Darwin's immersion in Lyellian geology convinced him that the earth had to be much older than previously thought. This idea would eventually be important to Darwin's evolutionary thinking, because the slow changes in species required vast amounts of time. The new geology seemed to supply an earth that was sufficiently ancient for evolution to do its work.

Darwin the Zoologist

When the *Beagle* reached South American waters and began its surveying work, Darwin, now free to explore on land for extended periods of time, began collecting specimens in earnest and keeping encyclopedic notes on his geologic and zoologic observations. By the end

---

[4] A modern form of catastrophism, minus the theological element, has gained adherents since the accumulation of evidence that comets or large meteors have occasionally struck the earth. It is estimated that one such meteor destroyed 95% of all marine species when it landed about 250 million years ago. More recently (a mere 65 million years ago), a huge meteor produced effects leading to the rapid extinction of about 70% of the earth's species, including the dinosaurs (Monastersky, 1997).

of the voyage he composed a 770-page diary, sent home in installments, 1383 pages of notes on geology, and 368 more pages on zoology. He also wrote a specimen catalog that included 1529 species of animals that had been preserved in spirits and another 3907 labeled items that were either bones, fossils, skins, or dried specimens (Desmond & Moore, 1991).

For at least a year into the voyage, Darwin firmly believed that he would return to England and become the Anglican priest/amateur scientist that he so admired in Henslow. He also assumed that his work would have no important bearing on the biblical account of creation; he was initially a believer in the argument from design. Yet his zoological observations gradually led to him to wonder about the species question. Why were there so many species of plants and animals? Why were some species similar to others, yet different in ways that suited them for survival in their own unique environments? Why did some species become extinct, their existence known only through their fossilized remains? Why did these fossils often seem to bear an uncanny resemblance to contemporary species living in the same geographical region? It began to occur to him that just as the earth evolved slowly, gradually, and according to uniform laws, perhaps the same was true of the organisms populating the earth.

The Galápagos Islands

On September 7, 1835, after spending more than three and a half years on its surveying mission, the *Beagle* left South America and headed across the Pacific. A week later, it made landfall at a remote series of about 20 volcanic islands owned by Ecuador, and located on the equator about 600 miles west of South America. They featured a variety of unusual species, including oversized, dinosaurlike lizards, and tortoises with shells up to five feet in diameter. The islands were named for the Spanish word for the giant tortoise, *galápagos*. They had little practical value, being used primarily as an Ecuadorian penal colony and as a stopping point for whaling vessels to replenish their stocks of food and water.[5] The lizards, tortoises, and numerous species of birds were oblivious to human presence, making it easy for crews to hunt them. Darwin was astounded to be able to push a large hawk off a tree branch by poking it with his gun.

The Galápagos were to give Darwin his most obvious clues to evolution, although at the time of the visit and for some time thereafter, he had no inkling of the importance of what he encountered there. During the five weeks spent on the islands, Darwin did some hiking and specimen-collecting, but he was not as systematic as he had been in South America. Nor did he pay much attention to the claim, made by the vice-governor of the penal colony, that it was possible to tell the home island of a tortoise merely by observing the design of its shell. He did notice differences from one island to another in the various bird populations, however, especially the mockingbirds, and it appeared that many of the species of birds and plants resembled those from the mainland, while having their own unique qualities. He later discovered that the shapes of the beaks of several species of finch provided an important clue to his theory, but while in the Galápagos he failed to notice these differences by mislabeling some of the finches as warblers, wrens, and "grossbeaks," and he was more intrigued by their coloration than their beaks (Sulloway, 1982). He even forgot to identify most of his finch specimens by their island of origin. These birds, now known as **Darwin's finches**, became an

---

[5] While accumulating the experiences that would eventually yield *Moby Dick*, Herman Melville was aboard a whaling vessel that reached the Galápagos shortly after the *Beagle*'s visit. Of the islands, Melville wrote, "Little but reptile life is here found; the chief sound of life is a hiss" (cited in Moorehead, 1969, p. 187).

important source of data for naturalists who followed Darwin to the Galápagos,[6] and they still contribute to evolutionary theory. For example, recent research has shown that dramatic changes in the finch species can occur in just a few years, if climatic changes are sufficiently drastic (Weiner, 1994).

After leaving the Galápagos, the *Beagle* sailed west across the Pacific and made stops at Tahiti, New Zealand, Australia, and South Africa before finally returning to England in October of 1836. Upon his return, Darwin was a changed man. He now seriously doubted that life as an Anglican priest was for him; a full-time devotion to science seemed more in the cards. During the voyage, he routinely shipped crates of specimens home to Henslow, and they had made a strong impression on the scientific community during his absence. By the time he returned, he was already a celebrity among zoologists and geologists and viewed as a rising young star. Darwin's reputation even impressed his father, who rewarded his son with a generous allowance and a healthy stock portfolio to enable him to continue his scientific work (Desmond & Moore, 1991).

THE EVOLUTION OF DARWIN'S THEORY

During the first few years after his return, Darwin set out to organize and classify his enormous collection of specimens, enlisting the help of other scientists and museum curators as much as possible. In 1837, he moved to London, and two years later he married his cousin, Emma Wedgwood. Their union was a long and happy one, even though Emma's strong religious beliefs eventually conflicted with her husband's gradual loss of faith. Emma was destined to become the family's source of strength, caring for the 10 children she would bear and for Darwin, who became ill soon after his return.

Darwin was a partial invalid for the remainder of his life, suffering from a variety of chronic digestive, headache, and cardiac symptoms. For months at a time until his death in 1882, he spent a significant portion of the day either in bed or being violently ill. The Darwins remained in London for three years, but the unrelenting street noise, coal-generated smog, and stench from the polluted Thames seemed to contribute to Darwin's declining health, so in 1842 they bought a country house at Down, about 15 miles south of London. Down became their permanent home and Darwin's laboratory. Today Down House serves as the Darwin Museum.

Despite his illness, Darwin produced. Within 10 years of his return to England, he published a journal (Darwin, 1839), books on the geology of coral reefs, volcanic islands, and South America, and several technical reports that were read to various scientific societies in London (e.g., the Geological Society). During this time he also formulated his theory on the evolution of species and wrote a brief abstract of it in 1842. Two years later he elaborated the sketch into a 200-page document, instructing his wife to publish it in the event that his ailments proved fatal (Desmond & Moore, 1991).

Darwin's theory developed out of his reflections on the *Beagle* voyage. He was perplexed by the "mystery of mysteries," and while he rejected the biblical account that God had created each species separately, he maintained (initially, at least) his belief in God by allowing for the divine creation of a set of laws to guide evolution. But what were those laws? Hints came to Darwin from two sources. First, in 1838 he read an essay on population by political economist Thomas Malthus (1766–1834), who championed the idea that government welfare for the poor would only increase their number, thereby decreasing Britain's overall standard of living. Instead, Malthus argued, society must recognize that life is a constant

---

[6] From 1905 to 1906, for instance, a project sponsored by the California Academy of Sciences collected 8691 finch specimens (Weiner, 1994).

"struggle for existence" and only those best suited for survival will do so. He pointed out that while food supplies grow at a relatively constant rate, population growth, if unchecked, occurs at a much more rapid geometric rate. Eventually, the population will outgrow its resources and its members will begin to die until a level of stability is achieved. For Darwin, this idea provided a model to be applied to species changes. For any species, the time will come when unchecked population growth will result in food shortages, especially when growth combines with severe environmental changes such as a prolonged drought. Under such circumstances, only those best suited to survive will do so. If those characteristics enabling survival could be passed on to off-spring, the next generation would be better suited for survival and would be different from previous generations. Over time, might these changes be sufficient to create a new species? Darwin began to think so.

Darwin's second clue came from his reflections on what he knew of breeding by farmers and hobbyists. For instance, pigeon breeders had been able to produce breeds of pigeons that hardly resembled each other. The breeders accomplished this by observing tiny variations that occurred naturally within a breed of pigeons, then developing those differences through generations of selective breeding. The results were such that if these pigeon varieties had been encountered in the wild, zoologists would have judged them to be different species! If such differences can be created artificially by pigeon breeders, could they not also be created naturally? Could there be a *natural selection* that was analogous to artificial selection? Darwin began to think so.

In the midst of these ruminations about population changes and selective breeding, Darwin learned from the famous ornithologist John Gould, who was classifying some of his *Beagle* specimens, that there was something very interesting about the birds from the Galápagos Islands. The birds that Darwin thought were finches, warblers, wrens, and "gross-beaks" were in fact different species of finches. Furthermore, Gould was "induced to regard them as constituting an entirely new group containing 14 species, and appearing to be strictly confined to the Galápagos islands" (Gould, cited in Weiner, 1994, p. 28). These finch species were distinguished by their size and by clear differences in the shapes of their beaks. Wondering about these differences, Darwin reexamined his sketchy notes on the islands of origin for the birds and supplemented the information by examining finch specimens that had been collected by Captain FitzRoy and others. He soon saw a distinct pattern—finches with specific beak shapes tended to cluster on islands that differed in terms of the sources of available food. For instance, finches living on islands with a large supply of certain types of hardshelled nuts and seeds had tough, blunted beaks, ideally suited for cracking open this food source. Other birds had thinner beaks, well-designed to spear the insects that populated their islands.

Darwin concluded that at some distant point in time, finches had arrived from the mainland as a single species and had dispersed throughout the islands. From generation to generation, the finches on each island produced offspring that varied slightly from each other, just as the domesticated pigeons did, and some of those variations would be beneficial, enabling certain finches to survive the kinds of periodic food shortages predicted by Malthus. Eventually, these variations produced new species. The theory was born.

Darwin's Delay

Much has been made of the fact that Darwin had outlined the essential features of his theory of evolution by the late 1830s, yet it took him another 20 years to publish the *Origin of Species* (Richards, 1983). Part of the reason was his health: he was often incapacitated for months at a time. A second reason for the delay was that he was concerned about the reactions of his peers. When the anonymously-authored and highly speculative *Vestiges of Creation* appeared in 1844, the same year that Darwin was entrusting his 200-page manuscript to his wife's care, it was ridiculed by the British community of zoologists, geologists, and botanists (including Lyell, for instance, who was now a close friend of Darwin's). Some of the reaction was to the vagueness in the proposed mechanism for evolutionary change in *Vestiges*, and Darwin knew that his model was better, but much of the negative response was to the idea of evolution itself. In a letter to the botanist Joseph Hooker, a close friend to whom he was disclosing his theory, Darwin wrote that proposing a theory of evolution was like "confessing a murder" (Colp, 1986). If he published in 1844, he feared that his theory would be confused with *Vestiges* and condemned by association.

A third reason for Darwin's delay was his conservative scientific nature. He knew he had a good theory and some data to support it, but he also knew that he needed much more evidence before he would be willing to go public. Thus, he spent much of the intervening years carefully gathering evidence to flesh out the theory. For instance, in 1846 he began an intensive eight-year study of the evolutionary history of barnacles, eventually publishing the results in four volumes. He also joined a local pigeon fanciers club and did some of his own pigeon breeding. And at Down House, one could always find a dozen experiments going on at the same time. For example, to determine how seeds could be spread over large distances, he hit on the idea that undigested seeds might be carried in the stomachs of birds. To test the idea he collected bird droppings, poking through them until he came across the occasional seed, which he planted. To his pleasant surprise, the seeds often germinated and grew.

Darwin's 20-year delay would have been even longer if not for a letter he received on June 18, 1858. It was from a fellow naturalist with an interest in evolution, Alfred Russel Wallace (1823–1913), who was at the time on the other side of the world in Malaysia. Wallace asked Darwin's opinion on a brief paper that he enclosed with the letter—the paper outlined a theory of evolution that was remarkably similar to Darwin's. Darwin was shaken, writing to Lyell that "If Wallace had my MS. sketch written out in 1842, he could not have made a better short abstract!" (cited in Desmond & Moore, 1991, p. 467).

After seeking the advice of Hooker and Lyell, Darwin agreed to a joint presentation at the July 1, 1858, meeting of the Linnean Society. Thus it occurred that the first public disclosure of Darwin's theory of evolution came at a professional meeting of botanists. The secretary of the society read Wallace's paper, an abstract of Darwin's 1844 essay, and a letter outlining the theory that Darwin had written a few years earlier to the American zoologist Asa Gray of Harvard. Darwin did not attend the meeting; neither paper attracted attention.

The Wallace letter sent a clear message to Darwin, however. To establish his legitimate priority, he needed to publish the complete theory, along with the supporting evidence that he had accumulated over the years. Despite continuing ill health and the death of one of his sons to scarlet fever, Darwin completed the work over the next 15 months and *On the Origin of Species by Means of Natural Selection or the Preservation of Favoured Races in the Struggle for Life* appeared in bookshops on November 22, 1859. The initial printing of 1250 copies sold out on the first day.

Elements of the Theory of Evolution

After a brief introduction, in which Darwin emphasized the importance of the *Beagle* voyage and gave credit to Wallace for his similar theory, the *Origin of Species* opens with two chapters establishing the fact that members of a given species vary from each other. In the first chapter, "Variation Under Domestication," Darwin showed how individual differences within a species could be accentuated through deliberate breeding—an artificial selection. This

**Key Date
1859**

This year marked the publication of Darwin's revolutionary *Origin of Species*, perhaps the most important book published in the nineteenth century.

These events also occurred:

- America's first oil well was drilled in Titusville, Pennsylvania
- The steamroller was invented
- Work began on the Suez Canal
- The French acrobat Charles Blondin crossed Niagara Falls on a tightrope
- Samuel Smiles published *Self-Help*, a manual on how to succeed in life
- Daniel Emmett composed "Dixie"
- These people were born:

    Arthur Conan Doyle, British creator of Sherlock Holmes

    Pierre Curie, French physicist

- These people died:

    Washington Irving, American author

    Alexander von Humboldt, German astronomer, geologist, and explorer

[handwritten margin note: deliberate selection (artificial selection) and "natural" selection; 1) artificial selection 2) Natural selection]

chapter prepared the way for him to argue later that just as there is deliberate selection by human breeders, there is also a "natural" selection by the conditions of normal existence. In Chapter 2, "Variation Under Nature," Darwin noted the universality of individual differences within species found in nature. He made the connection to Chapter 1 by pointing out that these differences "thus afford materials for natural selection to act on and accumulate, in the same manner as man accumulates individual differences in his domesticated products" (Darwin, 1859/1958, p. 59).

Because the science of genetics was yet to be born, Darwin had no concept of the phenomenon of genetic mutation, the primary means of creating individual differences within a species. Thus, he had to guess about the causes of variation. He believed that some variation was spontaneous and random, much like mutation, but he also allowed for the Lamarckian idea

that characteristics acquired during one's lifetime could be passed on to offspring.

Darwin's third and fourth chapters, the "Struggle for Existence" and "Natural Selection," contain the core of the theory. Citing Malthus, Darwin first argued that in nature, species face an inevitable struggle to survive because they produce offspring at a rate that outpaces the food supply. If that is the case, then those individuals having a variation that puts them at a slight advantage in the struggle will be "selected" by nature; those without the advantage will die. Over several generations, the "adaptive" variation will become more common. In Darwin's words:

> …Owing to this struggle [for life], variations, however slight and from whatever cause proceeding, if they be in any degree profitable to the individuals of a species,…will tend to the preservation of such individuals, and will generally be

inherited by the offspring.... This preservation of favorable individual differences and variations, and the destruction of those which are injurious, I have called Natural Selection. (Darwin, 1859/1958, p. 74, p. 88)

Darwin's finches illustrate the manner in which life's **struggle for existence** and **natural selection** combine to alter species. As mentioned earlier, Darwin believed that the original finches arrived as a single species from the mainland and settled in the various islands of the Galápagos. Because there is variation among members of a species in the wild, slight differences from one finch to another existed, including variations in the shapes of the birds' beaks. Suppose some of the birds happened to land on islands rich in certain types of seeds that are encased in hard shells. Those finches with slightly tougher and more blunted beaks would have an advantage in the hunt for these seeds. Finches with slightly thinner beaks would have a more difficult time getting at the seeds and would be more likely to die. Hence, the finches with the more "adaptive variation" would be "naturally selected" in the "struggle for existence." They would survive and pass on the advantage to their offspring. Over time, finches on that particular island would form a new species characterized by the specific beak shape. Similarly, on another island rich in insects, a species of finch with beaks thin enough to reach into small spaces would evolve.

Darwin believed that evolution by natural selection also explained extinction and the reason why modern species resemble fossils of extinct species found in the same geographical region. In South America, for example, Darwin had uncovered fossilized bones of animals similar to modern llamas but two to three times as large. Over time, he argued, the larger species had encountered environmental events (e.g., droughts) that reduced the food supply and favored the survival of smaller variations that did not need to eat as much.

In the remaining 11 chapters of the *Origin*, Darwin wrote of the evidence, both zoological and geological, in support of his theory, and tried to answer the objections he knew would be forthcoming. He recognized that most people believed in the divine creation of every single species, but asked his readers to consider the evidence he had placed before them.

Dennett (1995) has pointed out that evolution by natural selection, Darwin's "dangerous idea," created for the first time a reasoned argument for a reversal of the sequence proposed by the well-entrenched theological argument from design. For the Reverend Paley and others, an all-knowing Divine Mind created the intricate designs found in an orderly and predictable natural world. The sequence was Mind-Design-Order. The blindly-operating rules of natural selection, on the other hand, resulted in order, which in turn led to design, which could then produce a mind (hence the sequence Order-Design-Mind). Paley's watch and the watchmaker's mind, according to Dennett's scheme, would indeed be the result of design, but not necessarily design from above. Rather, it could be the outcome of what Dennett called the "Principle of the Accumulation of Design" (p. 68) resulting from the evolutionary process that produced visually oriented humans with the ability to build a watch.

After the Origin of Species

Reaction to Darwin's theory was not long in coming. Although he did not discuss humans in the *Origin*, the implications were clear and directly threatening to the Church of England. It might have been declining in power during the second half of the nineteenth century, but the Anglican Church was still capable of making its presence felt and Darwin was denounced from pulpits throughout England. To this day, evolution is a threat to the religious beliefs of some. The scientific community was a different matter, however. In his autobiography, Darwin argued that while there was some initial resis-

1877
√ Develop. 4

tance among some scientists (e.g., Lyell), general acceptance of the idea of evolution came quickly. While rejecting the idea that the success of his book demonstrated that the topic of evolution was "in the air," he did recognize the importance of Boring's zeitgeist: "What I believe was strictly true is that innumerable well-observed facts were stored in the minds of naturalists ready to take their proper places as soon as any theory which would receive them was sufficiently explained" (Darwin, 1892/1958, p. 45). By the end of the century, evolution had taken hold and the importance of Darwin's ideas eventually led some observers to refer to the entire century as "Darwin's Century" (Eiseley, 1958).

In the debates over evolution, Darwin himself stayed above the fray, preferring to have his case argued by others; he had work to do. He continued to collect evidence for his theory, publishing important works on topics ranging from orchids to earthworms. Although he avoided discussing human evolution in the *Origin of Species*, he addressed the topic head-on in *The Descent of Man, and Selection in Relation to Sex* (1871) and *Expressions of the Emotions in Man and Animals* (1872). In 1877, he published a pioneering article in child psychology in the British journal *Mind*, called a "Biographical Sketch of an Infant." It was based on extensive notes written years before on the physical and psychological development of his firstborn son, William (Figure 5.2).

Despite his ever-present illnesses, Darwin worked right up to the end of his life, which came on April 19, 1882. Although he wished to be buried quietly at Down, his cousin Francis Galton organized a successful campaign to have him interred among other British heroes at London's Westminster Abbey, just across the street from the Houses of Parliament. Today, the large rectangular stone marking Darwin's burial place can be found on the floor of the north side of the Abbey, just below the bust of Sir Isaac Newton.

DARWIN AND PSYCHOLOGY'S HISTORY

Darwin's primary contribution to psychology was his theory of evolution, which promoted a way of thinking among American psychologists that eventually became known as functionalism. This school of thought will be examined in Chapters 7 and 8; for now it is enough to say that the functionalists were interested in studying human behaviors and mental processes in terms of how they served to adapt the individual to an ever-changing environment. Consciousness, for instance, was said to serve the adaptive function of enabling the individual to assess a problem situation and solve it quickly. Similarly, habits served to free the individual's limited consciousness to concentrate on unsolved problems.

Two specific aspects of the theory also had a direct impact on psychology's history. First, an

Figure 5.2   Charles Darwin and his firstborn son, William (the subject of Darwin's "Biographical Sketch of an Infant") in 1842, from Desmond and Moore (1991).

2 Terms / Large in James' writing.

obvious implication of the theory, which Darwin made explicit in *The Descent of Man* (1871), was that a continuity of mental processes existed between humans and other species. This led to the creation of **comparative psychology**, the study of animal behavior. Second, the emphasis on individual variation led to the systematic study of **individual differences**, a research tradition that eventually led to the measurement of differences via intelligence and personality tests. These developments need some elaboration.

THE ORIGINS OF COMPARATIVE PSYCHOLOGY

Comparative psychology is a descendant of Darwin's argument for a continuity between species. Darwin himself may be considered one of the originators of the field, by virtue of his book on emotions. Originally intended as a chapter in *The Descent of Man* (1871), the topic of the origins of emotional expression took on a life of its own, and Darwin published it separately as the *Expressions of the Emotions in Man and Animals* in 1872. As the first scientific attempt to study emotional expressions, the book is Darwin's most important direct contribution to psychology's history. It includes accounts of the circumstances producing the various types of emotional response, detailed descriptions of the precise manner in which these emotions are expressed by the face, and a theory of how the expressions might have evolved.

DARWIN ON THE EVOLUTION OF EMOTIONAL EXPRESSIONS

Darwin opened his book by arguing for an evolutionary approach to the study of emotional expressions, pointing out that for humans, things such as "the bristling of the hair under the influence of extreme terror...can hardly be understood, except on the belief that man once existed in a much lower and animal-like condition" (Darwin, 1872, p. 12). He then described the problems encountered when studying emotions in normal adults. First, with the exception of the occasional extreme emotional reactions, most expressions are muted. Studying one's own emotions is not easy either, because the experience of a strong emotion is incompatible with a rational analysis of it. One cannot feel terror and dispassionately observe it in oneself at the same time. Investigating the forms and the causes of emotional expressions required a more creative strategy, and Darwin met the challenge by proposing several methods. For instance, he suggested studying children and the insane as a way to classify the precise patterns of emotional expression. Their expressions of such emotions as anger, joy, and fear, not restricted by normal adult inhibitions, would be more intense and their features more easily classified as a result. Another method was to use a technique called *galvanization*. As shown in Figure 5.3, electrodes touched the surface of the skin and stimulation produced recognizable muscle contractions. The idea was to establish exactly which muscles were involved in each emotional expression. Hence, Figure 5.3*a* shows an elderly man with a normal smile, whereas Figure 5.3*b* shows the result of stimulating the muscles to the sides of the mouth. Darwin used the example to show that laughter involves several sets of muscles. The galvanized smile

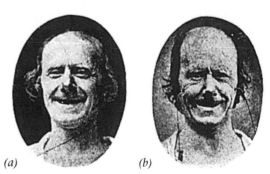

(a)   *(b)*

Figure 5.3   Expressing emotions, natural versus "galvanized" smiles, from Darwin (1872).

vaguely resembles the natural one, but the true smile also involved muscles around the eyes that were unaffected by the electrical stimulus.

Darwin also reasoned that if emotional expressions were the result of evolution, then the same basic expressions would be found around the world. By using a large network of correspondents, including many encountered on the *Beagle* voyage, Darwin conducted the first cross-cultural study of emotional expressions. Darwin asked his correspondents to examine the facial expressions displayed in cultures far and wide and answer questions like the following:

> Is astonishment expressed by the eyes and mouth being opened wide, and by the eyebrows being raised?…
>
> When a man sneers or snarls at another, is the corner of the upper lip over the canine or eye tooth raised on the side facing the man whom he addresses?…
>
> Is contempt expressed by a slight protrusion of the lips and by turning up the nose, and with a slight expiration?…
>
> Is the head nodded vertically in affirmation, and shaken laterally in negation? (Darwin, 1872, pp. 15–16)

Darwin's final method gave him clues for a theory about the origins of the various emotional expressions:

> …I have attended, as closely as I could, to the expression of the several passions in some of the commoner animals; and this I believe to be of paramount importance, not of course for deciding how far in man certain expressions are characteristic of certain states of mind, but as affording the safest basis for generalisation on the causes, or origin, of the various movements of Expression. (Darwin, 1872, p. 16)

After describing the techniques to be used in his study of emotions, Darwin described his theory about the evolution of emotion expression, which involved three basic principles. He devoted a chapter to each, then filled the bulk of the 366-page book with chapters devoted to the detailed descriptions of the various categories of emotion.

Principle one, the **principle of serviceable associated habits**, was the most important one. Incorporating the Lamarckian idea of the inheritance of acquired characteristics, Darwin argued that some emotional expressions were initially serviceable. That is, they originated in bodily actions that served some adaptive function, helping the organism to survive the struggle for existence. Those actions then became associated with situations similar to the ones in which they originally occurred. These acquired expressions were then inherited. Consider the expression of contempt. In exaggerated form, it includes a pronounced intake of air through the nose, accompanied by a lifting and turning away of the head. According to Darwin, the characteristic expression of this emotion derived from a situation in which our evolutionary ancestors reacted to a physically offensive odor. Through habit and inheritance, the same reaction now occurs whenever a person is confronted with a person or situation judged to be offensive: "We seem thus to say to the despised person that he smells offensively, in nearly the same manner as we express to him by half-closing our eyelids, or turning away our faces, that he is not worth looking at" (p. 255). Similarly, the emotional expression of a sneer, directed at an object of dislike, and characterized by the slight lifting of the lip to show the canine teeth, was said by Darwin to derive from the preparations for fighting an enemy.

> …We may readily believe from our affinity to the anthropomorphous apes that our male semi-human progenitors possessed great canine teeth…. We may further suspect…that our semi-human progenitors uncovered their canine teeth when prepared for battle, as we still do when feeling ferocious, or when merely sneering at or defying some one, without any real intention of making an attack with our teeth. (pp. 251–252)

Darwin's second principle for explaining the form of emotional expression was based on the idea that emotions that are just the opposite of each other are expressed in bodily reactions that are similarly opposed. He called it the **principle of antithesis**. As examples, Darwin pointed to numerous animal expressions. When faced with a perceived threat, for instance, a dog will strike a pose designed to make it look bigger and more of a danger to a potential enemy (e.g., the hair on its back bristles). The opposite of this threat gesture, however, is a gesture of submission. While a stranger might elicit the dog's threat gesture, the dog's master would elicit the gesture of submission.

Darwin's third principle concerned what he called the **direct action of the nervous system**. In effect, these expressions are side effects of the physiological arousal that accompanies strongly felt emotions. As an example of direct action, Darwin mentioned the unusual case of a person experiencing severe terror because he was about to be executed—his hair turned white almost immediately. As a more common example, Darwin cited the tendency to tremble, which could accompany any strong emo-

tion and would therefore not be associated with any specific one.

A theme that runs through Darwin's book is the universality of emotional expression. His questionnaire results, which anticipate the findings of modern cross-cultural studies, showed that all over the world, basic emotions were expressed in the same manner. A smile means the same thing everywhere. If emotional expressions are universal, the implication is that they are instinctive and consequently, that human emotional behavior can only be understood by knowing its evolutionary past.

Along with Darwin's *Descent of Man*, the emotions book made it clear that humans shared traits with animals, that a continuity of mental and emotional processes existed. Almost immediately, other naturalists began exploring the dimensions of continuum. Many people were involved, but the best known were two Britishers, George Romanes and Lloyd Morgan. Before reading about them, however, you should read the Close-Up which describes the contributions of a third Britisher, Douglas Spalding, normally ignored in histories of psychology, but worthy of special note.

▶ CLOSE-UP

Douglas Spalding and the Experimental Study of Instinct

An important but typically overlooked pioneer in the systematic study of animal behavior was Douglas Spalding. If he had lived a full life, he would almost certainly be known today as the founder of **ethology**, the study of instinctive animal behavior. Born in London of working class parents in 1840, he did not have the luxuries of inherited wealth and an Oxford/Cambridge education to support his scientific work. Instead, he earned his keep by repairing slate roofs and became educated through his own efforts. He did manage to complete a law degree in London in his early twenties, and it was during this time that he contracted the tuberculosis that would eventually kill him. While traveling for health reasons in southern Europe in the late 1860s, he met and came under the influence of the famous British philosopher John Stuart Mill (Chapter 2), who had by then retired to Avignon in the south of France. Mill recommended Spalding as a tutor for the two young sons of Lord and Lady Amberly, two ardent followers of Mill's liberal political philosophy. The younger son would become one of the best-known philosophers of the twentieth century, Bertrand Russell.

Spalding apparently began his animal research in the 1860s, influenced by the evolutionary fervor that swept through the intelligentsia of the day. Although he never wrote a book and his studies were scattered throughout several popular magazines of the day, his research was noteworthy enough to catch the attention of the famous American psychologist/philosopher William James (Chapter 6). In Volume II of his famous *Principles of Psychology*, James (1890/1950) described in detail "Mr. Spalding's wonderful article on instinct" (p. 396). He was referring to a piece that Spalding wrote for *Macmillan's Magazine* in 1873.

In the article, Spalding addressed the British empiricists' claim that such skills as depth and distance perception and sound localization were learned very early in life as the result of sensory experience. His results showed that experience was irrelevant—certain perceptual abilities, at least in animals, did not require experience, but were the result of **instinct**. Along the way, he anticipated the findings of the twentieth-century ethologists Konrad Lorenz and Niko Tinbergen, by demonstrating several phenomena that today would be called *species specific*.

Instinct. To determine whether sensory experience is necessary for depth perception in baby chicks, Spalding developed a clever procedure. In his words, "[t]aking eggs just when the little prisoners had begun to break their way out, I removed a piece of the shell, and before they had opened their eyes drew over their heads little hoods" (Spalding, 1873, reprinted in Haldane, 1954, p. 3). The hoods remained intact for several days, preventing the chicks from having any visual experiences. Other hatchlings had "gum paper" inserted into their ears to eliminate auditory experiences. When the hoods were removed, the chicks showed no ill effects. For example, after spending just a minute or two adjusting to light, they had no difficulty pecking accurately at the insects provided by Spalding. Those with plugged ears responded similarly—when the obstruction was removed, they immediately responded to the call from an unseen mother hen and ran in the proper direction. Spalding concluded that instinct played an important role in animal behavior and that the British empiricists had overstated the importance of sensory experience as a determiner of behavior.

Imprinting. A famous picture, found in virtually all general psychology texts, shows a fatherly Konrad Lorenz, the modern-day founder of ethology, walking through a field followed by a string of young goslings. Lorenz showed that the birds would follow the first object that they were able to detect moving, and he called the phenomenon **imprinting**. Although he did not label it, Spalding observed the same behavior:

> …Chickens as soon as they are able to walk will follow any moving object. And, when guided by sight alone, they seem to have no more disposition to follow a hen than to follow a duck, or a human being.
>
> Unreflecting onlookers, when they saw chickens a day old running after me, and older ones following me miles and answering to my whistle, imagined that I must have some occult power over the creatures, whereas I simply allowed them to follow me from the first. (Spalding, 1873, reprinted in Haldane, 1954, p. 6)

Critical Periods. Spalding also described behavior illustrating the modern ethological concept of a **critical period**—certain behaviors must develop within a limited time frame, if they are to develop at all. For example, Spalding found that if chicks were prevented from hearing the call of the mother hen for 8–10 days, they would never recognize the mother. Also, while the chicks became attached to him when they were hooded for up to three days, those hooded for four days were afraid of him.

Spalding continued his animal studies when he began tutoring the children of Lord and Lady Amberly in 1873. The sprawling country house in England's Wye Valley was soon filled with a variety of species. The unconventional Lady Amberly, a strong advocate for women's equality, served as Spalding's research assistant; according to some accounts (e.g., Boakes, 1984), she also tutored the naive Spalding in the human instinct of love. It was during this time that Spalding studied the *flight instinct*, demonstrating that birds did not have to *learn* how to fly. After hatching, he placed swallows and other nesting birds in wire mesh enclosures that prevented them from using their wings. Once released, they nonetheless flew immediately.

Spalding's idyllic life with the Amberlys came to an abrupt end in 1874, when both Lady Amberly and a young daughter died of diphtheria. A dispirited Lord Amberly also died within two years, naming Spalding as guardian to his two sons. Amberly's parents successfully contested the will, however, and Spalding was on his own (Gray, 1962). He soon left England and his tuberculosis reappeared. He was 37 when he died in France in 1877.

GEORGE ROMANES (1848–1894): THE ANECDOTAL METHOD

Like Darwin, George Romanes was wealthy, stumbled through an adolescence of minimal accomplishment, appeared headed for the priesthood but didn't get there, and became devoted to science as a result of his experiences at Cambridge (Lesch, 1972). A skilled researcher in physiology, Romanes became caught up in the prevailing excitement over Darwinian evolutionary theory and decided to investigate the levels of mental ability that could be found in other species. Darwin apparently considered the younger man to be his protégé, often entertaining Romanes at Down House; he even turned over his notes on animal behavior to the young scholar (Desmond & Moore, 1991).

Romanes combined Darwin's data with information he had been collecting on his own and in 1882, shortly after Darwin's death, he published *Animal Intelligence*, a detailed catalog of animal behavior, from insects to primates. The book has earned Romanes the title of founder of comparative psychology—he created the term and introduced it in the book as a way of drawing a parallel with comparative anatomy. Romanes argued that just as the specialist in that discipline made comparisons between the physical features of different species, in order to examine the evolution of physical structure, so the comparative psychologist would examine differences between the psychological (i.e., mental) features of different species, in order to examine mental evolution.

Traditional accounts of Romanes's work focus on his overuse of uncritical stories about animal behavior supplied by others, the so-called **anecdotal method**, which has great potential for exaggerating the mental abilities of animals. And during this time of evolutionary zeitgeist, the popular press was full of accounts of what appeared to be remarkable accomplishments by animals. Thus, Romanes's work is sometimes discredited. This is unfortunate, because Romanes was well aware of the problems with anecdotal evidence and took some care to include reliable reports of behavior in his book. For example, he tried to include accounts from observers known to be competent (e.g., Darwin), and he tried to accept unusual accounts of behavior only if they were independently reported by two or more persons. Nonetheless, Romanes himself recognized that the book, if considered by itself, might seem to be little more than a collection of animal stories. He expected that his subsequent books, outlining a theory of mental evolution, would be more important, and that this initial "fact" book would come to be viewed as a preliminary step to the more systematic treatises (Boakes, 1984). Romanes indeed published his theory books, but they have been largely ignored; his reputation, somewhat besmirched, rests on the fact book.

Romanes may have taken more precautions than are usually attributed to him, but *Animal Intelligence* does nonetheless rely mainly on stories told by others more than on direct observations. It also tends toward **anthropomorphism**, the attribution of human faculties to nonhuman entities. That is, Romanes rather uncritically sprinkled human characteristics among a vast array of species. For instance, he argued that ants are in the habit of keeping pets (p. 83), that spiders have a "fondness" for music (p. 205), that scorpions commit suicide when surrounded by fire (p. 222), that birds show sympathy and conjugal fidelity (pp. 271–273), and that beavers show "sagacity and forethought" when selecting sites for their lodges (p. 371) and have an intellectual appreciation for the architectural principles involved in dam-building (p. 376).

CONWY LLOYD MORGAN (1852–1936): THE PRINCIPLE OF PARSIMONY

The problems with Romanes's approach to animal behavior, with its emphasis on anecdotes and its excessive anthropomorphism, were noted by another British naturalist, C. Lloyd Morgan. Son of a lawyer, Morgan attended the School of Mines at the Royal College of Science in London to be trained as a mining engineer. At the School of Mines, he came under the influence of the evolutionist Thomas Huxley, one of Darwin's most ardent defenders. This led Morgan to an interest in zoology and geology, and eventually to a lifetime position as a professor of these topics at University College, Bristol, starting in 1883. He published several books on the geology of the Bristol region, but he is best known for his work in comparative psychology, reflected in books with titles like *Animal Life and Intelligence* (1890) and *An Introduction to Comparative Psychology* (1895).

Just as Romanes was a protégé of Darwin, Morgan started as a follower and admirer of Romanes, but eventually went beyond his mentor.

Morgan is best known today for arguing that explanations for animal behavior should be in the simplest terms possible. This appeal for "parsimonious explanations" is still called **Lloyd Morgan's canon**. As he put it: "In no case may we interpret an action as the outcome of the exercise of a higher psychical faculty, if it can be interpreted as the outcome of the exercise of one which stands lower in the psychological scale" (Morgan, 1895/1903, p. 59). Two of Morgan's examples illustrate the point. First, before beginning his long tenure at Bristol, Morgan taught in South Africa for five years, where he had the opportunity to observe scorpion behavior firsthand. Thus, he had the opportunity to examine Romanes's anthropomorphic claim about scorpions committing suicide when surrounded by fire. Could there be a more parsimonious explanation of the fact that scorpions occasionally sting themselves to death? Morgan thought so, and in contrast to Romanes, who relied on reports from others, Morgan made his own observations. What he discovered was that scorpions regularly used their tails to remove foreign substances and other irritants (e.g., smoke) from the surface of their bodies. It was a simple reflex action, not a deliberate, calculated response arising out of "despair." Every once in a while, Morgan observed, the reflex action would be just a bit too vigorous, resulting in the demise of a scorpion. There was no need to propose a "higher psychical faculty" (a decision to commit suicide) when the behavior could be seen as the result of some factor "lower in the psychological scale" (a reflex action).

A second example used by Morgan is a famous one, often credited with opening the way to the objective study of animal behavior and an important landmark on the road to behaviorism. Romanes had credited cats and dogs with the ability to plan and reason, based on the observation that some could open gates and consequently escape from yards. Morgan, however, believed that such behavior had a simpler explanation, and he used his fox terrier, Tony, as a case in point. As shown in the sketch in Figure 5.4, the dog could place his head through an opening in a gate and open the latch by lifting upward. The gate then swung open and Tony was free to leave the yard and "get out into the road, where there was often much to interest him; cats to be worried, other dogs with whom to establish a sniffing acquaintance, and so forth" (Morgan, 1895/1903, p. 292). To a naive observer, it might appear that the dog rationally "understood" the mechanics of the gate operation and the concept of lifting the latch as a planned means to a desired end. To Morgan, however, the behavior was simply the result of a three-week series of trial-and-error actions prompted by the dog's attempts to escape the yard for the romance of the road. He noted that before hitting on the correct solution, Tony had tried just about everything else, running back and forth along the fence, sticking his head between the bars at numerous locations, and eventually hitting upon the correct action by accident. After he had escaped one time, he quickly abandoned the unsuccessful behaviors and learned to repeat the successful one. As will be seen in Chapter 7, Morgan's description is very similar to the one used by the American psychologist Edward Thorndike, who used trial-and-error learning as an explanation for the results of his famous experiments with cats in puzzle boxes.

Morgan's law of parsimony is sometimes used to highlight an important shift in how comparative psychologists thought about animal behavior and Darwin's notion of the continuity between species. It is often argued that prior to Morgan, naturalists were overly anthropomorphic and searched for evidence of higher mental processes in virtually all species. After Morgan, researchers looked for simpler processes to explain an animal's actions, gradually resulting in the behaviorist dictum that behav-

Figure 5.4   Tony, Morgan's terrier, about to escape from the yard, adapted from Morgan (1895/1903).

iors, even human ones, are best understood in terms of simple conditioning processes. That is, Morgan is often seen as a pivotal figure in the progression from cute animal stories to sophisticated experimental research and a mechanical conception of animal behavior. Such an interpretation overstates the case, however. Morgan can indeed be credited for arguing that an understanding of animal behavior must go beyond a collection of anecdotes and embrace more systematic observational strategies. Yet to say that Morgan wished to rule out the existence of animal consciousness and intelligence is erroneous. As Morgan himself said, shortly after proclaiming the canon:

> …To this, however, it should be added, lest the range of the principle be misunderstood, that the canon by no means

excludes the interpretation of a particular activity in terms of the higher processes, if we already have some independent evidence of the occurrence of these higher processes in the animal under observation. (Morgan, 1895/1903, p. 59)

Thus, Morgan did not intend for the canon of parsimony to be an absolute prohibition against the idea of higher mental processes in animals; he was merely urging methodological caution. According to Costall (1993), Morgan's true purpose was to broaden the range of criteria on which to base a continuity between species. Rather than relying exclusively on a search for sophisticated rational reflection on the part of a variety of species, other types of mental processes, differing in degrees of complexity, could be included. Put in evolutionary terms, Morgan proposed that animals exhibited many levels of cognition, reaching a level of complexity just sufficient to enable them to survive their own unique struggle for existence. The point of the canon was to argue that there was no reason to suggest levels of mental capability beyond that needed to survive.

STUDYING INDIVIDUAL DIFFERENCES

A cornerstone of Darwin's theory, the raw material for natural selection, was the notion that individual members of a species varied from each other. For psychology, this fact led to the systematic study of **individual differences**, a research tradition that includes the creation of techniques to measure those differences. Today's intelligence and personality tests are just two outcomes of this tradition. The person most directly responsible for initiating the study of individual differences was Darwin's half-cousin, Francis Galton (1882–1911), whose

obsession with measurement led one scientist to refer to him as the nineteenth century's "apostle of quantification" (Gould, 1981, p. 75).

FRANCIS GALTON (1822–1911): JACK OF ALL SCIENCES

Like his more famous relative, Galton (Figure 5.5) was raised in affluence. Because he never found it necessary to earn a living, he was able to indulge an exceptionally wide range of interests. His insatiable curiosity, combined with a brilliant intellect that manifested itself at an early age,[7] resulted in a remarkably diverse list of accomplishments, only a small portion of which relates directly to psychology. For example, he became one of a number of famous British explorers of Africa during the Victorian era. From 1850 to 1852, he explored a little known territory in the south of Africa, mapping it accurately for the first time and displaying his devotion to the gods of precision in measurement. His exploits won him a gold medal from the Royal Geographical Society and he became a recognized public figure after publishing an account of his explorations and a highly successful (eight editions) travel guide for the inexperienced explorer. The latter included suggestions on everything from shelter to navigation to hunting to cooking, along with advice on dealing with native populations: "A frank, joking but determined manner joined with an air of showing more confidence in the good faith of the natives than you really feel, is the best" (Galton, 1855, cited in Forrest, 1974, p. 64).

In addition to geography and exploration, Galton made original contributions to several other fields. By gathering weather information from various locations at the same times during the day, for instance, he created the first systematic weather maps, and he was the first to observe the relationships between high and low pressure systems and how they influenced

---

[7] Galton resembled another child prodigy, John Stuart Mill, in this regard. Like Mill, Galton displayed adultlike abilities at a tender age. He could read and write English by age three, translate some Latin by age five, and quote from Shakespeare by his sixth birthday.

fingerprint

Figure 5.5   The ever curious Francis Galton.

the weather. By measuring the patterns of swirls on the fingertips of hundreds of different people, he demonstrated that every person had a unique pattern. Scotland Yard eventually started using this "fingerprinting" technique for identification purposes. This procedure, of course, is an example of looking for individual differences. Indeed, Galton's work in fingerprinting was just a small piece of his overall strategy of quantifying differences between people over a range of variables. And this leads to Galton's importance for psychology.

The Nature of Intelligence

As a wealthy, upper-class, Victorian-era, British white male, living at a time when England was the most powerful nation on earth, Galton and his cohort group had little difficulty believing themselves to be superior to those from other classes, countries, races, or the other gender. Furthermore, more a product of his environment than he cared to admit, Galton shared the widespread assumption among his peers that this preeminence was no accident, but based on an inherent superiority in ability. When his cousin published on evolution in 1859,

humans were not discussed, but Galton immediately saw the ramifications. If inherited individual variation, acted upon by natural selection, influenced the evolution of animal and plant species, it must have influenced humans as well. If human intelligence was a key trait enabling physically weak humans to survive the struggle for existence, then the more intelligent humans would naturally rise to the top of society. From this it was not hard for Galton to conclude that he and others of his class had achieved their lofty positions in society by virtue of their highly evolved and superior intellectual ability, rather than by the accident of being born to the right parents. He set out to collect evidence in support of his belief that intelligence was innate, producing *Hereditary Genius* in 1869.

To examine the question of whether intelligence was inherited, Galton relied on his proclivity for quantification and statistical analysis. First, by examining the contents of biographical dictionaries, which profiled people who had achieved eminence in some field, he estimated that the "rate of eminence" in Great Britain was about 1 person in 4000. He then looked at the family trees of these highly able people and discovered that talent tended to run in families. Of those noted in the dictionaries, about 10% had at least one relative who was also so noted, a rate much higher than could be expected by a one in four thousand probability for the general population. And talent within a family tended to be similar—lawyers related to lawyers, doctors related to doctors, and so on. Furthermore, if two relatives appeared in the dictionaries, they were four times more likely to be directly related (e.g., father-son) than related at a second level (e.g., uncle-nephew). Today, of course, we recognize that these patterns are just as likely to reflect environmental factors as genetic ones, but Galton was operating within the context of a social environment that was biased toward an assumption of inherited differences in ability and an intellectual environment that was dominated by the evolution discussion. For him, the signs all pointed to

surveys + twin studies

the same conclusion—intelligence was innate, the product of evolutionary forces.

Following *Hereditary Genius*, Galton continued his examination of talent by pioneering two methodological techniques in use today: surveys and twin studies. Although his cousin was using a similar technique to study emotional expressions at about the same time, Galton is credited with being the first person to use the **survey method**. Sometime in the early 1870s, he wrote a questionnaire and distributed it to 180 fellows of the Royal Society, the scientific elite of England. The survey asked its respondents to describe their personalities, physical attributes, family characteristics, and the details of their upbringing; it also asked them to describe the origins of their scientific interests and to indicate "How far do your scientific tastes appear innate" (cited in Forrest, 1974, p. 126). Galton received about 100 usable replies, and they formed the basis of his next book, which included a subtitle that popularized two words destined to become catchwords in the continuing debate over the origins of intelligence. The book was called *English Men of Science: Their Nature and Nurture* (Galton, 1874). While granting that some of the replies demonstrated that the environment (nurture) helped to shape the scientists, Galton believed that his respondents overwhelmingly supported the idea that talent in science was inherited (nature). This he concluded from making the questionable assumption that scientific ability could be considered innate if a subject reported being interested in science very early in life and could not point to any particular set of circumstances bringing about such an interest. It just seemed to be there from the start. As one of his respondents put it: "As far back as I remember, I loved nature and desired to learn her secrets" (cited in Forrest, 1974, p. 126).

Galton's second methodological innovation, **twin studies**, was on firmer scientific ground. He sent questionnaires to twins known to him, asking them to supply names of other twins; he eventually surveyed 94 pairs about their physical and psychological attributes. As might be

expected, he found support for his hereditarian beliefs—many similarities between pairs of twins, even in their later years, after they had been living in different environments. He reported the data anecdotally, and both his questionnaire wording and his interpretation of the results were affected by his preconceptions about intelligence, but the twin studies method itself has proven invaluable over the years as a way to evaluate the relative influences of nature and nurture.

The general conclusion that Galton reached on the basis of all these studies is clear from the opening sentence of *Hereditary Genius*: "I propose to show in this book that a man's natural abilities are derived by inheritance" (Galton, 1869/1891, p. 1). One implication of this statement, resulting from Galton's reading of Darwin's parallels between the artificial selection of the breeder and the natural selection of the wild, is spelled out in the book's second sentence. He wrote that just as it is possible "to obtain by careful selection a permanent breed of dogs or horses gifted with peculiar powers of running,…so it would be quite practicable to produce a highly-gifted race of men by judicious marriages during several consecutive generations" (Galton, 1869/1891, p. 1). This suggestion eventually led Galton to coin the term **eugenics** to promote the idea that society should take active steps toward improving its genetic material. This would include encouraging certain people to reproduce, sometimes known as "positive" eugenics. These individuals presumably would be those with great talent, people like Galton (ironically, Galton and his wife were childless). On the other hand, he also advocated a "negative" eugenics, arguing that the poor (i.e., intellectually inferior, otherwise they would not be so poor, he believed) should be discouraged from having children and that immigration should be restricted. He founded a Eugenics Society in 1908, a journal a year later, and spent his remaining years promoting a eugenics-based society. As will be seen in the chapter on mental testing (Chapter

8), he found a sympathetic audience, both in Great Britain and in the United States.

The Anthropometric Laboratory

In order to selectively breed for the intelligence that would keep Great Britain in its position as a world power, Galton knew that it would be necessary to have some means of identifying those best suited to improve the race. This meant developing ways to measure talent, a task close to Galton's quantitative heart. The measurement of ability was a natural outgrowth of his obsession with measuring all possible differences between people. His efforts reached their peak in the 1880s, when he established an Anthropometric Laboratory, initially as part of an international health fair held in South Kensington in 1884. It later moved to a nearby museum, where Galton collected data for another 10 years. Nearly 10,000 fair-goers were tested in 1884; about 17,000 were tested altogether (Forrest, 1974).

Each person entering the laboratory completed several tests, with many of the measuring instruments created by Galton. Some were simple physical measures: height, weight, arm span, and breathing capacity. Others tested basic sensory/motor capacities: reaction time, auditory and visual acuity, color naming, judgment of line lengths, how forcefully a target could be struck with the fist, and grip strength. After the lab moved from the health fair, head size was added as a measure. Although these might not appear to be valid measures of intelligence to us today, Galton argued that superior mental capacity was related to neural efficiency and sensory ability: "The only information

that reaches us concerning outward events appears to pass through the avenue of our senses; and the more perceptible our senses are of difference, the larger is the field upon which our judgment and intelligence can act" (Galton, 1883/1965, p. 421). Galton also argued that women were intellectually inferior to men, a widely-held nineteenth-century prejudice, and traced the deficiency to their inadequate senses. He noted that professions requiring sharp senses, such as piano-tuners, wine-tasters, and wool-sorters, were all populated by men. Deeply immersed in his times, of course, he failed to consider the fact that women would never be given the chance to be employed in these trades.

Galton's measures never proved to be useful indexes of intelligence and they were soon replaced by tests like those devised in France at the turn of the century by Alfred Binet (Chapter 8). Galton's effort is noteworthy, however, as the first serious attempt to measure individual differences in human abilities. It is also important for the history of statistics—in his attempts to determine whether scores on his various measures were associated with each other, he invented the statistical concept of **correlation**. In an 1888 paper entitled "Co-relations and their Measurement, Chiefly from Anthropometric Data," Galton argued that the strength of association between any two measures could be stated mathematically. This idea was soon refined into the modern concept of the correlation coefficient by one of his followers, the mathematician Karl Pearson, whose name is associated with the most common expression of a correlation coefficient, Pearson's r.

▶ ORIGINAL SOURCE EXCERPT

Galton on Measurement, Imagery, and Association

As a jack-of-all-sciences, Galton was continually on the lookout for new phenomena to measure. The following excerpt, taken from a collection of Galton papers that were published together as *An Inquiry into Human Faculty and Its*

Development (Galton, 1883), illustrate just a sample of his interests. First, one of his more famous inventions has come to be known as the Galton whistle. It was designed to measure auditory thresholds, and Galton's description of its use reveals something of his devotion to precision and his delight in making observations about behavior. His observation about age-related hearing loss for high-frequency sounds ("shrill notes") is now a well-established auditory phenomenon. The page references in the excerpt are from a collection of readings by Dennis (1948).

Whistles for Audibility of Shrill Notes

I contrived a small whistle for conveniently ascertaining the upper limits of audible sound in different persons.... I made a very small whistle from a brass tube whose internal diameter was less than one tenth of an inch in diameter. A plug was fitted into the lower end of the tube, which could be pulled out or pushed in as much as desired, thereby causing the length of the bore of the whistle to be varied at will. When the bore is long the note is low; when short, it is high. The plug was graduated, so that the precise note produced by the whistle could be determined by reading off the graduations and referring to a table.

On testing different persons I found there was a remarkable falling off in the power of hearing high notes as age advanced. The persons themselves were quite unconscious of their deficiency so long as their sense of hearing low notes remained unimpaired. It is an only too amusing experiment to test a party of persons of various ages, including some rather elderly and self-satisfied personages. They are indignant at being thought deficient in the power of hearing, yet the experiment quickly shows that they are absolutely deaf to shrill notes which the younger persons hear acutely, and they commonly betray much dislike to the discovery. Every one has his limit, and the limit at which sounds become too shrill to be audible to any particular person can be rapidly determined by this little instrument.

I have tried experiments with all kinds of animals on their powers of hearing shrill notes. I have gone through the whole of the Zoological Gardens, using an apparatus arranged for the purpose. It consists of one of my little whistles at the end of a walking stick—that is, in reality, a long tube; it has a bit of india-rubber pipe under the handle, a sudden squeeze upon which forces a little air into the whistle and causes it to sound. I hold it as near as is safe to the ears of the animals, and when they are quite accustomed to its presence and heedless of it, I make it sound; then if they prick their ears it shows that they hear the whistle; if they do not, it is probably inaudible to them. Still, it is very possible that in some cases they hear but do not heed the sound. Of all creatures, I have found none superior to cats in the power of hearing shrill sounds; it is perfectly remarkable what a faculty they have in this way. Cats, of course, have to deal with mice, and to find them out by their squealing. Many people cannot hear the shrill squeal of a mouse. Some time ago, singing mice were exhibited in London, and of the people who went to hear them, some could hear nothing, whilst others could hear a little, and others again could hear much.... Small dogs also hear very shrill notes, but large ones do not. I have walked through the streets of a town with an instrument like that which I used in the Zoological Gardens, and made nearly all the little dogs turn round, but not the large ones.... My attempts on insect hearing have been failures. (pp. 277–278)

One of Galton's many questionnaire studies concerned the nature of mental imagery, a topic of interest to twentieth-century cognitive psychologists. He asked his respondents to visualize some scene (e.g., the breakfast table) and answer questions about the qualities of their images. One outcome that surprised him was the apparent lack of imagery ability in the scientists he surveyed.

Mental Imagery

Anecdotes find their way into print, from time to time, of persons whose visual memory is so clear and sharp as to present mental pictures that may be scrutinised with nearly as much ease and prolonged attention as if they were real objects. I became interested in the subject and made a rather extensive inquiry into the mode of visual presentation in different persons, so far as could be gathered from their respective statements. It seemed to me that the results might illustrate the essential differences between the mental operations of different men, that they might give some clue to the origin of visions, and that the course of the inquiry might reveal some previously unnoticed facts....

The first group of the rather long series of queries related to the illumination, definition, and colouring of the mental image, and were framed thus:

"Before addressing yourself to any of the Questions on the opposite page, think of some definite object—suppose it is your breakfast-table as you sat down to it this morning—and consider carefully the picture that rises before your mind's eye.

1. Illumination. Is the image dim or fairly clear? Is its brightness comparable to that of the actual scene?
2. Definition. Are all the objects pretty well defined at the same time, or is the place of sharpest definition at any one moment more contracted than it is in a real scene?
3. Colouring. Are the colours of the china, of the toast, breadcrust, mustard, meat, parsley, or whatever may have been on the table, quite distinct and natural?"

The earliest results of my inquiry amazed me. I had begun by questioning friends in the scientific world, as they were the most likely class of men to give accurate answers concerning this faculty of visualising, to which novelists and poets continually allude, which has left an abiding mark on the vocabularies of every language, and which supplies the material out of which dreams and the well-known hallucinations of sick people are built.

To my astonishment, I found that the great majority of the men of science of whom I first applied protested that mental imagery was unknown to them, and they looked on me as fanciful and fantastic in supposing that the words "mental imagery" really expressed what I believed everybody supposed them to mean. They had no more notion of its true nature than a colour-blind man, who has not discerned his defect, has of the nature of colour. They had a mental deficiency of which they were unaware, and naturally enough supposed that those who affirmed they possessed it, were romancing. (pp. 279–280)

Galton had no difficulty uncovering descriptions of imagery in nonscientists, and he was able to classify the responses by the vividness of the images. Women and intelligent children seemed especially capable of vivid imagery, Galton thought, because they "take pleasure in introspection, and strive their very best to explain their mental processes" (p. 281).

Association was another mental process that caught Galton's attention. He was aware of the long history of philosophical speculation about the nature of association, of course, but he was unaware of the work that Hermann Ebbinghaus (Chapter 4) was doing at about the same time (Ebbinghaus's *On Memory* appeared two years after Galton's *Inquiry*). Galton's first concern was the difficulty in studying the associations in one's own mind—the very act of closely attending to the operation of the mind influences the sequence of ideas. Hence, the mind is not behaving naturally while under the careful examination required to meet the demands of science. He believed that he had succeeded in solving the problem:[8]

> …My method consists of allowing the mind to play freely for a brief period, until a couple or so of ideas have passed through it, and then, while the traces or echoes of those ideas are still lingering in the brain, to turn the attention on them with a sudden and complete awakening; to arrest, to scrutinize them, and to record their exact appearance….
>
> I must add, that I found the experiments to be extremely trying and irksome, and that it required much resolution to go through with them, using the scrupulous care they demanded. Nevertheless the results well repaid the trouble.
>
> …My first experiments were these. On several occasions, but notably on one when I felt myself unusually capable of the kind of effort required, I walked leisurely along Pall Mall, a distance of 450 yards, during which time I scrutinised with attention every successive object that caught my eyes, and I allowed my attention to rest on it until one or two thoughts had arisen through direct association with that object; then I took very brief mental note of them, and passed on to the next object. I never allowed my mind to ramble. The number of objects viewed was, I think, about 300, for I had subsequently repeated the same walk under similar conditions and endeavoured to estimate their number, with that result. It was impossible for me to recall, in other than the vaguest way, the numerous ideas that had passed through my mind; but of this, at least, I am sure, that samples of my whole life had passed before me, that many bygone incidents, which I never suspected to have formed part of my stock of

---

[8] In the Original Source Excerpt for Chapter 7, you will learn that this is precisely the approach taken by E. B. Titchener when trying to solve the problem of introspecting to emotional conscious content.

thought, had been glanced at as objects too familiar to awaken the attention. I saw at once that the brain was vastly more active than I had previously believed it to be, and I was perfectly amazed at the unexpected width of the field of its everyday operations. (pp. 285–286)

Galton noticed in subsequent walks that many of his associations repeated themselves, which led him to temper his initial impression of the richness and diversity of mental life. He next set out to study the association process with more precision, in the process inventing the **word association test**, in which he thought of a stimulus word and recorded the first word that came to mind. He even attempted to measure the time it took to produce an association:

...I selected a list of suitable words, and wrote them on different small sheets of paper. Taking care to dismiss them from my thoughts when not engaged upon them, and allowing some days to elapse before I began to use them, I laid one of these sheets with all due precautions under a book, but not wholly covered by it, so that when I leaned forward I would see one of the words, being previously quite ignorant of what the word would be. Also I held a small chronograph, which I started by pressing a spring the moment the word caught my eye, and which stopped of itself the instant I released the spring; and this I did so soon as about a couple of ideas in direct association with the word had arisen in my mind.... When the two ideas had occurred, I stopped the chronograph and wrote them down, and the time they occupied. I soon got into the way of doing all this in a very methodical and automatic manner, keeping the mind perfectly calm and neutral, but intent and, as it were, at full cock and on hair trigger, before displaying the word.... The list of words that I finally secured was 75 in number, though I began with more. I went through them on four separate occasions, under very different circumstances, in England and abroad, and at intervals of about a month. In no case were the associations governed to any degree worth recording, by remembering what had occurred to me on previous occasions, for I found that the process itself had great influence in discharging the memory of what had just been engaged in, and I of course, took care between the experiments never to let my thoughts revert to the words. The results seem to me to be as trustworthy as any other statistical series that has been collected with equal care. (pp. 286–287)

Galton's word association tests confirmed the tendency for associations to repeat themselves in one's mind. For example, after going through his list of 75 words four times, he found that in about 25% of the cases, the word gave rise to exactly the same association on all four trials.

...This shows much less variety in the mental stock of ideas than I had expected, and makes us feel that the roadways of our minds are worn into very deep ruts. I conclude from the proved number of faint and barely conscious thoughts, and from the proved iteration of them, that the mind is perpetually travelling over familiar ways without our memory retaining any impression of its excursions. Its footsteps are so light and fleeting that

it is only by such experiments as I have described that we can learn anything about them. (p. 288)

Galton concluded with the observation that we are only dimly aware of the
course of our mental life, strongly hinting at the unconscious mind that would
shortly become the focus of another famous nineteenth-century mind, Sigmund
Freud (Chapter 12):

...Perhaps the strongest of the impressions left by these experiments
regards the multifariousness of the work done by the mind in a state of
half-consciousness, and the valid reason they afford for believing in the
existence of still deeper strata of mental operations, sunk wholly below
the level of consciousness. (p. 289)

It has been estimated that a mere 25% of
Galton's research and writings were of direct
concern to psychology (Forrest, 1974). Yet his
contribution to the discipline is impressive: He
pioneered the study of individual differences in
human ability, introduced research methods
and statistical tools still in use, and made some
astute observations about human cognition.
Galton's lifelong devotion to British science
earned him a knighthood in 1909. Sir Francis
Galton died two years later.

DARWIN'S CENTURY
IN PERSPECTIVE

Although Darwin's major influence has been
on the biological sciences, modern psychology
cannot be properly understood without knowing about his theory and its implications. The
study of individual differences derives from his
observation about individual variation within a
species, and comparative psychology has its origins in an attempt to evaluate the claim of an
evolutionary continuity among species. As will
be seen in Chapter 12, Darwin's theory also
had a direct effect on Freud's thinking about
the importance of sexual motivation in directing the course of human behavior. Finally,
functionalism (to be encountered in varying
degrees in Chapters 6, 7, and 8), which examined behaviors and mental processes in terms

of their capacity for adapting the organism to
the environment, also had its roots in evolutionary thinking. Darwin, in effect, naturalized
the mind, causing it to be seen as the means by
which the human animal survives in the struggle for existence.

In recent years, some psychologists have
become even more explicit in looking toward
evolution as a means to explain human behavior, and the result is a new subfield called **evolutionary psychology** (Chapter 14).
Advocates (e.g., Wright, 1994) argue that if
evolutionary forces have been powerful
enough to create the physical characteristics
that make us human, then why not mental
characteristics as well? Evolutionary psychologists have paid special attention to social behaviors and to sexuality and gender differences in
behavior. Their general strategy is to describe
some behavior that has some regularity, then
look for an evolutionary justification for it.
They believe, for example, that much of the
behavior that surrounds male-female relations
reduces to an attempt to insure that one's
genetic materials make it to the next generation. Many of their ideas have been controversial, especially among psychologists who tend
to emphasize the importance of the environment in shaping human behavior. Yet their
increasing presence in the discussion about the
causes of human behavior is just another indication of the lasting power of Darwin's ideas.

SUMMARY

The Species Problem

- During the Enlightenment, some scientists began questioning the biblical account of how species were created. The species problem concerned the question of how species originated, why there were so many, and how extinction could be explained. The argument from design enabled scientists to continue to examine nature scientifically while maintaining religious beliefs.

- An early theory of evolution that omitted reference to the deity was proposed by Charles Darwin's grandfather, Erasmus. A more important theory was proposed by the French naturalist, Lamarck. His theory included the concept of the inheritance of acquired characteristics.

Charles Darwin (1809–1882) and the Theory of Evolution

- After several false starts, Charles Darwin found a vocation in science while a student at Cambridge. He initially thought of himself as a geologist, but he was also greatly interested in zoology. Two important mentors were the botanist John Henslow and the geologist Adam Sedgwick.

- During a five-year voyage aboard the *Beagle*, Darwin collected evidence that led to important contributions to both geology and zoology. He made discoveries that supported Charles Lyell's uniformitarian model of geological change (the earth changes gradually according to known principles, rather than as a result of periodic geological catastrophes) and he collected data that would eventually provide evidence for his theory of evolution. Evidence from the Galápagos Islands (e.g., finches) was especially important.

- In developing his theory. Darwin was influenced by the views of Thomas Malthus, who pointed out that because populations tend to grow faster than food supplies, a struggle for existence occurs among members of those populations. He also observed that hobbyists and farmers were able to bring about dramatic changes in species by careful breeding.

- Darwin created the essence of his theory in the late 1830s, but did not publish for 20 years. He was slowed by ill health, a concern over how his theory would be received by the scientific community, and a scientific cautiousness that led him to accumulate as much evidence as possible to support his theory. He was motivated to publish in 1859 by the appearance of a similar theory by Alfred Russel Wallace.

- Darwin's theory proposes that individual members of every species vary from each other, that some variations are more favorable in the struggle for existence than others, enabling the organism to adapt to the environment, and that nature "selects" (natural selection) those with the most favorable variations for survival.

The Origins of Comparative Psychology

- An implication of Darwin's theory was that there existed a continuity between species. This led to the development of comparative psychology, the study of differences between and similarities among species on various traits (e.g., intelligence). Darwin was an early pioneer, who examined the evolutionary history of emotional expressions and demonstrated that human expressions had evolutionary roots.

- George Romanes is considered the founder of comparative psychology and he provided extensive descriptions of the behavior of many species. He relied on anecdotal observations and was too anthropomorphic in his interpretations of the behaviors he described. A more experimental approach was taken by Douglas Spalding, who demonstrated that certain behaviors were the result of instinct, not experience. C. Lloyd Morgan took issue with the excessive anthropomorphism shown by other comparative psychologists and argued for more parsimonious explanations. For example, some behaviors were more parsimoniously explained as being examples of trial-and-error learning than rational thought.

Studying Individual Differences

- Individual variation is a cornerstone of evolutionary theory, and Francis Galton was the first to carefully examine these individual differences in humans. He studied individual differences in visual imagery, studying it through the first systematic use of the survey method (questionnaire). He also invented the word association method to study the nature of associations.

- Galton believed that intelligence was an inherited ability; nurture played no significant role. As evidence, he pointed to the fact that certain abilities tended to run in families. He argued for a eugenics-based society—only those who are *fit* should be encouraged to reproduce. To identify those who were most fit, he set out to measure individual differences in ability. This resulted in the first widespread attempt to measure and classify human abilities. His measures relied heavily on basic sensory/motor processes and did not prove very useful.

Darwin's Century in Perspective

- One modern indication of the power of Darwinian thinking is the development of evolutionary psychology, which aims to explain many social behaviors in evolutionary terms.

FOR FURTHER READING

BOAKES, R. (1984). *From Darwin to behaviourism: Psychology and the minds of animals.* Cambridge: Cambridge University Press.

Detailed yet highly readable treatment of the rise of comparative psychology from its evolutionary roots and its connection with behaviorism; notable for its collection of unique photos.

DESMOND, A., & MOORE, J. (1991). *Darwin: The life of a tormented evolutionist.* New York: W. W. Norton and Company.

One of several recent biographies of Darwin; as the subtitle suggests, the book deals extensively with Darwin's struggle to create and provide supporting evidence for his great theory; highly detailed account of the Beagle *trip.*

RUSE, M. (1979). *The Darwinian revolution: Science red in tooth and claw.* Chicago: University of Chicago Press.

Fits the development of Darwin's theory within the framework of nineteenth-century science and religion and within the historical context of Victorian England.

WEINER, J. (1994). *The beak of the finch.* New York: Vintage Books.

A scientific page-turner, and winner of a Pulitzer Prize; recounts the story of Darwin's finches and focuses on recent finch research, which provides direct evidence of evolutionary changes occurring in a relatively brief period of time.

6

AMERICAN PIONEERS

▼

When...we talk of "psychology as a natural science," we must not assume that that means a sort of psychology that stands at last on solid ground.... This is no science, it is only the hope of a science.

William James, 1892

▼

Preview

Having considered the philosophical and scientific contexts out of which modern psychology evolved, its origins and early development in Germany, and the far-reaching importance of Darwin's ideas, we are ready to shift our focus to the development of psychology in the United States in the nineteenth century. After a preliminary discussion of the influence of faculty psychology in pre-Civil War America, this chapter examines the life and work of America's first major psychologist: William James. Although he thought of himself more as a philosopher than a psychologist, his *Principles of Psychology* is arguably the most important book written in psychology's brief history and his ideas influence the field to this day. The Original Source Excerpt is by James and is a discussion of what came to be called the James-Lange theory of emotions; it is from an abbreviated version of *The Principles*. The chapter also considers the careers and contributions of several other members of the first generation of American psychologists, especially G. Stanley Hall and Mary Whiton Calkins. Hall exemplified the pioneering spirit said to characterize Americans: he spread the gospel of the New Psychology by founding laboratories, journals, and the American Psychological Association. Calkins was the best known of a handful of pioneering women psychologists who made their presence felt despite daunting odds.

PSYCHOLOGY IN NINETEENTH-CENTURY AMERICA

E. G. Boring (1950) once described American psychology as the offspring of the new psychology created in Germany (i.e., Wundt) and of British biology (i.e., Darwin), and he asserted that American psychology did not really begin until William James appeared on the scene. Boring influenced a whole generation of psychologists, of course, and one consequence has been the neglect of pre-Jamesian psychology. Yet while William James was clearly a towering figure during the formative years of modern scientific psychology in the United States, he was not the first American thinker to write about psychological issues or to teach psychology in an American university. Prior to James, psychology was taught in courses called "moral philosophy" or "mental philosophy," and it was dominated by **faculty psychology**, which derived from a Scottish philosophical movement called Scottish Realism.

FACULTY PSYCHOLOGY

As you recall from Chapter 2, empiricism and associationism, represented in the philosophies of Locke, Berkeley, Hume, Hartley, and Mill, were the dominant intellectual forces in Great Britain during the eighteenth and nineteenth centuries. Empiricists argued that knowledge resulted from our experiences in the world, with the structure of our minds being organized through the laws of association. The Empiricists also addressed the concept of reality, with Locke distinguishing between primary and secondary qualities of matter, Berkeley arguing that only the secondary qualities were real, and Hume extending the argument to the verge of skepticism by contending that we cannot be absolutely certain about the reality of anything. Thus, when we look at a tree, Locke would say that its basic shape and mass are pri-

mary qualities that have existence independent of our observations, but that color is a secondary quality, depending for its existence on the perceiving person. Berkeley would deny the distinction and say that all aspects of the tree rely on the subjective perception of the observer and we can only be sure of its existence by believing in God, the Permanent Perceiver. Hume would argue that we cannot even be 100% sure about the reality of our perception of the tree.

The Scottish Realist philosophers, most notably Thomas Reid (1710–1792) in the eighteenth century and Thomas Brown (1778–1820) in the nineteenth, took issue with the extreme Humean view of reality on the grounds that such an idea simply violates common sense. They believed that humans have an intuitive understanding that a real world truly exists—human existence would have no foundation otherwise. They also rejected the implication that mind is in essence nothing more than a collection of associated ideas based on experience. Instead, they argued that the mind has an independent existence in reality and is composed of various innate powers that they called *faculties*. Reid divided these faculties into two broad categories—intellectual and active (Evans, 1984). Intellectual faculties included such things as memory, abstraction, reasoning, and judgment, whereas active faculties concerned the emotions and the will. If the concept of faculty sounds familiar, it is because you encountered it in Chapter 3; Franz Josef Gall borrowed it when he developed the doctrine that eventually became known as phrenology. Reid identified more than 30 faculties; Gall and then Spurzheim tried to localize them in the brain. It is no coincidence that faculty psychology and phrenology were popular at the same time in America.

The Scottish influence in early American psychology arrived in the form of a wave of Scottish immigration in the eighteenth century. Many of the immigrants were educated—doctors, teachers, and ministers—and many played a role in the explosive growth of higher education in the United States in the years between the American Revolution and the Civil War. In the 140 years between the founding of Harvard in 1636 and the American Revolution of 1776, nine colleges had been created; by the start of the Civil War in 1861, 85 years later, students could choose from 182 colleges. Scottish Realism and faculty psychology dominated the curriculum of most of them.

American Psychology's First Textbook

Thomas Upham (1799–1872) of Bowdoin College in Maine is usually credited with authoring the first American psychology textbook when he organized his lecture notes and published them in 1827 as *Elements of Intellectual Philosophy*. The text eventually grew to three volumes and was given the broader title of *Elements of Mental Philosophy*. It quickly became the principal text in American colleges and universities for courses that today would be called introductory psychology (Evans, 1984). The book was organized along the lines of the Scottish faculty approach, although it included a healthy dose of associationism as well. It also included frequent references to the deity, and morality was a recurring theme. This is hardly surprising, given the fact that prior to the Civil War, most professors at American colleges (including Upham) were Protestant ministers. As will be seen shortly, the postwar rise of universities like Johns Hopkins, with its emphasis on the German model of research, created a need for a new type of textbook.

Upham subdivided Reid's "active" faculties, and his resulting book was organized into three main divisions: the intellect (cognition), the sensibilities (emotion), and the will (action). This "trilogy of mind" (Hilgard, 1980) was not unique to Upham, but represented a theme that can be traced back to the Greeks and ahead to the present day. Here is a sample of topics found under each of Upham's main divisions (cited in Evans, 1984, pp. 40–41):

Division I: The Intellect

- sensation, perception, consciousness, imagination
- concepts, abstraction, reasoning
- primary and secondary laws of association, memory
- disordered intellectual action: insanity (later expanded by Upham in 1849 into abnormal psychology's first textbook: *Outlines of Disordered Mental Action*)

Division II: The Sensibilities

- instincts, appetites, propensities
- the malevolent affections (e.g., anger, jealousy, revenge)
- the benevolent affections (e.g., love, patriotism, pity)
- the moral sensibilities or conscience

Division III: The Will

- laws of the will
- freedom of the will implied in man's moral nature
- on the power of the will

Upham's text was a best-seller on campuses well into the 1870s. By the end of the century, however, American psychology had changed dramatically, reflecting the mid-century influences identified by Boring: German psychology and British biology. The American system of higher education had also changed.

THE MODERN UNIVERSITY

The impressive growth of colleges prior to the Civil War was nothing compared with the revolution in higher education that occurred between the war and the turn of the century. During this time, the modern university was created, the result of a complex interplay of forces. One factor was the emergence of the public high school and the heightened expectation that education was a key to a successful career. An increase in high school graduates in turn meant a greater number of students eligible to attend college, and attend they did. There were an estimated 67,000 students attending college in 1870, 157,000 in 1890, and 335,000 in 1910 (Hofstadter & Hardy, 1952). This expanding college student population produced a need for teachers who had degrees beyond the bachelor's level, thereby creating a demand for graduate education. The initial lack of it in the United States was one reason why students flocked to Germany in the late nineteenth century. There they encountered an approach to education that emphasized graduate training, independent research, and a variety of courses from which to choose. The decade of the 1880s was the high point for Americans studying in Germany. By the 1890s, several good American universities were available, and some of the second-level German universities were developing the reputation of being mere diploma mills (two semesters for a Ph.D. at the University of Halle, for example) (Veysey, 1965).

The American universities began to develop shortly after the end of the Civil War. One major catalyst was the Morrill Land Grant Act of 1862, which gave every state a minimum of 30,000 acres of federal land. If the state built a university on the land within five years, it could keep the land; otherwise it reverted to the government. This, of course, produced the great state universities, which were run by laypeople rather than clergy and which emphasized science and practical applications (e.g., applying science to improve agriculture and mining). Also during this time, several of the Ivy League schools developed graduate training: Yale in 1860, Harvard in 1872. A third impetus was a consequence of the accumulation of great wealth by a handful of business tycoons in the second half of the nineteenth century. Several of them donated large amounts of money to found universities, motivated partly by a philanthropic desire to give something back to society, partly to blunt criticism of the exploitive manner in which they became wealthy, and partly to have their

names associated with an enterprise that was universally valued. Four of the better-known schools created in this way were Johns Hopkins University (1876), Clark University (1887), Stanford University (1891), and the University of Chicago (1891). All but the last, which was created with Rockefeller money, was named for the major benefactor.

Johns Hopkins University in Baltimore became the prototype of the new university in America. It was explicitly modeled on the German example that emphasized research and the accumulation of new knowledge, and although it had a small undergraduate division from the start, its main focus was on graduate education. Endowed with $3.5 million by its founder, wealthy Baltimore merchant Johns (correct spelling) Hopkins, it quickly became the most important American university of the 1880s, the only legitimate competitor to the German universities (Hawkins, 1960). Its innovative president, Daniel Coit Gilman, attracted good students by creating the concept of the competitive "university fellowship," which included a $500 stipend plus free tuition, and encouraging the development of laboratory training and the seminar, to supplement the traditional lecture course. Gilman also recognized the growing need to train educators, and Johns Hopkins became a leader in this area—during the school's first 10 years, 56 of its doctoral graduates were employed as professors in 32 different colleges and universities (Ryan, 1939).

The explosive growth of higher education at the end of the nineteenth century, accompanied by a willingness to experiment with new ideas, teaching methods, and the curriculum itself, made the new universities fertile ground for the creation of novel approaches to old problems. This was advantageous for psychology, which was of course undergoing a change from traditional faculty psychology to the new laboratory psychology. A major agent of this change was a troubled young man from a talented and wealthy Boston family.

WILLIAM JAMES (1842–1910): AMERICA'S FIRST PSYCHOLOGIST

William James did not establish a "school" of psychology, produced no meaningful research, and didn't leave behind a dedicated group of students to "carry on his work." Indeed, near the end of his life, he insisted on being referred to as a philosopher rather than as a psychologist. When delivering an invited address at Princeton in 1896, for instance, he was adamant about not being introduced as a psychologist (O'Donnell, 1985). In the quote that opens the chapter, taken from the closing pages of the briefer version of his monumental *Principles of Psychology*, he made it clear that psychology had a long way to go before it could claim the status of a science—it was "no science,…only the hope of a science" (James, 1892/1961, p. 335). And when he was just finishing the briefer version of the *Principles*, he expressed his disenchantment with psychology in a letter to his Wellesley student and colleague Mary Whiton Calkins, writing that he was "sick of the association of ideas and all things connected with psychology. The result of too unending an application to…the 'Briefer Course' of which the miserable proofs are not yet finished!… Treadmill work seems preferable" (James, 1891).

On the other hand, it is quite clear that James was crucial to the creation of modern psychology in the United States and that his role was recognized not just by historians but also by his contemporaries. When James McKeen Cattell asked psychologists to rank their peers for eminence in 1903, James was ranked first. In fact, he was ranked first on *every* return (Hothersall, 1995). His peers also elected him to the presidency of the American Psychological Association twice (1894 and 1904). Later, when second generation psychologists wrote chapters for the series *A History of Psychology in Autobiography*, at least a dozen explicitly mentioned James and/or his *Principles* as the main reason for their initial interest in psychology (King, 1992). Today, James's star continues to shine brightly. Several biographies have appeared (e.g., Croce, 1995; Lewis, 1991), and the 1990s saw the publication of two edited books celebrating the centennial of the *Principles* (Donnelly, 1992; Johnson & Henley, 1990). In a 1991 poll of historians, he ranked second (behind Wundt) on a list of the most important contributors to psychology (Korn, Davis, & Davis, 1991). Who was this person who did not want to be called a psychologist, yet is high on everyone's list of "most important psychologists of all time?"

THE FORMATIVE YEARS

William James was raised in a very unusual family. His father, Henry James, Sr., had sufficient income from an inheritance to avoid working,[1] and he devoted himself to the education and moral development of his five children, who were born within six years of each other in the 1840s. In addition to William, the oldest, there was Henry, Jr., the celebrated American novelist, two younger brothers, and a sister, Alice, the intellectual equal of her brothers, but unable to develop her creativity into a professional career because of prevailing nineteenth-century beliefs about the proper role for women. Henry James, Sr., who had been raised by a domineering father who demanded strict obedience, was determined to raise his own children in exactly the opposite manner. So he indulged them, allowing them to study whatever they wanted whenever they

---

[1] Henry's father lived the stereotypical American success story, an Irish immigrant who rose from store clerk to business tycoon, one of the wealthiest men of nineteenth-century America (Croce, 1995).

wanted to, taking them to Europe frequently to expand their horizons, and caring little about their formal education. His only expectation was that his children learn foreign languages. Consistent with his liberal philosophy of learning, he believed that "[t]o learn a language was not to enforce particular points of view, but to gain access to another realm of culture and thought; to be fluent was to see the world from another perspective" (Croce, 1995, pp. 43–44). Thus, William did not attend school before the age of 10 and attended only sporadically through adolescence. He made three trips to Europe before the age of 21 though, spending at least a year there each time. By age 18, he knew the essentials of Latin, had a reading knowledge of German, and was fluent in French. He would later add Greek and Italian to the list.

As he neared the end of adolescence, however, one other fact characterized William James—he was utterly at a loss about what to do with his life. He had a strong interest in art and some talent for it (Figure 6.1 is a self-portrait drawn during this time of his life), but after some lessons in Paris and a brief stint under the tutelage of the American artist William Morris Hunt, he realized that he would not achieve greatness. Despite abandoning a career in art, however, James never lost interest in it, and at least one biographer (Bjork, 1983) has maintained that James remained an artist in temperament for the rest of his life. Also, historian David Leary (1992) has pointed to James's recurring use of artistic metaphors in the *Principles*. For instance, he used the metaphor of a sculptor creating one result from the multitude of possibilities in a piece of stone to make the point that individual minds create different realities out of the varying experiences of life: "Other sculptors, other statues

Figure 6.1   Self-portrait sketch of William James, completed in the early 1860s.

from the same stone! Other minds, other worlds from the same monotonous and inexpressive chaos" (James, 1890/1950, v1, p. 289).

A LIFE AT HARVARD

In the fall of 1861, a 19-year old William James enrolled in the Lawrence Scientific School of Harvard University, much to the delight of his father. Although his philosophy of child rearing prevented him from forcing careers on his children, Henry Sr. had always hoped that his oldest son would become a "scientist."[2] At the Lawrence school, William first studied chemistry with Charles W. Eliot, soon to be one of Harvard's most innovative presidents. He quickly learned to hate the subject, especially

---

[2] He was also pleased that his son was able to avoid the Civil War, which began that same year. Henry, Jr., the novelist, also avoided the war, but the two younger brothers both fought for the North and one was severely wounded in the attack on Fort Wagner, near Charleston, South Carolina (the battle was dramatized in the 1990 film *Glory*).

what he viewed as the tedium and obsession with detail that characterized laboratory work. It was an attitude that would later lead him to disparage much of the laboratory work of the new experimental psychology.

After abandoning chemistry, James sampled several of the other sciences at Lawrence. One of his biology professors there was the famed Swiss naturalist Louis Agassiz, a fervent believer in a close relationship between science and religion and in the use of science to confirm religious truths. Thus, he was a strong advocate of the argument by design (Chapter 5) and an anti-Darwinian who believed that all species were created separately by God. James, of course, was a student at Lawrence during the height of the debates about Darwin's theory, which had been published in 1859. Initially awed by Agassiz, James eventually became a firm Darwinian and realized that history would judge his professor to be on the wrong side of the argument over evolution. Agassiz also confirmed in young James his distaste for the minutiae of science. He accompanied Agassiz on a collecting expedition to the Amazon in 1865, enjoying it about as much as chem lab, and for similar reasons. He also became ill during the voyage, beginning a long series of bouts with real and imagined illnesses that would plague him on and off for the remainder of his life (Lewis, 1991).

In 1864, James enrolled in the Harvard Medical School, completing his medical training in 1869, but not before taking yet another trip to Europe to (a) try recovering his health—he was afflicted with a bad back, severe headaches, and chronic gastritis after the Amazon trip, and (b) investigate the new experimental physiology that had been developing in Germany. In addition to health spas, his trip included stops at Heidelberg, where he met Helmholtz and learned of Wundt, and Berlin, where he attended lectures by the noted physiologist Emil du Bois Reymond (Chapter 3). The experience was educational, but it also deepened a profound depression that had been

haunting the edges of his psyche for several years. He was completing a medical degree, but had no desire to actually practice medicine. He was trained in science, but hated the details. And as a reflective person, he was disturbed by the overwhelming determinism and materialism of the science that he was learning. If all life reduces to physical matter moving through space, then what happens to free will? If freedom of choice is an illusion, then what is the basis for personal responsibility and morality? James was driven to the point of despair, and he even contemplated suicide (Croce, 1995).

Salvation came in the form of James's discovery of the French evolutionary philosopher Charles Renouvier. In an often-quoted diary entry from April 1870, James noted that his life had reached a crisis point when he encountered an essay by Renouvier and "saw no reason why his definition of free will—the sustaining of thought *because I choose to* when I might have other thoughts—need be the definition of an illusion. My first act of free will shall be to believe in free will" (cited in Bjork, 1983, p. 18, italics in the citation). The insight enabled James to continue studying physiology and psychology without being worn down by the implications. Free will might be an illusion, but by choosing to believe in it, the concept became *useful* for him, enabling him to continue his scientific work without despair. This "pragmatic" approach to the concept of free will, in which the truth value of the idea was a consequence of its functional value or utility, would become a cornerstone of James's **pragmatic philosophy** and a reason why he is considered a forerunner of those American psychologists who came to be known as functionalists.

In 1873, James accepted an offer from Charles Eliot, his old chemistry professor and now president of Harvard, to teach a course in physiology. Two years later, he taught his first psychology course, a class on the relationship between physiology and psychology. By incorporating the latest research from Germany, it differed radically from the typical mental philosophy course based on faculty psychology, thus inaugurating a new approach to the teaching of psychology in America. It was so new that James would later say that the first psychology class he ever attended was also the first one he taught! To help students understand some of the research he was describing, he set up some apparatus in a small room, thus creating in 1875 what would gradually become Harvard's laboratory of experimental psychology.[3] James remained at Harvard until his retirement in 1907. He died three years later of heart disease, two days after a return from one final trip to Europe.

CREATING AMERICAN PSYCHOLOGY'S MOST FAMOUS TEXTBOOK

In July of 1878, a 36-year-old William James married Alice Howe Gribbons, a 29-year-old teacher at Miss Sanger's School for Girls in Boston. Alice would become a stabilizing force in William's life, with a mind sharp enough to make her an intellectual colleague. Indeed, on their honeymoon in New York's Adirondacks, she helped him begin writing the *Principles of Psychology*, a book destined to become the classic among classics in psychology's history (Lewis, 1991). A month before the wedding, James had signed a contract with an aggressive young publisher named Henry Holt for a "manual" of psychology. Holt wanted the completed manuscript from James within a year, but reluctantly agreed on two years. The book seemed to take on a life of its own, however, eventually requiring *12 years* before it appeared in 1890. The book was encyclopedic, encompassing two volumes totaling nearly 1400 pages. It was an immediate best-seller, in part because the academic public knew what was coming—James published numerous articles based on it during the 1880s, and Holt began advertising it in 1881 (King, 1992). Shortly after its publication, James agreed to write a "briefer version" (referred to earlier in the letter to Calkins), which appeared in 1892. Over the years, Harvard students learned to refer to the massive two-volume text as the "James" and the briefer version as the "Jimmy."

In the *Principle's* opening sentence, James (1890/1950) defined psychology as "the Science of Mental Life, both of its phenomena and their conditions" (v1, p. 1). The phenomena of mental life included "such things as we call feelings, desires, cognitions, reasonings, decisions, and the like" (v1, p. 1). By "their conditions" he was referring to the physiological processes that accompany these phenomena, as well as the social, personal, and environmental circumstances in which they occur.

On Methodology

James was an eclectic, willing to include in his book the results of research using any methodological approach that could shed light on mental life. He was quite clear about what he believed to be the primary means of studying mental life, however: "Introspective Observation is what we have to rely on first and foremost and always" (James, 1890/1950, v1, p. 185). By **introspection** he meant careful self-observation, an examination and reflection on the states of consciousness that characterize one's mental life. He recognized the difficulties with the method—it was open to bias, one person's introspections could not be verified by a second person, and because it is impossible to experience a mental process and introspect to it at the same time, all introspection must rely on memory. Nonetheless, he believed that careful self-reflection was essential to gain insight into the workings of the human mind. One consequence of this belief was that

---

[3] This event has led some to argue that James created psychology's first laboratory, beating Wundt by four years. The lab was no more than a demonstrational adjunct to his lectures, however—Wundt's laboratory produced original research.

This year marked the publication of psychology's most famous textbook, *The Principles of Psychology* by William James.

These events also occurred:

- Rubber gloves were used in surgery for the first time, at Johns Hopkins Hospital, Baltimore
- The first entirely steel-framed skyscraper was built in Chicago by Louis Sullivan, mentor of Frank Lloyd Wright
- The Daughters of American Revolution was founded in Washington, DC
- Oscar Wilde wrote *The Picture of Dorian Gray*
- Japan held its first general election
- Idaho and Wyoming became states
- These people were born:

    Dwight David Eisenhower, American soldier and president

    Julius "Groucho" Marx, American comedic actor

    Agatha Christie, English mystery writer

- These people died:

    Vincent Van Gogh, Dutch painter

    Sitting Bull, Sioux chief on the winning side at the Battle of Little Big Horn

Key Date 1890

the book was reviewed harshly by psychologists enamored of the new laboratory approach that had emerged from Leipzig. Thus, Wundt thought it was more like literature than science and G. Stanley Hall (below), after writing that one's overall reaction to the book must be "gratitude and admiration" (Hall, 1890–1891, p. 578), criticized what he viewed as its "inconsistencies and incoherencies" (p. 589), and referred to James as an "*impressionist* in psychology (p. 585, italics in the original).

James did not ignore the new experimental methods. He gave a thorough description of reaction time methodology, for example, and he referred to the results of psychophysics research in numerous places. Nonetheless, his personal dislike of the tedium of laboratory work led him to declare that the German psychophysics and reaction time research "taxes patience to the utmost, and could hardly have arisen in a country whose natives could be *bored*" (James, 1890/1950, v1, p. 192, italics in the original). He later created a phrase that came to capsulize this laboratory approach, when he referred to it sarcastically as a **brass instrument psychology**.

In addition to introspective and experimental methods, James listed the "comparative method" as a third approach. This involved learning about mental life by comparing normal human consciousness with that of "bees and ants,…savages, infants, madmen, idiots, the deaf and blind, criminals, and eccentrics" (James, 1890/1950, v1, p. 194), and included the use of data derived from the kinds of questionnaires pioneered by Darwin and Galton. While James recognized the value of this kind of information, he once again disliked the tediousness of the survey method, suspecting that the next generation of psychologists might rank these questionnaires "among the common pests of life" (p. 194).

Consciousness

The chapter on **consciousness** shows James at his most eloquent. It is a central chapter, one in which James made it clear that he vehemently opposed the analytic approach that presumed to understand consciousness by reducing it to its basic elements. That strategy characterized "structuralism," which you will learn about in the next chapter, but it also formed the basis for the reaction time and psychophysics research imported from Germany, and it was an integral part of most British empiricist/associationist thinking. James believed that trying to identify the individual elements of consciousness, then seeing how they could be constructed to form "mind," was a meaningless, artificial exercise. In one of psychology's more frequently quoted passages, he argued that consciousness is not a set of interconnected units:

> Consciousness, then, does not appear to itself chopped up in bits. Such words as "chain" or "train" do not describe it fitly as it presents itself in the first instance. It is nothing jointed; it flows. A "river" or a "stream" are the metaphors by which it is most naturally described. *In talking of it hereafter, let us call it the stream of thought, of consciousness, or of subjective life.* (James, 1890/1950, v1, p. 239, italics in the original)

The chapter in which this quote appears is titled "The Stream of Thought," and it is the first of several dealing with the nature of consciousness. Using an artistic analogy, James told the reader that the chapter was introductory, with more detail to follow, describing it as being "like a painter's first charcoal sketch upon his canvas" (James, 1890/1950, v1, p. 225). His preliminary sketch included these additional attributes of consciousness:

It is *personal*; all consciousness includes an element of self-consciousness; thoughts don't exist independently of the person having them ("Consciousness of Self" was elaborated in a complete chapter).

It is *constantly changing*, as implied by the stream metaphor; no two states of consciousness are ever quite the same; once a state has disappeared, there will never be another one identical to it.

It is *sensibly continuous*; our perception of consciousness is that it is one continuous stream of thoughts; the stream may be temporarily interrupted, as in sleep, but upon awaking, the sleeper immediately reenters the same stream.

It is *selective*; out of the mass of sensory information available to it, it selects some for closer attention (James elaborated this in a chapter on "Attention").

It is *active*, rather than a passive collection of associated elements; it is goal-directed and purposive.

Elaborating on this last attribute, James used an example that provides a compelling description of the "tip-of-the-tongue phenomenon," anticipating some of the results of a well-known study later completed by Brown & McNeill (1966):

> Suppose we try to recall a forgotten name. The state of our consciousness is peculiar. There is a gap therein; but no mere gap. It is a gap that is intensely active. A sort of wraith of the name is in it, beckoning us in a given direction, making us at moments tingle with the sense of our closeness, and then letting us sink back without the longed-for term. If wrong names are proposed to us, this singularly definite gap acts immediately so as to negate them. They do not fit into its mold. (James, 1890/1950, v1, p. 251)

One final point about consciousness shows how James was affected by Darwinian think-

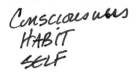
Consciousness
HABIT
SELF

ing. In addition to describing the features of consciousness, he was interested in understanding the function of consciousness. How did it enable us to adapt to our environment? What was its survival value? For James, the answer was that consciousness served individuals by enabling them to adapt quickly to new environments, to learn new things, and to solve new problems that present themselves.

Habit

Habits also had an adaptive function, according to James. Because they occurred more or less automatically, they enabled the consciousness to focus attention on other, more important (i.e., survival-related) problems. On a broader scale, habits serve as:

> ...the enormous flywheel of society, its most precious conservative agent.... It alone prevents the hardest and most repulsive walks of life from being deserted by those brought

up to tread therein. It keeps the fisherman...at sea through the winter; it holds the miner in his darkness, and nails the countryman to his log-cabin and his lonely farm through all the months of snow.... It dooms us all to fight out the battle of life upon the lines of our nurture or our early choice. (James, 1890/1950, v1, p. 121)

In his typical pragmatic fashion, James also had some advice on forming good habits. The first was motivational, an admonition to "launch ourselves with as strong and decided an initiative as possible" (James, 1890/1950, v1, p. 123). For instance, he recommended making a public pledge about the habit to be developed. Second, we must not allow for any lapses to occur: "Never suffer an exception to occur till the new habit is securely rooted in your life" (p. 123). Third, he urged readers to arrange their lives to increase the opportunities to act on the new habit; mere good intentions are not sufficient.

▶ ORIGINAL SOURCE EXCERPT

William James on Emotion

There are a number of quotations from the *Principles* in this part of the chapter, for the simple reason that James is so quotable. To get a closer look at his writing, however, and to see how he developed an argument, consider the following extended excerpt on emotion. It is taken not from the full *Principles*, but from the abridged version—*Psychology: The Briefer Course* (1892/1961). It describes one of the better-known of James's ideas, which he acknowledged borrowing from a Dutch physiologist, Carl Lange. Today's students recognize it as the **James-Lange theory of emotion**, and it can be found in every introductory psychology text.

James began the chapter by distinguishing emotions from instincts. The former he referred to as tendencies to feel, while the latter were tendencies to act. He recognized that emotions had bodily "expression," however, so the distinction was not absolutely clear-cut. He then distinguished between the "coarser" emotions (e.g., anger, fear, joy, grief) from the "subtler" ones (e.g., aesthetic appreciation of art), but with his characteristic dislike of classification, refused to go any further in categorizing the emotions, writing that he would prefer to "read verbal descriptions of the shapes of rocks on a New Hampshire farm"

(James, 1892/1961, p. 242). Instead, James proposed to look for general principles, with a focus on the coarser emotions:

> The feeling, in the coarser emotions, results from the bodily expression. Our natural way of thinking about these coarser emotions is that the mental perception of some fact excites the mental affection called the emotion, and that this latter state of mind gives rise to the bodily expression. My theory, on the contrary, is that *the bodily changes follow directly the perception of the exciting fact, and that our feeling of the same changes as they occur IS the emotion.* Common-sense says, we lose our fortune, are sorry and weep, we meet a bear, are frightened and run; we are insulted by a rival, are angry and strike. The hypothesis here to be defended says that this order of sequence is incorrect, that the one mental state is not immediately induced by the other, that the bodily manifestations must first be interposed between, and that the more rational statement is that we feel sorry because we cry, angry because we strike, afraid because we tremble, and not that we cry, strike, or tremble because we are sorry, angry, or fearful, as the case may be. Without the bodily states following on the perception, the latter would be purely cognitive in form, pale, colorless, destitute of emotional warmth. We might then see the bear and judge it best to run, receive the insult and deem it right to strike, but we should not actually feel afraid or angry. (pp. 242–243, italics in the original)

This paragraph might seem vaguely familiar—portions of it are often quoted in introductory textbooks. After beginning with such a bold assertion, he spent the remainder of the chapter defending it. He began with some anecdotal examples, including an autobiographical one, that supported his case:

> To begin with, *particular perceptions certainly do produce wide-spread bodily effects by a sort of immediate physical influence, antecedent to the arousal of an emotion or emotional idea.* In listening to poetry, drama, or heroic narrative we are often surprised at the cutaneous shiver which like a sudden wave flows over us, and at the heartswelling and the lachrymal effusion that unexpectedly catch us at intervals. In hearing music the same is even more strikingly true. If we abruptly see a dark moving form in the woods, our heart stops beating, and we catch our breath instantly and before any particular idea of danger can arise. If our friend goes near to the edge of a precipice, we get the well-known feeling of "all-overishness," and we shrink back, although we positively *know* him to be safe, and have no distinct imagination of his fall. The writer well remembers his astonishment, when a boy of seven or eight, at fainting when he saw a horse bled. The blood was in a bucket, with a stick in it, and, if memory does not deceive him, he stirred it round and saw it drip from the stick with no feeling save that of childish curiosity. Suddenly the world grew black before his eyes, his ears began to buzz, and he knew no more. He had never heard of the sight of blood producing faintness or sickness, and he had so little repugnance to it, and so little apprehension of any other sort of danger from it, that even at that tender age, as he well remembers, he could not help wondering how the mere physical presence of a pailful of crimson fluid could occasion in him such formidable bodily effects. (pp. 243–244, italics in the original)

James's argument was that the bodily changes that are the emotions are felt immediately, prior to the awareness of a cognitively recognizable emotion: Our heart pounds before we feel fearful. He also argued that we recognize different emotions because each one is associated with a unique pattern of bodily action:

> …When worried by any slight trouble, one may find that the focus of one's bodily consciousness is the contraction, often quite inconsiderable, of the eyes and brows. When momentarily embarrassed, it is something in the pharynx that compels either a swallow, a clearing of the throat, or a slight cough; and so on for as many more instances as might be named. The various permutations of which these organic changes are susceptible make it abstractly possible that no shade of emotion should be without a bodily reverberation as unique, when taken in its totality, as is the mental mood itself. (p. 245)

Research on the physiology of the emotions was not sufficiently advanced for James to realize that the preceding idea was a fatal flaw for his theory. For James-Lange to work, each emotion must have its own unique pattern of bodily reaction, and be recognized as such. We now know that this is simply not the case. Rather, although there are some physiological differences between emotions, most strong emotions are accompanied by similar patterns of physiological arousal in the autonomic nervous system. There is no question, however, that the emotions are closely tied to bodily arousal. James drove the point home by asking the reader to imagine the opposite:

> I now proceed to urge the vital point of my whole theory, which is this: *If we fancy some strong emotion, and then try to abstract from our consciousness of it all the feeling of its bodily symptoms, we find we have nothing left behind*, no "mind-stuff" out of which the emotion can be constituted, and that a cold and neutral state of intellectual perception is all that remains.… Can one fancy the state of rage and picture no ebullition in the chest, no flushing of the face, no dilation of the nostrils, no clenching of the teeth, no impulse to vigorous action, but in their stead limp muscles, calm breathing, and a placid face? The present writer, for one, certainly cannot. The rage is as completely evaporated as the sensation of its so-called manifestations, and the only thing that can possibly be supposed to take its place is some cold-blooded and dispassionate judicial sentence, confined entirely to the intellectual realm, to the effect that a certain person or persons merit chastisement for their sins. In like manner of grief: what would it be without its tears, its sobs, its suffocation of the heart, its pang in the breast-bone? A feelingless cognition that certain circumstances are deplorable, and nothing more. Every passion in turn tells the same story. A disembodied human emotion is a sheer nonentity. (pp. 246–247, italics in the original)

As always, James was pragmatic. In the case of emotions, practical application was a natural consequence of another argument for his theory:

> …If our theory be true, a necessary corollary of it ought to be this: that any voluntary and cold-blooded arousal of the so-called manifestations of

a special emotion should give us the emotion itself. Now within the limits in which it can be verified, experience corroborates rather than disproves this inference. Everyone knows how panic is increased by flight, and how the giving way to the symptoms of grief or anger increases those passions themselves. Each fit of sobbing makes the sorrow more acute, and calls forth another fit stronger still, until at last repose only ensues with lassitude and with the apparent exhaustion of the machinery. In rage, it is notorious how we "work ourselves up" to a climax by repeated outbreaks of expression. Refuse to express a passion, and it dies. Count ten before venting your anger, and its occasion seems ridiculous. Whistling to keep up courage is no mere figure of speech. On the other hand, sit all day in a moping posture, sigh, and reply to everything with a dismal voice, and your melancholy lingers. There is no more valuable precept in moral education than this, as all who have experience know: if we wish to conquer undesirable emotional tendencies in ourselves, we must assiduously, and in the first instance cold-bloodedly, go through the *outward movements* of those contrary dispositions which we prefer to cultivate. The reward of persistency will infallibly come, in the fading out of the sullenness or depression, and the advent of real cheerfulness and kindliness in the stead. Smooth the brow, brighten the eye, contract the dorsal rather than the ventral aspect of the frame, and speak in a major key, pass the genial compliment, and your heart must be frigid indeed if it do not gradually thaw. (pp. 249–250, italics in the original)

The idea that forcing emotions to occur by deliberately producing specific bodily reactions, which might seem a bit far-fetched, actually has been supported by some twentieth-century research on emotions. People whose facial muscles have been arranged to match certain emotions often experience those very emotions, at least to a degree (e.g., Izard, 1977).

James closed the chapter by considering the origins of emotions. Again showing his affinity for Darwinian thinking, his description is not very different from the one found in Darwin's book on emotional expressions (Darwin, 1872), which you read about in Chapter 5.

JAMES'S LATER YEARS

After completing the *Principles* in 1890 and the abridged version two years later, James (Figure 6.2) began to turn away from psychology and toward philosophy. In 1892, he convinced the German psychologist Hugo Münsterberg (Chapter 8) to emigrate to America and run the psychology lab at Harvard, thereby separating himself forever from the tedium of laboratory work. Although he continued to be involved in the American Psychological Association and was elected its president in 1894 and 1902,

James also supported the formation of the American Philosophical Association shortly after the turn of the century, and his publications after 1900 were mainly devoted to philosophy (e.g., *Pragmatism* in 1907) and religion (e.g., *Varieties of Religious Experience* in 1902).

Spiritualism

In addition to the shift from psychology to philosophy during his final two decades, James also became fascinated with **spiritualism**, a popular movement in the late nineteenth cen-

1892 Hugo Münsterberg

Figure 6.2   A healthy-looking William James in New York's Adirondack Mountains, taken in the 1890s when James was shifting his focus from psychology to philosophy, from Lewis (1991).

ing people could communicate over great distances via some mysterious invisible process, and if there was life after death, then why not a communication channel from the dead to the living (Coon, 1992)?

James became seriously interested in spiritualism in the 1880s, after discovering the Society for Psychical Research while on a trip to London (Benjamin, 1993). He helped establish a similar organization in the United States, and became a promoter of research into the phenomenon. He believed that psychologists, with their expertise in the powers of the mind, should be ideally suited for such investigations. And reflecting his pragmatic philosophy, in which the value of something is a consequence of its usefulness, he insisted on keeping an open mind about psychic phenomena—they might prove to be beneficial if they could be shown to be valid.

Starting in 1885, James began an extended study of Mrs. Leonore Piper, a popular Boston medium. Although most mediums, even in the nineteenth century, were easily shown to be frauds on careful investigation, James could find no trickery in Mrs. Piper's seances. In an article for the *Proceedings of the British Society for Psychical Research*, James wrote that he could not avoid concluding that in her seances, "knowledge appears which she has never gained by the ordinary waking use of her eyes and ears and wits. What the source of this knowledge may be, I know not, and have not the glimmer of an explanatory suggestion to make" (cited in Lewis, 1991, p. 494). On the other hand, James was skeptical about messages from the dead that were received by Mrs. Piper during seances. If the dead were truly communicating, surely they would have some rather important things to say—they might be expected to describe the afterlife for example. Instead, they tended to communicate inconsequential bits of information. In a letter to a colleague, James questioned the validity of Mrs. Piper's ability to reach the dead, pointing to the "extreme triviality of most of the communica-

tury. Spiritualists believed that consciousness survived death and that those who died could be contacted by certain people, called *mediums*. Mediums were also said to be able to predict the future and to know details of people's lives through telepathic means. The movement began at mid-century, but gained momentum after the Civil War—the war's appalling death toll dramatically increased the number of people desiring to contact deceased relatives and acquaintances. Furthermore, spiritualism was fueled by nineteenth-century technological advances such as the wireless telegraph. If liv-

tions. What real spirit, at last able to revisit his wife on this earth, [wouldn't] find something better to say than that she had changed the place of his photograph?" (cited in Benjamin, 1993, p. 83). Furthermore, Mrs. Piper's spirit-control (the intermediary between her and the dead spirits) was supposed to be a French doctor. He was unable to respond when James asked questions in French, however (Murphy & Ballou, 1960).

James was not rewarded for his open-mindedness by his peers in the medical and psychological communities. At a time when there was no formal licensure procedures for accrediting doctors, he was roundly criticized for opposing legislation to create such rules. His reason? The guidelines would prohibit mediums and "mental healers" from practicing without a license (Murphy & Ballou, 1960). The censure from psychologists was equally strong. At a time when psychology was trying to establish its identity as a legitimate scientific discipline, it was embarrassing for one of its stars to be regularly attending seances and publicly expressing faith in the veracity of a medium (Coon, 1992). In a letter to James published in his journal *Science*, for example, James McKeen Cattell wrote that the "Society for Psychical Research is doing much to injure psychology" (cited in Benjamin, 1993, p. 88); concerning James, Cattell pointed out that the psychological community "all acknowledge his leadership, but we cannot follow him into quagmires" (p. 88). Always independent, James was unmoved by the criticism, and in turn accused his critics of narrow and unscientific prejudgment. He continued to be fascinated by psychic phenomena for all of his remaining years.

WILLIAM JAMES IN PERSPECTIVE

In his lifetime, William James experienced the vast changes that characterized late nineteenth-century America. In his youth, America was an agricultural society, the western frontier was east of the Rocky Mountains, the possibili-

ty that Americans would kill each other in a Civil War was unthinkable, and higher education was limited mainly to the undergraduate college, which was aimed primarily at the training of ministers. In his last decade, America had entered the twentieth century an industrialized power, the western frontier had been declared closed, the trauma of the Civil War was becoming a memory, and higher education, which now included universities devoted to graduate studies, was producing professionals and Ph.D.'s in a variety of disciplines.

Psychology in America also changed significantly during this time, from mental philosophy to an independent discipline with aspirations to be a science. Despite his reservations about the new psychology, William James was a prime mover in bringing about its emergence. Trained in physiology, he saw how advances in that field could make a new laboratory psychology possible. At heart an artist and philosopher, he could see the problems inherent in a purely scientific attack on the human mind. His monumental *Principles of Psychology* stands at the transition point, artfully blending physiology, philosophy, and the new laboratory psychology. James was the acknowledged leader of the first generation of American psychologists, but he was not alone.

G. STANLEY HALL (1844–1924): PROFESSIONALIZING PSYCHOLOGY

G. Stanley Hall (Figure 6.3) had none of William James's reluctance about psychology. Rather, he was a vigorous promoter of the new field, and more than any other American, responsible for its evolving identity as a distinct academic discipline. Like Wundt did in Germany, Hall professionalized psychology in the United States by founding laboratories and journals. In addition, he institutionalized psychology's professional status by creating the American Psychological Association. As a psy-

Figure 6.3   G. Stanley Hall at Clark University, from Popplestone and McPherson (1994).

analysis (Chapter 12) to America. On the other hand, a consequence of his catholicity of interests was a failure to contribute a substantial body of research knowledge to any one of them. He also alienated his peers, including James, and some questioned the value of his work. In a letter to Clark University librarian L. N. Wilson in 1906, for instance, this is what Cornell's E. B. Titchener (Chapter 7) thought of Hall's ability to prepare graduate students:

> …you probably have no idea of the sort of contempt in which Hall's methods and the men trained solely by him are in general held in psychology, whether here or on the continent. Whenever his questionary papers [i.e., research using questionnaires] get reviewed, they get slightingly reviewed…. He has made no impression on the men of scientific training. (Titchener, 1906)

You will discover in the next chapter that Titchener had a rather narrow concept of what scientific training should be like; the criticism might be overstated, but it was not far from the mark.

If there was a common thread and guiding principle to Hall's various interests, it was evolution. In his autobiography, Hall (1923, p. 357) wrote that "[a]s soon as I first heard it in my youth I think I must have been almost hypnotized by the word 'evolution,' which was music to my ear." Most of his work can be classified under the heading of **genetic psychology**, which could be defined as the study of the evolution and development of the human mind, and included comparative, abnormal, and especially developmental psychology.

HALL'S EARLY LIFE AND EDUCATION

Hall was born in Ashfield, a small town in western Massachusetts, in 1844. His mother was a teacher and stern taskmaster and his father, who also had experience teaching, was mainly a farmer. The main benefit of being raised on a

chologist, Hall was a man of diverse interests, careening from one enthusiasm to another throughout his career, and aptly described by his biographer as a "prophet" for his zeal in promoting his ideas (Ross, 1972). He could be characterized as either creative and visionary or unsystematic and capricious. On the one hand, he pioneered the child study movement and the study of adolescence and aging, he demonstrated the importance of psychology to education, and he introduced Freud and psycho-

farm seemed to be the creation in Hall of a strong urge to leave it. He went to nearby Williams College and graduated in 1867, with a strong interest in philosophy and history and a desire to imitate many of his peers by studying for an advanced degree in Europe. Cost was a problem, however, and the most reasonable postgraduate option for a young man interested in philosophy, and unable to cross the ocean, was to study for the clergy, so Hall enrolled in New York's Union Theological Seminary (Ross, 1972).

New York was somewhat daunting for the farm boy from rural Massachusetts, but Hall took advantage of the cultural, educational, artistic, and social opportunities available to him. After a year at Union, however, he was able to borrow enough money to finally go to Europe, and there he stayed until 1871. His main goal was to study theology and philosophy, but he also encountered experimental physiology—like William James, he studied briefly with Emil du Bois Reymond in Berlin. Out of funds before he could complete a degree, Hall returned to New York and finished his education at Union. He was just going through the motions, however, and felt stifled by religious orthodoxy.[4] The ministry was out—Hall wanted to teach philosophy. After doing some private tutoring in New York, he landed a teaching position at Antioch College in Ohio, where he taught for four years. While there, he encountered Wundt's *Principles of Physiological Psychology* and resolved to return to Germany to study this new psychology. First, however, he moved to Cambridge to study at Harvard, feeding himself by teaching English composition to Harvard sophomores. He met William James, took several courses with him, and completed a doctoral thesis on "the muscular perception of space" in 1878. It was primarily a philosophical piece, with most of the work taking place in the library and between Hall's ears, but it also included some experimental work in perception, conducted in the physiology laboratory of H. P. Bowditch. Harvard had just begun offering the doctorate in philosophy, and Hall was the first person to complete one. Because the topic was in the area that would eventually become known as experimental psychology, Hall's doctorate is sometimes considered to be the first one in psychology.

Doctorate in hand, Hall returned to Germany and found himself in Leipzig in 1879, the "official" year of the founding of Wundt's laboratory. He later claimed to be Wundt's first American student, but he actually had very little contact with Wundt, completed no publishable research, and was in fact preceded by at least one other American (Benjamin, Durkin, Link, Vestal, & Accord, 1992). Hall was disappointed with his experience in Leipzig and was later critical of Wundt's status as both scientist and philosopher. He wrote to James that he considered Wundt's experiments "utterly unreliable and defective in method" (cited in Ross, 1972, p. 85). After Leipzig, Hall went to Berlin to study briefly with Helmholtz, although by then Helmholtz was more involved with physics than with physiology. While there, Hall became reacquainted with a young woman he knew from his days at Antioch, who was in Berlin to study art. They were married in Germany.

The Halls returned to Boston in the fall of 1880. Hall was 36 years old, highly educated, and devoted to his new bride. He was also poor and unemployed. Yet within 10 years, he would be a university president and one of the acknowledged leaders of psychology in America. His big break was an invitation from

---

[4] Hall (1923) probably embellished the story he told about how Union's president reacted to Hall's trial sermon, supposedly the culmination of one's theological development at Union. According to Hall (1923, p. 178), rather than critique the sermon, the president simply knelt on the floor and prayed for Hall's soul.

President Eliot of Harvard to give a series of lectures on education. Hall had already given considerable thought to how psychology might contribute to the educational reform that was occurring in the late nineteenth century. His lectures, given on Saturday mornings so that local teachers could attend, were highly successful. The publicity caught the attention of President Gilman of Johns Hopkins, eventually leading to Hall's being asked to give a similar series of talks in Baltimore in January of 1882. Their success led Gilman to offer Hall a position as part-time lecturer in philosophy. In 1884, Hall was hired as a professor at Hopkins at the generous (for the time) annual salary of $4000 (Ross, 1972). His apparent expertise at using psychological principles to make recommendations about education was reflected in his title—Professor of Psychology and Pedagogy. At age 40, then, Hall had his first real job!

FROM JOHNS HOPKINS TO CLARK

Hall did not stay long at Johns Hopkins, but while he was there, he significantly advanced the cause of psychology in America. In 1883, when still a part-time instructor, he created the first true research laboratory of experimental psychology in America and with the help of talented students such as James McKeen Cattell (Chapter 8), John Dewey (Chapter 7), and Edmund Sanford, he began to produce experimental research. In 1887, he founded the *American Journal of Psychology*, the first journal for the new psychology published in the United States. It served partly as a mechanism for publishing original research from Hall's lab and elsewhere, but it also included summaries and reviews of the psychological literature and sections devoted to "Notes and News" about psychology and psychologists. Journal finances were aided by a $500 donation from an advocate of spiritualism, who apparently thought the journal would be devoted to "psychic" research. This was an understandable confusion—the terms "psychic" and "psychological"

were used interchangeably in those days. Hall did not correct the donor's misperception and took the money. Over the years, articles on spiritualism occasionally appeared in the journal, but only to ridicule the scientific basis for it. Hall, for example, argued that what passed for telepathy, clairvoyance, and the like, was nothing more than magic tricks and other forms of deception. Indeed, Hall became an accomplished magician and used his skills to demonstrate how easily people could be fooled by deception (Ross, 1972).

Hall's journal was a bold and risky venture, undertaken at a time when nobody could have predicted psychology's future. In an opening editorial, he made it clear that the purpose of the *American Journal of Psychology* would be "to record the psychological work of a scientific, as distinct from a speculative character [and to] record the progress of scientific psychology" (Hall, 1887, pp. 3–4). The opening number included research on "The Variations of the Normal Knee-Jerk," "Dermal Sensitiveness to Gradual Pressure Changes," "A Method for the Experimental Determination of the Horopter," and "The Psycho-Physic Law and Star Magnitudes" (cited in Evans & Cohen, 1987).

In the late 1880s, an economic slowdown created financial difficulties for Johns Hopkins. It had invested heavily in B&O railroad stock, counting on dividends as income. These dividends essentially dried up starting in 1886, forcing a budget crisis (Hawkins, 1960). Facing dwindling resources, Hall began to look for greener pastures and found them in Worcester, Massachusetts. Jonas Clark, a merchant made wealthy by selling mining supplies to prospectors during the California gold rush, had decided to buy respectability in his hometown by opening a college to educate its youth. He recruited a distinguished group of eight trustees, who began the search for a president. Hall's name surfaced, and he seemed the perfect choice—ambitious, knowledgeable about higher education, and with a record of accomplishment in his brief time at Johns Hopkins.

Clark agreed and in April of 1888, Hall signed on as the new university's first president.

Jonas Clark wished to create a school for the youth of Worcester, but Hall had a grander vision, and managed to convince Clark that the school should offer graduate education, in the mold of Johns Hopkins, and that the focus should be on science. An undergraduate division could be added later. Thus, when Clark University opened its doors in the fall of 1889, it offered graduate training in five areas: psychology, biology, chemistry, physics, and mathematics. There were 18 faculty members and 34 graduate students in the initial group and almost all of the instruction took place by means of ongoing research—the teaching load was just two lectures per week (Ross, 1972).

For three years, Clark University approached Hall's vision of a true university. Faculty produced cutting-edge research, students came from as far away as Japan to join the elite group of scholars, and Hall developed an international reputation as a visionary leader in education. All was not well, however. At the end of the first year, Hall suffered a personal tragedy when his wife and eight-year-old daughter died in an accident. In the second year, faculty began to hear about new opportunities and larger salaries being offered at another new university being created in Chicago with Rockefeller money. And throughout the three years, Hall was constantly in conflict with his faculty. Things came to a head in 1892, when a combination of financial pressure, faculty unrest, and the lure of the University of Chicago almost closed the university. Approximately two-thirds of the faculty and students left Clark that year, leaving psychology as the only viable graduate department (Ross, 1972).

PSYCHOLOGY AT CLARK

Psychology survived after the fiasco of 1892 in part because Hall was deeply involved in the work of the department, and in part due to the loyalty of its two faculty members, Edmund Sanford and William Burnham. Both had been students of Hall at Johns Hopkins. In Clark's department of "psychology and pedagogy," Burnham was in charge of educational psychology and Sanford was in charge of the research laboratory. Hall was clearly the leader of the department, however, and dictated its general direction. He also directed the doctoral dissertations of most of the students, and his Monday evening seminars became legendary among Clark alumni. Held in the parlor of his home, they began at 7:30 and often lasted three hours. Students would make presentations, other students would contribute, then Hall would have the final word:

> ...for a half-hour or longer, depending on the importance he attached to the theme, he presented from his armchair in the central archway a masterly critique of the research just reported and added to it new illumination from fresh angles that sometimes left the [students] gasping....
>
> After the intellectually provocative evening was ended, many of the graduate students set off for their boarding-places but found themselves so moved by the galvanism of their emotions that only a long walk near midnight and a warm bath before retiring could relax them enough to permit them to sleep. (Averill, 1982, p. 342)

During the early 1890s, the laboratory at Clark was a state-of-the-art facility, in part because when Hall left Johns Hopkins, he took most of the research equipment with him. As a result the Hopkins laboratory disappeared and did not reopen until 1903; the Clark lab, meanwhile, was off to a flying start. Hall was also generous with expenditures in the first two years, giving Sanford all he needed to equip a lab fully. By 1892, for example, more than $10,000 had been spent on the laboratory (Goodwin, 1987); the abundance of costly "brass instrument" technology is evident from Figure 6.4a. This photo is one of a series taken in 1892 for display at a psychology exhibit at the Columbian Exposition in Chicago the following year. Figure 6.4b provides an inside look at the

(a)   *(b)*

Figure 6.4   The Clark Lab in 1892: (*a*) **"brass instruments," including timing devices and reaction time apparatus;** (*b*) **a voice reaction time study. (from the Clark University Archives)**

experimental psychology of the day—it illustrates an actual research project (voice reaction time) in action. Sanford gave students considerable leeway in the Clark laboratory; in addition, Hall was constantly suggesting ideas to students. Hence, although the research from Clark was unsystematic and scattered, it reflected the wide range of topics that interested American experimental psychologists in the 1890s.

In the mid-1890s, as part of his deep interest in evolution, Hall began supporting research in comparative psychology. One consequence was the creation of the first studies using what would become a standard piece of laboratory equipment—the maze. For details on the origins of the venerable rats-in-mazes tradition, read this chapter's Close-Up.

▶ CLOSE-UP

Creating Maze Learning

Ask psychologists to name famous pieces of apparatus in experimental psychology and mazes will be at or near the top of the list. The maze reached its peak of popularity from about 1920 to 1950, especially in the research of neobehaviorists Edward Tolman and Clark Hull (Chapter 11), and it remains in use today as a tool to investigate spatial abilities and in psychopharmacological and neuropsychological research. Literally hundreds of maze studies have been completed over the years, and one might ask how it all started. Credit is sometimes given to the Darwinian Sir John Lubbock, who used crude Y-shaped mazes in the 1870s to study how ants followed scent trails, or to E. L. Thorndike (Chapter 7), who observed chicks escaping from simple mazes created by placing books on end (see Figure 7.7). The research that launched the systematic study of rats-in-mazes, however, was completed by Willard Small of Clark University at the turn of the century.

Small arrived in Worcester in 1897 as a 27-year-old graduate student and was soon doing animal research with another student, Linus Kline. Kline completed the first general study of the abilities of rats (Dewsbury, 1984) and one of his interests concerned the rat's "home-finding" capacities. He discussed the problem with the lab's director, Edmund Sanford, who gave him the idea for a maze study and suggested a specific maze design. As Kline later told the story:

> I...described to [Sanford] runways which I had observed several years ago made by large feral rats to their nests under the porch of an old cabin on my father's farm in Virginia. These runways were from three to six inches below the surface of the ground and when exposed during excavation presented a veritable maze. Sanford at once suggested the possibility of using the pattern of the Hampton Court maze for purposes of constructing a "home-finding" apparatus. (Miles, 1930, p. 331)

One can only speculate about why the Hampton maze occurred to Sanford. That it was on his mind is clear from Kline's comment that "the readiness with which he direct-ed my attention to the Hampton maze is presumptive evidence that he had thought of its use before" (Miles, 1930, p. 331). One possibility is that Sanford may have been in the Hampton Court maze himself just prior to the conversation with Kline. He was on sabbatical in the spring of 1898 and visited a number of laboratories in Europe (Goodwin, 1987). His last stop was in England and it is at least conceivable that he visit-ed Hampton Court, which is just outside of London and is England's most famous hedge maze.

It is not clear why Small did the first maze study and not Kline. Kline reported that other work prevented him from pursuing the idea, and it was perhaps natural for his friend and laboratory coworker to take up the project. At any rate, in January of 1899, Small constructed three 6 × 8 foot mazes with wire mesh walls, using the Hampton Court design but adjusting it to a rectangular pattern, as shown in Figure 6.5. He then began his historic research on the manner in which rats learn mazes.

Sanford reported on Small's study at the December 1899 APA meeting, and Small published a highly detailed 33-page report in 1901. Modern accounts, perhaps inspired by Thorndike's rather caustic review of Small's earlier work (Thorndike, 1900), usually dismiss Small's description of the maze studies as a series of overly anthropomorphic comments about such things as the rat's alleged "disgust" over reaching a dead end. The criticism has some merit, but Small's report also gives a trial-and-error description of maze learning similar to other contemporary accounts by Thorndike and Lloyd Morgan (Chapter 5). Small also commented extensively on what he believed to be the mental processes involved, and he used blind rats to investigate the effects of sensory capacity on learning. These blind rats seemed to learn the maze as well as their sighted peers. Small concluded that "tactile motor sensations furnish the essential data for the recogni-tion and discrimination involved in forming the special associations at critical points" (Small, 1901, p. 237).

Small's work is less important for its conclusions than for the fact that it initiated a flood of similar research. In the next few years, versions of the Hampton Court maze were used by comparative psychologists to study species ranging from rhesus monkeys (Kinnaman, 1902) to English sparrows (Porter, 1904). With the white rat, research fol-lowed up on Small's ideas about the influence of the various senses on learning. The most famous of these were the studies by Watson and Carr at the University of Chicago (described in Chapter 10), who concluded, like Small, that the kinesthetic sense was most critical. Subsequent research, and there were dozens of such studies completed by 1920, showed the process to be much more complicated, but it is worth noting that the

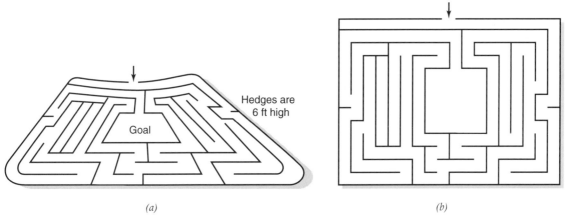

Figure 6.5   (*a*) Design of England's Hampton Court maze; (*b*) Small's readjustment of the Hampton Court maze to a rectangular configuration.

animal maze literature began by investigating the sensory and mental processes involved in maze learning and by investigating how organisms adapted to their environment. These of course were topics clearly in tune with the psychology of the early 1900s, which was the psychology of mental life and which reflected the pervasiveness of evolutionary theory.

In his remaining years at Clark University, Hall left his stamp on psychology in several ways. First, he continued to professionalize psychology by creating its first formal organization, the American Psychological Association (APA). He and about a dozen other psychologists held an organizational meeting in his study in July of 1892, at which time 31 charter members were identified (Sokal, 1992). As you might expect, Hall was elected the association's first president. Eighteen of the charter members convened in December 1892, at the University of Pennsylvania, for the APA's first annual meeting. The organization grew rapidly: 74 members after four years and 127 by the turn of the century (Ross, 1972). It adopted a constitution in 1894, making clear its role in creating disciplinary identity for a "scientific" psychology. The purpose of the organization was to be "the advancement of Psychology as a science. Those are eligible for membership who are engaged in

this work" (Cattell, 1895, p. 150). The APA also enhanced psychology's professional and scientific status by affiliating with older, more recognized associations, such as the American Association for the Advancement of Science (Camfield, 1973).

Hall and Developmental Psychology

In addition to activities connected with the journal and the APA, Hall contributed to American psychology by advancing his genetic psychology. He was a pioneer in developmental psychology, promoting the child study movement, writing the first textbook on adolescent psychology, and near the end of his career, writing a book on aging. He also continued to champion the importance of psychology for education, in part by establishing summer schools for the training of educators, but also by founding a second journal, *Pedagogical Seminary* (now the *Journal of Genetic Psychology*) in 1893.

Hall first became interested in child study while at Johns Hopkins, where he published the first in a series of studies about children using the results from questionnaires filled out by children, teachers, and parents (these were the "questionary" studies that Titchener disparaged in his letter to Wilson). His overall goal was identified in the title of his first research paper: "The Contents of Children's Minds" (Hall, 1883/1948). In this first survey, Hall accumulated data from more than 200 Boston children who were just beginning school. They were questioned by about 60 different teachers, who asked what they knew about a wide range of objects. The level of knowledge was not high. For instance, 75.5% could not identify what season of the year it was, 87.5% didn't know what an island was, and 90.5% couldn't locate their ribs. Hall also discovered that children reared in the country did much better than those raised in the city. As a farm boy himself, Hall did not find this surprising:

> …As our methods of teaching grow natural we realize that city life is unnatural, and that those who grow up without knowing the country are defrauded of that without which childhood can never be complete or normal. On the whole the material of the city is no doubt inferior in pedagogic value to country experience. A few days in the country at this age has raised the level of many a city child's intelligence more than a term or two of school training could do without it. It is there, too, that the foundations of a love of natural science are best laid. (Hall, 1883/1948, pp. 261–262)

In this quote can be seen the essence of Hall's philosophy of education. He ridiculed rote memorization and the rigid discipline of the classroom. Instead, he favored a more permissive approach that took for granted the child's "natural" curiosity about the world and encouraged what would be called "active learning" today—giving children problems to solve or activities to complete that would have some specific pedagogical value.

Hall was not only interested in children. Some of his questionnaire studies collected data from teenagers, and he reported the results, along with everything else then known about that age group, in his encyclopedic two-volume *Adolescence* (1904). It was the first book devoted to the study of teenagers, and Hall is the person most responsible for identifying adolescence as a distinct stage of development. The description of adolescence as a period of "storm and stress" has its origins in Hall's book. The book also contains the most thorough description of Hall's use of the theory of **recapitulation**. The theory originated with the German evolutionary biologist Ernst Haeckel, who proposed that an organism's stages of development, from cell to a fully formed individual, can be seen as a recapitulation of the evolution of the species.[5] Thus, at one stage of development, the human fetus resembles a fish, reflecting that point in evolutionary history where the human species had aquatic ancestors. Hall extended the idea beyond embryonic development, arguing for example that children's play often reflected earlier stages of mental evolution. For Hall, individual development up to adulthood shed light on the evolution of the race.

Toward the end of his life, Hall became interested in the middle and final stages of life, eventually writing about aging in *Senescence: The Last Half of Life* (1922). He once again relied on questionnaire data, asking the elderly their opinions about such topics as their fear of death and their ability to recognize the signs of aging. He also criticized the lack of retirement pension programs and recommended that the elderly organize politically.

---

[5] Haeckel's theory had been highly visible and heavily debated during Hall's first visit to Germany in 1868 to 1871 (Ross, 1972).

Hall and Psychoanalysis

A significant portion of Hall's *Adolescence* concerned sexual behavior, including an entire 50-page chapter entitled "Adolescent Love." Hall also offered a course at Clark entitled "The Psychology of Sex" (Rosenzweig, 1992), and consistent with his ideas on education, he believed that the natural expression of sexual behavior should not be inhibited. This attitude raised eyebrows among his peers, leading one of them to wonder: "Is there no turning Hall away from this d——d sexual rut? I really think it is a bad thing morally and intellectually to harp so much on the sexual string, unless one is a neurologist" (letter from F. Angell to E. B. Titchener on March 19, 1990, cited in Ross, 1972, p. 385).

Hall's preoccupation with sex, combined with an interest in abnormal behavior, led him to become fascinated by Freud's theories. In 1909, to celebrate the university's twentieth anniversary, Hall organized the Clark Conference, a series of public lectures by prominent psychologists. The centerpiece was a series of talks given by none other than Freud himself.[6] Accompanied by his younger colleague Carl Jung, who lectured on his new word association technique, Freud made his first and only visit to America and delivered five lectures that were soon published in the *American Journal of Psychology*, then separately in book form as *Introductory Lectures on Psychoanalysis* (some of this lecture material can be found in the Chapter 12 Original Source Excerpt). A grateful Freud later said that the Clark Conference was an important point in the history of psychoanalysis, constituting the first international recognition of his theories.

Hall retired from the presidency of Clark in 1920, but remained active in his remaining four years of life. He published his book on aging in 1922 and an autobiography, *Life and Confessions of a Psychologist*, a year later. In 1924, he was elected to a second term as president of the APA, only the second person ever to be elected twice (William James was the other). He died before he could assume his duties, however.

MARY WHITON CALKINS (1863–1930): CHALLENGING THE MALE MONOPOLY

Professional women in the late twentieth century often face discrimination in the workplace and find themselves unable to rise above the "glass ceiling." As frustrating as the problem is for modern women, it was many times worse 100 years ago. In the 1890s, women were widely believed to be intellectually inferior to men, and they had little standing in society (they could not vote until 1920, for instance). Combining marriage and a career was virtually impossible—marriage was assumed to be their career. Even if they didn't marry, they were expected to care for other members of their family, especially parents as they aged. Although women began attending college in increasing numbers in the late nineteenth century, and several colleges were founded for women (for instance, Smith, Vassar, Wellesley), higher education for women was looked on with skepticism by a male-dominated society. It was even believed that an education could harm women—their weak constitutions could be permanently damaged by the cerebral demands of college. One Harvard medical school professor urged women to abandon education after reaching puberty; too much mental activity after that stage could adversely affect the development of their reproductive

---

[6] Hall originally hoped for an all-star cast of international psychologists, including not just Freud, but also Wundt and Ebbinghaus. Wundt declined to come, however, and while Ebbinghaus accepted the invitation, he died just before the conference began.

organs, he warned (Scarborough & Furumoto, 1987). Of course, if undergraduate education could have such deleterious effects, education at the graduate level presumably would be much worse. Indeed, in the 1890s it was almost impossible for a woman to obtain a doctorate in psychology, a dilemma faced by Mary Whiton Calkins, easily one of the most important contributors to the new psychology in America.

CALKINS'S LIFE AND WORK

Mary Calkins grew up in Buffalo, New York, the oldest of five children in a close-knit family headed by a father who was a Congregationalist minister. He shared with William James's father a belief in the educational value of travel to Europe and in the importance of being multilingual. In fact, Mary's parents only spoke German in her presence during her first few years; by adulthood, Mary was fluent in English, German, and French (Furumoto, 1979). The Calkins fam-

Figure 6.6 Mary Whiton Calkins as a young instructor at Wellesley College, from Scarborough and Furumoto (1987).

ily moved to the Boston area when Mary was 17 and soon after that she entered Smith College in western Massachusetts, a recently founded women's college. She graduated in 1885, then went to Europe with her family for 16 months, where among other things she added Greek to her list of language competencies. Upon her return, she took a position teaching Greek at Wellesley College. Calkins (Figure 6.6) remained at Wellesley for the rest of her career.

By the late 1880s, Wellesley's leaders decided that to keep up with trends in modern science, the college needed to offer the new laboratory approach to psychology. Calkins had expressed some interest in teaching philosophy and had impressed her superiors in her first few years as a teacher, so she was given the opportunity to develop a course in laboratory psychology. It was understood, however, that she would take a year off to learn about this new field. Thus began her frustrating search for graduate education in psychology.

Graduate Education for Females

Calkins quickly learned that opportunities for advanced training were quite limited for women. After considering Europe and a few American schools (e.g., Yale, Michigan), she attempted to become a student at Harvard—it had William James to offer and it was close to home. She also looked into Clark University, 30 miles to the west of Boston. At Harvard, she was grudgingly allowed to attend seminars with James and the philosopher Josiah Royce, both of whom supported her application vigorously, but Harvard officials made it clear that she was merely an unofficial "guest" of the university. It was the same story at Clark. Women were not allowed in officially, but Edmund Sanford welcomed her into his new laboratory. Calkins later credited Sanford, who contributed time, advice, and apparatus, with being the true founder of the psychology laboratory at Wellesley (Calkins, 1930).

Calkins entered Harvard in the fall of 1890 and immediately encountered the educational opportunity of a lifetime. Calkins and four male students were enrolled in Philosophy 20a, Physiological Psychology, with William James, but the males dropped out within a few days. As Calkins (1930) later recalled, "...James and I were left...quite literally at either side of a library fire. The *Principles of Psychology* was warm from the press; and my absorbed study of those brilliant, erudite, and provocative volumes, as interpreted by their writer, was my introduction to psychology" (p. 31).

After her year of study at Harvard and Clark, Calkins returned to Wellesley, but her appetite for the new psychology had been whetted, and she was soon looking into further training. In 1892, when William James recruited Hugo Münsterberg from Germany to run the Harvard lab, Calkins returned to Cambridge, once more as an unofficial guest. Again the timing was perfect for Calkins—Münsterberg's English was poor, but she was fluent in German. They became colleagues immediately. For the next two years, Calkins worked in Münsterberg's lab part-time while continuing to teach 10 miles away at Wellesley. In the academic year 1894 to 1895, she took a leave from the college to complete her studies.

Calkins's Research on Association

Münsterberg treated Calkins just like any other doctoral student. For her thesis, she completed a brilliant series of experimental studies on association, publishing the research in two parts (Calkins, 1894; Calkins 1896), then writing an extended account as a *Psychological Review Monograph* paper in 1896. Traditional philosophical and introspective accounts often described how the strength of associations could be influenced by such factors as frequency, recency, vividness, and primacy. In the spirit of Ebbinghaus, Calkins was determined to go beyond "ordinary self-observation" and examine these factors experimentally. She did not go into detail about how her procedures developed, but it is clear that she went through considerable trial and error, what today we would

call "pilot studies," before arriving at her method. The procedure that evolved is an important one historically—although she did not use the name, she invented **paired-associate learning**, later to become a standard method in cognitive research. Her subjects first studied stimulus-response pairs comprised of sequentially presented color patches and numbers (each shown for four seconds), then tried to recall the number responses when shown the color stimuli. Calkins manipulated frequency by presenting the same color several times, once with one number, then either two or three times with a second number. Here's how she described series #89:

> I. Medium gray, 29; blue, 82; violet, 61 (n); red, 23; violet, 12 (f); peacock, 79; violet, 12 (f); strawberry, 47; violet, 12 (f); light brown, 53; dark gray, 34; light green, 72.

> II. Peacock, red, green, violet, medium gray, brown, strawberry, dark gray, blue. (Calkins, 1894, p. 478)

Thus, during presentation (I), violet was first paired with 61 (referred to by her as the "normal" pairing, or "n"), then three times ("f" = frequency) with the number 12. During recall (II), violet was the fourth color presented and the question was whether subjects would recall the number 61 or 12 (or both or neither). In like manner, Calkins studied recency by comparing the recall of two numbers paired with the same color, one pairing in the middle of the sequence and one at the very end. Vividness was examined by presenting a critical pair in some way that made it stand out from the other pairs, such as by altering the size of the numbers. Primacy was studied by looking at performance for the first pair in a series. In general, her results showed that recall was enhanced by each of the four factors: frequency, vividness, recency, and primacy. In subsequent trials in which she directly compared these factors by combining them within the same list, Calkins generally found that frequency was the most critical factor. She also ran some trials in which the colors and numbers were presented together on the same card. This enabled her to compare "simultaneous" associations with the earlier "successive" ones, thus examining the old British Empiricist distinction between simultaneous and successive forms of contiguity. She found no major differences.

Calkins did not mention the Ebbinghaus memory research, published in 1885 (and excerpted in Chapter 4), but she was clearly aware of it. She was fluent in German and very familiar with James's *Principles*, which includes a thorough description of the Ebbinghaus research in its chapter on "Memory." The Ebbinghaus influence is also apparent in Calkins's choice of materials when she altered her procedure to use auditory presentation. The stimuli in this case (and she used the term) were "nonsense syllables" instead of colors. Calkins found about the same outcome for both visual and auditory presentation, except that the recency findings were more striking with the latter.

Calkins (1896) summed up her overall results by emphasizing the importance of the frequency variable, but adding a caution that the laboratory results might not be completely "representative of ordinary trains of association" (p. 49). She even added a statement about the practical implications of her findings, referring to frequency as a "corrective influence.... The prominence of frequency is of course of grave importance, for it means the possibility of exercising some control over the life of the imagination and of definitely combating harmful or troublesome associations" (p. 49). Calkins was thinking along the same lines as her teacher, William James, and her research can be seen as providing some empirical evidence for James's suggestions about how to firmly entrench a habit (discussed earlier).

Madigan and O'Hara (1992) closely examined Calkins's research on memory, including some studies completed after her dissertation research. They found clear indications that

Calkins discovered a number of effects that would later be rediscovered half a century later, when psychologists once again became interested in studying cognitive psychology (Chapter 13). These included such immediate memory phenomena as the primacy, recency, and negative recency effects, the modality effect, and retroactive interference.

Although it was unofficial, Calkins completed a defense of her thesis and a Ph.D. examination in May of 1895. Münsterberg, James, and other examiners appealed to the Harvard authorities to grant her the Ph.D., with Münsterberg describing her as "superior...to all candidates of the philosophical Ph.D. during the last years" and "surely one of the strongest professors of psychology in the country" (cited in Scarborough & Furumoto, 1987, pp. 44–45). Harvard refused though—after all, Calkins was a woman. Later, when Radcliffe College had been created as a Harvard-for-women, Calkins was offered a Radcliffe Ph.D. This time it was Calkins who refused. She would have a doctorate from the school where she earned it or none at all. Although she would earn several honorary degrees, Harvard never did change its mind, and Calkins was never awarded the Ph.D.

From Psychology to Philosophy

After completing her non-degree from Harvard, Calkins returned to Wellesley, continued building her lab with Sanford's help, and produced a string of research publications through the turn of the century. In 1898, she turned over the laboratory to Eleanor Gamble, a new Ph.D. from Cornell (one of the few institutions that admitted women doctoral students). From about 1900 on, her publications became less research-oriented as she developed her major theoretical contribution to psychology, **self psychology**. It was a system that clearly showed the influence of her first mentor, William James. Calkins argued that psychology could be the study of mental life, as James had said, but that the central fact of psychology

SELF

must be that all consciousness contains an element of the self (Strunk, 1972).

At a time when strong disagreements were developing over the proper direction for the new psychology, Calkins saw her self psychology as a means of resolving disputes. For example, as will be clear from the next chapter, one conflict was between structural psychology, which emphasized analyzing consciousness into its basic elements, and functional psychology, which focused on how consciousness served to adapt the individual to the environment. When her peers elected her the fourteenth president of the APA in 1905, the first female so honored, Calkins (1906) delivered a presidential address called "A Reconciliation between Structural and Functional Psychology." In it she argued that both views could be accommodated within a system that recognized the self as the fundamental starting point. Thus, the structuralists could concentrate on discovering the elements that make up the self, while the functionalists could examine how the self relates to the environment.

Like James, Mary Calkins gradually shifted her interests over the years from psychology to philosophy. Shortly after her APA presidency, for instance, she wrote *The Persistent Problems of Philosophy* (1907), perhaps her most important work. In 1918, the American Philosophical Association elected her president of their organization, making her the first woman to be elected to the presidency of each of the APAs. Calkins retired from Wellesley in 1929 and died of cancer a year later.

OTHER WOMEN PIONEERS: UNTOLD LIVES

Calkins wasn't the only woman struggling against a male-oriented discipline at the turn of the century. In *Untold Lives: The First Generation of American Women Psychologists*, Elizabeth Scarborough and Laurel Furumoto (1987) have thoroughly documented the experiences of Calkins and several other pioneering women psychologists. Two of the better known were Christine Ladd-Franklin and Margaret Washburn.

Christine Ladd-Franklin (1847–1930)

Like Calkins, Ladd-Franklin was educated at a new women's college. She entered Vassar College in Poughkeepsie, New York, in 1866, a year after it had been founded. There she excelled in science and math and was inspired by the example of the astronomer Maria Mitchell, said to be the most eminent woman scientist in America at that time (Furumoto, 1992). She graduated in 1869, then taught in secondary schools for about 10 years before deciding to pursue a graduate education in math at Johns Hopkins. There she encountered the same roadblock that would later face Calkins—Hopkins did not admit women as official students. Nonetheless, she was allowed to attend classes and by 1882, she had completed all the requirements for a doctorate in math. It would be 1926, however, before Johns Hopkins officially awarded her the degree, which she accepted in person, at age 79 (Scarborough & Furumoto, 1987).

While at Johns Hopkins, Christine Ladd met, fell in love with, and married a faculty member in the math department, Fabian Franklin, and became Christine Ladd-Franklin. With her husband's active support, she was able to continue her interests in math and published several scholarly papers. In the mid-1880s she became interested in visual perception, a shift that led her to the new psychology. Her first publication, on binocular vision ("A Method for the Experimental Determination of the Horopter") appeared in 1887 in the very first issue of Hall's *American Journal of Psychology*. During her husband's 1891 to 1892 sabbatical, spent in Europe, she was able to conduct research on vision in the Gottingen lab of G. E. Müller. As you recall from Chapter 4, Müller's lab was one of the best in Germany. She also spent time in Helmholtz's lab in Berlin. It was during this time in Germany that she developed a theory of color vision that was grounded in evolutionary theory; it was an influential theory for several decades.

Of the three pioneer women considered here, Ladd-Franklin was the most outspoken about the lack of professional opportunities for women. For example, she directly challenged the "men only" rule of a group of psychologists known as the Experimentalists (see Chapter 7's Close-Up). Organized in 1904 by E. B. Titchener of Cornell, this select group met annually at various labs to discuss their current research. After being refused permission to attend in 1912, she wrote to Titchener that she was "shocked to know that you are still—at this year—excluding women from your meeting of experimental psychologists. It is such a very old-fashioned standpoint" (cited in Furumoto, 1988, p. 107). Two years later her persistence wore Titchener down somewhat and she presented her work on color vision at one of the Experimentalists' meetings. It was the only time a woman participated in a meeting during Titchener's lifetime.

Ladd-Franklin also vigorously campaigned for a faculty position at a research university, but never managed to obtain more than part-time lectureships, first at Johns Hopkins, then at Columbia when she and her husband moved to New York. She was seldom paid for her teaching. Nonetheless, she continued her work as a mathematician and expert on vision, never giving in to the prevailing belief that science was for men only.

Margaret Floy Washburn (1871–1939)

In addition to Ladd-Franklin, Vassar College also produced Margaret Washburn, then later reclaimed her. Washburn graduated from Vassar in 1890 with her interests divided between science and philosophy. She decided to pursue "the wonderful new science of experimental psychology" (Washburn, 1932, p. 338), because it seemed to combine her interests, so she applied for graduate studies at Columbia

University, where she ran into the same problems faced by Calkins and Ladd-Franklin. She was welcomed as a serious student by James McKeen Cattell, but as usual, was only permitted to attend his classes unofficially. Cattell saw her potential and encouraged her to apply to Cornell, which accepted women graduate students. There she encountered none other than E. B. Titchener (Chapter 7), who had just finished his doctorate with Wundt at Leipzig. Women might have been excluded from Titchener's Experimentalists, but they were accepted into his laboratory, and Washburn was Titchener's first Ph.D. student. She became the first woman to earn a doctorate in psychology when she completed the degree in 1894, a study of the effects of visual imagery on tactile sensitivity. It was one of the few studies published in Wundt's journal (*Philosophische Studien*) that was not completed at the Leipzig laboratory.

After leaving Cornell, Washburn held several teaching positions, then was asked to return to her alma mater, Vassar. This she did in 1903, and there she spent her remaining professional career. Despite the heavy teaching load and inadequate research facilities that invariably accompany faculty life at small colleges, Washburn fashioned a remarkable career that included an APA presidency in 1921, co-editorship of the *American Journal of Psychology* for more than a decade, and election to the prestigious National Academy of Sciences in 1931. When the Experimentalists reorganized after Titchener's death in 1927, she was one of two women elected as a charter member of the new group, and she hosted a meeting of the refashioned "Society of Experimental Psychologists" at Vassar in 1931.

As a psychologist, Washburn published in the areas of perception, imagery, "social consciousness" (empathy and helping behavior), and developed a motor theory of consciousness, but she is best known for her work in comparative psychology. She contributed some original research (e.g., on the perception of

handwritten notes in margin: Ph.D. production 1) germany 2) USA

color in fish) and summarized the field in her well-known text, *The Animal Mind*. First published in 1908, it went through four editions (1917, 1926, 1936) and became the standard textbook of its day (Dewsbury, 1992). It was notable for its exclusion of evidence based solely on anecdotal data; Washburn included only the results of experimental research. As implied by the title, its focus was on the cognitive processes of perception, attention, and consciousness, as exhibited by the behaviors of various species.

THE NEW PSYCHOLOGY AT THE MILLENNIUM

During the last 20 years of the nineteenth century, psychology in America changed dramatically. Prior to that time it had been dominated by traditional faculty psychology and taught as "moral" or "mental" philosophy. By the end of the century it was still being taught in philosophy departments for the most part, but it now reflected the influence of the new psychology of Germany and the revolutionary ideas of Charles Darwin. In the early 1880s there were no research laboratories of psychology in the

United States, and most American psychologists wishing to study the new laboratory psychology had to travel to Germany. By 1890, however, laboratories had been established at nine American universities, and by the end of the century, there were at least 41 (Hilgard, 1987). Although in the early 1890s a German Ph.D. in psychology held higher status than one earned in the United States, this was no longer true by the end of the decade.[7] The shift is reflected in the numbers: Between 1884 and 1892 the number of Americans earning Ph.D.s in America (n = 9) and Germany (n = 8), was about equal, but from 1893 to 1899, 63 American psychologists earned their doctorates in the United States, whereas only 10 earned theirs in Germany (O'Donnell, 1985).

Hall's Clark University was a leader in the production of Ph.D.s in psychology in the 1890s, but other young psychologists were being trained at several other up-and-coming universities. Foremost among them were Cornell, where students would find E. B. Titchener and structuralism, and Columbia and Chicago, two leading centers of a uniquely American movement that became known as functionalism. The story of these "isms" will occupy the next chapter.

handwritten notes in margin: Clark, Cornell, Columbia, Chicago

SUMMARY

Psychology in Nineteenth-Century America

- Prior to the Civil War, psychology in America was taught as mental or moral philosophy. It was taught following the precepts of faculty psychology, which was based on Scottish Realistic philosophy. Faculties were separate subcategories of the mind, normally falling into three categories: cognitive, affective, and behavioral.

- Thomas Upham's *Elements of Intellectual (Mental) Philosophy* (1827) is considered to be the first textbook of psychology, and it was organized around the concepts of faculty psychology.

- The post-Civil War period was one of great expansion in higher education. The modern university (e.g., Johns Hopkins), based on the German model which emphasized graduate education and independent research, began during this time.

---

[7] When Edmund Sanford of Clark was advising Mary Calkins about where to attempt her doctorate, he recommended Germany, partly because of prestige value. As he wrote to her in 1892, "I don't think that my [Johns Hopkins] Ph.D. is quite so impressive to the average person in authority as a Leipzig one would be" (cited in Scarborough & Furumoto, 1987, p. 41).

William James (1842–1910): America's First Psychologist

- Although he was trained in medicine and ultimately thought of himself as a philosopher, William James is considered America's first modern psychologist. He brought the new psychology to Harvard, and he wrote what is arguably the most important book in all of psychology's history, the *Principles of Psychology* (1890).

- Disturbed by nineteenth-century materialism and determinism, James decided to believe in free will because it was a useful belief for him to hold. Out of this emerged his general approach to philosophy, called pragmatism.

- In the *Principles*, James took issue with those who would analyze consciousness into its elements. Instead, he argued that it was more appropriately conceived of as analogous to a stream. Consciousness was personal, constantly changing, continuous, selective, and active, and it served individuals by enabling them to adapt quickly to new environments. Habit also had survival value, allowing individuals to avoid having to think about some activities so they could save their consciousness for more difficult and novel problems.

- According to the James-Lange theory of emotions, emotional responses were identified with the bodily reactions that accompanied the perception of some event. When trying to conceive of emotions without the physiological arousal, James argued, nothing remains. A problem with the theory is that it requires that a recognizably different pattern of arousal be associated with each different emotion.

- In his later years, James became interested in the possibility that there could be some validity to spiritualism. Despite criticism that he was harming the fragile scientific status of the new psychology, he believed that spiritualists and mediums should be investigated with an open mind.

G. Stanley Hall (1844–1924): Professionalizing Psychology

- Hall is best known for his efforts in professionalizing psychology. He founded the first psychology lab in America (at Johns Hopkins), America's first academic journal (the *American Journal of Psychology*), and the American Psychological Association.

- As the first president of Clark University, he copied the German ideal of graduate education that he first encountered at Johns Hopkins. For several years, Clark was a leader in graduate education in several scientific fields. After 1892, however, only psychology remained as a prominent field of study at Clark.

- Hall was interested in a wide range of topics, but they generally fall under the heading of genetic psychology, the study of the origins and development of consciousness and behavior. The importance of evolution was a consistent theme in Hall's work. At Clark, Hall encouraged research in developmental, abnormal, and comparative psychology. Under the direction of Edmund Sanford, Clark's laboratory produced important research throughout the 1890s, including the first studies of rats learning mazes.

- As a developmental psychologist, Hall pioneered the child study movement and is responsible for identifying adolescence as a distinct stage of development. He characterized adolescence as a time of "storm and stress." Later in life he wrote about the developmental changes associated with adulthood and aging. He believed in a theory of recapitulation—the development of the individual organism is a mirror of the evolution of the species.

- Hall's interests in development, sexuality, and abnormality led him to invite Freud to America for Clark's twentieth anniversary in 1909. It was Freud's only trip to America, and he believed that the invitation was the first sign that his ideas were developing an international reputation.

Mary Whiton Calkins (1863–1930): Challenging the Male Monopoly

- Mary Calkins was barred from being an official student at Harvard, but nonetheless completed an important experimental dissertation on association, during which she invented a memory procedure still in use, paired associate learning. In her thesis, Calkins investigated frequency, recency, vividness, and primacy as conditions that could strengthen associations, and found that frequency was the most important.

- In 1905, Calkins became the first woman elected president of the American Psychological Association; as her interests shifted to philosophy, she became (in 1918) the first woman elected president of the other APA, the American Philosophical Association.

- Calkins's major theoretical contribution was her self psychology, which was centered on the idea that all consciousness is personal. She used it as a way to reconcile competing theoretical schools of thought (e.g., structuralism and functionalism).

- Two other important women psychologists during this era were Christine Ladd-Franklin and Margaret Washburn. Both faced the exclusionary practices that made it difficult for women to become professional psychologists. Ladd-Franklin was a skilled mathematician and developed an evolutionary theory of color vision. Washburn was best known for her work in comparative psychology.

The New Psychology at the Millennium

- By the turn of the century, psychology in America had grown considerably and had shifted from faculty psychology to the new laboratory-based experimental psychology. Students also had numerous options for graduate study in America by 1900, and the number of students going to Germany quickly declined.

FOR FURTHER READING

CROCE, P. J. (1995). *Science and religion in the era of William James: Eclipse of certainty, 1820–1880.* Chapel Hill: University of North Carolina Press.

Documents the early intellectual development of William James; shows how James was at the center of the debate about the relationship between science and religion and how the debate was affected by evolutionary thinking; first of a two-part biography.

ROSS, D. (1972). *G. Stanley Hall: The psychologist as prophet.* Chicago: University of Chicago Press.

The definitive intellectual biography of American psychology's premier entrepreneur; also documents the development of psychology during Hall's time and sets it into its social and institutional context.

SCARBOROUGH, E., & FURUMOTO, L. (1987). *Untold lives: The first generation of American women psychologists.* New York: Columbia University Press.

Examines the lives, struggles, and contributions of several pioneering women psychologists, including detailed treatment of Mary Calkins, Milicent Shinn, Ethel Puffer, Margaret Washburn, and Christine Ladd-Franklin.

Special issue: The history of American psychology. (1992). *American Psychologist, 47(2),* 109–368.

Includes articles on the early years of the APA (Sokal), the founding of early laboratories (Capshew), spiritualism (Coon), William James (Leary), Mary Calkins's memory research (Madigan and O'Hara), Christine Ladd-Franklin (Furumoto), and G. Stanley Hall (Bringmann, Bringmann, and Early; Vande Kemp).

STRUCTURALISM AND FUNCTIONALISM

The first object of the psychologist...is to ascertain the nature and number of the mental elements. He takes up mental experience, bit by bit, dividing and subdividing, until the division can go no further. When that point is reached, he has found a conscious element.

E. B. Titchener, 1896

▼

Preview

This chapter begins with the story of a remarkable Englishman who came to a remote new university in America in 1892 and fashioned a unique and powerful but ultimately sterile system of psychology. Cornell's E. B. Titchener was trained by Wundt at Leipzig but had his own ideas about the proper definition of a scientific psychology. Its main goal was to analyze the adult mind into its fundamental structural elements, using a precise form of introspection that required extensive training. For Titchener, psychology was a pure positivist science that was centered in the laboratory; he was not interested in applications. Titchener was an influential and commanding presence in academic psychology's early years in America, but most American psychologists rejected structuralism. Reflecting the influence of Darwin and traditional Yankee pragmatism, they were more interested in how the mind functioned than in its structure, and they knew that for psychology to succeed in America, it had to be applicable to everyday life. While Titchener believed that the structure of mind had to be clarified before its functions could be studied, most American psychologists disagreed and adopted what came to be called functionalism. Functional psychologists were scattered throughout the academic landscape, but two schools became closely associated with the movement—Chicago and Columbia. The second half of the chapter examines how functionalism "evolved" at these locations, through the efforts of James Angell, John Dewey, and Harvey Carr at Chicago, and James McKeen Cattell, E. L. Thorndike, and Robert Woodworth at Columbia. This chapter's Original Source Excerpt is from one of Titchener's textbooks.

TITCHENER'S PSYCHOLOGY: STRUCTURALISM

In 1898, a paper appeared in the new journal *Psychological Review* entitled "The Postulates of a Structural Psychology." Its author, E. B. Titchener, was a young professor from Cornell University who had been in the United States for just six years, but already had a reputation as a talented laboratory psychologist with some clear and uncompromising ideas about the nature of the new psychology. In the article he named his approach a "structural" psychology, and he contrasted it with what he saw all around him at other American universities, which he labeled a "functional" psychology. Drawing an explicit parallel to biology, he wrote that **structuralism** is just like anatomy—the purpose is analysis. Just as the anatomist dissects the body into its fundamental elements, so would a structural psychologist analyze the human mind into its elementary units. **Functionalism**, on the other hand, is like physiology. The physiologist examines how the various parts of the body operate and the functions they serve; similarly, the functional psychologist studies how the mind serves to adapt the individual to the environment. Although not rejecting a functional approach outright, Titchener used the biology metaphor to argue that it was futile to study function before structure had been fully elucidated. Anatomy provides the foundation for physiology, Titchener contended. Similarly, a thorough understanding of the structure of the human mind was a necessary prerequisite to the study of its function. As Titchener had written two years earlier in his first text, *An Outline of Psychology*, the psychologist's goal "is to ascertain the nature and number of the mental elements. He takes up mental experience, bit by bit, dividing and subdividing, until the division can go no further. When that point is reached, he has found a conscious element" (Titchener, 1896/1899, p. 16). Titchener's system was never widely popular in America, but after he died, his best-known student, psychologist/historian E. G. Boring (Chapter 1 Close-Up), could make the somewhat overstated but valid claim that

...The death of no other psychologist could so alter the psychological picture in America. Not only was he unique among American psychologists as a personality and in his scientific attitude, but he was a cardinal point in the national systematic orientation. The clear-cut opposition between behaviorism and its allies, on the one hand, and something else, on the other, remains clear only when the opposition is between behaviorism and Titchener, mental tests and Titchener, or applied psychology and Titchener. His death thus, in a sense, creates a classificatory chaos in American systematic psychology. (Boring, 1927/1961, p. 246)

FROM OXFORD TO LEIPZIG TO CORNELL

Such a position of prominence in American psychology was a long journey from relatively humble beginnings in southern England. Edward Bradford Titchener (1867–1927) was born in Chicester, an hour's drive southwest of London and a few miles from the English Channel. His early years were a bit unsettling—his father, only marginally capable in business, died when Titchener was 13 and he was raised mainly by his paternal grandfather. Titchener's grandfather, a lawyer and stereotypical British country "gentleman," gave Titchener the set of attitudes and values that he never lost. Even after residing in America for many years, Titchener never stopped living according to the strict code of the behavior of a proper upper middle-class English gentleman (Leys & Evans, 1990).

Young Titchener was an industrious and talented student, good enough to win scholarships to attend Malvern, one of England's better "public" schools, and then Brasenose College of

Oxford University.[1] Titchener remained at Oxford from 1885 to 1890, where he excelled in the classics and philosophy. He also became fascinated with evolutionary biology, Darwinism, and through the acquaintance of George Romanes, comparative psychology. Recognizing that his background in science was weak, he spent most of his final year at Oxford in the physiology laboratory of John Scott Burdon-Sanderson. In that setting, Titchener showed himself to be just the opposite of William James in at least one respect—he discovered that he loved the precisely detailed work of the laboratory. For the rest of his life, he judged the quality of his peers by their standing as scientific "laboratory men," which accounts for his derogatory comments about Hall (refer to Chapter 6, p. 165) and his paradoxically close friendship with John Watson (Chapter 10). Watson derided Titchener's structuralism and Titchener disliked everything about Watson's behaviorism, but Watson was a true laboratory scientist in Titchener's eyes and that was sufficient grounds for respect and friendship. After first meeting Watson, Titchener wrote to a colleague: "I think that he has a big career, and I like him very much personally" (cited in Larson & Sullivan, 1965, p. 340).

While at Oxford, Titchener learned of the new laboratory approach to "physiological" psychology that was developing at Leipzig. Fluent in German and enamored of Germanic culture, Titchener applied to and was accepted for study in Wundt's new laboratory, which was only 11 years old at the time. There he encountered a group of like-minded laboratory devotees, including Oswald Külpe (Chapter 4), who was Wundt's assistant at the time (i.e., in charge of the day-to-day operation of the lab), and several Americans. Titchener completed a doctorate with Wundt in just two years and returned to Oxford to teach a summer course in biology. He hoped to remain at Oxford or move to Cambridge, but neither school seemed interested in the new psychology—the British empiricist/associationist philosophical tradition had too strong a hold and when an attempt was made to create a psychophysics laboratory in 1877, the Cambridge Senate rejected the proposal on the grounds that such a laboratory "would insult religion by putting the human soul on a pair of scales" (quoted in Farr, 1983). Fate intervened on Titchener's behalf, however, in the form of an offer to cross the Atlantic and teach at Cornell University. Titchener was recommended to Cornell's president by Frank Angell, one of the American psychologists befriended by Titchener at Leipzig. Angell had created a small lab at Cornell on his return from Leipzig in 1891, but was now leaving for the just-created Stanford University in California. Angell recommended his British friend as his replacement, the offer was made, and Titchener accepted.

Cornell University, founded in 1868 in Ithaca, sits high on a hill overlooking the southern end of Lake Cayuga, in New York State's beautiful Finger Lakes region. In 1892, it was in the middle of nowhere, barely accessible by the occasional train. Even today, residents refer to their town as "centrally isolated." If you can imagine finishing your education and deciding to take a job somewhere in a remote area of Australia, then you have some idea of what the decision must have been like for the young Britisher with his new doctorate. Yet he

---

[1] In England, the term "public school" actually refers to a highly select and very expensive private high school. Malvern was not among the top tier of public schools like Eton, Harrow, or Rugby, but it had a solid academic reputation. Only a small percentage of British schoolchildren attend public schools, but the majority of students at England's prestigious universities, Oxford and Cambridge (sometimes referred to collectively as Oxbridge) come from the public schools. Oxbridge graduates thus represent a small elite group, mostly male, of the British upper middle class. Brasenose is one of several independent colleges that constitute Oxford University.

took the risk, arrived in 1892, and never left.[2] Over the years, "Titchenerian psychology," "structuralism," and "the Cornell school of psychology" became interchangeable terms.

PROMOTING EXPERIMENTAL PSYCHOLOGY AT CORNELL

Titchener (Figure 7.1) moved quickly upon his arrival at Cornell, expanding the laboratory, attracting students, and starting his research program—by the turn of the century, he and his students had published more than 60 articles (Boring, 1927/1961). To ensure a forum for the research from the Cornell laboratory, he signed on with Hall in 1895 as editor of the *American Journal of Psychology*, enabling him to control one-third of the journal's pages (Hall and Sanford, the other editors, controlled the remaining two-thirds). In addition, Titchener spread the word about German psychology by translating books by Wundt and Külpe into English, and he began producing texts of his own. His *Outline of Psychology*, first published in 1896, went through several revisions and was rewritten and expanded as *A Textbook of Psychology* in 1909. It was the clearest overall statement of his structuralist system and portions of it are excerpted below. He also wrote a simplified *Primer of Psychology* in 1896, later revising it as *A Beginner's Psychology*. By 1900, Titchener was firmly established as a major player on the American psychological scene. His status was confirmed when he published "the Manuals."

The Manuals

In German laboratories, students learned laboratory procedures on their own, by participating in and running their own studies and by observing and questioning their more experienced

Figure 7.1   E. B. Tichener of Cornell, with ever-present cigar, from Popplestone and McPherson (1994).

peers, but American universities developed what came to be known as **drill courses**. Students in these courses did not produce original research but would repeat the classic studies, learn how to set up and work the "brass instruments," and in general become acclimated to the laboratory. As laboratory psychology expanded, these drill courses proliferated and even reached into the undergraduate level. Although some laboratory instructors were adequately trained, either in Germany or in one of the new American laboratories, many were not so knowledgeable about the new psychology.

---

[2] Titchener initially thought he would go to Cornell for a few years, then return to Oxford when it came to its senses about laboratory psychology. Oxford didn't, and Titchener never returned to England, even to visit home. He later considered offers from Clark University and Harvard, but turned down both.

Thus, a need developed for a text that could explain how to train students in basic laboratory procedures. Edmund Sanford of Clark wrote the first one in the early 1890s, and it started the process of standardizing laboratory instruction in the drill course (Goodwin, 1987). Titchener recognized the value of his close friend's manual, but he also knew that it was just a beginning and that it had some weaknesses. For instance, it was not always clear about how the instructor should proceed in the laboratory, seeming to take for granted more expertise than many instructors possessed. To remedy the problem, Titchener set to work on his own manuals and published them under the title of *Experimental Psychology: A Manual of Laboratory Practice*. They became his best-known work, serving for years as *the* guide into the complexities of laboratory investigation.

The Manuals, as they came to be known, were published in two volumes, in 1901 and 1905, each containing separate texts for students and instructors. Because of Titchener's concern that teachers might need to have procedures worked out step by step, the instructor manuals for both volumes were almost twice the length of the student manuals. The 1901 volume was subtitled "Qualitative Experiments" and it included experiments on basic sensory, perceptual, and affective processes. "Quantitative Experiments" filled the 1905 volume; these dealt mainly with psychophysics and reaction time procedures.

Students in drill courses worked in pairs, alternating between the roles of experimenter and **observer**, the latter being the person we would call the subject or research participant today. Observers were so-called because while they were participating in the experiment, they would be observing their own mental processes and would give a description of these processes at the close of the experiment. This introspective procedure will be described more fully below.

In the qualitative experiments, observers would experience some sensory, perceptual, or affective event, give an introspective account of

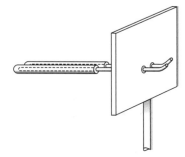

Figure 7.2   Sketch of an olfactometer, from Tichener's manual of qualitative experiments.

it, then answer some specific questions about it in their notebooks. For example, olfactory sensations were studied with the use of the double olfactometer sketched in Figure 7.2. The two thin glass tubes were bent at a 40° angle for insertion into the nostrils. Over their other ends were fitted slightly larger enclosed glass cylinders holding various odorous substances. These cylinders could be moved back and forth over the narrow tubes to vary the intensity of the smell. Titchener cautioned that the middle partition must be made of an odorless wood— he suggested "cherry wood, well-aired and sunned" (Titchener, 1901, pt. 1, pp. 79–80). In a typical experiment, observers smelled pairs of substances (e.g., iodine, beeswax, various herbs) with differing degrees of intensity, described the experience introspectively, and responded in their notebooks to questions about "compensation" (did one smell overwhelm the other?) and "smell mixture" (did the smells mix to form a new odor?).

As is clear from the label, the quantitative experiments involved numerical data, such as stimulus intensities identified as just noticeably different in psychophysics experiments or times to respond in reaction time experiments. Figure 7.3 shows detailed sketches of two different ways of responding in a reaction time experiment. The most common device was an ordinary telegraph key (7.3a); it would be held down, then released when the observer detected a stimulus. The right hand of the observer in

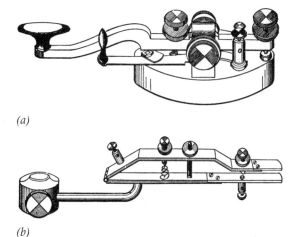

(a)

(b)

Figure 7.3   Reaction time apparatus: (*a*) a telegraph key; (*b*) a lip key. From Titchener's manual of quantitative experiments.

P.99

Figure 4.5 is depressing this type of key. The second device (7.3*b*) is a lip key, to be used in voice reaction time experiments. It is probably the same one shown in the Clark photo in Chapter 6 (Figure 6.4*b*). The right end would be inserted into the closed mouth; when observers opened their mouths to respond to a stimulus, the contacts separated from each other, breaking a circuit and stopping a clock.

Titchener's system of psychology faded rapidly after his death, but his encyclopedic manuals provided a lasting contribution to laboratory psychology. They remained in use well into the 1930s and trained several generations of experimental psychologists. Even today, they can provide wonderful demonstrations of sensory and perceptual phenomena. One final aspect of their timelessness is illustrated in Table 7.1. Titchener's half-serious recommendations to students about "how to fail" the drill course might remind you of some students you've known.

The Experimentalists

Titchener was one of the charter members of the American Psychological Association and although he was not at Hall's organizational meeting at Clark, he did attend the first annual

Table 7.1 How to Fail in Laboratory Psychology

In the Instructor's Manual for the Qualitative Experiments (1901, pp. xxvii–xxviii), Titchener described a program on how to fail that he routinely gave to students at the start of the drill course. He obviously hoped for students to avoid each point and he told instructors that students wouldn't take offense at the list as long as it was presented "tactfully and good-naturedly." In Titchener's words, here are some ways to fail in lab:

- Do not accept any general explanation, under any circumstances. Cherish the belief that your mind is different, in its ways of working, from all other minds....

- See yourself in everything. If the Instructor begins an explanation, interrupt him with a story of your childhood which seems to illustrate the point he is making.

- Call upon the Instructor at the slightest provocation. If he is busy, stroll about the laboratory until he can attend to you. Do not hesitate to offer advice to other students, who are already at work.

- Tell the Instructor that the science is very young, and that what holds of one mind does not necessarily hold of another. Support your statement by anecdotes.

- Work as noisily as possible. Converse with your partner, in the pauses of the experiment, upon current politics or athletic records.

- Explain when you enter the laboratory, that you have long been interested in experimental psychology.... Describe the telepathic experiences or accounts that aroused your interest.

- Make it a rule always to be a quarter of an hour late for the laboratory exercises. In this way you throw the drudgery of preliminary work upon your partner, while you can still take credit to yourself for the regularity of your class attendance.

meeting in the winter of 1892. He quickly became disillusioned with the organization, however, and resigned his membership (he rejoined the organization on two later occasions, only to resign twice more). Part of the problem was personal. Titchener felt like an outsider in an "American" Psychological Association, and the organization violated his strict code of proper behavior when it refused to censure an APA member accused by Titchener (with good cause) of plagiarizing portions of his translation of one of Wundt's books. More important, the organization did not represent Titchener's vision of a true experimental psychology and the format of its meetings did not advance psychology, he believed. In 1895, in a note for the *American Journal of Psychology*, he complained that the presentations of research were "hardly possible to follow intelligently...when method and results are thrown in lecture form and the lecture reduced to a compass of twenty minutes" (Titchener, 1895, p. 448). Instead, he suggested that "the meetings [be] allowed to take the form of a conversazione, the apparatus employed shown in their working, and the results made to speak for themselves in charts and diagrams arranged near the apparatus" (p. 448).

By 1904, Titchener was ready to correct the problem himself, and he proposed the creation of an informal "club" of experimental psychologists. He did not intend to rival the APA, but to provide a better means for researchers to present their work to peers. Thus was born a group that came to be known as the Experimentalists (Boring, 1967; Goodwin, 1985). They met for two or three days every spring, rotating from one laboratory to another. They discussed research in progress, tinkered with apparatus, and in general tried to keep the spirit of pure laboratory psychology alive. No formal papers were allowed and published descriptions of the meetings were discouraged. Titchener generally dominated the group; for instance, hosts would often check with him on who to invite. Figure 7.4 shows a group photo taken at the 1916 meeting at Princeton.

Those invited included laboratory directors and other researchers deemed satisfactory by Titchener. That is, they had to be committed to the laboratory, but it wasn't necessary that they be strict followers of Titchenerian structuralism. Also, to help ensure continuation of the ideal of a "pure" psychological science, talented graduate students often accompanied their mentors to meetings. The group was small but influential beyond its size. Correspondence among its members frequently resulted in the placement of experimentalist colleagues or their students in good academic positions.

One other important feature of the group was gender—all the Experimentalists were men. Part of the reason was the pervasive sexism described in the previous chapter. In Titchener's mind, however, the prohibition fol-

Figure 7.4 Titchener's Experimentalists (many with cigars) at Princeton in 1916, from Popplestone and McPherson (1994).

lowed from his code of gentlemanly conduct. His desire was to have something like an English club, where men could converse freely on any subject without being concerned about behaving properly in the presence of women. This meant being able to argue vociferously about some issue without either party taking offense; Titchener and other males of his time took it for granted that women would take such arguments personally (i.e., they would be too emotional). The club atmosphere also included smoking, and the social mores of the day usually excluded women from rooms where men smoked. These sentiments were summed up in a letter from Sanford to Titchener just before the group was formed. Probably thinking of Calkins, Washburn, and Ladd-Franklin (Chapter 6), he pointed out that several women "on scientific grounds have full right to be there and might feel hurt (in a general impersonal way) if women are not asked. On the other hand they would undoubtedly interfere with the smoking and to a certain extent with the general freedom of a purely masculine assembly" (cited in Furumoto, 1988, p. 104). Similarly, Lightner Witmer of the University of Pennsylvania (Chapter 12) wrote to Titchener that it would be impossible to have "an informal meeting of men and women.... We want a small vigorous association where we can speak our minds with perfect freedom.... I think that the presence of women...adds greatly to this danger [of mistaking argument for attack], owing to the personal attitude which they usually take even in scientific discussions" (cited in Furumoto, 1988, p. 105).

In defense of the charge that Titchener was antifemale, it has been pointed out that about one-half of his graduate students were female, his first doctoral student was Margaret Washburn, and on at least one occasion he argued for the hiring of a particular woman psychologist at Cornell over the objections of the administration (Leys & Evans, 1990). On the other hand, part of the reason for there being women in Titchener's laboratory was institutional—Cornell for years was about the only place for a woman to go in order to be an "official" student. At any rate, the exclusion of women from Titchener's club created a barrier to advancement and contributed to their difficulty in securing major academic positions. Even after the group reorganized following Titchener's death and technically included women, few were ever nominated for membership (Furumoto, 1988).[3]

► ORIGINAL SOURCE EXCERPT

Titchener's Structuralism

At the opening of the chapter, I pointed out that for Titchener, a prime goal for psychology was to analyze human consciousness into its basic elements or structural components. Thus, Titchener's psychology was the science of the structure of the human mind, and a primary purpose of research was to determine this structure. Titchener developed his system through his lectures, articles, and books. His *Text-Book of Psychology*, which first appeared in 1909 and was dedicated to his first physiology teacher, Burdon-Sanderson of Oxford, provides insight into the world of psychology according to Titchener. Boring (1927/1961)

---

[3] The noted physiological psychologist Donald Hebb (Chapter 14) resigned from the Society in 1953, mainly on the grounds that it seemed more like an exclusionary social club than a true honor society. His resignation letter included a handwritten note asking "Why no women? Charter admits them" (quoted in Glickman, 1996, p. 243).

considered it "the only thorough account of Titchener's psychology that we have in single covers" (p. 259). The following excerpts are from the first chapter of a 1916 reprinting of the book.

Titchener's opening chapter outlined his views on the nature of the discipline. He started with some general observations about science, then began describing psychology by comparing the viewpoints of psychologists and physicists, opening with a sentence that reveals his debt to the British empiricist philosophers:

> All human knowledge is derived from human experience; there is no other source of knowledge. But human experience...may be considered from different points of view. Suppose that we take two points of view...and discover for ourselves what experience looks like in the two cases. First, we will regard experience as altogether independent of any particular person; we will assume that it goes on whether or not anyone is there to have it. Secondly, we will regard experience as altogether dependent upon the particular person; we will assume that it goes on only when someone is there to have it....
>
> Take, to begin with, the three things that you first learn about in physics: space, time and mass. Physical space, which is the space of geometry and astronomy and geology, is constant, always and everywhere the same. Its unit is 1 cm., and the cm. has precisely the same value wherever and whenever it is applied. Physical time is similarly constant; and its constant unit is the 1 sec. Physical mass is constant; its unit, the 1 gr., is always and everywhere the same. Here we have experience of space, time and mass considered as independent of the person who experiences them. Change, then, to the point of view which brings the experiencing person into account. The two vertical lines in Fig. [7.5] are physically equal; they measure alike in units of 1 cm. To you, who see them, they are not equal. The hour that you spend in the waiting-room of a village station and the hour that you spend in watching an amusing play are physically equal; they measure alike in units of 1 sec. To you, the one hour goes slowly, the other quickly; they are not equal. Take two circular cardboard boxes of different diameter (say, 2 cm. and 8 cm.), and pour sand into them until they both weigh, say, 50 gr. The two masses are physically equal; placed on the pans of a balance, they will hold the beam level. To you, as you lift them in your two hands, or raise them in turn by the same hand, the box of the smaller diameter is considerably the heavier. Here we have the experience of space, time and mass considered as dependent upon the experiencing person. It is the same experience that we were discussing just now. But our first point of view gives us facts and laws of physics; our second gives us facts and laws of psychology....
>
> We find, then, a great difference in the aspect of experience, according as it is viewed from the one or the other of our different standpoints. It is the same experience all through; physics and psychology deal with the

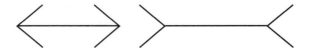

Figure 7.5

same stuff, the same material; the sciences are separated simply—and sufficiently—by their point of view. (pp. 6–8)

After making this distinction between experience as independent of or
dependent upon the individual, Titchener addressed the question of the relationship between mental and physical events—the mind-body problem. First,
he rejected the "common sense" view of the mind as a separate entity somehow
residing within us and directing our lives by interacting with the body. He
traced that idea to Descartes (Chapter 2). Instead, mind should be understood
as "the sum-total of human experience considered as dependent upon the
experiencing person" (p. 9), and its relationship to the body, he argued, is best
conceived of as a "psychophysical parallelism." Notice how Titchener tied the
parallelism to his dependent/independent distinction:

> Common sense says that we cry because we are sorry, laugh because we
> are amused, run because we are frightened;... Mind influences body and
> body influences mind. Our own position has been that mind and body, the
> subject-matter of psychology and the subject-matter of physiology, are sim-
> ply two aspects of the same world of experience. They cannot influence
> each other, because they are not separate and independent things.... This
> doctrine of the relation of mind to body is known as the doctrine of psy-
> chophysical parallelism: the common sense doctrine is that of interaction.
>
> From the point of view of psychophysical parallelism, then, it is not
> strictly true to say that we cry because we are sorry. If we look at the
> whole experience under its independent aspect, we find that certain phys-
> ical events, certain stimuli, affect the body; they set up in the body, and
> especially in the nervous system, certain physical changes; these changes
> cause the secretion of tears. This is an exhaustive account of the experi-
> ence, considered as independent of the experiencing person. If we look at
> the experience under its dependent aspect, we find that our consciousness
> has been invaded by grief or remorse or some kindred emotion. The two
> sets of events, physical and mental, are parallel, but they do not interfere
> with each other. (pp. 13–14)

Titchener next considered the distinction between mind and consciousness.
Then, without mentioning William James by name, he directly addressed
James's famous stream of consciousness metaphor (Chapter 6, p. 158), pointing
out that a precise science of consciousness is possible even if no two conscious
moments are exactly the same:

> ...We shall therefore take mind and consciousness to mean the same
> thing. But as we have the two different words, and it is convenient to
> make some distinction between them, we shall speak of mind when we
> mean the sum-total of mental processes occurring in the life-time of an
> individual, and we shall speak of consciousness when we mean the sum-
> total of mental processes occurring *now*, at any given "present" time.
> Consciousness will thus be a section, a division, of the mind-stream....
>
> While, therefore, the subject-matter of psychology is mind, the direct
> object of psychological study is always a consciousness. In strictness, we

can never observe the same consciousness twice over; the stream of mind flows on, never to return. Practically, we can observe a particular consciousness as often as we wish, since mental processes group themselves in the same way, show the same pattern of arrangement, whenever the organism is placed under the same circumstances. Yesterday's high tide will never recur, and yesterday's consciousness will never recur; but we have a science of psychology, as we have a science of oceanography. (pp. 18–19, italics in the original)

This last paragraph, especially the point about observing a particular consciousness "as often as we wish," led directly into a discussion of method. First, Titchener outlined the essence of any experimental procedure:

Scientific method may be summed up in the single word "observation";... And observation implies two things: attention to the phenomena, and record of the phenomena; that is, clear and vivid experience, and an account of the experience in words or formulas.

In order to secure clear experience and accurate report, science has recourse to experiment. An experiment is an observation that can be repeated, isolated and varied. The more frequently you can *repeat* an observation, the more likely you are to see clearly what is there and to describe accurately what you have seen. The more strictly you can *isolate* an observation, the easier does your task of observation become, and the less danger is there of your being led astray by irrelevant circumstances, or of placing emphasis on the wrong point. The more widely you can *vary* an observation, the more clearly will the uniformity of experience stand out, and the better is your chance of discovering laws. All experimental appliances, all laboratories and instruments, are provided and devised with this one end in view: that the student shall be able to repeat, isolate, and vary his observations. (pp. 19–20, italics in the original)

Next, Titchener outlined the essence of the method of introspection, which he believed was at the heart of experimental psychology. As you recall from Chapter 4, introspection was an important procedure in the Leipzig laboratory, but Wundt tended to limit it to simple verbal reports of the results of psychophysics ("this weight is heavier") and other sensory studies. His student (and Titchener's friend) Oswald Külpe, however, elaborated the procedure into **systematic experimental introspection**, in which observers would give detailed reports of the conscious events occurring while completing some task (e.g., word association). It was this latter approach that was taken by Titchener. He began by describing simple reports like the ones that Wundt would be likely to use. Then he moved to more complicated situations, showing that they nonetheless fit into the "repeat, isolate, vary" framework:

Now let us take some cases in which the material of introspection is more complex. (1) Suppose that a word is called out to you, and that you are asked to observe the effect which this stimulus produces upon consciousness: how the word affects you, what ideas it calls up, and so forth. The observation may be repeated; it may be isolated—you may be seated in a dark and silent room, free from disturbances; and it may be varied—different words may be called out, the word may be flashed upon a screen instead of spoken, etc. Here, however, there seems to be a difference between introspection and inspection. The observer who is watching the course of a chemical reaction, or the movement of some microscopic creature, can jot down from moment to moment the different phases of the observed phenomenon. But if you try to report the changes in consciousness, while these changes are in progress, you interfere with consciousness; your translation of the mental experience into words introduces new factors into that experience itself. (2) Suppose, again, that you are observing a feeling or an emotion; a feeling of disappointment or annoyance, an emotion of anger or chagrin. Experimental control is still possible; situations may be arranged, in the psychological laboratory, such that these feelings may be repeated, isolated, and varied. But your observation of them interferes, even more seriously than before, with the course of consciousness. Cool consideration of an emotion is fatal to its very existence; your anger disappears, your disappointment evaporates, as you examine it. (pp. 21–22)

Thus, Titchener was aware of the fundamental problem of introspection—it is impossible to have a conscious experience and reflect on it at the same time. To deal with the problem, he suggested three solutions. First, rely on memory:

> To overcome this difficulty of the introspective method, students of psychology are usually recommended to delay their observation until the process to be described has run its course, and then to call it back and describe it from memory. Introspection thus becomes retrospection; introspective examination becomes post mortem examination. (p. 22)

Titchener's second suggestion for reducing the memory load was to break the experience into stages, using the fractionation method associated with Külpe's laboratory (Chapter 4); his third, and most critical technique, was to acquire an **introspective habit**:

> …[T]he practiced observer gets into an introspective habit, has the introspective attitude ingrained in his system; so that it is possible for him, not only to take mental notes while the observation is in progress, without interfering with consciousness, but even to jot down written notes, as the histologist does while his eye is still held to the ocular of the microscope. (p. 23)

This is an important passage, for it is part of the reason why Titchener insisted that, for research purposes at least, observers had to be highly trained. In effect, they were to become introspective machines, behaving so automatically that problems of memory and any biasing influences would presumably disappear. Training was also important to avoid what Titchener referred to as the **stimulus error**. This was a tendency to report events by describing the stimuli presented rather than the conscious experiences resulting from those stimuli. For instance, when observing a tree, a proper introspective description would

[handwritten margin notes:]
3 solutions
1) rely on memory (Wundt did not wish to do this)
2) Break Experience into stages
3) acquire introspective habit.

stimulus error — describing stimulus not conscious experience include statements about the sensory elements present: shapes, colors, textures, and movements, along with the affective dimensions of pleasantness/unpleasantness and any accompanying images that came to mind. To commit the stimulus error would be to report simply that you were observing a large "tree." The "introspective attitude" is difficult for us to grasp today, because this type of laboratory training no longer exists. This chapter's Close-Up should give you some insight into what the introspective habit was like, however.

▶ CLOSE-UP

The Introspective Attitude

The absence of Titchenerian introspection in contemporary psychology makes it difficult for us to grasp what an introspective description was really like. One way to find out is to read articles summarizing this kind of research, because they often include verbatim introspective accounts. For example, consider the following study on attention. It was the doctoral thesis of Karl Dallenbach, one of Titchener's students, and later a colleague on the Cornell faculty. Using procedures similar to those found in modern research on attention, Dallenbach (1913) was interested in what happens to consciousness when attention is overloaded. One of his methods was to have observers listen to two metronomes set at different speeds and try to count the number of beats occurring between coincident beats. At the same time, they were to complete some mental task, such as continually adding numbers, singing, or saying the alphabet backwards. Each "experiment" lasted 90 seconds. Here's how one observer reported the experience. Note the presence of all the basic Titchenerian elements—sensations, images, and affect.

> ...The sounds of the metronomes, as a series of discontinuous clicks, were clear in consciousness only four or five times during the experiment, and they were especially bothersome at first. They were accompanied by strain sensations and unpleasantness. The rest of the experiment my attention was on the adding, which was composed of auditory images of the numbers, sometimes on a dark grey scale which was directly ahead and about three feet in front of me. This was accompanied by kinaesthesis of eyes and strains in chest and arms. When these processes were clear in consciousness the sounds of the metronomes were very vague or obscure. (Dallenbach, 1913, p. 467)

Reading articles full of introspective accounts like this can be revealing, but they tend to be long, repetitive, and boring enough to make one understand why psychologists eventually abandoned the method. A more interesting way to gain insight into the *introspective attitude* is to read the letters that experimental psychologists wrote to each other during this era (Goodwin, 1991). Introspective thinking was so ingrained that their correspondence is liberally sprinkled with informal introspections relating to their experiences. After returning from a holiday in New Hampshire, for instance, Edmund Sanford wrote to Titchener about his fear of thunderstorms. He wrote that he had:

> ...observed enough this summer to find that I cannot find anything in it but organic and other sensations unpleasantly colored and, on the cognitive side, a cramp of apperception towards a small group of ideas related to the thing dread-

ed with certain resultants in instinctive act and thought.... When the storm became imminent there would be cardiac and visceral symptoms to describe, etc. etc.—though when the thing was actually present these were as a general thing not so marked as in anticipation—i.e. as the storm approached. (Sanford, 1910)

A more dramatic example of how introspection was never far from the thoughts of turn-of-the-century psychologists comes from an 1893 letter from Lightner Witmer of the University of Pennsylvania to Hugo Münsterberg of Harvard. Witmer had been studying the psychology of pain firsthand in a rather unusual manner:

> ...I let a horse throw me from his back, allowing me to drop on my shoulder and head. I showed a beautiful case of loss of consciousness before the act.... I not only do not remember mounting and the horse running, but I forgot almost everything that happened.... [F]rom the time I got up in the morning till I regained complete consciousness..., I can form no continuous series of events. My head was bad for a while but is all right now, but my arm has served the purpose of quite a number of experiments as it still continues quite painful at times.... The psychological side of my afflictions will form the basis of at least three lectures next fall. (Witmer, 1893)

Titchener concluded the opening chapter of his *Text-Book* with a discussion of psychology's goals. The first two are descriptive: analysis and synthesis. Although analysis of consciousness into its elements was goal number one, it was not the only one:

> ...The psychologist seeks, first of all, to analyse mental experience into its simplest components. He takes a particular consciousness and works over it again and again, phase by phase and process by process, until his analysis can go no further. He is left with certain mental processes which resist analysis, which are absolutely simple in nature, which cannot be reduced, even in part, to other processes. This work is continued, with other consciousnesses, until he is able to pronounce with some confidence upon the nature and number of elementary mental processes. Then he proceeds to the task of synthesis. He puts the elements together, under experimental conditions: first, perhaps, two elements of the same kind, then more of that kind, then elementary processes of diverse kinds: and he presently discerns that regularity and uniformity of occurrence which we have seen to be characteristic of all human experience. He thus learns to formulate the laws of connection of the elementary mental processes. If sensations of tone occur together, they blend or fuse; if sensations of colour occur side by side, they enhance one another: and all this takes place in a perfectly regular way, so that we can write out laws of tonal fusion and laws of colour contrast. (pp. 37–38)

To the descriptive goals of analysis and synthesis, Titchener added the goal of explanation, which would be accomplished ultimately by understanding the operation of the nervous system.

Table 7.2 The Contents of Titchener's Text-Book of Psychology

Chapter Heading	No. of Pages	Percent
Subject-Matter, Method and Problem of Psychology	43	8

Sensation, subdivided into:
    vision
    audition
    smell
    taste
    cutaneous senses
    kinesthetic senses
    other organic sensations
    synaesthesia
    the intensity of sensation (psychophysics)
	179	33

Affection	39	7
Attention	38	7

Perception, subdivided into:
    spatial perceptions
    temporal perceptions
    qualitative perceptions
    composite perceptions
    the psychology of perception
	71	13

Association	22	4
Memory and Imagination	31	6
Action	42	8
Emotion	33	6
Thought	43	8
Conclusion—The Status of Psychology	3	<1

From its overall chapter organization, found in Table 7.2, you can see that the topics of sensation and perception dominated Titchener's *Text-Book*. There is little about the nervous system in it, but a great deal concerning the descriptive goals of analysis and synthesis. Note that fully one-third of the book is devoted to describing basic sensory processes.

THE ELEMENTS OF CONSCIOUS EXPERIENCE

On the basis of his introspective analyses, Titchener identified three types of elementary mental processes: sensations, images, and affections. Sensations were the basic elements of the more complex process of perception, images were the elementary components of ideas, and affections (feelings) were the elements of our emotions. These basic elements could not be reduced further, but they did have various features or **attributes**. All sensations, for instance, had the attributes of quality, intensity, duration, and clearness. Quality is what distinguishes one sensation from another: red from green, cold

Later 1920's

from warm, a high-pitched tone from a low-pitched tone. Intensity refers to the strength of the stimulus, decibel level for example. Duration is self-evident—all sensations last for some measurable period of time. And clearness "is the attribute which gives a sensation its place in a consciousness: the clearer sensation is dominant, independent, outstanding, the less clear sensation is subordinate, undistinguished in the background of consciousness" (Titchener, 1909, p. 53). According to Titchener, attention essentially reduced to this attribute of sensory clearness.

Images have the same four attributes, according to Titchener, but compared with sensations, the qualities are "relatively pale, faded, washed out, misty" (1909, p. 198).[4] In addition, he argued that the intensity and duration of images were "markedly less" (p. 198) than sensations. Affective states, the elements of our emotional life, differ from sensations and images in two important ways. First, although there are literally thousands of different sensorial and imaginal qualities, Titchener believed that affects have only two fundamental qualities—pleasantness and unpleasantness. Second, affects have the attributes of quality, intensity, and duration, but they lack clearness. If we want to experience pleasure at a concert, for example, we must attend to the sensory elements (i.e., the music), not to the feeling of pleasure itself; if we do so, the pleasure disappears. This point is the same one made earlier in the excerpt, when Titchener was describing the difficulty of introspecting to an emotional event—focus on it and the emotion goes away. Titchener rejected the James-Lange theory of emotion, on the grounds that he believed that by equating emotions with bodily reaction, James was reducing affect to sensation (Heidbreder, 1933). For Titchener, on the other

hand, pleasantness and unpleasantness could not be reduced to sensory qualities.

Titchener's structuralism continued to evolve over the years, and in the 1920s he moved away from an emphasis on elements and developed a more phenomenological model that described sensory processes in terms of dimensions. Thus, sensation shifted "from an observable entity to a classificatory term" (Evans, 1972, p. 172). Titchener also moved away from the idea that affects were separate elements after one of his students completed a dissertation that seemed to reduce the affective qualities of pleasantness and unpleasantness to the sensations of "bright pressure" and "dull pressure," respectively (Henle, 1974). Titchener was working on a major revision of his system along these lines, but his productivity dropped during the 1920s, possibly showing the early effects of the brain tumor that would kill him in 1927, and the final system was never completed. Some introductory chapters were published posthumously (1929) as *Systematic Psychology: Prolegomena*.

EVALUATING TITCHENER'S CONTRIBUTIONS TO PSYCHOLOGY

Psychology for Titchener was a pure laboratory science aimed at discovering the basic structure of human consciousness. Systematic experimental introspection was its prime method and because this form of introspection required extensive training, it was limited to highly motivated adult observers. Thus, according to Titchener, psychology was the science of the "generalized adult mind." Two immediate consequences of this rather limited definition of the field were that (a) Titchener was uninterested in individual differences between one

---

[4] Recall from Chapter 4 that Wundt identified two elements: sensations and affections. He believed, like Hume, that images were merely faint copies of sensations and ultimately reducible to them. Titchener was clearly thinking along similar lines, and even expressed some uncertainty about calling them separate elements, but nonetheless felt that sensations and images were sufficiently distinct to justify separate elementary status, at least at this stage of his thinking (Hindeland, 1971).

} Wundt

Excluded

mind and another and (b) he excluded all research using children, animals, and the insane—they could never introspect properly. Also, because the discipline was to retain the purity of the laboratory, Titchener omitted such applied concerns as industrial and educational psychology from his definition of the field. Although his vision of psychology was therefore quite narrow, it also led directly to his major lasting contribution—the promotion of an experimental psychology that featured the tight controls found in the laboratory. Although his particular introspective methodology has passed from the scene, his insistence on the value of basic laboratory research as the way to provide the foundation for psychological knowledge created a place for the laboratory in all colleges and universities with programs in psychology. As one historian put it, Titchener was "responsible for making psychology scientific—for setting psychology up in the laboratory and reaching his conclusions through experiment, under controlled conditions" (Hindeland, 1971, p. 28).

On the other hand, Titchener's psychology became as isolated from American psychology as Ithaca was from other centers of learning. Structuralism ultimately failed as a system, primarily because of the shortcomings of introspection as a method, but also because of Titchener's uncompromising insistence that his way was the only true way. Despite Titchener's belief that highly trained observers gained the "introspective habit," thereby avoiding bias and allowing for replication to occur, it quickly became apparent that serious problems existed with the method. The difficulty is illustrated in several controversies that surrounded Titchener. One was the imageless thought problem, described in Chapter 4. As you recall, introspectors in Külpe's lab at Wurzburg discovered situations in which conscious thoughts occurred in the absence of images. In a psychophysics weight-judging study, for instance, images occurred at various points in the process, but not at the exact moment of judgment. The judgment itself

seemed to be an "imageless" thought. This was a direct threat to Titchener's system, which held as dogma that images were the underlying elements of *all* ideas. To counter the assault, Titchener dismissed the Wurzburg outcome as a failure of experimental control and found that in *his* laboratory, observers were indeed able to detect images at all stages of the weight-judging experiment. Because of the inherently subjective nature of introspection, however, there was no independent means of determining who was right. It began to appear that introspection could not produce objective data.

A second controversy, concerning reaction time, produced a similar outcome—data congenial to Titchener's view from the Cornell laboratory, but a different result elsewhere. This time a researcher at Princeton, James Mark Baldwin (1861–1934), had uncovered what he believed were individual differences in the simple reaction experiment. His sin, in Titchener's view, was to use naive (i.e., untrained) observers. Such individual differences didn't occur at Cornell, of course, where introspectors were properly "trained." The details of this controversy, including the name-calling, can be found in an article by Krantz (1969), but for our purposes the controversy was another example of introspection's fundamental flaw.

Thus, psychologists began to suspect that the extensive training insisted on by Titchener produced bias rather than eliminated it—the training began to look like an indoctrination. In the paper that launched behaviorism, John Watson (Chapter 10) summarized introspection's problem with objectivity:

> …Take the case of sensation. A sensation is defined in terms of its attributes. One psychologist will state with readiness that the attributes of a visual sensation are *quality, extension, duration,* and *intensity.* Another will add *clearness.* Still another that of *order.* I doubt if any one psychologist can draw up a set of statements describing what he means by sensation which will be agreed to by three other psychologists of different

training.... I firmly believe that two hundred years from now, unless the introspective method is discarded, psychology will still be divided on the question as to whether auditory sensations have the quality of "extension," whether intensity is an attribute which can be applied to color, whether there is a difference in "texture" between image and sensation and upon many hundreds of others of like character. (Watson, 1913, p. 164, italics in the original)

The failure of introspection signaled the ultimate demise of structuralism, but the force of Titchener's personality provided one final contribution to psychology. As suggested by Boring's obituary at the start of the chapter, Titchener's death deprived American psychology of a focal point of opposition. Titchener, who lectured in his academic gown and said that the attire conferred on him the right to be dogmatic, insisted on the validity of introspective psychology and was a persistent and articulate critic of those who deviated from it. By so doing, he made it necessary for opponents to be intelligible about their own systems. If schools of thought in psychology gain momentum by virtue of their opposition to some established force, then Titchener's structuralism served the valuable purpose of giving movements such as functionalism and behaviorism a clear target.

AMERICA'S PSYCHOLOGY: FUNCTIONALISM

Titchener might not have been interested in applied psychology and individual differences, or in studying animals, children, or the insane, but practically every other psychologist in America was. Part of the reason for this derives from the historical context of late nineteenth-century America. During the final three decades of the century, following the Civil War, the United States entered a period of sustained growth. It was a time of reconstruction in the South, westward expansion, railroad building, technological innovation (e.g., telephone, typewriter), industrialization on a massive scale, and the amassing of great wealth by Gilded Age entrepreneurs with names like Rockefeller, Vanderbilt, Morgan, Carnegie, and Mellon. Of course, it was also a time when Native American populations were uprooted from their land and decimated, workers endured long hours and unsafe working conditions for pitiful wages, women and minorities were considered mentally inferior to white males, and an enormous gap developed between the very few rich and the very many poor. Nonetheless, most (white, male) Americans came to develop a concept of their national character that placed a high value on taking individual responsibility for success or failure, making something of oneself regardless of one's background, competing and winning in the marketplace, and always thinking of the usefulness or practical value of objects and ideas.

This emerging prototype of American pragmatic individuality was consistent with evolutionary thinking, although most Americans would have strongly denied that they were Darwinians. Nonetheless, Americans were attracted by the views of the British popularizer of evolution, Herbert Spencer (1820–1903), who promoted a brand of evolution congenial to Americans on the "winning" side of things. It was Spencer, not Darwin, who invented the phrase "survival of the fittest," but Spencer's idea of fitness was not the same as Darwin's.[5] Whereas any species attribute that furthered

---

[5] Another important difference between the men was that Darwin was scientifically conservative, unwilling to speculate in the absence of a large database. As discussed in Chapter 5, this unwillingness to go far beyond the data was one reason for his delay in publishing the *Origin of Species*. Spencer, on the other hand, did not hesitate to speculate far beyond available evidence. It was once said of Spencer that his "idea of a tragedy was a deduction killed by a fact." (cited in Boakes, 1984, p. 10)

the cause of survival (e.g., camouflage) would constitute fitness for Darwin, Spencer's use of the term implied that survivors were winners of fierce battles for limited resources. As Spencer used the phrase, survival of the fittest blended with and contributed to the developing American character of the nineteenth century. Spencer's system has come to be known as **social Darwinism**.

Social Darwinists believed that evolutionary forces were natural and inevitable and that any attempt on the part of humans to alter these forces was misdirected and harmful. Evolution must be left unchecked, Spencer argued, an attitude that had direct implications for the social, political, and economic contexts of the time. It meant, for example, that government should not interfere with business practices—losers in business failed simply because they weren't "fit." Those who accumulated enormous wealth, on the other hand, should not in any way be regulated or penalized (e.g., taxed)—their wealth was simply a sign of their fitness. Government also should not provide services to the poor—their poverty was obviously the outcome of a lack of fitness. If supported by the government, their lack of fitness would spread as they produced similarly unfit children. Social Darwinists took the notion "if fit, therefore successful," and made the logically flawed reversal "if successful, therefore fit." Thus, evolutionary fitness became a means of rationalizing the huge gap between rich and poor and of maintaining a belief in the superiority of the white male over all others (e.g., women, blacks, Native Americans). Most American psychologists, especially those interested in mental testing (see Chapter 8), were generally agreeable to social Darwinism.

The evolutionary thinking that psychologists found congenial led naturally to interests in studying individual differences, animal behavior, development, and abnormal behavior, and to the search for practical applications of psychological principles. This trend toward a more diverse psychology than Titchener's structural-

ism was clear from the work of James and Hall (Chapter 6), both of whom were influenced by Darwin and made important contributions before Titchener arrived from Leipzig. The movement came to be called functionalism, and while it was widespread enough to be called "America's psychology," it is normally associated with two schools, Chicago and Columbia. The remainder of the chapter will describe the work of several psychologists at these two schools. Chapter 8 will elaborate on the theme of application, a central component of functionalist thinking.

THE CHICAGO FUNCTIONALISTS

In May of 1889, John D. Rockefeller, pockets bulging with Standard Oil profits, donated an initial $600,000 to establish a Baptist university, contingent on the Baptists contributing an additional $400,00 (Ryan, 1939). It would be located in Chicago, a city already developing the reputation that would lead the poet Carl Sandburg to call it the "City of the Big Shoulders." Nearly destroyed by the famous fire of 1871 that burned 1688 acres, consumed buildings valued at $192 million, and bankrupted 64 different insurance companies (Cashman, 1993), Chicago was one of America's fastest growing cities in the late 1800s. Its hundreds of acres of cattle pens, slaughterhouses, and packinghouses made it the center of the beef industry, and its location made it a natural hub for railroads and a key location for industries (e.g., lumber, steel, agriculture) relying on transportation via rail and Great Lakes steamers. The university was a bold enterprise, far removed from the East Coast academic community, with its success entrusted to President William Rainey Harper, a biblical scholar who had earned a doctorate from Yale at age 18. Harper's main challenge was to hire a quality faculty, a task made easier by the troubles at Clark University. As you recall from the previous chapter, Harper filled a number of his faculty positions with disgruntled Clark University faculty and graduate students when financial problems and Hall's capriciousness as president led them to look for greener pastures.

The University of Chicago opened in 1892 and quickly became a leader in higher education, despite its remoteness from the East. It included separate colleges of liberal arts, practical arts, literature, and science, as well as a graduate school and a school of divinity. It began with a large staff of 120 faculty, and within three years they were teaching 534 graduate students, more than Johns Hopkins and Clark combined (Ryan, 1939).

Two years after the opening, Harper hired a young instructor from the University of Michigan to chair the philosophy department at Chicago. Although he would become better known for his philosophical writings on democracy and his innovative approach to education, John Dewey also wrote a paper that is often considered the official starting point for functionalism in America.

John Dewey (1859–1952): The Reflex Arc

John Dewey was born in Burlington, a small city in western Vermont that borders on Lake Champlain. There he was raised in a setting that shaped in him the traditional Yankee values of hard work, respect for others, thrift, simplicity, and a love of democracy. After completing high school at age 15, Dewey enrolled in the nearby University of Vermont, whose eight faculty members taught just a few dozen students; along with 16 peers, he graduated in 1879 (Barone, 1996). While at Vermont, he studied the traditional curriculum of the classics and humanities, but he also sampled evolutionary thinking by studying the new sciences of geology and zoology.

After graduating, Dewey taught high school for several years, then decided to continue his education. Johns Hopkins was the rising star in academia, and Dewey enrolled there to study philosophy in 1882. The new psychology was included in the Hopkins philosophy curriculum, so Dewey's schedule included work in G. Stanley Hall's brand new laboratory. After earning his doctorate in philosophy in 1884, Dewey's next stop was Michigan. There he taught both philosophy and psychology, working his notes into a text, *Psychology*, in 1886. The book was used on numerous campuses for several years and was the standard text at Michigan for a decade (Raphelson, 1973), but met its demise upon the 1890 publication of William James's instant classic. Dewey himself readily acknowledged *The Principles of Psychology* to be superior to his own effort.

As mentioned earlier, Harper hired Dewey to direct Chicago's philosophy program in 1894. His new department included traditional philosophy, laboratory psychology, and another area of great interest to Dewey—pedagogy. During his 10 years at Chicago, Dewey established the university as a center of functionalism, partly through recruiting colleagues sympathetic to the movement, but mainly through an article published in 1896 entitled "The Reflex Arc Concept in Psychology." In it, he took issue with the traditional manner of thinking about reflexes. Dating from Bell and Magendie's separation of the reflex into separate sensory and motor pathways (Chapter 3), physiologists thought of the **reflex arc** in terms of three separate elementary components: the stimulus producing sensation, central processing producing an idea, and the act or motor response. Dewey believed that dividing the reflex into these "elements" was artificial, however, resulting in a reflex concept that was "not a comprehensive, or organic unity, but a patchwork of disjointed parts" (Dewey, 1896/1948, p. 356). Instead, Dewey proposed a model of the reflex that substituted a functional for a structural analysis.

The reflex, Dewey argued, is best conceived of as an integrated, coordinated whole that serves the function of adapting the organism to its environment. Also, it is more like a continuous circuit than an "arc," the latter implying distinct starting and ending points. Consider a child reaching for a candle flame, for instance. Those using the reflex arc model would analyze the event into a series of stimulus-response elements—seeing the flame, reaching for it, feeling the heat, and withdrawing (S-R-S-R). For Dewey, though, such an analysis oversimplified a complex action. Reaching for something after seeing it, for example, can only make sense in the larger context of the child's learning history: "seeing and grasping have been so often bound together to reinforce each other, to help each other out, that each may be considered practically a subordinate member of a bigger coordination" (p. 356). The second part of the event, being seared by the flame and withdrawing the hand, is also part of the larger coordination that produces a learning event; the flame now takes on new meaning for the child. From that point on, seeing a burning candle is "no longer mere seeing; it is the seeing-of-a-light-that-means-pain-when-contact-occurs" (p. 357). Hence, the child has adapted to the environment as a result of experience. Furthermore, the sight of a burning candle now has a specific meaning that differs from the same sight viewed by a different child with different experiences. As will be seen in Chapter 9, the notion that actions result not from a specific stimulus but from a stimulus-as-perceived was central to the German gestalt psychologists. Dewey argued forcefully that psychologists studying human action should not be concerned with microscopic analysis into elements, but with how the act functions to promote the organism's well-being in the struggle to adapt to its ever changing world. That is, Dewey was proposing a change in emphasis about behavior, a shift in thinking from an emphasis on "what?" to a focus on "what for?"

America at the turn of the century was just entering the Progressive Era, a time of sweeping reform and the beginning of a reaction against social Darwinism. It was during this time that business monopolies were being attacked and their leaders were as likely to be called robber barons as heroes of the struggle for existence. Labor unions made significant gains on behalf of workers, the federal government enacted regulations to protect ordinary Americans from a variety of abuses (for instance, child labor, unsanitary conditions in food production industries), and social reformers set out to improve the welfare of those who used to be written off as "unfit." John Dewey fit perfectly into this context, making significant contributions to educational reform and launching the movement that came to be known as **progressive education**.

Dewey had been a schoolteacher for a brief time after graduating from college. He developed a strong dislike for the conventional approach to education, which emphasized rote learning, drill and practice, and strict discipline. Such an atmosphere made the classroom a place to avoid rather than a place to learn. Yet education was the key to an effective democracy, Dewey believed, because it offered everyone an equal opportunity to advance. At a time when public education was growing by leaps and bounds,[6] educational reform was essential. Dewey responded by creating a "Laboratory School" at Chicago in 1896 to study how children learned best in the classroom, and by writing *The School and Society* (1899), which established his reputation as a leading philosopher of education. He also implored psychologists to use their new knowledge of the mind to improve education, using his presidential address to the American Psychological Association in 1899 as a forum (Dewey, 1900). According to Dewey, children learn by interacting with their environment—they learn by doing. Consequently, the

---

[6] Attending school was compulsory in just six states in 1871, but was virtually universal by 1900. Between 1890 and 1910, the number of students in public schools increased by a factor of four (Cashman, 1993).

school must create an atmosphere that encourages children to explore on their own, to think critically and creatively, and to be actively involved in learning.

Dewey left Chicago for Columbia University in 1904, turning over departmental leadership to James Angell. At Columbia, he made no further contributions to psychology, but he continued to agitate for educational and social reform within the context of his democratic philosophy. He was a strong supporter of teachers' unions, helped found the American Association of University Professors, became a member of the American Civil Liberties Union, and actively campaigned for women's suffrage (Hilgard, 1987). He remained a committed activist for liberal causes well into his eighth decade.

James R. Angell (1869–1949): The Province of Functional Psychology

Like Dewey, James Rowland Angell was born in Burlington, Vermont, the son of the president of the University of Vermont. When his father took the same job at the University of Michigan in 1871, the Angells moved to the Midwest and James was raised in the academic environment of Ann Arbor. He went to school at his father's university, studying philosophy, the classics, and learning about natural science via courses in botany. His introduction to psychology came in a course with Dewey, using the professor's new textbook. Angell graduated from Michigan in 1890, then stayed another year to earn a master's degree in philosophy. During this last year his courses included a seminar with Dewey that used James's new *Principles of Psychology* as the text. As he later recalled, the text "unquestionably affected my thinking for the next 20 years more profoundly than any other" (cited in Raphelson, 1973, p. 120). To experience William James firsthand, Angell went to Cambridge and spent a year under James's tutelage, during which time he attempted some unsuccessful research into psy-

chic phenomena. He then decided to earn a German doctorate. By this time doctoral training in America was as good as if not superior to training in Germany, but there was still a high prestige value to a doctorate from the Continent. That Angell was aware of this status benefit is clear—his cousin Frank, with Leipzig credentials paving the way, had just been lured from Cornell to Stanford by an outstanding offer of $3000 annually (O'Donnell, 1985).

Angell intended to follow his cousin to Leipzig, but Wundt's laboratory was full, so he studied briefly with Ebbinghaus in Berlin before settling into the University at Halle. There he completed the work for his doctorate, but never finished the final version of it (he was asked to improve the German) after receiving an offer to teach at the University of Minnesota. The salary and the stability of real employment enabled him to marry the woman he had known since his Michigan days, and for the 24-year-old Angell, love and a new job were sufficient to offset the loss of what seemed to be a mere piece of paper. Thus, although he would go on to direct the doctoral projects of several prominent American psychologists, he never quite finished his own.

After a year at Minnesota, Dewey hired the young instructor to be in charge of the psychology portion of the philosophy curriculum and the Angells moved to Chicago in 1894. When Dewey moved on to Columbia a decade later, psychology became its own department, separate from philosophy, and Angell was made department chair. He moved further toward administration and away from psychology by being named Dean of the Faculty in 1911. He eventually followed in his father's footsteps and became a university president, leading Yale University for most of the 1920s and 1930s before retiring in 1937.

Angell's importance for psychology derives from his work in the period from 1894 to 1911. During this time he contributed valuable research in areas such as reaction time, imagery,

Key Date 1906	This year marked the publication date of James Angell's APA presidential address ("The Province of Functional Psychology") that brought functional psychology into clear focus.

These events also happened:

- The first U.S. Pure Food and Drugs Act was passed, after Upton Sinclair's description of the Chicago stockyards and slaughterhouses in *The Jungle*
- China and Britain agreed to a reduction in the production of opium
- The San Francisco earthquake killed 700 and produced $400 million in property loss
- Teddy Roosevelt visited the Panama Canal, the first trip outside the U.S. by a president in office
- U.S. troops occupied Cuba, remaining for three years
- The first running of the French Grand Prix motor race occurred
- These people were born:

  Greta Garbo, Swedish film actress

  Dmitri Shostakovich, Russian composer

  Gracie Allen, comedic actor and wife of George Burns
- These people died:

  Henrik Ibsen, Norwegian playwright

  Paul Cezanne, French artist

and sound localization,[7] and he built one of the top two or three departments in the country. He also became the most visible spokesperson for functionalism by writing a popular introductory textbook (Angell, 1904) and by delivering a memorable address after being elected to the presidency of the American Psychological Association in 1906 (Angell, 1907/1948). Dewey's reflex arc paper might have been the foundation paper for functionalist thinking, but it was not a "Here is what functionalism means" type of paper. Angell's was—he called it "The Province of Functional Psychology." In part, it was a response to Titchener's 1898 paper, "The Postulates of a Structural Psychology."

Angell opened the paper with the modest disclaimer that functional psychology was not a dogmatic "school" of psychology,[8] but rather "little more than a point of view, a program, an ambition" (Angell, 1907/1948, p. 439). He then

---

[7] Sound localization depends in part on sound waves reaching our ears at slightly different times. Angell, who was deaf in one ear, served as his own observer in a study on how localization was accomplished monaurally (Hunter, 1949).

[8] Traditionally, histories of psychology have been organized around the concept of "schools of psychology," a term referring to a major conceptual framework that includes statements about psychology's definition, its preferred methods, and its important concepts. Thus, structuralism, functionalism, behaviorism, gestalt psychology, and psychoanalysis are normally considered to be the predominant schools of psychology.

drew a sharp contrast between functional and structural psychologies. Whereas a structuralist is interested in mental contents, the "what?" of conscious experience, Angell stated, the functional psychologist wants to study mental operations, the "how?" and "why?" of consciousness. If the structuralist is asking *what is consciousness?* the functionalist is asking *what is consciousness for?* Furthermore, with a dig at what he considered to be the highly artificial nature of the results from Titchenerian-style research, Angell argued that a minute analysis of some hypothetical "moment of consciousness" fails to capture the importance of consciousness for everyday life:

> …If you adopt as your material for psychological analysis the isolated "moment of consciousness," it is very easy to become so absorbed in determining its constitution as to be rendered somewhat oblivious to its artificial character. The most essential quarrel which the functionalist has with structuralism…arises from this fact and touches the feasibility and worth of the effort to get at mental process as it is under the conditions of actual experience rather than as it appears to a merely postmortem [introspective] analysis. (p. 441)

Angell then explicitly rejected the analogy between psychology and biology that Titchener had used to argue for the primacy of a structuralist approach. As you recall, Titchener had likened structuralism to anatomy and argued that just as anatomy provides the basis for physiology, so must structuralism precede functionalism. But Angell would have none of it. Anatomy involves material objects that can be manipulated, observed, and measured with some precision, but mental contents are "evanescent" and "fleeting." We can attempt to isolate them, but they are fundamentally different from the materials being studied by anatomists. With the analogy between anatomy and structuralism shown to be faulty, Angell believed the supposed primacy of structuralism over functionalism to be meaningless.

Angell's functionalist approach to consciousness had the same evolutionary flavor found in James. Like James, Angell described the function of consciousness to be in allowing the individual to solve problems and therefore to adapt to novel situations. Near the close of his article, he pointed out the connections between functionalist thinking and the interests of American psychologists. If the psychologist is interested in the functions of consciousness, then it is important to understand how those functions develop, both ontogenetically and phylogenetically. Therefore, the psychologist has legitimate interests in developmental and comparative psychology. Similarly, an interest in failures to adapt leads naturally to the study of abnormal psychology, an interest in how some individuals adapt better than others leads one to study individual differences and develop mental tests to measure those differences, and an interest in how the individual learns to adapt and can be best trained to do so leads to the study of educational psychology and of learning in general. In short, all of the topics that were of interest to American psychologists could be gathered under the umbrella of functionalism. Furthermore, studying these diverse areas requires a liberal attitude about appropriate methods. Angell had no quarrel with introspection, but he believed that it had to be defined more broadly than Titchener would allow and that it must be supplemented with more direct observational methods.

In his productive years at Chicago, Angell mentored several individuals destined to become key figures in psychology's story. One was John Watson, normally considered the founder of behaviorism as a school of psychology (Chapter 10); another was Harvey Carr, Angell's successor as department head.

Harvey Carr (1873–1954): The Maturing of Functionalism

Carr was almost 30 when he landed in Chicago in 1902. The son of Indiana farmers, Carr's college education had been interrupted by financial problems and ill health, but he managed to complete both a bachelor's and a master's degree in psychology at the University of Colorado just prior to his arrival in Angell's department. At Colorado, he learned of the new psychology and its laboratory procedures from Arthur Allin, who had studied with Hall and Sanford at Clark. While at Chicago, he developed lifelong interests in two diverse topics, the perception of space and maze learning. His doctoral dissertation in 1905 was on the former topic and eventually led to a book (Carr, 1935). Most of his research publications concerned maze learning, however. Following Small's lead (refer to the Close-Up in Chapter 6) Carr investigated the sensory basis for maze learning, and two of his studies with John Watson are featured in Chapter 10. He was also interested in the general problem of maze standardization. In the early years of maze learning research, studies often failed to replicate because the mazes used from one study to the next varied considerably. Carr improved the situation substantially by inventing a type of maze that came to be called the "Carr maze" (Warner & Warden, 1927). Two examples are shown in Figure 7.6. As you can see, although each maze has a different solution, the number of choices per maze is held constant, as is the length of each pathway and cul de sac. Also, the mazes were constructed so that patterns could be changed quickly.

After earning his doctorate in 1905, Carr taught elsewhere for several years, then returned to Chicago in 1908. With Watson leaving for Johns Hopkins that year, Angell hired Carr to run the psychology laboratory. Carr remained at Chicago until his retirement in 1938, chairing the department for the second half of his years there. He contributed to the evolution of Chicago functionalism through his effect on students and by the publication of a popular textbook in the mid-1920s—*Psychology: A Study of Mental Activity* (Carr, 1925). In his years at Chicago, Carr had a hand in the doctoral work of no fewer than 131 students and he directed 53 dissertations, 18 in comparative psychology, 6 in space perception, and 29 in learning (Pillsbury, 1955). The 1925 text can be considered a statement of the "mature" functionalism, with the understanding that functionalism always remained more of an attitude than a systematic theoretical position.

THE COLUMBIA FUNCTIONALISTS

Because functionalism was more of a state of mind than a rigorous system, it existed well beyond Chicago. Indeed, elements of functional thinking could be found throughout the academic landscape, with the possible exception of Cornell. Even there, however, Titchenerian orthodoxy occasionally relaxed. For instance, E. G. Boring once ran a human maze learning study that featured blindfolded humans navigating an outdoor maze, their pathways marked by trails of flour leaking from sacks

Figure 7.6   Designs for two typical Carr mazes.

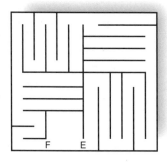 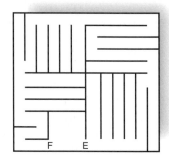

attached to their backs; Boring reported that the only significant outcome of the study was that he became infatuated with one of the maze-runners, later marrying her (Jaynes, 1969). Beyond Chicago, however, functionalism at the turn of the century was associated with Columbia University in New York. In its formative years, James McKeen Cattell headed the psychology program. You met him in the Chapter 4 discussion of reaction time, and you will learn more extensively of his work in the next chapter. While at Columbia from 1891 to 1917, Cattell created a vibrant graduate department, possibly the best in the country. Under his tutelage, dozens of historically important psychologists earned their doctoral stripes, and Cattell personally directed more than 50 dissertations (Jonçich, 1968). Two of his better known students were Edward Thorndike and Robert Woodworth.

Edward L. Thorndike (1874–1949): Connectionism

Thorndike spent practically his entire professional career making major contributions to educational psychology and psychological testing, but he is most often remembered among psychologists for studying how cats learned to escape from crudely constructed puzzle boxes. For this reason he is sometimes included in histories of comparative psychology as an example of what Lloyd Morgan had in mind as the proper way to do animal research, and at other times he can be found in the chapter on behaviorism as a precursor to the conditioning work of Pavlov and Watson. In a certain sense, then, he was a transition figure from the early comparative psychologists to the later behaviorists. More important, he was a leader of the functionalist movement, interested in studying how individuals adapted to their environments and how this knowledge could be applied to improve the human condition.

Thorndike's early life was somewhat nomadic; his father was a Methodist minister who moved his family from one New England

town to another as he was reassigned to different congregations every two or three years. Always the new kid in town, young Thorndike became terribly shy, but he also developed self-reliance, and under the stern eye of his puritanical and demanding mother, he became an excellent student. He gained easy acceptance to the Methodist-run Wesleyan University in Connecticut, graduating with honors in 1895. While there, he found his vocation by discovering James's *Principles of Psychology*, which electrified him as it had James Angell and countless others of their generation. Thorndike (1936) later described the book as more stimulating "than any book that I had read before, and possibly more so than any book read since" (p. 263). As Angell had done four years earlier, Thorndike entered Harvard's graduate program to experience James directly.

It is not clear exactly how Thorndike's interests in animal behavior developed, but a seminar taken with James used Wundt's *Lectures on Human and Animal Psychology* (which had just been translated by Titchener), and he probably attended public lectures given by the visiting C. Lloyd Morgan, Britain's premier comparative psychologist (Chapter 5). Like every educated person of his day, he was thoroughly familiar with evolutionary thinking; his knowledge of contemporary comparative psychology and its problems are evident from his half-hearted explanation for his choice of research topic: "My first research was in animal psychology, not because I knew animals or cared much for them, but because I thought I could do better than had been done" (cited in Jonçich, 1968, p. 89).

Thorndike first studied instinct and intelligence in baby chicks by asking them to escape from simple mazes formed by placing books on end. Figure 7.7 shows three of the patterns he used. Chicks would be placed in the maze at location A, then observed to see if they could find the exit. Thorndike reported that they initially jumped at the walls, made a lot of noise, and were just as likely to go more deeply into the maze than to escape from it. After several

Figure 7.7 Configurations of three mazes that Thorndike created by placing books vertically on a table.

trials, however, they eliminated the useless behaviors and learned their way out. Incidentally, some of this research was completed in the cellar of the William James household. Thorndike's landlord had evicted the animals, perhaps as a consequence of their noisy attempts to escape the mazes, and James had taken them in after being unable to secure space for them on campus. Thorndike believed that the "nuisance to Mrs. James was...somewhat mitigated by the entertainment to the two youngest children" (Thorndike, 1936, p. 264).

For reasons that were partly financial and partly the consequence of a romantic relationship that seemed to be going nowhere (with the woman who would become his wife, as it turned out; see Figure 7.8), Thorndike applied for and received a fellowship to Columbia. Cattell was impressed with the young comparative psychologist and Thorndike was awarded $700 a year in aid, more than the average annual income for most families at that time (Jonçich, 1968). At Columbia, he expanded his animal research to several different species, but his most important work was done with cats (and some dogs) in puzzle boxes, published as "Animal Intelligence: An Experimental Study of the Associative Processes in Animals" in 1898.

As is evident from his description of why he undertook the research, Thorndike was a strong critic of most comparative psychology, especially when it relied on nonrepresentative

Figure 7.8 Edward L. Thorndike during the time of his puzzle box studies, with his eventual spouse, Elizabeth Moulton, from Jonçich (1968).

anecdotal data to support claims of higher mental powers. With the brashness of youth, he sarcastically observed that

> …Dogs get lost hundreds of times and no one ever notices it or sends an account of it to a scientific magazine. But let one find his way from Brooklyn to Yonkers and the fact immediately becomes a circulating anecdote. Thousands of cats on thousands of occasions sit helplessly yowling, and no one takes thought of it or writes to his friend, the professor; but let one cat claw at the knob of a door supposedly as a signal to be let out, and straightaway this cat becomes the representative of the cat-mind in all the books. (Thorndike, 1898/1948, p. 379)

Disdaining the anecdotal strategy, Thorndike instead developed more systematic procedures to test claims for animal intelligence.

Thorndike was the exception to the rule that the early experimentalists were talented and creative apparatus builders. His books-on-end mazes hinted at a certain lack of mechanical aptitude; his puzzle boxes confirmed the handicap.[9] Photographs of several of these primitive devices have survived, and Figure 7.9 shows one of them, Box L (Burnham, 1972). Thorndike simply patched together pieces of used crates and built doors in each that could be opened in one of several ways—pulling a string, pushing a pedal, or moving a latch. Just as the chicks had been placed into the mazes to see if they could learn to escape, a cat would be put into a puzzle box and kept there until it hit upon the correct way of opening the door.

Despite appearances, there was a method to the apparent chaos in the box designs. Box L, for instance, was designed to combine responses that were the only ones necessary in each of three other boxes. It was used with cats that had learned each of the responses in the three

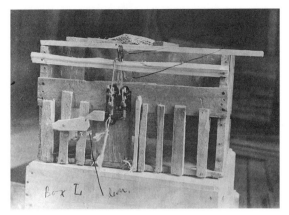

Figure 7.9   One of Thorndike's puzzle boxes, requiring three responses—wire pull, level press, knob turn. (From Burnham, 1972).

other boxes, to see if they could combine the information. They couldn't, leading Thorndike to conclude that the cats were not capable of the kind of reasoning attributed to them by less careful and more anthropomorphic animal researchers (e.g., Romanes). He also decided that imitation was beyond his cats' capabilities; cats observing other cats escape did not benefit from the experience. With reasoning and conscious imitation eliminated, then, what accounted for the cat's escape behavior?

Thorndike's explanation, which also applied to his chicks-in-mazes experiments, was the same as that given by Morgan to explain the behavior of terriers opening gates to escape from yards—**trial-and-error learning** (Thorndike preferred the phrase "trial and accidental success"). Because he believed that the cat learned to make connections between stimuli and responses during this trial and error learning, Thorndike's model is sometimes called **connectionism**. When first placed in the puzzle box, the cat exhibits behavior that is a random sequence of acts—clawing, biting, pushing, screeching, and so on. Eventually, the animal

---

[9] Also, Thorndike never learned how to use a typewriter or how to drive a car, and his son could never recall seeing his father "fix" anything (Thorndike, 1991).

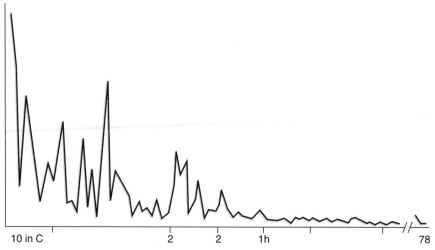

10 in C   2   2   1h   78

Figure 7.10 **Performance of cat #10 in puzzle box C. On the *X* axis, the unlabeled vertical dash meant a day, "2" meant two days, "1 h" meant an hour, and "78" meant 78 hours. (From Thorndike, 1911).**

hits upon the correct response (e.g., steps on a pedal), but its first solution is accidental. Nonetheless, that behavior has been successful, and such behaviors tend to be repeated, "stamped in" by their pleasurable consequences (escape), as Thorndike put it. On trial two, the cat continues to produce unsuccessful behaviors, but again hits on the correct one eventually. As trials continue, the failed behaviors are gradually eliminated and the successful one occurs earlier and earlier in the sequence. Before long, the animal is in and out of the box in a few seconds. Figure 7.10 charts the (erratic) progress of one of Thorndike's cats. Thorndike summarized the process by postulating his famous **Law of Effect**—behaviors leading to pleasurable consequences have the effect of being "stamped in," whereas behavior that produces annoying results is "stamped out." The process of learning, then, involves the creation of *connections* or associations between stimulus situations (e.g., a foot pedal) and the responses that are successful in those situations (e.g., step on it). Thorndike also proposed a **Law of Exercise**—the more frequently a response is associated with a situation, the stronger the connection between the two;

conversely, connections can be weakened if they aren't repeated. To account for the fact that every situation encountered in life is somewhat unique, Thorndike applied the results of some research on transfer that he completed with Woodworth (below). He proposed that if a new situation, S1, had some elements in common with an old situation, S2, then the response to S2 would transfer to some degree to S1. Children whose tantrums are successful in K-mart (S2) might give the same tactic a try on their first visit to Wal-Mart (S1).

Thorndike was excited about his results and willing to take on critics, writing to his future wife that his "thesis is a beauty.... I've got some theories which knock the old authorities into a grease spot" (cited in Jonçich, 1968, p. 146). One such authority who was not amused by Thorndike's youthful exuberance was Wesley Mills, a comparative psychologist who criticized Thorndike's research at the 1898 meeting of the American Psychological Association and followed it up with an article in *Psychological Review*. Mills started by criticizing Thorndike's lack of respect for his "elders," noting that "Dr. Thorndike has not been hampered in his

Ethological Approach also supported by J.J. Gibson + Ulric Neisser

researches by any of that respect for workers of the past…which usually causes men to pause before differing radically from them, not to say gleefully consigning them to the psychological flames" (Mills, 1899, p. 263). More important, Mills rejected the study's conclusions entirely because of the artificiality of the environment created by Thorndike. Cats placed in small enclosures, Mills argued, cannot be expected to act naturally. Thus, nothing about their normal behavior can be determined from their behavior in highly artificial, abnormal surroundings. Mills concluded that one might as well "enclose a living man in a coffin, lower him, against his will, into the earth, and attempt to deduce normal psychology from his conduct" (p. 266).

Far from being chastened, Thorndike (1899) offered a point-by-point rebuttal. He admitted to being unimpressed with animal research based on uncritical observation and anecdote and made no apology for it. He denied Mills's claim that his cats must have been in a panic, pointing out caustically that if Mills had acted like a genuine scientist and bothered to repeat the puzzle box studies, he would have discovered that little if any panic occurred. Furthermore, those cats that did show a higher "fury of activity" (p. 412) did not differ in learning speed from their more sanguine peers. As for the charge of "unnaturalness," Thorndike simply asked what Mills could mean by natural. Animals constantly face new situations; who is to say one is more "natural" than another? To drive home the point, Thorndike turned around an example that Mills had used, of the effects "of certain mental functions on the conduct of a kitten in gaining a certain resting place (in a bookcase, if I remember rightly), in spite of mechanical obstacles interposed. The situation here coped with is as 'unnatural' as that in…my experiments" (p. 414).

The Mills-Thorndike exchange is a good illustration of a difference of opinion about the appropriateness of laboratory methods that continues to this day. On the one hand are those who argue that understanding animal behavior requires the precision afforded by a controlled laboratory environment. In such a setting, the effects of various influences on behavior can be studied systematically. As will be seen, this approach was taken by the majority of American animal researchers who came to be known as behaviorists (e.g., Skinner). In contrast, other psychologists have followed Mills and argued that animal behavior can only be understood if it is studied outside of the artificial confines of the laboratory. Most twentieth-century European researchers have taken this route, producing a field known as **ethology**—the study of animal behavior in its "natural" surroundings. The best-known of these scientists are Konrad Lorenz, Karl von Frisch, and Niko Tinbergen, who shared the 1973 Nobel prize in biology for their work on instinctive animal behavior. Lorenz is familiar to most students from a photo of him being followed by ducklings. Although you know from the Chapter 5 Close-Up that Spalding anticipated this phenomenon, Lorenz is normally credited with the discovery of *imprinting*.

After earning his doctorate, Thorndike taught for a year at Case Western Reserve in Cleveland, then returned to Columbia's Teachers College, where he remained for the rest of his professional career. There he extended his research on learning to humans and became a leading educational psychologist. He also developed a series of aptitude tests for schoolchildren, thereby contributing to the psychological testing movement as well. Honors came his way in the form of an APA presidency in 1912 and election to the National Academy of Sciences in 1917. He was a prolific writer, averaging about a dozen articles a year. He also wrote numerous textbooks, including a three-volume *Educational Psychology* in 1913, which made his name "practically synonymous with the field of educational psychology for many years to come" (Goodenough, 1950, p. 295). Most of his texts were compilations of lecture notes, and as Titchener pointed out in a scathing review of an introductory text by Thorndike, publishing "lecture courses as soon as the lectures have been delivered…must inevitably show marks of hasty preparation and of immaturity of judgment" (Titchener, 1905). The criticism didn't slow Thorndike down for a minute, however, and by the 1920s his royalty earnings far exceeded his Columbia salary. In 1924, for instance, his royalty income of $68,000 was five times his faculty salary (Jonçich, 1968). Thorndike retired from Columbia in 1940 and died nine years later.

Robert S. Woodworth (1869–1962): A Dynamic Psychology

Woodworth, named Robert Sessions after an ancestor who participated in the Boston Tea Party, was born in the small western Massachusetts town of Belchertown. Like Thorndike, he was the son of a minister; his mother was an educator, a graduate of Mount Holyoke College and the founder of the Lake Erie Female Seminary in Ohio (Poffenberger, 1962). Considering a career in the ministry himself, Woodworth attended Amherst College, but emerged with an interest in teaching. After a few years of teaching high school science and math, he discovered (who else?) William James and the *Principles* and decided to pursue a career in either philosophy or psychology. Like Angell and Thorndike, Woodworth wanted to experience the master directly, so off he went to Harvard in the fall of 1895. Woodworth stayed in Cambridge for three academic years, earning a second bachelor's degree, a master's degree, and serving as assistant in physiology at the Harvard Medical School. During this time he developed two lifelong friendships, one with the noted physiologist Walter B. Cannon, whose work with Bard would eventually yield a theory of emotion to rival the James-Lange theory, and a second with Thorndike. This latter friendship contributed to Woodworth's next stop after Harvard—Cattell offered him a fellowship to Columbia, partly the result of being pestered to do so by Thorndike (Jonçich, 1968).

Woodworth completed his doctorate at Columbia in 1899 and was immediately appointed instructor in physiology there. After spending a productive year in England in the laboratory of the esteemed physiologist Charles Sherrington (Chapter 3), he accepted Cattell's invitation in 1903 to join the psychology department, where he remained until his retirement in 1939 at age 70. Retirement barely slowed him down, however, for he continued to teach part-time until he was 89 and to write until he was 91.

Woodworth was a modest man who once wrote this to a friend: "I rate my achievement very low, believing that I am one of the sort whose name will soon be forgotten, though of service during his lifetime" (cited in Poffenberger, 1962, p. 687). It was true that he did not contribute much in the way of original research and he did not create a school of thought that produced "Woodworthians," but he was quite wrong about his influence. He is remembered for (a) his research with Thorndike on transfer of training, (b) his "dynamic" psychology, with its emphasis on drives and organismic variables, and (c) his impact on students, both directly and through textbook writing, especially "The Columbia Bible." This latter achievement, by itself, was sufficient to insure his lasting importance to twentieth-century experimental psychology.

The research on **transfer** derived from a fundamental problem in higher education—the validity of claims made on behalf of the doctrine of "formal discipline." Rooted in faculty psychology, it was the mid-nineteenth century belief that the curriculum for higher education should be designed to "exercise" and strengthen the intellectual faculties. This was to be accomplished through the study of such disciplines as Latin, Greek, and classical literature. Once the faculties were in shape, the skills that had been developed were assumed to transfer to other disciplines learned later. The doctrine came under fire near the end of the century, when several schools copied Harvard's radical concept of an "elective" curriculum, which enabled students to avoid Latin and Greek if they wished. The debate generated much rhetoric, but little evidence accumulated for or against the idea that learning topic A (e.g., Greek) made it easier to learn topic B (e.g., zoology). Thorndike and Woodworth, in a series of coauthored publications (e.g., 1901), set out to find direct evidence for transfer of training. Their subjects practiced one simple task, then tried other tasks that varied in the degree of resemblance to the original task. After estimating the areas of rectangles, for instance, they estimated the areas of triangles (high resemblance) or the weight of objects (low). Briefly, what they found was that the amount of transfer occurring was directly proportional to the number of elements shared by the tasks. Although their tasks were quite different from curricular topics, Thorndike and Woodworth generalized their results to the issue of formal discipline, concluding that the doctrine had little merit. Because subjects like Greek bore minimal relationship to subjects like zoology, Thorndike and Woodworth predicted very little benefit to zoologists from studying Greek (except for some word origin information). As mentioned earlier, Thorndike also used the transfer concept to explain how cats that escaped from one box would find it easier to escape from a new box, assuming the two boxes shared some components.

Woodworth is often described as an "eclectic" when it came to theorizing, willing to incorporate the features of various diverse systems. In his popular introductory text, for example, he defined psychology as the study of both mental processes *and* behavior, thus blending the new behaviorism with the traditional psychology of consciousness. He also believed that psychologists should use a variety of methods, ranging from introspection to mental testing to the objective observation of behavior. He disliked those who would define psychology narrowly, naming both Titchener (structuralism) and Watson (behaviorism) as examples, and he revealed his basic philosophy by ending his popular history of psychology,

Contemporary Schools of Psychology, with a chapter called "The Middle of the Road" (Woodworth, 1931, pp. 205–219). He was especially critical of a simple mechanistic, stimulus-response psychology, arguing for what he referred to as an **S-O-R model**. That is, he insisted that psychologists must understand not just the stimulus and response, but also the organism (O) that stands in between. This includes studying what motivates or drives the organism. In his *Dynamic Psychology* (1918) and *Dynamics of Behavior* (1958), Woodworth established the importance of studying motivational factors influencing behavior. In the process he introduced the term **drive** to psychology.

Like his best friend Thorndike, Woodworth became wealthy by writing textbooks. His *Psychology*, with editions appearing in 1921, 1929, 1934, and 1940, introduced thousands of students to the field for over two decades. More important for research psychologists, his *Experimental Psychology* shaped the very definition the term "experiment." When the book made its initial appearance in 1938, it was already so well known that no psychologist was perplexed when the publisher announced that "The Bible is out" (Estes, 1981). As early as 1909, Woodworth had been distributing mimeographed handouts for his course in experimental methods, and by 1920 these had grown into a 285-page handout called "A Textbook in Experimental Psychology" (Winston, 1990). Columbia students who became professors used the materials in their own classes. By 1938, the eagerly anticipated volume finally appeared and was an immediate success, selling more than 44,000 copies by 1954, when it was revised and a coauthor added (Woodworth & Schlosberg, 1954). Historian Andrew Winston (1990) estimated that between 1938 and 1959, more than 100,000 psychology majors learned about research in psychology from Woodworth.

Woodworth's 1938 text was encyclopedic, with more than 823 pages of text and another 36 pages of references. After an introductory chapter, it was organized into 29 different research topics, including such diverse topics as memory, transfer of training, maze learning, reaction time, hearing, the perception of color, and thinking. Students using the text learned about the procedures related to each content area, as well as virtually everything there was to know in 1938 about each topic. They also learned some distinctions that were to have important ramifications for future psychologists.

Prior to Woodworth, the term "experiment" had been used broadly as a label for procedures ranging from the introspection of a mental event to a mental test to an observation under controlled circumstances. Woodworth, however, narrowed the definition and contrasted experimental research with what he referred to as correlational research. The defining feature of the experimental method was to be the manipulation of what Woodworth called an **independent variable**, and this variable would have its effects on what he called the **dependent variable**. Woodworth did not invent the terms, but he was the first to use them in this manner. While the experimental method manipulates independent variables, Woodworth wrote, the correlational method "measures two or more characteristics of the same individuals [and] computes the correlation of these characteristics. This method…has no 'independent variable' but treats all the measured variables alike" (Woodworth, 1938, p. 3). Furthermore, Woodworth originated the argument, now found in the opening chapter of every introductory text but not widely accepted during his time, that the experimental method was the only technique allowing causal conclusions; no causation could be inferred from correlations. Although Woodworth argued that correlational research should have the same overall status as experimental research, he omitted correlational findings from the remainder of the text. The reader could be excused for thinking that the experimental approach was superior. Indeed, the consequences of Woodworth's distinction were sufficient to become the focus of a cautionary APA presidential address in 1957. In "The Two Disciplines of Scientific Psychology," Lee Cronbach argued for reestablishing the status of correlational research.

Woodworth is a prime example of the reason why functionalism was less of a school of psychology than a set of attitudes about psychology. He would be surprised to find himself in a chapter on "functionalism"—like most of his peers, he considered himself simply a psychologist. The same can said for the other psychologists featured in this chapter and for those functionalists who extended their research interests into the areas of applied psychology. Their work occupies the next chapter.

SUMMARY

Titchener's Psychology: Structuralism

- E. B. Titchener earned a Ph.D. with Wundt at Leipzig, then came to Cornell University, where he established an approach to psychology called structuralism. Its main goals were to analyze human conscious experience into its elemental units, then show how these units could be synthesized into mental processes.

- Titchener promoted an experimental/laboratory approach to psychology by writing a series of highly detailed training manuals that introduced students and instructors to the particulars of precise laboratory work and by forming a close-knit group of fellow male researchers called the Experimentalists, who met annually to share the details of their ongoing research.

- Titchener's *Text-Book of Psychology* (1909) provides the best overall summary of his system. In it he defines psychology's subject matter as experience that is dependent on the experiencing person and proposed a parallelist solution to the mind-body question. He also identified introspection as psychology's primary method and defined experiments as observations that could be repeated, isolated, and varied. He believed that introspections could yield valid data only if introspectors were highly trained and capable of the introspective habit. Training was also needed to avoid the stimulus error, a tendency to describe a meaningful stimulus instead of the direct conscious experience of the stimulus.

- Titchener identified the main elements of conscious experience as sensations, images, and affects. Sensations and images have the attributes of quality, intensity, duration, and clearness, but images aren't as clear as sensations. Affects have but two qualities—pleasantness and unpleasantness—and they lack clarity.

- Titchener's primary contribution was to promote laboratory psychology, but his system omitted major topics of interest to most American psychologists, and his method of introspection was shown to be fundamentally flawed because of its lack of objectivity.

America's Psychology: Functionalism

- Most American psychologists, influenced by evolutionary theory and a generally pragmatic attitude, were interested more in the functions of consciousness than in its structure. Functionalism was widespread, but mainly associated with the University of Chicago and Columbia University.

- The origins of functionalism are often traced to a paper on the reflex arc by John Dewey of Chicago. Dewey argued against the analytic strategy of reducing the reflex to its elements and argued instead that the reflex needed to be seen in its broader context as a coordinated system that served to adapt the organism to its environment. Dewey was known primarily for his progressive views on education, believing that students should be active learners, and for his philosophical writings on democracy.

- The earliest clear statement of the functionalist philosophy came from the 1906 APA presidential address of James Angell, who succeeded Dewey at Chicago. Angell explicitly compared structuralism and functionalism, pointing out that structuralists were more likely to ask the question "What is consciousness?" whereas functionalists were more concerned with the question "What is consciousness for?" This led them to study topics ranging from developmental to abnormal psychology and led them to be interested in individual differences and how psychology could be used to solve everyday problems.

- Harvey Carr was Angell's successor at Chicago, bringing functionalism to its maturity there. He was known for his maze learning research and for developing Chicago into one of the country's best graduate programs.

- Functionalism at Columbia was led by James McKeen Cattell and associated with two of his students, Edward Thorndike and Robert Woodworth. Thorndike became a leading educational psychologist, but in his early years he was known for his studies of cats in puzzle boxes. He proposed that learning occurred through the creation of connections between situations and responses that were successful in those situations (Law of Effect). His debate with Mills reflected a fundamental disagreement between those advocating laboratory methods and those who preferred to study animals in their daily environments.

- Woodworth is remembered for his research with Thorndike on transfer, which called traditional educational practices into question, his dynamic psychology, which replaced an S-R model with an S-O-R framework and emphasized motivational influences on behavior, and his textbook writing, especially on methodology. His "Columbia Bible" institutionalized the distinctions between experimental and correlational research and between independent and dependent variables in experimental research.

FOR FURTHER READING

FURUMOTO, L. (1988). Shared knowledge: The Experimentalists, 1904–1929. In J. G. Morawski (Ed.), *The rise of experimentation in American psychology* (pp. 94–113). New Haven, CT: Yale University Press.

Examines the origins and development of Titchener's Experimentalists, with a focus on the consequences for female psychologists, who were excluded from the group during Titchener's lifetime, and only marginally included after his death.

HEIDBREDER, E. (1933). *Seven psychologies.* New York: Appleton-Century-Crofts.

A well-known early history of psychology that gives an especially strong description of the functionalism found at Columbia, written by a woman with firsthand experience as a student of Woodworth's.

KRANTZ, D. L. (1969). The Baldwin-Titchener controversy. In D. L. Krantz (Ed.), *Schools of psychology:* *A symposium* (pp. 1–19). New York: Appleton-Century-Crofts.

Details one of several controversies involving Titchener; technically concerning an issue in reaction time research, the controversy was actually over the adequacy of Titchener's introspective procedures and the basic question of how psychology should proceed—structurally (Titchener) or functionally (Baldwin).

WINSTON, A. S. (1990). Robert Sessions Woodworth and the "Columbia Bible": How the psychological experiment was redefined. *American Journal of Psychology, 103,* 391–401.

Documents the development and impact of Woodworth's text in experimental psychology, emphasizing how the impact of his distinction between experimental and correlational research consigned the latter to second-class status in psychology.

8

APPLYING THE NEW PSYCHOLOGY

▼

> Unless our laboratory results are to give us artificialities,
> mere scientific curiosities, they must be subjected to inter-
> pretation by gradual approximation to the conditions of
> life.

John Dewey, 1900

▼

Preview

In the discussion of historiography in Chapter 1, I pointed out that E. G. Boring's classic text, *A History of Experimental Psychology*, was written in part as a way for him to return laboratory research to what he saw as its rightful place at the forefront of American psychology. Boring's concern about the threat to "pure science" was justified—American psychologists in the 1920s seemed to be obsessed with finding new ways to apply psychological principles to everyday life. Actually, interest in application existed from the earliest days of psychology in America, and this chapter will explore both the roots and the development of applied psychology. Its origins lie deeply embedded in the American character and in the economic and institutional contexts of the late nineteenth and early twentieth centuries.

This chapter will examine several examples of applied psychology, starting with the mental testing movement. We will learn how Galton's approach was replaced by the strategy of Alfred Binet of France, how Binet's methods were brought to America, and how a hereditarian view of mental ability colored interpretations of intelligence. The major American mental testers discussed will be James McKeen Cattell, who brought the Galton tradition to America where it quickly failed; Henry Goddard, who brought Binet's test to America where it quickly succeeded; Lewis Terman, developer of the Stanford-Binet IQ test and chief architect of psychology's longest-running experiment; and Robert Yerkes, a comparative psychologist at heart, whose development of the Army testing program was a major reason for Boring's fear that the spread of applied psychology was a direct threat to "pure" experimental psychology.

A second major application of psychology took place in the area of business or industrial psychology. This part of the chapter will feature the work of Hugo Münsterberg, who earned his doctorate with Wundt and came to America to run the Harvard laboratory, but quickly developed applied interests. Münsterberg made contributions to several applied areas, but is best known for his text on industrial psychology. The Original Source Excerpt for this chapter is taken from Münsterberg's industrial psychology text. The chapter concludes with brief descriptions of the work of several other industrial psychologists. Clinical psychology, another important area of application, is considered in Chapter 12.

PRESSURES TOWARD APPLICATION

In 1895, Yale psychologist E. W. Scripture published *Thinking, Feeling, Doing*, a book that was intended to explain the new experimental psychology to the general public. He wrote in the preface that he hoped his effort would "be taken as evidence of the attitude of the science in its desire to serve humanity" (Scripture, 1895, p. iii). Perhaps to hold the reader's interest, he included 209 photos and drawings in the 295 pages of text. Most of the book described the basic laboratory procedures in vogue at the time—psychophysics, reaction time, basic sensory processes, and so on. What was unusual, however, was Scripture's attempts to convince the reader that basic laboratory techniques could improve everyday life. For example, after describing laboratory research in reaction time, Scripture pointed out that the method could be used to study the "psychological elements involved in sports, gymnastics, and all sorts of athletic work" (p. 57). He then proceeded to illustrate the point by adapting the reaction procedures to measure the reaction times involved in such activities as fencing. He used a similar approach for other standard laboratory methods, as is evident from these captions describing some of the photos found in the book:

Recording a Sportsman's Unsteadiness

Everyone is Somewhat Deaf. Finding the

Threshold of Intensity

Taking an Orchestra Leader's Record [of rhythmic action] with the Electric Baton

That Scripture believed it necessary to convince the public of psychology's usefulness is just one example of the pressures for utility felt by all of the early American psychologists. These pressures were recognized explicitly by John Dewey, in his APA presidential address (1900), when he warned of the dangers inherent in emphasizing pure laboratory research. It could "give us artificialities, mere scientific curiosities [unless] subjected to interpretation by gradual approximation to the conditions of life" (p. 119).

The need for application was partly the consequence of traditional American pragmatism, combined with the progressive drive for reform that infused the late nineteenth century. In an age of dramatic technological change, Americans were becoming accustomed to the idea that science should be used to improve their lives. In the last few decades of the century they had witnessed the arrival of such inventions as telephones, the telegraph, typewriters, electric lights (and chairs), skyscrapers, barbed wire, and the kinetoscope (for showing moving pictures). Railroads had expanded so dramatically that by 1900, virtually everyone in America lived within hearing distance of a train. The 35,000 miles of track that existed at the close of the Civil War had expanded to 193,000 miles by 1903 (Cashman, 1993). In the eyes of the public at that time, technology meant progress and progress meant a better life; for psychology to gain public support, it needed to produce useful results.

In addition to the general expectation that science ought to be practical, psychologists at the turn of the century faced institutional pressures for application. Most psychologists still taught within larger departments of philosophy, for instance, and while the philosophers needed little more than an adequate library budget and space for a decent office with an armchair, the psychologists among them needed significantly greater funds for equipment and physical space for their laboratories. To justify such costs, psychologists felt pressured to show that their new science could be helpful to society.

The pressure for application created strong internal conflicts for many laboratory psychologists. Most had been trained for basic research, conditioned to value the pursuit of knowledge for its own sake. They were also aware of the dangers inherent in promising more than they could hope to deliver. Yet reality forced them to adjust their activities toward application. For one thing, while laboratories proliferated in the decades before and after 1900, those with doctorates in laboratory psychology grew at an even faster rate. Historian John O'Donnell (1985) pointed out that in 1894 the number of psychology Ph.D.'s just about matched the number of available American laboratories, thus providing adequate employment opportunities for psychological scientists. By 1900, however, the number of Ph.D.'s outnumbered labs by three to one (90 to 33 by O'Donnell's count). Thus, not everyone was going to find the ideal job—directing the psychology laboratory at a college or university. Developing expertise as an applied psychologist enhanced one's résumé.

Some psychologists embraced the idea of using their laboratory training for applied ends, but others were torn by the belief that by engaging in applied work, they were somehow "selling out" their "pure laboratory" principles. For many, the selling was literal because low academic salaries forced them to supplement their income. Taking on extra courses and teaching in the summer were shortcuts to burnout, however, and only minimally useful in easing the financial burden. Hence, many psychologists adjusted their priorities and engaged in the more remunerative activities associated with applied psychology. The experience of Harry Hollingworth illustrates the dilemma. Although he became known as a leading applied psychologist, near the end of his life he wrote that he became one only to earn a living. His "real interest, now and always, has been in the purely theoretical and descriptive problems of my science, and the books, among the twenty I have written, of which I am the proudest, are the...ones which nobody reads" (cited in Poffenberger, 1957, p. 138).

Applied psychologists contributed their expertise to the areas of education, business, medicine, and the law. An activity that occurs in all of these areas is mental testing. Because psychological testing, especially intelligence testing, is a controversial issue even today, the early history of this movement is worth examining in some detail.

THE MENTAL TESTING MOVEMENT

Mental testing has its origins in the attempts by Galton to measure individual differences. As you recall from Chapter 5, one of his goals was to create measures that could identify those best able to further his eugenic vision. He believed that intelligence was inherited and that it was important to encourage procreation among the able and discourage it among those less capable of strengthening Britain's "racial stock." Galton's attitudes were generally shared by American psychologists and later caused controversy that continues to the present. The strongest American supporter of Galton in the nineteenth century was Cattell.

Remember Psych Cattell!

JAMES MCKEEN CATTELL (1860–1944): AN AMERICAN GALTON

You met James McKeen Cattell briefly in Chapter 4. His research on reaction time in Wundt's laboratory was representative of the technique of estimating the duration of mental events by adding "complications" to the simple reaction time procedure. Cattell earned his doctorate from Wundt, although as you recall from the chapter Close-Up, he did not hold a high opinion of Wundt's research operation. Instead, Cattell was enthused by Galton's work in mental testing and the study of individual differences, and he imported the Britisher's ideas to America.

Cattell (Figure 8.1) was raised in an academic environment similar to James Angell's—both had college presidents for fathers. Cattell's father presided over Lafayette College in Easton, Pennsylvania, just across the Delaware River from New Jersey. Young Cattell was schooled at home, then sent to Lafayette at age 16. There he found the type of education mentioned at the outset of Chapter 6—an emphasis on shaping students to reflect Protestant values (Presbyterian in this case) and a curriculum based in Scottish Realist philosophy, with its focus on strengthening the productive and moral "faculties." Cattell breezed through, graduating with honors in 1880. One lasting impact of this education resulted from courses taught by Francis Marsh, a well-known philologist (i.e., he studied the nature and history of language). Marsh was a dyed-in-the-wool Baconian inductivist, believing in the importance of collecting data exhaustively, with the assumption that once enough data were at hand, significant patterns and conclusions would become clear (Sokal, 1987). Cattell embraced this strategy, which prepared him to be awed by another Baconian, Francis Galton.

After graduating from Lafayette, Cattell traveled in Europe for a time, then spent a year (1882–1883) with Hall at Johns Hopkins, where he began the reaction time research that he would continue at Leipzig. In one of his studies, he measured the times taken to identify different letters, which led him to make the practical suggestion that the shapes of those letters taking the longest time to recognize should be altered to improve their legibility. Using himself as the only subject, Cattell also studied the effects of various drugs on behavior and consciousness, later writing that the amounts of caffeine, morphine, hashish, and opium he ingested were "perhaps the largest doses ever taken without suicidal intent" (cited in Sokal, 1971, p. 623).

Cattell planned to stay in Baltimore and perhaps complete a doctorate with Hall, but after a year his fellowship was not renewed; instead, it was given to another promising student, John Dewey (Chapter 7). Cattell then returned to

Figure 8.1   James McKeen Cattell as an intense young professor at Columbia, from Popplestone and McPherson (1994).

Europe, entered studies with Wundt, and completed his doctorate in 1886. While at Leipzig, he continued his reaction time research, improving technical aspects of the method while completing important studies on mental chronometry, and in keeping with his Baconian principles, contributing extensive data on the effects of such factors as attention, practice, and fatigue on reaction time (Sokal, 1987).

After completing the doctorate, Cattell went to England and briefly studied medicine at Cambridge, but the significant outcome of his time spent there was his exposure to the anthropometric testing being done at this time by Galton. Cattell never studied formally with Galton, but the two met, and for some time after they exchanged correspondence. Cattell later wrote that Galton was the greatest man he had ever known. The two shared the fundamental inductive belief that the more one could measure, the more one would know.

Cattell returned to America in 1889, after being appointed professor of psychology at the University of Pennsylvania. The title was unusual at a time when most psychologists were still considered professors of philosophy, and indicative of the changes that were starting to occur within departments of philosophy. He quickly established a laboratory and set out to continue his reaction time studies and to bring the Galtonian testing approach to America. In an 1890 article in the British journal *Mind*, he summarized the results of testing Penn students on 10 different tests (Cattell, 1890/1948). Some were borrowed from Galton, but Cattell eliminated the strictly physical measurements (e.g., height, weight, length of arm span), which led him to call his article "Mental Tests and Measurements." With this article, Cattell coined the term **mental test.**

The article's opening sentence revealed Cattell's inductivism: "Psychology cannot attain the certainty and exactness of the physical sciences, unless it rests on a foundation of experiment and measurement" (Cattell, 1890/1948, p. 347). He did not propose any specific purpose for the tests, merely indicating in vague terms that people might "find their tests interesting" (p. 347) and that the results might somehow be "useful in regard to training, mode of life or indication of disease" (p. 347). The 10 tests, which Cattell estimated to take an hour, are summarized briefly in Table 8.1.

Cattell spent just two years at Penn, then accepted (at a still youthful age of 31) an offer

Table 8.1 Cattell's Mental Tests

In his article on mental tests, Cattell (1890) described these procedures.

1. *Dynamometer pressure.* This was a measure of grip strength, which Cattell believed to be more than just a physical measure; mental effort and concentration were involved.

2. *Rate of movement.* How quickly one's hand could move across a 50 cm interval was determined; Cattell believed that mental effort and concentration also contributed to this measure.

3. *Sensation-areas.* Two-point thresholds on the back of the closed right hand were measured.

4. *Pressure causing pain.* The narrow (5 mm in radius) tip of hard rubber was pressed into forehead until pain was reported.

5. *Least noticeable difference in weight.* This was a traditional psychophysics procedure involving the lifting of small boxes that differed slightly in weight.

6. *Reaction-time for sound.* For Cattell, this was the most reliable variety of reaction time.

7. *Time for naming colors.* Ten colored papers were pasted adjacent to each other, to be named as quickly as possible.

8. *Bisection of a 50 cm line.* A movable line had to be adjusted until it was at a perceived midpoint.

9. *Judgment of 10 sec time.* After an experimenter tapped a pencil twice, with 10 sec between, those being tested had to repeat the task

10. *Number of letters repeated on once hearing.* This was an early version of a short-term memory test, to determine how many letters could be repeated verbatim.

to head the psychology program at Columbia, where he remained until being fired in 1917. At Columbia, his testing plans became even more ambitious as he expanded the number of tests beyond the original 10 and reinstated some of the physical measurements. Within a few years he was lobbying the authorities for permission to test every incoming Columbia freshman, suggesting that the results could be useful "to determine the condition and progress of students, the relative value of different courses of study, etc." (cited in Sokal, 1987, p. 32). Initially, he was not thinking of using the tests to predict the success of Columbia students. Instead, he was keeping to his Baconian program of accumulating as much data on individual differences as possible, and then seeing what could be concluded from them. He assumed that the results would eventually reveal relationships between different measures and provide some overall indication of mental capacity.

For the remaining years of the 1890s, Cattell and his students accumulated masses of data, but the project collapsed shortly after the turn of the century. Cattell, who was mathematically inept, had learned of Galton's correlational procedures. He asked one of his graduate students, Clark Wissler, to apply the new technique to the testing results, hoping to reveal strong mathematical relationships between the measures and to relate them to academic performance. Wissler completed the correlations and the outcome was devastating for Cattell— the tests were unrelated to each other and unconnected with anything academic. A student's performance in any one class (including gym!) correlated more highly with academic performance than did *any* of Cattell's tests (Wissler, 1901/1965). Table 8.2 shows some of these correlations. As you will learn shortly, Wissler's research appeared at the time when Alfred Binet was pioneering a different approach to mental testing in France. Almost immediately, the Binet approach succeeded and the Galton/Cattell strategy passed quietly from the scene.

After the testing debacle, Cattell turned his attention away from research and toward another of his interests, the professionalizing of psychology. A charter member of the American Psychological Association, he was an active participant and in 1895, its fourth president. In 1894, he helped to launch what would become one of psychology's more prestigious journals, *Psychological Review*, and a year later he took over the editorship of the financially ailing journal *Science* and rejuvenated it. By 1910, he had made it into the most important scientific journal published in America (Sokal, 1981b).

After the turn of the century, Cattell devoted most of his time to editorial and departmental administrative work. Always outspoken, he continually irritated the Columbia administration by arguing for greater faculty participation in academic decision making and for increased academic freedom (i.e., a faculty member's right to investigate and teach about controversial topics). In 1917, he finally pushed the administration over the edge by publicly protesting the government's policy of quickly sending conscientious objectors into combat in World War I. Columbia's president accused him of treason and fired him. Cattell sued for libel and won a large settlement, but his academic career was effectively over. He continued his editorial work, however, and returned to applied psychology by founding the Psychological Corporation in 1921. Designed to be an organization of psychologist-consultants, it began at a time when American psychologists had high expectations for the applicability of their knowledge. Cattell proved to be a poor administrator, however, and although the Psychological Corporation exists today as a profitable subsidiary of a major publishing house, it barely survived the 1920s under Cattell's leadership (Sokal, 1981a).

ALFRED BINET (1857–1911): THE BIRTH OF INTELLIGENCE TESTING

The Cattell/Galton strategy for assessing individual differences relied on an assortment of physical measurements and the results of simple sen-

Table 8.2 Sample Results of Wissler's Study on Mental Testing

Correlations among various mental tests
(those in Table 8.1 plus some additional ones):

	No. of Cases	Correlation
Reaction time and color naming	118	+.15
Reaction time and association	153	+.08
Marking A's and color naming	159	+.21
Rate of movement and color naming	97	+.19

Correlations between mental tests and "college standing":

	No. of Cases	Correlation
Reaction time	227	−.02
Marking A's	242	−.09
Association	160	+.08
Naming colors	112	+.02
Logical memory	86	+.19

Correlations between performance scores for different school subjects:

	No. of Cases	Correlation
Latin and math	228	+.58
Math and rhetoric	222	+.51
German and math	115	+.52
Latin and Greek	121	+.75
Gymnasium and average grade	119	+.53

Source: Wissler (1901/1965, pp. 443–445).

sory and perceptual tasks. A completely different approach, which focused on more complex mental phenomena and used children rather than college students or adults as subjects, developed in Europe. One advocate was Hermann Ebbinghaus, the famous memory researcher (Chapter 4), who developed a **completion test** in the mid-1890s as a way to assess the effects of mental fatigue in schoolchildren. He was responding to a practical problem—it seemed to the authorities in the German city of Breslau that the five-hour uninterrupted morning school session (8:00 to 1:00) was producing "fatigue and nervous irritability" (Ebbinghaus, 1897/1965, p. 433). City leaders appointed a commission to study the problem, and its first task was to determine the precise degree to which this five-hour school day affected children. Some research in the Galtonian tradition used two-point thresholds as a measure, finding that changes in the thresholds occurred during the course of the school day. Ebbinghaus was unimpressed with the method, however, questioning the connection between skin sensitivity and school performance: "Are children who show a deterioration [in sensitivity] also to be regarded as mentally exhausted in other respects, or have they merely become incapable of performing that fixed, relatively insignificant task to which they are not accustomed?" (p. 435). If the goal was to assess mental fatigue, he argued, then the measures ought to be of cognitive activities, not sensory ones. On the assumption that an important aspect of intellectual abil-

Ebbinghaus

ity involves taking incomplete information and forming it into a comprehensible whole, Ebbinghaus came up with the idea of giving students incomplete prose passages. That is, they were shown sentences that had syllables missing from words and in some cases whole words missing from sentences. Their job was to fill in the gaps to make the sentences complete and meaningful. Ebbinghaus was able to show that his completion tests distinguished between strong and weak students, but he did not find any consistent differences in performance over the five-hour school day, which remained intact.

Ebbinghaus did not develop his testing program further, but his basic strategy was the one taken by another European, Alfred Binet of France. Like Ebbinghaus, Binet responded to an educational dilemma. We have already seen that public education increased dramatically in the United States toward the end of the century. The phenomenon was not limited to America, however—the same thing was occurring in Europe. Compulsory education, however, meant that some children would be in school even though their lack of mental ability made it impossible for them to succeed in normal classes. By the turn of the century, school officials in Paris were faced with the problem of

how to identify these children so they could be placed in what we would call special education classes today. In 1904, a commission was formed to study the problem; it included Binet, one of France's leading psychologists.

Binet's status among his peers was not always so high. In the mid-1880s, he published some dubious research on hypnosis, claiming that hysteric symptoms displayed in that state could be transferred from one side of the body to another by reversing the polarity of a magnet held next to the patient. More sober researchers demonstrated that the effects were entirely the result of suggestion, and an embarrassed Binet was forced to retract his claim in print. He gradually resurrected his reputation, however, after becoming an unpaid research assistant at the recently created Laboratory of Physiological Psychology at the Sorbonne in Paris in 1891. He was successful enough to be named director of the laboratory in just three years, a position he held until his premature death in 1911 at the age of 54.

Even before starting his work at the Sorbonne, Binet had begun making careful observations of his two young daughters (Figure 8.2). The work shaped his belief in the value of conducting detailed case studies, and it

Figure 8.2   Alfred Binet, with his wife and the two daughters whose development he studied, from Popplestone and McPherson (1994).

diff. between children + adults

contributed to his lifelong interest in studying and measuring individual differences. Binet was aware of Galton's work and used some of Galton's sensory tests on his daughters. He was surprised to discover that there didn't seem to be much difference between his daughters' scores and the scores reported for adults. Adults appeared to be superior only on tasks that involved mental processing that went beyond sensory capacity. For example, compared with adults, his daughters did quite poorly on color naming, a task requiring memory and language, but very well on color matching, a purely perceptual task. These and other similar results led Binet to conclude that Galton's sensory measures were inadequate to assess mental ability.[1] He made the key insight that differences between the intellects of children and adults could only be determined by examining the more complex higher mental processes (Fancher, 1985).

During his years at the Sorbonne, Binet developed a program of research that focused on the study of individual differences. In an important paper coauthored with his assistant Victor Henri, he contrasted his **individual psychology** with a more general psychology. The latter is concerned with the discovery of general laws that apply to some degree to everyone (e.g., repetition strengthens memory), while individual psychology "studies the properties of psychic processes that vary from individual to individual—it has to determine the various properties and then study how much and in what ways they vary with the individuals" (Binet & Henri, 1895/1965, p. 428). Studying these differences required being able to measure them, of course, and that problem led Binet directly to his attempts to develop tests of mental processes. By 1904, when Paris school officials needed a way to identify students with low ability for special classes,

Binet already had some definite ideas about what kinds of tests to use.

The term retarded did not exist as a category of mental disability in Binet's time. Instead, children with limited capacity were divided into three overlapping and poorly defined categories. *Idiots* were severely handicapped and not capable of caring for themselves; *imbeciles* were somewhat more capable but still not able to be independent; the third level included children capable of learning, but not in normal school classes. These were the children to be identified for special education, and Binet labeled them *débiles* (translation: weak ones). He was appalled at existing diagnostic criteria and determined to develop a more reliable way of differentiating these "weak" children from the normal school population. He drew on a dozen years of his research into individual psychology, and the result was the first genuine intelligence test.

The Binet-Simon Scales

1st 1905
2nd 1908
3rd 1911

Along with his research assistant Theodore Simon, Binet published the first version of his test in 1905. They revised it three years later and again in 1911, just before Binet's death. They did not begin with a preconceived definition of intelligence, from which they derived the tests to be used. Rather, they developed the test empirically by identifying two groups of students, one normal and one clearly impaired, and giving them a long series of tests that appeared to be conceptually related to intelligence, looking for tests that differentiated between the groups. They eventually produced a series of 30 tests of increasing difficulty for their original 1905 test. By the 1908 revision, the number of tests grew to 58, and Binet and Simon incorporated age levels between 3 and 13. Table 8.3 lists some of the tests at different ages (note the contrast with Cattell's tests in Table 8.1).

---

[1] Cattell, during the time he was deeply immersed in his Galtonian program of testing at Columbia in the 1890s, knew all about Binet's work but rejected the new tests of "higher" mental processes as poorly defined and not capable of sufficient quantification (Sokal, 1987).

Table 8.3 A Sample of Binet & Simon's Tests of Mental Levels

The 1908 revision of the Binet-Simon scale contained 58 different tests, arranged within 11 different age levels (3–13). Here are some of the tests.

Three Years
show eyes, nose, mouth
repeat 6-syllable sentence
name objects in picture

Five Years
copy a square
compare 2 boxes, different wts.
repeat 10-syllable sentence

Seven Years
copy written sentence
repeat five digits
indicate omissions in drawings

Nine Years
name days of week
retain 6 memories after reading
arrange five weights in order

Eleven Years
criticize absurd sentences*
place 3 given words in a sentence
give abstract definitions

Thirteen Years
differentiate word meanings
solve reversed triangle problem
solve paper cutting problem

* For example: The body of an unfortunate girl was found, cut into 18 pieces. It is thought that she killed herself.
Source: Dennis (1948).

Adding age levels was Binet's way of solving the diagnosis problem. He believed that subnormal children could be defined in terms of how far behind they were in years. Thus, a normal 5-year-old could solve the tasks at the 5-year level, but a subnormal 5-year-old might only be able to score at the 4-year level. Where the child scored was called by Binet the **mental level**, a term later mistranslated as "mental age." He believed that children scoring at a mental level two years behind their actual age, a group he

estimated to include 7% of the population, should be considered débiles and placed in special classes (Fancher, 1985). In general, Binet defined intelligence in functional terms as "the faculty of adapting oneself. To judge well, to understand well, to reason well—these are the essential wellsprings of intelligence" (Binet & Simon, 1905, cited in Fancher, 1985, p. 74).

In light of how the concept of IQ evolved over the years, it is instructive to note Binet's attitudes about intelligence and its measurement. First, he believed that intelligence was multifaceted, composed of a variety of skills. Thus, while he reduced the outcome of the tests to a single unit, the mental level, he did so reluctantly. Had he lived, he would have been disturbed at the way in which the concept of IQ came to connote a unitary concept of intelligence. Second, he believed that within broad limits, mental levels could increase with training, and he developed a set of *mental orthopedics* to help children improve their intelligence levels. Binet was scornful of the prevailing opinion of his day, derived from evolutionary thinking, that intelligence was a fixed and unchangeable trait. Third, Binet believed that his scale was useful only within the narrow educational context of identifying weak students. He would have been surprised at how quickly the tool became much more widely used, as we are about to see.

HENRY H. GODDARD (1866–1957): BINET'S TEST COMES TO AMERICA

Henry Goddard (Figure 8.3) was a product of Hall's genetic psychology at Clark University, earning a doctorate there in 1899. After teaching for a few years at West Chester Teacher's College in Pennsylvania, he accepted an invitation from the Vineland Training School for the Feeble-Minded in southern New Jersey to develop a research program there. His initial efforts reflected his training—he set up a laboratory in imitation of the one he knew at Clark and began testing the children using standard

Figure 8.3   Henry Goddard, atop one of the pyramids of Egypt, from Popplestone and McPherson (1994).

laboratory tasks similar to the ones being used by Cattell. Goddard quickly learned that he was in a new environment and that using basic sensory tasks was easier said than done, however. His notes contain entries such as this: "A boy frightened at an insignificant thing so that it took six men to hold him could not squeeze a pound on the Dynamometer tho he clearly understood what was wanted" (quoted in Popplestone & McPherson, 1984, p. 242).

In search of better methods, Goddard discovered Binet's work while on a European tour of institutions for the feebleminded in 1908. He was unimpressed with the Binet-Simon tests at first, but brought the scale back with him anyway, translated it into English, and began administering it to the Vineland children. When the Binet-Simon results matched the expectations based on other observations of the children, Goddard became a convert. At a 1910 meeting of the American Association of the Feeble-Minded, he reported the results of testing 400 Vineland children and proposed a refinement of the existing classification system, based on Binet's mental level concept, which was now being called **mental age**. Idiots would now be defined as those scoring at mental ages 1 to 2, and imbeciles would be those with mental ages between 3 and 7. As for the third category, Binet's débile, Goddard proposed a new name. These children had sometimes been called feebleminded, but that term was also used to describe the entire spectrum of mental retardation. Yet it was important to have a clear category for these children, Goddard argued, "in order to make the public understand that there is a special group of children that requires special help" (Goddard, 1910, p. 395). Goddard proposed using the term **moron**, from the Greek word moronia, which means "foolish." These would be people with mental ages between 8 and 12.[2] Goddard's creation of the term and his promotion of its use helped to legitimize psychology as a professional discipline. Morons were believed to be responsible for many of society's ills, but to the average person they appeared to be normal. To identify them, therefore, society needed the help of highly trained experts. Psychologists such as Goddard made it clear that they were the ones best prepared for the role.

Over the next few years, Goddard became a leading advocate of the Binet-Simon tests, and many others were soon using it to identify and classify those with limited mental capacity. Vineland distributed about 20,000 copies of his translated Binet-Simon test between 1910 and 1914 (Watson & Evans, 1991). Goddard's ultimate goals, however, were very different from

---

[2] These terms—idiot, imbecile, and moron—did not carry the derogatory connotation they do today. They were meant to be clinical terms used for diagnostic purposes, not names to be tossed around derisively in schoolyards.

Binet's. Unlike Binet, Goddard was a strong believer in the widely held notion that intelligence was inherited and represented a fixed quantity. Well aware of the recent rediscovery of Mendel's work on genetics, Goddard came to believe that most feeblemindedness was caused by a single recessive gene. To support his hereditarian case, he published the results of a seemingly conclusive study of the family roots of one of the Vineland children. This famous study of the "Kallikaks" is examined in detail in this chapter's Close-Up.

▶ CLOSE-UP

The Kallikaks

Goddard made his case that feeblemindedness had a genetic basis in a 117-page book published in 1912 called *The Kallikak Family: A Study in the Heredity of Feeblemindedness*. In it he described an extensive genealogical study of one of his wards at Vineland. "Deborah Kallikak" was 22 at the time and had lived at Vineland for 14 years. She had been referred to Vineland when she was eight, supposedly because she "did not get along well at school and might possibly be feebleminded" (Goddard, 1912, p. 1). In reality, the refusal of her mother's third husband to provide support for several of the woman's younger children, including Deborah, contributed to the placement. At Vineland, Deborah was tested periodically with the Binet-Simon scales, never achieving a mental age greater than 9 years. Goddard considered her to be an illustration of the person ideally suited for Vineland. Although she had learned to sew, cook, and do competent woodworking, she could barely read or do math. If Deborah were to leave the safe and controlled environment of Vineland, Goddard believed,

> …she would at once become a prey to the designs of evil men or women and would lead a life that would be vicious, immoral, and criminal, though because of her mentality she herself would not be responsible. There is nothing that she might not be led into, because she has no power of control, and all her instincts and appetites are in the direction that would lead to vice. (p. 12)

How could one account for such an individual? For Goddard the answer was simple: "'Heredity'—bad stock. We must recognize that the human family shows varying stocks or strains that are as marked and breed as true as anything in plant or animal life" (p. 12).

Goddard routinely sent workers into the field to gather information about the backgrounds of those referred to Vineland. In Deborah's case, it soon became clear that many relatives lived close by and that the family was "notorious for the number of defectives and delinquents it had produced" (p. 16). Goddard's diligent assistants were able to trace six generations and "an appalling amount of defectiveness was everywhere found" (p. 16). On the other hand, field workers occasionally found themselves among relatives who were highly educated and living in comfortable environments. Further digging yielded a tale of a family that had branched in two decidedly different directions.

It seemed that a distant relative, a soldier in the Revolutionary War, behaved like soldiers sometimes do and had a brief affair with a young "feebleminded" girl that he met in a tavern. The result was a feebleminded son, Deborah's great-great grandfather, and the start of a long line of mental deficiency, the "bad" Kallikaks. Meanwhile, the soldier, unaware of the havoc he had created by sowing his wild oats, settled down, married "a respectable girl of good family" (p. 29), and began creating the "good" Kallikaks. Because the unfortunate girl at the tavern gave her young son the father's name, both sides of family bore the same surname.

Upon examining the Kallikaks, Goddard uncovered a stark contrast in the fates of those representing the two sides of the family. On Deborah's side, Goddard's field workers identified 480 descendants and on the basis of historical records, family histories, and some direct testing of living relatives, classified 189 of them: 143 were found to be feebleminded, while only 46 were normal. On the other hand, the descendants of the soldier and his respectable bride tended to be pillars of the community: doctors, lawyers, educators, and so on. Of 496 descendants, only 3 were found to be "somewhat degenerate, but...not [mentally] defective. Two of these were alcoholic, and the other sexually loose" (p. 29).

Despite the apparent thoroughness of the Kallikak study, it was seriously flawed. The most obvious problem was Goddard's failure to recognize that the environment had any significant effect on the fates of the two sides of the family. Nutritional and health care differences alone could have accounted for the large differences between the groups in infant mortality: 82 (bad side) versus just 15 (good side). Rather than a case study of the genetics of feeblemindedness, then, the Kallikak study could just as easily represent a case study of the differential effects of poverty and privilege. Goddard himself was of course highly intelligent; his inability to believe that the environment was important in the Kallikak family histories says more about the powerful influence of the contemporary zeitgeist than it does about his individual shortcomings. Indeed, the strong belief that intelligence level was a consequence of heredity, taken for granted by most turn-of-the-century psychologists, even led Goddard to argue that the environments of the two groups were about the same.

Goddard's bias also affected the way he interpreted his data. Much of the information about family members was secondhand and sketchy, with ambiguous events interpreted according to whether the person was on one side of the family or the other. Also, Goddard forgot some basic rules of logic. For example, a feebleminded person might be led into a life of crime or vice, but the reverse does not necessarily follow, for there are lots of other reasons to become a criminal (e.g., poverty). Yet any Kallikak from the "bad" side with questionable morals was automatically classified as moronic by Goddard and his assistants. At the very beginning of the story, Goddard merely assumed that the girl in the tavern was feebleminded, apparently on the questionable grounds that she was in a tavern and let herself be seduced by a soldier! In short, the Kallikak study, rather than being good science, is a classic illustration of how preconception can influence the collection and interpretation of data.

The name Kallikak was a pseudonym, of course, constructed by Goddard to protect Deborah's identity. He chose the name from two Greek words—*Kalos*, meaning "good," and *Kakos*, meaning "bad." He thought the name nicely captured the two sides of the unfortunate Deborah's family.

Goddard's conviction about the cause of mental defectiveness led him to an obvious solution to the problem—eliminate the gene. Hence, Goddard became a confirmed eugenicist, arguing that the mentally defective should be prevented from breeding. If this social engineering could be accomplished, then feeble-mindedness could be eliminated in just a few generations. Goddard's primary recommendation was that states build more institutions like Vineland, so that idiots, imbeciles, and morons could be properly diagnosed, removed from society, and prevented from having children by being carefully monitored. He also supported other prominent psychologists, including Thorndike, Yerkes, and Terman, in recommending the sterilization of the mentally unfit, pointing out that "[t]the operation itself is almost as simple in males as having a tooth pulled. In females it is not much more serious" (Goddard, 1912, p. 108). Sterilization was a relatively new procedure, however, so Goddard advised caution until its long-term effects were better known.

Thus, Goddard had a plan for dealing with feeblemindedness in America. But what about the importation of mental deficiency? In the early years of the new century, there was growing concern about an apparent threat to the American gene pool—rampant immigration. Goddard had a solution to this problem also.

Goddard and the Immigrants

The United States has always been a nation of immigrants, but a constant feature of American political life is that immigrants who have lived in America for a few generations often seek to restrict new immigration. This was true at the turn of the century when the number of immigrants increased dramatically, and these "new" immigrants seemed to be decidedly inferior to "old" immigrants. Throughout most of the nineteenth century, the majority of immigrants came from western and northern Europe. For instance, 788,992 hopeful men, women, and children arrived in 1882; of these 87% were from Germany, Great Britain, and Scandinavia, whereas a mere 13% were from southern and eastern European countries such as Italy, Poland, and Russia. By 1907, however, when the total number of arrivals grew to 1,285,349, the proportions had reversed—just over 80% now came from southern and eastern Europe (data from Cashman, 1993). With this shift came increased fears among those whose ancestors had arrived from northern Europe about the "quality" of the new immigrants. The old immigrants, generally Anglo-Saxon, Protestant, and at least moderately well-educated, contrasted strongly with the new immigrants, who were generally poor and uneducated, had larger families, were more culturally diverse, and were more likely to be Catholic or Jewish. Most Americans simply disagreed with the sentiments of the poet Emma Lazarus, who wrote that the Statue of Liberty, unveiled in 1886, symbolized a welcome to "your tired, your poor, your huddled masses yearning to breathe free."

New York was the main entry point for European immigrants and to handle the growing numbers of huddled masses, the federal government in 1892 built a large immigration station on Ellis Island, a mile southwest of Manhattan and within sight of the Statue of Liberty. Immigrants arriving there, as many as 10,000 a day in the early 1900s, had to go through a series of evaluations before being allowed to enter the country. Most immigrants passed through the Ellis Island inspections in a few hours, but about 20% were held for more detailed evaluations, and 1 to 2% were not allowed into the country (Schlereth, 1991). To be admitted, immigrants had to show that they were free from contagious diseases and mental illness, physically capable of working, not completely destitute, and not mentally defective. This latter criterion was difficult to measure, however, and Ellis Island examiners were concerned that "high-grade" defectives were slipping through the system.

It was in this context that Goddard, anxious to demonstrate the diagnostic usefulness of the Binet tests, appeared on the scene. He first visited Ellis Island in 1910, then returned with two research assistants in 1912. With one of his assistants picking out immigrants who "looked" defective and a second administering some of the Binet tests, Goddard contended that his team could quickly identify mental defectives with about a 90% accuracy. In one instance, Goddard's workers selected a young boy suspected of being defective and gave him the test with the aid of an interpreter. The boy scored an 8 on the Binet-Simon scale. Goddard reported that the "interpreter said 'I could not have done that when I came to this country,' and seemed to think the test unfair. We convinced him that the boy was defective" (Goddard, 1913, p. 105). Clearly, because of his naive faith in the technology of testing, Goddard failed to consider that the immigrants were undoubtedly intimidated and confused by the entire Ellis Island experience and that they probably failed to understand why they were being asked to complete these odd tests.

Officials at Ellis Island were impressed with the testing and invited Goddard to expand his operation. In 1913, two female assistants spent two and a half months at Ellis Island. Through interpreters, they tested 165 Russian, Hungarian, Jewish, and Italian immigrants on the Binet-Simon and several other tests. Goddard found that a disturbingly large proportion, about 80%, scored at a mental level of 12 or below (i.e., morons). Even after readjusting the scores to take cultural factors into account, he estimated that about 40% of the sample was feebleminded and concluded that "one can hardly escape the conviction that the intelligence of the average 'third class' immigrant is low, perhaps of moron grade" (Goddard, 1917, p. 243).

As a result of Goddard's work, mental testing became a part of the screening process at Ellis Island, contributing to an increase in the percentage of deportations over the next few years. Compared with the average number of deportations in the preceding five years, those occurring as the result of "mental deficiency" increased by 350% in 1913 and 570% in 1914 (Gould, 1981). No accurate estimate exists, but it is safe to say that thousands of hopeful immigrants, yearning to breathe free, were nonetheless sent back to Europe because they performed poorly on the Binet-Simon scales.

As for Goddard, he only remained at Vineland for a few more years. In 1918, the state of Ohio hired him to direct their Bureau of Juvenile Research, which had just been established to deal with the problem of juvenile delinquency. Four years later he became pro-

fessor of abnormal and clinical psychology at the Ohio State University where he remained until his retirement in 1938. While there, he broadened his interests by studying children at the other end of the spectrum from those at Vineland—the so-called gifted students. These later experiences led him to write a remarkable paper in 1928, in which he reversed many of his earlier views. He decided that a mental age of 12 did not necessarily mean feeblemindedness, that many of those diagnosed as morons could function in society and did not need to be institutionalized, and that the danger of them producing feebleminded offspring had been overstated. He considered the problem of the moron to be primarily one of education and argued that "when we get an education that is entirely right there will be no morons who cannot manage themselves and their affairs and compete in the struggle for existence" (Goddard, 1928, p. 224). By the end of his career, then, Goddard had moved closer to Binet's original vision for educating those of marginal ability.

LEWIS M. TERMAN (1877–1956): INSTITUTIONALIZING IQ

Like Goddard, Lewis Terman was a product of Hall's psychology program at Clark University. He arrived there in 1903, just after finishing a master's degree at Indiana University, not far from his boyhood home on a large farm in the Hoosier State. Indiana was rather like a midwestern branch of Clark University—its philosophy department featured three psychologists, William Bryan, Ernest Lindley, and John Bergström, who were all Clark graduates. In their classes, young Terman "became fired with the ambition to become a professor of psychology and to contribute something myself to the science" (Terman, 1932, p. 310). Lindley was especially influential and in a seminar with him, Terman wrote extensive papers on "degeneracy" and "great men." The projects brought him in contact with the writings of

Binet and Galton, and began to foreshadow his life's work (Minton, 1988). At Clark, his interests in intelligence and its testing only deepened, and his doctoral dissertation compared the mental and physical abilities of 14 preadolescent boys, "seven bright and seven dull" (Terman, 1906, p. 314). The former group outperformed the latter on all of the mental tests, which included Binet-like procedures such as problem solving, language, and memory, whereas the dull group did better on some motor coordination tasks. Perhaps influenced by his strong attraction to Galton's ideas, Terman believed that his study supported "the relatively greater importance of endowment over training, as a determinant of an individual's intellectual rank" (p. 372). Terman never wavered in his belief that heredity was the prime determiner of intelligence.

Terman suffered from periodic bouts with tuberculosis, both before and during his Clark years, which led him to search for warm-climate employment after completing his doctorate in 1905. He spent a year as a school superintendent in San Bernadino, California, then landed an academic position, teaching child psychology and pedagogy at Los Angeles State Normal School (which later became UCLA). The big break came in 1910, when he was asked to move north to Palo Alto and join the faculty at Stanford University. The opening was sudden and unexpected—Terman replaced his former Indiana teacher, John Bergström, who went to Stanford in 1908, but died two years later at age 42 (Capshew & Hearst, 1980). Within 12 years, Terman was chairing the psychology department, which he built into one of the premier departments in the country. Terman, three of his faculty recruits, and four of the doctoral students there during his tenure became APA presidents (Hilgard, 1957). He was much admired as a teacher, especially for the stimulating Monday evening seminars held at his home, recreating the atmosphere he had experienced as a student in Hall's famous Monday seminars. Terman retired from Stanford in 1941, but remained

professionally active until his death in 1956, just a few weeks before his eightieth birthday. His legacy to psychology includes (a) developing one of the world's best-known IQ tests, and (b) conducting the longest-running psychology study of all time.

The Stanford-Binet IQ Test

We have seen that Goddard translated the Binet-Simon scales into English and first introduced them to America. Terman, however, went far beyond translation, accomplishing a revision and the first standardization of the test. On the basis of some research with local schoolchildren, he determined that some of the Binet tests were too easy for young children and too hard for older children. For instance, average 5-year-olds often tested at a mental age greater than 5, while average 10-year-olds tested at a mental age less than 10. Terman added some new tests, including some of the ones created for his dissertation, revised others, and eliminated a few. Between 1910 and 1914, he standardized his test, using about 2300 subjects, mostly children and adolescents from middle-class environments, but also about 400 adults. He eventually arrived at a series of 90 test items, compared with 54 in Binet's final (1911) version. Along with a complete set of norms that resulted from his standardization effort, Terman published in 1916 what he called the Stanford Revision of the Binet-Simon test. It became known as the Stanford-Binet, and it quickly dominated the market and earned Terman a healthy income in royalties. Terman completely revised and restandardized it again in 1937. In a more recent version, it remains perhaps the best known individual test of intelligence.

The 1916 Stanford-Binet included a concept that Binet would have found disturbing—IQ. Terman borrowed it from a leader of the testing movement in Germany, William Stern. Stern had pointed out that an average 5-year-old should score at a mental level of 5, while a very bright 5-year-old might achieve a mental level of 6 or higher, and a slow 5-year-old could score lower than 5. He suggested that mental ability be capsulized in a "mental quotient" that represented the relationship between mental age and chronological age, found by dividing the former by the latter. For Terman, the idea meshed nicely with his norming procedures and with his growing belief that intelligence was a unitary trait. He changed Stern's "mental quotient" to **intelligence quotient** or IQ, multiplied the ratio by 100 to lose the decimal point, and built it into the revision. With the 1916 Stanford-Binet, then, the IQ was born. Three 5-year-olds with mental ages of 4, 5, and 6 would have IQs of 80, 100, and 120, respectively. The message was clear—mental capacity could be represented in a single number.

Terman Studies the Gifted

Binet's original purpose was to identify children in need of special training. Terman went beyond this vision, however, and believed that his IQ test could identify special children at both ends of the continuum. His long-standing interest in students at the upper end of the scale led him to design his best-known research, a study of giftedness. His original intent was to identify a group of talented children, then follow up on their lives at some later time to see if their promise had been fulfilled. Instead, the project took on a life of its own, continuing long after Terman himself died. It became psychology's longest-running longitudinal study.

In formulating his plans for the study, Terman was motivated by his hereditarian ideas about intelligence and his strong belief that America should be a **meritocracy**. That is, he believed its leaders should be those shown to be capable of leading. IQ testing, he suggested, would be a good way to identify such people; with the possible exception of one's morals, he once wrote, "nothing about an individual [was] as important as his IQ" (quoted in Minton, 1988, p. 99). Terman's vision of a true democracy meant equal opportunity, but only for those with the ability to profit from their opportunities. Those with low IQs, which Terman referred to as "democracy's ballast" (p. 99), could also reach fulfillment in life if properly identified, trained, and placed in jobs suitable for them. Thus, large-scale IQ testing could produce a classification system that would result in different types of education for different levels of ability. Terman believed this system would "go far toward insuring that every pupil, whether mentally superior, average, or inferior, shall have a chance to make the most of whatever abilities nature has given to him" (quoted in Minton, 1987, p. 102).

With this ideal meritocracy in mind, Terman set out to identify gifted children in 1921. His aim was to select the top 1% of all California schoolchildren, but because of logistical and financial problems, his team of field workers concentrated on just a few large and medium-sized urban areas. Teachers were asked to identify the three smartest children and the youngest child in their classes. These children were then tested with a group intelligence test and a brief version of the Stanford-Binet. Those scoring highest were given the full Stanford-Binet.

The outcome was a group of 1470 children, 824 boys and 646 girls. Most were in elementary school, but the group included 444 from junior or senior high school (sample size data from Minton, 1988, pp. 114–115). The average IQ was 151 for the younger children and 143 for the high schoolers. Interestingly enough, the student most likely to be chosen for the study was not one of the three smartest identified by teachers in a particular class, but the youngest. The sampling procedures appeared to be reasonable, but the resulting sample was not representative. Students tended to be middle- to upper-class, Protestant, and white, and their fathers tended to hold professional rather than working-class occupations. Jewish children were also overrepresented, while nonwhites and the poor were underrepresented (Cravens, 1992). The bias occurred in a number of subtle ways, from teacher selections to a reluctance of field workers to go to some schools in urban areas. For example, one of Terman's workers omitted 14 Los Angeles schools that had been set aside by authorities "to handle children who had been found guilty of minor offenses" (Minton, 1988, p. 114).

Having selected a sample, Terman's team compiled considerable information for each child, the result being the 600-page *Genetic Studies of Genius: Mental and Physical Traits of a Thousand Gifted Children* (Terman, 1925). Terman retested the group in the late 1920s and conducted major follow-ups 25 (Terman & Oden, 1947) and 35 years (Terman & Oden, 1959) after the original testing. After Terman died, Robert Sears, a member of the gifted group and by then a distinguished research psychologist himself, took over the project. He produced five additional follow-ups between 1960 and 1986 and was preparing *The Later Maturity of the Gifted* when he died in 1989 (Cronbach, Hastorf, Hilgard, & Maccoby, 1990).

The traditional view of gifted children is that while they are intellectually superior, they are physically weak, socially inferior, and they burn out at a young age, never quite fulfilling their childhood promise. Terman's research questioned all aspects of this stereotype, however. In follow-up after follow-up, his group appeared to be not just smarter than others but more successful, productive, well-adjusted, and physically healthy. Most entered professional life, but this was less likely to occur for the females in the group. Although more likely to be in a career than their nongifted peers, the women of Terman's group tended to be frustrated by the lack of opportunities for women in America at mid-century (Minton, 1988).

One final aspect of the study worth noting is Terman's devotion to the group and the corresponding loyalty of those who came to call themselves "Termites." A typical problem in longitudinal research is **attrition**—as time goes by, subjects drop out of the study for a variety of reasons. Attrition was not a problem

for Terman, however. Of those subjects who were alive for the follow-up studies done after 10, 25, and 35 years, the percentages of those participating were 92, 98, and 93, respectively (Minton, 1988). Terman corresponded regularly with hundreds of his Termites and cared very much about the progress of their lives. This is not too surprising, of course, for in Terman's mind, these were the meritorious people holding the key to America's future.

ROBERT M. YERKES (1876–1956): THE ARMY TESTING PROGRAM

You met Robert Yerkes briefly in Chapter 1, as an example of how an institutional context could influence the careers of early psychologists. As you recall, Yerkes began his academic career as a promising comparative psychologist at Harvard, his love of animals tracing from his childhood on a farm (Carmichael, 1957). But Harvard's interest in comparative psychology was never great—research in the topic was expensive, the laboratory smelled, and it didn't seem especially relevant or useful (Reed, 1987). Thus, Yerkes was pressured to produce more on the "human side" if he expected to advance through the ranks. Although comparative psychology remained his first love, he compromised by writing a mainstream introductory textbook that centered on the study of consciousness and even included introspective exercises at the end of each chapter (Yerkes, 1911). He further broadened his credentials by working part-time in the Psychopathic Department of Boston State Hospital from 1913 to 1917, where he first became familiar with intelligence testing by administering Binet tests to patients and improving the scoring system. Harvard still did not promote him, however, even though his reputation among peers was sufficient to get him elected to the presidency of the American Psychological Association in 1917. In that same year, perhaps tired of waiting for Harvard to promote him, he accepted an offer to chair the psychology department at the University of Minnesota. Fate inter-

This year marked the origins of the Army testing program during World War I that gave great impetus to applied psychology in the United States.

These events also occurred:

- A 100-in. reflecting telescope was installed at Mount Wilson, California
- Four women were arrested for picketing the White House on behalf of women's suffrage, and sentenced to six months in jail
- The actor Charlie Chaplin's annual salary reached $1 million
- The Allies executed dancer Mata Hari as a German spy
- Literacy requirements for U.S. citizenship were passed, over President Wilson's veto
- In World War I, German forces withdrew on the Western Front, a February revolution occurred in Russia, and Pershing arrived in Paris to lead American troops
- These persons were born:

    John Fitzgerald Kennedy, U.S. President

    I. M. Pei, Chinese-American architect

    Andrew Wyeth, American artist

- These people died:

    William F. ("Buffalo Bill") Cody, American cowboy and entrepreneur

    Auguste Rodin, French sculptor

vened, however, and Yerkes never made it to the upper Midwest.

In April of 1917, while Yerkes was cohosting a meeting of Titchener's Experimentalists (Chapter 7 Close-Up) at Harvard, the United States declared war on Germany and entered World War I. The group held an impromptu meeting to discuss how psychology might help the war effort and as APA president, Yerkes naturally took the lead. He later said that he had no real desire to take on the Army project, but did so out of a sense of duty (Dewsbury, 1996). Nonetheless, he quickly demonstrated superb organizational and persuasive skills, convincing the Army that psychological testing could aid the war effort.

By August of 1916, the Army had commissioned Yerkes as a major and placed him in charge of an elite group of psychologists (including Terman) charged with preparing mental tests. Their task was daunting. For one thing, the sheer number of people to be examined meant that traditional Binet-style testing, with examiners giving tests one at a time, had to be replaced by group testing procedures. Second, although part of the goal was in the Binet tradition of identifying those who were unfit, in this case for Army service rather than for normal schooling, Yerkes also had more ambitious plans. He hoped to create tests that would enable the Army to identify those with special skills so they could be placed where they could best serve the cause. For instance, he hoped to be able to select the best candidates for officer training. The tests were pilot tested at four Army camps in October and by the end of December, the Surgeon General decreed that psychological testing would be extended to all new recruits. The program was in full swing in early 1918 and by the time the war ended in November of that year, Yerkes and his team had tested 1,726,966 soldiers (Yoakum & Yerkes, 1920).

Army Alpha and Army Beta

Because nearly 30% of recruits could not "read and understand newspapers and write letters home" (Yoakum & Yerkes, 1920, p. 12), Yerkes developed two versions of his test. Recruits literate enough to read and follow written directions were given the **Army Alpha** test, while **Army Beta** was created for those with reduced literacy. Each took just under an hour to administer. Any soldier failing Alpha was to be given Beta, and those failing Beta were supposed to be tested individually. Logistical problems and time pressures usually eliminated both levels of retesting, however. Army Alpha comprised eight different tests, whereas Army Beta had seven (see Table 8.4). Soldiers given Army Alpha were told at the outset that the purpose of the test was to "see how well you can remember, think, and carry out what you are told to do. We are not looking for crazy peo-

ple. The aim is to help find out what you are best fitted to do in the Army" (Yoakum & Yerkes, 1920, p. 53). By contrast, those taking Army Beta were simply told to follow instructions and "ask no questions" (p. 82); they were not told why they were taking the exam.

To get an idea of what confronted soldiers, consider the first test in Army Alpha: the directions or commands test. Soldiers had the score sheet in Figure 8.4 in front of them and were told that in the Army it was important to be able to follow orders. The test would determine how well they could do so. For each of the 12 items, they were ordered to make specific marks on the page and given just a few seconds to do so. Here are three of the commands:

> 4. Attention! Look at 4. When I say "go" make a figure 1 in the space which is in the circle but not in the triangle or square, and also make a figure 2 in the space which is in the triangle and circle, but not in the square.—Go! (Allow not over 10 seconds)
>
> 7. Attention! Look at 7. When I say "go" *cross out* the letter just before C and also draw a line *under* the second letter before H—Go! (Allow not over 10 seconds)
>
> 11. Attention! Look at 11. When I say "go" draw a line through every even number that is not in a square, and also through every odd number that is in a square with a letter.—Go! (Allow not over 25 seconds) (Yoakum & Yerkes, 1920, pp. 55–56)

Table 8.4 Subtests for Army Alpha and Army Beta

Army Alpha Subtests	Army Beta Subtests
Commands Test	Maze Test
Arithmetic Problems	Cube Analysis
Practical Judgment	X-O series
Synonym-Antonym	Digit-Symbol
Disarranged Sentences	Number Checking
Number Series Completion	Pictorial Completion
Analogies	Geometrical Construction
Information	

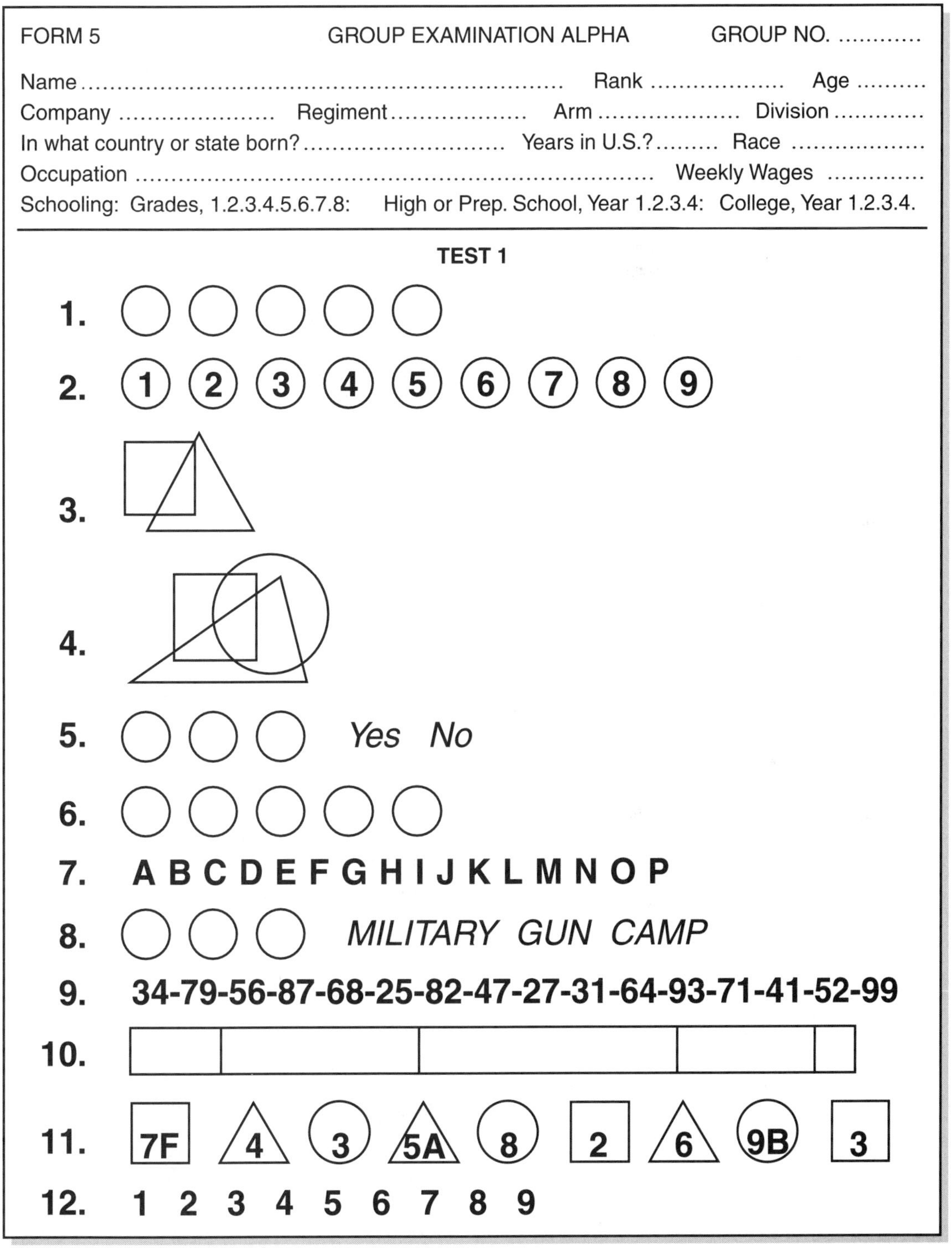

FORM 5   GROUP EXAMINATION ALPHA   GROUP NO. ....

Name... Rank .... Age ....

Company .... Regiment.................... Arm .... Division ....

In what country or state born?........................... Years in U.S.?......... Race ....

Occupation .... Weekly Wages ....

Schooling: Grades, 1.2.3.4.5.6.7.8:   High or Prep. School, Year 1.2.3.4: College, Year 1.2.3.4.

TEST 1

1. ○ ○ ○ ○ ○

2. ① ② ③ ④ ⑤ ⑥ ⑦ ⑧ ⑨

3. [square with overlapping triangle]

4. [square, circle, triangle overlapping with line]

5. ○ ○ ○   *Yes   No*

6. ○ ○ ○ ○ ○

7. **A B C D E F G H I J K L M N O P**

8. ○ ○ ○   *MILITARY GUN CAMP*

9. **34-79-56-87-68-25-82-47-27-31-64-93-71-41-52-99**

10. [rectangular boxes divided into segments]

11. 7F △4 ③ △5A ⑧ 2 △6 ⑨B 3

12. **1 2 3 4 5 6 7 8 9**

Figure 8.4   Test on following orders, a part of Army Alpha, from Yoakum and Yerkes (1920).

Test 1

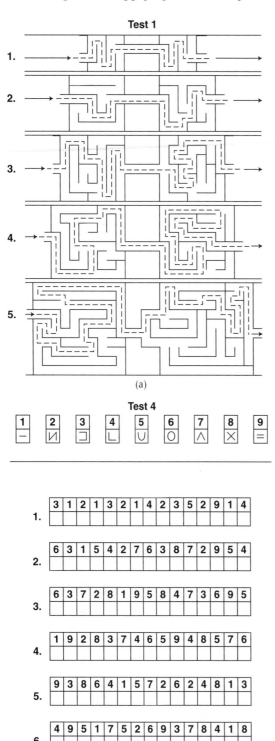

(a)

Test 4

1	2	3	4	5	6	7	8	9
—	N	⊐	L	∪	O	∧	✕	=

1.

3	1	2	1	3	2	1	4	2	3	5	2	9	1	4

2.

6	3	1	5	4	2	7	6	3	8	7	2	9	5	4

3.

6	3	7	2	8	1	9	5	8	4	7	3	6	9	5

4.

1	9	2	8	3	7	4	6	5	9	4	8	5	7	6

5.

9	3	8	6	4	1	5	7	2	6	2	4	8	1	3

6.

4	9	5	1	7	5	2	6	9	3	7	8	4	1	8

(b)

Figure 8.5   Subtests of Army Beta included (a) mazes, (b) digit-symbol, and (c) picture completion, from Yoakum and Yerkes (1920).

Test 6

(c)

Three of the Army Beta tests can be found in Figure 8.5. In the maze test, recruits had to draw a line to negotiate the maze accurately—the dashed lines are the correct answers. In test 4, digit-symbol, the symbols paired with each number had to be written into the blank spaces. In test 6, recruits were instructed to draw in the missing elements of each picture. They had two minutes to complete as many mazes and digit-symbols as they could, and three minutes to do the picture completion test.

Despite the fact that close to two million soldiers were given the tests, the war ended before they could be used effectively by the Army. Indeed, most historians conclude that the Army derived little if any benefit from the enterprise (e.g., Kevles, 1968). During the war, many within the military welcomed the tests as more efficient than traditional methods for placing soldiers. Yet others stubbornly refused to use the test results, some local commanders didn't cooperate with the examiners giving the tests, and testing conditions were often so poor as to render the results meaningless. At one point the Secretary of War polled camp commanders about the value of the testing program and most of the 100 responses were negative (Gould, 1981). That the Army discontinued the testing shortly after the war ended suggests that its top brass were less than impressed with the program's utility. On the other hand, the testing program laid the groundwork for a scientific approach to Army personnel work and a number of younger officers saw its potential benefits. And the program certainly gave psychology a boost. As one historian put it, "[w]hile testing may not have made a significant contribution to the war, the war had made a significant contribution to testing and as a by-product to psychology in general" (Minton, 1988, p. 74).

Yerkes believed the project showed that mental testing could be applied on a large scale, and after the war he spared no effort to propagandize the benefits of testing. Other psychologists soon joined in. Terman, for instance, claimed that testing had "brought psychology down from the clouds and...transformed the 'science of trivialities' into the 'science of human engineering'" (Terman, 1924, p. 106). Yerkes and Terman joined with other prominent psychologists (e.g., Thorndike) to create the "National Intelligence Tests" in 1920. The advertisement reproduced in Figure 8.6 shows how the alleged success of the Army testing program was used explicitly to promote group testing in schools.

The 1920s soon became known as "the heyday of the testing movement" (Goodenough, 1949, quoted in Dennis, 1948, p. 23), as mental testing spread into schools, business, and industry. Universities began using test scores to screen applicants, and informal tests of charac-

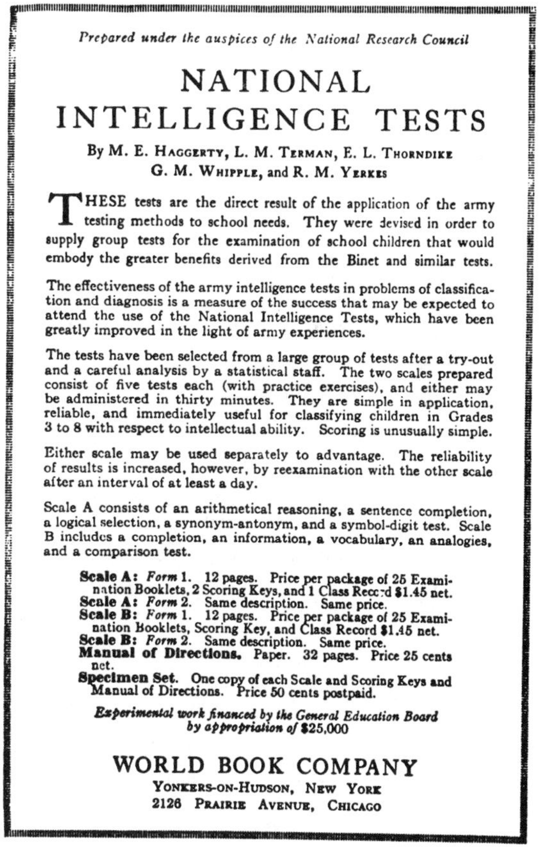

Prepared under the auspices of the National Research Council

NATIONAL
INTELLIGENCE TESTS

By M. E. Haggerty, L. M. Terman, E. L. Thorndike
G. M. Whipple, and R. M. Yerkes

THESE tests are the direct result of the application of the army testing methods to school needs. They were devised in order to supply group tests for the examination of school children that would embody the greater benefits derived from the Binet and similar tests.

The effectiveness of the army intelligence tests in problems of classification and diagnosis is a measure of the success that may be expected to attend the use of the National Intelligence Tests, which have been greatly improved in the light of army experiences.

The tests have been selected from a large group of tests after a try-out and a careful analysis by a statistical staff. The two scales prepared consist of five tests each (with practice exercises), and either may be administered in thirty minutes. They are simple in application, reliable, and immediately useful for classifying children in Grades 3 to 8 with respect to intellectual ability. Scoring is unusually simple.

Either scale may be used separately to advantage. The reliability of results is increased, however, by reexamination with the other scale after an interval of at least a day.

Scale A consists of an arithmetical reasoning, a sentence completion, a logical selection, a synonym-antonym, and a symbol-digit test. Scale B includes a completion, an information, a vocabulary, an analogies, and a comparison test.

Scale A: *Form* 1. 12 pages. Price per package of 25 Examination Booklets, 2 Scoring Keys, and 1 Class Record $1.45 net.
Scale A: *Form* 2. Same description. Same price.
Scale B: *Form* 1. 12 pages. Price per package of 25 Examination Booklets, Scoring Key, and Class Record $1.45 net.
Scale B: *Form* 2. Same description. Same price.
Manual of Directions. Paper. 32 pages. Price 25 cents net.
Specimen Set. One copy of each Scale and Scoring Keys and Manual of Directions. Price 50 cents postpaid.

Experimental work financed by the General Education Board by appropriation of $25,000

WORLD BOOK COMPANY
Yonkers-on-Hudson, New York
2126 Prairie Avenue, Chicago

Figure 8.6 Advertisement for National Intelligence Tests for schoolchildren, based on the Army tests, from Gould, 1981.

ter, personality, and ability began appearing in popular magazines. A writer in *Harper's* magazine, referring to the mental test as "this bright little device," noted wryly that "[i]n practically every walk of life…[it was] being introduced as a means of finding out what people don't know, and for what particular business they are specially unfitted" (quoted in Dennis, 1948, pp. 23–24). The glow soon faded, though, as the proponents and detractors of testing launched an acrimonious debate about the nature of intelligence and IQ that remains with us today. Before proceeding with the controversies over testing, however, let us close the book on Robert Yerkes.

After the war, Yerkes turned down the prewar offer from Minnesota, and remained in Washington as an administrator in the National Research Council, which had just been organized to promote science in America. In 1924, he returned to academia when his good friend, fellow "Harvard man," and now university president, James Angell, recruited him for the newly created Institute of Psychology at Yale. There he returned to his first love, the study of animal behavior, and began a campaign to create a research center to study primate behavior. The eventual result was the Anthropoid Experiment Station of Yale University, which opened in 1930 in Orange Park, Florida, near Jacksonville. When Yerkes retired in 1941, the center was renamed the Yerkes Laboratories of Primate Biology. It moved to Atlanta in 1965, and today the Yerkes Primate Center is perhaps the leading center of primate research in the world (Dewsbury, 1996).

THE CONTROVERSY OVER INTELLIGENCE

As leaders of the mental testing movement, Goddard, Terman, and Yerkes shared the beliefs that (a) mental capacity was primarily the result of genetic inheritance, (b) environment had little if any effect on this overall ability, (c) intelligence might be composed of a variety of skills, but underlying all of them was a single, unitary capability,[3] and (d) this capability was what intelligence tests measured. In the 1920s, the tests were at the forefront of the previously mentioned "heyday" of mental testing. By the middle of the decade, however, mental testing was under assault from several directions and Anne Anastasi, author of the best-known modern textbook on testing, would later write that "[t]he testing boom of the 1920s probably did more to retard than to advance the progress of testing" (Anastasi, 1992, p. 17). What happened?

An early sign of trouble was in Yerkes's 1921 report summarizing the Army testing program. Buried in the 890-page mass of data was this statement: "It appears that the intelligence of the principal sample of the white draft, when transmuted from Alpha and Beta exams into terms of mental age, is about 13 years" (Yerkes, 1921, p. 785). Combining the widely-held belief that the mental age of an average adult should be 16 and the Goddard scale of deficiency that considered those scoring between 8 and 12 to be morons, this was disturbing news indeed. If the Army testing program was valid and the sample representative (at 1.7 million it was certainly big enough), then it appeared that the United States was becoming a nation of morons. Even though critics later pointed out that problems like the abysmal testing conditions and the failure to implement the retesting scheme made the results virtually impossible to interpret, the report reinforced existing biases and created alarm. Could the fears of the eugenicists be coming true? Could all those years of unrestricted immigration and the failure to control the breeding of feebleminded

---

[3] In this regard, most Americans agreed with the British psychologist/statistician Charles Spearman, who argued that although separate intellectual skills might exist, underlying all of them was a unitary intellectual ability, which he called "g," for "general" intelligence.

people be reducing the overall intelligence of America? To add fuel to the fire, Yerkes observed in the *Atlantic Monthly* that on the basis of the Army tests, no more than 10% of Americans "are intellectually capable of meeting the requirements for a bachelor's degree" (quoted in Degler, 1991, p. 168).

Yerkes also presented data on intelligence as a function of national origin and found higher scores for native-born Americans. And in support of prevailing fears about the new immigrants, he reported that for soldiers of northern European origin, mental age was higher than for those with roots in southern or eastern Europe. The average mental age for this latter group was about 11. Carl Brigham, who participated in the Army project, highlighted the immigrant findings in his *A Study of American Intelligence* (1923), and warned that continued mass immigration from southern and eastern Europe, combined with the tendency of these groups to have large families, would threaten the national IQ. In a theme that would echo ominously in Germany in the 1930s, Brigham suggested that the fair-haired Nordic races were inherently superior to others.

All of this was happening at a time when the general political climate was characterized by an increasing **nativism**, a defensive nationalism that views all outsiders with suspicion and alarm. It was exacerbated in the 1920s by several factors. Immigration, which had declined during the war years, was surging again. The new immigrants, already disliked, seemed increasingly unwilling to join into the mythical American melting pot. They retained their own communities and language, and a large proportion had no intention of remaining in America—their goal was to make a sufficient amount of money to return home.[4] In addition, with the 1917 Bolshevik revolution in Russia

creating headlines, the 1920s witnessed the first genuine "Red Scare," and Americans often viewed immigrants from Russia as subversives rather than refugees from the harsh new Soviet regime. Thus, it came as no surprise when Congress passed the National Origins Act of 1924, which established immigration quotas with reference to 1890 data (i.e., before the shift from old to new immigration patterns). The American psychologists who led the mental testing movement have sometimes been portrayed as leading the charge for restrictive immigration, but they reflected the context of their times as much as they contributed to it.

While fears about immigration were widespread, not everyone was willing to accept the beliefs about IQ held by Goddard, Terman, Yerkes, and others (e.g., Thorndike). Although the popular press cranked out articles about the dangers of immigration that suggested unity among social scientists, there was in fact considerable disagreement within the professional community (Satariano, 1979). Noted anthropologist Franz Boas, for instance, was a strong critic of the hereditarian view, arguing instead for the effect of culture on mental abilities (Degler, 1991). Within psychology, behaviorism (Chapters 10 and 11), with its emphasis on the powerful effects of conditioning, was beginning to have a moderating effect, shifting opinion from nature to nurture. Furthermore, numerous psychologists (e.g., Freeman, 1922) urged caution when interpreting the Army data, pointed out that mental testing was still in its infancy and that the effects of upbringing on IQ scores could not be ignored when interpreting IQ data. In general, before behaviorism began shifting psychologists toward the nurture side of the issue, psychologists and biologists tended toward hereditarian explanations of mental capacity, whereas anthropologists and

---

[4] This was not the outcome for Nicola Sacco and Bartolomeo Vanzetti, immigrants from Italy, who were executed in 1927 after being found guilty of a payroll robbery. They were originally arrested because they "looked suspicious," and when witnesses were asked to identify them, no lineup was used. Rather, Sacco and Vanzetti were forced to pose as bandits (Davidson & Lytle, 1982).

sociologists leaned toward an environmental emphasis (Hilgard, 1987).

The most visible debate about intelligence and IQ testing in the 1920s resulted from a series of six articles in the *New Republic*, by its founder, the noted columnist Walter Lippmann, and replies in the same magazine from Terman. Neither Lippmann nor Terman minced words. Conceding that the tests might have some value in placing students or selecting employees, Lippmann ridiculed the notion that the tests were measuring innate general "intelligence," arguing that "[w]e cannot measure intelligence when we have never defined it, and we cannot speak of its hereditary basis after it has been indistinguishably fused with a thousand educational and environmental influences from the time of conception to school age" (Lippmann, 1922a, p. 10). Also, Lippmann was outraged at the possibility that testing could forever doom a child who happened not to perform very well for one 50-minute segment of his or her life. With the implications of Terman's meritocracy firmly in mind, he wrote that the result could be "an intellectual caste system in which the task of education had given way to the doctrine of predestination and infant damnation" (1922b, p. 298). Terman, who Lippmann mentioned by name when likening testing to other "fads" such as phrenology and palm reading, responded in an article that did not really answer Lippmann, but merely dismissed him as a rank amateur who should mind his own business and let the professionals deal with these complex issues. It was not one of Terman's better moments, part of a basic problem he experienced with being criticized (especially by non-scientists), and he later regretted writing the article (Minton, 1988). Indeed, although Terman is known as one of the most vocal proponents of the hereditarian view of intelligence, near the end of his life he had some second thoughts. In an autobiographical chapter for the series *A History of Psychology in*

Autobiography, Terman wrote that differences in IQ could never be completely accounted for by environmental factors—heredity was the key. However, in Terman's personal copy of the volume, this section of his essay is circled and he wrote in the margin "I am less sure of this now (1951)! And still less sure in 1955!—L. M. T." (quoted in Hilgard, 1957, p. 478). Questions about the relative influence of nature and nurture on intelligence, whether the IQ is a useful measure of intelligence, and the very nature of intelligence, continue to be debated today.

APPLYING PSYCHOLOGY TO BUSINESS

Its major impact was on education, but testing also came to be used frequently in business settings. Psychology applied to business went far beyond mere testing, however. As early as 1895, in *Thinking, Feeling, Doing*, Scripture pointed out that advertisers could benefit from what psychologists knew about attention and memory. Shortly after the turn of the century, Walter Dill Scott (1869–1955), who had been trained in traditional experimental psychology by Wundt at Leipzig, launched a distinguished career in applied psychology by writing *The Theory and Practice of Advertising* (1903). In it he argued that consumers were not rational decision makers and could be influenced by suggestion and appeals to emotion. Scott also wrote *Human Efficiency in Business* (1910), in which he applied psychological principles to suggest ways of increasing productivity. During this same time, Hugo Münsterberg, a young German psychologist, also a product of Wundt's laboratory and now at Harvard, was beginning to be involved in what he called "economic psychology." Although he became one of the most reviled public figures in America at the time of his death, he was psychology's most visible applied psychologist in the first decade and a half of the new century.

HUGO MÜNSTERBERG (1863–1916): THE DIVERSITY OF APPLIED PSYCHOLOGY

As one of Germany's rising stars in the new experimental psychology, Hugo Münsterberg attracted the attention of William James at a time when America's premier psychologist was shifting his interests from psychology to philosophy and desiring to distance himself from the laboratory. Young Münsterberg had earned both a Ph.D. with Wundt at Leipzig and an M.D. from Heidelberg, and he had established a productive laboratory of experimental psychology at Freiburg in the late 1880s. James was greatly impressed with Münsterberg's research, citing it frequently in his *Principles of Psychology*. With promises of a well-equipped laboratory and minimal teaching demands, James lured Münsterberg to Harvard in the same year that Titchener arrived at Cornell, 1892. Münsterberg stayed for three years while on leave from Freiburg, then returned home to Germany hoping to secure a professorship there. This was not forthcoming, however, and he came back to Harvard for good in 1897. There his career was nothing short of remarkable, although until recently his work has largely been ignored (Moskowitz, 1977). It included presidencies of both APAs (Psychological and Philosophical), a major position at Harvard as chair of the Philosophy Department from 1899 on, and status as a friend of the rich and famous.

Although he could barely understand English when he arrived in Cambridge and it took him two years before he could lecture adequately in it, Münsterberg managed to write more than two dozen books between his arrival in America and his death in 1916. He also became a well-known public figure by writing extensively in popular magazines such as *Harper's* and *Atlantic Monthly*. And he was a controversial figure: one of his goals was to explain the American temperament and personality to a German audience, and to an American audience, all the good qualities of Germans. His motives might have been pure, a simple desire to enhance intercultural understanding, and for a time his reputation as an ambassador of goodwill even earned him dinner at the White House with Teddy Roosevelt (Moskowitz, 1977). As World War I approached, however, his defense of German culture, and his attacks on what he saw as anti-German propaganda, changed public opinion about him. He was editorially condemned, hated by the general public, and accused of being a spy (Landy, 1992). After an editorial in the *London Times* labeled Harvard a center for pro-German agitation, Münsterberg became an outcast even among his colleagues and his sanity was questioned by former Harvard president Eliot (Spillman & Spillman, 1993). The effects of this vilification can only be guessed at, but the resulting stress probably contributed to the cerebral hemorrhage that killed the 53-year-old Münsterberg in the midst of a lecture at Radcliffe on December 16, 1916.[5]

During his productive years at Harvard, Münsterberg contributed substantially to the growth of experimental psychology in America. His research interests were eclectic, and his students found him willing to direct research on a wide range of topics. He welcomed anyone with an interest in research, even students, like Mary Calkins, whose gender prevented them from being there officially. Shortly after his arrival, he lobbied successfully for the construction of a new building to house a state-of-the-

---

[5] After Münsterberg's passing, psychology went into a decline at Harvard. Titchener was offered Münsterberg's position but declined and Cattell sought the job but was rejected. Harvard brought the British psychologist William McDougall to America, but he quickly became isolated and left. The department only began to recover when E. G. Boring was induced to leave Clark and come to Cambridge in 1922 (Hilgard, 1987).

art 24-room laboratory. It included facilities for both human and animal research, with Robert Yerkes placed in charge of the latter. By the turn of the century, however, Münsterberg was spending less time in the laboratory and more in developing his interests in applied psychology. One of his many interests was in **forensic psychology**, which examines how psychology applies to legal issues. His celebrated and best-selling *On the Witness Stand* (1908) included detailed descriptions of the reasons why eyewitness testimony often fails, many of which have been confirmed by modern research. He also warned against the use of hypnosis in the courtroom as a means of determining guilt or innocence, and in his final chapter on "The Prevention of Crime," he argued against the prevailing hereditarian view of human behavior and promoted the idea that the "prevention of crime is more important than the treatment of crime" (p. 233). For Münsterberg, criminals were made, not born.

In addition to writing about the law, Münsterberg contributed to clinical psychology, taking an approach to the treatment of insanity that was based on suggestion. In essence, his strategy was to assume that if he suggested to patients how they should behave and think, the power of his authority would lead them to obey and be cured. In his *Psychotherapy* (1909), he was also critical of the newly-popular Freudianism, with its belief in the importance of the unconscious. Münsterberg, often ahead of his times but behind them in this case, wrote that the subconscious mind had little if any impact on behavior. He did recognize the importance of Freud's emphasis on the early childhood determinants of later pathology, however.

It was in the area of industrial psychology, or "economic" psychology as he called it, that Münsterberg had his greatest impact as an applied psychologist. The following excerpt details just a few of the highlights of his best-known book.

▶ ORIGINAL SOURCE EXCERPT

Hugo Münsterberg and Employee Selection

As he did with most of his books, Münsterberg compiled his industrial psychology text from a set of lectures. He published it in German in 1912, then in English a year later as *Psychology and Industrial Efficiency* (Münsterberg, 1913). The wide range of topics can be seen in the Table of Contents, found in Table 8.5.

Münsterberg opened Chapter 1 with a rationale for the book and an overall description of its contents:

> Our aim is to sketch the outline of a new science which is to intermediate between the modern laboratory psychology and the problems of economics: the psychological experiment is systematically to be placed at the service of commerce and industry.... What is most needed today at the beginning of the new movement are clear, concrete illustrations which demonstrate the possibilities of the new method. In the following pages, accordingly, it will be my aim to analyze the results of experiments which have actually been carried out, experiments belonging to many different spheres of economic life. (pp. 3–4)

As the Table of Contents shows, after some introductory chapters, Münsterberg divided his book into three broad topics: the "best possible man,"

Table 8.5 Table of Contents for Münsterberg's
Psychology and Industrial Efficiency

the "best possible work," and the "best possible effect." In the first section, his concern was how psychological methods could be used to select workers. He argued for the importance of efficient selection of human resources by drawing an interesting parallel to the threats then existing to natural resources (which would soon lead to the creation of National Parks such as Yellowstone and Yosemite). Just as the country was beginning to recognize "how the richness of the forests and the mines and the rivers had been recklessly squandered without any thought of the future" (p. 38), so too were economists coming to believe that "no waste of valuable possessions is so reckless as that which results from the distribution of living force by chance methods instead of examining carefully how work and workmen can fit one another" (p. 38). Münsterberg's final two sections of the book concerned (a) ways to improve worker productivity, and (b) how to advertise and sell products.

To show how psychology could contribute to the process of fitting work and workers together, Münsterberg described three specific examples in Chapters 8 through 10. The first involved the hiring of conductors for the electric railways that provided the primary means of public transportation found in cities in those days, but now requires a trip to San Francisco to experience anything comparable. The job was not easy, for the conductor had to stay on schedule while watching out for the carriages, motorcars, and pedestrians that filled the typical city street, often crossing in front of the rail car. Mishaps were not uncommon—Münsterberg wrote that railway companies reported "up to fifty thousand accident indemnity cases a year" (p. 64)! Some conductors had better records than others, and Münsterberg was asked to identify the attributes of the competent ones. If he could, then the initial selection process would be improved. Münsterberg believed there were two different ways to proceed, either by simulating, as a whole, the essential processes involved in successful work, or breaking the work down into subprocesses and developing tests for each:

> …One way is to take the mental process which is demanded by the industrial work as an undivided whole. In this case we have to construct experimental conditions under which this total activity can be performed in a gradual, measurable way. The psychical part of the vocational work thus becomes schematized and is simply rendered experimentally on a reduced scale. The other way is to resolve the mental process into its components and to test every single elementary function in its isolated form. In this latter case the examination has the advantage of having at its disposal all the familiar methods of experimental psychology, while in the first case for every special vocational situation perfectly new experimental tests must be devised. (p. 59)

With regard to the "motormen," Münsterberg considered using the second, more analytic approach. Competent workers might be expected to have faster reaction times, for instance. He quickly discovered a ceiling effect: no differences in reaction time could be found between good and bad conductors. As Münsterberg put it, "the slow individuals do not remain in the service at all" (p. 65).

Having rejecting the piecemeal approach, Münsterberg turned to his other method—simulation. After observing several conductors, he identified what he thought to be the critical process:

> …I found this to be a particular complicated act of attention by which the manifoldness of objects, the pedestrians, the carriages, and the automobiles, are continuously observed with reference to the rapidity and direction in the quickly changing panorama of the street. Moving figures come from the right and from the left toward and across the track, and are embedded in a stream of men and vehicles which moves parallel to the track. In the face of such manifoldness there are men whose impulses are

almost inhibited and who instinctively desire to wait for the movement of
the nearest objects; they would evidently be unfit for the service, as they
would drive the electric car too slowly. There are others who, even with the
car at high speed, can adjust themselves for a time to the complex moving
situation, but whose attention soon lapses, and while they are fixating a
rather distant carriage, may overlook a pedestrian who carelessly crosses
the track immediately in front of the car. In short, we have a great variety
of mental types of this characteristic unified activity, which may be understood as a particular combination of attention and imagination. (p. 66)

But how could this "combination of attention and imagination" be simulated
in the laboratory? He ruled out using what he called "miniature situations," in
which subjects would have to maneuver tiny models of electric cars on models
of streets. Instead, he argued that a task should be created that catches the
essence of the mental processes being evaluated:

> ...The essential point for the psychological experiment is not the external
> similarity of the apparatus, but exclusively the inner similarity of the men-
> tal attitude. The more the external mechanism with which or on which
> the action is carried out becomes schematized, the more the action itself
> will appear in its true character.
>   In the method of my experiments with the motormen, accordingly, I
> had to satisfy only two demands. The method of examination promised to
> be valuable if, first, it showed good results with reliable motormen and bad
> results with unreliable ones; and, secondly, if it vividly aroused in all the
> motormen the feeling that the mental function which they were going
> through during the experiment had the greatest possible similarity with
> their experience on the front platform of the electric car. (pp. 68–69)

After several false starts, Münsterberg created a clever simulation, one that at
least met his second demand—his subjects indeed reported that the task was
similar to what they encountered "on the front platform." He created cards 4.5
inches wide and 13 inches long, divided into half-inch squares. Two parallel
lines ran down the middle, representing tracks, and the 26 squares between the
tracks were labeled with the letters of the alphabet. In the squares to either side
of the "tracks" were a random array of numbers:

> ...The digit 1 always represents a pedestrian who moves just one step, and
> that means from one unit to the next; the digit 2 a horse, which moves
> twice as fast, that is, which moves two units, and the digit 3 an automo-
> bile which moves three times as fast, that is, 3 units. Moreover, the black
> digits stand for men, horses, and automobiles which move parallel to the
> track and cannot cross the track, and are therefore to be disregarded in
> looking out for dangers. The red digits, on the other hand, are the dan-
> gerous ones. They move from either side toward the track. (pp. 69–70)

Münsterberg rigged an apparatus so that the card was covered except for an
area the width of the card and 2.5 inches long. By turning a crank, the conductors would successively expose various portions of the card and would be asked

to identify objects that could end up being on the track, and therefore be dangerous. Thus:

> ...a red digit 3 which is 4 steps from the track is to be disregarded, because it would not reach the track. A red digit 3 which is only 1 or 2 steps from the track is also to be disregarded, because it would cross beyond the track, if it took 3 steps. But a red 3 which is 3 units from the track...would land upon the track itself; the aim is to quickly find these points.... If the man to be experimented on turns the crank with his right hand, the window slips over the whole length of the card, one part of the card after another becomes visible, and then he simply has to call the letters of those units in the track at which the red figures on either side would land, if they took the number of steps indicated by the digit. (pp. 70–71)

Münsterberg tested each subject on 12 different cards, then combined time and errors into a weighted measure when describing the results. Unfortunately, his description of the outcome is incomplete. For example, the reader never learns how many men were tested, only that the company supplied "a number of the best motormen in its service," others "who had only just escaped dismissal," and a third group "neither especially good nor especially bad" (p. 74). Despite identifying these main groups, however, Münsterberg failed to report exactly how the groups differed on the simulation. Despite his claims for success, it appears that group differences might not have occurred, perhaps due to what researchers today would call a subject selection confound. That is, the reliable workers had also been with the company longer and were significantly older than the other workers. The fact that Münsterberg went out of his way to point out that older workers might be slower to pick up the simulation procedure suggests that these men did not do as well as he originally expected:

> ...We must consider...that those men whom the company naturally selects as models are men who have had twenty to thirty years of service without accidents, but consequently they are rather old men, who no longer have the elasticity of youth and are naturally less able to think themselves into an artificial situation like that of such an experiment. It is therefore not surprising, but only to be expected, that such older, model men, while doing fair work in the test, are yet not seldom surpassed by bright, quick, young motormen who are twenty years younger, even though they are not yet ideal motormen. (p. 75)

Despite the apparent lack of differentiation between the groups, Münsterberg proclaimed the simulation a success and made a series of recommendations about what score should be obtained before a conductor could be considered competent. Although he recognized that the "experiments could be improved in many directions" (p. 81), he concluded that

> ...an experimental investigation of this kind which demands from each individual hardly 10 minutes would be sufficient to exclude perhaps one fourth of those who are nowadays accepted into the service as motormen. (p. 81)

Münsterberg had better luck with his experiments on telephone operators. These underpaid and overworked women handled up to 300 calls per hour, which sometimes resulted in "fatigue and finally to a nervous breakdown of the employees and to confusion in the service" (pp. 98–99). The Bell Telephone Company spent a lot of time and money on training, so they were looking for a way to screen those most likely to have difficulty. Enter Münsterberg.

After observing operators for a time, Münsterberg decided to use his second strategy of breaking down a complex task into its elements and testing each component separately. He identified eight different "psychophysical" processes and developed tests for each. Thus, the women who participated in the study were tested in a group setting for "memory, attention, intelligence, exactitude, and rapidity" (p. 101). They were then tested individually on word association, card sorting, and accuracy in touching a pencil to crosses drawn on a page (i.e., similar to hitting the correct hole in the switchboard). After three months on the job, Münsterberg examined the work performance of the women ("about 30") he had tested. Once again, he failed to describe the results in any detail, but a sly move on the part of Bell Telephone provided some unexpected validation:

> …These three months had been sufficient to secure at least a certain discrimination between the best, the average, and the unfit. The result of this comparison [with the tests] was on the whole satisfactory. First, the skeptical telephone company had mixed with the class a number of women who had been in the service for a long while and had even been selected as teachers in the telephone school. I did not know, in figuring out the results, which of the participants…these particularly gifted outsiders were…. The results showed…that these women who had proved most able in practical service stood at the top of our list. (pp. 108–109)

The "motorman" and telephone operator selection examples are the best known of the studies reported in Münsterberg's pioneering book, but there are dozens more, examining such topics as the effects of monotony and fatigue on productivity, whether magazines should place ads together in one section or spread them throughout the magazine, and the effects of the size of ads on memory for products. He closed the book by recommending the creation of a "government bureau for applied psychology" (p. 306) and by painting a rosy picture of the "splendid betterments" (p. 308) resulting from the study of economic psychology:

> …We must not forget that the increase of industrial efficiency by future psychological adaptation and by improvement of the psychophysical conditions is not only in the interest of the employers, but still more of the employees; their working time can be reduced, their wages increased, their level of life raised. And above all, still more important than the naked commercial profit on both sides, is the cultural gain which will come to the total economic life of the nation, as soon as every one can be brought to the place where his best energies may be unfolded and his greatest personal satisfaction secured. The economic experimental psychology offers no more inspiring idea that this adjustment of work and psyche by which mental dissatisfaction in the work…may be replaced in our social community by overflowing joy and perfect inner harmony. (pp. 308–309)

OTHER LEADING INDUSTRIAL PSYCHOLOGISTS

Münsterberg was far from alone in his involvement with business and industry. The commercial world provided fruitful opportunities for many psychologists needing to supplement meager academic incomes. This part of the chapter began by mentioning one of them, Walter Dill Scott. Other prominent industrial psychologists included Walter Van Dyke Bingham, Lillian Gilbreth, and Harry Hollingworth.

Walter Van Dyke Bingham (1880–1952)

Bingham's career found him in direct contact with many of the psychologists who are or soon will be familiar to you. He was a graduate student at functionalist Chicago from 1905 to 1908, where he completed a dissertation on the perception of tones under James Angell and worked as John Watson's student assistant. In 1907, he traveled briefly in Europe, where he met the gestaltists Köhler and Koffka, then spent some time at Harvard getting to know James and Münsterberg while acquiring a minor in philosophy. His shift to applied psychology began to occur after he went to Columbia in 1908 to start his academic career. There he encountered Cattell and Thorndike, who sparked his interests in mental testing and educational psychology, respectively. After two years he moved to Dartmouth College, where he remained until 1915. For the next nine years, he presided over a unique academic enterprise, the Division of Applied Psychology at the Carnegie Institute of Technology, a school founded 10 years earlier and now known as Carnegie-Mellon University.

It was in Pittsburgh that Bingham established his reputation for applying psychological principles to business. With the aid of generous funding from local business executives (e.g., Westinghouse, Heinz), he established units within his division specifically oriented to business psychology. One example was the Bureau of Salesmanship Research, directed by Walter Dill Scott. On temporary leave from Northwestern University, Scott is believed to be the first person ever given the title of Professor of Applied Psychology (Landy, 1993). The bureau produced a useful guide for personnel directors called *Aids in the Selection of Salesmen*, which included a standardized application form, a set of questions for interviewers, and recommendations for tests to be given to applicants (Bingham, 1952). The sales bureau soon spawned a related enterprise, the Research Bureau for Retail Training. It was also generously underwritten, this time by department store magnate Edgar Kaufmann. The bureau "prepared employment tests, training manuals, merchandise manuals, and specific procedures for correcting defects of sales personality and of supervision" (Bingham, 1952, pp. 15–16). A third Bingham innovation was the School of Life Insurance Salesmanship, which trained a legion of sales reps to convince people that they were underinsured.

In addition to his work at Carnegie from 1915 to 1924, Bingham was also a key player in establishing the credibility of the Psychological Corporation. He replaced Cattell in 1926 when the temperamental founder was ousted as president of the corporation by its board (Sokal, 1981a). He also served with Yerkes in World War I, helping with the Army testing program, and he played a similar but even larger role in World War II. Given the title of Chief Psychologist by the War Department, he chaired a committee that produced the Army General Classification Test (AGCT), which was eventually given to 10 million soldiers (Hilgard, 1987). From the mid-1920s through the end of World War II, Bingham consistently promoted industrial psychology, making him the discipline's most visible advocate.

Lillian Moller Gilbreth (1878–1972)

The career of Lillian Gilbreth (Figure 8.7) can be divided into two segments by the early death of her husband, Frank, in 1924. Prior to this unfortunate event, she was able to combine the roles of mother and professional in ways seldom seen before or since. Frank Gilbreth, a former bricklayer without the benefit of a college education, was a pioneer in the new field of time-and-motion study. By carefully observing bricklayers, for instance, he identified wasteful motions and recommended more efficient ones, thereby increasing worker productivity. Lillian collaborated with this work, contributing equally to their successful consulting business, Gilbreth, Inc. In the process, she completed the requirements for a doctorate at Berkeley by writing a dissertation called "The Psychology of Management," but was not given the degree because she could not meet residency requirements. After the Gilbreths moved to Rhode Island, she finished a *second* doctorate at Brown University, with a dissertation on how worker efficiency principles could be applied to the teaching profession. Her Ph.D., awarded in

1915, is the first ever granted in industrial psychology (Perloff & Naman, 1996). During this time she also published her initial dissertation in book form, after reluctantly bowing to pressure from her publisher to disguise her gender by having the book attributed to "L. M. Gilbreth." Together, the Gilbreths published books on ways to eliminate fatigue (1916) and on the uses of time-and-motion study (1917).

These achievements, remarkable by any measure, approach the incredible when one realizes that during the 20 years of their marriage, Frank and Lillian Gilbreth raised 12 children, six boys and six girls. You might be familiar with this part of the story from the book or the movie *Cheaper by the Dozen*, written by two of the children (Gilbreth & Carey, 1949). It is a marvelous tale about living in a large family run by principles of worker efficiency (e.g., "shave" a few seconds off the morning's whisker removal by using two blades, one in each hand). Their family also became the focus of a paper written by one of Terman's students in 1923 called "IQ Farming." With both parents and all the children testing in the "gifted" range, the Gilbreths were the prototypical example of the kind of family destined to lead Terman's meritocracy (Minton, 1988).

After her husband's fatal heart attack, Lillian Gilbreth's accomplishments increased, even though she was now raising a dozen children on her own, while continuing to run the consulting business and teaching part-time at Purdue and MIT. She became a pioneer in the field of **ergonomics**, the study of how systems and products can be made most efficient for human use. Her ideas included the redesign of household tasks, based on her own ample experiences; for instance, she became largely responsible for modern kitchen design: pop-up trash cans and side-door shelves for refrigerators are among her innovations (Perloff & Naman, 1996). She was also a major force in helping people with physical handicaps become productive citizens—she considered this her most important work. When she died in 1972

Figure 8.7   Lillian Gilbreth, mother of 12 and pioneer in ergonomics and industrial psychology.

at age 94, Gilbreth had added 16 honorary doctorates to her two earned ones.

Harry Hollingworth (1880–1956)

You met Hollingworth earlier in the chapter, as the psychologist who confessed to being involved with applied psychology only to put food on the table. Regardless of his motives, however, he is justly recognized as a leader in the field of industrial psychology. As an undergraduate at the University of Nebraska, Hollingworth encountered the new psychology in a laboratory course taken with T. L. Bolton, who had recently finished his doctorate with Hall at Clark University. He left Nebraska in 1907 to pursue graduate studies at Columbia, where he studied with Cattell, Thorndike, and Woodworth. After a year, he married fellow Nebraskan Leta Stetter, destined to become a well-known psychologist herself. Leta planned to teach, but married women were not allowed to teach in New York City.

Hollingworth finished his doctorate in 1908, then took a position as instructor at nearby Barnard College. The plan was for Leta to begin graduate studies at this point, but the increasingly frustrated young couple barely managed on Harry's $1000 annual salary. Salvation came in the form of an offer from the Coca-Cola company, which hired both Hollingworths in 1911 to conduct research on the effects of caffeine. The company had been charged by the government with adding an element to its formula, caffeine, that had unhealthy stimulant properties. The Hollingworths completed an elaborate series of studies, using sophisticated double-blind procedures, and Harry was able to testify in court that the amount of caffeine in the cola had no discernible adverse effects, except that relatively large amounts taken late in the evening could interfere with sleep (Benjamin, Rogers, & Rosenbaum, 1991).

The Coca-Cola project provided enough money for Leta to complete her own doctorate at Columbia's Teachers College and launched Harry onto the path of applied psychology. He became inundated with consulting opportunities from businesses ranging from railroads, that wanted to know what color to paint their cars, to city planners, who wanted to know how to improve the legibility of traffic signs, to chewing gum manufacturers, who wanted some evidence that gum chewing provides useful relaxation (Benjamin, 1996). While he took advantage of many of these requests, he did so reluctantly, seeing himself first as a "psychologist," and only secondarily as an applied psychologist, writing that "[i]t has been my sad fate to have established early in my career a reputation for interests that with me were only superficial" (quoted in Benjamin, 1996, p. 134).

Despite his desire to be known as more than an applied psychologist, Hollingworth's other research has been generally forgotten. His doctoral dissertation on motor accuracy in reaching, however, emphasized the importance of the overall context within which the reaching behavior occurred. The gestalt psychologist Kurt Koffka once told him that the study had been a "cornerstone" of the Gestalt movement, our next topic.

SUMMARY

Pressures Toward Application

- From the time when the new psychology first appeared in America, in the late nineteenth century, psychologists have been concerned with how psychological knowledge could be put to good use. The concern over application was partly a natural consequence of traditional American pragmatism, and the belief that scientific progress should result in beneficial technology.

- Psychologists also experienced institutional pressures to justify their existence within departments of philosophy and their needs for fully-equipped laboratories.

The Mental Testing Movement

- Galton's approach to mental testing, which emphasized physical and basic sensory measures, was imported to America by James McKeen Cattell, who created the term "mental test" and developed an elaborate testing program at Columbia. The program failed when the measurements could not be correlated with academic performance, however. Cattell played an important role in the professionalization of psychology in America, primarily through his editorial work.

- Modern intelligence testing, with its emphasis on measuring cognitive rather than sensory processes, originated with the Ebbinghaus completion tests and the creation of the Binet-Simon test. Binet's goal was to identify students who were academically weak (débiles), so that special programs could be developed for them. The test was scored in terms of mental level (later called mental age) and children in need were considered to be those scoring two mental levels below their actual age. Binet's approach to psychology, which he called individual psychology, was to emphasize the study of individual differences rather than the search for general laws.

- The Binet tests came to America when they were translated by Henry Goddard of Vineland Training School. Goddard used the tests to classify degrees of feeblemindedness in terms of mental age and created the term "moron" to identify those with mental ages between 8 and 12. He believed that mental deficiency was inherited, and supported his case with the methodologically flawed Kallikak study, which traced the lineage of one of the Vineland children. Goddard also used the tests to help officials at the Ellis Island immigration center try to identify those who were mentally unfit. His results added to the perception that immigrants from southern and eastern Europe were mentally inferior to those from northern and western Europe.

- Lewis Terman institutionalized intelligence testing by revising and standardizing the Binet tests, thereby creating the Stanford-Binet, one of the best-known tests of intelligence. The test was scored in terms of William Stern's concept of IQ, a ratio of mental age to chronological age. To support his belief in a meritocracy, Terman conducted an extended study of gifted children, finding that they broke the stereotype that such children are intellectually superior but socially and physically inferior.

- Robert Yerkes, a comparative psychologist at heart, became involved in mental testing in World War I by organizing the Army testing program. He and his team developed two group intelligence tests, one for literate soldiers (Army Alpha) and one for illiterates (Army Beta). The program was minimally useful to the Army, but launched intelligence testing as big business and made testing a popular enterprise in the 1920s. After the war, Yerkes's report on the program, which suggested that the typical American soldier was scored barely higher than moron level, generated much controversy over mental testing, IQ, and the question of how much intelligence resulted from nature and nurture.

Applying Psychology to Business

- The first psychologists to apply psychological principles to business were Walter Dill Scott, who wrote books on advertising and how to improve business practices, and Hugo Münsterberg, who came from Germany to run the laboratory at Harvard, but soon developed interests in several applied areas, including forensic psychology, educational psychology, psychotherapy, and industrial ("economic") psychology.

- Münsterberg's *Psychology and Industrial Efficiency* included several examples of how psychological principles could be used to select employees. He recommended two approaches to measurement: simulations of critical features of the worker's task, as in driving an electric railcar, and analysis into component skills, as in being a telephone operator. The book also included research-based advice on improving the workplace and on how to market products.

- Other pioneering industrial psychologists include Walter Van Dyke Bingham, whose Division of Applied Psychology at the Carnegie Institute developed programs for training people in sales and retailing, Lillian Moller Gilbreth, an efficiency expert and one of the first to study ergonomics, and Harry Hollingworth, a reluctant applied psychologist, but an effective one who applied sophisticated experimental design to applied problems such as the effects of caffeine on performance.

FOR FURTHER READING

FANCHER, R. E. (1985). *The intelligence men: Makers of the IQ controversy.* New York: W. W. Norton.

An excellent history of the testing movement, with detailed descriptions of the work of Galton, Cattell, Binet, Goddard, Terman, and Yerkes; brings the controversy up to date by examining modern descendants of the hereditarian side of the issue—Burt, Eysenck, and Jensen—and the debate over the alleged fabrication of twin study data by Burt.

GOULD, S. J. (1978). *The mismeasure of man.* New York: W. W. Norton.

A highly readable but presentist history of how intelligence has been conceptualized and measured over the years, and used as a means of perpetuating stereotypical beliefs about various groups; includes an excellent layman's overview of factor analysis, the statistical tool used to examine whether intelligence is unitary or multifaceted.

SOKAL, M. M. (Ed.). (1987). *Psychological testing and American society.* New Brunswick, NJ: Rutgers University Press.

A collection of essays written by leading experts on the history of testing; includes chapters about Cattell, Goddard, Yerkes, Terman, and the origins of the multiple-choice testing format.

BENJAMIN, L. T., JR., ROGERS, A. M., & ROSENBAUM, A. (1991). Coca-Cola, caffeine, and mental deficiency: Harry Hollingworth and the Chattanooga trial. *Journal of the History of the Behavioral Sciences, 27,* 42–55.

A description of Hollingworth's research of the effects of caffeine, set nicely into its historical context; shows how Hollingworth was reluctantly drawn into the project, how he tried to protect his scientific integrity while doing the research, and how his experiments, still cited today, were models of experimental design.

9

GESTALT PSYCHOLOGY

> There are wholes, the behaviour of which is not determined by that of their individual elements, but where the part-processes are themselves determined by the intrinsic nature of the whole.
>
> *Max Wertheimer, 1924*

Preview

Advocates of a new way of thinking often find that they must speak loudly in order to be heard. Such was the case for those who became known as gestalt psychologists. With missionary zeal, these German psychologists promoted an approach to psychology that objected deeply to the prevailing analytical strategy that characterized certain aspects of other German psychologies, Titchenerian structuralism, American behaviorism, and any theory derived from associationist principles. The gestaltists argued that understanding mind and behavior could not be achieved by trying to identify the basic sensory elements of conscious experience, or by reducing complex behavior to elementary stimulus-response units. Rather, their emphasis was on wholes and before long their movement came to be identified with this catch-phrase: the whole of an experience is different from the sum of its parts. The first section of this chapter highlights the work of three Germans who established the gestalt movement: Max Wertheimer, normally considered the founder by virtue of his elegant yet simple demonstrations of apparent motion; Kurt Koffka, who first introduced gestalt concepts to an American audience and extended gestalt ideas into developmental psychology; and Wolfgang Köhler, whose research on learning and problem solving in apes challenged behaviorism. The chapter's Original Source Excerpt is from Köhler's problem-solving studies.

All three gestalt pioneers emigrated to the United States, two of them (Wertheimer and Köhler) as a consequence of Adolph Hitler's dismantling of German science in the 1930s. The gestalt psychology that arrived in America was sometimes associated only with perception, but the gestaltists also made important contributions to the psychology of thinking and problem solving, and their ideas influenced the later development of cognitive psychology.

The final portion of the chapter describes the life and work of Kurt Lewin. He was for a time associated with the gestaltists in Germany, and like Wertheimer and Köhler, he emigrated to the United States to escape the Nazi menace. Lewin went beyond gestalt psychology, however, and developed a complex theory of human behavior that led him to make important contributions to developmental, social, and industrial psychology. Impatient with abstract laboratory studies, he developed "action research," aimed at making a direct impact on people's lives and solving social problems.

THE ORIGINS AND DEVELOPMENT OF GESTALT PSYCHOLOGY

The starting date for gestalt psychology is normally thought to be somewhere between 1910 and 1912, the years when German psychologist Max Wertheimer looked at a common perceptual phenomenon from a new angle. Like all intellectual movements, however, this one had roots. The gestaltists were influenced indirectly by the German philosophical tradition of Kant, with its emphasis on how a priori perceptual and cognitive categories shape our experiences (see Chapter 2), and by the late nineteenth-century phenomenology of Edmund Husserl, which stressed the importance of relying on direct descriptions of our experiences over the artificial introspective accounts that attempted dissection when trying to understand the nature of these events. The gestaltists were also influenced by contemporary physics, especially the work of Max Planck, an important pioneer of field theory in physics, which emphasized how overall fields of force determined the nature of the relationships among components of the field. A magnetic field, for instance, represents a force that produces an overall pattern of interrelations among elements that cannot be understood by analyzing each of the elements within the total field.

Three direct influences on the creation of gestalt psychology were the physicist Ernst Mach (1838–1916), and the philosopher/psy-chologists Christian von Ehrenfels (1859–1932) and Carl Stumpf (1848–1936). In a book on sensation written in 1886, Mach argued that certain "space-forms" resisted analysis into more basic elements. For example, a square has the essential spatial feature of "squareness" that cannot be further reduced. The four lines that compose it can change in size, but the relationship among the four lines must stay the same for squareness to occur. The overall relationship is what counts when identifying squares, not the individual components. The Austrian von Ehrenfels, in an 1890 paper called "On Gestalt Qualities," came to a similar conclusion. There are certain qualities of experience, he contended, that go beyond individual sensory elements and persist even if the elements are altered. A talented musician, von Ehrenfels used melody as an example. By playing a song in a different key or with a different instrument, the physical properties of every single note (element) might change, yet the melody itself does not change—it has a **form-quality** ("Gestaltqualitat") that is different from the sum of the individual notes. Stumpf, like von Ehrenfels a talented musician, was a noted experimentalist who contributed important work on the auditory perception of tones. He also engaged in a spirited debate with Wundt over who was best qualified to be an "observer" in experiments about judging musical tones. At issue was an auditory phenomenon with a distinct gestalt theme. When listening to two pure tones simultaneously, the experience is of a unique third tone that does not seem to be a combination of its two components. Wundt believed that suitably trained laboratory workers would be capable of analyzing the phenomenon into its elements, but Stumpf contended that skilled musicians were better observers and that the phenomenon resisted analysis. If a laboratory analysis contradicted the phenomenal experience of a trained musician, Stumpf argued, then the analysis was in error. While not denying the importance of laboratory work, Stumpf and his followers urged the primacy of direct experience over an abstract reduction to elements (Ash, 1985). As will be seen, two of the original three gestaltists took their doctorates with Stumpf, and the third studied with him for a time.

MAX WERTHEIMER (1880–1943): FOUNDING GESTALT PSYCHOLOGY

Max Wertheimer (Figure 9.1) was born in Prague and initially studied law at its university, before his broad interests led him to switch to philosophy. He took courses with von Ehrenfels, where he undoubtedly learned of his teacher's concept of Gestaltqualitat, then studied in Berlin for three semesters, where he encountered Stumpf, and Würzburg, where he completed a doctorate with Oswald Külpe (Chapter 4) in 1904. His dissertation derived from an earlier interest in criminal law and used a word association technique to discern characteristic patterns of thinking (Newman, 1944). The next few years following 1904 are not well documented, but family wealth apparently made it possible for Wertheimer to indulge his varied interests in philosophy and psychology.

Somewhere around 1910, Wertheimer became fascinated by the perceptual problem of

Figure 9.1   Max Wertheimer, gestalt psychology's founder.

apparent motion. The phenomenon was well-known at the time and the basis for the newly created motion picture industry. It can be illustrated with a simple example. In a darkened room, two adjacent small circles are flashed on and off in sequence. If the interval between the flashing of the two lights is just right (about 60 msec), the perception is that a single light moves back and forth. Thus, two separate sensory events occur, but the perception is that of a single continuous event.[1] In the space between the lights, the circle is perceived even though there is no sensory basis for this perception. How could this occur?

Traditional explanations for apparent motion centered on sensory-motor events or higher cognitive inferences. The first idea was

---

[1] If the interval between the flashing of the lights is too short, about 30 msec or less, the perception is that both lights are on at the same time and neither is moving. If the interval is above 200 msec, two separate flashing lights will be seen. The precise timing also depends on the intensity of the lights and the distance between them (Goldstein, 1996).

that as the circles flashed alternately, the person would shift the eyes from left to right, over and over. Sensory stimulation resulting from the eye movements was said to produce the perceptual "fusion" that was experienced as movement. The second explanation, in the spirit of Helmholtz, was that the individual made an unconscious logical inference that if a light was in position A then in position B, it must have moved there. The perception, held to be illusory, was the result of this "reasonable" inference.

With the cooperation of Max Schumann, laboratory director at the University of Frankfurt (and coinventor, with G. E. Müller, of the memory drum), Wertheimer was able to acquire laboratory space and equipment to develop his ideas about apparent motion into a program of research. He was aided by two young psychologists then working in Schumann's lab, Wolfgang Köhler and Kurt Koffka (Figure 9.2), who served as subjects in the experiments (as did Koffka's wife). The outcome was a 1912 paper, "Experimental Studies on the Perception of Movement," often considered the founding event of gestalt psychology. In the research, Wertheimer and his colleagues demonstrated the phenomenon under a variety of conditions and raised serious questions about prevailing explanations. In one of their studies, for example, three lights in a straight line, A, B, and C, were used. If lights A and C were flashed on and off simultaneously, then B was flashed after 60 msec, the perception was that two lights (A and C) had moved at the same time to the center point. This demonstration eliminated the eye movement explanation, because the eyes cannot move in two directions at the same time. The inference explanation was rejected on the grounds that the movement perception occurred too quickly to involve such a complicated sequence of mental events and that the perception of motion was real, not illusory. Instead, Wertheimer argued that the phenomenon must stand on its own as a valid example of an immediately given phenomenological experi-

Figure 9.2   Kurt Koffka (left) and Wolfgang Köhler at 9th International Congress of Psychology, held at Yale University, 1929, from Popplestone and McPherson (1994).

ence that does not require any reference to constituent parts. Indeed, because perception occurred in areas devoid of any sensory information (i.e., the space between the flashing lights), analysis into sensory elements could not possibly explain the phenomenon. Wertheimer referred to the perceived motion as the **phi phenomenon**; he disliked the term "apparent" motion because it implied that the motion was not really perceived (Henle, 1980). As he later concluded, we perceive whole, meaningful figures, not elements that somehow combine to form wholes. Not only is the whole different from the sum of its parts, but "the part-processes are themselves determined by the intrinsic nature of the whole" (Wertheimer, 1924/1967, p. 2). The assault on elementism had begun.

Wertheimer lectured and continued doing research at Frankfurt until 1916, then went to Berlin, where he became a central figure at the

Berlin Psychological Institute until 1929.[2] In that year Schumann retired from Frankfurt, and Wertheimer returned there to chair the department. He probably would have remained at Frankfurt until his own retirement, but world events intervened with the rise of Nazi Germany. After Hitler came to power in 1933, academic freedom in German universities quickly disappeared and Jewish professors, including such luminaries as Wertheimer's close friend, Albert Einstein, began to be dismissed from their positions. In response to the argument that Germany would be losing an invaluable resource, Hitler is said to have replied: "If the dismissal of Jewish scientists means the annihilation of contemporary German science, then we shall do without science for a few years!" (quoted in Henle, 1986, p. 226). At least with regard to psychology, Hitler was correct. The effects of his leadership effectively destroyed psychology in Germany for a generation.

Shortly after Hitler came to power, Wertheimer, who was Jewish and could see the writing on the wall, gathered up his wife and three children and emigrated to the United States, settling in New York.[3] There he joined with a number of other German refugee-scientists at the recently created New School for Social Research. For the remaining 10 years of his life, he continued to work on perception and expanded an earlier interest in problem solving. The outcome was *Productive Thinking* (1945/1982) published posthumously, which will be described later in the section on the gestalt approach to cognition and learning.

KOFFKA (1886–1941) AND KÖHLER (1887–1967): THE CO-FOUNDERS

Kurt Koffka was born in Berlin and, except for a year spent at the University of Edinburgh in Scotland, educated there as well. He earned a Ph.D. from Carl Stumpf at the University of Berlin in 1908. Under Stumpf, Koffka developed research in the perceptual topics of color contrast and auditory rhythm that would prepare the way for his acceptance of gestalt psychology (Harrower-Erickson, 1942).

After completing his doctorate, Koffka studied physiology, then went to Würzburg for several years where he worked in Külpe's laboratory. Starting in 1910 he spent three semesters in Schumann's lab at Frankfort, and it was during this time that he encountered Wertheimer, participated in the famous apparent motion studies along with Köhler, and became a convert to gestaltist thinking. As he later wrote, the three young researchers "were thrown into the closest contact which resulted in lasting collaboration" (quoted in Harrower-Erickson, 1942, p. 279). Koffka left Frankfurt in 1911 to begin his first professorial job at the University of Giessen. He remained there until 1924, producing a modest but steady flow of experimental papers on such topics as sound localization and memory. During World War I, he studied the cognitive consequences of severe brain injury in soldiers. In 1921, he extended gestalt ideas into the realm of developmental psychology by writing *The Growth of the Mind*.

Of the three early gestaltists, Koffka was primarily responsible for introducing the movement to America. He accomplished this first by writing an article in 1922 for the *Psychological Bulletin* called "Perception: An Introduction to Gestalt-Theorie" (Koffka, 1922). It was an unfortunate choice of a title, however. Although the gestaltists thought of their movement as a new theory applicable to all psychology, the article implied that gestalt psychology was merely a new approach to the study of *perception*. This "misperception" lingers today—in modern introductory texts, discussion of gestalt psychology occurs mainly in the perception chapter.

---

[2] For a sense of the geography, refer again to the map of Germany in Chapter 4 (Figure 4.1).

[3] One of the children, Michael Wertheimer, is currently a professor of psychology at the University of Colorado. He is a prominent historian of psychology, nationally recognized as a master teacher by the APA, and a leader in Psi Chi, psychology's national honor society for students.

Koffka also spread the gestalt word in person starting in 1924, in a 30-campus lecture tour, in an invited address to the annual meeting of the APA in 1925, and in a pair of visiting professor appointments at Cornell and Wisconsin (Sokal, 1984). In 1927, he accepted a full-time academic position at Smith College in western Massachusetts, a private liberal arts college for women, where he remained until his death in 1941. At Smith, the absence of a graduate program effectively curtailed Koffka's research productivity, but he influenced the careers of several talented women psychologists, including Eleanor Gibson, who later invented the visual cliff as a means of studying the development of depth perception in infants (see Chapter 14). In 1935, Koffka wrote his most important book, *Principles of Gestalt Psychology*. It established his reputation as gestalt psychology's major theorist, but also contributed to a growing impression among Americans that the gestaltists were more interested in theory than data. At a time when most American psychologists were firmly in the positivist camp, this tendency was seen as a weakness. Koffka's arguments in his highly abstract book were also somewhat difficult to follow. The works of his more erudite gestalt colleague, Köhler, were more widely read.

Wolfgang Köhler was just a year younger than Koffka and 7 years younger than Wertheimer, but he outlived his peers by 25 years and 23 years, respectively. This longevity, combined with his deliberate promotion of gestalt ideas, made him the best-known gestaltist of the three originators, especially in America. In 1958, he became the only one of them to be elected president of the APA. His early career was not unlike Koffka's—he earned a doctorate from Stumpf in 1909. He then became Schumann's assistant at Frankfurt, just in time for the arrival of Wertheimer and Koffka and their fateful collaboration (Asch, 1968).

In 1913, an intriguing opportunity came Köhler's way in the form of an invitation to direct the research at a primate colony that the Prussian Academy of Sciences had created at Tenerife, largest of the Canary Islands, which lie off the northwest coast of Africa. He accepted, arriving just before the outbreak of World War I, which effectively marooned him on the island with his family and his small colony of apes. As the Close-Up relates, though, research might not have been his only activity during these years—some think he could have been a German spy. Regardless of the espionage claims, the Tenerife years made Köhler's reputation as a scientist. There he produced his most famous research, the studies of problem solving in apes. This research will be examined in more detail later in this discussion when you will encounter an excerpt from Köhler's book-length account of his studies—*The Mentality of Apes* (1917/1926).

▶ CLOSE-UP

A Case of Espionage?

Wolfgang Köhler's research on the Canary Island of Tenerife during World War I established his scientific reputation. The insight studies are widely cited, even today, and not just in history texts. But was research into the mental capabilities of apes Köhler's only interest during these years? No, according to psychologist Ronald Ley. During a visit to the island in 1975, in an attempt to locate the original site of Köhler's Research Station, he happened to meet 87-year-old Manuel González y García, who was none other than the animal handler and caretaker during Köhler's years on Tenerife! Despite the passage of years, González y García's memory of the work done at the Research Station and of the behavior of the apes appeared to be cogent. For instance, his recollections of the apes weren't all fond. He remembered that Köhler's most famous ape, Sultan, almost bit off a finger, and he showed Ley the scars from encounters with other apes in the colony. Concerning Köhler, he revealed that the German scientist seemed to enjoy working with the animals, but that he never went into the animal enclosures alone; he made most of his observations from outside the cages. And one other thing—Köhler was a German spy.

Naturally, the espionage claim astounded the initially skeptical Ley, who eventually wrote *A Whisper of Espionage: Wolfgang Köhler and the Apes of Tenerife* (Ley, 1990), a scientific detective story that describes his search for information to verify the assertion by González y García. It took him from Tenerife to archival collections throughout Europe to the homes of Köhler's wife and son. Ley failed to find direct evidence that Köhler was a spy, but he was able to piece together circumstantial evidence suggesting that Köhler might have contributed to the German war effort. Located close to allied shipping lanes, the mountainous Canary Islands had strategic importance. Observers could easily spot allied shipping and convey information about it to German U-boats. Throughout the war, the British, who had numerous ships sunk in the area, made repeated claims to Spain that German spies on the island were doing just that. The islands were owned by Spain, supposedly a neutral country. Nonetheless, the British claimed that German scientists on the island had the means (wireless radio) to conduct espionage. According to Ley, Köhler, who kept a wireless radio at the Research Station, was one of those scientists.

Ley's espionage claim is intriguing, but it has been criticized. According to Pastore (1990), the radio might simply have been for general communication with the mainland, Köhler's research and writing output would not have left much time for active spying, and the whole story might be nothing more than a rumor that eventually turned into a "fact" in an old man's mind. Köhler himself referred to such a rumor in some of his correspondence: "certain Englishmen…take us for German spies, and are even so kind as to spread the rumors that the animals are just a pretext" (quoted in Pastore, 1990, p. 369). On the other hand, it would not be unusual for any young patriotic scientist, given the opportunity, to pass along information that might be of use to the homeland.

Ley's espionage claim is debatable, but his research uncovered interesting details about Köhler's years on Tenerife, including the role played by his first wife Thekla. While raising two young children, she managed to contribute substantially to the research. She was apparently more at ease with the apes than Köhler, and according to her daughter, "the one who pressed to continue the work during times when things were going poorly" (quoted in Ley, 1990, p. 226). A talented artist, she drew the profile sketch of one of the apes that appeared as the frontispiece for *The Mentality of Apes* (Figure 9.3), and she filmed the research. Her photos, including the famous picture of Sultan that appears in this chapter, appear in the book. Köhler recognized her value: he wrote to German authorities that Thekla was capable of running the Research Station herself, and he indicated that he wished her to be a coauthor of the book that summarized the research. He apparently changed his mind on the latter point, however. Thekla's initials below the sketch in the frontispiece are the only tangible sign of her contribution to the book.

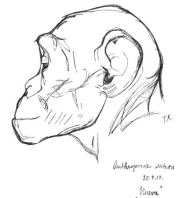

Figure 9.3   Sketch of one of Köhler's apes, drawn by his first wife Thekla, and appearing as the frontispiece to *The Mentality of Apes* (Köhler, 1917/1926).

Köhler returned to a war-ravaged Germany in 1920 and was initially unable to find full-time employment. In 1922, however, his status as a rising star in academia was confirmed when he was named to succeed the venerable Stumpf, his former mentor, as Director of the Psychological Institute at the University of Berlin. Wertheimer was also there, as was a young Kurt Lewin (below). Along with a talented group of students, the gestaltists created a "golden age" for their movement that lasted for about a decade (Henle, 1986). They produced important research, founded the journal *Psychologische Forschung* (*Psychological Research*) to promote their work, and sent their students throughout Germany to expand their base of operations. It all ended with the Nazis, however.

Of the three founding gestaltists, Köhler was the last to leave Germany when he emigrated in 1935. Because he was not Jewish, he did not face the kind of threat encountered by Wertheimer (and Lewin), but he was nonetheless appalled by the Nazi destruction of academia and he spoke out publicly about it. In April of 1933, for instance, he wrote the last anti-Nazi article to be published during the Hitler years, denouncing the dismissal of Jewish professors. In the article, he argued that "only the quality of a human being should determine his worth, that intellectual achievement, character, and obvious contributions to German culture retain their significance whether a person is Jewish or not" (quoted in Henle, 1986, p. 228). Although Köhler was not arrested for writing the article (somewhat to his surprise), his situation deteriorated steadily. He was forced to open his lectures with a Nazi salute (which he did with notable sarcasm), Nazi sympathizers began to "monitor" his lectures, and on one occasion troops appeared outside his classroom and students had their identification papers examined. By early 1935, after refusing to sign a loyalty oath to Hitler, Köhler had had enough. He resigned his beloved directorship and accepted a position at Swarthmore College in eastern Pennsylvania, where he remained until his retirement in 1958. He died nine years

later. In addition to his ape book, he wrote *Gestalt Psychology* in 1929. It was shorter, easier to read, and more popular than Koffka's gestalt book. It is notable for its assault on American behaviorism. Just as the structuralists and associationists had faltered by trying to analyze consciousness into its elements, Köhler argued, so would behaviorism fail because of its similar atomistic strategy of reducing behavior to artificial stimulus-response units.

GESTALT PSYCHOLOGY AND PERCEPTION

Wertheimer launched gestalt psychology with his research on a perceptual phenomenon, apparent motion, and the study of perception became a central focus of the gestalt program. Much of their effort went into describing the basic rules determining how phenomena become organized into whole, meaningful figures. These so-called **gestalt organizing principles**, first articulated by Wertheimer (1923/1967), are now familiar fixtures in the perception chapters of general psychology texts. Here are some of the more important ones.

PRINCIPLES OF PERCEPTUAL ORGANIZATION

One of our most basic perceptual tendencies is to separate whole figures from their backgrounds. It provides the foundation for all object perception (Goldstein, 1996). This **figure-ground** segregation was first described in detail in 1915 by Edgar Rubin, a Danish psychologist who studied with G. E. Müller at Göttingen and was also known for establishing the phenomenon of "paradoxical warmth" (Prentice, 1951). Rubin was not a gestalt psychologist, but the gestaltists used his figure-ground phenomenon to support their cause. According to Rubin's phenomenological description, figures have several distinct features that enable them to be isolated from backgrounds. The border seems to "belong" to the

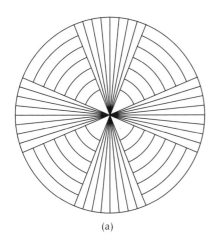

(a)

(b)

Figure 9.4
Reversible figure-ground illustrations, from Rubin (1915/1958).

figure, for example, while the ground seems to extend behind the figure, and this perceptual impression is a powerful one, even though we "know" otherwise. Also, the figure is more memorable than the ground and seems to have a substance that is lacking in the ground (Rubin, 1915/1958). In Figure 9.4a, for instance, observers usually perceive the segments with the straight, radiating lines as a figure against a background of fully concentric circles. The result is an overall perception of a type of cross. With effort, it is possible to reverse the figure-ground relations in Figure 9.4a, making a cross with each arm composed of arcs. This reversal is more easily accomplished in Figure 9.4b, the most famous portion of Rubin's 1915 paper. By changing the focus of attention, the figure can either be a vase or two faces in profile. Note that only one of these perceptions can occur at a time. When the vase is the figure, the black area cannot be perceived as anything but an unformed background. When the faces are figures, the reverse happens. If you stare at Figure 9.4b, you will find your perception switching rapidly from one "whole" to another.

Three other gestalt organizing principles are illustrated in Figure 9.5, taken from Wertheimer's 1923 paper on "Laws of Organization in Perceptual Forms" (Wertheimer, 1923/1967). In Figure 9.5a, the first two dots, a and b, seem to belong together, as do the next

two and the final two. They are organized by the principle of **proximity**. Wertheimer (1923/1967, p. 72) demonstrated the power of

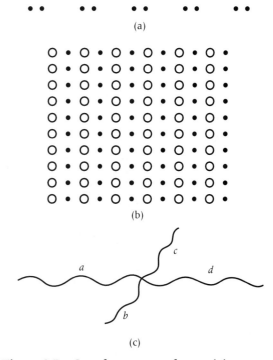

Figure 9.5   Gestalt perceptual organizing principles of (a) proximity, (b) similarity, and (c) good continuation, from Wertheimer (1923/1967).

this simple principle by challenging readers to perceive the dots as *a/bc/de/f* rather than *ab/cd/ef*, a task he considered impossible. If proximity is held constant, then stimuli might be organized according to **similarity**, as shown in Figure 9.5*b*, and we are compelled to perceive alternating vertical columns of open and closed dots. The third principle, **good continuation** is a tendency to organize our perceptions in smoothly flowing directions. Thus, we perceive Figure 9.5*c* as two wavy lines *a-d* and *b-c*. It is difficult to perceive the figure as two lines that sharply change direction, *a-b* or *c-d*.

All of the organizing principles have in common what is sometimes called the law of simplicity or what the gestaltists called **Prägnanz** (rough translation: "good figure"). It refers to the basic tendency for our perceptions to mirror reality as closely as possible. When the situation is ambiguous, the organizational principles work to provide the most reasonable guess about the nature of what is being perceived. Thus, even though Figure 9.6 could have been created in several different ways, we tend to perceive the figure as being composed of a rectangle and a triangle, the simplest and most

likely hypothesis. Similarly, when we encounter incomplete figures, we often construct a "good figure" by filling in the gaps, a phenomenon called **closure**. You might recognize the law of Prägnanz as the perceptual equivalent of Lloyd Morgan's Canon of Parsimony.

One final point about these organizing principles is that psychologists have often referred to them when making the claim that the gestaltists were nativists with regard to perception. On the contrary, they argued that the organizing principles had nothing to do with the nature-nurture issue. Rather, these principles were considered to be inherent in the nature of objects in the world; our perceptual systems are designed to make the best guess about what is out there. As Wertheimer (1923/1967) put it, "one recognizes a resultant 'good Gestalt' simply by its own 'inner necessity'" (p. 83).

BEHAVIORAL VERSUS GEOGRAPHIC ENVIRONMENTS

The organizing principles might be designed to help us perceive the world as it is, but that is

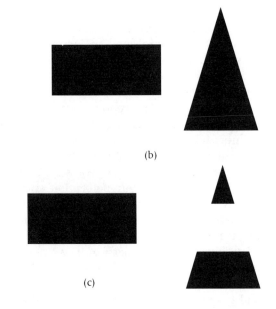

(a)

(b)

Figure 9.6   The gestalt principle of Pragnänz. The figure on the left could have been created in several ways. We tend to perceive it as being composed of a rectangle and a triangle, the simpler of the two possibilities shown on the right.

(c)

not to say that our perceptions mirror physical reality. The gestaltists, most notably Koffka in his *Principles of Gestalt Psychology* (1935) made an important distinction between the world as it is, what he called the **geographical environment**, and the world as we perceive it, the **behavioral environment**. It is the latter perception that determines how we act. Koffka used an old German folktale to drive home the point. It concerned a weary traveler in the dead of winter who reached an inn after riding on horseback for hours over what seemed to be an open snow-covered plain. When he arrived, the innkeeper asked from which direction he had come. The rider pointed to the plain and the innkeeper, "in a tone of awe and wonder, said: 'Do you know that you have ridden across the Lake of Constance?' At which the rider dropped stone dead" (p. 28). Apparently, realizing that the behavioral environment ("this seems to be a wide open plain") does not match the geographical environment ("a frozen lake that could easily crack under the weight of a horse—I could have drowned!") can be rather stressful.

This distinction between physical reality and reality as perceived led Koffka to a point that would soon be elaborated by Kurt Lewin, with his concept of "life space" (below). If the behavioral and geographic environments differ, then two people in the same geographic environment might perceive it differently. Thus, the descriptions of a walk in the woods by a geologist and a botanist might vary considerably.

PSYCHOPHYSICAL ISOMORPHISM

The gestaltists did not limit themselves to phenomenological descriptions of perceptual events; they also theorized about the relationship between perception and underlying brain processes. Their position on this ancient mind-body problem was a version of psychophysical parallelism that Köhler (1929/1947) called **isomorphism**: "in a given case the organization of experience and the underlying physiological

facts have the same structure" (p. 300). That is, for a given experience, the underlying brain processes mirror the experience in some fashion. This does not mean that brain processes duplicate experience—Köhler was not suggesting that when we experience a circle that a circular area of our brain fires. Rather, there is a functional isomorphism between the two. A geographical metaphor illustrates the point: The actual terrain over a 20-square mile-area looks nothing like the map of the area and represents a different kind of experience altogether, but the map is structurally isomorphic to the terrain. Similarly, the gestaltists believed that brain activity was isomorphic to phenomenological experience.

The gestaltists' model of brain function was speculative (and attacked by American physiological psychologists such as Lashley), but it was consistent with their orientation. It suggested that the brain operated as a field of force and that cortical activities were interrelated in complex ways and parallel with experience.

THE GESTALT APPROACH TO COGNITION AND LEARNING

Although the title of Koffka's 1922 landmark article in *Psychological Bulletin* gave the impression that gestalt psychology was concerned only with perception, such was not the case. Rather, the gestalists conceived of their system as a *general* psychology, and they made specific contributions to the study of thinking, problem solving, and learning. The two best-known examples are Köhler's research on problem solving in apes and Wertheimer's posthumous book on *Productive Thinking* (1945/1982). A portion of Köhler's *The Mentality of Apes* (1917/1926) is excerpted here. The book was first published in German in 1917, then translated into English and expanded slightly in 1924. The excerpt is from a 1926 printing.

►ORIGINAL SOURCE EXCERPT

Köhler on Insight in Apes

Köhler and his family lived on Tenerife from 1913 to 1920, but most of the research reported in *The Mentality of Apes* was completed within the first full year on the island. Early in the book, Köhler took dead aim at Thorndike's puzzle box experiments. As you recall from Chapter 7, Thorndike concluded that learning and problem solving was a process of trial and error, with unsuccessful behaviors gradually being eliminated in favor of behaviors that worked. Köhler, however, strongly disagreed that problem solving was such a mechanical, step-by-step process. Instead, in keeping with his gestalt orientation, he argued that solutions to problems occur when individuals can view the entire problem field and rearrange the elements of the problem into a new configuration. Solutions have a perceptual quality to them, then, and they occur quickly, once the components have been reconfigured. Köhler used the term **insight** to label such a process. The main procedural problem with Thorndike's research, according to Köhler, was that the animals could never perceive the entire field. Hence, they were unable to see how the components of the apparatus related to each other in an overall configuration.[4] Thorndike's studies, Köhler wrote,

> ...were designed as intelligence tests of the same type as our own..., and ought, therefore, to have conformed to the same general conditions, and above all, to have been arranged so as to be completely *visible* to the animals. For if essential portions of the experimental apparatus cannot be seen by the animals, how can they use their intellectual faculties in tackling the situation? It is somewhat astonishing to find that (in Thorndike's experiments) cats and dogs were frequently placed in cages containing the *extreme end* only of one or the other mechanism, or allowing a view of ropes or other parts of the mechanism, but from which a survey over the *whole* arrangement was not possible. (p. 23, italics in the original)

Köhler, of course, was determined not to make the same mistake in his research. His animals would have the entire field in front of them, and all of the elements needed to solve the problems would be in full view. Furthermore, his problems would take advantage of the animals' natural hand-eye coordination and not force them to behave in ways unnatural to them. That is, Köhler was keenly aware of what we would today refer to the biological constraints on behavior:

> ...[T]he response of the chimpanzee...will always be limited and determined by his own very pronounced natural proclivities. For I must most

---

[4] Köhler criticized maze learning studies for the same reason, complaining that "American animal psychology makes animals (or people) seek their way out of mazes, over the whole of which there is no general survey from any point inside" (p. 18).

emphatically state, after a full acquaintance with chimpanzees, that it may perhaps be possible...by beating or such means, to compel them to an action, to a habit, an omission, or a method of procedure which is not spontaneous and the natural anthropoidal response to the particular conditions; but so to *weld* an alien nature into his own that the chimpanzee will continue to exhibit it when not under pressure, appears to me difficult in the extreme, and probably impossible. I should have the highest admiration for a pedagogic talent which could achieve such a result. It is a continuous source of wonder, and often enough of vexation, to observe how every attempt to re-mould his biological heritage "runs off" an otherwise clever and ductile animal of this species "like water from a duck's back." (p. 70, italics in the original)

The Mentality of Apes includes descriptions of dozens of experiments on problem solving. One of the most famous occurs in a chapter called "The Making of Implements" and concerned a problem in which bananas lying outside a cage were to be retrieved. Two hollow bamboo sticks with different diameters were available, each too short to reach the food. Köhler wondered if one of his smartest chimpanzees, Sultan, could solve the problem by joining the sticks. Traditional accounts of this famous experiment portray a thoughtful animal who carefully examined the elements of the situation and suddenly hit upon the insight that solved the problem. Actually, the animal tried several other strategies first, each doomed to failure, and he even failed to take the hint when the essence of the solution was shown to him directly!

> ...Beyond the bars lies the objective, just so far away that the animal cannot reach it with either rod.... Nevertheless, he takes great pains to try to reach it with one stick or the other, even pushing his right shoulder through the bars. When everything proves futile, Sultan commits a "bad error," or, more clearly, a great stupidity, such as he made sometimes on other occasions. He pulls a box from the back of the room toward the bars; true, he pushes it away again at once as it is useless, or rather, actually in the way. (pp. 130–131)

Sultan's "bad error," dragging a box over to the bars of the cage, was probably the result of an earlier experiment, in which a banana was suspended from the ceiling of the cage and could be reached by dragging a box under it, climbing on the box, and jumping. Sultan had solved this problem quickly (pp. 40–41). After recognizing that the box would not work in this new situation, Sultan tried a different strategy:

> ...Immediately afterwards, he does something which, although practically useless, must be counted among the "good errors": he pushes one of the sticks out as far as it will go, then takes the second, and with it pokes the first one cautiously towards the objective, pushing it carefully from the nearer end and thus slowly urging it towards the fruit. This does not always succeed, but if he has got pretty close in this way, he takes even greater precaution; he pushes very gently, watches the movements of the

stick that is lying on the ground, and actually touches the objective with its tip. Thus, all of a sudden, for the first time, the contact "animal-objective" has been established, and Sultan visibly feels (we humans can sympathize) a certain satisfaction in having even so much power over the fruit that he can touch and slightly move it by pushing the stick.... But although, in trying to steer it cautiously, he puts the stick in his hand exactly to the cut (i.e., the opening) of the stick on the ground, and although one might think that doing so would suggest the possibility of pushing one stick into the other, there is no indication whatever of such a practically valuable solution. Finally, the observer gives the animal some help by putting one finger into the opening of one stick under the animal's nose (without pointing to the other stick at all). This has no effect; Sultan, as before, pushes one stick with the other towards the objective, and as this pseudo-solution does not satisfy him any longer, he abandons his efforts altogether, and does not even pick up the sticks when they are both again thrown through the bars to him. The experiment has lasted over an hour, and is stopped for the present, as it seems hopeless, carried out like this. As we intend to take it up again after a while, Sultan is left in possession of his sticks; the keeper is left there to watch him. (pp. 131–132)

When Sultan did manage to solve the double-stick problem, Köhler was not there to see it. Instead, he had to rely on the description given by the animal's keeper (presumably the same Manuel González y García mentioned in the Close-Up). In a footnote, Köhler vouched for the keeper's honesty. There was "no suspicion that the keeper quickly 'trained the animal'; the man would never dare it" (p. 132). The keeper's description is one of psychology's most quoted passages:

Keeper's report: "Sultan first of all squats indifferently on the box, which has been left standing a little back from the railings; then he gets up, picks up the two sticks, sits down again on the box and plays carelessly with them. While doing this, it happens that he finds himself holding one rod in either hand in such a way that they lie in a straight line; he pushes the thinner one a little way into the opening of the thicker, jumps up and is already on the run towards the railings, to which he has up to now half turned his back, and begins to draw a banana towards him with the double stick." (p. 132)

Sultan's famous solution was captured about a month later on film and appears in Köhler's book; it is reproduced in Figure 9.7. Despite the drama of the keeper's report, the suddenness of the solution is less impressive in the context of what preceded it. In addition, the solution was far from ideal—the sticks kept falling apart. Nonetheless, Sultan persevered, using the double-stick solution to drag everything within reach into his cage. Shortly after the initial solution, Köhler returned to the scene to observe Sultan himself:

...Sultan is squatting at the bars, holding out one stick, and, at its end, a second bigger one, which is on the point of falling off. It does fall. Sultan pulls it to him and forthwith, with the greatest assurance, pushes the thin-

Figure 9.7   Köhler's ape Sultan, solving the two-stick problem, from Köhler (1917/1926).

ner one in again, so that it is firmly wedged, and fetches a fruit with the lengthened implement. But the bigger tube selected is a little too big, and so it slips from the end of the thinner one several times; each time Sultan rejoins the tubes immediately.... The proceeding seems to please him immensely; he is very lively, pulls all the fruit, one after the other, towards the railings, without taking time to eat it, and when I disconnect the double-stick he puts it together again at once, and draws any distant objects whatever to the bars. (p. 133)

That the solution depends on the perceptual aspects of the situation is clear from the following. Even after solving the problem many times, Sultan hesitated when he saw the sticks in certain configurations:

Sometimes, however, he experiences a difficulty, where one would least expect it. Holding both tubes in his hand and wanting to proceed as usual to connect them, he hesitates for a few minutes and seems strangely uncertain; this is when the tubes lie in his hand in certain positions, namely almost parallel, or else across each other in the shape of a very narrow "X." This difficulty has now almost disappeared, but at first it occurred frequently. (pp. 135–136)

In addition to the double-stick problem and the problem of using a single box to reach bananas, Köhler's chimps also retrieved suspended fruit by stacking several boxes. They learned the task gradually, as Köhler raised the fruit higher and higher. They first learned to use a single box, then two, then three. Hence, the procedure was similar to one later called "shaping" by behaviorists. In one experiment, Sultan was once again center stage:

The objective hangs still higher up; Sultan has fasted all the forenoon and, therefore, goes at his task with great zeal. He lays the heavy box flat underneath the objective, puts the second one upright upon it, and, standing on the top, tries to seize the objective. As he does not reach it, he looks down and round about, and his glance is caught by the third box, which may have seemed useless to him at first, because of its smallness. He climbs down very carefully, seizes the box, climbs up with it, and completes the construction. (p. 142)

Köhler declined (p. 194) to develop a new theory of intelligence to explain his findings, but he spent the bulk of a chapter refuting the "theory of chance," his phrase for the approach taken by Thorndike and other American psychologists wedded to a strategy based on associationist and reductionist principles. In so doing, he described several attributes of what he considered to be insightful behavior. For example, in the early stages, the problem solver systematically surveys the field:

> We can…distinguish sharply between the kind of conduct which from the very beginning arises out of a consideration of the characteristics of a situation, and one that does not. Only in the former case do we speak of insight, and only that behaviour of animals definitely appears to us intelligent which takes account from the beginning of the lie of the land, and proceeds to deal with it in a smooth, continuous course. Hence follows this characteristic: *to set up as a criterion of insight, the appearance of a complete solution with reference to the whole lay-out of the field.* (p. 198, italics in the original)

Another feature of insightful problem solving is that it is goal-directed. Contrary to Thorndike's "chance" theory, which had the animal behaving randomly at first, Köhler believed that animals behaved quite differently, unless placed in a situation (e.g., Thorndike's puzzle boxes) in which the inability to survey the field made it impossible for the animal to see the objective clearly:

> …It is certainly not a characteristic of the chimpanzee, when he is brought into an experimental situation, to make any chance movements…. As long as his efforts are directed to the objective, all distinguishable stages of his behavior (as with human beings in similar situations), tend to appear as complete attempts at solutions, *none* of which appears as the product of accidentally arrayed parts. This is true, most of all, of the solution which is finally successful. Certainly, it often follows upon a period of perplexity or quiet (often a period of survey), but in real and convincing cases, the solution never appears in a disorder of blind impulses. It is one continuous, smooth action, which can be resolved into its parts *only by the imagination* of the onlooker…. (pp. 199–200, italics in the original)

According to Köhler, then, when placed in a problem situation, the animal first surveys the whole field with reference to some clear objective. Eventually, the animal will insightfully reorganize the problem elements in the field into a new configuration which quickly solves the problem. The necessary condition for insight is that all aspects of the problem must be within the animal's field of view.

Köhler's explanation did not go unchallenged by American psychologists, who questioned the methodological sophistication of Köhler's demonstrations and pointed out that a careful reading of the descriptions finds ample evidence of trial-and-error learning. Some attempts to replicate the research produced ambiguous results and suggested that the more prior experience the animal had with similar problems, the more likely a "quick" (i.e., insightful) solution would appear (Windholtz & Lamal, 1985). On the other hand, Köhler's research introduced a new way of thinking into the debate about learning and problem solving and extended animal methodology beyond puzzle boxes and mazes.

WERTHEIMER ON PRODUCTIVE THINKING

Köhler was not the only gestaltist studying cognition. Max Wertheimer had a long-standing interest in thinking and problem solving that culminated in *Productive Thinking* (1945/1982), which he sent to the publisher just before his death in 1943. Its topics ranged from how children learn arithmetic to how Einstein developed his theory of relativity. A good example of his use of gestalt principles can be found in his description of how to teach children about geometry. Wertheimer deplored the traditional approach to teaching math, which relied heavily on asking students to memorize rules and formulas without giving them true insight into the concepts behind the symbols.

Early in the book, Wertheimer described his visit to a class in which the teacher was explaining how to find the area of parallelograms. Using the example in Figure 9.8a, the teacher explained the rules:

> "I drop one perpendicular line from the upper left corner and another perpendicular from the upper right corner."

> "I extend the baseline to the right."

> "I label the two new points e and f." (Wertheimer, 1945/1982, p. 14)

Because students had already memorized the rule for finding the area of rectangles, they could now determine the area of the parallelo-

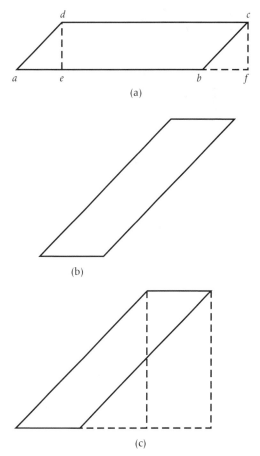

Figure 9.8   The area of a parallelogram: (a) diagram used to teach by formula; (b) problem presented by Wertheimer that caused difficulty for students taught by formula; (c) one solution attempt from students taught by formula, from Wertheimer (1945/1982).

gram by multiplying its base (*e-f*) by its height (*d-e*). The teacher then gave the students several more problems, which they solved by going through the same steps. More problems were assigned for homework.

The next day, Wertheimer again visited the class, and with the teacher's permission, gave students a slightly different parallelogram—the one in Figure 9.8*b*. Most students could not find its area. Some gave up immediately—"Teacher, we haven't had that yet" (Wertheimer, 1945/1982, p. 15)—while others tried applying the rules they had been taught, producing drawings like Figure 9.8*c*, but being unsure of how to proceed from that point. A minority rotated the parallelogram 45°, then applied their rules successfully. The teacher was not amused, claiming that Wertheimer had given his students "a queer figure. Naturally they are unable to deal with it" (p. 16).

Wertheimer believed that children would be more productive thinkers if they truly understood the concept of area. He suggested that teachers start with simple concrete examples. For instance, students could easily grasp the idea that two equivalent square fields would produce the same amount of some crop. Next, rectangular surfaces could be understood as combinations of square fields. With that knowledge, students could be shown that any parallelogram could be transformed into a rectangle by chopping off one end and attaching it to the other. He demonstrated that children with such an insightful understanding had no trouble (a) solving area problems like those in Figure 9.9*a*, what he called "A-Figures" and (b) recognizing instantly that the procedure would fail for the problems in Figure 9.9*b*, the "B-Figures." For students who memorized the traditional base by height routine for parallelograms, however, *none* of the problems in Figure 9.9 seemed to be solvable.

For Wertheimer, then, productive thinking in the classroom went far beyond the memorization of sets of rules and formulas for "correct" solutions. True understanding involved a

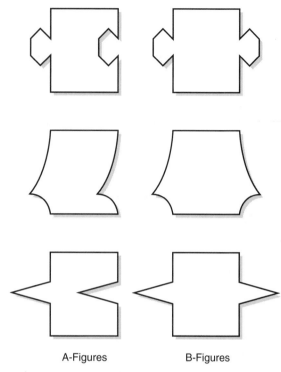

A-Figures   B-Figures

Figure 9.9   Sketches used by Wertheimer to illustrate productive thinking. Students with productive knowledge of area solve A-Figures and recognize the problem with B-Figures. For students who have learned area by rote, both types of figures seem unsolvable, from Wertheimer (1945/1982).

complete restructuring of the problem in order to gain insight into its solution. By moving a portion of the parallelogram from one end to the other, children accomplished this "restructuring" and thereby created a "good gestalt," a simpler figure (rectangle) from which their understanding of squares and rectangles could be used to calculate area.

OTHER GESTALT RESEARCH ON COGNITION

As mentioned earlier, while at Berlin in the 1920s, the gestaltists attracted a talented group of students. Among them were Hedwig Von Restorff and George Katona, who made important contributions to the study of memory, and Karl Duncker, whose studies of problem solving and insight are routinely found in general psychology texts today. All three ran afoul of the Nazi regime, and while Von Restorff remained in Germany after her dismissal from Berlin and died sometime before the end of World War II (Henle, 1980), Katona and Duncker joined the emigration of scholars to the United States.

Hedwig Von Restorff (1901–unknown) discovered that if people learned lists with a three-digit number embedded in a series of nonsense syllables, the number would almost always be recalled better than the syllables. In good gestaltist fashion, she interpreted the result as an illustration of the figure-ground relationship—the number provided a sharp figure against the background of nonsense syllables (Baddeley, 1990). Today, her result is called the **Von Restorff effect**. Anytime a stimulus in an information array stands out in some fashion, it will be recalled more easily than the remaining information. George Katona (1901–1981) had a long and distinguished career. His contribution to memory research came in the form of his 1940 book, *Organizing and Memorizing*, in which he applied gestalt organizational principles to the memory process. Like Wertheimer, he considered rote learning to be useless. Instead, he argued that memory would be enhanced if the information could be organized in meaningful patterns. The importance of organization in memory would be rediscovered by cognitive psychologists in the 1960s, most of whom were unaware of Katona's pioneering efforts.

Karl Duncker (1903–1940) was a student of Köhler's who followed his mentor to Swarthmore College during the Nazi years. Although he died young (suicide), he managed to produce a major work on thinking, extending his teacher's ideas about insight into the area of human problem-solving behavior. His

innovative *On Problem Solving* appeared in German in 1935 and was translated into English and reprinted in *Psychological Monographs* 10 years later (Duncker, 1935/1945). It has been called by Hilgard (1987) "the most careful and analytical account of insight ever published" (p. 233). Duncker studied the cognitive processes of college students by asking them to think out loud while they were trying to solve problems. He then analyzed the written transcripts of their protocols, searching for patterns of thinking and typical problem-solving strategies. He discovered, for instance, that students often solved problems creatively if they were able to imagine uses for objects that differed from typical uses. Duncker's famous candle problem illustrates the point. Subjects must mount a candle vertically on a wall so that it won't scorch the wall. They are given several objects, including a box of tacks. The correct solution involves seeing the box not as serving its normal function as a container, but as a platform on which to mount the candle. Subjects who failed to solve the problem were said by Duncker to show **functional fixedness**, an inability to think beyond the typical function of an object. Similarly, in his "tumor" problem, he asked subjects to figure out how to destroy an inoperative stomach tumor using radiation. The difficulty was that radiation of sufficient intensity to destroy the tumor would also destroy surrounding tissue. The solution was to expose the tumor to several rays from different directions that would focus on the tumor. Each individual ray would be relatively weak, leaving healthy tissue intact, but when the rays combined at the point of the tumor, they would be strong enough to kill it. Duncker found that when he showed students the diagram in Figure 9.10, only 9% solved the problem. On the other hand, 37% arrived at the solution when the diagram was not shown (Mayer, 1992). Duncker concluded that the diagram induced functional fixedness by making subjects think about using a single direction for the radiation.

Figure 9.10   Diagram used by Duncker to induce functional fixedness in the tumor problem, from Duncker (1945).

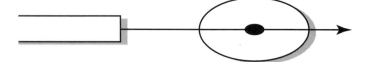

KURT LEWIN (1890–1947): EXPANDING THE GESTALT VISION

Kurt Lewin[5] was a contemporary of gestalt psychology's "big three," Wertheimer, Koffka, and Köhler, and although he did not consider himself a gestalt psychologist per se, he recognized his debt to "these outstanding personalities.... The fundamental ideas of gestalt theory are the foundation of all our investigations in the field of the will, of affect, and of the personality" (quoted in Marrow, 1969, p. 76). Like the gestaltists, Lewin built his theory around concepts taken from field theory, and he borrowed freely from gestalt perceptual and cognitive ideas. While the gestaltists tended to focus on perception, learning, cognition, and their neurological correlates, however, Lewin was more interested in motivation, emotion, personality and its development, and the influence of social forces on human action. Researchers investigating those topics today, especially developmental and social psychologists, all claim Lewin as a pioneer in their fields.

EARLY LIFE AND CAREER

Lewin was born on September 9, 1890, in the small Prussian village of Mogilno, now a part of Poland. The son of a merchant, he was raised in an environment that combined the relative comfort of middle-class status with a pervasive

and state-approved anti-Semitism. Being on the receiving end of sanctioned discrimination created in Lewin a strong sense of social justice that characterized his career. The Lewins moved to Berlin in 1905, where Kurt's intellectual potential blossomed. After graduating from the Kaiserin Augusta Gymnasium, a traditional school emphasizing the classical languages (Greek and Latin), philosophy, and math, Lewin spent a semester each at Freiburg and Munich, studying medicine and biology but unsure of a vocation. At some point he decided to emulate his professors and be one himself, and he returned to Berlin, where he completed a doctorate on association with this chapter's most recognizable mentor—Carl Stumpf. That Lewin thought highly of his teacher is clear from an obituary that he later wrote, in which he placed Stumpf and G. E. Müller (Chapter 4) at "the highest rank...within the pyramid of psychologists participating in research" in Germany (Lewin, 1937, p. 189). Stumpf earned Lewin's high regard despite the fact that they had little personal contact. During the years spent on his doctoral research, for example, Lewin did not recall discussing his thesis with Stumpf until he defended it! Lewin generously characterized this aloofness as an indication of Stumpf's willingness to give his students considerable leeway in their own work. Lewin greatly admired Stumpf, but he was just the opposite in this regard, always taking a very active role in directing his students' research (Marrow, 1969).

---

[5] The correct German pronunciation of Lewin is "La-*Veen*" but he began pronouncing it "*Loo*-in" after arriving in America. Apparently, his children's peers and schoolmates used the latter Americanized pronunciation and Lewin decided to save his children the aggravation of continually "explaining to their friends why the family name was spelled 'Lewin' but pronounced 'Laveen'" (Marrow, 1969, p. 177).

Lewin finished his dissertation at a momentous time—the outbreak of World War I. As a loyal citizen, he enlisted in the Army in 1914, and spent the next several years trying to survive the brutal trench warfare that decimated a generation of young European men. He entered as a lowly private, left as an officer, was wounded once, and earned Germany's Iron Cross. While on furlough to recover from his wounds in 1917, he reflected on his experiences and wrote "The War Landscape," an article containing the seeds of many of his later concepts. In a distinction similar to the one made later by Koffka between geographical and behavioral environments, Lewin pointed out that the same objects in the environment can be phenomenologically different, as a function of whether they are part of the war landscape or the peace landscape. A narrow path in the woods, for example, which might produce enjoyment and relaxation under peaceful circumstances, becomes potentially deadly in the war landscape because it can provide cover for the enemy. That is, the same physical environment can be perceived in two completely different ways.

Lewin returned to Berlin's Psychological Institute at the end of the war (1918), became an instructor in 1921, and remained there until 1933. During these years, he developed his ideas and his research program, attracted many talented graduate students, and began establishing an international reputation. He also befriended his Berlin colleagues Wertheimer and Köhler during these years, and he got to know Koffka. As his biographer wrote, although "he was never a completely orthodox Gestaltist, he did become a vital force in the new movement and contributed to it his own special insights" (Marrow, 1969, p. 13).

Lewin remained in Berlin until 1933, when his status as war hero was not sufficient to overcome the liabilities of his Jewish heritage.[6] He was already well-known in the United States, after giving a stirring invited address at the 1929 International Congress at Yale and spending a six-month leave as visiting professor in Terman's department at Stanford. Cornell's Robert Ogden, an early convert to the gestalt vision and as responsible as anyone for bringing the gestaltists to America (Freeman, 1977), arranged for Lewin to spend two academic years in Ithaca. In 1935, he and his family moved from New York to Iowa, where Lewin joined the Child Welfare Research Station, a research institute connected to the University of Iowa, but separate from the psychology department. The institute was created in 1917 to study the development of normal children and train child development researchers (Ash, 1992). Lewin remained there for nine years, then moved back east to Boston in 1944 after successfully lobbying for funding to create a Research Center for Group Dynamics, to be housed at the Massachusetts Institute of Technology. His work there had just begun when he died suddenly of a heart attack in February of 1947.

FIELD THEORY

Lewin contributed more empirical research than the three gestalt founders combined, but like them he was first and foremost a theory builder—in response to the criticism that theories are sometimes far removed from useful applications, he once said that "[t]here is nothing as practical as a good theory" (quoted in Marrow, 1969, p. 128). Lewin called his theory a **field theory** because he believed that understanding a person's behavior required knowing about all the forces acting on a person at a given moment. Lewin named the particular field within which the person operates the **life**

---

[6] While in America, and with the Nazi menace becoming more evident, Lewin tried desperately to arrange for his mother's emigration, first to the United States, then to Cuba, but was unsuccessful. Sometime in 1943 she perished in one of the Nazi death camps (Marrow, 1969).

space. It is the pivotal concept in his theory, and he defined it as a psychological field that includes the "totality of facts which determine the behavior (B) of an individual at a certain moment.... [It] includes the person (P) and the environment (E)" (Lewin, 1936, p. 216). Person factors include such things as personality variables, needs, goals, and beliefs, while environmental factors include things external to the person that directly affect him or her. Furthermore, it is not simply the physical environment, but the environment as perceived by the individual that influences behavior. Thus, all behavior is a joint function of the characteristics of the person behaving and the features of the psychological environment in which the person is behaving. Or as Lewin summarized it in a now-famous formula:

$$B = f(P, E)$$

Lewin symbolized the life space concept by borrowing from **topology**, a nonquantitative spatial geometry. He represented life space with various ovals, which contained symbols of features influencing the individual. Two examples of these, which his students came to call "Lewin's eggs," are drawn in Figure 9.11. Figure 9.11*a* is a simple representation of the basic formula. Life space includes everything within the oval (i.e., the person, P, and the environment, E). Outside the oval, which Lewin referred to as the **foreign hull**, could be found all the events, circumstances, and stimuli that were having no effect on a person at a particular moment.

A major difference between the original gestaltists and Lewin was the latter's emphasis

(a)

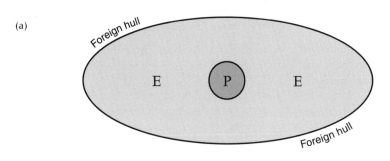

Life space = everything within oval

(b)

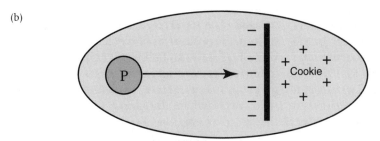

Figure 9.11   Two examples of Lewin's "eggs": (a) basic life space; (b) a child desiring an out-of-reach cookie.

on motivational constructs and goal-directed behavior. He believed that the person is a complex energy system, in which individual actions can be predicted with reference to the amount of tension in the system, which in turn is the consequence of the predominant needs being felt, the strengths of those needs, and the various obstacles in the life space. When all needs are satisfied, the individual is said to be in a state of **equilibrium**. The creation of a need produces a disequilibrium, and a person is therefore motivated to satisfy the need in order to return to a steady state. Consider Figure 9.11*b* as an illustration. It represents a situation in which a hungry child desires a cookie, which resides in an out-of-reach jar. The desire has created a tension in the life space. The cookie is the desired object, or in Lewin's terms, it has a positive **valence** (symbolized by the plus signs). The arrow pointing from the child (P) is a **vector**—these arrows symbolize a push that is directed toward a specific desired goal, an approach tendency, or away from a goal to be avoided, an avoidance tendency. The arrow's length is proportional to the strength of the need. The vertical bar is a barrier (the cookie jar), which has a negative valence.

Lewin used his topological system to analyze conflicts, one of his best-known contributions. He described three common situations in which a conflict between needs occurs. In Lewin's scheme, a conflict exists whenever there are at least two vectors that are exerting pressure in different directions. In an **approach-approach conflict**, there are two desirable goals of equal strength from which to choose. For instance, a diner might have to decide between steak and lobster. Two equally undesirable goals characterize **avoidance-avoidance conflicts**, as when a student might be faced with the choice of studying one of two disliked topics. Third, in an **approach-avoidance conflict**, the person experiences simultaneous approach and avoidance tendencies with reference to a single goal. Thus, our decision about whether to order the hot fudge sundae

will be influenced by both approach (it's good) and avoidance (it's fattening) tendencies.

The Zeigarnik Effect

Lewin's system was highly theoretical, and it has been criticized for being merely descriptive. That is, the diagrams might be able to describe virtually any event, but they are said to be of little use in predicting behavior (Frank, 1978). Lewin and his students did conduct considerable research, however, and their studies produced results consistent with the theory (of course, many of the outcomes could have alternative, non-Lewinian explanations). One example is a series of studies completed by one of Lewin's first students, the Russian psychologist Bluma Zeigarnik (1927/1967).

Ideas for research often come from everyday observation, and that appears to have been the case for Zeigarnik's research. In Berlin, Lewin gathered a team of active graduate students around him. From about 1924 on, his group typically consisted of 12 to 15 doctoral candidates (Marrow, 1969). Because the German university system did not prescribe a rigid set of course requirements, a major element of doctoral education was a continuous small-group seminar, characterized by discussions of work in progress, what research to do next, and so on. Lewin's group often met informally for hours at a time at a café across the street from the Institute, keeping their table by occasionally ordering refills on coffee and pieces of cake. In that setting, Lewin was impressed by a waiter who seemed to be able to keep track of what each student had ordered, without writing it down. Soon after the bill was settled, however, the waiter had no memory of it. To Lewin the explanation was simple. As long as the bill was unpaid and the students remained at the café, the waiter's life space had a tension to it. Once the bill was paid, the tension resolved and closure had been achieved.

Zeigarnik's study tested Lewin's interpretation directly. In her main experiment, she individually tested 164 teachers, students, and children by giving them between 18 and 22 simple tasks, each requiring a few minutes to finish. They included such things as constructing a cardboard box, making a clay figure, completing puzzles, and performing arithmetic and other mental tasks. Each subject was allowed to complete half of the tasks, but was interrupted and not allowed to finish the other half. To ensure that the interruption was clearly felt to be a disruption, Zeigarnik "always chose a time when the subject was most engrossed in his work" (1927/1967, p. 303). What she found was that the interrupted tasks were 1.9 times as likely to be recalled as the uninterrupted ones. In Lewinian terms, the enhanced memory was the result of the unrelieved tension of the incomplete task. This phenomenon, that memory is better for incomplete rather than complete tasks, is today called the **Zeigarnik effect**.

Zeigarnik and other members of Lewin's team, like good scientists everywhere, did not stop with the original finding. For example, to counter the possibility that the improved memory was due more to the "shock" of being disturbed rather than the lack of completion, Zeigarnik did a follow-up study that replicated the two conditions of her first experiment, while adding a third condition in which some tasks were briefly interrupted, but then allowed to be resumed to completion. Recall was the same as for the uninterrupted tasks, leading Zeigarnik to conclude that it was the lack of completion that produced the better memory, not just the interruption. In a related study, Maria Ovsiankina, another of Lewin's Russian students, interrupted her subjects as Zeigarnik had done, then gave them some free time following the interruption. She found that they resumed the tasks on their own, especially if they had almost completed them prior to the interruption (Marrow, 1969, pp. 245–246). Thus, incomplete tasks remain in memory, and people are motivated to complete them.

LEWIN AS DEVELOPMENTAL PSYCHOLOGIST

Lewin arrived in New York in the fall of 1933, at a time when the United States was in the depths of its worst economic crisis, the Great Depression. His position at Cornell, made possible through limited grant funds from a committee to help displaced European scholars, was not in the psychology department but in the School of Home Economics, and it was not a faculty appointment. This might not seem very impressive, in light of Lewin's growing international status, but it must be seen in light of the academic job market in the 1930s. One effect of the Depression was that few families could afford college and with low enrollments, few colleges could afford new faculty. As a result, finding an academic position was virtually impossible. The depth of the problem was revealed in an APA survey which found that in 1932, there were 32 positions available for 100 new psychology Ph.D.'s; the prospects looked even worse in 1933—46 fewer jobs than the year before and 146 newly minted Ph.D.'s competing for them (Napoli, 1981). In this context, Lewin's appointment is perhaps an indication of his elevated stature rather than a puzzling loss of status.

When Lewin arrived in the United States, he was perceived by American psychologists as a developmental psychologist whose approach contrasted sharply with (a) the developing behaviorist movement, and (b) an increasing tendency to study groups of children and take statistical averages of their behavior (Ash, 1992). In contrast, Lewin believed that the behaviorists overemphasized the environment at the expense of personality factors. That is, in contrast to his balanced B = f(P,E), the behaviorists had too much E and not enough P. Methodologically, Lewin criticized the strategy of trying to identify some mythical average child; he preferred nonstatistical in-depth case studies of individual children.

This year marked the convening of the Ninth International Congress of Psychology at Yale University, which included important talks by Köhler and Lewin that helped advance the gestalt cause.

Key Date 1929

These events also occurred:

- The term "apartheid" was used for the first time
- The German *Graf Zeppelin* airship circled the globe in 20 days
- The U.S. stock market crashed on October 28 ("Black Friday"), signaling the start of the Great Depression
- Kodak introduced 16mm color movie film
- Herbert Hoover was inaugurated as thirty-first U.S. president
- Six notorious Chicago gangsters were machine-gunned by a rival gang in the "St. Valentine's Day Massacre"
- These people were born:

    Martin Luther King, Jr., American civil rights leader

    Arnold Palmer, American golfer

    Jacqueline Bouvier Kennedy Onassis

- These people died:

    Thorstein Verblen, American social scientist

    Katherine Lee Bates, American author and composer (wrote "America the Beautiful")

    Wyatt Earp, legendary figure of the American West

The impression of Lewin as a developmentalist was based on his much-discussed presentation at the Yale International Congress in 1929 and a chapter on developmental psychology that he wrote for the first edition of the *Handbook of Child Psychology* (Lewin, 1931). In the latter, he introduced his $B = f(P,E)$ formulation to the American audience. His Yale talk was highlighted by a film that he showed of an 18-month-old girl trying to sit on a rock. She apparently thought that she would miss the target if she took her eyes off the stone, so she circled the rock several times trying to figure out how to sit on it accurately without removing her eyes from it. She finally devised the creative solution of putting her head between her knees and slowly backing up to the stone before sitting. In that way she could watch the stone while depositing herself on it. In his talk, Lewin described this simple event in terms of field forces, vectors, and valances, and tied it to other research on reaching goals by making detours. Older children solve detour problems, according to Lewin, because they perceive the problem as a whole and recognize that the first step, a movement away from a goal (to get around the detour), is part of the overall structure of the solution. Thus, a solution can be achieved even if the initial vector points away from a goal. An older child would solve the rock-sitting problem as a detour problem, by recognizing that taking one's eyes off the goal, while seeming to be a step away from the goal, could be organized as part of the solution. The

18-month-old could not make that detour step, however, and was forced to rely on maintaining a simple goal-directed vector by not letting the rock out of sight. The difference between the younger and older child, according to Lewin, was that the older child had a greater degree of **differentiation**. Within the child, this means that the life space becomes more complex over time. Thus, development proceeds from less to greater differentiation.

Lewin's two years at Cornell were busy ones. In addition to acclimating himself to an environment vastly different from Berlin and polishing his weak skills in English, Lewin plunged into a research program on how social pressure affected the eating habits of children, and with the help of translators, published a collection of essays on personality theory (Lewin, 1935) and a book on his topological theory (Lewin, 1936). He also organized a loose confederation of former and current students and colleagues into the "Topology Group." It first met in 1933 as a reunion of sorts, hosted by Koffka at Smith College. Its success produced its replication, and except for a few years during the World War II era, it met annually until 1965. In a manner reminiscent of Titchener's meetings of experimental psychologists, the sessions were marked by informality, camaraderie, and discussions of work in progress. (Unlike Titchener's group, though, women were welcome.)

It was not until he moved to Iowa, however, and developed a research team at the Iowa Child Welfare Station, that Lewin was able to recreate the environment that reminded him of Berlin. Just as in the old days, his research group combined seminars with informal sessions. Lewin even found a substitute for the Berlin café where his observation of a waiter's memory inspired Zeigarnik's research. In Iowa City, Lewin and his students congregated at the Round Window Restaurant, where they dubbed their group the "Hot-Air Club" (Marrow, 1969).

Lewin's research on children continued at Iowa and yielded one of his best-known studies—"Frustration and Regression: An Experiment with Young Children" (Barker, Dembo, & Lewin, 1941). Roger Barker came to Iowa from Stanford, where he had been a student during Lewin's brief time there as visiting professor. Tamara Dembo was one of Lewin's most loyal students, with him at Berlin, Cornell, and Iowa. The experiment evolved from some earlier research by Dembo in which children in detour problems sometimes became frustrated at not being able to reach the goal and gave up trying. Barker, Dembo, and Lewin decided to study the problem more systematically, the goal being to determine the effects of frustration on the quality of play for children just under four years of age.

Each of the 30 children in the study first encountered a "free play" period in a room where they could play with some simple play materials, while the experimenter took notes on their behavior. After a half-hour, a partition was raised revealing a much richer play environment which included a large doll house and "toy lake" complete with real water and boats. Each child spent up to 15 minutes in this enriched environment, then was led back to the front of the room and a wire mesh partition was lowered and secured with a padlock). The child then spent a second 30-minute session with the same toys found in the original free play session. Unlike the first session, however, they could now see what they were missing! In Lewinian terms, the toys on the other side of the room had a much higher valence than the ones now available to them; the barrier had a negative valence and was producing real tension. And the behavior of the children reflected their frustration. They spent some of their time trying to get around the barrier or out of the room entirely. Failing that, their play deteriorated significantly from that of the original free play situation. They became more destructive in their play, easily distracted by what they could see across the room, and more emotionally upset. Under high frustration, then, their behavior regressed to less constructive patterns than shown just a few minutes earlier.[7] Although increased age produces differentiation, Lewin pointed out that under stress, a temporary shift in the opposite direction, what he called **dedifferentiation**, could occur. The Barker, Dembo, and Lewin study has become a classic in the developmental psychology literature.

LEWIN AS SOCIAL PSYCHOLOGIST

Lewin's American colleagues might have identified him as a developmental psychologist, but his self-identity was much broader, as reflected in his general theory, his "action research" (below), and his research on such topics as prejudice, group influence, and leadership. These latter studies are the reason why he is considered a founder of modern social psychology. The leadership research, still frequently cited, grew out of his reflections on the state of the world in the mid-1930s. Mindful of the contrast between the democracy of his new home and the increasingly dictatorial environment of his old one, Lewin became interested in the consequences of different leadership styles. Along with Ronald Lippitt and Ralph White, he completed several experiments on the problem (Lewin, Lippitt, & White, 1939; Lippitt & White, 1943).

The basic procedure in the leadership research was to create different environments for five-person groups of 10-year-old boys who were given various craft-making projects (e.g., making masks) to complete. The main experiment contrasted three different leadership styles—authoritarian, democratic, and laissez-faire. Table 9.1, taken from Lippitt and White (1943), describes the three approaches. Each group of boys experienced all three styles, and their behavior was dramatically influenced by how they were guided. When led by an autocratic leader, the boys quickly became submissive, failed to take any initiative, did not produce high-quality products, and showed no real interest in the tasks. They also tended to be aggressive when the leader was out of the room, and they often made fun of disliked group members, a form of scapegoating. Those in the laissez-faire group did not fare much better. Because they were in an "unstructured field," they spent a great deal of time unsuccessfully trying to decide what to do. The lack of adult direction often led to confusion, frustration, and hostility. Under this form of leadership, nothing was accomplished. On the other hand, under a more democratic leader, the group became cohesive, task-oriented and motivated, and they produced more high-quality products. One disturbing finding was that when the boys switched from a democratic to an authoritarian environment, they quickly and with minimal protest succumbed to the tyranny. As Lewin later described it, "[t]here have been few experiences for me as impressive as seeing the expression on children's faces during the first day under an autocratic leader. The group that had formerly been friendly, open, cooperative, and full of life, became within a short half-hour a rather apathetic-looking gathering without initiative" (quoted in Marrow, 1969, p. 127). On the other hand, and equally troubling, those shifting from authoritarian to democratic settings had a difficult time overcoming the effects of being told what to do.

The broader implications of the leadership studies were obvious to Lewin. Although he recognized the problem of generalizing beyond the experimental setting, he saw the results as a strong endorsement of the democratic form of government and an indictment of anything

---

[7] Although the experiment occurred long before the APA adopted an ethics code, Lewin was sensitive to the emotional states of his young subjects. After they finished the final 30 minutes of observation, the barrier was again raised, and the children were allowed to play with the high-valence toys for as long as they wished.

Table 9.1 Leadership Styles Compared by Lewin's Research Group

Authoritarian	Democratic	Laissez-faire
1. All determination of policy by the leader.	1. All policies a matter of group discussion and decision, encouraged and assisted by the leader.	1. Complete freedom for group or individual decision, with a minimum of leader participation.
2. Techniques and activity steps dictated by the authority, one at a time, so that future steps were always uncertain to a large degree.	2. Activity perspective gained during discussion period. General steps to group goal sketched, and where…advice was needed, the leader suggested…alternative procedures from which choice could be made.	2. Various materials supplied by the leader, who made it clear that he would supply information when asked. He took no other part in work discussion.
3. The leader…dictated the particular work task and work companion of each member.	3. The members were free to work with whomever they chose, and the division of tasks was left up to the group.	3. Complete nonparticipation of the leader.
4. The dominator tended to be too "personal" in his praise and criticism of each member; remained aloof from active group participation except when demonstrating.	4. The leader was "objective" or "fact-minded" in his praise and criticism and tried to be a regular group member in spirit without doing too much of the work.	4. Infrequent spontaneous comments on member activities unless questioned and no attempt to appraise or regulate the course of events.

Source: Lippitt & White (1943, p. 487).

short of it. They also reinforced his belief that scientists needed to be "in the arena" rather than confined to the rarified atmosphere of their laboratories. To that end, he became the prototype of the scientist-activist. He became a committed Zionist, vigorously advocating the creation of an independent Jewish state in Palestine, as a place for Jews to establish their own democratic system.[8] He also lobbied (unsuccessfully) for the creation of a psychological research institute at Hebrew University in Jerusalem. Third, Lewin became an early leader in the APA-affiliated Society for the Psychological Study of Social Issues (SPSSI), founded in 1936 and concerned with applying psychological knowledge to the solution of social problems. Activism pervaded his work

and much of his research was designed specifically to solve some real-world problems (Heims, 1978). He called this work "action research."

Action Research

The leadership research is just one example of a constant theme in Lewin's work—using science as a means of bringing about productive social change. Psychology must do more than simply explain behavior, Lewin argued; it must "be equally concerned with discovering how people can change their ways so that they learn to behave better" (quoted in Marrow, 1969, p. 158). During his Iowa years, which extended into the World War II era, he was involved in several studies designed to solve immediate

---

[8] The state of Israel was created in 1948, a year after Lewin's death.

real-world problems, several of which involved group processes. During World War II, for instance, in a project with anthropologist Margaret Mead, Lewin looked at the effects of group processes on convincing people to include more visceral meats (e.g., liver, kidney) in their diets. Such a change would help the war effort; by expanding the range of foods eaten, shortages in more preferred foods could be avoided. Lewin and Mead found that people were more likely to change following group discussions than after hearing lectures on nutrition.

Much of Lewin's group research occurred in work settings, and for this reason he is an important historical figure for industrial psychologists. For example, in a series of studies designed to increase worker productivity in an industrial setting, Lewin showed that letting workers set production goals after meeting in groups had the twofold effect of improving morale and increasing worker output. Group processes could also be used effectively to train managers and to overcome male prejudice against women workers.

To further his mission of using science to promote social change, Lewin in the late 1930s began planning for the creation of a research institute devoted to action research that would be affiliated with a university, yet autonomous. He began the search for funds, recognizing the dangers involved—donors might expect tangible results sooner than science typically provided them. Nonetheless, Lewin was determined, writing that he was "ready to go to any lengths to find a productive solution. Social action is part of the changing social world. Security, I realize, will have to be established every day anew. But I am ready to take the risk" (quoted in Marrow, 1969, pp. 163–164).

Lewin's aggressive pursuit of private funding paid off, and in late 1944, he founded the Research Center for Group Dynamics, to be affiliated with the Massachusetts Institute of Technology (MIT) in Cambridge. There he quickly assembled an enthusiastic research team, most of them from the Iowa Hot-Air Club, and set out to study group processes and social action. At the same time, he accepted an invitation from the American Jewish Congress to organize a second action research initiative, the Commission on Community Interrelations (CCI), to be centered in New York City. Under Lewin's leadership, the CCI sponsored research on discrimination and prejudice, attempting to answer questions such as these (cited in Marrow, 1969, pp. 175–176):

> Which procedures in giving jobs to minority members serve to increase, and which to decrease, group tension?
>
> Under what circumstances and to what degree is the building of self-respect among minority members a prerequisite for improvement?
>
> What problems develop in a community with the arrival of minority group members?
>
> Which methods of dealing with these problems resolve them most readily?

For the remaining two years of his life, Lewin immersed himself in the work of his two parallel projects, the MIT center for group dynamics and the CCI. The resulting studies, combined with his other work on leadership and group dynamics, provide the foundation for modern experimental social psychology. The graduate students and colleagues who conducted the studies, such as Leon Festinger, Harold Kelley, Morton Deutsch, and Fritz Heider, are among the recognized leaders of the field. Even today, their names figure prominently in the author indexes of social psychology textbooks. Here are a few examples of the kind of work completed by Lewin's group:

1. *Interracial housing.* Morton Deutsch and Mary Collins compared integrated housing projects, in which blacks and whites both lived in the same building, with partially integrated projects, in which each building housed either blacks or whites, with the buildings organized in a "checkerboard" pattern. While the first arrangement reduced prejudice, the second enhanced it.

2. *In-group loyalty.* Leon Festinger formed small groups of female Catholic and Jewish college students, then had them nominate group leaders by secret ballot after forming first impressions. The students, especially the Catholics, had a tendency to nominate those of their own religion.

3. *Leadership training.* In response to a request from the Connecticut State Interracial Commission, Lewin and his team developed procedures for training effective leaders and reducing group conflict. The first training workshop was held in New Britain, Connecticut, where 41 participants, mostly educators and social agency workers, formed three groups that met intensively over a two-week period. Out of the experience emerged the "Training Group" or "T-group" concept. In T-groups, ancestors of the so-called encounter groups of the 1960s, participants were encouraged to express themselves freely and honestly, give and receive nonjudgmental feedback from other group members, and try to achieve an empathic understanding of the viewpoints of other group members. Leaders were trained to facilitate such an environment. They were expected to create a democratic environment, of course, not an autocratic or laissez-faire one. The initial Connecticut workshop was a success and eventually led to the creation of the National Training Laboratories (NTL) in Bethel, Maine, in 1946, as a permanent center for leadership training.

EVALUATING LEWIN

When asked to describe Lewin's appeal for students, Jerome Frank, who studied with Lewin in Berlin, summed up his mentor's overall personality with a single word—"zest." He went on to describe Lewin as "a little man with an apparently inexhaustible supply of energy and a ruddy complexion that suggested vigorous health. Although he must often have been seated in my presence, in my memories he is almost always in motion" (Frank, 1978, p. 223). Other students had similar recollections of Lewin's passion for his work, their memories usually including images of Lewin filling the blackboard with his graphic representations of life space, "the air...heavy with chalk dust" (Marrow, 1969, p. 137).

Lewin's topological theory, along with his egg-shaped illustrations of it, has disappeared from modern psychology, yet the research it generated makes him one of the leading psychologists of the twentieth century. During his years in the United States, Lewin never landed a full-time academic position in the psychology department of a major university, yet he was able to surround himself with enthusiastic students who turned his ideas into experimental reality and perpetuated his unique blend of basic and applied research long after his premature death in 1947. Ralph White, a Lewin student and one of the authors of the famous study of leadership styles, acknowledged in a symposium in 1976 that field theory in its strictest sense was a thing of the past—few psychologists refer to "valences" or "vectors" anymore, and "one doesn't often see diagrams consisting of goals, paths, barriers, and little arrows, all within an elliptically-shaped outline" (White, 1978, p. 245). On the other hand, White argued that Lewin's influence could still be clearly felt:

> ...It is alive in the form of paying continual attention to the patterns of motivation and cognition that directly determine behavior.... It is alive in the form of a selective but fairly widespread use of Lewin's more specific theories and concepts, such as the approach-avoidance conflict and the differentiation of the cognitive field. It is alive in the very frequent quoting of Lewin's famous formula: $B = f(P,E)$. In other words, much of the substance of his field theory, though not usually in his words, is still very much alive. (pp. 245–246)

IN PERSPECTIVE: GESTALT PSYCHOLOGY IN AMERICA

During the 1920s, gestalt psychology flourished in Germany, especially at Berlin, but as seen in the biographical sketches of its leaders, it also made its first inroads into American psychology in that same decade. In Germany, the gestaltists established themselves by opposing what they believed to be the wrong way to study human experience. It was fruitless to attempt an analysis of experience into elementary units, they argued, because the whole of an experience had properties not evident in a description of component parts. When they came to America, the gestaltists perceived in behaviorism another form of the same elementist foe, and much of their writing was directed at the perceived shortcomings of this American psychology that seemed interested in analyzing behavior into S-R units. Gestalt psychology failed to become a major force in American psychology, but its influence was felt and is still being felt in many ways. Modern cognitive psychology (Chapter 13), for example, which investigates such topics as the "organization" of information in memory, owes much to gestalt thinking.

Gestalt psychology's failure to become America's mainstream psychology stems in part from the historical circumstances of its early leaders. Its three originators found themselves in small schools without graduate programs to give birth to gestalt heirs, and of the four men highlighted in the chapter, three died in their early or mid-50s. More fundamentally, however, the gestaltists were simply unable to convert most American psychologists to their message. While a number of psychologists found the gestalt approach an appealing *addition* to the mix of competing viewpoints in psychology, few were convinced that *all* of psychology could be organized under the gestalt banner, and many were caught up in the new wave of behaviorism, the topic of the next two chap-

ters. And pragmatic American psychologists, more comfortable with the concrete than the abstract, also viewed the gestalt movement as being long on theory and philosophy and short on data and science. Furthermore, American psychologists were put off by the gestaltists' missionary zeal. Köhler, for example, recalled this about a conversation he once had with Karl Lashley (Chapter 3), who was generally supportive of the gestalt position: "Once when we discussed the main tenets of gestalt psychology, he suddenly smiled and said, 'Excellent work—but don't you have religion up your sleeve?'" (Köhler, 1967/1969, p. 79).

Most American psychologists, reflecting a functional attitude receptive to any approach that helped explain human actions, tended to be more eclectic than would be acceptable to the gestaltists (Ash, 1985). Thus, when describing the new German movement in his *Schools of Contemporary Psychology*, first published in 1931, Robert Woodworth (Chapter 7) applauded their "great vitality" while at the same time gently chastising them for oversimplifying the ideas of their opponents. Specifically referring to Thorndike's trial-and-error learning and its law of effect, Pavlov's conditioned reflex research, and Köhler's insight studies, Woodworth argued that some truth could be found in all three and that "supporters of each interpretation could make out a plausible case for explaining all the facts in their own way" (Woodworth, 1931, p. 124). He closed the chapter by referring to gestalt psychology as "a strong and valuable addition to the varieties of psychology" (p. 125), and helped to perpetuate the idea that the movement was concerned mostly with perceptual phenomena by applauding them for emphasizing "the importance of the topic that has usually been called perception, neglected by the behaviorists and handled very meagerly by the [structuralists]" (p. 125).

In the final analysis, Wertheimer, Koffka, Köhler, and Lewin added considerable "insight" into our knowledge of the human experience and provided an important caution to those building psychological theories on the foundation of associationist principles. The tradition of understanding complexity through analysis was a strong one, however, as will be seen in the next two chapters.

SUMMARY

The Origins and Development of Gestalt Psychology

- The gestalt movement had it roots in the philosophical traditions of Kant and Husserl and in nineteenth-century developments in physics, in particular the work of Max Planck, a pioneer of field physics. Force fields can only be understood in terms of the overall patterns of relationships among objects in the field.

- The physicist Ernst Mach argued that some of our sensory experiences are of forms (e.g., squareness) that cannot be further reduced. Similarly, Christian von Ehrenfels used the example of a melody that changes key to illustrate the concept of form-qualities. A melody played in a new key retains its form-quality even though all the individual elements are different. The prominent philosopher/psychologist Carl Stumpf directed the dissertations of three of the four men featured in the chapter, and briefly taught the fourth.

- Gestalt psychology was founded in 1910 to 1912 when Max Wertheimer, with the help of Kurt Koffka and Wolfgang Köhler, completed research on apparent motion, which Wertheimer called the phi phenomenon. By flashing separated lights at certain intervals, the observer perceives one light in motion, and the whole experience cannot be analyzed into its component parts. Wertheimer concluded that the whole is different from and determines the nature of its parts.

- When the Nazi party came to power in the early 1930s, posing a direct threat to Jewish scientists, Wertheimer emigrated to America and spent his remaining years at the New School for Social Research in New York.

- Kurt Koffka, one of Wertheimer's observers in the apparent motion study, earned his doctorate under Stumpf. He is known for introducing the gestalt movement to America, both through his publications and visits. He was the first gestaltist to move to the United States permanently, accepting a position at Smith College in 1927. He was gestalt's major theorist, and he extended gestalt ideas into the area of developmental psychology.

- Wolfgang Köhler also earned a doctorate with Stumpf, and he also aided Wertheimer in the apparent motion study. From 1913 to 1920 he studied primate behavior at a German research station in the Canary Islands, where he completed research on insightful problem solving. He moved to the United States permanently in 1935, where he became gestalt's most influential spokesperson.

Gestalt Psychology and Perception

- Wertheimer described a number of basic principles that determine how our perceptions are organized. These gestalt organizing principles included figure-ground, grouping by proximity and similarity, and good continuation. Our perceptions are governed by pragnänz, a tendency to organize perceptions into the simplest meaningful whole. We often construct such good figures by filling in gaps, a phenomenon called closure.

- Koffka made an important distinction between the world as it exists in reality, the geographical environment, and the world as perceived by the individual, the behavioral environment. Our behavior is most clearly influenced by the latter.

- Köhler's principle of isomorphism stated that phenomenal reality and the underlying physical reality of the nervous system were functionally equivalent to each other.

The Gestalt Approach to Cognition and Learning

- Köhler's *Mentality of Apes* summarized his research on problem solving in animals. He criticized Thorndike's mechanical trial-and-error explanation of animal learning and argued instead that animals could show insight and solve problems quickly if they were able to perceive all elements of the problem situation. Köhler's apes were able to solve problems by stacking boxes to retrieve fruit suspended from a ceiling and by building crude instruments to retrieve other fruit. Sultan, for example, joined two sticks to reach beyond his cage for fruit.

- Wertheimer's *Productive Thinking* described how thinking could be inhibited by an educational system that relied on rote learning and rule memorization. Alternatively, the productive thinker had a true understanding of relationships and could solve novel problems. He used the example of figuring the area of a parallelogram as one illustration of the weakness of rule memorization and the advantage of his more insightful productive thinking approach.

- Other gestaltists who worked on cognition included Hedwig Von Restorff, who showed that memory would be improved for information that stood out from the background (Von Restorff effect), George Katona, who studied the effects of organization on memory, and Karl Duncker, who investigated factors that inhibit insightful problem solving, such as functional fixedness, a tendency to think only of the normal uses for objects.

Kurt Lewin (1890–1947): Expanding the Gestalt Vision

- Like Koffka and Köhler, Lewin earned a doctorate in Stumpf's laboratory, then joined Köhler and Wertheimer at Berlin during the 1920s. He emigrated from Nazi Germany in 1933, and spent his remaining years at Cornell, the Child Welfare Research Station at Iowa, and the Research Center for Group Dynamics at MIT, which he founded shortly before his death.

- Lewin's field theory is centered on the concept of the life space, which includes all of the factors influencing a person's actions in a given moment. These factors include those within the person (P) and those in the environment (E). Thus, B = f (P,E). Lewin borrowed from topology to represent various life spaces symbolically. He emphasized the importance of motivation and the goal-directedness of behavior.

- Lewin used his system to describe various conflict systems (e.g., approach-avoidance). One of his students, Bluma Zeigarnik, showed that unresolved tension in the system could have behavioral consequences. The Zeigarnik effect states that memory will be greater for uncompleted than completed tasks.

- As a developmental psychologist, Lewin argued for the study of individual cases over the "average child," and he considered development to be a process of increased differentiation. He studied the effects of frustration by giving children the opportunity to play with attractive toys, then removing the toys. The frustration resulted in the deterioration (regression) of their behavior.

- Lewin is often considered a founder of modern social psychology. His most famous work in this area involved studying the consequences of different types of leadership styles. Adolescent boys were more effective when led by a democratic leader, than by either an autocratic or a laissez-faire leader.

- Much of Lewin's research has been called "action research" because of its social relevance. A committed activist, Lewin always believed that his research should contribute to the improvement of society. Examples of his action research include studies of prejudice and its reduction, in-group loyalty, and the effectiveness of group processes. Interest in the dynamics of group action led to the development of Training-groups (T-Groups), designed to improve in-group communication and leadership skills.

In Perspective: Gestalt Psychology in America

- Gestalt psychology was a vigorous movement that continually criticized psychologies that were based on the idea of understanding behavior and mental processes through analysis into constituent parts. In America, they were regular critics of behaviorism.

- American psychologists tended to be more eclectic than the gestaltists liked, willing to learn from gestalt principles but not willing to commit themselves entirely to gestalt psychology. Americans were also critical of the gestaltists' tendency to rely more on theory than research and application.

FOR FURTHER READING

HENLE, M. (1986). One man against the Nazis—Wolfgang Köhler. In M. Henle (Ed.), *1879 and all that: Essays in the theory and history of psychology* (pp. 225–237). New York: Columbia University Press.

A sobering portrayal of the effect of Nazi policies on German science, as seen through the particular experiences of a courageous Wolfgang Köhler; includes an excerpt from the protest letter sent by Köhler, as well as other correspondence concerning the matter.

LEY, R. (1990). *A whisper of espionage.* Garden Park, NY: Avery Publishing Group.

An intriguing and readable account of Ley's search for information about Köhler's alleged espionage activities while on the island of Tenerife; a circumstantial case is built, but Ley found no smoking gun; includes an interesting account of Köhler's life on Tenerife.

MARROW, A. J. (1969). *The practical theorist: The life and work of Kurt Lewin.* New York: Basic Books.

A flattering and uncritical biography of Lewin; provides solid information on the events in Lewin's life and provides good descriptions of his research and theories; weak as a historical account, however (overly internal and personalistic).

SOKAL, M. M. (1984). The Gestalt psychologists in behaviorist America. *American Historical Review, 89,* 1240–1263.

A detailed account of the arrival of gestalt thinking and the gestalt psychologists in America during the 1920s and 1930s; excellent treatment of the contemporary historical context and the shifting opinions of American psychologists about the quality of the gestalt movement.

10

THE ORIGINS OF BEHAVIORISM

In a system of psychology completely worked out, given the response the stimuli can be predicted; given the stimuli the response can be predicted.

John B. Watson, 1913

▼

Preview

In the first two decades of the new century, psychologists in America became increasingly immersed in the kinds of applications described in Chapter 8. In addition, a new force arrived on the scene—behaviorism. The behaviorists set out to alter the direction of psychology in America and, to a large extent, they succeeded. The founder of behaviorism as a school of thought in American psychology was John Broadus Watson (1878–1958). Like Wundt, Watson has been awarded the title of "founder" by historians, not because he was an originator, but because he was a self-conscious promoter. For Watson, the thing to promote was a program with the seemingly impossible goal outlined in the quote that opens this chapter, taken from his 1913 "Behaviorist Manifesto."

This chapter will document the trends toward increased objectivity that led to the eventual acceptance of behaviorism by most American psychologists. Then it will chronicle the life and work of the renowned Russian physiologist Ivan Pavlov, whose conditioning research provided an approach to learning that some American behaviorists adopted. Third, the chapter will look at Watson's life and work in some detail. Trained by the Chicago functionalists, he quickly rose to the top of his profession as head of the psychology department at Johns Hopkins University, only to be forced out of academia at the height of his career. The chapter will examine his Behaviorist Manifesto and the reaction to it, his ideas about learning, and his research, including the (in)famous Little Albert experiment, which will be this chapter's Original Source Excerpt. Most of Watson's middle adult years were spent in the world of advertising, where he became a living example of applied psychology.

BEHAVIORISM'S ANTECEDENTS

American behaviorists often trace their roots to John B. Watson and in particular to his so-called **Behaviorist Manifesto**, a paper he tried out in a talk at Columbia University in February 1913, and soon published (Watson, 1913). Yet history seldom turns dramatically on such events—they are usually individual chapters of a more complex narrative. Long before Watson saw the inside of the psychology laboratory at the University of Chicago, forces were at work paving the way for behaviorist thinking to become accepted as the norm by American psychologists. Furthermore, the psychological world did not convert to behaviorism just because of Watson's "revolutionary" pronouncements. Rather, Watson contributed a strong voice to the growing dissatisfaction with introspective psychology. Few psychologists, however, were immediately converted to Watsonian behaviorism (Samelson, 1981). Indeed, it was not until Watson was far removed from the scene that behaviorism became the central force in American experimental psychology.

Behaviorism has a clear affinity with several of the philosophical movements described in Chapters 2 and 3. For example, the behaviorist's belief in the importance of the environment in shaping behavior resonates with the British empiricist/associationist dictum that experience is the all-important determiner of one's mind and character. There are also parallels between the behaviorist's stimulus-response connections and the concept of association. In Chapter 3, you learned about the influence of nineteenth-century mechanistic and materialist thinking on physiologists; these philosophies are also congenial to behaviorist thinking. During the nineteenth century **positivism** also emerged, normally associated with the French philosopher Auguste Comte (1798–1857), and eventually taken as an article of faith by behaviorists. Comte argued that we can only be certain of knowledge that results

from publicly observable events. *Positive* knowledge was said to be the result of *objective* observations using the systematic methods of science, to be made by unbiased (i.e., machine-like) observers. Truth, then, amounted to agreement among observers. Metaphysical speculation about the fundamental nature of events (including behavioral ones) in the universe was considered to be a worthless exercise, according to the positivists, because such speculations could never be verified objectively. Positivists also valued "practical" knowledge, believing that an intimate connection existed between understanding nature and controlling it. Indeed, Comte argued that the ability to control nature was evidence that it was understood—creating an effective steam engine, for instance, demonstrated an understanding of a number of principles of physics. Comte's faith in science even led him to recommend the deliberate redesign of society. This theme of controlling nature, virtually identical to arguments made 200 years earlier by Sir Francis Bacon (Chapter 2), later became a centerpiece of behaviorist thinking, evident in such works as Skinner's *Walden Two* (1948), a description of an ideal community based on principles of behavioral control (see Chapter 11). John Watson's prescriptions about child rearing, which you will encounter near the end of this chapter, also fall under the heading of using science to exert control over nature.

At the start of the twentieth century, psychologists were beginning to turn toward increased objectivity in their measures of psychological phenomena. One important influence was the rapid acceptance of evolutionary thinking among scientists and the resulting growth of animal psychology, as documented in Chapter 5. Animals cannot introspect, of course, so studying the relationship between human and animal consciousness required the creation of objective, behavioral measures. Most nineteenth-century descriptions of animal behavior were unduly anthropomorphic, but as we have seen, Morgan established the principle that parsimonious explanations for animal behaviors were to be favored over unnecessarily complex ones. Explaining a dog's ability to open a gate in terms of trial and error learning, rather than by means of intelligence and planning, moved comparative psychology from anecdotes to objective descriptions of stimuli and responses. Thorndike's puzzle box research in the late 1890s (Chapter 7) is perhaps the clearest manifestation in America of this movement toward increased objectivity in animal psychology. In Czarist Russia at the same time, however, an even greater level of precision could be found in the laboratory of Nobel Laureate Ivan Pavlov. American psychologists did not immediately realize the value of Pavlov's research for their own growing desire for objectivity, but his approach to research eventually became a model for many American behaviorists to emulate.

As the new century unfolded, the trend toward greater objectivity led a number of American psychologists to become disillusioned with the state of experimental psychology, especially its reliance on introspective procedures. The imageless thought controversy, described in Chapters 4 and 7, is a good illustration of this developing uneasiness. It came as no surprise to some American psychologists that an observer at Würzburg would experience imageless thoughts, while another at Cornell would fail to find them. Because introspective data were ultimately subjective, no independent way of evaluating each claim existed. In an address delivered at the 1904 World's Fair in St. Louis and later published in *Popular Science Monthly*, James McKeen Cattell declared that psychology should not be limited to the study of conscious experience and that introspection need not be the dominant method used by psychologists. In fact, "the rather widespread notion that there is no psychology apart from introspection is refuted by the brute argument of accomplished fact" (Cattell, 1904, cited in Woodworth, 1931, p. 48). In his own research, according to Cattell,

introspection played a minimal role. And reflecting the positivist thinking just described, he said that he saw "no reason why the application of systematized knowledge to the *control of human nature* may not in the course of the present century accomplish results commensurate with the nineteenth century applications of physical science to the material world" (Cattell, 1904, cited in Woodworth, 1931, p. 49, italics added).

In the same year that Cattell addressed the St. Louis World's Fair, another event marked a milestone in a career that was shifting from a fascination with the digestive system to a passion for discovering how the brain works. The event was the awarding of a Nobel Prize for physiology to the Russian scientist Ivan Petrovich Pavlov.

PAVLOV'S LIFE AND WORK

Pavlov earned the Nobel Prize for his long years of painstaking and ingenious investigations of the physiology of digestion. In particular, he was known for inventing or perfecting a number of surgical techniques that facilitated this research. Yet when the 54-year-old scientist delivered his acceptance address in December of 1904 at the Nobel awards ceremony in Stockholm, Sweden, he did not have much to say about the work that won him the prize. Rather, in an address entitled "The First Sure Steps Along the Path of a New Investigation" (Babkin, 1949), Pavlov described the research that had interested him for the past several years and would occupy the rest of his life. This research is familiar to you, of course, and probably brings to mind images of dogs salivating. Pavlov's conditioning research eventually provided an important model for American behavioral scientists, despite the fact that Pavlov himself always insisted that he was a physiologist, not a psychologist, and he had little regard for those who called themselves psychologists. He once pointed out that while the study of reflexes had been dominated historically by those taking a psychological (by which he meant introspective) approach, his more objective strategy offered the hope of these investigations of the reflex "being liberated from such evil influences" (Pavlov, 1906, p. 618).

THE DEVELOPMENT
OF A PHYSIOLOGIST

Ivan Petrovich Pavlov (1849–1936) was born into relative poverty in the small farming village of Ryazan in west central Russia in 1849. His father was a priest and his mother was the daughter of a priest, but despite their resulting social status, both parents had to work as peasant farmers to feed their large family. Ivan was the firstborn of 11 children, six of whom died in childhood. His early schooling was geared toward following in his father's clerical footsteps, but while studying at the Ryazan Ecclesiastical Seminary, an interest in science blossomed from his discovery of (a) Darwin's *Origin of Species* and (b) *Reflexes of the Brain*, published in 1863 by Russia's leading nineteenth-century physiologist, Ivan Sechenov (1829–1905). Sechenov argued that all cortical processes involved complex relationships between excitatory and inhibitory processes in the nervous system and that "psychical" (psychological) events could be reduced to and explained by reflex action in the cortex. It was a model very much in tune with the mechanistic and materialistic climate of nineteenth-century science, and it was influenced by Sechenov's direct contact with some of Europe's leading physiologists. In turn, these ideas eventually became the cornerstone of Pavlov's model of nervous system functioning.

Pavlov left the seminary and enrolled as a student of physiology at the University of St. Petersburg in 1870, thereby trading a simple rural life for the glamour of Russia's most important city.[1] St. Petersburg, located in northwest Russia near the Gulf of Finland, was the cultural, political, and intellectual center of Russia in the late nineteenth century. It was also Russia's capital city until it was replaced by Moscow in 1918, following the Soviet Revolution. In this high-powered setting, Pavlov completed a degree in medicine in 1883 and became a research physiologist. After additional years of study, several low-level research positions, and financial hardship, he was named the first director of the physiology division of St. Petersburg's Institute of Experimental Medicine in 1891. It was during the 1890s that he systematically investigated the physiology of the digestive system; this was the research that led to the Nobel Prize in 1904.

Pavlov studied digestion by isolating various parts of the digestive system and extracting digestive fluids. The quantities of the various fluids secreted were measured as a function of the type of substance fed to the animal. The research was noted for its precision and for the development of several surgical techniques to isolate and collect digestive secretions in dogs that were otherwise functioning normally. The best known was the so-called Pavlov pouch. It was created by segregating a small section of stomach (about one-tenth of it) and redesigning it as a miniature stomach. It was situated so that food could not enter when it reached the stomach from the esophagus. A small tube or fistula led from the pouch to the exterior, thereby providing a means to collect the fluids secreted by the mini-stomach. Uncontaminated by food, these fluids could be measured accurately (Gray, 1979).

In addition to investigating gastric secretions, Pavlov also studied salivary responses, relating them to the type of substance placed in the dog's mouth. He measured salivation with another fistula, this time a small tube directly connected to a salivary duct. Inevitably, dogs

---

[1] After Lenin's death in 1924, the Soviets renamed the city Leningrad; in 1991, following the collapse of the Soviet Union, it was rechristened St. Petersburg.

would begin to salivate before food would reach their mouths, however, which presented Pavlov with a dilemma. On the one hand, these "psychic" secretions were a nuisance, reducing the accuracy of Pavlov's attempts to measure an exact amount of saliva in response to a specific amount of a certain type of food. On the other hand, the animal's behavior was predictable, and these and other "psychic" secretions (e.g., the flow of gastric juices before food reached the stomach) intrigued Pavlov, suggesting an objective way to study those "reflexes of the brain" that Pavlov had read about in Sechenov's book. Whereas a less creative scientist might have tried to control the secretions to focus on the problem at hand, the basic physiology of digestion, Pavlov chose to examine this new phenomenon directly. After the turn of the century it became his life's work.

WORKING IN PAVLOV'S LABORATORY

In a biography of Pavlov, Babkin (1949) sketched a fascinating account of life within Pavlov's laboratory. As a student of Pavlov at the turn of the century, Babkin was present during the early years of the research on conditioning. The Institute of Experimental Medicine was about a dozen years old and although it was prestigious within Russia, it was not very impressive to the international visitor in those early years: Babkin described Pavlov's original laboratory as "small and dirty" and as a "mere hovel" (p. 68). Although its budget was fairly large by Russian standards, Pavlov found it necessary to raise additional money through the sale of gastric juices taken from the dogs during "sham feeding" experiments. Dogs would eat normally, but a fistula connected to the esophagus redirected the food to a collection tube. The dog would eat and swallow, but the food never made it to the stomach, which nonetheless secreted gastric fluids in anticipation of the food's arrival. Another tube in the stomach collected the juices. Pavlov marketed

the vile-tasting fluid as an elixir for those suffering from various digestive ailments, especially those resulting from "an insufficient flow of the [their] own gastric juice" (p. 69).

Despite the difficult conditions, Pavlov managed to institutionalize demanding controls in the laboratory and gradually created a world-class research environment. He was especially rigorous in creating an antiseptic environment for his surgical procedures. That, combined with Pavlov's skill as a surgeon, produced an environment that dramatically reduced infection and ensured the survival of virtually all of the animals in Pavlov's care. He also developed a systematic method to train the dozens of research assistants who passed through his laboratory. Most of the assistants, who were already qualified as physicians, were looking to add a doctorate in physiology to their medical degree (Todes, 1997). Whenever a new worker would enter the lab, Pavlov would assign this person a problem that had already been investigated. Thus, the student would learn experimental procedures without being under pressure to produce new findings, while also providing an ongoing program of **replication**. Once the earlier research had been replicated successfully, the worker would be given a new problem to investigate. A failure to replicate would trigger additional research (by yet a third worker) to clear up the contradiction. Replication, of course, is a cornerstone of sound scientific research; results that cannot be repeated are of no value.

Beginning in 1910 (but not fully equipped until 1925), the Institute built a special laboratory for Pavlov's conditioning research. Later known as the Tower of Silence, it featured extensive soundproofing techniques to ensure that the dogs would respond only to the stimulus being studied at the time and not to any extraneous stimuli. As Figure 10.1 shows, there were eight experimental chambers, four on each of two floors that were separated by an intermediate floor. Each research chamber was fully insulated and separated from other cham-

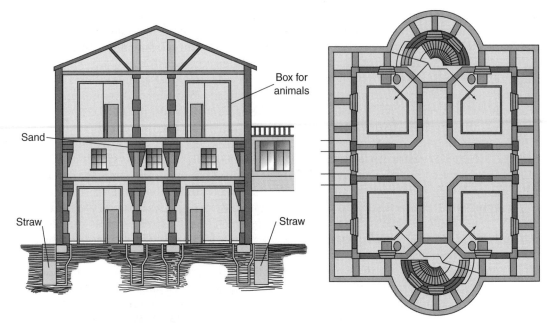

Box for
animals

Sand

Straw

Straw

Figure 10.1 Cross-section and floor plan of Pavlov's laboratory at St. Petersburg, from Pavlov (1928).

bers by a corridor. To further reduce noise and vibration, the building itself was supported by beams immersed in sand and surrounded by a sand- and straw-filled moat! Experimenters were separated from the dogs by the double wall that is evident in Figure 10.2.

PAVLOV'S CLASSICAL CONDITIONING RESEARCH

In the spring of 1924, Pavlov organized a series of lectures that summarized about 25 years of his work on conditioning. He gave the lectures

Figure 10.2 Apparatus arrangement in Pavlov's laboratory, around 1915, from Pavlov (1928).

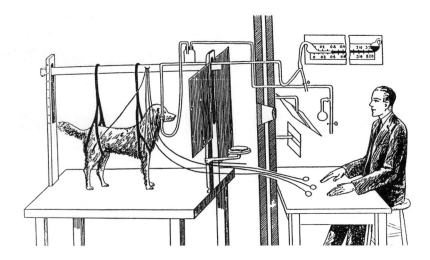

at the Military Medical Academy in St. Petersburg and then rewrote them for publication. They were translated into English by G. V. Anrep, a British researcher and another former student of Pavlov's, and published as *Conditioned Reflexes: An Investigation of the Physiological Activity of the Cerebral Cortex* by the British Royal Society in 1927 (Pavlov, 1927/1960).

In his opening lecture, Pavlov acknowledged his debt to Sechenov and Darwin, credited the American psychologist Thorndike with doing the first systematic work on the relationship between "visual and tactile stimuli on the one hand and the locomotor apparatus on the other" (p. 6), then described the start of his own inquiries and his recognition that the problem had to be attacked from a purely physiological rather than a psychological standpoint. Pavlov believed that restricting the investigation to specific external stimuli and measurable physiological responses was the only scientifically defensible strategy to use. The "psychological approach," on the other hand, implied a dualism of mental and physical processes that Pavlov was not willing to accept. He often referred to an episode from the early years of his laboratory when one of his students, Anton Snarskii, investigated the effects of severing the facial nerves on the development of a conditioned response. Despite opposition from Pavlov (or so Pavlov later claimed), Snarskii interpreted his results in mentalistic terms and referred to such processes as "visual association" and "recognition" (Windholtz, 1986). Pavlov believed such an approach to be unnecessarily speculative.[2]

After a detailed description of basic reflex action, Pavlov concluded his opening lecture by referring to the accidental demonstrations of salivary conditioning that launched him into his 25 years of research. First describing how salivation occurs automatically if either food or some objectionable substance is placed into the dog's mouth, to begin the process of digesting the food or to wash out the offending stimulus, Pavlov then pointed out that a similar reflex can occur "when these substances are placed at a distance from the dog and the receptor organs affected are only those of smell and sight;... further, the secretion may be provoked even by the sight of the person who brought the vessel, or by the sound of his footsteps" (Pavlov, 1927/1960, p. 13).

In his second lecture, Pavlov began by describing some of the technical details of his procedures and the measures taken to control experimental conditions. He explained that the dog presented with food shows both secretory (i.e., salivary) reflexes and motor reflexes. It drools, but it also turns its head, moves its mouth, and so on. That Pavlov decided to study the secretory reflex and ignore the motor reflexes is another indication of his concern over precise measurement and a desire to avoid anthropomorphic speculation about what the animal might be "trying" to do.

Conditioning and Extinction

Having set the stage, Pavlov described the basic procedure for the acquisition of a conditioned response. The essence of the technique is to pair a stimulus known to produce a particular response (i.e., salivation) with a neutral stimu-

---

[2] Pavlov often told the Snarskii story, using it as an illustration of the failure of a purely "psychological approach." Todes (1997) examined the original episode carefully, however, and discovered that Pavlov's memory had become distorted over the years. At the time of the Snarskii research (1901), Pavlov was actually the one thinking in more subjective terms, whereas Snarskii was proposing a more mechanistic and associationistic model. As the years went by, Pavlov apparently felt the need to distance himself from his earlier psychological theorizing. For some reason, he apparently convinced himself that he had been objective and Snarskii had been subjective, when the reverse was closer to the truth. The interesting historiographic point here is that you cannot always rely on the veracity of autobiographical accounts.

lus, such as a tone or a metronome. During acquisition, then, the starting point is an already existing reflex. For Pavlov, this reflex was the **unconditioned reflex** (UCR) of salivating when food (the **unconditioned stimulus**, or UCS) was presented to the animal. Conditioning involved presenting a neutral stimulus, then the UCS. This neutral stimulus Pavlov called a **conditional stimulus** (later mistranslated as condition*ed* stimulus), or CS, because the resulting reflex depended on (was "conditional" on) the CS-UCS pairing. This resulting reflex was called a **conditioned reflex**, or CR.

After describing acquisition, Pavlov showed how a CR could undergo **extinction** if the metronome (the CS) was sounded without being accompanied by food (the UCS). Pavlov let the metronome run for 30-second intervals every two minutes, recording the amount of saliva secreted and what he called the "latent period"—the amount of time between the starting of the metronome and the beginning of salivation. As Pavlov described it, the "weakening of the reflex to a conditional stimulus which is repeated a certain number of times without reinforcement may appropriately be termed experimental extinction of conditioned reflexes" (Pavlov, 1927/1960, pp. 48–49). An indication of Pavlov's concern for precision can be seen from his results, which he presented as follows (p. 49):

Latent period in seconds	Secretion of saliva in drops during 30 seconds
3	10
7	7
5	8
4	5
5	7
9	4
13	3

With successive extinction periods, then, it took longer (i.e., greater latency) for the animal to begin salivating, and there was a steady decline in the amount of salivation.

Generalization and Differentiation

Pavlov's subsequent lectures describe his procedures for demonstrating a wide range of conditioning phenomena, including many of the ones you learned about in your introductory psychology course. Two of the most familiar are generalization and discrimination (the latter referred to as differentiation by Pavlov). **Generalization** is in evidence when a response conditioned to stimulus A also occurs, to some degree at least, in response to stimuli that are similar to stimulus A. So if the CS of a 60 cps tone produces eight drops of saliva, the animal will also respond to a 70 cps tone, perhaps with six drops. A generalization gradient also exists—the amount of saliva secreted is proportional to the similarity of the CS and the tested stimulus. **Differentiation** results from pairing the 60 cps tone with food, while presenting the 70 cps tone without the food. Eventually, the dog salivates only to the 60 cps tone.

Pavlov also went to great lengths to incorporate Sechenov's constructs of cortical excitation and inhibition into his descriptions. For example, excitatory processes were said to be involved in acquisition and generalization, whereas inhibitory cortical processes contributed to extinction and differentiation. In general, Pavlov was not interested in the conditioning phenomena per se, but only in terms of the light they shed on how the brain operated.

Experimental Neurosis

One interesting outgrowth of Pavlov's research on generalization and differentiation was his discovery of how a breakdown in differentiation could produce **experimental neurosis** or "pathological disturbances," as he put it in the title of his Lecture 17. He first projected a circle onto a screen in front of the dog's face, pairing its presentation with food. Soon, the circle became a normal CS for the CR of salivation. After creating this conditioned reflex, Pavlov then trained the dog to make an easy differentiation between the circle and an ellipse that had a 2:1 ratio between its two axes. The shape of the ellipse was then changed gradually until it reached a 9:8 ratio; that is, the ellipse was made to look more and more like the circle. The dog showed a slight ability to discriminate at first, but it failed to improve after three weeks of training, and eventually its behavior deteriorated to the point where it even had some difficulty distinguishing the original 2:1 ellipse from the circle, as Pavlov's results (Pavlov, 1927/1960, p. 292) make clear (key trials in boldface):

Time	Conditioned stimulus applied during 30 seconds	Salivary Secretion in drops during 30 seconds
Experiment of 4th August, 1914		
4.10 pm	Circle	4
4.22 pm	Circle	6
4.37 pm	**4:3 ellipse**	**0**
4.55 pm	Circle	4
Experiment of 2nd September, 1914		
1.10 pm	Circle	2
1.27 pm	Circle	8
2.6 pm	Circle	10
2.16 pm	**9:8 ellipse**	**1**
2.30 pm	Circle	6
2.48 pm	Circle	8
Experiment of 17th September, 1914		
3.20 pm	Circle	4
3.31 pm	Circle	7
3.54 pm	**9:8 ellipse**	**8**
4.9 pm	Circle	9
Experiment of 25th September, 1914		
2.17 pm	Circle	9
2.47 pm	**2:1 ellipse**	**3**
3.8 pm	Circle	8
3.22 pm	Circle	8
3.46 pm	**2:1 ellipse**	**3**

In the experiments on August 4, then, the animal had no difficulty differentiating between the circle and the 4:3 ellipse. In experiment 2, the animal showed an apparent ability to discriminate between the circle and the 9:8 ellipse, but the performance deteriorated dramatically in experiment 3 (September 17), and even spilled over into experiment 4, when the animal could not even successfully avoid salivating to a 2:1 ellipse. For Pavlov, then, neurotic behavior meant a breakdown in the ability to make normal differentiations. The neurosis also manifested itself in other ways. As Pavlov described it,

> …At the same time the whole behavior of the animal underwent an abrupt change. The hitherto quiet dog began to squeal in its stand, kept wriggling about, tore off with its teeth the apparatus for mechanical stimulation of the skin, and bit through the tubes connecting the animal's room with the observer, a behavior which never happened before. On being taken into the experimental room the dog now barked violently, which was also contrary to its usual custom; in short it presented all the symptoms of an acute neurosis. (Pavlov, 1927/1960, p. 291)

During the course of his research on experimental neurosis, Pavlov noticed that although all the dogs were adversely affected, they displayed individual differences in how they displayed their pathology. Furthermore, these variations seemed to reflect overall differences in the temperaments of the dogs. Thus, some dogs were generally more excitable than others—they tended to respond to the experimental neurosis procedure like the dog just described. Others, however, who were ordinarily of a more placid temperament, reacted to the procedure by becoming even more withdrawn. As he did with all of his results, Pavlov interpreted these outcomes in terms of excitatory and inhibitory cortical processes. He believed that the individual differences in temperament related to whether excitatory or inhibitory processes were more dominant in them. Hence, he concluded that the first category of dog had a relatively higher proportion of excitatory than inhibitory processes, whereas the reverse was true for the second type of dog.

Pavlov's research over the years is a classic example of how experiments never occur in isolation, but are always embedded within an ongoing systematic program of research. The outcome of one study has interest in itself, but it also raises new questions and leads invariably to the next study. For instance, the acquisition research led naturally to the question of the precise timing of the CS and UCS, and Pavlov and his students completed dozens of studies that carefully varied the timing and the sequencing of the CS-UCS interval. Similarly, research developed over the years on such topics as (a) higher order conditioning, which involved pairing a new CS with an already conditioned one, (b) the durability of extinction, in which it was found that if a dog was returned to the laboratory several days after extinction, the CR would occur to some degree (i.e., spontaneous recovery occurred), and (c) the effectiveness of various types of conditional stimuli, in terms of how quickly conditioning could be established.[3]

PAVLOV AND THE SOVIETS

Pavlov was the prototype of the scientist whose life was his work, a philosophy reflected in an article he wrote near the end of his life for a Soviet youth organization. He told them that scientists must be systematic, modest, and passionate about their work, and that "science demands of a man his whole life. And even if you could have two lives, they would not be sufficient. Science calls for tremendous effort and great passion" (cited in Babkin, 1949, p. 110). While in the laboratory, and from

September through May he was there seven days a week, Pavlov was totally absorbed in the research at hand, and expected everyone else to share his passion. Thus, he was occasionally a stern taskmaster and was known for his frequent but short-lived outbursts of temper when mistakes were made. Nonetheless, his workers were intensely devoted to him, knowing that his anger passed quickly and was not directed at them personally.

One famous story about Pavlov provides an indication of his single-minded devotion to his work. Although the story might be more mythical than real, it clearly illustrates Pavlov's priorities. Pavlov is said to have admonished a worker for being 10 minutes late during the height of the 1917 Russian Revolution. When the worker told of bloody skirmishes in the streets of St. Petersburg, causing him to take a more circuitous route to the laboratory, Pavlov was not impressed. After all, he had made his customary three-mile walk to the lab, arriving safely and promptly at nine o'clock. Pavlov made it clear to the worker that a mere revolution was not to interfere with the important work of the laboratory. The assistant was told to leave home earlier during the next revolution (Babkin, 1949).

Of course, the revolution of 1917 had a profound effect on everything in Russia, including Pavlov's work. Pavlov was initially hostile to the winners of the Soviet Revolution, Lenin's Bolsheviks, once saying publicly that if "that which the Bolsheviks are doing with Russia is an experiment, for such an experiment I should regret giving even a frog" (cited in Babkin, 1949, p. 161). He also protested directly to Stalin in the late 1920s about a policy to admit only communist professors to the Russian Academy of Science, telling the Russian leader: "On account of what you are

---

[3] Ironically, although most students think that Pavlov's typical CS was a bell, Pavlov reported that "the violent ringing of a bell" was seldom effective as a CS, because the dog tended to be startled by it (Pavlov, 1906, p. 616).

doing I am ashamed to be called a Russian" (cited in Gantt, 1973). Pavlov's ambivalent attitude was not hard to understand: the Soviets had confiscated his Nobel Prize money and when he requested permission to emigrate in 1923, they refused. Yet by the end of his life, Pavlov had adjusted to the reality of the Soviet Union, and on one public occasion in the 1930s, even proposed a toast to "the great social experimenters." According to Babkin, Pavlov's change of heart came about primarily because of the developing threat of the Nazis in Germany, who came to power in 1933. Fiercely patriotic, Pavlov recalled the huge Russian losses at the hands of Germany in World War I and feared (accurately) that the Nazis would bring more suffering to his beloved homeland. In that context, the Soviets appeared to be the lesser of two evils.

Pavlov's accommodation to the reality of the Soviet state also was aided by the strong backing the government gave to his work. As early as 1921, when Russia was immersed in civil war and conditions were generally chaotic, the Soviets saw to it that Pavlov's research continued with full support. For example, it was officially decreed that a special committee be formed "to create as soon as possible the most favorable conditions for safeguarding the scientific work of Academician Pavlov and his collaborators" (cited in Babkin, 1949, p. 165). These conditions included extra rations and a guarantee to fully equip Pavlov's laboratory.

It is easy to see why the Soviets were so enamored of Pavlov. A major theme of his research was that behavior could be changed by controlling the environment—actions could be "conditioned." That, of course, was exactly what the Soviets hoped to do on a broad scale. The essence of their "great social experiment" was to bring about changes in behavior to accomplish the Marxist-Leninist ideal whereby each should produce according to one's abilities and receive according to one's needs. Thus, although Pavlov had no interests beyond

understanding the physiology of the brain, his research had great propaganda value for the Soviets. This tolerance by the Soviets is shown in a brief notice in *Time* magazine, which the American psychologist Walter Miles cut out and pasted into his diary in late 1929. It said that Pavlov had

> refused an official celebration of his 80th birthday.... Said he: "I deplore the destruction of cultural values by illiterate Communists." Mindful that upon his research rests the behavioristic "Science of Marxism"..., the Soviet tolerates his slaps gently and without reproach, babies him. Birthday gifts from the Soviet to him include $50,000 endowment of his laboratory and an assurance that traffic would be diverted from the street near it so as not to disturb the conditioned reflexes of some six score dogs, kept there for experimental purposes. (Miles, 1929)

After Pavlov's death from pneumonia in 1936, the Soviets treated him like a war hero. A monument to him was erected in St. Petersburg (at that time renamed Leningrad), the Medical Institute was renamed the Pavlov Institute, his wife was given a generous pension, and his brain was preserved.

PAVLOV AND THE AMERICANS

Western scientists knew about Pavlov because of the Nobel Prize, but the impact of his conditioning research was slow in being felt. Most American psychologists were introduced to Pavlov through an article published in *Psychological Bulletin* in 1909 by Robert Yerkes, whose interests at that time were mainly in comparative psychology (see Chapters 1 and 8), and Sergius Morgulis, a Russian student. One feature of the article was a series of apparatus sketches that eventually resulted in mistaken portrayals of Pavlov's apparatus which continue to this day. See the Close-Up for this story.

► CLOSE-UP

Misportraying Pavlov's Apparatus

You probably recognize the sketch in Figure 10.3a. It shows up in one form or another in most general psychology texts, probably including the one you used, and it is usually identified as Pavlov's conditioning apparatus. It wasn't. Rather, it was devised by a German physiologist, G. F. Nicolai, who worked for a brief time in Pavlov's laboratory (Goodwin, 1991). He wished to improve on how the saliva was recorded in the early years in Pavlov's lab, when the drops of saliva were simply counted as they fell into the graduated cylinder portrayed in Figure 10.3b. The early apparatus was cumbersome, a problem recognized by Pavlov, who eventually developed the more sophisticated apparatus shown in Figure 10.2. How did the mistaken attribution of Nicolai's apparatus occur?

The article by Yerkes and Morgulis (1909), which introduced Pavlov's research to American psychologists, included both the sketches in Figure 10.3. Neither was labeled, but the text of the article described Figure 10.3b as showing a dog prepared for conditioning research in Pavlov's lab, whereas Figure 10.3a was described as showing "the modification of experimental technique *which has been devised by Nicolai in Berlin*" (p. 259, italics added).

The distinction between Nicolai's and Pavlov's procedures was recognized by John Watson, who reproduced and correctly labeled both drawings in his well-known comparative psychology text of 1914. The first erroneous attribution seems to have been in a popular introductory textbook by Hunter (1919); it included only Figure 10.3a, referred to it as Pavlov's apparatus, and cited the Yerkes and Morgulis article. From this point on, the sketch of Nicolai's experimental setup became the standard depiction of Pavlov's apparatus, partly because it is consistent with Pavlov's eventual separation of dog and experimenter into two separate rooms, but also because it is simply a more interesting sketch than Figure 10.3b.

The perpetuation of this error over the years provides an important lesson for any textbook writer: beware of relying too heavily on secondary sources. Many subsequent writers probably included the wrong drawing simply because it had become so widely used in other texts. Seeing the same drawing over and over, it is easy to assume it must be accurate.

Despite the detailed descriptions in the Yerkes and Morgulis (1909) article, Pavlov's research had little immediate impact on American psychologists. The work was of interest to those studying animal behavior, but at a time when American psychology was still the study of human conscious experience, salivating dogs did not seem especially pertinent. Most introductory psychology textbooks prior to 1920 either failed to mention Pavlov at all (including a 1911 text by Yerkes) or mentioned his work just briefly (Goodwin, 1991). Even John Watson, whose proclamation of behavior-ism you will read about shortly, did not see the immediate relevance of Pavlov's work for his model of learning. Instead, he was initially more influenced by the conditioning work of another Russian physiologist and rival of Pavlov's, Vladimir Bekhterev (Skinner, 1981). Bekhterev investigated motor rather than salivary conditioning, in which muscle movements were conditioned to various stimuli. This lent itself more readily to Watson's interests in overt behavior.

Pavlov's major impact on American psychology began in the 1920s, when much of his work

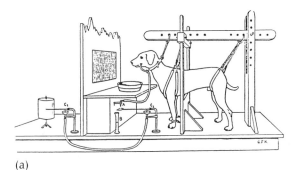

(a)

(b)

Figure 10.3   (a) Conditioning setup developed by German physiologist Nicolai, but usually attributed to Pavlov; (b) Early device used by Pavlov for recording salivary responses (both from Nicolai, 1907).

was translated into English for the first time. Pavlov also visited the United States twice, once in 1925 for a conference and lecture series at Rockefeller Institute in New York, and again in 1929 for the Ninth International Congress of Psychology at Yale University. There he delivered one of the major addresses (Duncan, 1980), an impassioned description (in Russian) of his research on conditioning to a large audi-

ence of American and international psychologists. As one observer noted, "the audience was spellbound, and the following standing ovation brought little smiles and bows of appreciation from the Guest of Honor of the Congress" (Withington, cited in Duncan, 1980).

American psychologists, especially behaviorists, eventually understood the importance of Pavlov's research for their own theories of learning. A passage from Ernest Hilgard's well-known *Theories of Learning* (1948) shows that Pavlov's importance was taken for granted by the late 1940s. Hilgard pointed out that research on "conditioned salivary responses in dogs was carried out systematically by Pavlov over many years, and he discovered most of the relationships which later studies have more fully explored. The translations of his terms have become common in the literature of learning" (Hilgard, 1948, p. 55).

Finally, Pavlov had a direct impact on the career choice of a young B. F. Skinner (Chapter 11), whose decision to pursue behavioral research was strongly influenced by reading a translation of Pavlov's *Conditioned Reflexes* (1927/1960). Skinner once wrote that a guiding principle in his scientific life was Pavlov's simple dictum that if you "control your conditions…you will see order" (Skinner, 1956, p. 223). Skinner was also excited by the writings of an American psychologist who shared with Pavlov a passion for systematic research grounded in measurable behavior. This person was John B. Watson, usually considered to be the founder of the American school of thought that came to be known as behaviorism.

JOHN B. WATSON AND THE FOUNDING OF BEHAVIORISM

Near the beginning of the chapter it was mentioned that at the start of the twentieth century, a number of American psychologists were arguing that psychology should adopt a more "objective" methodology than introspection.

One example was the 1904 address by Cattell to an audience at the World's Fair in St. Louis. Also at St. Louis and probably in the audience for Cattell's address was John B. Watson, a young psychologist with a brand new Ph.D. from the University of Chicago. The developing trends toward objectivity in psychology were beginning to crystallize in the thinking and writing of this young man, and he would shortly become the mouthpiece for the movement that came to be called behaviorism.

THE YOUNG FUNCTIONALIST AT CHICAGO

Watson was born in 1878 in the rural area just outside of Greenville, South Carolina, into a family that would earn the label "dysfunctional" today. His father was a marginally successful farmer whose interests included consuming large amounts of alcohol, brawling, and committing adultery. He frequently left home for extended periods of time. Watson's mother was fiercely religious, enough so to name her son after a well-known fundamentalist Baptist preacher, John Broadus, and to insist that he aspire to the ministry. Growing up in this environment, Watson understandably developed behavior problems of his own; by mid-adolescence he was a known troublemaker and had been arrested at least twice. Nonetheless, he was known to be an intelligent young man when he entered Furman University in Greenville at the age of 16. He graduated with a master's degree in 1900.

Watson's mother died during his final year at Furman, releasing him from any obligation to pursue the ministry. Instead, influenced by one of his professors at Furman, he applied to and was accepted at the University of Chicago. Eight years old in 1900, the university was established with Rockefeller oil money, and was presided over by William Rainey Harper. As you recall from Chapter 7's discussion of functionalism, Harper envisioned a "practical" university that would produce leaders for an emerging class in America—the professional elite, experts who would manage society's improvement and industry's productivity. Watson's initial intention was to study philosophy and psychology, which coexisted in the philosophy department at Chicago. He quickly discovered that neither philosophy nor introspective psychology appealed to him (he had no talent for introspection), but he was comfortable with the general precepts of a functionalist psychology. He was especially attracted to comparative psychology—not a surprise considering his rural background and familiarity with animals. Many years later, Watson's son rather painfully recalled that his father "preferred the company of animals to people most of the time" (Hannush, 1987, p. 150).

Watson's interests in animal behavior began to shape his beliefs about psychology in general. When reflecting on his Chicago years, he later wrote that he was always uncomfortable with introspective methods and human subjects but that with animals, he was "at home.... More and more the thought presented itself: Can't I find out by watching their behavior everything that the other students are finding out by using [human subjects]?" (Watson, 1936, p. 279). This belief was reinforced by Watson's contacts with Jacques Loeb and Henry Donaldson. Loeb was a German physiologist who studied **tropisms**, movements of plants or animals that are forced automatically by some aspect of the environment. For example, a flower that always faces the sun is said to be showing a positive heliotropism (helio = sun). Loeb was an uncompromising materialist and mechanist who believed that all organic life could be understood as a series of automatic responses to stimuli. Donaldson was a neurologist specializing in the nervous system of white rats.

Watson's doctoral dissertation, codirected by Donaldson and James Angell, was a study of the relationship between cortical development and learning in young white rats. It was an important study because at the time many leading physiologists believed that rats were incapable of true "associative learning" because their brains contained few if any "medullated" fibers.[4] Through a painstaking series of studies that showcased his talents as a careful scientist, Watson demonstrated that rats showed minimal learning ability for approximately the first three weeks of their lives, but that their ability to form associations improved dramatically in their fourth week. Furthermore, during this same time, the number of medullated fibers increased significantly. Thus, Watson concluded that associations could be formed in young white rats and that these associations were correlated with cortical development. Watson borrowed $350 from Donaldson and had his results published as *Animal Education: An Experimental Study of the Psychical Development of the White Rat, Correlated with the Growth of its Nervous System* (Watson, 1903). It earned him the doctorate and an offer to remain at Chicago as an instructor. Watson accepted.

The Watson/Carr Maze Studies

Watson remained on the faculty at Chicago from 1903 to 1908. During that time he began to build a reputation as a good teacher and a careful scientist. His most important research during this time involved studying rats in mazes; it was completed with Harvey Carr, then a graduate student at Chicago, later an important leader in the functionalist movement, and eventually chair of Chicago's psychology department (Chapter 7).

The goal of the Watson/Carr studies (Carr & Watson, 1908; Watson, 1907) was to determine which senses were needed for a rat to learn a maze. Watson was intrigued by the maze studies done at Clark by Willard Small (see the Close-Up in Chapter 6), but believed that Small had not been very systematic when trying to identify the factors contributing to the rat's ability to learn a maze. For example, Small's willingness to let the rats live in the maze at night made it impossible to evaluate how the

learning occurred. Watson and Carr remedied that problem and others, producing a methodologically brilliant series of studies that established (at least for a time) the importance of the kinesthetic sense for maze learning.

In their first study (Watson, 1907) Watson and Carr systematically eliminated the ability of the animals to use their senses when solving a version of the Hampton Court maze. Displaying skillful surgical techniques, Watson removed the eyes from some rats, the middle ears from others, and the olfactory bulbs from a third group. Deprived of their various senses, the rats nonetheless learned the maze with ease. Watson and Carr also found that learning ability was not markedly hindered by removing the rats' whiskers, or by anesthetizing the rats' feet. By a process of elimination (literally!), they concluded that the only important factors in the formation of learned associations were "the kinesthetic impressions coupled with certain other intra-organic impressions" (Watson, 1907, p. 84). That is, the animals were learning to associate sequences of muscle movements with the various turns in the maze. In essence, they learned to take 10 steps, then turn right for another five steps, then turn left, and so on.

Having ruled out one sense after another, Watson and Carr set out to provide direct evidence of their remaining hypothesis about the kinesthetic sense. In their second study (Carr & Watson, 1908), they hit on the clever idea of shortening or lengthening the mazes that their rats had already learned. Figure 10.4 shows the maze they used, in its full-length version, with the piece that could be removed shaded. The effects were dramatic—rats initially trained in the full-length maze literally ran into the walls of the shortened maze. For example, according to Watson's lab notes, one rat "ran into [the wall] with all her strength. Was badly staggered and did not recover normal conduct until she had gone 9 feet" (Carr & Watson, 1908, p. 39). Similarly, rats trained in the shortened maze and

---

[4] Today such fibers would be called "myelinated axons."

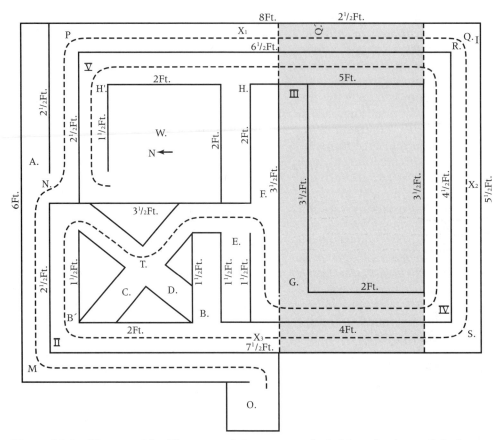

Figure 10.4   Maze used by Watson and Carr to test their kinesthetic model of maze learning; shaded piece could be removed to produce a shorter version of the maze, from Carr and Watson (1908).

tested in the long version often started to turn at the point where the correct turn used to be.

The Watson/Carr studies are models of scientific research, arriving at an empirical conclusion by first eliminating one alternative hypothesis after another, then producing a direct demonstration of the viability of the remaining (kinesthetic) hypothesis. They also provide a good illustration of how scientists can be naive about how their research will be accepted in the public eye. Watson might have thought he was simply pursuing an important question about learning, but in the public eye he became a target for antivivisectionists[5] and was portrayed in the *New York Times* on December 30, 1906, as a butcher of helpless white rats, chopping out bits and pieces of them in order to satisfy some idle scientific curiosity.

---

[5] Like today's animal rights activists, antivivisectionists protested the use of animals for research purposes; their influence on early comparative psychology has been documented by Dewsbury (1990).

OPPORTUNITY KNOCKS
AT JOHNS HOPKINS

By 1908, Watson was known among his professional colleagues as an up-and-coming star in the world of experimental psychology (see Figure 10.5). He was also beginning to feel unappreciated at Chicago, where he still held the low academic rank of instructor after five years. Thus, when offered a full professor position, control of a laboratory, and more than double his salary from Johns Hopkins University, he could hardly refuse. Furthermore, within a year of his arrival in Baltimore, the head of the psychology department, James Mark Baldwin, was fired for moral reasons (arrested in a police raid on a house of prostitution, he claimed he was doing research). Barely into his third decade, then, Watson found himself in charge of psychology at Johns Hopkins University. Over the next 12 years, before he would himself be fired for moral reasons, he would (a) cement his reputation as a leading researcher in the world of animal psychology, (b) proclaim behaviorism, and (c) develop a program of research in devel-

Figure 10.5   John B. Watson in 1908, at age 30.

opmental psychology, with an emphasis on the study of emotional development.

Watson and Animal Behavior

Once settled into his new position at Johns Hopkins, Watson launched a wide-ranging program of research in animal behavior. Like his dissertation and the maze studies with Carr at Chicago, some of the research was of the basic laboratory variety and included work in animal psychophysics. For example, he studied the visual abilities of several species by training them to make choices between pairs of slightly different stimuli (e.g., Watson, 1909), and by using the motor conditioning procedures of Pavlov's Russian colleague Bekhterev (Watson, 1916). The logic of Watson's psychophysics research was simple—if an animal could be trained or conditioned to respond correctly to one stimulus (e.g., light red) while not responding to another (e.g., a darker shade of red), then the animal must be able to perceive the difference between the two.

Outside of the laboratory, Watson continued a series of naturalistic studies begun while he was still at the University of Chicago. He spent several summers on a small island near the Florida keys (Bird Key, one of the Dry Tortugas) observing the behavior of several species of terns. In contrast with Watson's later writings, which downplayed the importance of the instinctive control of behavior, especially human behavior, this research reads like an early version of the kind of ethological research later associated with names like Konrad Lorenz and Niko Tinbergen, emphasizing the importance of instinctive behavior for species survival (Dewsbury, 1994). He carefully documented the mating behaviors of the terns on Bird Key, their nest building and territoriality, and their behavior relating to the care of offspring, before and after their hatching (Todd & Morris, 1986). He also observed that recently hatched birds would often persistently follow him around the island. This of course is the same behavior studied by Spalding (see the

Close-Up in Chapter 5) and later called **imprinting** by Lorenz.

The Behaviorist Manifesto

In 1913, Watson accepted an invitation from Cattell to speak at Columbia University. By then he believed he had sufficient stature to proclaim what he had believed for at least 10 years—that it was time for the field to move away from an introspective psychology that studied consciousness and toward a psychology of behavior. His Columbia lectures, published with the provocative title "Psychology as the Behaviorist Views It" (Watson, 1913), have come to be called the Behaviorist Manifesto. What did Watson proclaim? The opening paragraph, one of the most widely quoted passages in psychology's history, set the tone:

> Psychology as the behaviorist views it is a purely objective experimental branch of natural science. Its theoretical goal is the prediction and control of behavior. Introspection forms no essential part of its methods, nor is the scientific value of its data dependent upon the readiness with which they lend themselves to interpretation in terms of consciousness. The behaviorist, in his efforts to get a unitary scheme of animal response, recognizes no dividing line between man and brute.... (p. 158)

Watson quickly elaborated on his theme of discarding introspection and consciousness, pointing out the absurdity of a method that produced results that could never be independently verified (i.e., could never be objective) and where a failure to replicate some introspective result would be blamed on the inadequate training of introspectors. Concerning the introspective analysis of sensation, for example, he doubted whether "any one psychologist [could] draw up a set of statements describing what he means by sensation that would be agreed to by three other psychologists of different training" (p. 164); consequently, Watson believed the time had come "when psychology

must discard all reference to consciousness" (p. 163) and turn to behavior as the data to be observed. His attack was most clearly directed at the Titchenerian structuralists, but he was also critical of his mentors, the functionalists. Although the functionalist approach had increased the scope of psychological research, it nonetheless had failed to reject introspection and the study of consciousness. They might be studying consciousness in a way that differed from the structuralists, Watson pointed out, but they were still studying it.

In place of psychology as the study of consciousness, Watson proposed that psychology become the science of behavior. Just as behavioral methods had increased our understanding of animals, he argued, so could they enhance our knowledge of humans. He set as a goal for psychology the prediction and control of behavior and boldly proclaimed that in a mature S-R system, "given the response the stimuli can be predicted; given the stimuli the response can be predicted" (Watson, 1913, p. 167). Even such activities as thinking could be reduced to stimuli and responses. According to Watson, thinking was in essence nothing more than **subvocal speech**, and the subject of this thinking would be determined by habits that he referred to as "laryngeal habits." He later suggested (Watson, 1926) that some evidence in support of his position was the observation that our thinking tended to suffer when we experienced a sore throat!

One thing that eventually made behaviorism popular among American psychologists was its insistence that behavioral principles must have applications to real life. Watson made the point in his manifesto as a way of contrasting his approach with introspective psychology, which seemed to him to be devoid of application. A behavioral strategy, he argued, was already making contributions to such applied topics as advertising, drug effects, the law, and education.

Watson's behaviorist manifesto was a powerful statement, sometimes seen as the starting point for a behaviorist "revolution" in psychol-

This year marked the publication of Watson's behaviorist manifesto, "Psychology as the Behaviorist Views It."

These events also occurred:

- Niels Bohr formulated his theory of atomic structure
- Albert Schweitzer opened his hospital in the French Congo
- Henry Ford pioneered new assembly line procedures in his car factory
- Grand Central Station opened in New York
- Federal income tax was introduced via the 16th Amendment to the Constitution
- Mahatma Ghandi, leader of Indian passive resistance movement, was arrested
- These people were born:

    Richard Nixon and Gerald Ford, U.S. presidents

    Albert Camus, French author and philosopher

    Rosa Parks, pioneer in American civil rights movement
- These people died:

    Harriet Tubman, American abolitionist and reformer

    J. Pierpont Morgan, wealthy American industrialist

ogy and as the vehicle that catapulted Watson to the presidency of the APA in 1915. Yet Samelson (1981) has shown that the immediate effect of the manifesto was that most psychologists ignored it or saw it as just one more instance of a growing number of assaults on introspection. Only two psychologists— Titchener (1914) and Calkins (1913)— responded in print to it, and both were highly critical.[6] As for Watson's APA presidency, it was more likely the outcome of his already-existing status among his peers, earned by virtue of a decade of research, his friendships with influential APA members, his position as chair at Johns Hopkins, and his editorship of *Psychological Review*. Also, his nomination for the APA presidency occurred before the manifesto had been delivered (Samelson, 1981). On the other hand, while the manifesto might not have been a revolutionary event, it certainly energized Watson. For the remainder of the decade, he vigorously advocated behaviorism, and eventually elaborated the manifesto into a book-length treatise—*Psychology From the Standpoint of a Behaviorist* (1919). According to historian James Todd (1994), it was this book and Watson's promotional efforts in the 1920s, more than the earlier manifesto, that were

---

[6] Despite the obvious contrast between the psychologies of Titchener and Watson, they maintained a mutual respect for each other—both were "laboratory men." They corresponded with some regularity, and when Watson hosted a meeting of Titchener's Experimentalists in 1910, Titchener was Watson's houseguest. When Watson was fired from John Hopkins in 1920, Titchener was one of the few psychologists who lent public support to his colleague (Larson & Sullivan, 1965).

3 infant Emotions

responsible for the increased influence of behaviorism among American psychologists as the 1920s drew to a close.

Studying Emotional Development

In the manifesto and elsewhere, Watson made some large claims about the ability of behaviorism to deliver applications that would improve the quality of life. Yet at the time of the manifesto, Watson's own research had been limited largely to animals. Thus, when an opportunity arose to study infants, Watson saw this as a major chance to apply behaviorism in a way that would convince skeptics and more important, secure Watson's position as a leader in the application of psychological principles to improve society. Furthermore, Watson was feeling some of the same pressure felt by other comparative psychologists who were finding it increasingly difficult to maintain institutional support for their basic research in animal behavior. University administrators were becoming reluctant to supply budgetary support for research that seemed esoteric, of little practical value, and required facilities with strong, unpleasant odors (Buckley, 1989).

The opportunity came to Watson in the form of an invitation from Adolf Meyer, a well-known psychiatrist, to set up a human laboratory in Meyer's clinic at the Johns Hopkins Medical School. The new lab was adjacent to the medical school's obstetrical ward, thereby providing Watson with a supply of infants for his research. The result was a series of studies investigating reflexes, basic emotional responses, and conditioned emotional responses.

The work on basic emotions was coauthored with J. J. B. Morgan. They set out to identify the fundamental human emotional responses and the stimuli that produced these responses. They identified three: fear, rage, and love. According to Watson and Morgan (1917), the fear response, defined behaviorally as "a sudden catching of the breath, clutching randomly with the hands,…blinking of the eye lids, puckering of the lips, then crying" (p. 166), occurred in response to either of two classes of stimuli: sudden loud noises and loss of support (the latter produced by dropping the infant or pulling out the infant's blanket just as the infant is falling asleep!). The second emotion, rage, resulted from hindering the infant's movements: "If the face or head is held crying results, quickly followed by screaming. The body stiffens and fairly well coordinated slashing or striking movements of the hands and arms result" (pp. 166–167). The third emotion, love, defined as smiling, gurgling, or cooing, resulted from gently stroking the infant's skin or gently rocking or patting the child.

▶ ORIGINAL SOURCE EXCERPT

Watson & Rayner's Little Albert Study

From the infant research, Watson concluded that only a few stimuli would elicit the three instinctive emotions of fear, rage, and love. Why do older children show these emotional responses to a much wider range of stimuli? For Watson, the answer was simple: conditioning. His attempt to demonstrate this directly resulted in what has come to be called the Little Albert study. It was published as "Conditioned Emotional Reactions" in the *Journal of Experimental Psychology* in 1920 and it was coauthored by Watson and Rosalie Rayner, a graduate student at Johns Hopkins. As will be seen shortly, she was to play a pivotal role in another important event for Watson in 1920—his forced resignation from Johns Hopkins.

Watson and Rayner (1920) opened the article by stating their belief that emotional reactions develop through conditioning but that "direct experimental evidence in support of such a view has been lacking" (p. 1). Hence, the goal of their study was to provide just such evidence, using a young child by the name of Albert B., whose attributes and suitability for the experiment they described in the following terms:

> Experimental work has been done so far on only one child, Albert B. This infant was reared almost from birth in a hospital environment; his mother was a wet nurse at the Harriet Lane Home for Invalid Children. Albert's life was normal: he was healthy from birth and one of the best developed youngsters ever brought to the hospital, weighing twenty-one pounds at nine months of age. He was on the whole stolid and unemotional. His stability was one of the principal reasons for using him as a subject in this test. We felt that we could do him relatively little harm by carrying out such experiments as those outlined below. (pp. 1–2)

Before the experiment began, the nine-month old Albert was put through a series of tests—the same ones used in Watson's earlier infant research with Morgan. Albert showed no fear when presented "with a white rat, a rabbit, a dog, a monkey, with masks with and without hair, cotton wool, burning newspapers, etc." (Watson & Rayner, 1920, p. 2). Unlike other infants, Albert did not show a fear response to the stimulus of a loss of support. Like the others, however, he *was* afraid of a loud, unexpected noise:

> ...The sound was made by striking a hammer upon a suspended steel bar four feet in length and three-fourths of an inch in diameter. The laboratory notes are as follows:
> One of the two experimenters caused the child to turn its head and fixate her moving hand; the other, stationed back of the child, struck the steel bar a sharp blow. The child started violently, his breathing was checked and the arms were raised in a characteristic manner. On the second stimulation the same thing occurred, and in addition the lips began to pucker and tremble. On the third stimulation the child broke into a sudden crying fit. This is the first time an emotional situation in the laboratory has produced any fear or even crying in Albert. (p. 2)

Having established that Albert feared the loud noise, Watson and Rayner outlined the four areas of research they hoped to explore: conditioning the fear to a new stimulus, seeing if the fear would transfer to other stimuli, seeing if the fear would dissipate after a period of time, and determining whether techniques could be developed to remove the fear. Before describing the research, however, they attempted an ethical justification for it. In essence, this amounted to pointing out that the child would learn to be afraid of new stimuli *anyway*, during the course of daily life, so why not do it under controlled conditions, thereby increasing the body of knowledge about emotional behavior?

> ...At first there was considerable hesitation upon our part in making the attempt to set up fear reactions experimentally. A certain responsibility

attaches to such a procedure. We decided finally to make the attempt, comforting ourselves by the reflection that such attachments would arise anyway as soon as the child left the sheltered environment of the nursery for the rough and tumble of the home. We did not begin this work until Albert was eleven months, three days of age.... (p. 3)

Thus, the conditioning phase of the study began two months after the initial testing of Albert. It was reported in detail in Watson and Rayner's laboratory notes:

11 Months 3 Days

1. White rat suddenly taken from the basket and presented to Albert. He began to reach for rat with left hand. Just as his hand touched the animal the bar was struck immediately behind his head. The infant jumped violently and fell forward, burying his face in the mattress. He did not cry, however.

2. Just as the right hand touched the rat the bar was again struck. Again the infant jumped violently, fell forward and began to whimper.

   In order not to disturb the child too seriously no further tests were given for one week.

11 Months 10 Days

1. Rat presented suddenly without sound. There was steady fixation but no tendency at first to reach for it. The rat was then placed nearer, whereupon tentative reaching movements began with the right hand. When the rat nosed the infant's left hand, the hand was immediately withdrawn.... It is thus seen that the two joint stimulations given the previous week were not without effect. He was tested with his blocks immediately afterwards to see if they shared in the process of conditioning. He began immediately to pick them up, dropping them, pounding them, etc. In the remainder of the tests the blocks were given frequently to quiet him and to test his general emotional state. They were always removed from sight when the process of conditioning was under way.

2. Joint stimulation with rat and sound. Started, then fell over immediately to right side. No crying.

3. Joint stimulation. Fell to right side and rested upon hands, with head turned away from rat. No crying.

4. Joint stimulation. Same reaction.

5. Rat suddenly presented alone. Puckered face, whimpered and withdrew body sharply to the left.

6. Joint stimulation. Fell over immediately to right side and began to whimper.

7. Joint stimulation. Started violently and cried, but did not fall over.

8. Rat alone. *The instant the rat was shown the baby began to cry. Almost instantly he turned sharply to the left, fell over on one side, raised himself on all fours and began to crawl away so rapidly that he was caught with difficulty before reaching the edge of the table.*

> This was as convincing a case of a completely conditioned fear response as could have been theoretically pictured. In all seven joint stimulations were given to bring about the complete reaction. (pp. 4–5, italics in the original)

Modern textbook accounts of the Albert study often describe it as a human example of classical conditioning, labeling the loud noise an unconditioned stimulus (UCS) and the fear of the noise an unconditioned response (UCR). The rat is the conditioned stimulus (CS) that comes to produce the conditioned response (CR) of fear through the pairing of CS and UCS, just as pairing a tone (CS) with food (UCS) yields salivation to the tone in the standard Pavlovian procedure. A close reading of Watson and Rayner's lab notes, however, suggests that an operant punishment procedure might have occurred instead, at least on the first two trials. The baby's behavior of reaching for the rat resulted in the immediate consequence of the loud noise. Whether the same sequence of events occurred on other trials that are simply labeled "joint stimulation" is not clear. It is clear that Albert was affected by the procedures and became afraid of the rat, but the ambiguity over precisely what happened is one reason why the study has been criticized (Harris, 1979).

After conditioning (by whatever procedure) Albert to fear the rat, Watson and Rayner's second goal was to see if the response would "transfer" to other stimuli (or "generalize," as Pavlov would say). Five days after the famous trials just described, Albert was returned to the lab and tested first with blocks and the rat. He played with the former and continued to be afraid of the latter. After showing that the conditioned response still existed, Watson and Rayner presented other stimuli, alternating them with occasions for the child to play with his blocks:

> ...The rabbit was suddenly placed on the mattress in front of him. The reaction was pronounced. Negative responses began at once. He leaned as far away from the animal as possible, whimpered, then burst into tears. When the rabbit was placed in contact with him he buried his face in the mattress, then got up on all fours and crawled away, crying as he went. This was a most convincing test.
>
> ...The dog did not produce as violent a reaction as the rabbit. The moment fixation occurred the child shrank back and as the animal came nearer he attempted to get on all fours but did not cry at first.... The dog was then made to approach the infant's head (he was lying down at the moment). Albert straightened up immediately, fell over to the opposite side and turned his head away. He then began to cry.
>
> ...Fur coat (seal). Withdrew immediately to the left side and began to fret. Coat put close to him on the left side, he turned immediately, began to cry and tried to crawl away on all fours.
>
> ...Just in play W. put his head down to see if Albert would play with his hair. Albert was completely negative. Two other observers did the same thing. He began immediately to play with their hair. W. then brought a Santa Claus mask and presented it to Albert. He was again pronouncedly negative. (pp. 6–7)

After another five days, Albert was again tested, and while he showed some aversive reactions to the rat, rabbit, and dog, the responses were less extreme. Watson and Rayner decided to "freshen up the reaction" (p. 7) by sounding the loud noise again, pairing it not just with the rat, but also with the rabbit and the dog. They also decided to test the fear response in a different room, larger and more brightly lit than the initial testing room. The results? Albert showed moderate fear reactions to the rat, rabbit, and the dog, but a second presentation of the dog produced an unanticipated event.

> ...Dog alone. At first the dog did not produce the pronounced reaction. The hands were held high over the head, breathing was checked, but there was no crying. Just at this moment the dog, which had not barked before, barked three times loudly when only about six inches from the baby's face. Albert immediately fell over and broke into a wail that continued until the dog was removed. The sudden barking of the hitherto quiet dog produced a marked fear response in the adult observers! (p. 9)

From the testing with stimuli such as the rabbit, dog, and fur coat, Watson and Rayner concluded that the fear generalized beyond the original stimulus of the rat. As you probably noticed, however, the "freshening up" of the response by banging the steel bar several times, along with the dog's sudden barking, introduced what amounted to new learning trials, thus contaminating a pure test for generalization. Nonetheless Watson and Rayner believed that transfer had been effectively demonstrated, so they moved to their third research question: Would the response be retained for a significant period of time? The retention interval was limited by a practical consideration:

> ...In view of the imminence of Albert's departure from the hospital we could not make the interval longer than one month. Accordingly no further emotional experimentation was entered into for thirty-one days.... The notes on the test given at the end of this period are as follows:

Albert's Age → **1 Year 21 Days**

1. Santa Claus mask. Withdrawal, gurgling, then slapped at it without touching. When his hand was forced to touch it, he whimpered and cried....

2. Fur coat. Wrinkled his nose and withdrew both hands, drew back his whole body and began to whimper as the coat was put nearer....

3. Fur coat...He began immediately to fret....

4. Blocks. He began to play with them as usual.

5. The rat. He allowed the rat to crawl toward him without withdrawing. He sat very still and fixated it intently. Rat then touched his hand. Albert withdrew it immediately, then leaned back as far as possible but did not cry. When the rat was placed on his arm he withdrew his body and began to fret, nodding his head....

6. Blocks. Reaction normal.

7. The rabbit. The animal was placed directly in front of him.... Albert showed no avoiding reactions at first. After a few seconds he puckered up his face, began to nod his head and look intently at the experimenter. He next began to push the rabbit away with his feet, withdrawing his body at the same time. Then as the rabbit came nearer he began pulling his feet away, nodding his head, and wailing "da da."...

These experiments would seem to show conclusively that directly conditioned emotional responses as well as those conditioned by transfer persist, although with a certain loss in the intensity of the reaction, for a longer period than one month. Our view is that they persist and modify personality throughout life. (pp. 10–12)

At the start of this section on the question of the fear's duration, Watson and Rayner mention that they knew about Albert leaving the hospital within a month. In the final section of their paper, they addressed the question of how Albert's fear might have been alleviated, if additional time had been available. Although they gave the impression that they wish they could have had more time with Albert, it is clear that they knew of his forthcoming departure and chose to test the persistence of the fear rather than to attempt its reversal. Nonetheless, they did make several suggestions about how the fear might be removed.

(1) Constantly confronting the child with those stimuli which called out the responses in the hopes that habituation would come in corresponding to "fatigue" of reflex when differential reactions are to be set up. (2) By trying to "recondition" by showing objects calling out fear responses (visual) and simultaneously stimulating the erogenous zones (tactual). We should try first the lips, then the nipples and as a final resort the sex organs. (3) By trying to "recondition" by feeding the subject candy or other food just as the animal is shown. This method calls for the food control of the subject. (4) By building up "constructive" activities around the object by imitation and by putting the hand through the motions of manipulation. (pp. 12–13)

Although Watson and Rayner made no attempt to alleviate Albert's fear, Watson later redeemed himself to some extent by supervising the research of Mary Cover Jones (Figure 10.6). Watson was by then out of academia and working in advertising (below), but his research with children inspired Jones, a young Columbia graduate student and friend of Rosalie Rayner. Working with several children who feared various objects, Jones tried a number of methods (1924a), most of them unsuccessful. For example, fears were not reduced (a) simply through the passage of time, (b) through the method of verbal appeal (i.e., trying to convince the child that the fear was groundless), or (c) by having peers ridicule the child. What did work, however, was the third method suggested by Watson and Rayner. In a study that is often cited as a pioneering example of the behavior therapy technique of *systematic desensitization*, Jones (1924b) reduced a young boy's fear of rabbits by placing the animal at some distance from the boy while he was eating, then gradually moving the rabbit closer. The pleasurable responses associated with eating apparently replaced the fear response associated with the rabbit.

Watson and Rayner closed their Little Albert article by detailing some additional observations about the boy (e.g., thumb sucking seemed to reduce his fear somewhat) and by taking issue with Freud, whose theories were widely known and popular in 1920 (Chapter 12). Watson and Rayner argued that their research showed that sex ("love" for Watson) was not the primary motivator, as claimed by the Freudians. Rather, there were three fundamental emotions and the Little Albert study showed that fear was "as primal a factor as love in influencing personality" (Watson & Rayner, 1920, p. 14). They also took the opportunity to poke some fun at Freudians, suggesting that some future psychoanalyst might attempt to trace the adult Albert's fear of a "seal skin coat" to an unresolved Oedipal complex.

The Little Albert study can be found in the chapters on learning in virtually all modern introductory psychology texts. The study is often thought of as a "classic," displaying the power of behavioral principles to condition our emotions. If learning is a change in behavior brought about by experience, then clearly the study illustrated learning of some kind. Albert was certainly affected by his encounter with Watson and Rayner. Yet the study had some serious flaws. First, there is some question about whether the initial procedure actually produced a strong fear of animals in Albert (Harris, 1979). During the start of generalization testing ("transfer"), his reactions were often so weak that they needed to be "freshened up" with additional pairings of the animals with the loud noise. Second, as noted earlier, these additional pairings constituted further learning trials, thus rendering the generalization test meaningless. Third, even if one concedes that the child developed a fear, just what he was afraid of is not clear. As you were reading the study, especially the place when Watson "just in play" put his head down for Albert to play with his hair, did it occur to you that perhaps Albert became afraid, not of the animals, but of Watson himself? A similar impression of some relatively rough treatment of infants on the part of Watson comes from viewing the films that he made of his infant research. Fourth, it is inappropriate to draw a general conclusion about fear conditioning on the basis of a study using a single baby. Research limited to individual subjects is acceptable, and represents an important tradi-

Figure 10.6   Mary Cover Jones of Columbia, during the time of her studies on the unlearning of fears.

tion in psychological research, but confidence in the generality of results only comes with continued replication of the basic finding. Several attempts to produce conditioned emotional responses in the 1920s and 1930s produced ambiguous results, however. For instance, English (1929) failed to condition a 14-month old to fear a wooden duck, primarily because the child did not react adversely to the loud noise. Also, Valentine (1930) failed to condition a child to fear opera glasses, but apparently succeeded with a caterpillar. Similarly, Bregman (1934) failed to condition fear to biologically-neutral stimuli, including a curtain and some wooden blocks. Both the Valentine and Bregman studies were seriously flawed methodologically, however, making it difficult to determine if replication occurred or not (Todd, 1994).

In summary, then, the Little Albert study cannot be considered a conclusive demonstration of the widespread applicability of conditioning principles. Why has it become so well known? One reason is political. For behaviorism to become recognized as an important force in American scientific psychology, it needed examples of the power of conditioning. It was one thing for Watson to proclaim behaviorism, but proof of its viability was needed. The Little Albert study seemed to fit the bill, and in subsequent descriptions of it by Watson and others sympathetic to behaviorism, the methodological weaknesses were ignored and it eventually achieved the status of an unambiguous case of "conditioning in action" (Prytula, Oster, & Davis, 1977). A second reason for the study's popularity, related to the first, is that it has a certain dramatic appeal and applicability to one of life's importance tasks: how we raise our children. If their lives can be affected so strikingly by the experiences they encounter, then managing the child's environment becomes an important way to shape the child's future.

Thus, the Little Albert study served the important function of legitimizing the new behavioral approach that within a decade would become a dominant force in American psychology. Watson was not destined to be a major player during that decade of the 1920s, however. The year that the Little Albert study was published also marked the year that Watson was fired from Johns Hopkins.

A NEW LIFE IN ADVERTISING

While a young bachelor instructor at the University of Chicago, Watson fell in love with Mary Ickes, a student in his introductory psychology class; he eventually married her. As an established experimental psychologist at Johns Hopkins, he had a similar experience with two major differences. This time the student was a graduate student (Rosalie Rayner) rather than an undergraduate; more important, this time Watson was already married—to the same woman who had been that undergraduate some 17 years earlier. The details of this unhappy situation can be found elsewhere (e.g., Buckley, 1989). It is enough to say that Watson's love for Rayner led to (a) his highly publicized divorce from Mary Ickes Watson, which featured the publication of love letters written by Watson to Rosalie and discovered by Mary, (b) his forced resignation from Johns Hopkins, and (c) his marriage to Rosalie.

The dismissal from Johns Hopkins was a devastating blow to Watson. Furthermore, the attendant publicity ruined any chance that he would secure another academic position. Instead, through the intercession of a friend, he entered the business world by joining the J. Walter Thompson advertising agency in New York City. After an apprenticeship, during which Watson served in all departments of the agency, he rose to the position of vice-president within four years (Buckley, 1989).

As an advertising executive, Watson had the opportunity to put into practice some of his claims about the applicability of behaviorism. For instance, he developed a number of advertising campaigns around themes derived from his research on the three basic emotions of fear, rage, and love. To sell a product to a consumer, Watson suggested, one must "tell him something that will tie [him] up with fear, something that will stir up a mild rage, that will call out an affectionate or love response, or strike at a deep psychological or habit need" (cited in Buckley, 1989, p. 137). For example, an ad campaign for Johnson & Johnson baby powder sent a clear message designed to scare young parents into buying the product: if they failed to use baby powder, they risked exposing their children to serious infection. Watson also relied heavily on the use of testimonials by well-known personalities and experts to sell products. The baby powder campaign used testimony by doctors, for example.

Watson brought to his new career the same passion for scientific method that characterized his life in academia. In an autobiographical statement, for example, he claimed that "it can be just as thrilling to watch the growth of a sales curve of a new product as to watch the learning curve of animals or man" (Watson, 1936, p. 280). Indeed, his major contribution to consumer psychology was not the introduction of new advertising techniques—historian Deborah Coon has shown that he merely adopted strategies in use at the time and pioneered by Walter Dill Scott (Chapter 8). Rather, his more lasting impact was in the application of scientific thinking to the areas of marketing (e.g., using demographic data to target certain consumers) and in the development of training programs and productivity evaluations for sales personnel (Coon, 1994).

Advertising did not occupy all of Watson's time during the 1920s, however. He lectured on behaviorism in New York at the New School for Social Research, joined the board of directors of Cattell's Psychological Corporation, and renewed his work on infants by supervising research financed through a grant from the Laura Spelman Rockefeller Memorial Fund (Buckley, 1989). The Fund provided $15,000 to Columbia University to continue the research begun at Johns Hopkins, and the experiments funded by the grant included the famous study mentioned earlier by Mary Cover Jones that successfully eliminated a learned fear in a young boy. Watson also continued writing about behaviorism during the 1920s, securing his reputation as behaviorism's popular voice.

POPULARIZING BEHAVIORISM

Watson began communicating with the general public early in his academic career, by publishing articles in popular magazines (e.g., *Harper's Monthly*) with titles like "The New Science of Animal Behavior" (1910), but this activity blossomed in the 1920s, with additional magazine articles, radio broadcasts, and two books: *Behaviorism* (1924/1930) and *Psychological Care of Infant and Child* (1928). The former became the most widely known statement of Watson's ideas. Although Columbia's Robert Woodworth (1931) aptly described it as "certainly not one of [Watson's] most scientific books from the psychologist's point of view" (p. 91), the *New York Times* said that it would begin "a new epoch in the intellectual history of man" (cited in Buckley, 1989, p. 173). It was the book that first interested a young B. F. Skinner in behaviorist thinking. The book included one of Watson's most famous quotations, a reflection of his belief in the importance of the environment in shaping our lives:

> Our conclusion, then, is that we have no real evidence of the inheritance of traits. I would feel perfectly confident in the ultimately favorable outcome of careful upbringing of a healthy, well-formed baby born of a long line of crooks, murderers and thieves, and prostitutes....
>
> I should like to go one step further now and say "Give me a dozen healthy infants, well-formed, and my own specified world to bring them up in and I'll guarantee to take any one at random and train him to become any type of specialist I might select—doctor, lawyer, artist, merchant-chief and, yes, even beggar-man and thief,

regardless of his talents, penchants, tendencies, abilities, vocations, and race of his ancestors." (Watson, 1924/1930, pp. 103–104)

Watson admitted that he was going beyond the data in making his "dozen infants" claim and he was probably overstating the case to contrast his views with those psychologists, including most of the mental testers (see Chapter 8), who were promoting the role of inherited traits in individual behavior. Although Watson always recognized the interaction of nature and nurture in the production of behavior, his "dozen infants" quote has become a regular feature of introductory textbooks in psychology, and Watson is routinely but inaccurately portrayed as someone who completely denied the significance of the nature side of the nature-nurture dichotomy (Todd, 1994).

Watson's reputation as an extreme environmentalist was enhanced by many of the recommendations in his *Psychological Care of Infant and Child* (1928), written "with the assistance of Rosalie Rayner Watson" (frontispiece). The book contains Watson's strongest statements about how the technology of behavior could be brought to bear on that most important of tasks, the raising of children. He dedicated it to "the first mother who brings up a happy child" and began by stating the urgency of the task: Healthy babies can overcome the short-term effects of physiological deprivation, but "once a child's character has been spoiled by bad handling which can be done in a few days, who can say that the damage is ever repaired?" (p. 3).

In a chapter entitled "The Dangers of Too Much Mother Love," Watson warned against being overly affectionate with children. The result would be "invalidism"—a failure of the child to become responsible, independent, and ultimately successful in life. He warned that there were "serious rocks ahead for the over-kissed child" (p. 71). What to do instead?

> There is a sensible way of treating children. Treat them as though they were

young adults. Dress them, bathe them with care and circumspection. Let your behavior always be objective and kindly firm. Never hug or kiss them, never let them sit in your lap. If you must, kiss them once on the forehead when they say goodnight. Shake hands with them in the morning. Give them a pat on the head if they have made an extraordinarily good job of a difficult task. Try it out. In a week's time you will find how easy it is to be perfectly objective with your child and at the same time kindly. You will be utterly ashamed of the mawkish, sentimental way you have been handling it. (Watson, 1928, pp. 81–82)

Watson (1936) later said that he regretted writing the book, that it was not sufficiently supported by data. Yet it stands as a perfect example of the faith that he had in the ability of behaviorism to affect daily living. More broadly, it illustrates the positivist belief that understanding and control go hand in hand.

EVALUATING WATSONIAN BEHAVIORISM

In a certain sense, Watsonian behaviorism was a magnificent failure. The grand scheme of being able to predict all responses, given the stimulus, was never realized. Most of Watson's proclamations went far beyond the available empirical evidence—the data never caught up with the excessive claims. What, then, was the impact of Watson's system?

Watson's lasting importance for psychology derives from his propagandizing on behalf of his strong beliefs. As mentioned previously, behaviorism certainly did not take hold immediately. Indeed, the initial reaction in academia was decidedly mixed. But Watson's forceful and repeated arguments started a process that by 1935 brought behaviorism to the center of American experimental psychology. Thus, he deserves the title "founder" of behaviorism.

Second, by attacking introspective psychology directly and exposing its Achilles' heel, its lack of objectivity, Watson contributed to the gradual shift from psychology as the study of immediate conscious experience to psychology as the study of behavior. By making observable and measurable behavior the dependent variable, rather than an introspective report, Watson ultimately helped place the field of psychology on firmer scientific ground.

Third, Watson's popularity with the general public suggests that his ideas struck a responsive chord with Americans. His belief that the environment could be arranged to shape someone's future development was consistent with the American ideal that through proper child-rearing and education, people could aspire to any goal. As we have seen before (Chapter 3), this optimistic attitude helped maintain the popularity of phrenology long after the scientists had given up on it. It was an especially appealing message in the 1920s, a time of prosperity in America and a time when average Americans were generally optimistic about their futures and unable to imagine the Great Depression that was to come at the end of the decade. Watson himself was a living example of this attitude, a poor farm boy who rose to the top of his profession twice—once in psychology and once in the business world. This message was much more inviting for average Americans than the one they were receiving from the mental testers. As you recall from Chapter 8, the advocates of mental testing were agitating for a meritocracy based on an IQ that was assumed to be largely innate.

Finally, Watson's behaviorism effectively bridged the gap between basic and applied psychology. Laboratory work in areas like conditioning and maze learning gradually became scientifically rigorous, thereby fulfilling the promise of a scientific psychology. At the same time, the possibilities for application, repeatedly stressed by Watson, also bore fruit as behaviorist ideas eventually influenced child rearing, education, industry, and even psychotherapy.

And what of Watson himself? His productivity as an advertising executive and as a popularizer of psychology declined precipitously in 1935 with the sudden death of Rosalie, the great love of his life. In that same year, he left J. Walter Thompson for a similar position with the William Esty Company and retired 10 years later. In his remaining years he became increasingly reclusive. In 1957, a year before his death, the American Psychological Association honored Watson at their annual convention and although he traveled to the meeting in New York from his home in Connecticut, he backed out at the last moment and did not attend the ceremony, sending his son in his place. According to his biographer, "Watson was afraid that in that moment his emotions would overwhelm him, that the apostle of behavior control would break down and weep" (Buckley, 1989, p. 182).

SUMMARY

Moving Toward Greater Objectivity

- Prior to Watson, many psychologists were becoming concerned about the objectivity of their measures. One influence was evolutionary theory, which led to the study of animal behavior. Studying animals meant developing behavioral measures, and American psychologists did just that (e.g., Thorndike's puzzle box studies).

- The philosophies of empiricism and associationism, which both emphasize the importance of experience, provided a foundation for behavioral thinking. Positivism, which argued that the only valid knowledge is obtained through inductive, systematic observations, also contributed.

- Many psychologists became interested in more objective measures of psychological phenomena because they were becoming increasingly critical of introspection.

Pavlov's Life and Work

- Pavlov thought of himself more as a physiologist than psychologist, and his 1904 Nobel prize was for research on the physiology of digestion. He was especially known for developing surgical procedures (e.g., the Pavlov pouch) that allowed the digestive processes of live, intact animals to be studied.

- Pavlov's work on conditioning developed out of the digestion research, when he decided to investigate why his dogs would often salivate before food reached their mouths. He systematically examined a large number of conditioning phenomena, including acquisition, extinction, generalization, differentiation, and experimental neurosis (a breakdown in the ability to differentiate stimuli). He interpreted these phenomena in terms of the reciprocal brain processes of excitation and inhibition.

- Although initially hostile to the Soviet government, Pavlov eventually accommodated when the threat from Nazi Germany developed. The Soviets saw Pavlovian conditioning as a foundation for shaping the modern communist citizen; consequently, Pavlov's research was heavily subsidized by the government.

- Pavlov's work was generally known to American psychologists from the early years of the twentieth century, but not widely known and appreciated until his research was translated into English in the 1920s.

John B. Watson and the Founding of Behaviorism

- Watson was trained at the functionalist University of Chicago, where he developed a distaste for introspection and a love of animal research. His dissertation on the relationship between cortical development and the learning abilities of rats was followed by several important studies on how rats learned mazes by relying on their kinesthetic sense.

- After teaching at Chicago for several years following his doctorate, Watson moved to Johns Hopkins in 1908, where he stayed until 1920. In his behaviorist manifesto (1913), he proclaimed that introspective psychology should be replaced by a psychology that specified the relationships between stimuli and responses. In his APA presidential address (1915), he showed how behaviors could be conditioned using procedures similar to Pavlov's.

- In his final years at Johns Hopkins, Watson studied newborns and young children, especially their emotional development. He argued that fear, rage, and love were the three fundamental emotions, each resulting from specific stimuli. More elaborate emotional responses resulted from conditioning.

- Watson attempted to demonstrate the conditioning of emotional responses in the famous Little Albert experiment. By pairing a loud noise with a white rat, Watson and Rayner created a fear of the latter. The fear generalized to similar stimuli (e.g., rabbits) and lasted at least a month. Later, Mary Cover Jones demonstrated that fears could be unlearned.

- Watson spent his final professional years as an advertising executive, applying behavioral principles to marketing. During this time, he also became a popularizer of behaviorist philosophy, especially in the area of child rearing.

FOR FURTHER READING

Babkin, B. P. (1949). *Pavlov: A biography.* Chicago: University of Chicago Press.

Provides a unique glimpse into Pavlov's life and his research, through the eyes of a former student. It is especially effective in portraying life inside Pavlov's laboratory during the early years of the twentieth century.

Buckley, K. W. (1989). *Mechanical man: John Broadus Watson and the beginnings of behaviorism.* New York: The Guilford Press.

The only existing scholarly biography of Watson; a thorough and critical analysis of how his ideas were shaped, and how they in turn influenced American psychological thought. A good example of a biography that fits its central character into the social, cultural, and institutional context of the times.

HARRIS, B. (1979). Whatever happened to Little Albert? *American Psychologist, 34,* 151–160.

A critical examination of how the Little Albert study became a "classic study" of the application of conditioning principles, despite the fact that the study was seriously flawed and that replication efforts were not successful. Textbook descriptions of the experiment are often inaccu-rate, mainly because writers rely on secondary sources rather than on the original article.

O'DONNELL, J. M. (1985). *The origins of behaviorism: American psychology, 1870–1920.* New York: New York University Press.

Scholarly but highly readable description and analysis of American psychology's formative years, and the factors leading to the development of behaviorism; excellent example of an external, historicist, contextual history.

11

THE EVOLUTION OF BEHAVIORISM

I believe that everything important in psychology...can be investigated in essence through the continued experimental and theoretical analysis of the determiners of rat behavior at a choice-point in a maze.

Edward Chace Tolman, 1938

▼

Preview

This chapter continues to describe the development of behaviorist thinking by focusing on the work of three research psychologists who have come to be known as "neobehaviorists"— Edward Tolman, Clark Hull, and B. F. Skinner. But first it opens by examining the fate of Watsonian behaviorism and describes several trends (e.g., operationism) that prepared the way for American experimental psychologists to be receptive to the behaviorism that conquered the discipline in the 1930s and remained dominant until the late 1950s . Each of the learning theories to be considered here differed from each other substantially—concerning the definition and role of reinforcement, for instance. All were grounded in research using animals as subjects, however, and all focused their research efforts on discovering the essential laws of conditioning. Although not discounting the importance of biological factors, the neobehaviorists, in the tradition of the British empiricists, believed that understanding human action largely meant discovering how life's experiences (i.e., conditioning history) shaped the individual. This chapter's Original Source Excerpt will give you some insight into B. F. Skinner's beliefs about the nature of psychological science.

POST-WATSONIAN BEHAVIORISM

Traditional accounts of psychology's history often refer to Watsonian behaviorism as revolutionary. The legend goes something like this: Before Watson, there was the darkness of introspective psychology. Because of its intensely subjective nature, it prevented psychology from being a truly objective science. Then along came Watson and his brilliant 1913 "behaviorist manifesto." Except for a few narrow-minded holdouts, psychologists everywhere saw the light, and psychology dramatically changed from the almost-science of consciousness to the true science of behavior. After Watson, behaviorism quickly became the dominant way of thinking among experimental psychologists. It is a dramatic plot, but not what happened. The actual story is infinitely more complex and considerably at odds with the legend.

As mentioned in the previous chapter, Watson's behaviorism did not catch on immediately, and the initial response to his 1913 manifesto was more likely to have been indifference or criticism than support (Samelson, 1981). Most psychologists simply went about their business: if they were interested in imageless thoughts, they continued to study them by combining cognitive tasks with introspection; if they were interested in the functioning of the visual system, they continued to study phenomena like afterimages and illusions; if they were interested in comparative psychology, they continued to study animal behavior. And after World War I, of course, many psychologists became involved in the mental testing movement (Chapter 8). Indeed, more can be learned about the nature of psychology in 1920s America by examining the growth of mental testing than by studying the development of behaviorist thought (Samelson, 1985). Furthermore, nonbehavioral approaches to psychology did not simply disappear after the manifesto and during the 1920s. At least a dozen varieties were examined in Murchison's

Psychologies of 1925 (1926) and *Psychologies of 1930* (1930), and gestalt psychology (Chapter 9) attracted as much attention as behaviorism. As late as 1931, Robert Woodworth's widely-read *Contemporary Schools of Psychology* preceded the chapter on behaviorism with one on introspective psychology, and followed it with chapters on gestalt psychology, Freudian psychoanalysis, and "hormic" (i.e., focused on instincts) psychology. Woodworth correctly predicted that after 50 years, historians would assign much significance to the behaviorist movement, but he was "puzzled to guess exactly where [the historian] will find its significance to lie" (p. 89). He granted that behaviorism had an appeal to some of the younger psychologists, but he also pointed out that advocating objective methods was not unique to Watson, and that despite his arguments, introspective studies were still being carried out.

Beginning in the decade of the 1930s, however, behaviorism did begin to take hold in American experimental psychology. Watson certainly played a role, especially with his consistent proselytizing on behalf of behaviorism, even after leaving academia. During the 1920s, his child-rearing advice and his *Behaviorism* (1924/1930), while "not one of his most scientific books from the psychologist's point of view" (Woodworth, 1931, p. 91), made great claims about shaping the future during a decade of great optimism in America. In the Roaring 20s, the United States had emerged from World War I as a world power and it was not until the end of the decade that its confidence was shaken by the stock market crash that brought on the Great Depression. The normally conservative *New York Times* said Watson's book "marks an epoch in the intellectual history of man" (cited in Woodworth, 1931, p. 92). Woodworth believed that behaviorism's significance would lie primarily in its appeal to those who believed that science could be used to improve the common good. To some extent, then, the development of behaviorism as a force in American psychology derived from an optimistic public's belief that a way had been found to raise their children efficiently, to improve their marriages and their businesses, and in general to help them lead more productive lives.

Public enthusiasm for behaviorism cannot account for the whole story of its rise to power, however. Other events in the 1920s played an equally important role in bringing behaviorism to the forefront of American psychology. First, as pointed out in the preceding chapter, a substantial amount of Pavlov's research was translated into English for the first time. Americans knew about Pavlov, but before the 1920s, they had little idea about the scope of his work, its precision, and its implications. If American psychologists were looking for a model of a systematic research program focusing on overt, measurable behavior, this was it. As discussed in the previous chapter, by the time of the International Congress at Yale in 1929, Pavlov was widely recognized by American psychologists as a major figure. Another event that paved the way for behaviorism was the publication of a book by a Harvard physicist. In *The Logic of Modern Physics* (1927), Percy Bridgman introduced American psychologists to operationism. Along with its close relation, logical positivism, operationism provided the intellectual foundation for neobehaviorism.

LOGICAL POSITIVISM AND OPERATIONISM

Operationism appeared at about the same time a small group of philosophers, mathematicians, and scientists began meeting Thursday evenings in a Viennese coffee house to discuss the logic and philosophy of science. Known as the Vienna Circle, they promoted a version of positivist thinking that came to be known as **logical positivism** (Gillies, 1993). Since the nineteenth century, positivists had taken a strictly empiricist stance, maintaining that certain knowledge about natural phenomena could only result from the public observation of mea-

surable events. This philosophy suited Watson just fine, because it was consistent with his belief that psychology must be the study of objectively observable behavior rather than subjectively produced introspections. The difficulty was that even by focusing on observables, it is difficult if not impossible to avoid discussing unobservable concepts when developing a theory. For example, if you believe, along with Clark Hull, that human behavior can be motivated by the need to reduce a strong drive such as hunger, you are forced to address the question of just what is meant by hunger and how does it function to motivate behavior. Yet hunger is an unobservable event, seemingly limited to an introspective description ("my stomach just feels empty and I feel a bit lightheaded"). The logical positivists, dealing with this problem in the context of physics—magnetism or gravity as forces are also not observed directly—resolved the issue to their satisfaction by distinguishing between observable and theoretical events, but insisting that the two be closely tied to each other. Specifically, they were willing to allow abstract concepts into a scientific theory, as long as these concepts were closely tied to some observable event(s). Thus magnetism could be proposed as a theoretical force having specific properties if certain objects (e.g., metal filings) behaved in a predictable fashion and could be observed and measured objectively. Similarly, hunger could be used in a theory of motivation if it could be tied to observable behaviors. Operationism provided the link.

The essential idea of **operationism** was that scientific concepts were to be defined, not in absolute terms, but with reference to the operations used to measure them. The concept of length, for instance, would be defined by agreed-upon procedures. As Bridgman put it, in his *The Logic of Modern Physics* (1927), the "concept of length is…fixed when the operations by which length is measured are fixed; that is, the concept of length involves as much as and nothing more than a set of operations" (p. 5). Bridgman also discussed what he called "pseudo-problems," questions that might be interesting, but were unanswerable by means of scientific observations. Whether or not time has a beginning or an end is an example.

A Harvard colleague of Bridgman's, experimental psychologist S. S. Stevens, was the most vocal promoter of operationism within psychology. Stevens was a doctoral student of E. G. Boring in the early 1930s and became the best-known twentieth-century researcher in psychophysics. He also developed the classification scheme for measurement scales (nominal, ordinal, interval, ratio) recognized by all those who have survived a statistics course. His 1935 paper, "The Operational Definition of Concepts," was the first of several attempts to convince psychologists of the wisdom of adopting an operational strategy. For Stevens, operationism provided an answer to the problem confronted by the logical positivists—how to define scientific concepts that could not be observed directly. By using **operational definitions**, that is, definitions involving precise descriptions of procedures for measurement and for specifying the variables in an experiment, psychologists could study such seemingly invisible concepts as hunger, anxiety, aggression, and memory while remaining faithful to the dictates of a positivist philosophy. Researchers could now define a motivational state like hunger or a perceptual quality like loudness in terms of the set of operations that were assumed to bring them about. Thus, hunger could be defined as the outcome of a certain number of hours without food, perceived loudness could be defined as a series of discriminations of quantitatively different tones made by subjects, and so on.

Stevens also saw the relevance of Bridgman's pseudo-problems for experimental psychology. One of Bridgman's examples was the problem of whether person A's sensation of blue is the same as person B's sensation of blue. That can never be known for certain; all that can be done is to determine if similar discriminations are made by person A and B to a series of visual stimuli of known wavelengths. Thus, one outcome of operational thinking was to raise additional questions about the validity of introspective observations and to argue that they should be replaced with behavioral observations (i.e., discriminations between stimuli).

Operational definitions continue to be widely used among psychological scientists, but a rigid operationism did not last long in psychology. One of operationism's implications is that the meaning of a concept does not go beyond the operations used to measure it. Thus, hunger is nothing more than 24 hours without food. The problem was that researchers often disagreed on the "best" operational definition of a term. The idea that one definition could be better than another necessarily meant that researchers believed that the meaning of terms like hunger went beyond a mere set of operations. To complicate matters further, many of psychology's concepts resisted simple operational definitions. For instance, researchers studying aggression have created operational definitions ranging from the delivery of shocks from one subject to another to horn honking among drivers at intersections. Is aggression being studied in both cases? Do widely different measures of a phenomenon measure the same thing? A strict operationist would have to argue that different operations measure different phenomena. Consequently, either all researchers would have to agree on a single definition of aggression, or all would have to agree that they are investigating different phenomena when using different measures.

Hilgard (1987) has argued that the essence of operationism was simply to force experimental psychologists to define their terms more precisely. The chief advantage is **replication**. If terms are defined clearly enough, other researchers can repeat a particular study. Successful replications produce increased confidence in some research outcome; unsuccessful replications generate additional research to clear up the inconsistency. Furthermore, if researchers using slightly different operational definitions of terms nonetheless produce the same outcome (e.g., frustration tends to be accompanied by aggression), the generality of the outcome is increased. The phrase **converging operations** refers to this idea that our understanding of some psychological phenomenon is enhanced when several studies, each using different operational definitions, "converge" on the same basic conclusion. According to Hilgard, metaphysical arguments over the "real" meaning of phenomena in the world could be left to philosophers. Thus, he contended that the debate over the merits of operationism, and its philosophical cousin, logical positivism, was largely ignored by psychologists (Hilgard, 1987, p. 779). For them, the necessity of precisely defined measures came to be taken for granted. To this day, operational definitions are a standard feature of any text in research methodology.

NEOBEHAVIORISM

Public enthusiasm for the promise of behaviorism, a recognition of the importance of Pavlov's long series of conditioning studies, and the general acceptance of operationism and logical positivism, along with the emergence of several hard-working and highly creative experimental psychologists, converged in the late 1920s and early 1930s to produce a movement in psychology called **neobehaviorism**. This movement became the dominant one in experimental psychology, lasting roughly from 1930 to 1960. It was not a unified school of thought by any means; large differences existed between the three examples of neobehaviorism that you are about to study. Nonetheless, there was a certain consensus among the neobehaviorists.

First, all neobehaviorists took for granted the evolutionary assumption of a continuity between species. Laws of behavior that apply to one species should apply, at least to a degree that can be calibrated, to other species as well. Consequently, phenomena relevant for human behavior could be examined by using nonhu-

man subjects in research. For experimental psychology, the result was a dramatic increase in the use of animal subjects for basic research on learning/conditioning during the period 1930–1960. Although said partly tongue-in-cheek during his APA presidential address, Edward Tolman's comment—"I believe that everything important in psychology…can be investigated in essence through the continued experimental and theoretical analysis of the determiners of rat behavior at a choice-point in a maze" (cited in Hilgard, 1978, p. 364)—reflected the neobehaviorist faith in the lessons to be learned by studying animal behavior. Tolman (1932) even dedicated his most important book to "M.N.A." (Mus Norvegicus Albinus—the white rat).

The second belief held in common by neobehaviorists was that learning was central to an understanding of behavior. In simple terms, neobehaviorists leaned heavily toward the nurture end of the nature-nurture continuum, arguing that knowing why people do what they do requires a thorough analysis of the basic principles of how things are learned. This, of course, was one of Watson's guiding principles and the motivation for the Little Albert experiment. The emphasis on learning also provided a bridge between behaviorism and British empiricist thought. When John Locke resurrected the Aristotelian concept of the mind as a blank paper and proclaimed that "experience" was the writer, he was arguing the same point made by Watson when he claimed that fears were the result of learning.

An emphasis on learning was also consistent with American psychology's obsession with practical applications. Watson's appeal with the general public was a result of his genius in showing how the principles of learning could be applied to improve education, child rearing, and sales figures. If we are what we learn, and if learning is the result of specific experiences in certain environments, then by arranging environments in certain ways, behavior can be shaped in any number of productive directions.

It is one thing to herald the importance of learning; it is quite another to know precisely how such learning comes about. Thus, during the era of neobehaviorism, the focus of research and theory was on the manner in which learning occurred. This fundamental issue produced the sharpest divisions among the neobehaviorists, but eventually yielded important knowledge about a variety of learning phenomena. We will examine the ideas of the three most important neobehaviorists: Tolman, Hull, and Skinner.

EDWARD C. TOLMAN (1886–1959): A PURPOSIVE BEHAVIORISM

Edward Chace Tolman was born into an upper-middle class environment in Newton, Massachusetts, a suburb of Boston. As a youth, he learned the virtues of perseverance and hard work from his father, a successful business executive, and the need for a reflective life with a strong moral foundation from his mother, who had a Quaker background. Although under some pressure to enter the family business, Tolman enrolled at the Massachusetts Institute of Technology (MIT) and graduated in 1911 with a degree in electrochemistry. He did not pursue a career in this field, however, partly because he did not wish to compete with his talented brother, Richard, who had preceded him by five years at MIT (Crutchfield, 1961). Richard Tolman became a well-known physicist who contributed to the development of the atomic bomb during World War II. A second reason for Edward's shift away from physics and chemistry was his discovery of William James during his senior year. The *Principles* gave Tolman's life a new direction.

Immediately following graduation from MIT in 1911, Tolman enrolled in two summer classes at Harvard, a philosophy course and an introductory psychology course, the latter taught by Robert Yerkes. Yerkes sold him for good on psy-

chology, and he entered the graduate school at Harvard, earning his doctorate in 1915. While taking a second course from Yerkes, he worked his way through Watson's *Behavior: An Introduction to Comparative Psychology* (1914), and although he did not become immediately converted to the behaviorist point of view, he saw behaviorism as an attractive alternative to the traditional introspective psychology he was encountering in Hugo Münsterberg's laboratory. As he later put it, he was troubled by the problems with introspection, and the "introduction in Yerkes' course to Watson's behaviorism came as a tremendous stimulus and relief" (Tolman, 1952, p. 326). During his graduate years, while visiting Germany to prepare for his foreign language competency examination, he met Kurt Koffka and was introduced to gestalt psychology (Chapter 9). The gestalt concept of "wholes" later played an important role in his theorizing about behavior (Figure 11.1 shows Tolman with Lewin and Koffka at a 1935 meeting of Lewin's Topology Group.) A final impor-

Figure 11.1   Tolman at a meeting of the Topology group in 1935, with Lewin and Koffka, from Marrow (1969).

tant influence on Tolman during his Harvard years was another of his teachers, psychologist Edwin Holt (1873–1946), whose leanings toward behaviorism were infused with the notions of goals and purpose. Holt believed that Watsonian behaviorism was too reductionistic, that behavior could not meaningfully be reduced to simple physical stimuli and muscular or glandular responses. He argued instead that behavior should be defined more broadly as actions that serve some purpose. That is, behavior is purposive and goal-directed. These ideas would become the core of Tolman's theory of learning.

Tolman taught for three years at Northwestern University during the World War I years. He was dismissed in 1918, allegedly for a lack of teaching skills, but more likely because of his visible antiwar stance (Tolman, 1952). It would not be the first time that his moral convictions, reflecting his mother's Quaker influence, would affect his career.

Tolman joined the faculty at Berkeley in 1918 and remained there for the rest of his academic career. When given an opportunity to develop a new course shortly after his arrival, he remembered "Yerkes' course and Watson's textbook [and] proposed 'comparative psychology.' And it was this that finally launched me down the behavioristic slope" (Tolman, 1952, p. 329). The course led to some research in animal maze learning, and Tolman was soon attracting talented graduate students to his laboratory. He began developing his unique form of behaviorism in the early 1920s, publishing articles with titles like "A New Formula for Behaviorism" (Tolman, 1922). His major work, *Purposive Behavior in Animals and Men*, was published in 1932. For the remainder of his career at Berkeley, he continued to develop and revise his system and to generate research support for it.

TOLMAN'S SYSTEM

Tolman's writings illustrate the complex interplay between empirical research and theorizing in the tradition of logical positivism. A theory makes testable predictions that lead to research, the outcome of which supports or reshapes the theory, which leads to more research, and so on. Because such theories evolve as a consequence of research outcomes, Tolman's theory of learning in 1932, when he produced *Purposive Behavior in Animals and Men*, was different from his theory in 1959, when he contributed a chapter ("Principles of Purposive Behavior") to Sigmund Koch's seven-volume series, *Psychology: A Study of a Science*. Nevertheless, there are some constant themes in Tolman's writings. His theories emphasized (a) molar over molecular behavior, (b) the purposiveness or goal-directedness of behavior, and (c) the use of intervening variables.

Molar Versus Molecular Behavior

Taking cues from his gestalt friends and one of his Harvard mentors, Edwin Holt, Tolman argued that the unit of study had to be larger than the "molecular" muscle movements, glandular responses, or neurological responses emphasized by Watson. One of Tolman's students, for example, showed that rats taught to swim through a maze were later able to run through it accurately (Macfarlane, 1930). Hence, what was learned could not be simply a series of individual kinesthetic responses. Rather, the animal must come to some general understanding of the pattern of the maze and the response needed to be conceived of in terms of whole behavior patterns that had meaning beyond component movements. As a gestaltist would say, the whole behavior is more than the sum of its parts. **Molar behavior**, then, referred to broad patterns of behavior that, as will be seen shortly, were directed at some goal. Tolman provided several examples:

> A rat running a maze; a cat getting out of a puzzle box; a man driving home to dinner; a child hiding from a stranger...—*these are behaviors (qua molar)*. And it must be noted that in mentioning no one of them have we referred to, or, we blush to confess it,

Key Date 1932	This year marked the publication date of Tolman's influential *Purposive Behavior in Rats and Men*, dedicated to Mus Norvegicus Albinus—the white rat.

These events also occurred:

- Amelia Earhart became the first women to fly solo across the Atlantic, traveling from Newfoundland to Ireland in 13.5 hours
- Work began on the Golden Gate Bridge in San Francisco
- Jack Sharkey (U.S.) defeated Max Schmeling (Germany) to capture the world heavyweight boxing crown
- Austrian-born Adolph Hitler was granted German citizenship
- Aldous Huxley published *Brave New World*
- Johnny Weissmuller made his first Tarzan movie and 4-year-old Shirley Temple made her movie debut
- These people were born:

  John Updike, American author

  Andrew Young, U.S. civil rights leader, politician, and diplomat

  Sylvia Plath, American author
- These people died:

  George Eastman, American inventor of photographic materials

  John Philip Souza, American composer of marches

  William Wrigley, American founder of chewing-gum empire

for the most part have known, what were the exact muscles and glands, sensory nerves, and motor nerves involved. (Tolman, 1932, p. 8, italics in the original)

Tolman called his theory a **field theory** to distinguish it from the more molecular approach of the stimulus-response model, which he likened to a telephone switchboard. Learning did not involve the mere strengthening and weakening of connections between incoming calls (stimulus information) and outgoing ones (motor responses). Instead, he proposed that the brain is more like a "map control room than it is like an old-fashioned telephone exchange" and that during learning the animal develops a "field map of the environment" (Tolman, 1948, p. 192).

Goal-Directedness

The preceding examples of molar behavior all have another feature: they are directed toward some goal. For Tolman, goal-directedness or **purposiveness** was a universal feature of the behavior that we learn. Although the term "purpose" seems like a return to a subjective, even introspective psychology, Tolman merely meant that behavior "always seems to have the character of getting-to or getting-from a specific goal-object" (1932, p. 10). Tolman was obviously influenced by evolutionary thinking here; goal-directed behavior is adaptive and therefore has survival value for the species. As a term, Tolman used "purposiveness" as descriptive, not causal. That is, it is merely a label for that which can be inferred from an observation of behavior, as when a hungry rat consistently works its way through a maze until food is reached. The causes of such behavior are to be found elsewhere, in the animal's specific learning history and its instinctive behaviors.

Intervening Variables

To Tolman belongs credit for introducing a concept that has been widely used in psychology: the intervening variable. Stimulus conditions, or independent variables, are under the direct control of the experimenter; behaviors, or dependent variables, can be measured with precision by the experimenter. **Intervening variables** are hypothetical factors that are not seen directly but are inferred from the manner in which independent and dependent variables are defined. They are assumed to "intervene" between stimulus and behavior, in such a way as to influence learning. For instance, "thirst" is an intervening variable. It is never seen directly, but can be inferred to exist as a consequence of (a) creating some stimulus condition, such as not allowing an animal to drink water for 12 hours, or (b) measuring the completion of some behavior that leads to water, which is consumed by the animal. As you might guess from the earlier discussion, Tolman's intervening variables clearly reflect the influence of logical positivism, with its insistence that abstract, theoretical terms be closely tied to observable events.

Tolman's intervening variables were usually mentalistic in nature and followed from his field theory. For example, when exploring a maze, Tolman believed that the rat gradually learned a set of "expectancies" about how the maze was organized. As it would encounter various parts of the maze, it would learn that certain environmental cues (visual, olfactory, tactile, etc.) were associated with certain outcomes. Tolman used the term **sign-gestalt** to refer to learned relationships between these cues and the animal's expectations about what would happen if it chose path A instead of path B. Eventually, the rat developed an overall field map or "cognitive map" of the maze that direct-

ed its future goal-oriented behavior. Sign-gestalts, expectancies, and maps are all examples of kinds of cognitive intervening variables that decorate Tolman's theory.

Just as the term "purposiveness" strongly implies a subjectivity that seems foreign to behaviorist thinking, so do terms like "expectancy" and "cognitive map." Tolman, however, again reflecting the dictates of logical positivism, carefully tied these cognitive intervening variables to operationally defined stimulus situations and behaviors. That is, he did not believe nor was he interested in whether a rat somehow had a map in its brain. Rather, he inferred the existence of this hypothetical map from the specific stimulus conditions he created and the subsequent behaviors that he observed and measured.

As an example, consider the cognitive intervening variable of expectancy. Tolman believed that one result of learning was that certain expectations were created. Rats finding food at the end of a maze expect to find food there in the future. Furthermore, it is reasonable to assume that they come to expect a particular type of food, an assumption tested in a clever study in Tolman's lab by Elliott (1928). Using the 14-unit T-maze shown in Figure 11.2a, Elliott taught two groups of rats the maze. The experimental group found bran mash in the goal box, whereas the control group found sunflower seeds there. Over the first nine days of the study (i.e., nine trials, one per day), both groups improved, although performance was better for the group fed with bran mash. On the tenth day, Elliott changed the reward for rats in the experimental group—they now found sunflower seeds at the goal instead of bran mash. As Figure 11.2b shows, their behavior was disrupted. In Tolman's terms, they had come to expect bran mash; when that expectancy was violated, their behavior changed. In short, expectancy is a process intervening between stimulus and response, but is closely tied to the clearly defined stimulus features of the experiment and the observed and easily measured behaviors.

Figure 11.2 (*a*) **Fourteen-unit multiple T-maze, used by Elliott to study latent learning;** (*b*) **Results of Elliott's latent learning study, from Tolman (1932).**

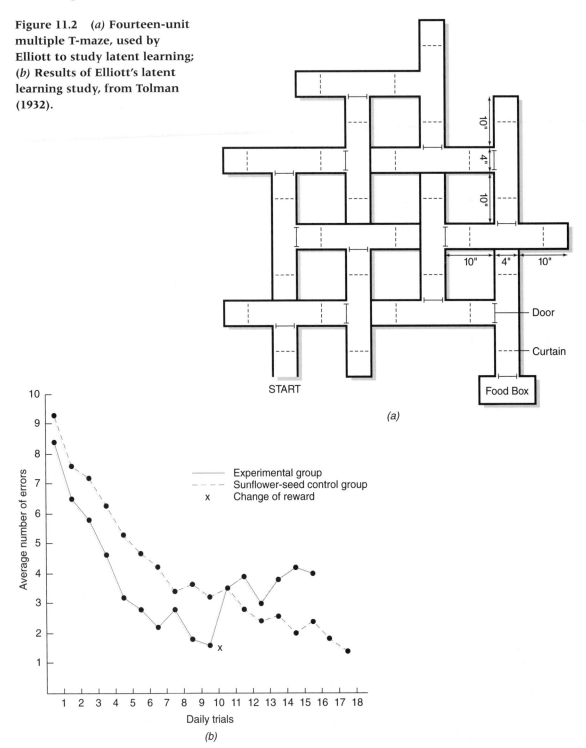

(*a*)

(*b*)

TOLMAN'S RESEARCH PROGRAM

Tolman and his students completed dozens of important studies of rats learning mazes. These were reported in a series of *University of California Publications in Psychology* during the 1920s and 1930s, in the *Purposive Behavior* book (1932), and in a famous *Psychological Review* paper entitled "Cognitive Maps in Rats and Men" (1948). The bulk of the research was theory-related, but Tolman also spent considerable time and effort standardizing maze learning procedures.

In the early 1920s, psychologists were beginning to question the **reliability** of the maze as a research tool. Any measurement is reliable to the extent that repeated measures yield approximately the same results, and the issue was a vital one. Mazes had evolved into a wide variety of shapes and sizes since the days of Small and his adaptation of the Hampton Court design (Chapter 6 Close-Up). Different mazes often produced different outcomes, however, and sometimes even the same maze would yield inconsistent data. In a long series of studies, Tolman and his students (e.g., Tolman & Nyswander, 1927) set out to examine the issue, identify the factors that reduced reliability, and develop a standardized procedure for maze learning that would ensure optimal reliability. On the basis of their research, they recommended that error scores be used rather than time-to-completion scores, that mazes have uniform choice points (e.g., a left-right choice at a "T"), numerous choice points (e.g., a 14-unit T-maze), and gates that closed once an animal had made a correct choice, to prevent retracing. They even developed an automated system for delivering animals from their home cages to the start points of mazes and removing them from the end points, so as to eliminate the element of human handling of the rats (Tolman, Tryon, & Jeffress, 1929).

Having established procedures for improving the reliability of maze learning data, Tolman and his students focused their attention on the meatier issues related to the evolving theory.

What follows are examples of his better-known studies.

Latent Learning

In his studies on latent learning, Tolman attacked the notion that reinforcement was necessary for learning to occur. He believed that food discovered by the rat at the end of the maze did not affect learning directly; it merely influenced the animal's motivation to complete the maze as quickly and accurately as possible. That is, learning needed to be distinguished from performance, and reinforcement affected the latter but not the former. Learning occurred more or less automatically whenever the animal was experiencing the maze, even if no food was to be found in the goal box. Tolman termed the phenomenon **latent learning** because it occurred "below the surface," that is, without being immediately apparent in the animal's performance.

Testing for latent learning required showing that learning occurred even if reinforcement didn't, and Tolman and Honzik (1930) accomplished this by testing three groups of rats (one trial per day) in the same 14-unit T-maze shown in Figure 11.2. The first group of rats (no reward or "NR") was never given food reward after completing the maze. The second group ("R") was always rewarded with food. As you can see from Figure 11.3, the error scores for these two groups during the course of just over two weeks was about what you would expect—lots of errors for NR and steady improvement for R. The third group was the key one, however. As suggested by their label—"NR-R"—rats in this group were not rewarded initially (i.e., during the first 10 days), but starting on day 11, they found food in the goal box. Tolman reasoned that if reinforcement was necessary for learning, then no learning would occur on days 1–10 and that performance would gradually begin to improve, starting on day 11. That did not happen, though, as is clear from the graph. Instead, performance improved immediately after day

Figure 11.3   Results of Tolman and Honzik's study of latent learning, from Tolman (1932).

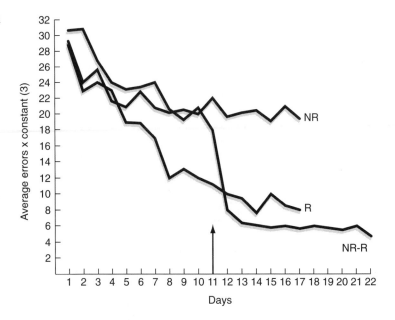

11. For Tolman, the evidence was clear—the maze was being learned during those first 10 days, even though the learning was not reflected in performance. That is, the learning was "latent."

Cognitive Maps

As mentioned earlier, Tolman did not believe that rats learned stimulus-response connections when learning a maze. Rather, he argued that they created a **cognitive map** of the maze—an overall knowledge of the maze's structure and spatial pattern that gave them a general sense of where to go in the maze. A pair of clever studies by Tolman, Ritchie, and Kalish (1946a; 1946b) demonstrated the operation of these maps.[1] In one study, rats encoun-

tered the maze found in Figure 11.4 and were started at either S1 or S2. Some rats, the "response learning" group, always found food by turning to the right. Others, the "place learning" group, always found food in the same place, F1. Tolman, Ritchie, and Kalish (1946a) found that rats in the place learning group learned faster, a result that is of course congenial with Tolman's theory.[2]

In the second study (Tolman, Ritchie, & Kalish 1946b), rats first learned to run the simple maze in Figure 11.5a. Starting at A, they ran across an open circular table to C, the only part of the maze with side walls, then eventually to the goal box, G. A light was on at H. There were no errors to be made, so the rats soon learned to move quickly from A to G. After 12 trials, the

---

[1] Tolman's ideas about cognitive maps were similar to those of Karl Lashley (see Chapter 3), and in his "Cognitive Maps in Rats and Men" paper, Tolman specifically referred to Lashley's observation about "a couple of his rats who, after having learned an alley maze, pushed back the cover near the starting box, climbed out and ran directly across the top to the goal-box where they climbed down in again and ate" (Tolman, 1948, p. 203).

[2] "Place" versus "response" learning became a contentious issue, with Tolman's outcome not always replicated, especially by those supportive of Clark Hull's learning theory. Restle (1957) eventually concluded that both types of learning are possible, the outcome depending on whether place or response cues are more dominant in a particular situation.

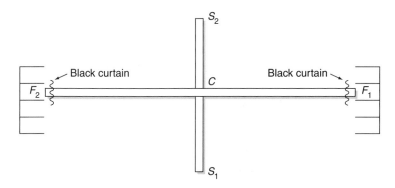

Figure 11.4   Maze used in place learning experiment by Tolman, Ritchie, and Kalish (1946a).

simple maze was replaced with the one in Figure 11.5*b*. Now the path down C was blocked and the rats had to choose another route to the food. An S-R behaviorist might expect the rats to choose either 9 or 10, the routes most similar to the original path at C, but Tolman, Ritchie, and Kalish reported that path 6, the best choice to get

to the general location of the food, was the most frequently chosen. Tolman (1948) argued that "the rats had…acquired not merely a strip-map to the effect that the original specifically trained-on path led to food but, rather, a wider comprehensive map to the effect that food was located in such and such a direction in the room" (p. 204).

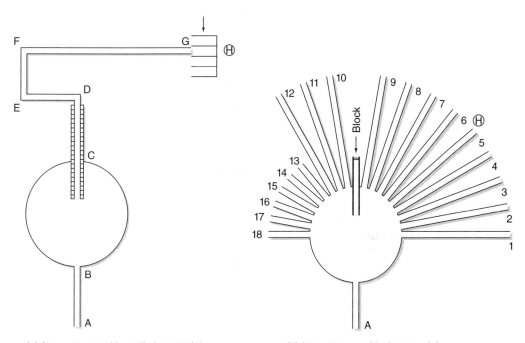

(a) Apparatus used in preliminary training   *(b)* Apparatus used in the test trial

Figure 11.5   (*a*) Apparatus used in the first phase of Tolman, Ritchie, and Kalish's experiment on the spatial abilities of rats; (*b*) "Sunburst" apparatus for studying spatial learning, from Tolman (1948).

Tolman elaborated on this distinction between narrow "strip-maps" and wider "comprehensive maps" in the last section of his 1948 "Cognitive Maps in Rats and Men" paper and tried to show how all of this had relevance for human behavior. According to Tolman, narrow strip-maps, which are maladaptive in the long run, result from too much mindless repetition on the original path, an environment too limited to see the whole picture, and levels of motivation or frustration that are too high. Comprehensive maps are to be preferred. Revealing the idealism and moral sensitivity that were never far from his thoughts, as well as his penchant for viewing the world as a large maze, Tolman (1948) closed his paper with an appeal to the

> ...child-trainers and world-planners [to] see to it that nobody's children are too over-motivated or too frustrated. Only then can these children learn to look before and after, learn to see that there are often round-about and safer paths to their quite proper goals—learn, that is, to realize that the well-beings of White and of Negro, of Catholic and of Protestant, of Christian and of Jew, of American and of Russian (and even of males and females) are mutually interdependent....
>
> We must, in short, subject our children and ourselves (as the kindly experimenter would his rats) to the optimal conditions of moderate motivation and of an absence of unnecessary frustrations, whenever we put them and ourselves before that great God-given maze which is our human world.... (p. 208)

EVALUATING TOLMAN

During the heyday of neobehaviorism, Tolman's research and his theorizing commanded attention, especially from the followers of Clark Hull (below), with whom Tolman disagreed on practically everything except the usefulness of intervening variables and the general precepts of logical positivism. The complexity of his theory

contributed to its lack of lasting influence, but Tolman's research program was creative and helped to institutionalize the maze as standard research apparatus. His students were intensely loyal to him and he in turn treated them as equals. On the other hand, despite their loyalty and devotion, few of Tolman's students continued doing research in "the Tolman tradition" when they left Berkeley. While academia became crowded in the 1940s, 1950s, and 1960s with Hullians and Skinnerians, the "Tolmanian" was a rare creature indeed. Furthermore, Tolman's research with rats in mazes did not produce much in the way of practical application. His plea for training children to have broad cognitive maps, for instance, gave little explicit guidance to parents. Instead of demonstrating the applicability of Tolman's work for everyday problems, the example seemed more like a good illustration of the dangers inherent in extrapolating too far beyond one's data.

Tolman's emphasis on purposiveness and his heavy use of mentalistic variables were both criticized by his contemporaries. Tolman was careful to tie these terms operationally to stimulus conditions and responses, but some critics saw his use of such subjective terms as a step backward. One learning theorist, Edwin Guthrie, complained that Tolman's theory proposed so many intervening cognitive factors that a rat faced with a choice in a maze would be overwhelmed: "In his concern with what goes on in the rat's mind, Tolman has neglected to predict what the rat will do. So far as the theory is concerned the rat is left *buried in thought*" (Guthrie, 1935, p. 172, italics added). The criticism is unfair—Tolman's writings are full of data showing rats doing quite a bit of behaving—but it illustrates the preference of many neobehaviorists for observable action over hypothesized internal states. On the other hand, Tolman's willingness to propose cognitive intervening variables makes him an important link between behaviorism and cognitive psychology (Chapter 13). More specifically, among those studying animal behavior,

Tolman's cognitive theory resonates with today's widespread interest in animal cognition. Olton's research on spatial behavior and short-term memory in rats (e.g., Olton, 1979), using a radial maze reminiscent of Tolman's sunburst maze, is an example.

Perhaps Tolman's lasting importance results not from his specific theory of learning but from a set of attitudes and values that he displayed. As a researcher, he was serious about his work and careful in executing it. He was persistent and passionate about developing and supporting his theory. Yet he also had a remarkable sense of perspective that enabled him to be fully absorbed in his research while not taking himself too seriously. He knew that better theories than his were bound to come along and that newer research would supersede his. As he said in one of the last pieces he wrote, published the year he died,

> The system may well not stand up.... But I do not much care. I have liked to think about psychology in ways that have proved congenial to me. Since...psychology [is] still immersed in such tremendous realms of the uncertain and the unknown, the best that any individual scientist...can do seems to be to follow his own gleam and his own bent, however inadequate they may be. In fact, I suppose that actually this is what we all do. In the end, the only sure criterion is to have fun. And I have had fun. (Tolman, 1959, p. 152)

In addition to his healthy sense of perspective, Tolman had one other enduring trait—his strong sense of morality. It led him to protest the U.S. involvement in World War I, thus contributing to his dismissal from Northwestern in 1918. In the midst of World War II, his strong feelings about war resurfaced, this time motivating him to write *Drives Toward War* (1942), in which he combined some of his ideas with those of Freud to explain what leads to warfare and to make some recommendations to eliminate the problem.[3] One of his suggestions, which he granted was unlikely to occur, was the creation of a "World-Federation" that would replace nationalist boundaries and encourage cooperation among the peoples of the world rather than competition. The histories of the League of Nations and of the United Nations have made it clear just how difficult it is to overcome nationalist sentiment.

Near the end of his active career, Tolman's convictions faced a final test. In the early 1950s, America was at the beginning the so-called cold war, its long ideological struggle with the Soviet Union. The Soviets' expressed desire to spread the gospel of Marxist/Leninist doctrine created images of one country after another being subverted and falling (like dominoes) into Communist hands. Holding the line against Communism meant defending South Korea in the 1950s and South Vietnam in the 1960s.

It was also feared that Communists would infiltrate the United States, corrupt its youth, and eventually take over the country. These fears were fueled by an obscure Wisconsin senator, Joseph McCarthy, who claimed to know of Communists who had infiltrated the government. Senate hearings, laced with rumor and innuendo, ruined the careers of anyone who was merely accused of being a "Red." McCarthy also hinted that Communists were infiltrating the film industry (dangerous because movies influence attitudes) and higher education (even greater influence).

In this climate, professors at California universities were told by those running the university system to sign oaths of loyalty to the United States and to declare that they were not members of the Communist Party. Professors were told to sign or resign. As a senior faculty member at Berkeley and by then one of America's leading experimental psychologists,

---

[3] My copy, originally belonging to psychologist Nevitt Sanford and signed by Tolman, carries the inscription "May the ghost of Freud haunt not my dreams."

Tolman could easily have left Berkeley and been welcomed anywhere. He courageously refused to sign the oath, however, on the general principle that it violated the First Amendment's right of free speech. And out of concern for younger, more vulnerable (i.e., not tenured) faculty members, he also refused to leave Berkeley. Rather, he led a fight that successfully repealed the oath in California and preserved the concept of academic freedom. In 1957, Tolman received the Distinguished Scientific Contribution Award from the APA and just before his death in 1959, the Board of Regents of the University of California recognized the significance of his fight for academic freedom by awarding him an honorary degree (Crutchfield, 1961).

CLARK HULL (1884–1952): A HYPOTHETICO-DEDUCTIVE SYSTEM

The life and career of Clark Leonard Hull is a case study in how perseverance and hard work can overcome seemingly insurmountable odds. Born into poverty in a log cabin on a farm in New York, raised on a "good but unimproved" farm in Michigan, and educated in a one-room schoolhouse, Hull grew up under "pioneer conditions" (Hull, 1952, p. 143). In addition to these trying circumstances, he almost died from typhoid fever just before starting college, and after his second year at Alma College, a small Presbyterian school in Michigan, he contracted polio, which left him partially paralyzed at age 24. At the time, he was aiming for a life as a mining engineer, but the polio made it impossible for him to meet the physical demands of that career.

After spending a year at home, during which he regained some degree of health, he decided

on a career in psychology. Why psychology? In his words, he was searching for a field related to philosophy that would involve theoretical work, and "one which was new enough to permit rapid growth so that a young man would not need to wait for his predecessors to die before his work could find recognition, and…would provide an opportunity to design and work with automatic apparatus" (Hull, 1952b, p. 145). The quote reveals two of Hull's enduring features: his strong ambition and his talent with the design and construction of experimental apparatus. The latter first manifested itself during the polio episode, when Hull designed his own leg brace.

Following two years of high school teaching and a marriage, Hull entered the University of Michigan. His most memorable experience was a yearlong course in experimental psychology, taught jointly by John Shepard, who had studied briefly with Watson, and Walter Pillsbury, a doctoral student of Titchener's. More teaching followed graduation, this time at a Normal School in Kentucky. Hull then applied to graduate school and was rejected at Cornell and Yale, but taken in at the University of Wisconsin, where he earned a Ph.D. under the tutelage of Joseph Jastrow, a former Johns Hopkins student of G. Stanley Hall's.

Doctoral dissertations often find their way into the far reaches of filing cabinets, but Hull's (1920) eventually became a well-known study of the processes involved in learning new concepts.[4] For stimuli, Hull used Chinese characters, including the ones in Figure 11.6. Notice that the characters in each row have a common feature, called a "radical." Hull's subjects had to learn to associate a nonsense sound with each radical (e.g., "oo" for the radical that looks like a large check mark). Over the course of several sets ("packs") of stimuli, subjects learned to

---

[4] The study was initially ignored by other researchers, which discouraged Hull greatly. However, a brief description of it appeared in a popular general psychology text in the late 1920s, and due to the tendencies of textbook authors to borrow from each other, it became increasingly cited thereafter (Hilgard, 1987).

Six of the Chinese radicals that Hull used are shown here. First, the subject was shown a Chinese character and guessed its "name" (for example, oo), then the experimenter gave the correct name, and so on. Characters with the same radicals always were given the same name so that after going through several packs of characters, the subjects improved their performances and were eventually able to correctly name characters they had never seen before.

From Hull (1920)

Concept Formation

Figure 11.6   Chinese characters used as stimulus materials in Hull's doctoral dissertation on concepts learning, from Hull (1920).

Aptitude TESTING

look at a character and give the correct nonsense sound; eventually they could identify stimuli they had not seen before. There were a number of findings in the study, but the one that impressed Hull the most was the shape of the learning curve—performance improved gradually but steadily. The idea of learning being the result of a gradual increase in "habit strength" eventually became a salient feature of Hull's learning theory.

Hull completed the doctorate in 1918 at age 34, and remained at Wisconsin for another decade. While there he developed two very different interests, both resulting from courses

that he taught. Early in his career, he was asked to teach a course in psychological testing. Although he knew little about testing, the subject interested him, especially the mathematics involved in test validation. He immersed himself in the literature of testing, especially that aspect of it concerning tests for vocational guidance, and within a few years produced an authoritative text called *Aptitude Testing* (Hull, 1928). Displaying his mechanical aptitude again, he built a machine to automatically calculate correlations. This saved him the tedium of calculating by hand the numerous correlations (e.g., between test scores and some measure of performance) needed to validate tests. The machine was delicate, however, a problem that prevented widespread use.[5]

Shortly after Hull began teaching the testing course, he was assigned a section of introductory psychology being taught to premedical students. Because he believed that suggestion and physician authority influenced the outcome of many medical treatments, he decided to incorporate the topic into his lectures. This led him to his second interest, hypnosis, and to the understatement that "the subject has largely tended to attract experimenters with a peculiarly unscientific type of approach" (Hull, 1952b, p. 152). Determined to correct the problem, Hull spent about 10 years examining the phenomenon systematically, eventually producing *Hypnosis and Suggestibility: An Experimental Approach* (Hull, 1933). He concluded that hypnosis was a state of hypersuggestibility and a reduction in analytical thought, brought on by hypnotically induced relaxation. He believed that hypnosis was not qualitatively different from normal consciousness, but only differed in degree. Thus, given the proper instructions, the various hypnotic phenomena (e.g., pain reduction) could be demonstrated in nonhypnotized subjects. Hull also believed that the medical community overestimated the therapeutic value of hypnosis. For example, he found that, contrary to the medical community's widely-held belief, memory was not notably improved by hypnosis.

Although working primarily on aptitude testing and hypnosis in the 1920s, Hull did not lose sight of his dissertation topic of learning. Indeed, while Hull's interests in aptitude testing, hypnosis, and learning are often portrayed as three distinct periods in his life, they were intertwined and all three reflected Hull's systematic, analytic approach to research (Triplett, 1982). During the 1920s, Hull was well aware

of Watson's writings and was familiar with the research being done by Tolman. Learning became the primary focus of his life, however, after he read the translations of Pavlov's research in the late 1920s. The topic captured his full attention soon after 1929, the year he left Wisconsin to undertake (at age 45) a major new challenge at Yale University.

When he arrived as president of Yale University in 1921, James Angell, one of the leaders of the original Chicago functionalist group (Chapter 7), found that psychology at Yale could only be described as moribund. The psychologists were still part of the philosophy department, virtually no research was being done, and only eight psychology doctorates had been awarded between 1903 and 1921, compared with 46 at Columbia and 51 at Chicago (Morawski, 1986). With the aid of Robert Yerkes, Angell established the Institute of Psychology in 1924. Generous funding from the Laura Spelman Rockefeller Memorial, headed by a psychologist with close ties to both Yerkes and Angell, enabled the Institute to recruit first-class researchers and equip laboratories. In 1929, the Institute expanded into the multidisciplinary Institute of Human Relations (IHR), which had as its lofty goal "to correlate knowledge and coordinate technique in related fields that greater progress may be made in the understanding of human life" (Angell, 1929, cited in Morawski, 1986, p. 219). It was composed of Yale professors taken from a range of disciplines, including psychology, law, sociology, anthropology, and economics; their teaching duties at Yale were reduced to a minimum in order for them to devote the bulk of their time to the Institute. One of the Yale psychologists assigned to IHR was Clark Hull, who had just been recruited from Wisconsin for the now-defunct Institute of Psychology. Hull spent the rest of his career at

---

[5] In a diary entry after traveling by train with Hull to a conference in 1928, Walter Miles of Stanford reported that Hull had built three of the machines but "they are hard to keep in shape and [he] will not send one far away." Consequently, an order that Miles had placed for one had to be canceled (Miles, 1928).

Yale, dying of a second heart attack just three weeks from retirement. While there, he developed his theory of learning, tested it extensively in the laboratory, and created a small army of "Hullians," students (and their students) and colleagues who extended the research program far beyond New Haven. The best known was Kenneth Spence (1907–1967), who got to know Hull while studying at Yale with Yerkes. Spence made contributions significant enough for Hull's theory to become known as the Hull-Spence theory among devotees. At the University of Iowa, Spence perpetuated the Hullian legacy by producing no fewer than 73 Ph.D. students between 1940 and 1963 (Hilgard, 1967).

HULL'S SYSTEM

One of Hull's heroes was Sir Isaac Newton. He kept a copy of Newton's *Principia* on his desk, and he urged graduate students to read it so they would understand that Hull's approach to psychological research mirrored Newton's approach to physics. Newton viewed the universe as a giant machine controlled by precise mathematical laws; Hull thought of humans in the same mechanical fashion. Indeed, he believed that an ultimate understanding of human behavior could only occur if a machine could be built that would be indistinguishable from a human. The attitude was undoubtedly influenced by Hull's own highly developed skill as a machine-builder.

Newton also affected Hull's beliefs about progress in science; it proceeded by developing sophisticated theories, then testing them, modifying them, testing the revisions, and so on. This system, also used by Tolman and consistent with the dictates of logical positivism, is called a **hypothetico-deductive system**. At the core of this type of theory of human behavior is a set of postulates: These are statements about behavior based on accumulated knowledge from research and logic that are assumed to be true, but cannot be tested directly. From these postulates specific theorems can be logi-

cally deduced, however, and these lead directly to experiments. The results of these experiments support or fail to support the theorems, which in turn strengthen or weaken the basic theory and eventually modify its postulates. Consequently, the theory evolves over time on the basis of empirical support or nonsupport.

Hull worked on the theory right up to his death, and the final account of it, *A Behavior System* (1952a), appeared posthumously. The best known version of the system, however, can be found in *Principles of Behavior* (1943); it includes a set of 16 postulates, presented both verbally and mathematically, along with descriptions of research supporting the theory. A complete description of Hull's theory is well beyond the scope of this chapter segment, but some insight can be gained from an examination of his most famous postulate, number 4.

Postulate 4: Habit Strength

Postulate 4 reveals the core of Hull's belief about the conditions necessary for learning to occur. It also illustrates the extent to which Hull aimed for theoretical precision and formality—*Principles of Behavior* was not meant to be read at the beach. Here is how Hull stated the first part of the fourth postulate:

> Whenever an effector activity ($r \rightarrow R$) and a receptor activity ($S \rightarrow s$) occur in close temporal contiguity ($_sC_r$), and this $_sC_r$ is closely associated with the diminution of a need (G) or with a stimulus which has been closely and consistently associated with the diminution of a need ($\check{G}$), there will result an increment to a tendency (Δ_sH_R) for that afferent impulse on later occasions to evoke that reaction. The increments from successive reinforcements summate in a manner which yields a combined habit strength ($_sH_R$) which is a simple positive growth function of the number of reinforcements (N).... (Hull, 1943, p. 178)

The key elements here are contiguity and reinforcement. According to Hull, learning occurs when there is a close contiguity between stimulus and response. A rat learns to associate a location X in a maze, for instance, with the response "turn right." Contiguity is necessary, but it is not sufficient, however. In addition, reinforcement must be present for learning to occur. Reinforcers for Hull were stimuli that reduce drives; food reduces hunger, for example. Together, S-R contiguity and reinforcement gradually increase $_SH_R$, or **habit strength**. Thus, by repeatedly reaching X, turning right, and finding food, the rat accumulates habit strength with each reinforced trial. To learn is to increase $_SH_R$. That learning is incremental rather than sudden echoes the results of Hull's dissertation on concept learning. The importance to Hull of the ideas in postulate 4 may be inferred from Figure 11.7, a portrait completed late in Hull's career. The graph in the background is an idealized learning curve in which habit strength increases as a function of the number of reinforced trials.

For Hull, then, reinforcement was defined in terms of drive reduction ("diminution of a need"), and his theory is sometimes known as a **drive reduction** theory. Primary drives are those connected directly with survival, and they can be reduced with **primary reinforcers** like food and water. But Hull also described **secondary reinforcers**, stimuli he described in postulate 4 as those that have been associated with primary reinforcers. A tone that has been paired with the primary reinforcer of food can itself become a reinforcer, for instance.

Reaction Potential

Although Hull rejected the type of intervening variables used by Tolman, he acknowledged that he borrowed the concept from his fellow neobehaviorist (Hull, 1943, p. 31). An important intervening variable for Hull was what he called **reaction potential**, or $_SE_R$. Introduced in postulate 7, $_SE_R$ refers to the probability that a response will occur at a given time. It is influenced by several factors, with drive and habit strength being the most important. That is, a

Figure 11.7   Portrait of Clark Hull, from Popplestone and McPherson (1994).

response will be most likely to occur if both habit strength and drive are high. Hull believed the relationship to be multiplicative ($_SE_R = D \times _SH_R$) rather than additive. Thus, if either drive or habit strength is zero, the response won't occur. Rats will run a maze correctly only if they are motivated (e.g., hungry) *and* if they have a sufficient number of reinforced trials under their belts. Figure 11.8*a* shows how Hull envisioned the theoretical effects of drive and habit strength (i.e., number of reinforced trials) on reaction potential. For empirical support, Hull included data from two studies (Perin, 1942; Williams, 1938) and combined them to form Figure 11.8*b*.

EVALUATING HULL

Throughout the 1940s and into the early 1950s, Clark Hull was arguably the dominant research psychologist in America. His work was cited more often than that of any other psychologist (far more frequently than Tolman's work), and his students (and their students) spread the gospel far and wide. Between 1941 and 1950, for example, approximately 70% of all research articles published in the areas of

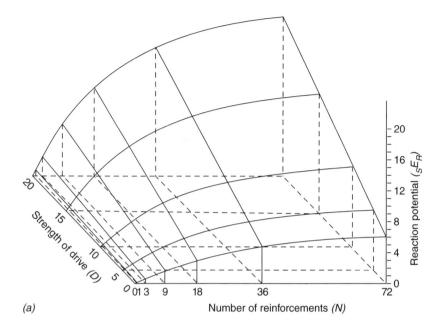

(a)

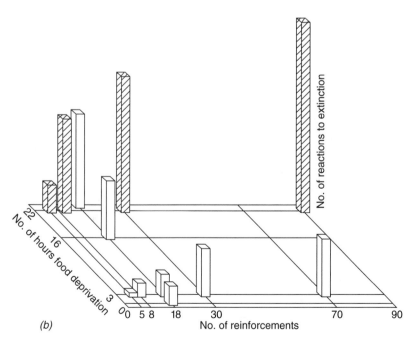

(b)

Figure 11.8   (a) Theoretical effects of habit strength and drive on reaction potential; (b) Data from studies research showing the effects of habit strength and drive on reaction potential, from Hull (1943).

learning and motivation referred to and cited Hull's work (Spence, 1952). For the psychologists of Hull's era, his theory met the need for a clear direction into the future. Introspective psychology had met its demise in the 1920s, but there was nothing to replace it. Watsonian behaviorism appeared, but so did gestalt psychology, Freudianism, mental testing, and a host of other variants. Searching for maturity and respectability as a science, psychologists seized on what appeared to be just the kind of formalized theory that characterized the older sciences, especially physics.

Paradoxically, today's college students not only fail to appreciate Hull's stature, they seldom even recognize his name. Hull's rise and fall is illustrated by an analysis done by Guttman (1977). He examined the reference sections of all of the articles published in the *Journal of Experimental Psychology* in 1940, 1950, 1960, and 1970, counting up the number of references to the work of Hull or his best-known collaborator, Spence. For those four years, respectively, the percentages of articles citing Hull and/or Spence were 4%, 39%, 24%, and 4%.

There are several reasons for the collapse of Hull's theory. For one thing, it was overambitious, attempting to build a theory of extraordinary complexity and mathematical precision on what turned out to be a very narrow empirical base—the behavior of simple organisms in artificial, highly controlled, simple environments. Hullians countered that other sciences do the same thing; biologists, for instance, use isolated tissue cultures to study cellular processes, even though those cultures are "artificial" relative to real-life biological environments. Also, Hull was planning a major work that extended his system to complex human behavior, but was never able to get very far with it before his death. On the other hand, several of his students, along with other members of Yale's IHR, did manage to combine Hullian and Freudian ideas into a testable theory of aggression. In *Frustration and Aggression* (Dollard, Doob, Miller, Mowrer, & Sears, 1939),

Hull's students developed the well-known frustration-aggression hypothesis and tested it with both animal subjects and children. The same group later produced *Social Learning and Imitation* (Miller & Dollard, 1941), which launched modern social learning theory.

Another criticism of Hull's theory was that it overlooked the very human nature of research. Consistent with his underlying assumption of human as machine and developed in the context of logical positivism, Hull took it for granted that disputes over the empirical support for the theory would be resolved by dispassionate and completely objective scientists listening to their data. There was faith that "crucial experiments" would decide the "truth" of some issue, but contentious issues never seemed to go away. For example, during the 1930s and 1940s Hull and Tolman engaged in a series of skirmishes over the nature of learning. Tolman's group would produce a study that seemed to refute some aspect of Hull's theory; Hull's group would then rush to the barricades and produce some data that seemed to explain away Tolman's results while simultaneously maintaining the Hullian model. Followers of each theorist felt they had the data on their side; to those outside both camps, it appeared that little was resolved. Furthermore, the failure to settle these disputes about learning contributed to the growing suspicion that behaviorism was fundamentally flawed as a system, and questions about the adequacy of behaviorism contributed to the development of cognitive psychology in the 1960s (Segal & Lachman, 1972), as will be seen in Chapter 13.

Although Hull's theory might not have survived, his positivist approach to research remains. There might not be any Hullians out there trying to shore up postulate 4 anymore; nonetheless there is a *legacy* of programmatic research being maintained by Hull's intellectual descendants. In graduate schools of experimental psychology, they are taught to do research systematically; that is, they learn to derive testable hypotheses from working theories, to define terms operationally, to collect data bearing on the hypotheses, and to adjust the theory based on the empirical outcome. The theories are no longer as formal or as mathematical as Hull's, but the same kind of thinking occurs.

One final problem for Hull was also shared by Tolman and was perhaps the most important reason why both men faded into relative obscurity in the latter half of the twentieth century. The problem was the rising star of B. F. Skinner, who combined the brashness and entrepreneurial spirit of John Watson with the scientific creativity, work ethic, and ability to attract talented students to match both Hull and Tolman.

B. F. SKINNER (1904–1990): A RADICAL BEHAVIORISM

Burrhus Frederick Skinner was a product of small-town America (Susquehanna, Pennsylvania) during the Progressive era. He grew up at a time when optimism within the emerging middle class was high in America—the country had just emerged from difficult economic times in the 1890s, and it had just beaten the over-matched Spanish in the Spanish-American War. The president, Theodore Roosevelt, was the dashing hero of the war and the youngest man ever to hold the office at that time. Parents, unless poor and/or nonwhite, had every reason to expect great opportunities for their children. Skinner's father was a moderately successful lawyer; his mother stayed at home and cultivated in young Fred the Protestant values of (a) hard work, and (b) constant concern about "what other people might think."

Hard work indeed characterized Skinner's life, but concern about what others thought of his behavior did not become one of his enduring features. On the contrary, independent thinking and an unwillingness to accept the "wisdom of elders" unless accompanied by sound evidence was more his style. It emerged

early: his high school principal wrote him a strong recommendation to New York's Hamilton College, but cautioned that young Fred was "passionately fond of arguing with his teachers. He is quite a reader and although I do not think he actually supposes himself wiser than his teachers, I have found him [to give] that impression..." (cited in Bjork, 1993, p. 28).

Skinner was initially unhappy in the fraternity/sorority-dominated atmosphere of Hamilton, but he soon found his niche and developed a passion for creative writing. He even sent some short stories to the poet Robert Frost, whom he had met at a writers conference. Frost's high praise led to a career decision. Determined to be a famous writer, Skinner informed his parents that he wished to take a year off after his 1926 graduation and simply write. This of course created problems for Skinner's parents, who were naturally concerned about what people would think of the new college graduate who was living at home but did not seem to have an actual job. It's not hard to imagine the pressure he felt from his parents to be productive ("And what did you write today, Fred?"), and as the year passed he also had a growing sense that he would never match the achievements of the famous writers whose works he was reading. Although Skinner later referred to this time as his "Dark Year," some of what he read started a sequence of events that eventually led to graduate studies in psychology at Harvard. For instance, during this time he read a number of popular articles on behaviorism, and this led him to Watson and Pavlov. He became intrigued by behaviorism and in the fall of 1928, he was off to Cambridge, Massachusetts. Figure 11.9 shows Skinner working in the Harvard laboratory two years later.

Skinner developed his system of behaviorism while at Harvard, first as a graduate student, then as a prestigious University Fellow. There was no noticeable change in his general attitude toward authority. He was not impressed by the work of E. G. Boring, the head of the laboratory and as we have seen,

Figure 11.9 B. F. Skinner as a graduate student at Harvard in 1930, from Malone (1991).

Boring spent three entire lectures explaining a single visual illusion. Boring, in turn, was not inclined toward behaviorism and removed himself from Skinner's doctoral committee. During the defense of his doctoral dissertation, when the noted personality theorist Gordon Allport asked him to describe what he thought to be the shortcomings of behaviorism, Skinner replied that he could think of none (p. 75).

Skinner's first important book, *The Behavior of Organisms* (1938), summarized his eight years of research at Harvard. After nine years at the University of Minnesota and another three chairing the psychology department at Indiana University, Skinner returned to Harvard in 1948, where he remained active, even after his retirement in 1974. Just eight days before his death from leukemia in 1990, he addressed the opening session of the APA's annual meeting in Boston. I was in the audience that evening and recall that he needed assistance getting on stage and walking to the podium, but once there he barely glanced at his notes while delivering an articulate and impassioned plea for his brand of behaviorism and an attack on what he viewed as the misguided efforts of cognitive psychologists. The talk was published shortly after Skinner's death as "Can Psychology Be a Science of the Mind?" (Skinner, 1990).

Titchener's best-known student. He referred to Boring's perception course as "simply painful" (Skinner, 1979, p. 47) and lamented that

▶ ORIGINAL SOURCE EXCERPT

Creating the Skinner Box

Skinner's approach to science was very different from both Tolman's and Hull's. Rather than deducing hypotheses from theoretical statements, then designing studies to test the hypotheses, Skinner preferred a more informal, inductive approach to research in the tradition of Sir Francis Bacon. A delightful illustration of Skinner's attitudes about doing research, and a realistic depiction of life as an experimental psychologist, can be found in his "A Case History in Scientific Method" (Skinner, 1956). It describes the steps leading to the development of Skinner's most famous invention. He eventually came to call it an operant chamber, but everyone else used the eponymous label first created by Clark Hull—the Skinner box. Although you might think that Skinner built the apparatus to have a means to demonstrate his ideas about operant conditioning, it is clear that the device developed in a trial and error fashion simply as the result of the sequence of experiments attempting to discover orderly behavior. Each study was characterized by a slight change in the apparatus, following several "unformalized principles of scientific practice." It was only *after* the final apparatus was created that Skinner began to see its widespread applicability to operant phenomena.

The case history begins with Skinner's assertion that the day-to-day experiences of a scientist do not resemble the highly structured logical system said to characterize traditional theory building and theory testing. Neither Hull nor Tolman is mentioned by name, but their presence in Skinner's thoughts is clear:

> ...But it is a mistake to identify scientific practice with the formalized constructions of statistics and scientific method. These disciplines have their place, but it does not coincide with the place of scientific research. They offer a method of science but not, as is so often implied, *the* method.... It is no wonder that the laboratory scientist is puzzled and often dismayed when he discovers how his behavior has been reconstructed in the formal analyses of scientific method. He is likely to protest that this is not at all a fair description of what he does.
>
> But his protest is not likely to be heard. For the prestige of statistics and scientific methodology is enormous.... Many [methodologists] are zealous people who, with the best of intentions, are anxious to show the nonstatistical scientist how he can do his job more efficiently and assess his results more accurately....
>
> Against this, the practicing scientist has very little to offer. He cannot refer the young scientist to a book which will tell him how to find out all there is to know about a subject matter, how to have the good hunch which will lead him to devise a suitable piece of apparatus, how to develop an efficient experimental routine, how to abandon an unprofitable line of attack, how to move on most rapidly to later stages of his research....
> (p. 221, italics in the original)

Skinner first presented this case history at the Eastern Psychological Association in 1955, when the Hull-Spence system was at its zenith (its "prestige...is enormous"). The tone of these opening comments makes it clear that Skinner, characteristically, had no hesitation about taking on the establishment. Indeed, by 1955, he had been arguing for an inductive, descriptive strategy for 20 years, and he was making converts.

The "case history" portion of Skinner's paper describes how five "unformalized" principles shaped his own behavior as a scientist, using his doctoral research as the case example. He mentioned his introduction to behaviorism via Watson and Pavlov, then described what he found at Harvard in September of 1928:

> When I arrived at Harvard for graduate study, the air was not exactly full of behavior, but Walter Hunter was coming in once a week from Clark University to give a seminar, and Fred Keller, also a graduate student, was an expert in both the technical details and the sophistry of Behaviorism.... I soon came into contact with W. J. Crozier, who had studied under Loeb.

> It had been said of Loeb, and might have been said of Crozier, that he "resented the nervous system." Whether this was true or not, the fact was that both these men talked about animal behavior without mentioning the nervous system and with surprising success. (pp. 222–223)

A constant theme in Skinner's writings, dating from his dissertation, is that behavior can be understood, predicted, and controlled without reference to underlying events in the nervous system. That is, it is not necessary to reduce behavior to neurological events; as far as Skinner was concerned, behavioral events and neurological events were merely correlated. The causes of behavior lie elsewhere, in the environment. Skinner seems to have been affected by Crozier in much the same way that Loeb influenced Watson (Chapter 10). In both cases the pupil came away skeptical about nervous system explanations for behavior.

The sequence of events that eventually yielded the first Skinner box began:

> ...simply by looking for lawful processes in the behavior of the intact organism. Pavlov had shown the way, but I could not then, as I cannot now, move without a jolt from salivary reflexes to the important business of the organism in everyday life. Sherrington and Magnus had found order in surgical segments of the organism. Could not something of the same sort be found, to use Loeb's phrase, in "the organism as a whole"? I had the clue from Pavlov: *Control your conditions and you will see order.* (p. 223, italics added)

Skinner began by creating a "silent release box," a device that could be used for introducing rats into mazes. Skinner, however, was not interested in maze learning but in how a rat adapted to sounds. A rat would be released from a holding chamber:

> ...at the far end of a darkened tunnel from which it emerged in exploratory fashion into a well-lighted area. To accentuate its progress and to facilitate recording, the tunnel was placed at the top of a flight of steps, something like a functional Parthenon. The rat would peek out from the tunnel,... then stretch itself cautiously down the steps. A soft click (carefully calibrated, of course) would cause it to pull back into the tunnel and remain there for some time. But repeated clicks had less and less of an effect. I recorded the rat's advances and retreats by moving a pen back and forth across a moving paper tape.
>
> The major result of this experiment was that some of my rats had babies. I began watching young rats. I saw them right themselves and crawl about very much like the decerebrate or thalamic cats and rabbits of Magnus. So I set about studying the postural reflexes of young rats. Here was the first principle not formally recognized by scientific methodologists: *When you run onto something fascinating, drop everything else and study it.* I tore up the Parthenon and started over. (p. 223, italics added)

Skinner studied these postural reflexes by developing a series of devices, eventually constructing an eight-foot elevated runway designed so that the animal's progress down its length could be monitored and its postural reflexes (e.g., freezing) could be noted when Skinner sounded a click. To induce the animal to begin the journey, Skinner placed some bran mash at the end of the runway. He soon tired of picking the animal up after each trial and returning it to the start, however:

> Now for a second unformalized principle of scientific practice: *Some ways of doing research are easier than others.* I got tired of carrying the animal back to the other end of the runway. A back alley was therefore added [making a circuit]. Now the rat could eat a bit of mash..., go down the back alley...around the end,...and back home [again]. The experimenter...could collect records...in comfort. In this way a great many records were made of the forces exerted against the substratum [below the alley] as rats ran down the alley and occasionally stopped dead in their tracks as a click sounded. (p. 224, italics added)

Next, Skinner noticed that instead of returning quickly to the starting point at the end of a trial, the rats often delayed after reaching the food. He measured the delays and discovered that they were orderly. Invoking unformalized principle 1, Skinner:

> ...forgot all about the movements of the substratum and began to run rats for the sake of the delay measurements alone. But there was now no reason why the runway had to be eight feet long and, as the second principle came into play again, *I saw no reason why the rat could not deliver its own reinforcement.*
>
> A new apparatus was built. In Figure [11.10] we see the rat eating a piece of food just after completing a run. It produced the food by its own action. As it ran down the back alley A to the far end of the rectangular runway, its weight caused the whole runway to tilt slightly on the axis C and this movement turned the wooden disc, permitting a piece of food in one of the holes around the perimeter to drop through a funnel into a food dish.... The rat had only to complete its journey by coming down the homestretch B to enjoy its reward. The experimenter was able to enjoy *his* reward at the same time, for he had only to load the magazine, put in a rat, and relax. (pp. 224–225, first italics added, second italics in the original)

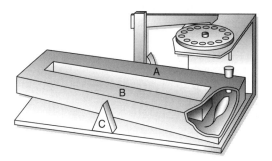

Figure 11.10   Precursor to the Skinner box, from Skinner (1956).

Figure 11.11 does not yet look like the modern Skinner box, but it shares the fundamental principle that it is a self-contained unit in which the animal's behavior leads to predictable consequences (i.e., food). Skinner next discovered, by accident, a means of recording the data that eventually became the cumulative recorder. This step also marks the point where Skinner first noted the importance of using rate of response as a measure:

> A third unformalized principle of scientific practice: *Some people are lucky.* The disc of wood from which I had fashioned the food magazine was taken from a storeroom of discarded apparatus. It happened to have a central spindle, which fortunately I had not bothered to remove. One day it occurred to me that if I wound a string around the spindle and allowed it to unwind as the magazine was emptied [Figure 11.11], I would get a different kind of record. Instead of the mere report of the up-and-down movement of the runway, as a series of pips as in a polygraph, I would get a *curve....* The difference...may not seem great, but as it turned out *the curve revealed things in the rate of responding, and in changes in that rate,* which would certainly otherwise have been missed. (p. 225, first and third italics added, second italics in the original)

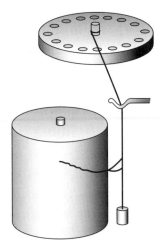

Figure 11.11   Precursor to the cumulative recorder, from Skinner (1956).

Skinner soon discarded the runway as unnecessary (principle 2 again) and refined the apparatus so that the rat would be reinforced by pushing open the door to a food bin. Each movement of the door moved a pen one step in a cumulative curve. This did not prove to be entirely satisfactory, however:

> ...The behavior of the rat in pushing open the door was not a normal part of the [rat's] ingestive behavior. The act was obviously learned but its status as part of the final performance was not clear. It seemed wise to add an initial conditioned response connected with ingestion in a quite arbitrary way. *I chose the first device which came to hand—a horizontal bar or lever placed where it could be conveniently depressed by the rat to close a switch which operated a magnetic magazine.* (p. 225, italics added)

Here at last is the prototype for the Skinner box. The animal presses down a bar, food is delivered, the animal eats, presses the bar again, and so on. With his new apparatus, Skinner at last had a result that would have satisfied Pavlov: He had controlled conditions, and he had seen order. It is worth noting that although Skinner abandoned the door-opening procedure as awkward, he observed that the conditioning which occurred was similar to that found when asking the rat to press a bar. That is, the form of the response was not important—the contingencies of reinforcement were (Coleman, 1996). Like Tolman, then, Skinner's definition of behavior was molar rather than molecular.

Two more important "unformalized principles of scientific practice" remained in the case history:

> Now, as soon as you begin to complicate an apparatus, you necessarily invoke a fourth principle of scientific practice: *Apparatuses sometimes break down.* I had only to wait for the food magazine to jam to get an extinction curve.... I can easily recall the excitement of that first complete extinction

curve.... I had made contact with Pavlov at last! Here was a curve uncor-
rupted by the physiological process of ingestion. It was an orderly change
due to nothing more than a specific contingency of reinforcement. It was
pure behavior! (pp. 225–226, italics added)

In his autobiography, Skinner related the almost childlike excitement over finding his first extinction curve. He reported that it happened late on a Friday afternoon and there was no one around to share in the discovery. As he put it, "[a]ll
that weekend I crossed streets with particular care and avoided all unnecessary
risks to protect my discovery from loss through my death" (Skinner, 1979, p. 95).

Skinner soon built several more boxes, and was on his way "to an intensive
study of conditioned reflexes in skeletal behavior" (Skinner, 1956, p. 32).
Another problem appeared, however. Skinner was making his own pellets, and
while he once again showed his ingenuity by creating an efficient device, it was
nonetheless time-consuming. His solution: Don't feed the rat for every bar
press. Orderly behavior occurred and Skinner applied principle 1 again—he
began to study the effects of partial reinforcement. Initially, his study of partial
reinforcement was motivated by the problem of controlling the level of hunger
(i.e., food deprivation) in his rats. It occurred to him that by reinforcing the animal periodically, he could develop a steady state of responding while at the
same time keeping the level of hunger more or less constant:

> ...By setting the reinforcements at a given number of responses it should
> even be possible to hold the rat at any given level of deprivation. I visual-
> ized a machine with a dial which one could set to make available, at any
> time of day or night, a rat in a given state of deprivation. Of course, noth-
> ing of the sort happens. This is "fixed-ratio" rather than "fixed-interval"
> reinforcement and, as I soon found out, it produces a very different type
> of performance. This is an example of a fifth unformalized principle of sci-
> entific practice, but one which has at least been named. [It is called]
> *serendipity—the art of finding one thing while looking for something else.* (p. 227,
> first italics in the original, second italics added)

Looking for a means to control deprivation, then, Skinner discovered something unexpected and new—different schedules of reinforcement yield different
patterns of behavior. This serendipitous finding led to years of research examining the effects of different schedules, eventually resulting in the 739-page
Schedules of Reinforcement (Ferster & Skinner, 1957). It is perhaps the best example of Skinner's belief in a descriptive, inductive approach to research and his
faith in relying on the intensive study of individual animals. The book is not
really meant to be read; rather, it is a vast catalog of how the various schedules
affect behavior. It includes 921 different cumulative records.

Skinner summed up his version of how research actually occurs with another broadside at the hypothetico-deductive method:

> This account of my scientific behavior up to the point at which I published
> my results in a book called *The Behavior of Organisms* is as exact in letter and

spirit as I can now make it.… I never faced a Problem which was more than the eternal problem of finding order. I never attacked a problem by constructing a Hypothesis. I never deduced Theorems or submitted them to Experimental Check. So far as I can see, I had no preconceived Model of behavior—certainly not a physiological or mentalistic one and, I believe, not a conceptual one.… Of course, I was working on a basic Assumption— that there was order in behavior if I could only discover it—but such an assumption is not to be confused with the hypotheses of deductive theory. It is also true that I exercised a certain selection of facts but not because of relevance to theory but because one fact was more orderly than another. If I engaged in Experimental Design at all, it was simply to complete or extend some evidence of order already observed. (p. 227)

The remainder of Skinner's case history article is filled with specific examples of operant research from his and other laboratories, designed to show its wide applicability. He ends with an insightful observation on the control of behavior:

The organism whose behavior is most extensively modified and most completely controlled in research of the sort I have described is the experimenter himself. The point was well made by a cartoonist in the Columbia *Jester*. The caption [of a cartoon showing two rats in a Skinner box] read: "Boy, have I got this guy conditioned! Every time I press the bar down he drops in a piece of food." The subjects we study reinforce us much more effectively than we reinforce them. I have been telling you simply how I have been conditioned to behave. (p. 232)

THE EXPERIMENTAL ANALYSIS OF BEHAVIOR

Do you still have your introductory psychology text? If you examine the chapter on learning, I guarantee that you will find a major section on "classical" conditioning (probably accompanied by the wrong picture of Pavlov's apparatus) followed by a section on "operant" conditioning. The relationship between the two is actually quite complex and beyond the scope of this chapter, but Skinner is responsible for making the distinction, and operant conditioning is sometimes referred to as Skinnerian conditioning.

In *The Behavior of Organisms* (1938), Skinner distinguished between Type S and Type R conditioning. **Type S conditioning** is the Pavlovian model: an identifiable stimulus *elicits* an identifiable response through the procedure of pairing two stimuli, one that initially elicits the response (e.g., food) and one that doesn't

(e.g., tone). It is called Type "S" because in this case the reinforcer (food) is correlated with the eliciting **s**timulus (tone). Skinner also referred to this as **respondent conditioning**, because the behavior is a response to a specific stimulus. Type S conditioning accounts for some behavior, but Skinner argued that it cannot explain a great deal of behavior that seems to have no easily identifiable stimulus. That is, some behavior is *emitted* by the organism and is controlled by the immediate consequences of behavior. Even if an eliciting stimulus exists, it may be impossible to identify it accurately. In **Type R conditioning**, or **operant conditioning**, a behavior occurs, is followed by some consequence, and its future chances of occurring are determined by those consequences. It is called Type "R" because in this case the reinforcer (e.g., food) is associated with an emitted **r**esponse (e.g., bar pressing). For example, in a Skinner box, the rat presses a lever and receives food. Lever pressing has therefore been reinforced and is now likely to occur again. If lever pressing results in the animal being shocked, a negative consequence called punishment, the chances of that behavior occurring again decline. Skinner (1953) called this type of conditioning "operant" conditioning, because "the behavior *operates* upon the environment to generate consequences" (p. 65, italics in the original).

Skinner believed that psychology should have but two goals—the prediction and control of behavior. This could be accomplished through an "experimental analysis of behavior," that is, a full description of behaviors (e.g., bar pressing), the environments in which they occurred (e.g., Skinner box), and the immediate consequences of the behaviors (e.g. reinforcement). While recognizing that these relationships would be influenced by the animal's innate behavioral tendencies and capabilities, Skinner focused on how behaviors were shaped by the environment. In that sense, then, he makes contact with the environmentalism of Watson and fits into neobehaviorism's emphasis on the importance of learning.

We have learned that both Tolman and Hull felt it necessary to propose the existence of intervening variables to account for learned behavior. These variables were carefully tied to stimuli and responses via operational definitions. Skinner rejected the concept, however, mainly because it opened the door to what he called **explanatory fictions**. These refer to a tendency to propose some hypothetical internal factor mediating between observable stimuli and measurable behaviors and then to use the factor as a pseudo-explanation for the behavior. It is something that we do all the time, at least informally. For example, suppose you discover that your new roommate stays up late at night studying and seems to spend more time in the library than anyone else you know. You ask his friends about him. They say that he has a high need for achievement. According to Skinner, at this point we might make the mis-

take of thinking that we have explained the studying behavior by attributing it to the high need for achievement. In fact, however, this "need for achievement" is merely a label that summarizes the studying and library-going behaviors and adds nothing to the explanation of them. The explanation, Skinner would contend, lies in the person's overall learning history and the specific reinforcement contingencies in evidence at the time the behavior occurs.

The problem with explanatory fictions led Skinner to be critical of physiological psychologists, who sought to explain behavior by reducing it, in his view, to nervous system activity. Although Skinner recognized the importance of studying brain function and nervous system activity, he was certain that a full description of behavior, together with the ability to predict and control it, was possible without reference to the nervous system. In this regard, Skinner mirrored the attitude of Crozier. Similarly, he rejected most of contemporary cognitive psychology, on the grounds that it also resorted to explanatory fictions (e.g., attributing memory failures to short-term memory limitations). In his final address to the APA in 1990, he sarcastically referred to cognitive psychology as the equivalent of scientific creationism in biology.

This is not to say that he denied the obvious fact that thinking, memory, and language occur. However, he rejected the idea that there was a qualitative distinction between public and private events and that, as some behaviorists argued, private events cannot be studied scientifically. He argued instead that both public and private events are essentially the same and can be understood through an experimental analysis of them (Skinner, 1953). Running is a public event and problem solving is a private event, but they are both things that humans *do*, and are therefore subject to the contingencies of reinforcement. A Skinnerian analysis of problem solving, for instance, would focus on how different problem-solving behaviors occur in different environments and how these behaviors have been reinforced in the individual's learning history. Skinner first outlined his views about public and private events in a 1945 paper called "The Operational Analysis of Psychological Terms." In that paper he explicitly labeled his approach a "radical behaviorism," a label that continues to be associated with his system.

THE TECHNOLOGY OF BEHAVIOR

As mentioned earlier, one of Skinner's heroes was Sir Francis Bacon, whose inductive approach to science was described in Chapter 2. Bacon provided the prototype of what Smith (1992) has referred to as the technological ideal—a scientist who desires not merely to understand nature but to control it. In fact, Bacon argued that true understanding only occurred if one could demonstrate control over some phenomenon, either by manipulating some aspect of the environment and observing a predicted outcome, or by creating some technology that worked effectively. Thus, a thorough understanding of physics can be demonstrated by creating machines that rely on various physical laws. For Skinner, the extrapolation to psychology was easy. He would show that behavior could be predicted, and he would create a technology of behavior based on reinforcement principles.

Skinner's first full-scale attempt to develop a behavioral technology was known as Project Pigeon (Skinner, 1960). During World War II, he obtained modest funding from government and private sources to pursue the development of a guidance system using pigeons to direct missiles toward targets. Along with a dedicated team of students, he was able to train pigeons to key peck at a target screen. As they pecked at the target, the missile would change direction until the target remained in the crosshairs of the screen. As a

backup measure, each nose cone was fitted with three pigeons, each with its own target. The pigeons, of course, would make just one trip. Skinner was able to build a sophisticated prototype and to demonstrate its effectiveness, but the military eventually killed the project.[6] Nonetheless, the experience convinced Skinner that his brand of behaviorism was applicable far beyond the laboratory. At a 1947 symposium on current trends in psychology, he pointedly argued for "extending the practices of an experimental science to the world at large. We can do this as soon as we wish to do it" (quoted in Capshew, 1996, p. 144).

Despite the setback suffered as a result of Project Pigeon, Skinner was encouraged by the experience, and as the preceding quote makes clear, was more determined than ever to show that operant technology could bring about useful results. In subsequent decades he would (a) follow Watson's lead and delve into the areas of child development and parenting, (b) challenge educational practice and develop a programmed teaching machine to facilitate learning, and (c) satisfy his long-held desire to write fiction with *Walden Two* (Skinner 1948), the account of a utopian community based on operant principles. It is described more fully in this Chapter's Close-Up. His ideas would also be extended by others into the areas of psychotherapy (Chapter 12) and business.

Finally, although Skinner was not directly involved, operant technology did manage to find its way into a missile program. On at least two of the early flights that were part of the NASA space program, chimpanzees spent their time in space learning various operant tasks. One psychologist involved in the project wrote that "[e]very technique, schedule, and programming and recording device we used then and subsequently can be traced to [Skinner] or his students" (Rohles, 1992, p. 1533).

---

[6] One of the persons involved in killing Project Pigeon was Tolman's physicist brother, who was involved with the National Defense Research Committee. Skinner apparently believed that Richard Tolman's "lack of respect...for his brother's behavioral psychology" (Bjork, 1993, p. 123) contributed to the demise of the project.

▶ CLOSE-UP

A Skinnerian Utopia

If behavior is inexorably controlled by the contingencies of reinforcement, then why not manipulate those contingencies to create happy, useful, and productive people? Skinner certainly found no good reason not to do so, and he was not shy about calling for the redesign of society according to operant principles. His first attempt at proposing a behavioral technology to improve the world came in 1948, with the publication of *Walden Two*, a story about a community built on operant conditioning ideas.

Like all utopian novels, the story line is thin, merely a device allowing the author to describe the brave new world. In *Walden Two*, a professor named Burris visits the rural community of a thousand or so members in the company of two former students, their girlfriends, and a philosopher colleague. They spend some time at Walden Two, mostly in the company of Frazier, the community's founder and designated tour guide. The philosopher (of course) is skeptical throughout the novel, convinced that Walden's inhabitants have been brainwashed and are under the diabolical control of Frazier. Burris is initially skeptical, but becomes convinced and at the end of the novel, he decides to give up academia and stay at Walden Two

Life in Walden Two seemed idyllic. Members could choose the kinds of work they would do, within the limits of their ability. To receive all the community's benefits (e.g., free health care, education, cultural opportunities), each member had to earn a certain number of labor credits per year; less attractive jobs like collecting the trash earned more credits than more enjoyable ones like tending the gardens. Most members could earn all their credits by working no more than four hours per day. A rotating board of six "Planners" managed the community, along with a larger group of "Managers," who were experts in areas like nutrition or child care, and "Scientists," whose research fed into community decision-making. Everyone, regardless of their position in the community, performed some physical labor each day.

Child rearing at Walden Two was not entrusted to individual parents but was shared by the community—echoing Watson, Frazier declared that "[h]ome is not the place to raise children" (p. 132). Children's productive behaviors were shaped through positive reinforcement—aversive conditioning was not used. For example, children learned frustration tolerance by being exposed to a very minor frustrating experience that they could handle and be praised for handling. They then experienced a series of slightly more frustrating events, gradually developing their skills at frustration management.

Two other aspects of the community show that Skinner, like all good utopian authors, anticipated movements that were years from developing. First, at Walden there was a strict equality of the sexes, maintained by always having three male and three female Planners, and reflected in the community concept of child rearing. Women could pursue anything that interested them. Second, great care was taken to protect the natural resources of the environment around Walden. The values of living the simple life and protecting the earth pervade the book, and is one reason why Skinner believed his book had a connection with Thoreau's original *Walden*.

Sales of *Walden Two* were initially sluggish. At a time when they were just emerging from World War II and were entering the cold war, Americans apparently weren't interested in an idea that sounded vaguely communistic and seemed to deny the importance of the competitive spirit and individual initiative. Sales increased during the 1960s and 1970s, however, a time of protest against war and the "establishment," when America's youth embraced countercultural alternatives to conventional behavior. The book has always been controversial, especially concerning the inseparable issues of freedom and the control of behavior. Skinner makes his position clear through the voice of Frazier, who takes up the issue with the philosopher:

> ...If man is free, then a technology of behavior is impossible. But I'm asking you to consider the other case.... I deny that freedom exists at all. I must deny it—or my program would be absurd. You can't have a science about a subject matter which hops capriciously about. Perhaps we can never prove that man isn't free; it's an assumption. But the increasing success of a science of behavior makes it more and more plausible. (Skinner, 1948, pp. 241–242)

Skinner repeated this message for the rest of his life. Freedom of choice is illusory and contrary to the assumption that behavior follows predictable laws and is under the control of reinforcement contingencies. If behavior is going to be controlled *anyway*, why not do it for the general good? Skinner never seemed to grasp the importance of the question "Who controls?" though, which was seized on by critics who blasted *Walden Two* as a totalitarian treatise that treated people like rats in Skinner boxes. Skinner argued that behavioral scientists should naturally play a leading role in the design of society, given their expertise, but it was never very clear just how this was to be accomplished.

EVALUATING SKINNER

Unlike Tolman and Hull, Skinner was never elected president of the American Psychological Association. His research is seldom cited in mainstream APA journals like the *Journal of Experimental Psychology*. Although he attracted many enthusiastic graduate students, few remained operant researchers for long, and there aren't many pure Skinnerians left today (Robinson & Woodworth, 1996). Skinner himself was concerned about the longevity of his brand of behaviorism, fearing that it would fade after his death. As early as 1974, he wrote about what he perceived to be "the lack of young operant conditioners" (cited in Bjork, 1993, p. 224) and the difficulty they had in finding jobs during a time when cognitive psychology was "in." Yet it is clear that his impact on psychology surpasses that of Tolman and Hull, as well as most of the psychologists encountered in this text. In a survey by Korn, Davis, and Davis (1991), for example, department chairpersons and historians were asked to rank order psychologists in terms of eminence.

Two sets of rankings were obtained: one for the top 10 "contemporary" psychologists and another for an "all-time" top 10. Among contemporary psychologists, both chairpersons and historians ranked Skinner no. 1; on the "all-time" list, Skinner again ranked no. 1 among chairpersons, but dropped to no. 8 among historians. Although Skinner's rating might have been inflated by the proximity of the survey to his death in 1990, it is nonetheless clear that psychologists and historians alike consider him to be one of the discipline's premier figures. Incidentally, neither Tolman nor Hull made any of the final top 10 lists.

Throughout this history of modern psychology, we have seen that American psychologists have felt pressured to show that their systems could be applied to improve the general welfare. This is one reason for the failure of Titchenerian psychology and the general success of functional and behavioral psychologies. In this regard, Skinner's contributions are unmatched in the history of psychology. His early research at Harvard, leading to *The Behavior of Organisms*, and his work in the 1950s, which produced

Schedules of Reinforcement, fall into the category of basic laboratory research, but the bulk of his writing has been directed at convincing the world that an experimental analysis of behavior is the only hope for the future welfare of the human species. This, of course, makes Skinner the true heir to Watson, who also labored long and hard to spread the "good word" of behaviorism. The proselytizing made Skinner a controversial figure, but it also resulted in his ideas being applied in more ways than ever imagined by either Tolman or Hull.

BEHAVIORISM IN PERSPECTIVE

In the opening paragraph of his book on the alleged mid-twentieth century cognitive revolution in psychology, Bernard Baars (1986) makes the observation that behaviorism "is often referred to in the past tense" (p. 1) and that not too many psychologists refer to themselves as behaviorists anymore. There is a grain of truth to this assertion—as we will learn in Chapter 13, behaviorism with a capital "B" has been on the wane for decades and cognitive psychology,

which returned the study of mental processes to scientific respectability, has to a certain extent replaced behaviorism as American psychology's predominant conceptual framework. Yet Baars's assertion overstates the case. It overlooks the fact that research on learning and conditioning continues to occur at virtually every major university in America, and that behavioral principles continue to form the basis for many successful applications (e.g., behavior therapy). More important, and an indication of just how influential behaviorism has been, the central message of behaviorism is now taken for granted by every research psychologist. That is, regardless of whether researchers consider themselves behaviorists, they all are careful to define psychological concepts in behavioral terms, and even if they are interested in internal, unobservable processes (e.g., insight in problem solving), they limit their evidence to behavioral phenomena (e.g., solutions to problems). Furthermore, I know of no introductory textbook that fails to include the term "behavior" in its definition of psychology. Baars recognized this himself in the preface to his book, writing that in the sense just described, "we are all behaviorists" (p. ix).

SUMMARY

Post-Watsonian Behaviorism

- Contrary to traditional historical accounts, American psychology did not become predominantly behaviorist as the immediate result of Watson's program. Behaviorism did begin to take hold in the 1930s, however, partly because of Watson's continued propagandizing but also because full translations of Pavlov's research became available for the first time.

- Logical positivism, which allowed for theories to include abstract concepts but insisted that these concepts be tied to observable events, created a fertile climate for the evolution of behaviorism. Operationism, originating in physics in the late 1920s, also helped to create an environment conducive to objective, behaviorist thinking. Operational definitions define concepts in terms of a set of operations, under the control of the researcher, that are assumed to bring about the term in question (e.g., 24 hours without food brings on hunger). Confidence in the generality of some research outcome increases when various studies, each using a slightly different operational definition, nonetheless converge on the same outcome.

- Neobehaviorists disagreed on a number of issues, but agreed that (a) continuity between species allowed for general rules of behavior to be derived from nonhuman species, (b) understanding behavior required a thorough knowledge of how the organism learns, and (c) research results should have practical applications.

Edward C. Tolman (1886–1959): A Purposive Behaviorism

- Much of Tolman's research used maze learning, and he investigated both the general reliability of the maze as an apparatus and the manner in which rats learn mazes. According to Tolman, rats in a maze do not learn a series of S-R connections; rather, they learn an overall cognitive map of the maze. This spatial ability can be shown in latent learning studies, in which animals can be shown to be learning a maze even though the learning is not reflected in their performance until reinforcement is made available, and in place learning, in which animals learn to go to a location more quickly than they learn to make a specific response.

- Tolman believed that all important behavior was goal-directed or purposive and that molar rather than molecular behavior should be the unit of study. He did not think that reinforcement was necessary for learning to occur. He developed the concept of the intervening variable, a hypothetical factor internal to the organism that intervenes between stimulus and response and is defined operationally. Many of the intervening variables in Tolman's system (e.g., expectancy) were cognitive.

Clark Hull (1884–1952): A Hypothetico-Deductive Behaviorism

- Although he is known primarily for his theory of learning based on animal studies, Hull also studied the development of concept learning in humans, aptitude testing, and experimental hypnosis, producing a doctoral dissertation on the first and books on the latter two topics.

- Modeled on Newtonian physics and consistent with the dictates of logical positivism, Hull's hypothetico-deductive system of behavior involved the development of a theory in which specific experiments were created to test hypotheses that were derived from highly formalized postulates. Research outcomes would then strengthen faith in the postulates or bring about their revision.

- Hull's learning theory is a drive-reduction theory. Postulate 4 proposes that learning (i.e., an increase in habit strength) involves stimulus-response contiguity accompanied by reinforcement. Reinforcers are stimuli that reduce drives. They can be primary or biologically based (e.g., food), or secondary (i.e., learned through association with primary reinforcers).

- Hull used a large number of intervening variables. The most important one was reaction potential, $_sE_R$, the probability that a response will occur at a given time. It was said to be influenced by a number of factors, including drive (D) and habit strength ($_sH_R$), both of which Hull believed were necessary for behavior to occur.

B. F. Skinner (1904–1990): A Radical Behaviorism

- Skinner rejected the more formal theories of both Tolman and Hull and argued for a more inductive, descriptive behaviorism that simply looked for evidence of behavior that could be predicted and controlled. He is best known for developing the distinction between classical (Type S) and operant (Type R) conditioning and for investigating the latter. To do so, he created the Skinner box, an experimental chamber in which the rate of some response (e.g., bar pressing) is recorded continuously by a cumulative recorder. Operant conditioning occurs when behavior is shaped by its immediate consequences. If the consequences are positive, the behavior occurring in a specific environment is more likely to occur in that environment in the future; if they are negative, the behavior becomes less likely to occur.

- He rejected the use of what he called explanatory fictions, hypothetical factors that appear to explain a phenomenon but actually do nothing more than relabel it. Hence, he was critical of nervous system explanations of behavior, and he never accepted the idea that explanations for behavior would be found by cognitive psychologists.

- Skinner called for a technology of behavior to improve child rearing, education, and society as a whole through the use of behavioral techniques. In *Walden Two*, he outlined how an entire community could function according to operant principles.

FOR FURTHER READING

BORING, E. G., LANGFELD, H. S., WERNER, H. & YERKES, R.M. (Eds.), *A history of psychology in autobiography Vol. 4.* Worcester, MA: Clark University Press.

Part of a series of autobiographies. Volume 4 includes interesting autobiographical chapters written by Hull (pp. 143–162) and Tolman (pp. 323–339).

BJORK, D. W. (1993). *B. F. Skinner: A life.* New York: Basic Books.

A brief and readable biography of Skinner. Not very detailed in treating Skinner's research or that of other operant scientists, but an excellent treatment of Skinner's early development as an operant scientist and his crusade for behavioral engineering.

DELPRATO, D. J., & MIDGLEY, B. D. (1992). Some fundamentals of B. F. Skinner's behaviorism. *American Psychologist, 47,* 1507–1520.

A solid introduction to the essentials of Skinnerian psychology, designed to counter some of the misconceptions of his work. This is just one of 25 articles on Skinner to be found in the November 1992, special issue of American Psychologist.

MALONE, J. C. (1991). *Theories of learning: A historical approach.* Belmont, CA: Wadsworth Publishing Company.

Provides thorough descriptions of the major theories of learning, written from a historical standpoint. In addition to Tolman, Hull, and Skinner, the book covers other important learning theories (i.e., Thorndike, Pavlov, Watson, Guthrie).

12

PSYCHOANALYSIS AND CLINICAL PSYCHOLOGY

▼

...I should like to formulate what we have learned so far as follows: Our hysterical patients suffer from reminiscences. Their symptoms are residues and mnemic symbols of particular (traumatic) experiences.

Sigmund Freud, 1909

▼

Preview

When students first begin to explore psychology, they typically identify the discipline with the diagnosis and treatment of "mental illness." Of course, they quickly discover that psychology is a much broader subject—in a normal introductory course, they must wade through a dozen or so chapters on such topics as the brain and behavior, perception, learning, and cognition, before they get to the chapters on psychopathology and its treatment. Similarly, most histories of psychology, including this one, focus on how the discipline began applying scientific methods to age-old questions and how it developed as a "science" in the academic environment. Nonetheless, no history of psychology can be complete without describing, if briefly, the various ways that psychopathology has been conceived of and treated over the years. Most of this chapter is devoted to Sigmund Freud's creation and promotion of psychoanalysis, the name he gave both to his theory of personality and to his method for treating disordered personalities. We will explore the origins and evolution of some of his well-known concepts. Moreover the Original Source Excerpt in this chapter is from a famous series of lectures that Freud gave during a visit to the United States in 1909. Preceding the discussion of Freud, however, the chapter examines some early conceptions of mental illness and various attempts at the reform of mental institutions, and briefly discusses the intriguing history of hypnosis as a therapy tool.

The final portion of the chapter traces the history of clinical psychology in the United States from its modest origins to its emergence as a major force in psychology after World War II. Unlike psychoanalysis, which developed in a medical context, an early form of clinical psychology emerged from the laboratory environment that characterized the new psychology of the late nineteenth century. Pioneers such as Lightner Witmer adapted existing laboratory procedures and created new ones to diagnose and treat children with various problems that were hindering their school performance. Modern clinical psychology evolved from these early clinics, as well as from the mental hygiene and mental testing movements of the early twentieth century. Clinical psychologists held second class status among professionals treating mental illness until after World War II, when the number of psychological casualties dramatically increased the need for competent therapy. Psychology responded by developing standardized doctoral programs to train clinicians and by developing forms of therapeutic intervention different from traditional psychoanalytic approaches.

EARLY TREATMENT OF THE MENTALLY ILL

Every society has had to confront the need to deal with people whose thought processes, emotions, and behavior mark them as deviant from the norm. For much of recorded history, such persons, so different from the rest of "us," have sometimes been a source of fear and loathing, their treatment less than humane. They have been regarded as evil or possessed by the devil, to be punished by being tortured and put to death, perhaps by being burned at the stake or drowned as a "witch." Alternatively, they have been considered either morally deficient and dangerous to society because of their transgressions, or incurable nuisances, and in need of being locked away from decent folks, perhaps chained to a wall, with no hope of being freed. Out of sight, out of mind. On the other hand, the picture is not as uniformly bleak as is normally portrayed in standard histories of mental illness (e.g., Zilboorg, 1941). Treatises proposing reasonable biological causes for mental illness existed in medieval times, at the same time that demonology was a competing hypothesis, and there is accumulating evidence that the insane were frequently treated with compassion in their communities and through organized governmental intervention (Neugebauer, 1978; Kroll, 1973). As is true today, however, community size and socioeco-

nomic status were important predictors of care. The poor, especially those living in the larger population areas, received the worst treatment, if they received any help at all.

"ENLIGHTENED" REFORM: PINEL, TUKE, AND RUSH

Several efforts at improving treatment of the mentally ill occurred in the late eighteenth and early nineteenth centuries, a product of the closing years of the Enlightenment, a time of "spreading light into the dark corners of the human mind" (Appleby, Hunt, & Jacob, 1994, p. 36). As you recall from Chapter 3, the hallmark of Enlightenment thinking was a belief in the ideas of progress and reform and a strong faith in the ability of science to improve society. It was the kind of thinking that helped produce political revolutions both in the United States and France, and it elevated "science," the engine of progress, to the status of religion. In that context, mental illness came to be viewed in naturalistic terms as being biologically based and amenable to treatment.

The best-known reformer during this era was the French physician Phillipe Pinel (1745–1826), who instituted humane reforms in Paris, first at the Bicêtre asylum for men (1793), then at the Salpêtrière asylum for women (1795). Pinel's most dramatic action was to remove the chains from patients who had been restrained, in some instances, for years. Although it has been shown (e.g., Weiner, 1979, cited in Micale, 1985) that the number of liberated patients was relatively small (about 15% of the total asylum populations), and that for many patients, the chains were simply replaced by more modern forms of restraint (e.g., an early version of the straitjacket), Pinel nonetheless deserves credit for bringing the concept of reform to mental institutions. He called his overall program *traitement moral* ("moral treatment"), and it featured improvements in patient nutrition, hygiene, and general living conditions, and an early form of behavior modification using rewards and punishments to bring some order into the lives of patients. Pinel's efforts, occurring in the context of the French Revolution, provide a clear example of the combined effects of an "enlightened" approach to insanity and an assault on institutions perceived to be repressing freedom. His reforms reflected the Enlightenment faith in progress and the revolutionary desire to liberate the oppressed.

While Pinel was effecting change in France, similar reforms were occurring in England, led by the work of William Tuke (1732–1822). A Quaker, Tuke was predisposed toward providing relief for subjugated groups (the Society of Friends also became leaders in the antislavery movement). In 1792, a year before Pinel was named director of the Bicêtre, Tuke founded the York Retreat in the north of England, which was dedicated to the benevolent treatment of the insane. Set in a rural environment and designed to resemble a working farm more than a prison, the Retreat established a program of treatment similar in spirit to the one used by Pinel. Patients who behaved well were given greater freedom of movement, allowed more visitors, and given more opportunities for recreation and work; on the other hand, those

behaving badly or out of control were punished, usually through isolation from other patients, but sometimes by being tied to their beds (Bell, 1980). Its religious origins in the Society of Friends meant that the York Retreat and its philosophy of treatment would be known to Quakers in other parts of the world who had similar reform motives. According to Grob (1994), Tuke's York Retreat became the model for at least half of the private mental hospitals created in the United States in the first quarter of the nineteenth century.

The person credited with being the first in America to bring a scientific approach to the treatment of the mentally ill was Benjamin Rush (1745–1813), a prominent signer of the Declaration of Independence and surgeon general to the Continental Army of the American Revolution. He has been called the "father" of modern psychiatry, largely because of his *Medical Inquiries and Observations upon the Diseases of the Mind*, which went through five editions between 1812 and 1835. One of the few "doctors" of this era with actual university training in medicine,[1] Rush became a strong advocate of a contemporary belief that many illnesses derived from problems with the blood and circulatory system. Accordingly, a common remedy was to remove diseased or excess blood, and Rush became a promoter of bloodletting as a cure for a wide range of illnesses. These included mental ones, which Rush believed stemmed from "hypertension in the brain's blood vessels" (Bell, 1980, p. 9). Reducing the tension, then, involved opening veins and removing blood until the person reached a more tranquil state. This often worked rather well as a temporary means of calming violent patients, undoubtedly because these unfortunate individuals, minus a few pints, were too weak to be hyperactive. Rush reported one case in which a violent patient

---

[1] His medical training included a stop at the university in Edinburgh, Scotland. As was mentioned in Chapter 5, Edinburgh was Great Britain's foremost center for medical education, the locus of Darwin's unsuccessful attempt to become a doctor.

was given 47 different bleedings, involving a total loss of between 400 and 500 ounces of blood. He was eventually pronounced cured and was returned to the community. He wrote a glowing testimonial thanking Rush for the therapy, but then relapsed and hung himself not long after his release (Bell, 1980).

In addition to bloodletting, Rush also created two devices for calming the blood. The *gyrator* was a revolving board on which a patient would be spun rapidly, the idea being to redistribute blood toward the head. The *tranquilizer*, shown in Figure 12.1, was a chair with straps for restraining arms and legs, and a boxlike device that fit tightly over the head. By eliminating movement, the goal was to reduce the pulse rate. Both devices became standard forms of treatment in postrevolutionary asylums, and while they might seem cruel and unusual to us today, they reflected an important new idea at the time—a belief that the mentally ill could benefit from therapy.

REFORMING ASYLUMS: DIX AND BEERS

During the first third of the nineteenth century, a number of private mental asylums were founded in the United States, influenced by the reforms of men such as Pinel, Tuke, and Rush. Because they were private, however, their patients tended to be relatively affluent and the asylums were seldom overcrowded. For example, the McLean Asylum in Boston, one of the first, housed a yearly average of about 50 patients during its first dozen years of existence and developed a progressive moral treatment program based on the York model (Grob, 1994). The mentally insane poor, on the other hand, usually wound up in jails or "almshouses" (poorhouses) or were left to wander the countryside. As the population of the United States expanded, however, and urban areas in particular began to grow, the number of mentally ill patients increased proportionally, and the need for public support for them became

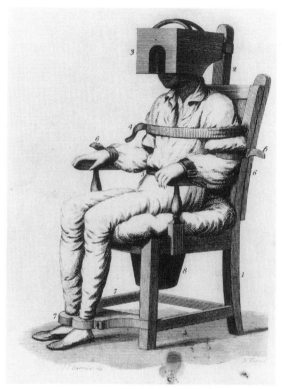

Figure 12.1   The tranquilizer chair, devised by Benjamin Rush for restraining and "calming" agitated mental patients, from Bell (1980).

increasingly evident. The response was the creation of large, state-funded asylums, designed for both the affluent and the poor, but eventually housing mostly the latter. They tended to be located in rural areas, often in the geographical centers of states (i.e., equally accessible to all citizens, but also "out of sight"), and because they tended to house the powerless, they quickly became underfunded, overcrowded, filthy beyond imagining, and custodial rather than therapeutic.

Improving the care given in these asylums became the focus of a spirited crusade by Dorothea Dix (1802–1887). Dix (Figure 12.2) was a New England educator whose general concern for the less fortunate led her to examine the conditions for treating those housed in

Figure 12.2   Dorothea Dix, crusader for mental health reform, from Viney, 1996.

public institutions. In Massachusetts in 1841, she began an 18-month tour of the state's jails, hospitals, and almshouses, and any other location that might house the mentally ill poor. What she encountered was an alarming level of abuse and neglect, with the mentally ill being treated no better than animals. They were often chained to the walls of unheated closet-sized rooms filled with their excrement, poorly fed and clothed, often beaten into submission, and generally abandoned. On her return home, she wrote a scathing indictment of the system and did not mince words when describing the details of what she had seen. Her case was presented to the Massachusetts legislature and led to a series of reforms, including an increase of funds to improve the state's public asylum in Worcester. This success prompted her to repeat her modus operandi in other states—a system-

atic tour of institutions followed by a lengthy and detailed exposé. By 1848, the Dix crusade had found its way to every state except North Carolina, Texas, and Florida, and Dix had logged some 60,000 miles of travel, observing in the process "more than nine thousand idiots, epileptics, and insane,...destitute of appropriate care and protection" (Dix, 1848, quoted in Viney, 1996, p. 22). Her efforts played a role in the creation of 47 mental hospitals and schools for the feebleminded (Viney & Zorich, 1982). Although many of these institutions over the years grew to sizes that prevented effective care and led in the twentieth century to a renewal of problems with overcrowding and abuse, her efforts on behalf of the mentally ill poor dramatically improved the living conditions of those powerless to help themselves. That she was able to accomplish what she did in the face of poor health (probably tuberculosis), difficult traveling conditions, and the generally accepted belief that women were not worth listening to, is nothing less than extraordinary.

Dorothea Dix and other nineteenth-century reformers focused their efforts on the treatment of those already mentally ill and living in institutions. Often, even in the best of circumstances, the improvement in care amounted to better living conditions for those doomed to spend most or all of their lives in these places. Shortly after the turn of the century, however, another reform movement began that was based on the related ideas that (a) mental illness could be cured, and (b) with proper care, it might even be prevented. It was called the Mental Hygiene movement and it was launched by Clifford Beers (1876–1943). As a former mental patient himself, he was uniquely qualified to discuss the issue. Beers was a graduate of Yale and apparently had settled into a job in New York with an insurance company when a suicide attempt, followed by a year of depression, landed him in the first of three mental institutions that he would inhabit for just over three years. After being released from the third one in 1903, he compiled his notes into a book describing what life was like for a hospitalized mental patient. *A Mind That Found Itself* appeared in 1908, complete with a prefatory letter from William James, who had read the manuscript and wished to support Beers's cause. Other contemporary exposés of life in mental institutions existed, but Beers's book had special impact because it was written by someone who had lived through the ordeal. Beers was critical of the psychiatrists he had encountered, believing them to be generally incompetent and too willing to use punitive measures, but he saved his heaviest invective for the attendants in charge of the day-to-day operation of the wards. He documented the constant verbal and occasional physical abuse suffered at the hands of the staff, and called for improved conditions and professional training for attendants.

Because Beers had experienced mental institutions and lived to write about them, a second message of his book was that mental illness was curable. This was an important idea at a time when the medical community generally believed that there was little hope for the institutionalized mentally ill. In 1909, Beers founded the National Committee for Mental Hygiene to further the cause of prevention, and he spent his remaining years informing the public of his beliefs about mental illness, promoting programs to enhance mental health, and lobbying for the creation of mental hygiene clinics (Williams, Bellis, & Wellington, 1980).

MESMERISM AND HYPNOSIS

At the same time that the various reforms just described were occurring, philosophers, psychologists, and medical doctors were developing theories about the causes and defining features of mental illness, and evolving methods for treating the afflicted. We have seen that bloodletting was a popular medical practice in the late eighteenth and early nineteenth centuries and that in several private asylums, various forms of "moral treatment" were instituted to manage behavior through rewards and punishments. A major breakthrough in psychological treatment occurred when Freud developed psychoanalysis, as will be seen shortly. First, though, it is necessary to set the stage for Freud by briefly describing the history of hypnosis, a technique that Freud learned about in Paris and tried briefly before abandoning it for other procedures. The origins of hypnosis lie with an eccentric Viennese physician who created an occasionally effective therapy based on the idea that illness, mental or otherwise, was the consequence of misaligned magnetic forces within the distressed person.

MESMERISM AND ANIMAL MAGNETISM

The start of Franz Anton Mesmer's (1734–1815) professional career was conventional enough. He earned a medical degree at the prestigious University of Vienna in 1766 and quickly established a thriving practice. Through a fortunate marriage, he entered into Vienna's highest social circles, counting the young composer Wolfgang Amadeus Mozart among his friends. As a scientist, Mesmer was aware of current developments and was especially intrigued by the recent discoveries of forces such as electricity and magnetism. He became convinced that magnetic powers affected humans directly, with good health being the consequence of properly aligned internal magnetic forces. Were these forces to become misaligned, however, ill health (either physical or mental) would result. If you can imagine the effects of trying to push together the plus poles of two magnets, you can get an idea of Mesmer's disease concept. Illness resulted from the disharmony of forces opposing each other. The cure, then, involved straightening out these forces within the body. Mesmer found that he could help many of his patients, especially those suffering from disorders with psychological roots, by giving them medicine containing heavy doses of iron, then passing magnets over their bodies.

Patients would fall into a "crisis state," a type of trance, and when they emerged, would find their health improved. He called his theory of illness and cure **animal magnetism**. He did not know it, of course, but he had inadvertently demonstrated the power of suggestion on human behavior, and he had discovered what would later be renamed hypnosis.

Mesmer soon discovered that he could effect cures without the magnets. Convinced that he had special magnetic powers himself, he discarded the magnets and began treating patients directly by passing his hands over them. He would also massage parts of a patient's body causing distress (e.g., an apparently paralyzed arm), following the path of the nerves and suggesting that things would improve (Winters, 1950). Mesmer had some success, became convinced that he really was quite special, and as a result aroused the ire of the generally conservative medical community in Vienna. After becoming embroiled in several heated controversies over the effectiveness of his magnetic cures, he found himself no longer welcome in Vienna. In May of 1777, the powers that be expelled him from the medical faculty of the University of Vienna and ordered him to stop practicing medicine in the city (Hoffeld, 1980). It was time to move on.

Hoping to find a more open-minded environment, Mesmer moved his magnetic therapy to Paris in 1778, the same year that Pinel first arrived there (Zilboorg, 1941). Aided by his promotional skills and his "magnetic" personality, he soon began attracting more patients than he could easily handle. His solution to the overcrowding was to create a form of group therapy. In an expensively decorated clinic in one of the most fashionable neighborhoods in Paris, small groups of patients would congregate around Mesmer's famous *baquet*. This was a type of wooden chest or tub that contained various chemicals and had iron rods protruding from it in all directions. Patients would join hands and encircle the *baquet*, while Mesmer, often dressed in a flowing lilac-colored robe,

would pass among them and encourage them to enter the crisis state. There was much swooning and moaning, with many individuals undoubtedly influenced by a kind of group contagion effect. Once the mass crisis passed, patients recovered their composure, pronounced themselves much better, then left the clinic to spread the good word of its effectiveness. Indeed, many patients seemed to be cured, especially those suffering from a variety of what we would today call psychosomatic complaints (e.g., headaches, fainting spells, digestive problems).

As in Vienna, however, the medical community was not impressed with Mesmer. Paris in the prerevolutionary years was a place of much uncertainty and flux, and it was full of faith healers and others promising simple answers to the anxieties of the day (Hoffeld, 1980). In this context, Mesmer seemed to be just another quack. The question of the validity of **mesmerism**, as Mesmer's technique was now called, was taken up by a distinguished commission of the French Royal Academy of Sciences, appointed by the king. At its head was the renowned Benjamin Franklin, the American ambassador to France and a distinguished scientist in his own right, a pioneer in the study of electricity and the inventor of a remarkable new device, the lightning rod (Cohen, 1995). The commission also included the eminent chemist Lavoisier, the discoverer of oxygen, and the physician Joseph Guillotin. The latter would soon give his name to an execution device that creatively applied Newtonian gravitational principles concerning the accelerated motion of a falling blade of steel.

As might be expected from Mesmer's experience in Vienna, the Franklin commission's 1784 report concluded that his form of therapy had no foundation in science. It recognized that patients had been helped by Mesmer, but shrewdly attributed any cures to the patient's beliefs rather than to Mesmer's "magnetizing" powers. As Benjamin Franklin put it in a letter to a sick friend contemplating a visit to a mesmerist, if hypochondriacs who overuse medication "can be persuaded to forbear their drugs in expectation of being cured by only the physician's finger or an iron rod pointing at them, they may possibly find good effects tho' they mistake the cause" (quoted in Hoffeld, 1980, p. 380). Mesmer ignored the commission report and continued to practice for a time, but left Paris in 1792 and lived briefly both in London and Germany, practicing mesmerism until his death in 1815.

FROM MESMERISM TO HYPNOSIS

Mesmer gradually faded from the scene after the Franklin commission's report, but mesmerism itself continued to spread throughout Europe, although mainly at the level of entertainment. Much like today's stage hypnotists, mesmerists toured the countryside giving dramatic demonstrations that awed the locals. Few scientists paid attention, but one who did was John Elliotson (1791–1868), a professor of medicine at University College, London, and senior physician at the teaching hospital affiliated with the college. He was intrigued by the demonstrations of apparent anesthesia, during which mesmerized people would show no signs of pain, even while being poked with sharp needles. Elliotson was one of those open-minded scientists who often antagonizes the establishment—he was already under suspicion for promoting a new contraption that other doctors refused to use, the stethoscope (Boring, 1950). Thus, eyebrows were raised when he began mesmerizing patients, and when he proposed a systematic study of the anesthetic effects of mesmerism in the late 1830s, the storm broke. He was denied permission by his hospital board, which also outlawed any use of mesmerism at the hospital. Elliotson resigned in protest and spent his remaining years promoting mesmerism.

Meanwhile other physicians were starting to use mesmerism to reduce the pain of surgery. In the 1840s, for example, there were numer-

ous reported cases of amputations being done while the patient was in a trance. The largest study was completed by James Esdaile (1808–1859), a Scottish surgeon working in India. In 1845, he summarized the results of several hundred surgeries using mesmerism-induced anesthesia. He reported a mortality rate of less than 5% as a result of the surgery, at a time when mortality was normally 40% (Gravitz, 1988). Keep in mind that these were the days before the existence of chemical anesthetics such as ether, and surgery was a brutal business that prized speed over precision, with screaming patients firmly secured to the operating table. Thus, any procedure for pain reduction was a welcome development. Nonetheless, the medical community was slow to change, and the prevailing medical wisdom was that pain, because it was a naturally occurring phenomenon, was good and even necessary for surgery to succeed.

Mesmerism finally began to gain respectability in the late 1840s, in part by changing its name. The Scottish physician James Braid (1795–1860), a respected member of the conservative medical establishment, initially set out to demolish mesmerism, but was led by the studies he conducted to recognize the validity of some of its effects. Because he thought of the trance state as being similar to a state of sleep, he coined a new term for the phenomenon. **Neurypnology**, a contraction of "neuro-hypnology," combined Greek terms for nervous (neuro) and sleep (hypnos) and was defined by Braid as a "nervous sleep." Soon the initial part of the term began to be dropped, and the phenomenon came to be called hypnology or **hypnotism**. Braid discovered that the hypnotic trance could be induced by having patients stare fixedly at an object just above their line of vision, and he came to believe that a general fixation of attention was behind the phenomenon. He also emphasized the importance of suggestion in producing hypnotic effects, and he hinted at a recognition of the importance of unconscious processing when he found that memories could persist from one hypnotic session to the next, even though the person had no recollection during the intervening periods of normal consciousness (Boring, 1950). By 1860, when the discovery of ether and chloroform rendered surgical use of hypnosis unnecessary, the phenomenon was recognized in the scientific community as legitimate and worthy of study. Further developments, and controversy, occurred in France.

THE HYPNOTISM CONTROVERSIES

Hypnotism achieved a degree of legitimacy with Braid, but little consensus existed over its explanation. Two opposing views about the nature of hypnotism developed in France, with a pair of physicians working in the provincial city of Nancy (180 miles east of Paris) on one side of the sometimes acrimonious debate, and the powerful director of the famous Salpêtrière Hospital in Paris on the other.

The so-called Nancy School of hypnosis originated from the curiosity of Auguste Liebeault (1823–1904), an unassuming country doctor practicing just outside of Nancy, who decided to give hypnosis a try after being intrigued by an old book on animal magnetism. He recruited patients for hypnotic treatment by charging no fees for it, and his success produced a legendary local reputation. He soon attracted the attention of a nationally known physician living nearby in Nancy, Hippolyte Bernheim (1840–1919), who traveled to Liebeault's clinic expecting to discover and expose fakery. Instead, he became a convert and the leading voice of the Nancy school.

The central feature of the Liebeault-Bernheim theory of hypnosis was the concept of **suggestion**, which they defined as the ability to uncritically accept an idea or a command suggested by a hypnotist and transform it into an action (Ellenberger, 1970). They considered suggestibility to be a personality trait like any other, with every person having it to some degree. Hypnotic susceptibility was therefore considered to be a normal phenomenon, experienced by different people with varying degrees of strength. In their medical practices, Liebeault and Bernheim induced hypnosis by having the patient stare into the doctor's eyes while being told to deeply relax. Once in a sleeplike trance, the doctor would suggest to the patient that the symptoms (e.g., headache) would go away. The symptoms often did just that.

Meanwhile, the sprawling Salpêtrière Hospital in Paris had become the European center for the study of hypnosis. Its director, Jean-Martin Charcot (1825–1893), was known throughout Europe for his pioneering work on epilepsy; he was the first to identify the features of grand mal seizures and to distinguish them from petit mal seizures. Charcot was also an expert in the study of **hysteria**, a disorder characterized by a wide range of symptoms that appeared to indicate neurological malfunction, but without apparent physical damage to the nervous system. Some patients experienced epilepsy-like seizures, others developed paralyses that were neurologically impossible (e.g., only the hand), and still others had nervous tics, severe headaches, sensory loss (e.g., deafness), or memory lapses.[2] The term "hysteria" derives from the Greek word for uterus, and for a time it was thought that the disorder was experienced only by females. By Charcot's time, however, numerous cases of male hysteria had been demonstrated (Sulloway, 1979). Charcot's contribution was to take hysteria seriously as a disorder and search for its cause. Contemporary medical opinion, grounded in the materialistic belief that true disorders had a physical basis, was that hysterics were simply malingerers, making up their symptoms. Charcot's willingness to tackle the problem head-on eventually earned him the title of "Napoleon of the Neuroses" (Ellenberger, 1970, p. 95).

---

[2] Today, most of these symptoms would earn the patient a diagnosis of conversion disorder.

Figure 12.3   Painting of Charcot lecturing on hysteria at the Salpêtrière, with Blanche Wittman as the hypnotized patient, from Gay (1988). Freud bought an engraving of the piece and hung it in his consulting room.

Because Charcot observed that many of the symptoms of hysteria were the same as the phenomena demonstrated under hypnosis, he came to believe that hysteria and the ability to be hypnotized shared the same underlying pathology. Thus, although the hypnotists at Nancy considered suggestibility a normal trait and therefore generally useful as a therapy tool, Charcot declared that hypnotism was dangerous if it was used indiscriminately. Furthermore, he argued, susceptibility to hypnosis was an indication of underlying hysteric tendencies, which Charcot believed were the result of an inherited nervous system disorder. Hypnotism, then, was an "innately predisposed reaction on the part of [hysterics] to stroking, fixations of the sensory apparatus, and various other means of hypnotic induction" (Sulloway, 1979, p. 46). Hypnotism could be useful, Charcot proclaimed, primarily as a means of investigating and influencing the symptoms of those suffering from hysteria. Furthermore, because some patients were indeed malingerers, hypnosis was the means of separating the true hysterics from the fakes. Only true hysterics could be hypnotized, Charcot believed.

At the Salpêtrière, Charcot was famous for his elaborate and spectacular clinical demonstrations of hysteria. He would pick his "best" hysteric patients, hypnotize them, and suggest various symptoms to them. Charcot's patients apparently competed with each other for the privilege of being "on stage." Predictably, they performed as expected. Figure 12.3 portrays Charcot giving a clinical demonstration of hypnosis on Blanche Wittman, whose dramatic performances earned her the title among her peers of "Queen of the Hysterics" (Fancher, 1990). Charcot also used hypnosis to suggest the removal of hysteric symptoms in his patients, and claimed some success.

The doctors from Nancy disagreed sharply with Charcot's beliefs about hypnosis, arguing that his dramatic clinical demonstrations merely showed the effects of suggestion. Charcot's patients knew exactly what was expected of them, it was argued, and they delivered. A fierce debate erupted in the mid-1880s and between 1888 and 1893, one bibliographic source listed 801 publications in journals and magazines on the nature of hypnosis

(Sulloway, 1979)! By the mid-1890s, most observers had rejected Charcot's ideas about hypnosis in favor of the Nancy model.[3]

During the height of his fame, young physicians from all over Europe came to the Salpêtrière to experience Charcot and learn from his brilliant lectures and demonstrations. One such man was a young doctor from Vienna whose ideas have reverberated through the twentieth century.

SIGMUND FREUD (1856–1939): FOUNDING PSYCHOANALYSIS

That Freud has had a profound influence on Western culture is widely recognized. What is less known is the manner in which his ideas evolved and the sources of influence on him. Indeed, students in introductory and personality courses often encounter a distorted description of Freud that perpetuates what science historian Frank Sulloway (1979) has called the "myth of the hero." The Freudian myth encompasses two components, according to Sulloway. First, it includes the image of Freud as a solitary heroic figure fighting for his ideas against all odds, in a uniformly hostile environment. Second, it maintains the illusion that the hero's theories were absolutely original to him, without serious precedent. Both aspects of this Freudian myth have been brought into question by recent historical scholarship. As will be seen: (a) Freud was indeed controversial but his ideas were not nearly as revolutionary as is normally portrayed, and (b) all of his major concepts have traceable origins to related or identical ideas in existence in the late nineteenth century. Freud's genius was not in creation but in synthesis and advocacy—in weaving ideas together into a unified theory of

human behavior and in vigorously promoting this theory in the medical community.

Interestingly enough, Freud played a role in creating his own myth, in part by hand-picking his first biographer, Ernest Jones, but also by destroying his papers and correspondence on at least two occasions (1885 and 1907), thereby making it difficult to trace the roots of his ideas. After the first of these events, which occurred long before he began to make a name for himself, Freud wrote to his fiancée that her letters were safe and to make his purpose clear:

> One intention...I have almost finished carrying out, an intention which a number of as yet unborn and unfortunate people will one day resent...: my biographers. I have destroyed all my notes of the past fourteen years, as well as letters, scientific excerpts, and the manuscripts of my papers. As for letters, only those from the family have been spared. Yours, my darling, were never in danger.... As for the biographers, let them worry, we have no desire to make it too easy for them. Each one of them will be right in his opinion of "The Development of the Hero," and I am already looking forward to seeing them go astray. (quoted in Sulloway, 1979, p. 7)

This is a remarkable letter. Who was this 31-year-old young man who was certain that he would someday have biographies written about him?

EARLY LIFE AND EDUCATION

Freud spent most of his life in Vienna, Austria. His father moved a growing family there in 1860, when young Sigmund was four, and Freud left only when the Nazi threat to his personal safety took him to London in 1938, a year before his death. Freud's intellectual promise

---

[3] Chapter 8 briefly described some research on hypnosis that embarrassed a young Alfred Binet, in which his apparent success in producing effects with magnets was shown to be the result of suggestion. This study was conducted under Charcot's direction at the Salpêtrière, and the patient was none other than Blanche Wittman (Fancher, 1990).

appeared early. He was a precocious young child in a large household of moderate means, the only one of his siblings given a room of his own for study. He was also given a generous book-buying allowance, and legend has it that when he once complained about the distractions of a younger sister's noisy piano lessons, they ended and the piano was banished from the house.

Freud was the first of eight children produced by the marriage of Jacob and Amalia Freud. Amalia was Jacob's third wife and half his age (20 versus 40). Freud developed a strong emotional attachment to his young mother, while his father was more distant and appeared more grandfatherly than fatherly—the family dynamics undoubtedly played a role in Freud's later thinking about parent-child relationships. Although the Freud family was Jewish, religious practice was not at the center of family life, and Freud would later recall that his father "allowed [him] to grow up in complete ignorance of everything that concerned Judaism" (quoted in Gay, 1988, p. 6). One aspect of Judaism that Freud did manage to experience, however, was Vienna's pervasive anti-Semitism. The period of Freud's youth saw a steady rise in the Jewish population in Vienna, from 2% of the population in 1857, to 10% by 1880 (Gay, 1988). Although liberal reforms made life easier for Jews in the 1860s, a serious economic depression in 1873 led to the all too familiar scapegoating scenario—Jews were blamed for Vienna's problems and became the objects of political (and physical) attack and discrimination. In that same year, Freud entered the University of Vienna's famed medical school after graduating with high honors from the gymnasium (high school). He quickly became aware of his status as a Jew in a setting dominated by non-Jews, but he refused to feel inferior to his peers. In fact, as might be expected from his early promise, he quickly became an academic star.

When he began medical school, Freud had no intention of eventually practicing medicine—his passion was for research. His mentor, one of the most important influences in his life, was Ernst Brücke, director of the university's Physiological Institute. Through Brücke, Freud became immersed in the nineteenth century materialist-mechanist-determinist zeitgeist in physiology (see Chapter 3). Brücke had been a student of the great Johannes Müller, and together with Helmholtz and other students of Müller, he was a leader in the movement that sought to explain all living action by reducing it to physical, mechanical forces. Although Freud's interest in searching for the physiological mechanisms underlying psychological processes diminished over the years, he never wavered in his belief that all events have causes that can be identified through science. His later idea that dreams were not random events, but had deep underlying meanings, is just one example of his strong faith in the essential orderliness and predictability of psychological events.

Freud's immersion in research was the main reason why it took him eight years instead of the typical five to earn his medical degree. Working in Brücke's laboratory from 1876 to 1882, he published articles on the nervous systems of various species and the gonadal structure of eels; he also developed an important research technique for staining nerve fibers. Much of his comparative neurological research carried with it strong evolutionary implications, for Darwin's monumental text was less than 20 years old and its ideas affected the thinking of all physiologists during the era. Indeed, Darwin's thinking would eventually influence Freud profoundly. First, Darwin's basic insight that human nature is rooted in its animal past provided support for Freud's beliefs about the importance of biological instincts in motivating behavior and the fact that behavior is not always "rational." Second, Freud's belief in the central importance of sexual motivation follows logically from the rather obvious point that sex and the resulting perpetuation of the species provides the very foundation for evolution.

Freud had every intention of continuing as a researcher when he completed his medical degree in 1883, but by then he was also deeply in love and faced with a financially uncertain future as a laboratory researcher. And as a Jew, few academic positions would be open to him. If he wished to marry, establishing a medical practice would be necessary. Hence, on Brücke's advice, he reluctantly began to prepare for life as a practitioner by taking three years of instruction at Vienna's General Hospital. For five months of this time, he came under the tutelage of Theodor Meynert (1833–1893), a famous brain anatomist and professor of psychiatry. Freud's earlier research with Brücke led him to be especially interested in disorders of the nervous system, and the time spent with Meynert confirmed in him the decision to specialize in that area. Patients with neurological problems also included hysterics, of course, and it was through his experience with Meynert that Freud first began to encounter the type of patient who would soon become the focus of his life's work. In 1885, he broadened his knowledge of hysteria, and began to learn something about hypnosis, when he earned a six-month travel grant to study with Charcot at the Salpêtrière. He later used hypnosis in the early years of his practice, but eventually abandoned it as an ineffective technique for exploring the unconscious mind.

Breuer and the Catharsis Method

Another important contact that Freud made while in medical school was with the eminent physician/neurologist Joseph Breuer (1842–1925), known for his research on the self-regulatory processes in breathing and his discovery of the role played by the semicircular canals of the inner ear in maintaining balance and equilibrium. From 1880 to 1882, while Freud

was still finishing medical school, Breuer had treated a perplexing case of hysteria that was destined to become one of the defining events in the history of psychoanalysis: the **Anna O. case**. It is also just one example of how the story of psychoanalysis has become distorted over the years.

Anna O. (Figure 12.4) was the pseudonym that Breuer created for Bertha Pappenheim, an intelligent woman in her early twenties with a bewildering array of hysteric symptoms.[4] At various times her right (then her left) side appeared to be paralyzed and anesthetic, she had a persistent nervous cough, experienced both visual and auditory deficits, developed bizarre eating habits (e.g., living solely on oranges for a period of several weeks), lost the ability to speak German for a time (while retaining the ability to speak English), and experienced dissociative states that she called "absences" (Sulloway, 1979). The problems appeared to be precipitated by the long-term nursing care she had given to her dying father, although Anna's general frustrations about her situation in life contributed as well. An intelligent young woman, Anna was raised in a family context that consistently stifled her intellect and ambitions.

According to the traditional description of the case, Breuer found success with what he called the **method of catharsis**. He discovered that if Anna could be made to trace a particular symptom back to the occasion of its first appearance, she would experience an emotional release, which Breuer referred to as a "catharsis," and she would gain relief from the symptom. Anna referred to it as her "talking cure." For example, for a time she was unable to drink water from a glass and thought the practice disgusting. Breuer got her to trace her "hydrophobia" back to a situation in which Anna had wit-

---

[4] The family of Bertha Pappenheim (1859–1936) was not pleased when Ernest Jones revealed her true identity in the first volume of his biography of Freud (Jones, 1953). After recovering her health, Bertha became a leader in the women's movement in Germany and once wrote that "if there is any justice in the next world, women will make the laws and men will bear the children" (quoted in Sulloway, 1979, p. 57). The West German government issued a stamp in her honor in 1954.

Figure 12.4   Bertha Pappenheim (Anna O.) at the time of her therapy with Breuer, from Sulloway (1979).

nessed a woman who shared the same glass of water with her dog. Once the initial memory had been retrieved, she achieved a catharsis and the hydrophobia disappeared. In like manner, so the story goes, Breuer worked his way laboriously through Anna's remaining symptoms, seeing her *every* evening for more than a year.

The Anna O. case is a compelling story, but clever detective work by Ellenberger (1972) showed that the case was not as straightfor-

ward as it appears in most descriptions. Although the cathartic method had some success, relief of Anna's symptoms was often just temporary; the initial diagnosis of hysteria was only a small part of her problem (she also had psychotic symptoms and possibly a multiple personality disorder). She truly began to recover only after spending more than a year in an asylum *after* Breuer ended her treatment, and several of the events reported in traditional descriptions were factually wrong. For example, according to the account in the Jones biography of Freud, Breuer's wife was not happy about the amount of time he was spending with this attractive young woman, and when Anna developed a false pregnancy and named Breuer as the father, he did his catharsis magic to relieve the symptom and then terminated the therapy in a mild panic. The very next day he whisked his wife off to a second honeymoon to Venice where they conceived a daughter (and they all lived happily ever after). Ellenberger, however, showed that none of Breuer's case notes mentioned a false pregnancy, and the birth date of his daughter conflicts with the second honeymoon story.

Breuer told his younger colleague Freud about the case, and it eventually became featured as the first of several cases described in their coauthored *Studies on Hysteria* (1895/1955). This book is often considered the founding event for psychoanalysis. For Freud, the case showed that (a) memory of a traumatic event might be actively repressed into the unconscious, but it will continue to influence the person's behavior as a hysteric symptom; (b) the form of a hysterical symptom bears a symbolic relationship to the traumatic event that caused it, as in the hydrophobia example; and (c) a symptom can be alleviated if the person gains insight into the originating event. As Freud would later say in the first of a series of lectures given at Clark University, "[o]ur hysterical patients suffer from reminiscences. Their symptoms are residues and mnemic symbols of particular (traumatic) events" (1909/1992, p. 16).

Freud also thought he detected a strong undercurrent of sexuality in the case. Anna seemed to be unusually attached to her father and near the end of therapy, developed a strong attachment to Breuer as well. Freud would eventually refer to this attachment for the therapist as **transference**, and would consider it an important step on the road to recovery. Breuer, however, rejected the sexual implications of the case and split with Freud over the issue, thus ending a long friendship. It would not be the first time that Freud's insistence on the importance of sexual motivation would cost him a colleague.

CREATING PSYCHOANALYSIS

From the mid-1880s to the mid-1890s, Freud developed his neurology practice, specializing in the treatment of hysteria. He was not at a loss for patients. Vienna was like other European cities in the Victorian era—sex in marriage was considered a necessary evil, good only for producing heirs, whereas sex for pleasure was confined to males visiting prostitutes. The results included frustrated sexual needs for the faithful wife, lingering guilt for the wandering husband, and good incomes for therapists like Freud. The picture was more complicated, of course—historians continue to debate whether the Victorian female was sexually inhibited (e.g., Sterns, 1985). Nonetheless, neurotic symptoms seemed plentiful at a time when Freud was trying to establish his practice. He tried everything with his patients, from conventional treatments such as hydrotherapy (i.e., similar to a modern whirlpool bath, presumably designed to soothe the nerves) to hypnosis to a procedure in which he pressed on a patient's forehead while insisting that they retrieve repressed memories. He eventually discovered a technique that became the centerpiece of psychoanalytic practice—**free association**. Patients were placed in a relaxed position (hence, the famous couch) and encouraged to say whatever came into their minds, without

censoring anything. This often proved difficult for patients, who would display what Freud called **resistance**—they would be unable or unwilling to mention something that had occurred to them. Freud welcomed resistances, believing they were a sure sign that he was getting to the root of the patient's problem. For example, if a depressed female patient resisted telling the therapist that she was attracted to her brother-in-law, who looked a bit like her father and shared some of Dad's mannerisms, Freud would immediately begin thinking about how her problems might stem from unresolved feelings toward her father.

In addition to free association, Freud also used **dream analysis** as a means to explore the unconscious. He first hit upon the idea while searching for a way to perform psychoanalysis on himself, a task he undertook in the late 1890s. He could recall his dreams in great detail, and he discovered that they provided a rich source of information, both on their own and as a starting point for further free association. He published what is widely considered his most important book, *The Interpretation of Dreams*, in 1900. Freud's dream theory will be elaborated on later in the excerpt from his Clark lectures.

The Importance of Sex

As Freud's experience with hysteria grew, he became convinced that unresolved sexual problems were at the heart of the matter. Patients working their way into their pasts by means of free associations and dream reports often seemed to have experienced some type of sexual trauma at a young age. By the mid-1890s, Freud had heard enough of this theme to propose what became known as his **seduction hypothesis**. Hysteria, he argued, was the result of childhood sexual abuse by a parent or other adult. Because the young child had no understanding of what was happening, Freud believed, the experience was forgotten, buried deep in the unconscious mind. Sometime after puberty occurred and the person began to

This year marked the official publication date of Freud's *Interpretation of Dreams*. It appeared a year earlier, but Freud wanted the millennium publication date on his book.

These events also occurred:

- Physicist Max Planck formulated quantum theory   1900
- F. E. Dorn discovered radon
- The Commonwealth of Australia was created
- D. F. Davis was presented an international lawn tennis cup bearing his name
- Puccini's opera, *Tosca*, made its debut in Rome
- Boxer uprisings in China, protesting European influence, occurred
- These people were born:

    Spencer Tracy, American actor

    Aaron Copeland, American composer

- These people died:

    Oscar Wilde, English author

    Friedrich Nietzsche, German philosopher

Key Date 1900

understand about and experience mature sexuality, the long-buried memory would resurface in the form of one or more hysterical symptoms.

Freud first presented his seduction theory in public at an 1896 meeting of the Vienna Society for Psychiatry and Neurology, which was presided over by Richard von Krafft-Ebbing, the era's leading authority on sexual pathology. The talk was not well received by the medical community, and Krafft-Ebbing even called Freud's theory a "scientific fairy tale" (Gay, 1988, p. 93). Freud himself soon began to doubt the universality of the abuse-hysteria connection, partly because some of his patients' stories didn't seem to stand up to other evidence. Also, Freud was bothered by the idea that it was only sexual traumas in childhood that led to later problems. What about all the other, nonsexual traumas (e.g., severe illness, bad falls) that children experience? Why didn't they lead to later psychopathologies? It seemed impossible, Freud later wrote, "to suppose that distressing sexual affects so greatly exceed all other unpleasurable affects in intensity. It must be another characteristic of sexual ideas that can explain how it is that sexual ideas are alone subjected to [pathological] repression" (quoted in Sulloway, 1979, p. 111).

Tradition has it that Freud's great intellectual breakthrough was to abandon his seduction theory and replace it with the idea that sexual events in childhood were not real but *imagined* and that sexuality did not begin in adolescence but existed in some form from infancy. This insight about universal childhood sexuality supposedly emerged from Freud's famous self-analysis in the late 1890s, in which he recognized that the guilt he felt over his father's recent death was a consequence of what he would later call the Oedipal complex. Freud thought he recognized some repressed sexual fantasies in his own childhood, directed toward his attractive young mother, accompanied by feelings of hostility toward his father and a desire to replace

Handwritten margin notes:
Sig Freud 1856-1939
Wed. Evening group. ORIGINAL 5 1902
By 1908 There were 20.
Alfred Adler 1870-1937 out of group 1911

him in his mother's affections. This led him to wonder if his patients were also reporting fantasies; perhaps the sexual memories were imagined, not real. There is surely some truth to Freud's "heroic" account of how he came to abandon his seduction hypothesis and develop his famous Oedipal complex. However, this is an area where the Freudian myth has also been at work. Freud was not operating in an intellectual vacuum here, creating ideas that were unique. For instance, several other noted "sexologists" (e.g., Havelock Ellis) were also proposing that sexual strivings extended into infancy and that repressed sexuality was connected with later psychopathology. Indeed, the 1890s witnessed an outpouring of books on sex, childhood and otherwise, and Freud was fully knowledgeable about them (Sulloway, 1979). Hence, the origins of the concept of infantile sexuality include Freud's self-analysis, but go much deeper to include the intellectual context of late nineteenth-century Europe.

Psychoanalysis Enters the Twentieth Century

By the turn of the century, Freud was launched on his career as a psychoanalyst specializing in the treatment of hysteria. With *The Interpretation of Dreams*, he also began developing his general theory of behavior, which continued to evolve for the rest of his life. A year after the dream book, in 1901, he published *The Psychopathology of Everyday Life*, and in 1905 two books appeared: *Three Contributions to the Theory of Sex* and *Wit and Its Relation to the Unconscious*. Also during this time, he began attracting a small group of followers, the best-known being Alfred Adler and Carl Jung. The story of Freud and the sometimes stormy relationships with his "disciples" is elaborated in the Close-Up.

▶ CLOSE-UP

Freud's Inner Circle: Loyalty and Dissent

By the turn of the twentieth century, Freud had begun attracting the interest of other physicians in Vienna. In 1902, he asked four of them to join him on Wednesday evenings to discuss issues related to psychoanalysis. The group expanded to about 20 by 1908 and began calling itself the Vienna Psychoanalytic Society. Discussions were spirited, but the authoritarian and dogmatic Freud dominated the meetings and made it clear that his word was to be law. As might be expected, while some members remained intensely loyal to Freud for years, others were not so compliant. The first major defector was one of the original five who met in 1902.

Alfred Adler (1870–1937) was trained in ophthalmology and general practice at the University of Vienna medical school, graduating in 1895. He was apparently attracted to Freud's ideas on reading the *Interpretation of Dreams*, and became an enthusiastic charter member of the Wednesday evening group. Soon, however, he began to question Freud's seeming obsession with sexual motivation. Instead, he drew on his own troubled childhood, which included illness and feelings of inferiority when compared to an older brother, and created the **inferiority complex** as the basis for an alternative theory. All infants are inherently inferior in their abilities, he argued, and life could be viewed as an attempt to compensate for this inferiority. He also pointed out that as we grow, the social environment places obstacles in our paths that also create feelings of inferiority to be overcome. Adler's emphasis on the importance of social factors over biological ones, along with his writings on inferiority and his belief that behavior was determined as much by conscious planning for the future as by the repressed events of one's past, alienated him from Freud. The official break came in 1911, when he was tossed out of the Vienna Psychoanalytic Society, taking several followers with him. He went on to create a rival school of psychoanalysis that he called **individual psychology**. Adler and Freud never reconciled; indeed Gay (1988) described their subsequent relationship as one of mutual hate, and when Adler died suddenly in 1937, Freud was delighted to learn that he had outlived his rival.

An equally bitter split occurred between Freud and the Swiss psychiatrist Carl Jung (1875–1961), known for his pioneering work with schizophrenia. The two met in Vienna in 1907 after exchanging some earlier correspondence in which Jung's praise for Freud's dream theory was matched by Freud's enthusiasm for a **word association** task that had been developed by Jung (1919). The procedure involved giving patients a prepared list of words and asking them to respond to each with the first word that came to mind. Also, their reactions were timed and some physiological measures were recorded (Watson & Evans, 1991). Jung assumed that longer reaction times and arousal (e.g., increased breathing) would indicate that a particular word had important emotional implications, a rationale similar to the one later used to justify the polygraph's validity as a lie detector.

Jung accompanied Freud to America and the Clark conference of 1909, where he lectured on his word association procedure. In 1911, Freud arranged to have Jung named the first president of the newly formed International Psychoanalytic Society, in part because Freud believed that naming Jung, who was neither Viennese nor Jewish, would make the association appear to be more international and broad-based than it really was. Meanwhile, Freud began thinking of Jung in father–son terms, even writing to him as his "successor and crown prince" (quoted in McGuire, 1974, p. 218). But trouble was looming on the horizon and by 1913, Jung went the way of Adler, expelled from the inner circle.

Like Adler, Jung (a) questioned Freud's emphasis on sex and (b) had some ideas of his own. Over the rest of his career, he developed what came to be called **analytical psychology**, to be distinguished from Freud's psychoanalysis. He went beyond Freud in some ways. For example, to the concept of a "personal" unconscious, similar to Freud's use of the term, he added the evolutionary concept of the **collective unconscious**, said to include the collective experiences of our ancestors. He believed that the common themes found in mythology reflected a shared human legacy. Jung also contributed to personality theory with his distinction between what he saw as two major types: introverts and extroverts.

After the defection of Adler, Jung, and another analyst named Stekel, Freud closed ranks. At the suggestion of Ernest Jones, destined to be Freud's hand-picked biographer, Freud formed a secret group of eight called the "Committee." He even gave each member of his new inner sanctum a gold ring. Their task was to safeguard orthodox Freudianism, respond to critics, control the various psychoanalytic organizations, and as it turned out, perpetuate the Freud myth. (Sulloway, 1979).

Freud's loyal followers are too numerous to mention, but none was more devoted than the youngest of his six children, his daughter Anna (1895–1982). Apparently oblivious to the risks, Freud psychoanalyzed her himself as part of her preparation for a career as analyst. Anna survived the analysis and went on to a distinguished career. She was a pioneer in extending psychoanalytic practice to children through the use of play therapy. Children lack the verbal fluency for normal analysis, of course, so Anna probed children's psyches by giving them various materials (e.g., Mommy and Daddy dolls) and asking them to just play. She also helped her father develop his own theory, especially the relationship between anxiety and defense. In fact, the lists of defense mechanisms (projection, reaction formation, etc.) normally found in introductory texts are more the outcome of her work than her father's. She articulated them in *The Ego and Mechanisms of Defense* (A. Freud, 1937).

Freud's reputation grew, slowly but steadily, throughout the first decade of the twentieth century. In America, his theories caught the enthusiastic attention of G. Stanley Hall of Clark University. As you recall from Chapter 6, Hall's enormous range of interests included the study of children and adolescents, including their sexual development. He described Breuer and Freud's work on hysteria in his two-volume tome on adolescence, and he was offering courses on sexuality as early as 1904 (Rosenzweig, 1992). In 1909, to celebrate the twentieth anniversary of Clark University's founding, Hall invited Freud to Worcester to receive an honorary degree and lecture on psychoanalysis. Several other "behavioral scientists" also gave talks and were awarded degrees at the celebration, including Jung, Titchener, and the noted anthropologist Franz Boas. Still other psychologists came to hear the talks, including James, Cattell, and Goddard. It was Freud's only visit to the United States and he returned with a healthy dislike of the country, especially its food. Nonetheless, he was forever grateful to Hall, crediting him with enhancing the international reputation of psychoanalysis and providing "the first official recognition of our endeavors" (quoted in Gay, 1988, p. 207).

►ORIGINAL SOURCE EXCERPT

Freud's Lectures on Psychoanalysis at Clark University

From Tuesday, September 7, 1909 through Saturday, the 11th, Freud gave five improvised lectures, in German, to the assembled audience of educators, scientists, and press. In the opener, he paid homage to Breuer and described the origins of psychoanalysis in the Anna O. case. The lecture included the quote about hysterics suffering from their memories that begins this chapter. Lecture 2 focused on the related processes of resistance and repression and described how Freud shifted from hypnosis to free association as a method for searching the unconscious. The following excerpt comes from lectures 3 and 4, and is taken from a 1977 translation by James Strachey.

Lecture 3 included Freud's dream theory, with its distinction between the manifest and latent content of dreams, and his ideas about slips of the tongue and other so-called accidents. After opening the talk with some further discussion of free association and Jung's related word association procedure, Freud began to discuss dreams, starting with an acknowledgment of American pragmatism:

> I must admit, Ladies and Gentlemen, that I hesitated for a long time whether, instead of giving you this condensed general survey of the whole field of psycho-analysis, it might not be better to present you with a detailed account of dream-interpretation. I was held back by a purely subjective and seemingly secondary motive. It seemed to me almost indecent in a country which is devoted to practical aims to make my appearance as a "dream interpreter," before you could possibly know the importance that can attach to that antiquated and derided art. The interpretation of dreams is in fact the royal road to a knowledge of the unconscious; it is the securest foundation of psycho-analysis and the field in which every work-

er must acquire his convictions and seek his training. If I am asked how one can become a psycho-analyst, I reply, "By studying one's own dreams." Every opponent of psycho-analysis hitherto has, with a nice discrimination, either evaded any consideration of *The Interpretation of Dreams*, or has sought to skirt over it with the most superficial objections. If, on the contrary, you can accept the solutions of the problems of dream-life, the novelties with which psycho-analysis confronts your minds will offer you no further difficulties. (p. 33)

Freud's comment about critics "evading any evaluation" of the dream book or superficially dismissing it, combined with his complaints at other times that nobody would read the book, helped further the Freudian myth. Sales were indeed slow at first—it took six years to sell the first printing of 600 copies (Jones, 1953)—but the book was neither ignored nor condemned. In fact, it was widely reviewed and generally praised as "epoch-making" (Decker, 1975).

After proclaiming the importance of dreams, Freud introduced the central idea that dreams serve the function of wish fulfillment. This is easy to see in children's dreams, but disguised in adult dreams:

In the first place, note all dreams are alien to the dreamer, incomprehensible and confused. If you inspect the dreams of very young children, from eighteen months upwards, you will find them perfectly simple and easy to explain. Small children always dream of the fulfillment of wishes that were aroused in them the day before but not satisfied. You will need no interpretative art in order to find this simple solution; all you need do is to enquire into the child's experiences on the previous day (the "dream day"). Certainly the most satisfactory solution of the riddle of dreams would be to find that adults' dreams too were like those of children—fulfillments of wishful impulses that had come to them on the dream-day. And such in fact is the case. The difficulties in the way of this solution can be overcome step by step if dreams are analyzed more closely.

The first and most serious objection is that the content of adults' dreams is as a rule unintelligible and could not look more unlike the fulfillment of a wish. And here is the answer. Such dreams have been subjected to distortion; the psychical process underlying them might originally have been expressed in words quite differently. You must distinguish the *manifest content of the dream*, as you vaguely recollect it in the morning and laboriously (and, as it seems, arbitrarily) clothe it in words, and the *latent dream-thoughts*, which you must suppose were present in the unconscious. This distortion in dreams is the same process that you have already come to know in investigating the formation of hysterical symptoms. It indicates, too, that the same interplay of mental forces is at work in the formation of dreams as in that of symptoms. The manifest content of the dream is the distorted substitute for the unconscious dream-thoughts and this distortion is the work of the ego's forces of defense—of resistances. In waking life these resistances altogether prevent the repressed wishes of the unconscious from entering consciousness; and during the lowered state of sleep they are at least strong enough to oblige them to adopt a veil of disguise. Thereafter, the dreamer can no more understand the meaning of his dreams than the hysteric can understand the connection and significance of his symptoms.

...The manifest dream, which you know from your memory when you wake up, can therefore only be described as a *disguised* fulfillment of *repressed* wishes.

You can also obtain a view, by a kind of synthetic work, of the process which has brought about the distortion of the unconscious dream-thoughts into the manifest content of the dream. We call this process the "dream-work." It deserves our closest theoretical interest, since we are able to study in it, as nowhere else, what unsuspected psychical processes can occur in the unconscious, or rather, to put it more accurately, *between* two separate psychical systems like the conscious and the unconscious. Among these freshly discovered psychical processes those of *condensation* and *displacement* are especially noticeable. The dream-work is a special case of the effects produced by two different mental groupings on each other—that is, of the consequences of mental splitting; and it seems identical in all essentials with the process of distortion which transforms the repressed complexes into symptoms where there is unsuccessful repression....

I should like you to notice, too, that the analysis of dreams has shown us that the unconscious makes use of a particular symbolism, especially for representing sexual complexes. This symbolism varies partly from individual to individual; but partly it is laid down in a typical form and seems to coincide with the symbolism which, as we suspect, underlies our myths and fairy tales. It seems not impossible that these creations of the popular mind might find an explanation through the help of dreams. (pp. 34–36, italics in the original translation)

Hence, the manifest content of the dream includes images that serve as symbols for the deeper, more meaningful latent content. For Freud, as you might guess, many of the symbols had sexual content. Elongated objects symbolized male sexuality, while anything symbolizing containers represented females. (A Freudian would have no difficulty interpreting a dream about a train going in and out of a tunnel!) Both condensation and displacement involve symbolism. In **condensation**, two or more latent or unconscious thoughts combine to form a single thought that is symbolized in an image reported in the manifest dream. For example, a dream in which a person hesitates about going into a church with a large (i.e., elongated) steeple might symbolize the conflict between sexuality and morality. In **displacement**, a minor part of the manifest content might be the major part of the latent content, and vice versa. Thus, a long dream about a golf match might include a single moment of indecision about which club to choose. That small part of the manifest content, for a Freudian, might in fact symbolize a deeper problem about the lack of direction in one's life (and because a "club" is involved, sex would surely find a way into the interpretation).

At the end of the third lecture, Freud discussed events that appear to be trivial, yet provide another glimpse of the unconscious mind. He also made his determinist beliefs clear—even the simplest of accidents points to some predictable unconscious motive:

The phenomena in question are the small faulty actions performed by both normal and neurotic people, to which as a rule no importance is attached: forgetting things that might be known and sometimes in fact *are* known (e.g., the occasional difficulty in recalling proper names), slips of the tongue in talking, by which we ourselves are so often affected, analogous slips of the pen and misreadings, bungling the performance of actions, losing objects or breaking them. All of these are things for which as a rule no psychological determinants are sought and which are allowed to pass without criticism as consequences of distraction or inattention or similar causes. Besides these there are the actions and gestures which people carry out without noticing them at all, to say nothing of attributing any psychological importance to them; playing about and fiddling with things, humming tunes, fingering parts of one's own body or one's clothing and so on. These small things, faulty actions and symptomatic or haphazard actions alike, are not so insignificant as people, by sort of conspiracy of silence, are ready to suppose. They always have a meaning, which can usually be interpreted with ease and certainty from the situation in which they occur. And it turns out that once again they give expression to impulses and intentions which have to be kept back and hidden from one's own consciousness, or that they are actually derived from the same repressed wishful impulses and complexes which we have already come to know as the creators of symptoms and the constructors of dreams. They therefore deserve to be rated as symptoms, and if they are examined they may lead, just as dreams do, to the uncovering of the hidden part of the mind....

As you already see, psycho-analysts are marked by a particularly strict belief in the determination of metal life. For them there is nothing trivial, nothing arbitrary or haphazard. They expect in every case to find sufficient motives where, as a rule, no such expectation is raised. Indeed, they are prepared to find *several* motives for one and the same mental occurrence, whereas what seems to be our innate craving for causality declares itself satisfied with a *single* psychical cause. (pp. 37–38, italics in the original translation)

Freud did not give any examples of these **Freudian slips** in the Clark lecture, but *The Psychopathology of Everyday Life* is full of them. For instance, when a lecturer referred to the "Freuer-Breudian" theory of hysteria instead of "Breuer-Freudian," when referring to their jointly authored hysteria book, Freud suggested that a hostile motive was behind the mistake. In another case, a patient who couldn't recall (i.e., had repressed) where a man had touched her, quickly changed the subject to her summer home. When asked where it was located, she said "near the mountain loin" instead of "mountain lane."

Freud's fourth Clark lecture was a summary of his *Three Contributions on the Theory of Sexuality,* and it included a discussion of childhood sexuality and the Oedipal complex. He began by asserting that:

First and foremost we have found out one thing. Psycho-analytic research traces back the symptoms of patient's illnesses with really surprising regularity to impressions from their *erotic life.* It shows us that the pathogenic wishful impulses are in the nature of erotic instinctual components; and it forces us to suppose that among the influences leading to the illness the predominant significance must be assigned to erotic disturbances, and that this is the case in both sexes. (p. 40, italics in the original translation)

Freud next tried to convince his audience of his assertion that sexual motivation reached back into childhood and defined this sexuality broadly as any pleasurable activity related to the "erogenous" zones, which included:

Put away your doubts, then, and join me in a consideration of infantile sexuality from the earliest age. A child's sexual instinct turns out to be put together out of a number of factors; it is capable of being divided up into numerous components which originate from various sources. Above all, it is still independent of the reproductive function, into the service of which it will be later brought. It serves for the acquisition of different kinds of pleasurable feeling, which, basing ourselves on analogies and connections, we bring together under the idea of sexual pleasure. The chief source of infantile sexual pleasure is the appropriate excitation of certain parts of the body that are especially susceptible to stimulus: apart from the genitals, these are the oral, anal and urethral orifices, as well as the skin and other sensory surfaces. Since at this first phase of infantile sexual life satisfaction is obtained from the subject's own body and extraneous objects are disregarded, we term this phase (from a word coined by Havelock Ellis) that of *auto-erotism*. We call the parts of the body that are important in the acquisition of sexual pleasure "erotogenic zones." (p. 43–44, italics in the original translation)

As examples of autoerotic behaviors, Freud mentioned such things as thumb-sucking and innocent genital manipulation. He then turned to the question of object-choice, which led him to the Oedipal complex:

…Children's relations to their parents, as we learn alike from direct observations of children and from later analytic examination of adults, are by no means free from elements of accompanying sexual excitation. The child takes both of its parents, and more particularly one of them, as the object of its erotic wishes. In so doing, it usually follows some indication from its parents, whose affection bears the clearest characteristics of a sexual activity, even though of one that is inhibited in its aims. As a rule a father prefers his daughter and a mother her son; the child reacts to this by wishing, if he is a son, to take his father's place, and, if she is a daughter, her mother's. The feelings which are aroused in these relations between parents and children and in the resulting ones between brothers and sisters are not only of a positive or affectionate kind but also of a negative or hostile one. The complex which is thus formed is doomed to early repression; but it continues to exercise a great and lasting influence from the unconscious. It is to be suspected that, together with its extensions, it constitutes the *nuclear complex* of every neurosis, and we may expect to find it no less actively at work in other regions of mental life. The myth of King Oedipus, who killed his father and took his mother to wife, reveals, with little modification, the infantile wish, which is later opposed and repudiated by the *barrier against incest*. Shakespeare's *Hamlet* is equally rooted in the soil of the incest-complex, but under a better disguise....

It is inevitable and perfectly normal that a child should take his parents as the first objects of his love. But his libido should not remain fixated to these first objects; later on, it should merely take them as a model, and should make a gradual transition from them on to extraneous people when the time for the final choice of an object arrives. The detachment of the child from his parents is thus a task that cannot be evaded if the young individual's social fitness is not to be endangered. During the time at which repression is making its selection among the components instincts, and later, when there should be a slackening of the parent's influence, which is essentially responsible for the expenditure of energy on these repressions, the task of education meets with great problems, which at the present time are certainly not always dealt with in an understanding and unobjectionable manner.

You must not suppose, Ladies and Gentlemen, that these discussions on sexual life and psychosexual development of children have led us too far from psycho-analysis and the problem of curing nervous disorders. You can, if you like, regard psycho-analytic treatment as no more than a prolongation of education for the purpose of overcoming the residues of childhood. (pp. 47–48, italics in the original translation)

Freud's fifth and final lecture described the importance of transference for the successful outcome of psychoanalysis and held out the hope that the individual's **libido**, the psychic energy associated with the sex drive, could be directed toward socially useful activities, a process he referred to as **sublimation**.

THE EVOLUTION OF PSYCHOANALYTIC THEORY

Freud was already 54 years old when he delivered his lectures at Clark, but he was just beginning to develop what he referred to as his **metapsychology**—his general theory of human behavior and mental processes. Over the next 20 years, this metatheory evolved considerably; indeed, many of the concepts most frequently associated with Freud did not appear until after World War I, when he was in his late sixties. One major postwar change in Freud's metapsychology was his conviction that destructive tendencies were just as powerful as sexual ones in motivating behavior.

Freud did not ignore aggression in the years prior to World War I. Male feelings of hostility toward the father were an integral part of the Oedipal complex and the sex act itself contains elements of male aggression, he believed. Yet the war, with its seemingly unending brutality and appalling loss of life, had a profound impact on Freud's thinking (Gay, 1988). In 1920, he produced *Beyond the Pleasure Principle*, in which he proposed a distinction between **eros**, the life instinct, manifested in sexual motivation, and **thanatos**, a death instinct, which showed itself in the form of aggression and self-destruction. Hence, he came to believe that human behavior was jointly motivated by life-enhancing (sexual) and life-destroying (aggressive) instincts.

Although his reflections on the world war were the immediate stimulus for his proposal that we all have instinctive destructive tenden-

Topographical Theory (Uncs. Precon. Consc.) gives way to STRUCTURAL THEORY Ego, Id, Superego

Anxiety
Objective: Realistic fear
Neurotic
Moral

382   Chapter 12 / Psychoanalysis and Clinical Psychology

cies, the concept of a death instinct was also rooted in a lifelong preoccupation that Freud had with death, and his conviction of its reality was strengthened by events in his life during the 1920s. Shortly after he wrote *Beyond the Pleasure Principle*, one of his three daughters died during an influenza outbreak. Soon after that, a favorite grandson died and a niece committed suicide. Then in 1923, Freud, who smoked up to 20 cigars a day, was diagnosed with cancer of the mouth and saw his own demise on the horizon. Over the next 16 years, he endured 33 painful surgeries and had to live with a series of increasingly bulky denture-like prostheses to replace parts of his palate and jaw. Freud saw all of these events as confirmation that death instincts go hand in hand with life instincts.

1923 The Ego + The Id.

Other well-known Freudian concepts also developed in his later years. These include his structural analysis of personality into id, ego, and superego components, and his description of the relationship between anxiety and ego defense mechanisms. Freud first wrote about his familiar tripartite structure of personality— id, ego, and superego—in *The Ego and the Id*, a short book that appeared in 1923. The **ego**, partly conscious and partly unconscious, lies at the center of personality, Freud wrote, trying to maintain a balance between three conflicting forces: the **id**, the superego, and reality. The **id**, repository of the instinctive drives of sex and aggression, constantly demands that its needs be satisfied. On the other hand, the **superego**, the person's learned moral values, works to inhibit the free expression of the instincts. The ego must also take into account the environmental factors operating in the real world, which enter the system through what Freud called the "perception-consciousness" system. The properly functioning ego, according to Freud, serves as a mediator, channeling id-based needs in directions that are realistic and consistent with moral values.

The demands made on the ego necessarily produce some tension. Freud's approach to anxiety was to distinguish three forms of it, one for each of the forces pressuring the ego. **Objective anxiety** (or "realistic" anxiety) is a normal reaction to a perceived threat from the external world, based on the person's memories of past situations of danger. Thus, sailors observing a "red sky in the morning" know they must "take warning" because it means a storm is on the horizon. This perception, combined with memory, would create an understandable level of objective anxiety. More interesting to the psychoanalyst, however, were the other two forms of anxiety, neurotic and moral. In **neurotic anxiety**, the person fears that id-based impulses will get out of control. Memories of being punished for acting out impulsively in the past lead to the feeling of anxiety. In the closely-related **moral anxiety**, feelings of guilt and shame arise from a sense that one is about to violate the strict moral code of the superego.

The feeling of anxiety serves as a signal to the ego that it is under attack, Freud reasoned, and it responds through defense. The response to objective anxiety is to deal with the situation realistically (e.g., the sailors prepare the ship for a storm) or to use the fight/flight reflex if a true danger is at hand. Because neurotic and moral anxieties are generated internally, however, the responses must also come from within, and they do so in the form of ego **defense mechanisms**. The most common form of defense is **repression**, accomplished by that portion of the ego that is unconscious. In repression, unwanted impulses are actively forced from awareness and into the unconscious. Repression is also an element in other defenses. In **projection**, for example, personal faults cannot be accepted, so they are attributed to some other person. People who cannot accept the hostility within them, for example, might convince themselves that those around them are the hostile ones. That is, they repress their own hostility and project it onto others. Another common defense is **reaction formation**, in which unacceptable impulses are repressed and replaced with the opposite ones. For instance, feelings of hatred toward an

Figure 12.5   Freud and his daughter Anna, in 1928, the year of Anna's book on child psychoanalysis, from Gay (1988).

unwanted child, unacceptable to the superego, are transformed into an exaggerated level of attention and an unwillingness to allow any negative feelings about the child to surface (Hall, 1954). Freud's thinking about defense mechanisms was aided greatly by his daughter, Anna, who became his closest collaborator in the 1920s and became a pioneer herself in the area of child psychoanalysis (e.g., A. Freud, 1928; see Figure 12.5 and the Close-Up).

THE RECEPTION OF PSYCHOANALYSIS AMONG AMERICAN PSYCHOLOGISTS

The Clark lectures put Freud on the intellectual map in America, but not all of those in attendance were impressed. An ailing William James, within a year of his death from heart disease, traveled to Worcester to hear Freud's fourth lecture and the two men spent some time together in private. James later wrote to a colleague expressing the hope that Freud would push his interesting ideas to the limit because they "can't fail to throw light on human nature." On the other hand, James had to "confess that [Freud] made on me personal-ly the impression of a man obsessed with fixed ideas. I can make nothing in my own case with his dream theories, and obviously 'symbolism' is a most dangerous method" (quoted in Rosenzweig, 1992, p. 174).

Over the next few years, American psychologists had the opportunity to learn more about Freud. Reviews of Freud's work and articles on psychoanalysis appeared in the *Journal of Abnormal Psychology* with some regularity, but many academic psychologists found psychoanalysis either tangential to their research interests, or annoyingly "unscientific." Robert Woodworth of Columbia (Chapter 7), who might have been congenial to the Freudians because of his own interest in motivation and his general eclecticism, attacked psychoanalysis as being more religion than science (Woodworth, 1917). He was especially annoyed at a clever strategy used by analysts; whenever attacked, they would attribute the criticism to an unconscious resistance on the part of the attacker, thereby providing support for a key Freudian concept. It was a perfect Catch-22: analysts could claim support for Freud's ideas regardless of whether critics praised or condemned them. For Woodworth, this attitude was unconscionable. Equally galling to American psychologists was the analysts' claim that to truly understand psychoanalysis and to criticize it, one had to undergo a complete psychoanalysis oneself (Hornstein, 1992).

As mentioned in the previous chapter, some behaviorally inclined psychologists (i.e., John Dollard and Neal Miller) in the late 1930s tried to assimilate psychoanalysis by reinterpreting it in terms understandable to them. Repression, for instance, rather than being some mysterious force that wrestled with unacceptable ideas and shoved them into the deep void of the unconscious, could be considered "more rationally" as a response of nonthinking about certain events that were associated in one's learning history with negative emotions. It was simply a matter of avoidance conditioning—nonthinking about some event was reinforced by the elimination of anxiety associated with that event. Other psy-

in U.S.A. Early work of Freud translated (+ commented on) by A. A. Brill
Later in 50's + on The Psychoanalytic Assn. - appointed Frank Stachey

chologists tried to bring Freudian concepts into the laboratory and subject them to operational definitions. Repression, for example, could be defined in terms of whether or not people recognized "dirty words" that were flashed at threshold level (e.g., McGinnies, 1949). This research on perceptual defense was interesting in its own right, but whether it adequately tested Freud's ideas was another question.

Freudian psychoanalysis might not have played well within academia, but it had a strong impact on the medical practice of psychiatry, and it caught the imagination of the general public. Between 1912 and 1918, some 170 articles relating to psychoanalysis appeared in medical journals, and about 50 articles appeared in popular magazines ranging from *Ladies' Home Journal* to *The New Republic* (Green & Reiber, 1980). By the 1920s, psychoanalysis was popular enough to be the subject of light satire. In "A Manual of the New Mentality," for example, Stephan Leacock (1924) noted that "[i]n every direction one sees references to psychoanalysis, auto-suggestion, hypnosis, hopnoosis, psychiatry, inebriety, and things never thought of a little while ago" (p. 471). A more sarcastic tone was taken by Grace Adams, a former student of Titchener, in an *Atlantic Monthly* article. Referring to the Clark conference, she noted that the psychologists in the audience didn't realize they were listening to the wave of the future; rather, they thought "they were merely listening to a bearded foreigner make some altogether preposterous remarks" (1934, p. 85). Adams went on to lament the intrusion of psychoanalysis into everyday life, with "its majestic verbiage and high-minded meddlesomeness" (p. 88). Analysts might know nothing about the details of housekeeping, acting, or banking, for instance, "yet from the mastery of their own special subject they were accepted as being able to tell a housewife, an actress, or a banker just how to perform his (sic) tasks" (pp. 86–87).

Despite the criticism and the satire, psychoanalysis persevered. It made significant inroads in the medical community and by the 1930s, training in psychiatry and neurology typically included a strong dose of Freud (Hale, 1971). In addition, psychoanalytic institutes were created in urban areas, especially in the eastern United States, and catered to M.D.s who wished further certification as professional psychoanalysts. Over the years, reflecting differences in institutional contexts and the focus of their interests, academic psychologists and psychoanalysts have tended to go their separate ways.

FREUD IN PERSPECTIVE

Near the end of his life, Freud was once again reminded of his Jewish heritage. Ominous signs occurred soon after the Nazis rose to power in 1933. As you recall from the gestalt chapter, Jewish professors were routinely dismissed from their positions. In addition, psychoanalysis was branded "Jewish science" and outlawed within Germany. Soon, Freud's writings were publicly burned, along with other books by Jews (e.g., Einstein). Freud wryly noted that the world seemed to be making progress: "In the Middle Ages they would have burnt me; nowadays they are content with burning my books" (quoted in Gay, 1988, pp. 592–593). Then in March of 1938, the Nazis occupied Austria. Vienna, that great city of culture and the arts, became a scene of beatings and even of cold-blooded murders of Jews on its streets. Freud was reluctant to leave Vienna, but became convinced that it was time to go, after Nazi sympathizers searched his home and the Gestapo briefly detained his daughter Anna. He left Vienna with his family in June of 1938 and resettled in London, where his cancer finally claimed him on September 23, 1939.[5]

[5] Freud never seemed to grasp the precariousness of his situation and like most people living during that era, he had no idea of the extent of the evil to come. Included among the six million killed in the Nazi death camps were four of his sisters (Fancher, 1990).

The value of Freud's contributions to psychology has been a matter of some debate in recent years. One critic went so far as to refer to psychoanalysis as "the most stupendous intellectual confidence trick of the twentieth century...[and] a vast structure of radically unsound design and with no posterity" (Medawar, 1975, quoted in Sulloway, 1979, p. 499). Scholars dissecting Freud's published case histories have found scant evidence of the effectiveness of psychoanalysis as therapy; he has been chastised for missing the opportunity to expose widespread childhood sexual abuse when he abandoned his original seduction theory, and he has even been accused of plagiarism (Gay, 1988). Defenders, on the other hand, argue that Freud is responsible for some of the most important ideas of the twentieth century and that his influence spreads beyond psychology and deeply into Western culture. This issue will not be resolved here, of course, or at any time in the near future. What can be enumerated are some aspects of Freud's influence and some of the typical criticisms that are made of his work.

Contributions

Modern scholars have uncovered many of the sources and antecedents of Freud's ideas. As a result, his ideas are recognized as less original than once thought. Nonetheless, any attempt to understand human nature must include serious consideration of his work. First, although Freud did not discover the unconscious, he told us more about the hidden causes of behavior than anyone before or since. Aspects of unconscious thinking such as repression, defense, and the "Freudian slip" have become an accepted part of the psychological lexicon. Freud's emphasis on unconscious motives also raised awareness of the general need to study motivational processes. Second, we now take it for granted that the events of early childhood can significantly affect later development. We might take issue with the Freudian model of early development, including the Oedipal complex, but there is no

question that he made us more aware of the malleability of the young mind. Third, at a time when the medical community favored biological explanations of mental disorders and their treatment, Freud showed that some problems were psychological in origin and, therefore, could be treated with psychological means (i.e., through psychotherapy).

Criticisms

As the Close-Up in this chapter documents, many of Freud's conflicts with peers concerned the degree of emphasis he placed on sexual motivation. Breuer, Jung, and Adler all disagreed with him over the issue, and we now recognize that human behavior is too complex to be reduced to single broad motives. Psychoanalysts in the post-Freudian era have paid increasing attention to the roles of interpersonal relationships ("object relations") and the social environment in shaping personality (Pervin, 1991). The criticism of Freud's overemphasis on sex is part of a broader problem—he often overstated the case. Thus, while childhood is clearly an important determiner of later personality, it is an exaggeration to say, as Freud did, that the personality structure is essentially fixed during the first five or six years of life. A third frequent criticism of Freud, often delivered by those accustomed to laboratory control over variables, concerns the "scientific status" of his work. Freud has been criticized for relying on a limited sample of case studies, for excessive bias in bending the data from his patients into shapes that suited him, and for defining terms too loosely for his theory to be adequately tested. Freud's dogmatic insistence on his point of view and his demands of loyalty from his followers have also been said to be at odds with the "objectivity" expected of scientists in the positivist tradition. Finally, Freud has been widely criticized for his theoretical views about female psychology, although one must be careful to recognize that few people can step away from the social context in which they live. Thus, Freud was a typical Victorian male with a typical Victorian attitude about the second-class status of most women, and it showed in his work. He believed, for example, that superego development was never complete in women, that they envied the status of men and would even prefer to be male if that were possible, and that a woman's best hope for fulfillment was to produce male children. Anatomy, Freud declared, was destiny. In fairness, Freud never hindered and even encouraged the development of competent female analysts, most obviously his daughter Anna. And he occasionally acknowledged his meager understanding of the female psyche, once asking plaintively "What does a woman want?" (quoted in Gay, 1988, p. 501).

Freud's grand theory, his metapsychology, may not have held together over the years, but many of his specific insights have stood the test of time. As early as 1910, this conclusion about Freud was recognized by his contemporary, Havelock Ellis, and is a fitting way to close this section of the chapter: "But if...Freud sometimes selects a very thin thread [in tying together his theoretical arguments], he seldom fails to string pearls on it, and these have value whether the thread snaps or not" (Ellis, 1910, quoted in Sulloway, 1979, p. 500).

CLINICAL PSYCHOLOGY IN AMERICA

Today, clinical psychologists specialize in the diagnosis and treatment of all types of mental disorders, and they are at the forefront of research concerning these problems. In contrast with psychiatrists, clinical psychologists train in graduate school rather than medical school and earn Ph.D.s rather than M.D.s. Many have their own private practice, while others work in Veterans Administration (VA) hospitals or in private clinical settings. Some combine their practice with academic positions at colleges and universities. Some incorporate Freudian concepts into their practice, but most

do not. They comprise the elite group among those providing mental health service. This type of clinical psychologist began to emerge at the end of World War II, when the number of psychological casualties created a need that the medical community, in particular psychiatry, could not meet. In one sense, then, **clinical psychology** as we know it today is about 50 years old.

On the other hand, a portion of the APA's 1996 annual meeting was devoted to a celebration of clinical psychology's *centennial*. Much was made of a clinic created on the campus of the University of Pennsylvania in 1896 by the director of the psychology laboratory there, Lightner Witmer. The event was undoubtedly important, as will be elaborated shortly, and it set in motion circumstances that eventually produced modern clinical psychology. Yet the clinical psychology that existed prior to World War II was quite different from the discipline that emerged in the postwar era. The APA's centennial celebration is an interesting example of how the historical significance of some event can be created long after the event has occurred, through the decisions of historians and others (e.g., convention planners) who may be motivated by more than just a desire for historical truth. Thus, although the centennial of Witmer's clinic deserved a celebration on its own merits, it is probably no coincidence that it came at a time when clinicians are struggling to maintain their status in the face of cost-conscious health care providers who sometimes question the value of paying for adequate clinical services. One hundred years as a profession looks more substantial than 50.

LIGHTNER WITMER (1867–1956): CREATING PSYCHOLOGY'S FIRST CLINIC

Like a number of other American psychologists, Witmer was trained in basic laboratory research, but made his reputation by applying psychology to solve real-world problems. A native Philadelphian, Witmer stayed close to home for most of his life, earning a bachelor's degree at nearby University of Pennsylvania in 1888, then taking graduate courses there while teaching at a local college preparatory school. His shifting interests eventually settled on psychology, and for a time he served as the laboratory assistant for Penn's new psychology professor, James McKeen Cattell (Chapter 8). He then followed Cattell's example and went to Leipzig, completing a doctorate in Wundt's laboratory in 1892. On his return to the United States, he was named laboratory director at the University of Pennsylvania, Cattell having moved to Columbia the year before. Witmer became a vigorous advocate of the new laboratory psychology, to the point of encouraging (without success) experimental psychologists to form their own organization separate from the APA, which he thought supported too many nonscientific (i.e., philosophy) interests (Goodwin, 1985). Witmer revealed his passion for research in an amusing letter to Hugo Münsterberg in 1893 (quoted in the Chapter 7 Close-Up), in which he described a study on the psychology of memory and pain that he had undertaken on a very personal level by deliberately letting a horse throw him (Witmer, 1893). The episode apparently was in character; one friend later recalled that when on holiday in New York's Adirondacks, Witmer liked to ride his brakeless bicycle "down steep hills...with [his] legs on the handlebar" (Collins, 1931, p. 9).

Although fiercely committed to a scientific psychology, Witmer, like most American psychologists, believed that psychology should be able to improve people's lives. Thus, he was intrigued when a local schoolteacher, who knew Witmer from taking a summer course with him, came into the laboratory in March of 1896. She brought along one of her students, a 14-year-old who couldn't seem to learn how to spell, even though he was reasonably competent otherwise. Witmer, always willing to try something new, agreed to help and quickly discovered that part of the problem was poor eyesight; once corrected, the boy was able to undertake a training program and his spelling improved somewhat. This episode, and a second one involving a child with a speech disorder, turned a portion of Witmer's laboratory into a clinic and launched clinical psychology, the eventual outcome being several days of symposia and celebrations at the 1996 APA convention.

Word of the new clinic spread, and soon Witmer began seeing other cases of children with physiological, cognitive, and behavioral problems related to school performance, about two dozen during the remainder of 1896 (McReynolds, 1987). In December of that year, he read a paper at the APA's annual meeting in Boston, in which he called for increased research on the kinds of problems he was encountering and the development of training programs to increase the number of experts able to solve such problems. In 1907 he founded the journal, *The Psychological Clinic*, which included descriptions of case studies, research reports, and theoretical articles. The first issue contained a lead essay penned by Witmer; its title, "Clinical Psychology," gave a name to the emerging new specialty (Witmer, 1907/1931). In the article, he described the first 10 years of the clinic's development and called once more for increased research and training. He urged the creation of "a new profession—that of the psychological expert, who should find his career in connection with the school system, through the examination and treatment of mentally and morally retarded children" (p. 346). Thus, clinical psychology began with a relatively narrow focus—diagnosing and treating children with school-related problems. Today, that area of expertise is associated with **school psychology**. In fact, school psychologists also consider Witmer one of their pioneers, and the APA's Division for School Psychology still gives an annual "Lightner Witmer Award" to a promising young school psychologist (Baker, 1988).

By 1909, Witmer's clinic had expanded and had developed a team approach. A child entering the program would be given a thorough medical examination by a consulting physician, a social worker would compile a family and school history, and Witmer or one of his assistants would do the mental testing, using a battery of tests for such things as memory, attention, and motor coordination (Fernberger, 1931). Witmer disliked paper-and-pencil tests of intelligence, and although he believed that assessments like the Binet tests could yield interesting information about various abilities, he thought they were overused and he saw little value in the IQ scores themselves (McReynolds, 1996). After compiling all the information, the children would be classified as (a) experiencing some correctable medical condition (e.g., defective vision) but not needing special training, (b) possibly experiencing some medical problem but more clearly requiring some special program or other environmental intervention (e.g., improved nutrition), or (c) being severely retarded, untreatable, and requiring custodial care (Baker, 1988).

Unlike most of his contemporaries, Witmer was skeptical of the claims being made for the heritability of traits like mental defectiveness. He clearly recognized individual differences in ability in the students he saw, and he conceded that some degree of deficiency was inherent and unalterable. Severely retarded children, he believed, should be segregated from society in special institutions and prevented from having children. Yet the very existence of his clinic demonstrated his firm belief that some deficiencies could be corrected through proper training and/or control of the environment.

Hence, Witmer shared with behaviorists the belief that the environment could shape behavior. He believed that if past environmental influences produced the problem behavior observed in the clinic, then future environmental intervention could alter behavior and make the child more productive as a student. He considered his approach to be an optimistic one, arguing that to emphasize heredity is to give up hope of change: "To ascribe a condition to the environment, is a challenge to do something for its ameliorization or cure; to ascribe it to heredity often means that we fold our hands and do nothing" (Witmer, 1911, p. 232). Witmer introduced the term **orthogenics** to refer to this strategy of "investigat[ing] retardation and deviation and the *methods of restoring to normal condition* those who are found for one reason or another to be retarded or deviate" (Witmer, 1909, p. 122, italics added).

Witmer's clinic grew rapidly in the early decades of the twentieth century, its total case files numbering just under 10,000 by 1931 (Fernberger, 1931). It also added several specialized functions to its general role of diagnosing and treating problems in school-aged children. One was a clinic for speech disorders, developed by E. B. Twitmyer in 1914.[6] Another was a vocational clinic where adolescents and adults could go for testing and advice about careers. It was created by Morris Viteles, who could be added to the Chapter 8 list of pioneers in industrial psychology. Witmer's clinics also spawned numerous copies and variants, about two dozen by the start of World War I (Sexton, 1965). Meanwhile other forces were at work that would eventually yield modern clinical psychology.

---

[6] Twitmyer's dissertation, under Witmer's direction, was an examination of the knee-jerk reflex (Twitmyer, 1905). During the course of his investigation, he discovered that knee jerks could be elicited by stimuli associated with stimulation of the patellar tendon. That is, shortly after Pavlov discovered classical conditioning in Russia, Twitmyer was making the same discovery in the United States. Pavlov justifiably gets the credit, however, because of the massive research program that he undertook. Twitmyer, on the other hand, after being ignored when presenting his research at the 1904 APA meeting, abandoned conditioning and became involved in Witmer's clinic.

CLINICAL PSYCHOLOGY PRIOR TO WORLD WAR II

Chapter 8 chronicled the evolution of the mental testing movement, and this chapter briefly described the drive for mental hygiene that originated with Clifford Beers's efforts. Both developments contributed to clinical psychology's history. In addition, starting in the post-World War I era, there were several organizational efforts within the APA to professionalize the work of the clinician. It was a difficult struggle. One problem was that psychology's increasing popularity and the apparent success of the war's testing program prompted many unqualified people to claim that they could deliver psychological services. In addition, clinicians did not always feel welcome in an APA that was centered in the academic environment and maintained strict scholarly requirements for membership. An illustration of the dilemma was the effect of a resolution the APA passed in 1915 requiring that testing be done only by those trained to do so. Most people administering the tests did not belong to APA, however, so the resolution had no effect (Napoli, 1981). A final problem for clinicians was that unless they worked in clinics like Witmer's, they generally had low status in their work environments, which were often hospitals or private clinics. They were usually limited to performing basic testing duties; the major diagnostic and therapy work was done by psychiatrists, and the medical community had no wish to yield its authority or status.

The first serious effort toward forming an identity for clinicians within the APA was taken at the 1917 annual convention, when J. E. Wallace Wallin organized a meeting "to consider the advisability of establishing a new association to 'encourage and advance professional service in the field of clinical psychology'" (Wallin, 1966). The seven people who met that winter in Pittsburgh formed the American Association of Clinical Psychologists (AACP). The leadership of the APA was not amused,

1917

however, fearing the eventual disintegration of the APA. A compromise was reached in 1919 when the APA created a "section" for clinical psychology within the Association and the AACP members abandoned their new organization and joined it. During the 1920s, the Clinical section pursued a number of professional issues, including proper training, certification, and ethics, but little came of their efforts. The only major effect of their growing presence was that the APA relaxed its membership requirements in the mid-1920s, creating two categories: full member and associate member. By the end of the decade, associates outnumbered full members (Napoli, 1981).

usually those with less than Ph.D.

During the 1930s, clinical psychologists (and other psychologists with applied interests) kept pushing for recognition in an APA that continued to be dominated by academic interests. Even the most firmly entrenched academician had to face the reality of the Great Depression, however. As you recall from the discussion of Lewin's experiences in the 1930s (Chapter 9), academic positions became increasingly difficult to find during the Depression years, making nonacademic employment a growing necessity for young psychologists. The APA created such committees as the Committee on the Social Utilization of Unemployed Psychologists and the Committee on Psychology and the Public Service. It also became more open to the professionalizing efforts of applied psychologists, who created their first successful national organization for practitioners in 1937—the American Association for Applied Psychology (AAAP).

1937

The AAAP remained in existence until the end of World War II, independent of, yet affiliated with, the APA. It made some progress on the issues of training and standards, but the advent of a second world war within a generation once more transformed psychology. The national spirit of unity and interdependence fostered a cooperation between academicians and practitioners that had not existed before (and has not existed since). The outcome was a

[handwritten margin notes: Psychologists After WWII 1) Psychoanalysis 2) Behavior Therapy 3) Client Centered Therapy.]

[handwritten margin note left side: 1943 Special Interest Divisions]

complete reorganization of the APA to incorporate both scientific and applied interests. It emerged from an "intersociety" convention held in New York in 1943 (chaired by E. G. Boring) that brought together 25 delegates from several different organizations, but mainly the APA and AAAP. They approved a new structure for the APA which still exists today. The new structure was an umbrella organization that included special interest "Divisions," and a revised purpose. Whereas the original APA described its primary goal as the advancement of psychology as a "science," the expanded vision added advancement as a "profession" and as a "means of promoting human welfare" (Napoli, 1981, p. 127).

CLINICAL PSYCHOLOGY AND PSYCHOTHERAPY AT MID-CENTURY

Besides producing a level of cooperation that created the modern APA, World War II also had the effect of transforming clinical psychology. We have learned that prior to the war, clinicians struggled to establish their status as professionals. The cruel circumstances of war, however, created a permanent place for clinicians, who were among those providing professional services to the mentally wounded. Organized psychiatry, which had controlled the delivery of therapeutic services to the mentally ill prior to the war, was overwhelmed by the need for therapy. As in the first world conflict, applied psychologists continued to contribute their services through various testing programs, but in the second war they also gained experience treating those who were damaged psychologically by their war experiences. When the war ended, there were approximately 44,000 veterans who were in Veterans Administration hospitals suffering from various mental disorders resulting from the war, compared with 30,000 hospitalized with physical wounds (Sexton, 1965). Psychiatry simply could not cope with the caseload and was forced to abandon its therapeutic monopoly. In addition, the

federal government, perceiving the increased need, launched an aggressive program to support the training of graduate students in clinical psychology.

Out of these circumstances the modern clinical psychologist emerged—no longer limited to testing, but gradually recognized as an expert diagnostician and therapist; no longer limited to children and juveniles in school settings, but now capable of delivering services to anyone in need of them; no longer restricted to a clinic setting, but now more likely to develop a private practice; no longer under the supervision of psychiatrists, but increasingly on a par with them. Furthermore, the ability of clinicians to deliver effective psychological service was enhanced by the development of new forms of psychotherapy in the postwar era. Two of these approaches, behavior therapy and client-centered therapy, prospered in the context of a developing perception that traditional psychoanalytic and related "insight" therapies were of doubtful validity. The doubts were magnified in the early 1950s by a British psychologist, Hans Eysenck, who examined the effectiveness of traditional psychoanalytic therapy by combining the results reported in about two dozen articles (Eysenck, 1952). He concluded that the chances of improvement were a little better than 50–50 for those in therapy; more important, the rate of spontaneous improvement among those not in therapy was even higher. Thus, what Eysenck appeared to find was that traditional Freudian-based therapy simply did not work. Later research (e.g., Bergin, 1971) questioned Eysenck's conclusion, but the damage was done. Throughout the 1950s and 1960s, psychologists proposing alternatives to traditional psychoanalysis often pointed to Eysenck's work as evidence that new ideas were needed.

Behavior Therapy

We learned in Chapter 10 that a reason for the popularity of the behaviorist ideas of promoters like Watson was the promise of application to daily life, through such things as the improvement of child-rearing practices. If behaviors are primarily the result of learning, then presumably dysfunctional behaviors could be unlearned and replaced with more adaptive ones. This rationale was part of Watson's thinking as he formulated the Little Albert study. As you recall from Chapter 10, although he and Rayner made no attempt to remove Albert's fear of rats, they had several proposals about how to do so, based on their beliefs about conditioning. Furthermore, some of these ideas were tested in the 1920s, especially by Mary Cover Jones, who is often credited with pioneering behavior therapy. She tried all of Watson's suggestions and several of her own ideas on a number of different children, and is remembered for one particular case in which she removed a young boy's fear of rabbits by gradually moving the rabbit closer to the child while he was eating, using a procedure that she called "direct conditioning."

During the 1920s and 1930s, there were several other demonstrations of how conditioning could be used to alter behavior in a clinical setting. In Russia, for example, researchers applied Pavlovian principles to treat alcoholism by pairing alcohol (CS) with electric shock (UCS), and hysteria by conditioning movement in limbs that appeared initially to be paralyzed (Kazdin, 1978). In the United States, O. Hobart and Willie M. Mowrer developed a treatment program for bed-wetting based on conditioning principles by creating a crib pad that rang a bell as soon as it became wet. The Mowrers used the success of their procedure to attack psychoanalytic concepts of bed-wetting, which relied on the usual deep-seated conflicts to explain the problem. Instead, the Mowrers argued, it is much simpler to assume that the problem results from a failure to recognize the cues connected with bladder tension. If conditioning is the problem, they believed, then it is also the solution (Mowrer & Mowrer, 1938).

Behavior therapy gained major impetus in the 1950s through the development of a technique descended from the work of Mary Cover Jones. Joseph Wolpe, a South African at the University of Witwatersrand, created the procedure and called it **systematic desensitization** (Wolpe, 1958). It remains one of the best known behavior therapy techniques. Wolpe, a medical doctor, was trained in traditional psychoanalytic procedures but became dissatisfied with them. He began studying learning theory, especially Hull's, and benefited from the presence in South Africa of an American psychologist who had studied with Kenneth Spence, Hull's alter ego.

Wolpe began exploring behavioral techniques by studying the phobic reactions of cats. After creating fears by shocking the animals whenever they reached for food, he tried to eliminate the fear. Like Jones, he assumed that fear and eating were incompatible responses, so he tried to replace the fear responses by substituting eating responses. Wolpe accomplished this by feeding the animal first in a room that vaguely resembled the original room where the shock occurred, then in a room that more closely resembled the original room, and so on. That is, the fear response was gradually weakened, replaced by the approach to food (Kazdin, 1978).

Wolpe discovered a way to apply this procedure to phobic humans after reading a book by the Chicago physiologist Edmund Jacobson, which described a technique called **progressive relaxation** (Jacobson, 1929). Jacobson had been using relaxation to treat patients with nervous disorders; Wolpe viewed the procedure as a substitute for the eating response he had used in cats. In essence, Wolpe's systematic desensitization procedure involved relaxation training, then the creation of an "anxiety hierarchy," a list of situations that created increasingly greater levels of anxiety. Patients would become relaxed and imagine the situation of least anxiety, then gradually ascend the hierarchy. Wolpe found that after just a few sessions, patients could remain relaxed in the presence of their most feared objects.

1. unconditional acceptance
2. Empathic Understanding
3. Congruence

With additional modifications over the years, Wolpe's procedure has been shown to be highly effective with certain types of anxiety problems. A number of other behavior therapy techniques have evolved, ranging from token economy/reinforcement systems based on a Skinnerian model, to cognitive-behavior therapy, which synthesizes learning theory and the insights from cognitive psychology. A good summary can be found in Kazdin (1978).

Client-Centered Therapy

Another psychologist who became disillusioned with psychoanalysis, but also became skeptical about behavioral approaches, was Carl Rogers (1902–1987). As the label implies, his **client-centered therapy** assumes that the potential for positive change resides within the individual in therapy; the function of the therapist is to create an atmosphere conducive to that change. The therapist must display what Rogers called "unconditional positive regard," a basic acceptance of the person as fundamentally worthwhile, and "empathy," an understanding of what the person is feeling and thinking, from the person's standpoint. In addition, the therapist must be a model of a psychologically healthy, "congruent," person. If all three factors are in evidence, Rogers believed, then the client would be able to achieve positive therapeutic change. He rejected both psychoanalytic and behavioral approaches to therapy on the grounds that both (a) involve a therapy relationship in which the therapist has all the power and directs the client toward some "cure," and (b) assume that the individual's current behaviors and ways of thinking and feeling are dictated by his or her past history. In the world of client-centered therapy, the client is the person responsible for taking control and the past, while not ignored, is not considered a barrier to change (Hall & Lindzey, 1970).

Rogers was himself the product of a highly controlled environment, but managed to shape a career despite his early experiences. The fourth of six children, he was raised in a Chicago suburb in an extremely conservative Protestant family that valued hard work and considered all pleasures sinful. As Rogers (1961) later recalled: "[E]ven carbonated beverages had a faintly sinful aroma, and I remember my slight feeling of wickedness when I had my first bottle of 'pop'" (p. 5). When Rogers was 12, his father moved the family to a large farm in Wisconsin, partly to remove his children from the evils of suburbia. He was determined to run the farm according to the principles of "scientific agriculture," and Carl developed a keen appreciation for science out of the experience. It led him to enroll in the college of agriculture at the University of Wisconsin, but the enthusiasm soon faded as the sheltered young man discovered a bright new world of people and ideas. He switched to studying history and, determined to be a minister, entered New York's Union Theological Seminary after graduating from Wisconsin in 1924. The theology students at Union were encouraged to think for themselves in this liberal environment, and Rogers (1961) "thought [himself] right out of religious work" (p. 8) and into psychology.

Rogers began taking courses across the street from Union at Columbia's Teachers College, where he came under the influence of Leta Hollingworth (Chapter 8). She sparked his interest in doing child guidance work, and he began for the first time to think that he might like to be a clinical psychologist. He completed an internship at the Freudian-based Institute for Child Guidance in New York, where he developed a distaste for psychoanalysis, and earned a doctorate from Columbia in 1931. Rogers then took a position as a staff psychologist at a child guidance clinic in Rochester, New York, where he remained for a dozen years. It was there that he began developing his unique brand of therapy. Professionally, he attended APA meetings, but found them "full of papers on the learning processes of rats and laboratory experiments which seemed...to have no relation to what [he] was doing" (Rogers, 1961, p. 12). When the

American Association for Applied Psychology (AAAP) formed in 1937, however, he became an active member, and in 1939 he advocated a training model for clinicians that reduced the heavy emphasis on research and enhanced the opportunities for supervised practice in the craft of diagnosis and therapy. Academia ignored his proposal, but the idea was in essence identical to the one that emerged 30 years later at the University of Illinois in the form of the Psy.D. degree (Napoli, 1981). Most clinicians continue to earn the Ph.D., but the Psy.D. has become a popular alternative route to clinical practice, and although the Illinois program no longer operates, it became the model for some two dozen other programs in existence today (see Chapter 14).

Rogers entered academia himself in 1940, accepting a position at the Ohio State University. There the stimulus provided by critically thinking, assertive graduate students sharpened his ideas about therapy and the nature of personality, and resulted in his first book, *Counseling and Psychotherapy*, in 1942. Three years later he went to the University of Chicago as a professor of psychology and director of the counseling center. In 1946 he was elected president of the APA, the second president following the big postwar reorganization, and a clear sign to research-oriented academicians that the APA had truly changed. Rogers spent 12 years at Chicago, then 4 back at Wisconsin, where he had a joint appointment in psychology and psychiatry. The Wisconsin years were not happy ones—client-centered therapy had come under attack as being relevant only for articulate people with mild problems, and Rogers wanted to show that more seriously disturbed clients could benefit as well. He launched an ambitious project to apply the therapy to schizophrenic patients at a local hospital, but the results were at best "equivocal" (Lakin, 1996). That outcome, combined with a generally cool reception from the experimentally oriented psychology department at Wisconsin, led Rogers to look for greener pastures. He found them in California in 1961,

where he accepted the invitation of a former student to join the staff at the Western Behavioral Sciences Institute at La Jolla. Several years later, he founded the Center for the Study of the Person in La Jolla, where he extended his client-centered therapy to a group setting.

As an alternative to Freudian-based therapies, Rogers's client-centered therapy (first called nondirective therapy) quickly became popular among clinical psychologists. In contrast with analytic approaches, it was easier to grasp conceptually, took less time, and actually seemed to help people. It was also based on a more optimistic assessment of human potential for change, reflecting Rogers's own ability to take control of his life and a general Midwestern faith that things can be improved if one works at it hard enough. Finally, Rogers was able to argue for the therapy's effectiveness on the basis of a program of research that he and his students developed. Perhaps stemming from his earlier experiences with scientific agriculture, Rogers took great pleasure in undertaking empirical research on therapy outcomes, complete with comparisons between those in treatment and those in waiting list control groups, demonstrating that his approach brought about positive changes in people's lives (e.g., Rogers, 1954).

Carl Rogers is often considered a pioneer in the **humanistic psychology** movement. It has been called psychology's "third force," an alternative to behaviorism and psychoanalysis. Humanistic psychologists criticized the ideas that human behavior could be reduced to simple conditioning processes or repressed biological instincts, and proposed instead that the qualities that best characterize humans are free will, a lifelong search for meaning, and a basic potential to become what Rogers called a "fully functioning person."

Abraham Maslow (1908–1970), whose concepts of self-actualization and the hierarchy of needs are familiar to students in introductory psychology, is another well-known humanistic psychologist. Maslow was trained as an experimental psychologist and researched primate behavior, but rejected what he saw as a sterile scientific approach for the humanistic strategy. Humanistic psychology enjoyed a brief period of popularity in the 1960s and 1970s, and Maslow was even elected to the APA presidency in 1968. Nevertheless, the movement has been on the fringe of psychology. It has been faulted for overemphasizing the self at the expense of the community and for being clear-er about what it is against than what it proposes as an alternative (e.g., Farson, 1978; Wertheimer, 1978).

Behavior therapy and client-centered therapy are just two of many developments in the professional practice of psychology that have occurred since World War II. More developments will be discussed in the closing chapter, but first we must explore the most important intellectual movement in postwar psychology—cognitive psychology.

SUMMARY

Early Treatment of the Mentally Ill

- Near the end of the eighteenth century, Enlightenment thinkers pressed for reform in the ways of treating the mentally ill. In France, Phillipe Pinel introduced the concept of "moral treatment," in which institutional living conditions were improved, the tendency to rely exclusively on physical restraint of patients was reduced, and direct efforts were made to improve the behavior of patients. Similar reforms were undertaken at the York Retreat in England by William Tuke. His model was copied extensively in the United States in the nineteenth century. Benjamin Rush, considered to be the founder of modern psychiatry, introduced a medical model as a way of explaining mental illness and developed an approach to treatment that emphasized "improving" the condition of patients' blood and circulatory systems.

- In the middle of the nineteenth century, Dorothea Dix successfully urged the reform of large public asylums and better treatment for the mentally ill poor. At the turn of the twentieth century, Clifford Beers, a former mental patient, agitated for similar reforms; he was also a pioneer in the Mental Hygiene movement, which emphasized prevention.

Mesmerism and Hypnosis

- In the mid-1700s, Franz Anton Mesmer developed a procedure for treating hysteria (apparent nervous system disorders with no true organic damage), based on his belief that the disorder was the result of disturbed magnetic forces within the body. Believing that he had magnetic powers, he treated patients and effected some cures by "mesmerizing" them. Although he didn't know it, his successes were the result of the power of suggestion, and Mesmer had discovered a procedure that would eventually be known as hypnotism.

- Before the discovery of such drugs as ether in the nineteenth century, mesmerism was championed by the British doctor John Elliotson as an anesthetic for surgery and used extensively in India by another British doctor, James Esdaile. It gained further scientific credibility in the hands of James Braid, who renamed the procedure "neurypnology," which soon came to be called hypnology or hypnotism.

- In France in the mid-nineteenth century, two schools of thought developed about the nature of hypnotism. According to Liebeault and Bernheim of the "Nancy" school, hypnotism was a normal phenomenon that had its effects through the power of suggestion; people differed in their levels of suggestibility. According to Charcot in Paris, however, hypnotic effects mirrored the symptoms of hypnosis and suggestibility was a sign of hysterical neurosis.

Sigmund Freud (1856–1939): Founding Psychoanalysis

- Freud is one of psychology's best-known figures. Over the years, a Freudian myth has developed, a false belief that Freud was the solitary hero fighting for his ideas against overwhelming opposition, and that his ideas were original to him, without important antecedent. Recent scholarship has questioned both aspects of the myth.

- Freud was trained in neurology and influenced, through his contact with Ernst Brücke, by the prevailing materialism of nineteenth-century physiology. Financial problems led him to the private practice of neurology, where he became interested in the treatment of hysteria. In the 1880s, he studied with two of the leading experts of the problem, Meynert and Charcot. He was also greatly influenced by Darwin's work.

- Through his association with Joseph Breuer, Freud learned of the Anna O. case, in which hysteric symptoms were shown to be related to repressed memories and successful treatment occurred (apparently) if the patient would retrieve memories of the events surrounding the first appearance of a symptom. The recall produced an emotional release or catharsis. With Breuer, Freud published *Studies on Hysteria* in 1895, normally considered the founding event for psychoanalysis.

- Freud believed that hysteria resulted from the repression of trauma, real or imagined, into the unconscious, and the purpose of psychoanalysis was to bring repressed memories back to the surface so that insight into the causes of the patient's problem could be gained. To explore the unconscious, Freud developed the procedures of free association, in which a person said whatever came to mind, and dream analysis, in which the surface or "manifest" content of a dream was examined to discover the underlying or "latent" content of the dream. All dreams reflected some disguised wish fulfillment, Freud argued. He also believed that all events have causes; even accidents or slips of the tongue (Freudian slips) can be traced to unconscious purposes.

- Freud believed that sexual problems were a critical determinant of hysteria. He initially believed that hysteria resulted from the effects of childhood sexual abuse, but he later abandoned this "seduction" hypothesis, arguing that the memories of abuse were actually the results of imagined sexual feelings originating in childhood. This led to his theory of infantile sexuality and the Oedipal complex.

- International recognition for psychoanalysis came when Freud was invited to deliver a series of five lectures at Clark University in 1909. His lectures included descriptions of Anna O., his dream theory, Freudian slips, and infantile sexuality.

- Freud cultivated an inner circle of followers loyal to psychoanalysis. Two early converts, Alfred Adler and Carl Jung, both broke with Freud over the issue of sex and established their own schools of thought, individual psychology (Adler) and analytical psychology (Jung). One of Freud's most loyal followers was his daughter Anna, known for extending psychoanalysis to the treatment of children.

- After World War I, Freud's theory evolved to include the proposals (a) that both life (sex) and death (aggression) instincts are a part of human nature; (b) that personality structure centers on the ego, which mediates between the instinctive demands of the id, the moral restrictions of the superego, and the constraints placed on behavior by reality; and (c) that each of the three sources of pressure on the ego can create anxiety, and the ego reacts through defense mechanisms such as repression, projection, and reaction formation.

- Freud's ideas were treated with some skepticism by academic psychologists, and were more influential, at first, in the medical community and in the general public. His contributions include the concepts of the unconscious and repression, his emphasis on the importance of early childhood, and his insistence on the psychological nature of mental disorders. Critics have cited his overemphasis on sex, problems with the scientific status of psychoanalysis, and his description of female psychology.

Clinical Psychology in America

- Lightner Witmer is usually credited with establishing, in 1896, the first clinic for the treatment of psychological disorders in the United States. His clinic focused on "psycho-educational" problems similar to those encountered by modern school psychologists—physiological, cognitive, and behavioral problems related to school performance. He called his treatment program orthogenics.

- Prior to World War II, clinical psychologists for the most part provided mental testing services and did not have high status, either in clinical settings, which were dominated by psychiatrists, or in the APA, which was controlled by academics. The American Association for Applied Psychology was formed in 1937 as a way of professionalizing the practice of psychology.

- Alternatives to psychoanalysis proliferated in the postwar years, with behavior therapy and client-centered therapy being the prime examples. Behavior therapy derived from learning theory, and assumed that positive change resulted from relearning rather than insight into the unconscious. The best-known behavior therapy technique is Joseph Wolpe's systematic desensitization, which is similar to a procedure used by Mary Cover Jones in the 1920s. Desensitization has been shown to be useful in the treatment of anxiety disorders; clients are trained to replace anxiety responses with relaxation responses.

- Client-centered therapy is the creation of Carl Rogers, and is based on the idea that positive psychological change results from a therapeutic atmosphere in which the therapist shows unconditional positive regard for the client, empathy, and congruence. Rogers's approach to therapy assigns responsibility for change to the client rather than to the therapist, and his faith in the individual's ability to take control of his or her life made him a leader (along with Abraham Maslow) in the humanistic psychology movement.

FOR FURTHER READING

HORNSTEIN, G. A. (1992). The return of the repressed: Psychology's problematic relations with psychoanalysis, 1909–1960. *American Psychologist, 47,* 254–263.

An excellent analysis (and for a scholarly article, witty) of how American psychologists reacted to psychoanalysis over the years; shows how the Americans first rejected analysis outright then tried to incorporate it into mainstream experimental psychology.

ROSENZWEIG, S. (1992). *The historic expedition to America (1909): Freud, Jung, and Hall the kingmaker.* St. Louis: Rana House.

The definitive source for information about Freud's trip to America; lacks contextual analysis, but its extensive footnoting provides a wealth of detail; a translation of Freud's lectures gives the reader a chance to read Freud in the original and provides a good summary of Freud's thinking, circa 1909.

SEXTON, V. S. (1965). Clinical psychology: An historical survey. *Genetic Psychology Monographs, 72,* 401–434.

A bit dated, but a good summary of clinical psychology in America; includes information on mental testing, mental hygiene, and clinical psychology's efforts at achieving professional status; also useful is a similar, but even older, article by Watson (1953).

SULLOWAY, F. J. (1979). *Freud: Biologist of the mind.* New York: Basic Books.

One of several biographies of Freud, and an excellent one, focusing on an analysis of the Freudian myth; includes extensive treatment of the contemporary sources of ideas often thought to be original to Freud (e.g., infantile sexuality); more critical than another first-rate biography by Gay (1988).

13

THE POSTWAR EMERGENCE
OF COGNITIVE PSYCHOLOGY

The basic reason for studying cognitive processes has
become as clear as the reason for studying anything else:
because they are there.... Cognitive processes surely exist,
so it can hardly be unscientific to study them.

Ulric Neisser, 1967

Preview

The most important development in academic psychology since World War II has been the
advent of modern cognitive psychology. During the 1950s and especially the 1960s, American
psychologists began to shift their research and theoretical interests. Whereas in the 1930s and
1940s behaviorism and the search for basic laws of conditioning occupied the attention of most
researchers, the postwar period saw a reemergence of interest in studying cognitive processes
such as perception, memory, attention, imagery, and thinking. The shift was evolutionary rather
than revolutionary—many psychologists were interested in cognition during the heyday of
behaviorism, and behaviorists, especially Skinnerians, remained active and productive in the
face of the shift toward cognitive psychology. Nonetheless, the academic psychology of 1970
was quite different from the 1950 version. This chapter will examine the rise of postwar cognitive psychology and its spread to other subdisciplines of psychology. The Original Source
Excerpt is from Ulric Neisser's milestone 1967 text, aptly titled *Cognitive Psychology*.

COGNITIVE PSYCHOLOGY ARRIVES (AGAIN)

When psychology began to identify itself as a separate discipline in the latter half of the nineteenth century, it aimed at a scientific understanding of human conscious experience, and Ebbinghaus, Wundt, Külpe, Wertheimer, Titchener, and other pioneers studied such mental phenomena as memory, attention, perception, and thinking. Psychologists in America also took up these same topics, gave them a functional twist, and investigated them vigorously in the early years of the twentieth century. Then Watson appeared and said that the study of mental life was unscientific and that everyone should be a behaviorist, studying the relationships between environmental stimuli and the individual's responses. Not everyone listened, of course, and as we learned in Chapter 10, Watson's message took a long time to produce significant effects. By the mid-1930s, however, behaviorism had become a force in American psychology, and the most compelling image of the psychology laboratory in those days included rats and mazes. After World War II, however, interests began to shift again, and the study of cognitive processes came once more to the forefront. This time the methods were slightly different and more rigorous, and the models were based on a new technological breakthrough—the computer. But the topics of interest remained the same. Some psychologists began calling themselves cognitive psychologists, and a new movement, which was in a sense a return to an old one, was born. In the latter half of the twentieth century, cognitive psychology has been the dominant conceptual framework in American psychology.

THE ROOTS OF COGNITIVE PSYCHOLOGY

Despite Watson's best efforts at promotion, American psychology did not become behaviorist overnight, and even when behaviorism was "in" among American psychologists, not everyone joined the party. In the 1930s and 1940s, the pages of the leading journals still contained numerous articles describing research on such cognitive topics as memory, perception, attention, language, and thinking. Among others, they included one of psychology's most famous papers, a summary of three experiments by an obscure graduate student at George Peabody College in Tennessee, J. Ridley Stroop (1935/1992). The "Stroop effect," a problem in which color naming is hindered by interference from automatic reading processes (e.g., the word "red" is printed in green ink and the subject must respond "green"), has been called psychology's most replicated finding (MacLeod, 1992). Books dealing with cognitive topics also appeared during behaviorism's heyday, even including one with the title *Cognitive Psychology* (Moore, 1939). Although its treatment of cognition was more of a look back to the earlier years of the century than a call for a new approach to cognition (Knapp, 1985), it dealt with many of the same topics that would concern cognitive psychologists two decades later. And on the theoretical front, the gestaltists promoted the study of cognition and argued with behaviorists throughout the 1930s and 1940s.

Behaviorism was a distinctly American phenomenon, and hence it is not surprising to learn that (a) there were several important European psychologists doing cognitive work during behaviorism's glory years, and (b) most American experimental psychologists, focused intently on whether their rat was going to turn left or right at a choice point in a maze, paid little attention to this ongoing cognitive research. These Europeans included the famous Swiss developmental psychologist, Jean Piaget, whose ideas about cognitive development first appeared in the 1920s (Piaget, 1923/1959), but weren't influential in the United States until the 1960s, and England's Sir Frederick Bartlett, who took memory research in a distinctly non-Ebbinghaus direction in the 1930s (Bartlett, 1932/1967).

Jean Piaget (1896–1980)

All students who have taken a course in developmental psychology will recognize Piaget's name and will probably recall seeing a photo in their text of a 6- or 7-year-old schoolchild staring at the water levels in two different-sized containers. Piaget was a master at creating simple demonstrations of complex cognitive phenomena, and his conservation of volume task, in which "preoperational" children typically fail to recognize that the volume of a liquid remains constant when it is transferred to a taller or shorter container, is among the better-known of them.

Jean Piaget (Figure 13.1) was a native of Switzerland, and except for a few brief interludes, spent most of his life there. Much like John Stuart Mill and Francis Galton before him, he was a precocious child. He developed a strong interest in the biological sciences as a schoolboy, and at the age of 10, he managed to publish a one-page description of an albino sparrow in a local natural history journal. He spent most of his adolescence collecting and classifying mollusks, publishing several articles and even being offered a job as curator of mollusks at a reputable museum in Geneva, which he had to decline on the grounds that he still had two years of high school remaining (Piaget, 1952). He completed his college degree at age 18. Within another three years, in 1918, he had earned a Ph.D. in biology and an international reputation as an expert on mollusks.

During these school years, Piaget also became interested in the philosophical problems of epistemology, especially the question of how we obtain our knowledge of the world. He read widely in philosophy and psychology (including William James and Sigmund Freud) and after finishing his biology doctorate, decided to examine the problem more closely. An opportunity arose in 1919 when he met Théodore Simon of Binet-Simon fame, who asked the young biologist to work on an intelligence testing project in the Binet laboratory in Paris. Consequently, Piaget spent the next few years studying verbal intelligence in school-aged children. His initial task was to standardize a reasoning test developed by British psychologist Cyril Burt, but while doing so, he discovered that he was less interested in whether the children answered questions correctly than in the thinking processes they used to answer the questions. Especially revealing were the cognitive processes involved when children got the wrong answers. To explore these strategies, Piaget began interviewing the children about how they solved the problems. From this experience, he concluded that children's cognition differs from adult cognition not just quantitatively, but qualitatively. That is, children do not just know less than adults, they think in an

Figure 13.1   Jean Piaget, with two of his favorite research subjects, from Popplestone and McPherson (1994).

entirely different manner. Eventually, this insight led to Piaget's well-known stage theory of cognitive development.

Following the experience in the Binet lab and on the basis of the resulting publications, Piaget was offered a position as director at a research institute for the study of children in Geneva in 1921. During the 1920s, he also taught at the Universities of Geneva and Neuchâtel (his hometown) and published numerous articles and five books. The first of the five, *The Language and Thought of the Child* (1923/1959), gave Piaget an international reputation while he was still in his late twenties (Brainerd, 1996).

Piaget and his wife also had three children during this time, daughters in 1925 and 1927, and a son in 1931. Piaget was not about to miss an opportunity, so he and his wife made systematic observations of their three children as they grew. One important lesson for Piaget was that the verbal interviews he used in the Binet laboratory were useless for preverbal infants—other observational procedures had to be used. For instance, he inferred that infants were learning about cause and effect by observing their tendency to systematically repeat their actions, and he developed his famous concept of "object permanence" by noting whether or not infants would search for objects that were out of sight. It was during these years, the decade of the 1930s, that Piaget developed some of his most famous demonstrations of children's cognition and formulated his stage theory (Brainerd, 1996).[1] He referred to his approach as a **genetic epistemology**, using the term "genetic" to refer to developmental processes, not heredity (i.e, in the same way that G. Stanley Hall had used the term a generation earlier). That is, Piaget's focus was on determining precisely how knowledge, as represented by hypothetical mental structures that he called "schemas," developed within the individual. He believed that children were active formulators of their knowledge rather than passive recipients of their experiences, and he believed that knowledge structures formed "wholes" that could not be reduced to their elements. This latter point connects with gestalt psychology (Chapter 9), of course, and Piaget was well aware of and generally appreciative of the gestaltists for showing him that he was not alone in formulating a theory based on "structures-of-the-whole." As he put it, "contact with the work of Köhler and Wertheimer made [an]…impression on me.… I had the distinct pleasure of concluding that my previous research was not sheer folly, since one could design on such a central hypothesis of the subordination of the parts to the organizing whole not only a consistent theory, but also a splendid series of experiments" (Piaget 1952, p. 248).

In the early 1950s, Piaget established a research institute of his own at the University of Geneva, the International Center for Genetic Epistemology, and remained its director for all of his remaining years (Voyat, 1981). Despite his reputation in Europe, however, he was still relatively unknown in the United States, partly because not all of his work was being translated into English, but also because of the American preoccupation with behaviorism. He was not completely unknown in America—he had been among the group of young international psychologists participating in the 1929 international congress at Yale (others: Pavlov and Lewin), and Harvard had given him an honorary degree at a conference celebrating its three-hundredth birthday in 1936 (Kessen, 1996). Also, as you might have noticed from the citation in the last paragraph, the editors of the prestigious *History of Psychology in Autobiography* series (including E. G. Boring) saw fit to include Piaget in their fourth edition, which appeared in 1952. Nonetheless, his work

---

[1] As you may recall, the stages are sensorimotor (0–2), preoperational (2–7), concrete operational (7–11), and formal operational (11–adult). For details, refer to any textbook of developmental psychology.

was not widely known in the United States until the 1960s, just when cognitive psychology was coming to the forefront of American experimental psychology. Following a 1960 conference devoted to his work in Dedham, Massachusetts, sponsored by the Social Science Research Council (Kessen & Kuhlman, 1962) and the publication of John Flavell's *The Developmental Psychology of Jean Piaget* (1963), Piaget's ideas exploded onto the scene, and he began accumulating the status he retains today as one of the century's most influential psychologists (Kessen, 1996). Piaget died in 1980.

Frederick C. Bartlett (1886–1969)

In 1932, a brief book with the simple title of *Remembering: A Study in Experimental and Social Psychology* appeared, authored by a psychologist from England's Cambridge University, Frederick Bartlett. In the United States, the book was ignored, and an American reviewer of the book, writing three years after its publication, concluded his generally dismissive review by saying that the book would "find a place upon the shelves of those who study remembering, but it will not be in the special section reserved for those investigators whose writings have become landmarks in the advance towards the comprehension of this important problem" (Jenkins, 1935, p. 715). The reviewer probably had Ebbinghaus in mind as a "landmark." Today, Bartlett's book is recognized as being equal to Ebbinghaus's in importance.

Frederick Bartlett was born and raised in the rural Cotswolds region of England, northwest of London and near Oxford and Stratford-upon-Avon. Much of his early education was at home, and his first formal higher degree was by correspondence course from London University. He then completed a more traditional undergraduate program at Saint John's College of Cambridge University in 1914. He remained at Cambridge for graduate studies and completed

the research on memory as his doctoral thesis, shortly after World War I. Thus, the studies in *Remembering* were completed about 15 years before they were published (Oldfield, 1972). During the 1920s, Bartlett became head of the Psychology Laboratory at Cambridge, and set about establishing one of the few centers of experimental psychology in Great Britain. He directed the laboratory until his retirement in 1952, producing, with his students, research on topics ranging from pilot fatigue to animal learning. He also adapted some of the methods used in his memory book to the study of thinking, the result being *Thinking: An Experimental and Social Study*, which appeared in 1958. It was the memory book that makes him a pioneer cognitive psychologist, however.

Bartlett opened the memory book by questioning the usefulness of research in the Ebbinghaus tradition, with its emphasis on the effects of rote repetition on the memorization of highly artificial stimuli, the famous nonsense syllables, and its theoretical basis in associationism. Instead, Bartlett argued that memory must be understood in the context of more realistic situations using everyday materials. He also believed that the memorizer, rather than passively accumulating associative strength as the result of practice and repetition, actively organizes the material into meaningful wholes called **schemas**.[2] Bartlett defined these schemas (sometimes called schemata) as "active organisation[s] of past reactions, or of past experiences, which must always be supposed to be operating in any well-adapted organic response" (1932/1967, p. 201). For example, as a result of our experiences, we will develop a schema relating to the concept of death. This schema will in turn influence our current and future perceptions of death and dying and affect our memory of these experiences. People with different experiences and from different cultures will have different schemas about death.

---

[2] Thus, independently of Piaget, Bartlett arrived at a similar conclusion about cognitive structures and used the same term.

To provide empirical support for his arguments, Bartlett developed a series of tasks, the best-known being his "method of repeated reproduction." Subjects were given a 330-word story to read through twice at their own speed. The story was a Native American folk tale called "The War of the Ghosts." Thus, the story reflected a culture quite different from that of the typical upper class British student reading it. It tells of a pair of young seal hunters from "Egulac," one of whom reluctantly joins a war party "going up the river to make war on the people." There is a fight, and many are killed. Then,

> ...the young man heard one of the warriors say: "Quick, let us go home: that Indian has been hit." Now he thought: "Oh, they are ghosts." He did not feel sick, but they said he had been shot.
>
> So the canoes went back to Egulac, and the young man went ashore to his house, and made a fire. And he told everybody and said: "Behold I accompanied the ghosts, and we went to fight. Many of our fellows were killed, and many of those who attacked us were killed. They said I was hit, and I did not feel sick."
>
> He told it all, and then he became quiet. When the sun rose he fell down. Something black came out of his mouth. His face became contorted. The people jumped up and cried.
>
> He was dead. (Bartlett, 1932/1967, p. 65)

Unless you are a member of this particular culture, I suspect that you found the passage to be a bit odd. So did Bartlett's subjects. Fifteen minutes after reading the story, they were asked to reproduce as much of it as they could. Additional reproductions were elicited at later intervals ranging from hours to months (Bartlett even found one subject six years later and asked him to recall the story). Total recall declined with the passage of time, of course, a result that even Ebbinghaus would find unsurprising. What was more intriguing, however,

was the quality of the reproductions. Bartlett's subjects did not just recall less; what they recalled was shaped by their need to form a coherent, understandable story within the context of their own culture-bound schemas. Thus, "something black coming out of his mouth," was transformed to "foaming at the mouth" for one subject and the Indian's face becoming "contorted" became convulsions leading to death for another. Also, the ambiguity about the ghosts (if they are already ghosts, how come they can be killed?) led some to decide that "Ghosts" was just a label for a particular tribe. Others recalled erroneously that the "ghosts" appeared only after some Indians were killed in the battle. In all, then, subjects recalled the story within the framework of their own cultural ideas about battle and death. For Bartlett, this was evidence that memory was more of a constructive process than a mere reproductive one. Recall is not the replaying of a recording of some experienced event, he argued, but an active process of fitting recalled information into already existing schematic wholes. This notion of memory as constructive is now widely accepted and central to the understanding of such phenomena as eyewitness memory (e.g., Loftus, 1979).

A CONVERGENCE OF INFLUENCES

Neither Piaget's nor Bartlett's work had much impact in the United States at the time of their publication. It was only in the 1960s, after cognitive psychology had emerged from multiple sources, that the significance of their work began to be appreciated. The influences that produced modern cognitive psychology came both from within psychology, in the form of a growing suspicion about the widespread applicability of conditioning and associationist principles, and outside of psychology, through several disciplines that received their initial impetus in the context of World War II or developed after the end of the conflict (Segal & Lachman, 1972).

1. growing rejection of conditioning, association + behaviorism as "Panaceas"
2. Development of other Areas
   —Neurophysiology, linguistics, computers, cultural anthropology, philosophy

Cognitive Psychology Arrives (Again)   403

Influences Within Psychology

Among psychologists during the 1940s and 1950s, there was growing concern that conditioning and associationist principles could not adequately account for all human behavior, especially language behavior. Although the radical behaviorists had either reduced mental events to subtle muscular responses to stimuli (Watson), or viewed them merely as other types of behavior under the control of reinforcement contingencies (Skinner), Tolman and Hull had attempted to address the problem of "representation." That is, both recognized that individuals acted as if they were influenced by representations or conceptions of the external world (e.g., memories). Hull dealt with the issue by avoiding mentalistic concepts and proposing internal sequences of stimuli and responses that became chained together through reinforced experiences. Tolman went further and proposed that such internal constructs as cognitive maps and expectancies served to guide behavior. Both approaches fell short when it came to explaining distinctly human behavior such as language, however, and attempts to force language into conditioning terms failed.

The adequacy of associationism's principles was also called into question, most notably by the neuropsychologist Karl Lashley (Chapter 3), a former research colleague of Watson's at Johns Hopkins but a longtime critic of simple Watsonian S-R formulations. In 1948, Lashley participated in the Hixon Symposium, an interdisciplinary meeting that brought together psychologists, mathematicians, neurologists, and psychiatrists to consider the general topic of the relationship between the cerebral cortex and behavior. Lashley's talk, published three years later in the collected symposium papers, dealt with the problem of serial order and the gener-

al failure of association theory to account for it (Lashley, 1951). Simply stated, the serial order problem concerns the question of how to explain, in terms of cerebral mechanisms, linear sequences of behavior, ranging from the series of finger movements while playing the violin to the memorization of a list of words to the production of language in sentences. A basic tenet of association theory was that adjacent elements in a sequence become associated or "chained" together because they are experienced together (i.e., contiguously). Lashley argued that such a formulation was inadequate. In complex motor skills such as playing the violin, for example, the sequence of behaviors occurs much too rapidly for one element to depend on the neurological analysis of the preceding element and be the stimulus for the next element. Also, the oral production of a sentence is more complex than a simple sequencing of words, as illustrated by (a) the rules of syntax and (b) slips of the tongue. Thus, two sentences, one in the active voice and the other in the passive, have completely different syntactical orders yet convey the same meaning. And certain errors of speech, called Spoonerisms, involve anticipations of words or word segments that were meant to occur later in the sentence.[3] Instead of a cortical model based on the concept of linear associative chains, Lashley argued that the brain was a system that exercised organizational control over patterns of behavior.

Lashley's paper was well-received, but like Piaget's and Bartlett's work, its significance for the development of cognitive psychology was not immediately recognized, as shown in a careful citation analysis by psychologist/historian Darryl Bruce (1994). References to the article accumulated at a leisurely pace throughout the 1950s and then increased dramatically in the mid-1960s, the decade in which cognitive

---

[3] An example of a Spoonerism might be saying "Let me sew you to your sheets" instead of the intended "Let me show you to your seats."

Computers

psychology achieved its greatest momentum. Thus, the serial order paper was a bit ahead of its time. Nonetheless, it contributed to the critical mass that was developing in the postwar years that eventually led to cognitive psychology's appearance.

Influences External to Psychology

Other events relevant for the cognitive movement took place in disciplines far removed from psychology. One of the most critical was the development of computer science, which was accelerated in the 1940s by the military needs of World War II, with its demands for such things as automated radar-tracking systems (Baars, 1986). Of course, philosophers and psychologists have a long history of using contemporary technology as metaphors relating to human behavior. Examples range from Descartes' use of hydraulic garden figures in his model of the nervous system to Watson's belief that the telephone switchboard paralleled the S-R connections underlying the relationship between stimulus and action. In the postwar era, it wasn't long before scientists began to see parallels between the computer and the brain.

The computer is essentially a device for taking in information from the environment, processing it internally, and producing some output. By analogy, the brain could be seen as doing the same thing. The mathematician John von Neuman explicitly developed this metaphor in the opening address given at the Hixon Symposium in 1948. It reappeared on occasion in the 1950s, and by the 1960s it was commonplace to hear cognitive phenomena described in computer language and its models portrayed as computer flowcharts. The best-known example, soon to be a regular feature in the memory chapters of introductory psychology books, was the model proposed by Atkinson and Shiffrin (1968). Some form of the flowchart in Figure 13.2, a simplified version of theirs, is probably familiar to you. It introduced the well-known distinctions between the limit-

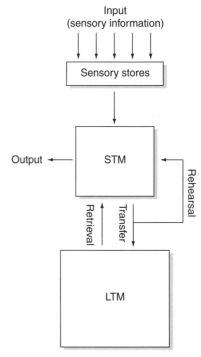

Figure 13.2   A typical example of the use of a flow chart to illustrate the two-stage model of memory like the Atkinson and Shiffrin (1968) model.

ed capacity short-term memory (STM), analogous to a computer's RAM, and long-term memory (LTM), likened to a computer's permanent memory stores, and it freely used computer jargon. Thus, humans don't just memorize things, they "transfer information from STM to LTM," and they don't just recall things, they "retrieve information from LTM."

One advantage of the computer metaphor was that it provided a scientifically respectable way to discuss complex internal mental processes, thus muting behaviorism's criticisms that psychological scientists shouldn't be dealing with mysterious unobservable entities that intervene between stimulus and response, and avoiding the old problems with introspection. As George Miller put it, "[c]omputers give us an existence-proof of the complexity that is possible in information-processing systems. This made us all feel a lot freer" (quoted in Baars, 1986, p. 212). Further respectability came from a refinement in the way of describing the flow of information through the system. This occurred in 1949 with the publication of *The Mathematical Theory of Communication* by Shannon and Weaver, which introduced **information theory** and the concept of the **bit**, an abbreviation of "binary digit." An electrical engineer, Shannon recognized a connection between the logical operators of "true" and "false" and the two states, "on" and "off," of any electromagnetic relay. Working with Weaver, he defined the bit as the amount of information that would enable a decision between two equally likely alternatives. Thus, information reduces uncertainty. A coin toss, for instance, contains one bit of information because it tells us which of two possible outcomes is true. Each time the number of alternatives doubles, one additional bit of information is added: with four alternatives, it takes two bits of information to reduce uncertainty, with eight alternatives, it takes three bits, and so on. The significance of the concept was that it provided a way of standardizing units of information, regardless of the form that the information took (e.g., coin toss, dice throw, numbers, letters, etc.). The bit wound up being more important for computer science than for cognitive psychology, but in the 1950s it added further legitimacy to the scientific study of the mind.

A third area of development outside of psychology, but relating to the assault on behaviorism within psychology, was linguistics. Led by Noam Chomsky (b. 1928) of the Massachusetts Institute of Technology (MIT), theories of language structure and language production began to proliferate in the 1950s, and they went beyond anything conceivable to behaviorists. Chomsky came to the attention of psychologists in 1959, when he wrote a highly

Chomsky

critical review of *Verbal Behavior*, B. F. Skinner's (1957) creative attempt to put language into operant terms (Chomsky, 1959). Language development occurs too rapidly for conditioning to be relevant, he argued. Even if we could learn a sentence per second, there are not enough seconds in a lifetime to learn all the sentences that we are capable of producing. Furthermore, people routinely create and/or understand sentences they have never experienced before. Language was simply too complex for what Chomsky took to be an overly simplistic behaviorist explanation.

As the result of the work of Chomsky and other linguists, language came to be viewed not as verbal behavior that was the outcome of conditioning and associative learning, but as the result of the application of a hierarchical set of rules called a **grammar**. These rules allow the individual to generate a virtually infinite number of grammatical sentences, while also enabling the person to immediately identify nongrammatical sentences. For instance, to use one of Chomsky's favorite examples (Gardner, 1985), we easily recognize "Colorless green ideas sleep furiously" as perfectly grammatical, if silly, while we have no difficulty rejecting these same words in a different order, "Sleep ideas green colorless furiously," as ungrammatical. The sentences we use cannot be the result of simple learning, Chomsky argued, but must follow from the systematic application of a grammar. Furthermore, this ability to use a grammar is instinctively human—Chomsky believed that language was the attribute that most clearly distinguished humans from other species. He believed that all languages shared common principles which he called **linguistic universals** and that the human brain is structured to be able to understand these universals automatically (Chomsky, 1966). Chomsky and other linguists supported their nativist arguments about language by pointing out that (a) as with other species-specific behaviors, there appears to be a critical period for language development, and that (b) attempts to teach language skills to other species (e.g., through the use of sign language) have failed.[4]

Questions about behaviorism/associationism, along with developments in computer science, information theory, and linguistics, helped to change the intellectual climate among experimental psychologists. Then during the 1950s and early 1960s, several landmark publications led to a recognition that experimental psychology was somehow different than it had been before. Some have referred to the events at this time as a "revolution" in psychology, an issue that is examined in this chapter's Close-Up. Whether revolutionary or evolutionary, however, it is clear that several events reflected a change in direction of experimental psychology.

Thomas Kuhn

▶ CLOSE-UP

What Revolution?

There is little doubt that more experimental psychologists in America were interested in studying cognitive processes in the 1960s than in the prior two decades, and that except for dedicated diehard Skinnerian holdouts, behaviorism began to decline as a force at the same time. Some have referred to the change as a "revolution" in psychology (e.g., Segal & Lachman, 1972; Sperry, 1993), and at least two books chronicling the shift to cognition include "cognitive revolution" in their titles (Baars, 1986; Gardner, 1985). On the other hand, psychologist/historian Thomas Leahey (1992) contends that the development of cognitive psychology does not meet any of the accepted criteria of a scientific revolution. Clearly, resolving the issue requires some understanding of what is meant by a "revolution" in science.

In 1962, a brief (172 pages) but momentous book entitled *The Structure of Scientific Revolutions* appeared on the academic scene, proposing a new way to look at progress in science. Its author, physicist-turned-historian Thomas Kuhn, argued against the traditional Enlightenment-based notion that scientific progress involves a gradual accumulation of objective knowledge over time. Rather, in Kuhn's version, science proceeds through history by establishing agreed-upon "paradigms" that guide scientists, and then shifts from one paradigm to another. When such a shift occurs, a revolution has happened.

According to Kuhn, all sciences begin in a "preparadigmatic stage." During this time there are competing schools of thought within a disciple, and they argue over fundamental conceptual and definitional issues. Eventually, one of those schools gains a majority of adherents and becomes established as a **paradigm**. A Kuhnian paradigm is an all-embracing worldview within the scientific community that organizes what is known into a grand theory, determines how terms are defined and what problems are to be solved by scientists, and dictates appropriate research methods. Newtonian physics is the typical example. Once a paradigm has been established, there exists a period of **normal science**, during which the paradigm guides research designed to provide empirical evidence for it. Because all paradigms have some truth to them, much of this research indeed supports the paradigm, but not all of it does. Anomalous findings can usually be ignored or explained away, but sometimes predictions keep failing and the science enters

---

[4] Chimpanzees and other primates have been quite successful at learning to use sign language and communicating their needs symbolically, but the general consensus among both linguists and experimental psychologists is that their learning is imitative and does not show evidence of the use of a true rule-bound grammar (see Anderson, 1990, for a review).

a "crisis" period, during which confidence in the paradigm starts to wane. Eventually, a creative scientist or two will come up with a new idea that explains the anomalies along with everything else explained by the paradigm-in-crisis. If this new idea is sufficiently powerful and well promoted, it can become a new paradigm, replacing the old one. If so, a revolution is said to have occurred. The replacement of Newtonian physics with Einsteinian physics is the typical example.

Kuhn's ideas have been applied to the history of psychology. Kirsch (1977), for example, claimed that psychology's first paradigm could be called "mentalism," and it encompassed Wundtian, structuralist, and functionalist thinking. Its guiding interest was the scientific study of the human mind. Problems with introspection led to a paradigm crisis, however, leading to the behaviorist revolution. Similar arguments were made by Palermo (1971), who believed that psychology in the 1960s and 1970s was in the midst of a second revolution, from behaviorism to cognitive psychology. The shifts from mentalism to behaviorism and then to cognitive psychology have a certain intuitive appeal and there is a degree of truth to the broad overview.

According to Leahey (1992), however, clothing psychology's history in Kuhnian garb can oversimplify complex events and perpetuate myths. Concerning the so-called cognitive revolution, for instance, he argued that (a) behaviorists disagreed on too many basic issues (e.g., S-R or S-O-R?) for behaviorism to be anything close to a Kuhnian paradigm, (b) any shift from behaviorism to cognition was too gradual for the term "revolutionary" to have any meaning, (c) the early research in cognition was not motivated by the perception of a "crisis" in behaviorism, but by a variety of other factors, and (d) cognitive psychologists themselves disagreed on too many fundamentals for cognitive psychology to resemble a Kuhnian paradigm.

Leahey (1992) also made the interesting suggestion that the 1962 appearance of Kuhn's book *by itself* helped to create the "myth" that a cognitive revolution was in progress. Reflecting on that era, researcher James Jenkins recalled it as a "tremendously exciting time. The basic assumption was that things were boiling over, and...a new day was coming. And of course, everyone toted around their little copy of Kuhn's [book]" (quoted in Baars, 1986, p. 249). Although not denying that changes were indeed occurring, Leahey concluded that *"there was no awareness of revolution until Kuhn's book suggested it"* (p. 315, italics in the original). It is worth noting that all of this was going on during a particularly turbulent time in American history. In the 1960s, protests against the war in Vietnam and the civil rights movement produced a climate in which talk of overthrowing the existing order, not trusting anyone over 30, and rejecting institutional authority was commonplace on university campuses. As a graduate student in cognitive psychology myself at that time, I can recall how Kuhn's message of revolutionary change seemed to resonate with my professors and peers. For instance, the book was the first one we had to read in a seminar on "higher mental processes," and it colored the discussion for a whole semester. By formulating a new way of looking at the history of science, then, in a culture awash with calls for change, Kuhn's book might have helped to *create* the idea of a "cognitive revolution."

MAGICAL NUMBERS, SELECTIVE FILTERS, FOCUS GAMBLING, AND TOTE UNITS

Perhaps the first psychologist to recognize the relevance of information theory to psychology was George A. Miller (b. 1920). As a research fellow in Harvard's Psycho-Acoustic Laboratory from 1944 to 1948, Miller (Figure 13.3) investigated speech perception, a problem that derived from a military context—the difficulty in hearing spoken messages while sitting in loud air-

Figure 13.3   George Miller, from Thorne and Henley (1997).

planes (Hilgard, 1987). Out of this research came a course offered to Harvard undergraduates called "The Psychology of Speech and Communication," and from the course came Miller's first book, *Language and Communication* (1951). Shortly after Shannon and Weaver produced their groundbreaking work (above), Miller introduced information theory to psychologists in a *Psychological Review* article (Miller & Frick, 1949). Then, seven years later, he published an article with a title more whimsical than normally found in stuffy academic journals—"The Magical Number Seven, Plus or Minus Two: Some Limits on Our Capacity for Processing Information" (Miller, 1956/1994). The conclusions of the paper were destined to become a standard feature in the memory chapters of introductory textbooks, and the article

itself has become the most frequently cited paper in the 100-year history of the *Psychological Review* (Kintsch & Cacioppo, 1994).

In the article, which was a printed version of an address given at the Eastern Psychological Association the year before, Miller showed how information theory concepts such as bits and channel capacity could be used to describe limits on our ability to process information in several kinds of tasks. The last portion of the paper contains the most frequently cited information, Miller's analysis of the limited capacity of immediate memory. Depending on the type of information being memorized, he argued that people could only process between five (for monosyllabic words) and nine (for binary digits) items at a time. Recognizing that the amount of information in bits varies dramatically, depending on the type of material being studied, Miller introduced a new term, the **chunk**, to refer to the information being held in immediate memory. Hence, the capacity limit on short-term memory was identified as seven, plus or minus two, chunks of information, the chunk being a small, meaningful unit of information. Further, Miller applied the information theory concept of **recoding** to take into account the fact that humans have the ability to reorganize data, thereby squeezing in more information per chunk. In his words, because "the memory span is a fixed number of chunks, we can increase the number of bits of information that it contains simply by building larger and larger chunks, each chunk containing more information than before" (Miller, 1956/1994, p. 349). Miller used the example of learning Morse code to drive home the point. The learner first hears each *dit* and *dah* as individual units. With experience, however, combinations of these sounds are recoded ("chunked") as whole letters, then words, then phrases, so that the experienced operator can, in effect, keep many more *dits* and *dahs* in immediate memory than the novice.

The mid-1950s also saw the publication of several works from England that applied information theory ideas to attention, a cognitive phenomenon largely neglected since Wundtian times. The prime mover was a student of Bartlett's at Cambridge, Donald Broadbent (1926–1993), who first became interested in psychology during World War II, while being trained as a pilot in the Royal Air Force. Although impressed by the technical complexity of the aircraft he was flying, he was frustrated by the failure of engineers to take the human pilot into account when designing the cockpit instrumentation and controls. The similarity of gauges often induced perceptual and attentional errors—for instance, Broadbent recalled that while landing on one occasion, he thought he was flying at 2000 feet, only to discover that he was attending to the wrong gauge and that he was actually flying at 2000 rpm (Broadbent, 1980).

After the war, Broadbent went to Cambridge, studied with Bartlett, and was eventually named director of Bartlett's laboratory there, the Applied Psychology Unit. During the 1950s, he and Colin Cherry, a professor of telecommunications, pioneered modern research on attention by using a "dichotic listening" procedure, in which subjects would experience two channels of information at the same time, one sent to each ear via headphones. They were able to document limits on the ability to use multiple communication channels, showing, for instance, that while attending to one message, very little of a second message could be recalled (e.g., Cherry, 1953). Broadbent summarized this research in *Perception and Communication* (1958) and proposed a simple **selective filter** model of attention. When confronted with two streams of information, he suggested, our limited capacity system separates the information on the basis of physical characteristics, enabling us to filter out one message and select the other for attention and further processing. The problem of selective attention, which introductory textbooks soon began labeling the "cocktail party phenomenon" because the task resembled that of trying to listen to two conversations at once, remains an important and vigorous area of research in cognitive psychology.

A third major development in the 1950s was a series of studies on the thinking strategies people used while trying to identify concepts, culminating in the 1956 publication of *A Study of Thinking*, by Harvard's Jerome Bruner and his colleagues (Bruner, Goodnow, & Austin, 1956). Bruner (b. 1915), who has also made important contributions to perceptual, social, and developmental psychology, became interested in an old problem in psychology, but was determined to look at it from a new angle. The task that he studied was concept identification, in which subjects are given stimuli that vary along several dimensions and have to identify the common features of predefined "correct" stimuli. Bruner's goal was to determine "what happens when an intelligent human being seeks to sort the environment into significant classes of events so that he may end by treating discriminably different things as equivalents" (Bruner, Goodnow, & Austin, 1956, p. viii). The traditional approach to such a problem was grounded in behaviorism, with its assumption that concept learning proceeded as a result of the reinforcement or nonreinforcement of specific responses to specific stimulus dimensions. Bruner, however, in keeping with one of the themes of the evolving cognitive approach, preferred to think of the subject as an active searcher for concepts, rather than the passive recipient of environmental events and reinforcement. Throughout the book, then, the reader encountered descriptions of the strategies pursued by subjects when trying to identify concepts.

Two of these schemes, "conservative focusing" and "focus gambling," can be illustrated with reference to Figure 13.4, the stimulus array used in the research. The 81 stimuli combine four "attributes" (number of figures, shape of figures, color of figures, and number of borders), with each attribute having three values (e.g., cross, circle, and square are the three values of the attribute "shape"). On a given trial, the subject would identify a stimulus, the experimenter would indicate whether it was an

Figure 13.4   Stimulus materials used by Bruner, Goodnow, and Austin (1956) in their research on the strategies used in concept identification.

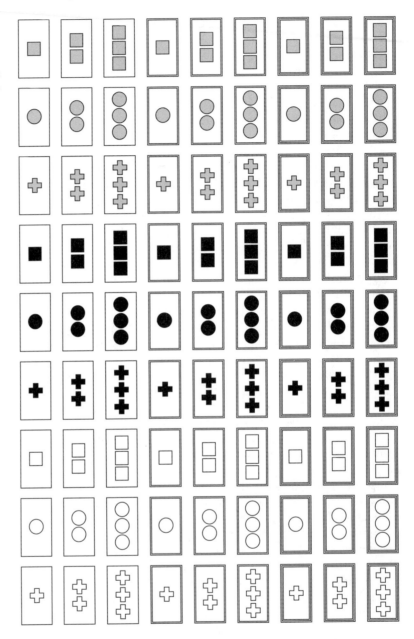

example of the sought-after concept, the subject would point to the next stimulus, and so on until the subject could name the concept. Suppose, for example, that the concept is the conjunctive one of "two circles," for which nine of the stimuli are examples. In a **conserv-** **ative focusing** strategy, according to Bruner, the subject first identifies a positive example, then varies one attribute at a time in order to determine if it is essential to the concept being sought. For example, such a subject might make these choices:

1. 2W01b (read this as "2 white circles, 1 border")—positive instance

2. 2WO2b—positive instance

3. 1WO2b—negative instance

Note what the subject can conclude from trial to trial. After trial two, it is reasonable to infer (but not conclusive: 2WO3b could be negative) that the number of borders is not relevant to the sought-after concept. After the third trial, however, it is clear that the number of stimuli *is* relevant. A few more trials should yield the answer. In **focus gambling**, the subject alters two attributes at a time, instead of just one. It is a gamble because if the outcome is a positive instance, then two attributes can be ruled out on a single trial, abbreviating the overall search; but if it is a negative instance, then each of the attributes has to be checked individually, lengthening the search.

The Bruner study was later criticized for using artificial stimuli in concept tasks that had unambiguously correct outcomes, whereas the concepts found in real life are often ill-defined and concept learning proceeds less systematically. Nonetheless, with its emphasis on the person as an active information processor and its unqualified belief in the functional reality of mental representations, the book marks an important advance in the study of the "higher" cognitive processes.

One final example of the shift toward cognitive psychology also took the form of a book. Entitled *Plans and the Structure of Behavior*, it appeared in 1960, the outcome of a collaboration between George Miller, of 7+2 fame, Eugene Galanter, a Harvard experimental psychologist with expertise in math and computers, and Karl Pribram, a well-known neuroscientist. The book centered on the idea of a "Plan," defined as "any hierarchical process in the organism that can control the order in which a sequence of operations is to be performed" (Miller, Galanter, & Pribram, 1960, p. 16). In keeping with the computer metaphor that was rapidly coming into vogue, the authors explicit-ly likened these Plans to the program written for a computer. The second main concept was that of the "Image," which the authors defined broadly as "all the accumulated, organized knowledge that the organism has about itself and its world" (p. 17). The main problem for the book was said to be to "explore the relationship between the Image and the Plan" (Miller, Galanter, & Pribram, 1960, p. 18).

The book is perhaps best remembered for borrowing the concept of feedback from the field of **cybernetics** (i.e., the study of the principles involved in controlling any living or non-living system). In a radical departure from behaviorist/associationist tradition, they proposed that a feedback system could be substituted for the reflex arc as the basic unit of behavioral control. In a feedback system, the operation of one part of the system produces results that are fed back and monitored by the system, thereby affecting its future operation. The thermostat and furnace, for instance, operate together as a simple feedback system. On a cold day, the thermostat sends a signal to the furnace to start, which increases the air temperature, which is read by the thermostat, which eventually tells the furnace to stop. The temperature then drops, triggers another signal from the thermostat to restart the furnace, and so on. In the long run, the feedback system produces a "steady state," a temperature that does not vary much from the thermostat setting. For human feedback systems, Miller and his colleagues created the basic concept of the **TOTE unit**, TOTE being an acronym for Test-Operate-Test-Exit. It is shown in Figure 13.5. It begins with a Test phase that looks for incongruities in the system (e.g., in the thermostat example, a difference between the desired temperature and the actual temperature). If there are no incongruities, nothing happens, but if there are, an operation occurs to reduce the incongruity. Another Test then occurs, and so on until no incongruity exists. For humans, these TOTE units are organized hierarchically, as in the example shown in Figure 13.6, which

Key Date 1960

This year marked the publication of Miller, Galanter, and Pribram's influential *Plans and the Structure of Behavior*.

These events also occurred:

- U.S. scientists developed a LASER device (Light Amplification by Simulated Emission of Radiation)
- The American Heart Association issued a report relating heavy smoking to increased health risks
- Columbia professor Charles Van Doren was charged with perjury after lying about being given the answers on the quiz show "Twenty-One"
- After three historic TV debates, John F. Kennedy narrowly defeated Richard Nixon for the presidency
- The Pittsburgh Pirates won the World Series from the Yankees on a home run by Bill Mazerowski
- These films premiered: *Exodus* and *Psycho*
- These people were born:

    Kenneth Branagh, English Shakespearean actor

    John Elway, professional football player

    Cal Ripkin, professional baseball player

- These people died:

    W. E. B. DuBois, civil rights leader and cofounder of the NAACP

    Clark Gable, American actor

    Oscar Hammerstein, American songwriter

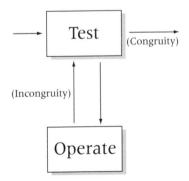

Figure 13.5 The basic TOTE (Test-Operate-Test-Exit) unit proposed by Miller, Galanter, and Pribram's *Plans and the Structure of Behavior* (1960).

represents the authors' example of a two-level system for hammering a nail. The first Test is to see if the nail is sticking up; if not, no hammering is needed; if so, the second level TOTE units engage to alter the state of the nail.

Miller's 7±2 paper, the British work on attention, Bruner's work on thinking, and *Plans* were just four prominent examples of events that marked an important shift in experimental psychology, legitimizing the study of heretofore frowned-on mentalistic topics. The momentum continued to build in the 1960s, a tumultuous decade in which change from the existing order became a familiar theme (refer again to this chapter's Close-Up). In addition, experimental

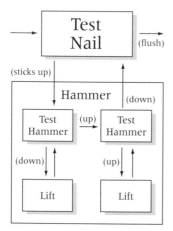

Figure 13.6   TOTE units arranged to illustrate a hierarchical plan for hammering nails, from Miller, Galanter, and Pribram (1960).

psychology benefited from increased government funding of all scientific research, part of the attempt during the cold war to reestablish American scientific supremacy in the wake of Soviet successes in space (e.g., launching the first satellite—"Sputnik"—into orbit in 1957). By the mid-1960s, sufficient research existed to warrant book-length summaries of it, and texts in cognitive psychology began to appear, most notably Ulric Neisser's *Cognitive Psychology* in 1967, which gave a specific name to the converging ideas of such people as Miller, Broadbent, and Bruner. Neisser (Figure 13.7)

Figure 13.7   Ulric Neisser, from Thorne and Henley (1997).

would later recall getting "letters from people saying that they were glad that I had given [the movement] a name, because they were interested in all the topics I considered, but the area had not had a theoretical identity" (quoted in Baars, 1986, p. 278). After Neisser, it did.

▶ ORIGINAL SOURCE EXCERPT

Neisser on Cognitive Psychology

As an undergraduate at Harvard, Ulric Neisser (b. 1928) studied with George Miller, later recalling that Miller's course on speech and communication "covered some pretty unusual topics…[such as] linguistics, acoustics, articulatory physiology, and engineering mathematics" (Neisser, 1988, p. 82). Neisser's interest in cognition was aroused by the experience, and he followed his undergraduate degree with a master's degree from Swarthmore, adopted home of the Gestaltist Köhler, and further graduate study at MIT before earning a doctorate in psychoacoustics at Harvard in 1956. He subsequently taught at Brandeis, Cornell, and Emory, before returning to Cornell, where he now teaches.

The following excerpt is from the introduction to Neisser's landmark text. After some opening remarks, he described what he meant by cognition:

> ...One of Freud's papers on human motivation is entitled "Instincts and their Vicissitudes" (1915). The title reflects a basic axiom of psychoanalysis: that a man's fundamental motives suffer an intricate series of transformations, reformulations, and changes before they appear in either consciousness or action. Borrowing Freud's phrase—without intending any commitment to his theory of motivation—a book like this one might be called "Stimulus Information and its Vicissitudes." *As used here, the term "cognition" refers to all the processes by which the sensory input is transformed, reduced, elaborated, stored, recovered, and used.* It is concerned with these processes even when they operate in the absence of relevant stimulation, as in images and hallucinations. Such terms as sensation, perception, imagery, retention, recall, problem-solving, and thinking, among many others, refer to hypothetical stages or aspects of cognition.
>
> Given such a sweeping definition, it is apparent that cognition is involved in everything a human being might possibly do; that every psychological phenomenon is a cognitive phenomenon. But although cognitive psychology is concerned with all human activity rather than some fraction of it, the concern is from a particular point of view. Other viewpoints are equally legitimate and necessary. (p. 4, italics added)

The "other viewpoints" referred to by Neisser include dynamic psychology (concerned with motivation) and behaviorism. He recognized the close relationship between cognition and motivation, but in the manner of other researchers during this era, he was critical of behaviorism's onetime monopoly on experimental psychology, and somewhat smug about how the climate had changed:

> ...From Watson to Skinner, radical behaviorists have maintained that man's actions should be explained only in terms of observable variables, without any inner vicissitudes at all. The appeal to hypothetical mechanisms is said to be speculative at best, and deceptive at worst. For them, it is legitimate to speak of stimuli, responses, reinforcements, and hours of deprivation, but not of categories or images or ideas. A generation ago, a book like this one would have needed at least a chapter of self-defense against the behaviorist position. Today, happily, the climate of opinion has changed, and little or no defense is necessary. Indeed, stimulus-response theorists themselves are inventing hypothetical mechanisms with vigor and enthusiasm and only faint twinges of conscience. The basic reason for studying cognitive processes has become as clear as the reason for studying anything else: because they are there.... Cognitive processes surely exist, so it can hardly be unscientific to study them. (p. 5)

Neisser next referred to another way of examining psychological questions, that of the physiologist. Recognizing that behavior and consciousness "depend entirely on the activity of the brain" (p. 5), he nonetheless made it clear that the reader would find little information on the brain and nervous system in his book. He used the example of memory and worked the computer metaphor into the narrative to explain why:

> No one would dispute that human beings store a great deal of information about their past experiences, and it seems obvious that this information must be physically embodied somewhere in the brain. Recent discoveries in biochemistry have opened up a promising possibility. Some experimental findings have hinted that the complex molecules of DNA and RNA, known to be involved in the transmission of inherited traits, may be the substrate of memory as well. Although the supporting evidence so far is shaky, this hypothesis has already gained many adherents. But psychology is not just something "to do until the biochemist comes" (as I have recently heard psychiatry described); the truth or falsity of this new hypothesis is only marginally relevant to psychological questions. A pair of analogies will show why this is so.
>
> First, let us consider the familiar parallel between man and computer. Although it is an inadequate analogy in many ways, it may suffice for this purpose. The task of a psychologist trying to understand human cognition is analogous to that of a man trying to discover how a computer has been programmed. In particular, if the program seems to store and reuse information, he would like to know by what "routines" or "procedures" this is done. Given this purpose, he will not care much whether his particular computer stores information in magnetic cores or in thin films; he wants to understand the program, not the "hardware." By the same token, it would not help the psychologist to know that memory is carried by RNA as opposed to some other medium. He wants to understand its utilization, not its incarnation.... (pp. 5–6)

Neisser's second analogy, to show why he was uninterested in brain physiology, was between psychology and economics (the economist is interested in the "flow" of capital, not in the physical attributes of currency). He then described the relevance of information theory for modern psychology.

> Psychology, like economics, is a science concerned with the interdependence among certain events rather than with their physical nature. Although there are many disciplines of this sort (classical genetics is another good example), the most prominent ones today are probably the so-called "information sciences," which include the mathematical theory of communication, computer programming, systems analysis, and related fields. It seems obvious that these must be relevant to cognitive psychology, which is itself much concerned with information. However, their importance for psychologists has often been misunderstood, and deserves careful consideration.
>
> Information, in the sense first clearly defined by Shannon, is essentially choice, the narrowing down of alternatives. He developed the mathematical theory of communication in order to deal quantitatively with the transmission of messages over "channels." A channel, like a telephone line, transmits information to the extent that the choices made at one end

determine those made at the other. The words of the speaker are regarded as successive selection from among all the possible words of English.
Ideally, the transmitted message will enable the listener to choose the
same ones; that is, to identify each correctly. For practical purposes, it is
important to measure the amount of information that a system can trans-
mit, and early applications of information theory were much concerned
with measurement. As is now well known, amounts of information are
measured in units called "bits," or binary digits, where one "bit" is represented by a choice between two equally probable alternatives. (p. 7)

Recognizing the importance of information theory, Neisser nonetheless questioned the value of trying to reduce the information found in psychology experiments to "bits," arguing that such a notion fails to account for the human's
active participation in the processing of information. On the other hand, the
computer metaphor had been quite useful, and Neisser spent some time elaborating it. Note that while acknowledging the significance of Bartlett's work,
Neisser argued that the information processing approach was superior to one
grounded in the idea of a "schema":

...The "bit" was developed to describe the performance of rather unselec-
tive systems: a telephone cannot decide which portions of the incoming
message are important. We shall see throughout this book that human
beings behave very differently, and are by no means neutral or passive
toward the incoming information. Instead, they select some parts for
attention at the expense of others, recoding and reformulating them in
complex ways.

Although information measurement may be of little value to the cognitive psychologist, another branch of the information sciences, computer
programming, has much more to offer. A program is not a device for measuring information, but a recipe for selecting, storing, recovering, combining, outputting, and generally manipulating it. As pointed out by [others],
this means that programs have much in common with theories of cognition. Both are descriptions of the vicissitudes of input information.

...A program is not a machine; it is a series of instructions for dealing
with symbols: "If the input has certain characteristics...then carry out certain procedures...otherwise other procedures...combine their results in
various ways...store and retrieve various items...depending on prior
results...use them in further specified ways...etc." The cognitive psychologist would like to give a similar account of the way information is
processed by men.

This way of defining the cognitive problem is not really a new one. We
are still asking "how the mind works." However, the "program analogy"
(which may be a better term than "computer analogy") has several advantages over earlier conceptions. Most important is the philosophical reas-
surance which it provides. Although a program is nothing but a flow of
symbols, it has reality enough to control the operation of very tangible
machinery that executes very physical operations....

There were cognitive theorists long before the advent of the computer.
Bartlett, whose influence on my own thinking will become obvious in

later chapters, is a case in point. But, in the eyes of many psychologists, a theory which dealt with cognitive transformation, memory schemata, and the like was not *about* anything. One could understand theories that dealt with overt movements, or with physiology; one could even understand (and deplore) theories which dealt with the content of consciousness; but what kind of a thing is a schema? If memory consists of transformations, what is transformed? So long as cognitive psychology literally did not know what it was talking about, there was always a danger that it was talking about nothing at all. This is no longer a serious risk. *Information* is what is transformed, and the structured pattern of its transformations is what we want to understand.

A second advantage of the "program analogy" is that, like other analogies, it is a fruitful source of hypotheses. A field which is directly concerned with information processing should be at least as rich in ideas for psychology as other fields of science have been before. Just as we have borrowed atomic units, energy distributions, hydraulic pressures, and mechanical linkages from physics and engineering, so may we choose to adopt certain concepts from programming today. This will be done rather freely in some of the following chapters. Such notions as "parallel processing," "feature extraction," "analysis-by-synthesis," and "executive routine" have been borrowed from programmers, in the hope that they will prove theoretically useful. The rest of their value, of course, is strictly psychological. We will have to see how well they fit the data. (pp. 7–9, italics in the original)

The content chapters of Neisser's *Cognitive Psychology* are full of rich experimental detail about some of the ways that information is transformed by the human information processor. Reflecting the newness of cognitive psychology, about 60% of the book's 321 references are to research published in the decade of the 1960s (Weaver, 1998). The bulk of the book concerns the initial processing of visual and auditory information, but there are also chapters on memory, language, and a brief concluding chapter on the relationship between memory and thought.

THE SPREAD OF COGNITIVE PSYCHOLOGY

Interest in cognitive psychology continued to grow after the publication of Neisser's 1967 book. Psychology departments rushed to create cognitive laboratories and to hire cognitive psychologists, conferences on cognition were held, their contents later published in edited books (e.g., the Loyola Symposium, in Solso, 1973), and informal networks such as S.W.I.M. (Southeastern Workers in Memory) were formed. Traditional journals such as the *Journal of Experimental Psychology* featured more cognitive research, and new journals appeared— *Cognitive Psychology* in 1970, *Cognition* in 1972, *Cognitive Science* in 1977, and *Memory and Cognition* in 1983. In addition, cognitive psychology spread to psychology's other subdisciplines, such as developmental, social, personality, and abnormal psychology. Even animal psychology was not immune—researchers began investigating "animal cognition" (e.g., Flaherty, 1985). Here is just a sampling of how cognitive psychology swept through related areas in psychology.

1. In *developmental psychology*, Piaget's theories of cognitive development were rediscovered in the 1960s and led to an explosion of research on how various cognitive skills develop, from infancy through adolescence (e.g., Kail & Hagen, 1977). Following from the linguist's arguments about the unique nature of human language, the psychological study of children's language—developmental psycholinguistics—became a hot topic of research in the 1970s (e.g., Brown, 1973).

2. In *social psychology*, Leon Festinger's theory of cognitive dissonance (1957) arrived in the 1950s, showing that social psychology was less affected by behaviorism than other subdisciplines. This should not be surprising, knowing what we do about the influence of Kurt Lewin on social psychology (Chapter 9). Festinger was a student of Lewin, and dissonance theory, which generated an enormous amount of research in the 1960s and 1970s, relates to Lewin's field theory of behavior. Just as Lewin proposed that the individual seeks to produce equilibrium by reducing tensions in the life space, so Festinger based his theory on the notion that people try to maintain an internal consistency between their thoughts and actions, and that a failure to do so produces "cognitive dissonance" and an attempt to reduce that dissonance. More recently, there has been a great deal of interest among social psychologists in a variety of topics under the general heading of "social cognition," the study of how we interpret our own actions and those of others in social environments (e.g., Fiske & Taylor, 1984), and in "attribution theory," which examines the ways in which we attempt to explain the reasons for behavior, our own and that of others (e.g., Kelley, 1973).

3. *Personality psychology* has seen the development of Walter Mischel's cognitive theory of per-

sonality, which proposes that the key factors differentiating one person from another are cognitive variables such as processing competencies, expectations, and encoding strategies (Mischel, 1984). Similarly, Rotter (1966) proposed that an important determinant of personality is whether one's "locus of control" is "internal" or "external." Those with an internal locus of control believe that they are in control of the events in their lives, whereas those with an external locus believe that the environment causes things to happen to them and that they exert minimal effective control. And cognitive concepts have become central to the social learning theory of Albert Bandura (e.g., Bandura, 1977). To Bandura, a student of Kenneth Spence and therefore trained in the Hull-Spence tradition (Chapter 11), learning in humans is a complex process that requires certain cognitive processes. Thus, Bandura's theory emphasizes observational learning, which requires such cognitive processes as memory and internal practice, over traditional operant or classical conditioning. In recent years, a focus of Bandura's evolving theory has been the cognitive concept of **self-efficacy**, a general conception of our ability to deal with the problems that we encounter in life (Bandura, 1986). To students, Bandura is perhaps best known for his studies of imitative aggression, in which children attack the famous "Bobo" doll after seeing films of adults doing so (e.g., Bandura, Ross, & Ross, 1963).

4. In *abnormal psychology*, cognitive theories of depression (e.g., Beck, 1967) attribute the disorder to inappropriate cognitive interpretations of the events in our lives. Research on schizophrenia shows that some of its symptoms involve breakdowns in the normal processes of attention and language.[5] And in the realm of psychotherapy, an important elaboration of behavior therapy is cognitive-behavior therapy, in which faulty belief systems are challenged and people are taught to alter what they say to

---

[5] Recall that Wundt's student Emil Kraepelin proposed an attention-based theory of schizophrenia in the late nineteenth century.

Neisser in 1976 : ecological validity ← influence of J. J. Gibson
called for Ecological validity
(Earlier text : 1967)

Cognitive Psychology Arrives (Again)   **419**

themselves and how they interpret the events in their lives (e.g., Beck, 1979).

PRAGMATISM REVISITED: THE PROBLEM OF ECOLOGICAL VALIDITY

Within cognitive psychology itself, changes occurred in the 1970s, once again led by Ulric Neisser. In *Cognition and Reality* (1976), he argued that the laboratory tradition in cognitive psychology, while producing important results, nonetheless had failed to yield enough useful information about information processing in real-world contexts. He was even critical of his own 1967 text for being top heavy with pure laboratory research. Instead, explicitly recognizing the influence of Bartlett, he called for more research concerning what he referred to as **ecological validity**—research with relevance for the everyday cognitive activities of people trying to adapt to their environment. Experimental psychologists, Neisser (1976) urged, "must make a greater effort to understand cognition as it occurs in the ordinary environment and in the context of natural purposeful activity. This would not mean an end to laboratory experiments, but a commitment to the study of variables that are ecologically important rather than those that are easily manageable" (p. 7).

Neisser's call to arms was embraced by many (but not all, of course) cognitive researchers, and the 1980s and 1990s saw increased research in such topics as eyewitness memory (e.g., Loftus, 1979) and the long-term recall of topics learned in school, such as Spanish (e.g., Bahrick, 1984). Although these events are too close to the present for detached historical analysis, the turn to everyday cognition should not be surprising, given what we know about the history of functionalist thinking in American psychology. Research that helps us to understand how the individual adapts to the environment and has practical applications is the type of research that has always resonated with American psychology's functional/pragmatic spirit.

COGNITIVE SCIENCE

In addition to the interest in ecological validity, another aspect of the evolution of interests among research psychologists has been the creation of **cognitive science**, an interdisciplinary field that includes cognitive psychology, linguistics, computer science, cultural anthropology, and even epistemology. Gardner (1985) defined the field broadly as an "empirically based effort to answer long-standing epistemological questions—particularly those concerned with the nature of knowledge, its components, its sources, its development, and its deployment" (p. 6). The term "cognitive science" began to appear in the mid-1970s and became institutionalized with the naming of a journal devoted to it in 1977. In the opening editorial for *Cognitive Science*, Collins (1977) pointed out that the discipline could have been called "applied epistemology or intelligence theory, but someone on high declared it should be cognitive science and so it shall" (p. 1).

It is worth noting, of course, that while the label is relatively new, cognitive science is not. The initial stirrings of the new discipline can be seen in the postwar era, when the above-mentioned "influences external to psychology" (information theory, computer science, linguistics) contributed to the emergence of what psychologists began calling "cognitive psychology." From a broader perspective, however, it is clear that something more than a new psychology was developing and that some of the key players were aware of it. George Miller, for instance, traced the origins of cognitive science to a 1956 symposium on information theory, held at MIT (Baars, 1986), and in 1960, Miller and Jerome Bruner cofounded the Center for Cognitive Studies at Harvard, designed explicitly to foster the interdisciplinary study of cognition. Bruner later recalled that he and Miller decided "that psychology was too complicated a field to leave to the psychologists, [so] what we needed was an alliance with colleagues from other disciplines who were, each in his or her own context, concerned about how humans acquired and used knowledge" (Bruner, 1988, p. 92).

Artificial Intelligence

One important focus of interest among cognitive scientists has been in the applied computer science area of **artificial intelligence** (AI), which may be defined simply as the field that attempts to examine whether machines can act with some degree of intelligence. Workers in AI are interested in a variety of topics, but they generally fall into two broad categories. Some researchers are mainly interested in understanding human intelligence, studying it by attempting to write computer programs that simulate human cognitive processing. Consider human problem solving, for example. The idea is that if a computer can be made to solve problems in the same way that humans solve problems, then the problem-solving strategies built into the computer program can be seen as analogous to human strategies. This was the approach taken by two nonpsychologist pioneers in AI, Herbert Simon (b. 1916) and Alan Newell (1927–1992). Simon, whose work on decision making produced a Nobel Prize in economics in 1978, and Newell, a physicist, collaborated on computer simulations of thinking and problem solving in the 1950s and 1960s. Their first effort, the Logic Theorist (LT), was designed to solve problems in formal logic, while their later and more ambitious project, the General Problem Solver (GPS), was aimed at a broader range of problems (Newell & Simon, 1972).

Both LT and GPS illustrate an important distinction in computer science between algorithms and heuristics. An **algorithm** is a set of rules guaranteed to produce a solution by working systematically through all possible steps. A **heuristic**, on the other hand, is a more creative strategy or "rule of thumb" that, while not guaranteeing a solution, is more efficient

than an algorithm. A common anagram problem can illustrate the difference. When asked to rearrange the letters "LTEAGST" so that a real word is formed, an algorithmic approach would try every possible combination of letters until a solution was reached. This would not present a problem for a computer, which performs operations very quickly and does not get bored in the process. Humans, however, would probably attempt to solve the anagram by using heuristics, such as "do not consider uncommon combinations of pairs of letters." Thus, the solver would try the combination "ST" but not "GT", on the way toward solving the anagram (hint: it's a word found throughout Chapter 9).

The primary heuristic built into Simon and Newell's GPS was called a **means-ends analysis**. A feedback system, it involved assessing the current state with the goal state, identifying a difference between the two, identifying and applying an operator (some behavior) to reduce the difference, reassessing the new state with the goal, and so on, until the current state became the goal state. Newell and Simon (1972) developed the program by giving problems (e.g., algebra problems) to people and asking them to externalize their thinking by describing their thought processes as they occurred, a procedure bearing an interesting similarity to introspection. They then wrote the GPS program in a way that attempted to simulate what their human subjects were doing. Hence, the goal was to understand human thinking, on the assumption that if they could simulate it, with the computer producing solutions just like human solutions, then they would increase their understanding of it. This simulation strategy was used in attempts to study cognitive processes ranging from pattern recognition to memory to thinking, although interest in such simulations reached its peak in the 1970s, in part because of the abandonment of GPS when it failed to be as "general" a problem solver as originally hoped (Gardner, 1985).

The second approach to AI, and the more dominant one since the 1980s, is to create a computer program that will perform some task in the most efficient way possible, regardless of how humans might approach the task. That is, the goal is to create expert systems that deal with problems intelligently. The outcome has been such things as computerized chess programs that can beat world-class human players, robots, and interactive tutoring systems. This second usage of AI has raised the question of whether computers can be said to think, which in turn has led to debates on the nature of thinking and what it is to be human. That is, AI has perpetuated some of the issues that have always been of interest to psychologists.

The question of whether true intelligence can be found in computers was posed as early as 1950, in an article entitled "Computing Machinery and Intelligence," by Alan Turing (1912–1954), a brilliant English mathematician. Turing was instrumental in ensuring the allied victory in World War II by helping to break the supposedly unassailable "Enigma" code of the Germans, thereby informing allied strategists of German troop movements, strategies, and the like. In his 1950 article, Turing described an "imitation game" that provided a set of criteria to determine whether computers could be said to think. This has since been called the **Turing test**. Imagine, wrote Turing, a situation in which a person in one room can ask a series of any questions to a human and a computer, both located in a second room. On the basis of the two sets of answers, the questioner must try to distinguish between the human and the machine. The human tries to convince the questioner that he or she is human, as does the computer. If the questioner cannot discriminate human from machine on the basis of the answers, according to Turing, then it must be concluded that no significant differences exist between computer intelligence and human intelligence—that is, computers can think just like humans.

The idea of the computer as thinker equivalent to the human as thinker, sometimes referred to as **strong AI**, has been sharply crit-

icized, most cogently by John Searle. Proponents of strong AI believe that thinking is essentially rule-bound symbol manipulation, a skill possessed by both humans and computers. Searle, while accepting the validity of what is called **weak AI**, the idea that computers can yield important insights about the nature of human thinking, argued that strong AI was not justified. To illustrate the point, Searle described a thought problem that has come to be called the **Chinese Room problem** (1990). Imagine that you are isolated in a room with a massive rule book that specified all of the combinations of markings that comprise Chinese writing. This book enables you to examine a sequence of such markings presented to you in the form of a written question from a native Chinese speaker and accurately produce a written response using other Chinese symbols. That is, a Chinese speaker could write a question to you in Chinese symbols and you could use your rule book to generate a response that would be acceptable to the questioner. Indeed, your responses might be indistinguishable from those given by a native speaker of Chinese, which means that you would pass the Turing test. The question is whether this means that you understand Chinese, and for Searle the answer is no. Thinking involves more than just symbol manipulation according to fixed rules, he has argued; it also includes semantics—a deeper level of understanding that goes beyond the rules for organizing the symbols. Computers can manipulate symbols in remarkably complex ways, but they have no understanding of what they are doing for the same reason that you would have no understanding of Chinese while in the Chinese room.

Your growing knowledge of psychology's history can help put the AI debates about thinking in some perspective, for the problem is not new, but merely an extension of the age-old mind-body (or mind-brain) problem. One of psychology's recurring issues has concerned whether purely mechanical explanations are sufficient for an understanding of human

The Backside of Positivism : The Turing Test

behavior and mental processes. From the time of Descartes' fascination with the hydraulically driven figures in the gardens of French royalty, to the nineteenth-century physiologists who believed that all living function could be reduced to the movements of material objects, to Watson's mechanistic S-R model that likened human functioning to a telephone switchboard, mechanical metaphors for human functioning have been commonplace. It is not likely that the AI debates will resolve the issue.

COGNITIVE PSYCHOLOGY IN PERSPECTIVE

Although some have considered cognitive psychology to be an all-encompassing framework, even a "paradigm," for modern psychology, the movement has also been sharply criticized. Understandably, the most vocal critic was B. F. Skinner (Chapter 11), the leading behaviorist of the second half of the twentieth century. Skinner objected to the creation of hypothetical mental mechanisms (e.g., short-term memory), which all too easily could become reified, he believed. That is, instead of looking for the causes of behavior in the environment and one's learning history, where they belonged (in Skinner's view), the cognitive psychologist turned these hypothetical mechanisms into real, causal entities. Attributing failures of recall to limited short-term memory capacity hardly explains the phenomenon, he argued. Skinner deplored the spread of cognitive ideas throughout the field of psychology, sarcastical-

ly observing that a graph showing the use of the term "cognitive" in psychology's literature would show exponential growth after 1960— "Is there any field of psychology today in which something does not seem to be gained by adding that charming adjective to the occasional noun?" (Skinner, 1987, p. 783).

A second general criticism of cognitive psychology derives from the computer metaphor, with its human-as-machine implication. Such a view ignores significant aspects of human behavior, critics charge, such as emotion and motivation (e.g., Zajonc, 1980), or intentionality (Searle, 1980). Hilgard (1980), referring back to the eighteenth-century tripartite division of mental activities—the cognitive, the affective (emotional), and the conative (motivational/behavioral)—made a similar argument that cognitive psychology addresses only a portion of the whole. A related criticism has been that cognitive psychologists sometimes ignore neurological reality, building models of mental processing that contradict what is known about how the nervous system operates.

Despite the problems, the study of cognitive processes has worked its way into virtually every area of psychological investigation. The pervasiveness of cognitive variables is perhaps an indication of how important such processes have always been to psychology, even when their importance may have been questioned by prominent behaviorists, and how central they are to the very definition of what it means to be human.

SUMMARY

Cognitive Psychology Arrives (Again)

• After World War II, psychologists became increasingly involved in studying mental processes, a topic that had been a central interest for psychology's earliest pioneers. This cognitive psychology movement in America developed gradually dur-

ing the 1950s, 1960s, and 1970s, while behaviorism became a less powerful force. The change was more evolutionary than revolutionary.

• During the period when behaviorism dominated American psychology (1930s and 1940s), some American researchers (e.g., Stroop) still investigated cognitive topics and European psychologists, who never became as enamored of behaviorism as the Americans did, made important contributions to the understanding of mental processes. The Swiss psychologist Jean Piaget, whose genetic epistemology and stage theory of cognitive development eventually became influential in America, is a prime example. Another is England's Frederick Bartlett, who was critical of the laboratory, nonsense-syllable type of memory research being done, and proposed instead that research on memory should emphasize real-life situations. He believed that memory was constructive and was influenced by schemas, that is, one's basic concepts about the phenomenal world. His "war of the ghosts" research showed that memory is affected by schemas unique to one's culture.

- Within psychology, the cognitive movement gained momentum from problems that developed within the behaviorist/associationist tradition. At the Hixon Symposium in 1948, Lashley showed that associationist principles could not explain the problem of serial order, and behaviorism seemed incapable of explaining language behavior.

- Outside of psychology, developments in computer science, information theory, and linguistics contributed to the evolution of cognitive psychology. Researchers began to create models of cognitive processes that used the computer program as a metaphor and emphasized the concept of the individual as an information processor rather than as a responder to stimuli. Chomsky argued that Skinnerian behaviorism was not relevant for the study of language and proposed a nativist account of language development.

- During the decade of the 1950s, several landmark papers and books appeared. These included Miller's paper on the limited capacity of information processing in immediate memory (7±2), Broadbent's research on selective attention, Bruner, Goodnow, and Austin's book on strategies in concept identification, and the book by Miller, Galanter, and Pribram on "plans," which featured the idea of information feedback in the form of TOTE units as a replacement for the reflex arc concept.

- The first major summary of laboratory research in cognitive psychology appeared in 1967 with Neisser's book; the book also produced a self-identification of the field as "cognitive psychology." About a decade later, Neisser questioned cognitive psychology's emphasis on basic laboratory research and in the spirit of Bartlett, called for an increase in research on cognitive processes as they operate in the everyday world to help individuals adapt to their environments (i.e., research having ecological validity).

- Cognitive psychology has spread to other specialty areas within psychology, including developmental, social, personality, and abnormal psychology. In addition, the interdisciplinary field of cognitive science evolved in parallel with cognitive psychology. Cognitive science includes psychology, computer science (e.g., artificial intelligence), linguistics, anthropology, and epistemology. The field of artificial intelligence includes the study of computer simulations of human cognitive processes and the development of expert systems in which the computer acts intelligently. Researchers disagree on the extent to which machine thinking resembles human thinking.

FOR FURTHER READING

Baars, B. J. (1986). *The cognitive revolution in psychology.* New York: Guilford Press.

A detailed description of the cognitive movement, taken from the standpoint that cognitive psychology represents a revolutionary shift away from behaviorism; noteworthy for containing extensive interviews with key figures, including B. F. Skinner, George Miller, Ulric Neisser, and Noam Chomsky.

Bruce, D. (1994). Lashley and the problem of serial order. *American Psychologist, 49,* 93–103.

A highly readable description of Lashley's paper on serial order given at the Hixon Symposium, its impact at the time and later on different audiences; shows that Lashley's paper was not immediately recognized as a breakthrough for cognitive psychology, but its importance was eventually recognized, once cognitive psychology had become more established.

Gardner, H. (1985). *The mind's new science: A history of the cognitive revolution.* New York: Basic Books.

A comprehensive history of cognitive science; includes a great deal of information on developments in psychology, but also documents the history of artificial intelligence and weaves together the various other disciplines (e.g., linguistics, anthropology) that comprise this interdisciplinary field.

Leahey, T. H. (1992). The mythical revolutions of American psychology. *American Psychologist, 47,* 308–318.

A careful description of several models of the criteria necessary for there to be a "revolution" in science, followed by an analysis of why both behaviorism and cognitive psychology, while important developments in psychology's history, cannot be considered revolutionary.

14

LINKING PSYCHOLOGY'S
PAST AND PRESENT

▼

The seats on the train of progress all face backwards: you
can see the past but only guess about the future. Yet a
knowledge of history, although it can never be complete
and fails miserably to foretell the future, has a huge capacity
for adding significance to the understanding of the present.

E. G. Boring, 1963

▼

Preview

This chapter will of necessity be incomplete—the growth of psychology has been exponential
over the past half century and would require its own book just to tell the story in broad outline
(700-page introductory psychology texts barely scratch the surface). The more modest goal for
the chapter will be to highlight some of the important developments that have occurred in the
discipline since the end of World War II, other than the rise of cognitive psychology, which was
considered in the preceding chapter. These changes include increased diversity. Women and
minority groups have found it difficult to make inroads into a field dominated historically by
white males, but some improvements have occurred in the postwar years and especially during
the past 20 years. Other significant changes in psychology over the past half century will be
sketched in the second part of the chapter by linking contemporary trends to earlier events in
psychology's history. The focus will be on increased interest in the relationship between the
brain and behavior, the developing specialty of evolutionary psychology, which "evolved" out of
sociobiology, and the growth of the professional practice of psychology. The chapter closes with
a discussion of whether modern psychology can be considered a unified discipline.

THE GROWTH AND DIVERSITY OF PSYCHOLOGY

One indication of organized psychology's growth over the past 100 years lies in the membership data for its major professional organization, the American Psychological Association. From its origins in G. Stanley Hall's study in 1892 until the mid-1920s, the APA showed steady but unspectacular expansion. The initial 31 charter members rose to about 125 by the turn of the century and to about 375 by the end of World War I (Fernberger, 1932, p. 5). With the creation of the associate member status in 1925, however, the growth curve changed direction, as can be seen in Figure 14.1. After World War II, the total membership stood at approximately 5000, and as Figure 14.2 shows, it has climbed steadily since that time, reaching the 70,000 mark by 1990 (Bulatao, Fulcher, &

Evans, 1992). As the twentieth century closes, APA membership is rapidly approaching 100,000. And the future promises continued growth—psychology is among the most popular majors on campus, new graduate programs appear each year, and applications to graduate school far outnumber available places.

Along with the expansion reflected in APA membership rolls, psychology has also become more diverse over the years. One form of this diversity has been specialization. Psychologists are no longer just psychologists, they are developmental psychologists, social psychologists, industrial psychologists, counseling psychologists, and personality psychologists, among many others. Even these labels are too broad. Developmental psychologists, to take just one example, cannot hope to be knowledgeable about their entire subfield, but must specialize further within it, perhaps by establishing

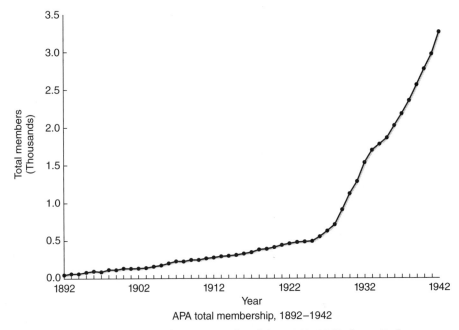

Figure 14.1   **The growth of APA membership, 1892–1942, from Bulatao, Fulcher, & Evans (1992).**

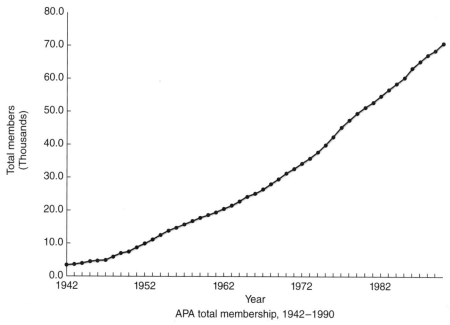

Figure 14.2   The growth of APA membership since 1942, from Bulatao, Fulcher, & Evans (1992).

expertise in infant memory, adolescent peer relations, or reasoning processes in the elderly. A second form of psychology's increased diversity is in various types of persons who enter the field. In the 1990s, psychologists are more likely than ever to be female and/or nonwhite.

WOMEN IN PSYCHOLOGY'S HISTORY

The problems for women in psychology have been touched on earlier. From Chapter 6, you recall the difficulties experienced by such pioneering women as Mary Calkins, Margaret Washburn, and Christine Ladd-Franklin, who were either unable to secure full-time academic positions (Ladd-Franklin) or were limited to teaching at small women's colleges without

graduate programs (Calkins and Washburn). This latter problem actually got worse in the 1920s, when many of these small colleges began replacing female professors with males to "enhance" their prestige (Diehl, 1992). Another long-standing barrier to advancement was that women were excluded from the all-important informal communication network of scientific psychologists, as described in Chapter 7. Although allowing some women into his graduate program at Cornell, E. B. Titchener kept them out of his Experimentalist "club." After Titchener's death in 1927, the group reorganized as the Society of Experimental Psychologists (SEP) and voted to include women, but the de facto obstacles remained. Two women, Washburn and June Downey of Wyoming (who died before attending any meetings), were made charter members of the new group, and Washburn even hosted an SEP meeting at Vassar in 1931.[1] Yet photos of the group in the 1940s and 1950s seldom include female faces, and no other woman was elected until 1958 (Furumoto, 1988). Although relatively small in number, the SEP constituted a closed network that influenced academic hiring and advancement (Goodwin, 1985). Hence, the exclusion of women from the group made it virtually impossible for them to fashion successful scientific careers. Some did, despite the odds, and a good postwar example is one of developmental psychology's most celebrated scientists.

Eleanor Gibson (b. 1910)

In a Rose Garden ceremony in June of 1992, George Bush awarded the National Medal of Science, the highest honor a president can confer on a scientist, to Eleanor Gibson (Figure 14.3). The award was for a lifetime of research on topics ranging from the development of depth perception to the basic processes involved in reading. Only nine other psychologists had earned this award up to that time (Kent, 1992). Gibson is also the person referred to above as the first woman since Downey and Washburn to be elected to the SEP. Today, students recall Gibson best for creating the "visual cliff," used to study depth perception in infants. Her career is a case study in perseverance.

Gibson first became interested in psychology at Smith College, a liberal arts college for women in western Massachusetts, where she learned to run rats in mazes from a student of Harvey Carr and studied psychology's history with a student of E. G. Boring. In her senior year, she took a course from Smith's new German professor, Kurt Koffka, but found the experience less than enthralling—the gestaltist did little more than read notes from his forthcoming book on gestalt psychology (Koffka, 1935). She had better luck in a laboratory course taught by a newly-minted experimental psychologist from Princeton, James Gibson, later to become one of the best-known twentieth-century researchers in perception. Eleanor fell in love with both the lab course and the professor. She remained at Smith for a year after graduation, earned a master's degree, and married her favorite teacher.

Full of enthusiasm for research in psychology, Gibson went to Yale in 1935, eager to work in the primate lab of the famous Robert Yerkes (Chapter 8). There, however, she quickly encountered a world very different from the sheltered one of Smith. She managed with some difficulty to get an appointment to see Yerkes, who seemed curious about why she was there. When she said that she wished to work for him, "[h]e stood up, walked to the door, held it open, and said, 'I have no women in my laboratory'" (Gibson, 1980, p. 246). Although angered and somewhat disillusioned, Gibson stubbornly refused to leave Yale, and eventually managed to convince Clark Hull (Chapter 11) of her abilities and earned a doctorate under his direction in 1938. After a brief return to Smith, she moved to Ithaca, New York, when her husband was hired by Cornell University. Antinepotism rules, a major problem for many women psychologists married to professors, kept her from employment at Cornell, yet she persevered once again. For 16 years, she labored as an unpaid "research associate," earning her keep by winning a series of competitive and prestigious research grants. It was during these years that she created the visual cliff and completed the pioneering stud-

---

[1] Walter Miles of Stanford attended the 1931 Vassar meeting and recorded an interesting comment made by Washburn about Titchener. Miles's diary for April 1, 1931, includes this entry: "Washburn's attitude toward T. He never discovered anything, he did not create any apparatus, or methods, he was simply not an experimenter…. His great points were his learning and his ability to give a lecture." Washburn apparently also believed that part of the reason why Titchener "gave her but little" was that "they were too near the same age" (Miles, 1931).

Figure 14.3   Eleanor Gibson receiving the National Medal of Science in 1992.

ies on depth perception with Richard Walk (e.g., Gibson & Walk, 1960). When Cornell removed its nepotism rules in 1966, Gibson was immediately made a full professor. In 1974, she was named the Susan Linn Sage Endowed Professor of Psychology and while she never actually retired, she was named Professor Emeritus in 1980 (Pick, 1994). Since then she has continued to be an active scholar and as late as 1994, she addressed the question of psychology's future by vigorously arguing for a theory of organism-environmental interaction that was grounded in a developmental approach (Gibson, 1994).

Eleanor Gibson is just one example of a highly talented scientist who faced barriers to advancement simply because she was a woman. The situation improved somewhat in the 1960s, when the women's movement emerged as part of the drive for civil rights. The Civil Rights Act of 1964 prohibited discrimination against women as well as minorities and in 1972, Title IX specifically prohibited gender discrimination in higher education (Russo, 1988). Within the APA, committees on the status of women were formed in the 1960s and 1970s, and in 1973 the APA created the Division for the Psychology of Women (Division 35). Today, women under-

graduate majors in psychology outnumber men by about two to one, and about 60% of doctorates in psychology are awarded to women. Although most faculty continue to be male, changes are beginning to occur—the proportion of women faculty in graduate departments of psychology shifted from one-fifth in the mid-1980s to one-third a decade later ("Sex, Race/Ethnicity Data," 1995).

MINORITIES IN PSYCHOLOGY'S HISTORY

Like women, members of minority groups have been on the outside looking in for most of psychology's history. Unlike the advancement for women, however, significant gains have not been made in the postwar years, and minorities continue to be underrepresented in psychology. In 1991, for example, only 14% of all bachelor's degrees, 11% of master's degrees, and 9% of doctoral degrees were granted to minorities ("Sex, Race/Ethnicity Data," 1995). Of these, about one-half went to African-American students, a quarter to Hispanic students, and the remainder to Asian-Americans and Native Americans. The APA is currently addressing the issue with a Commission on Ethnic Minority

Recruitment, Retention, and Training, and the APA's Board of Educational Affairs has a Task Force on Diversity.

Despite barriers at least as high as those confronting women, minority psychologists have made contributions to psychology's history. We have already seen that displaced European Jewish psychologists such as Wertheimer and Lewin became major figures in American psychology. They did so in the face of an anti-Semitism that, though less virulent than the version found in Nazi Germany, occurred in subtle ways nonetheless. The gestaltists were already well enough known to secure positions, but job searches were not quite so easy for other Jewish psychologists, especially during the Great Depression when all jobs were scarce. As Winston (1996) has shown, for example, letters of recommendation during the 1930s frequently reinforced the stereotype of Jewish persons as being shrewd and calculating, oversensitive to perceived slights, argumentative, clannish, and defensively aggressive. Candidates for academic positions could be doomed by a letter indicating that they possessed these attributes, and their chances were hardly improved if they were praised by saying, in effect, that while they might be Jewish, they were not like a "typical" Jew. In recommending one of his students, for example, Robert Woodworth wrote that "as his name indicates, [he is] a Jew, but I am sure you would find him a very satisfactory colleague...cooperative and eager to fit into the group" (quoted in Winston, 1996, p. 30).

The difficulties faced by Jews paled in comparison to those encountered by African-Americans, however. At least nobody accused Jews of lacking intellectual ability. Blacks, on the other hand, have often had their basic abilities questioned, and this was especially true during psychology's formative years. As seen in Chapter 8, one of the Darwinian legacies was the belief, shared by virtually all of the pioneering mental testers, that intelligence was an inherited trait. It was also widely believed that group differences in intelligence existed, with

white males being inherently superior to other racial groups (and to women). The belief in the intellectual superiority of white males was so strong that it even colored the interpretation of research that might have suggested otherwise. For example, an early study by Bache (1895) comparing the reaction times of whites, blacks, and Native Americans found that whites had the *slowest* overall times. Ignoring the Galtonian idea that reaction time was assumed to be related to mental quickness and therefore to intelligence, the author concluded that the results provided evidence for the mental superiority of whites because it showed that whites, a "higher" human form, could be characterized as "reflective," while the swifter reactions of the more "primitive" blacks and Native Americans showed an immature and intellectually backward impulsiveness. Similarly, in a study comparing 500 white children with a like number of black children, Stetson (1897) found no differences in their ability to memorize poetry. Rather than conclude that the groups were similar in this type of cognitive skill, however, Stetson decided that his study simply showed that memorization was useless as a test of intelligence. In short, strongly held prejudices rendered some scientists immune to data that might have called their beliefs into question.

One consequence of the prejudice against African-Americans was inferior education and reduced opportunities for higher education. On the assumption that education would put ridiculous ideas like "freedom" into their heads, black slaves in the South were barred from formal education by "black codes" in the pre-Civil War years. After the war, conditions improved only marginally. Blacks were segregated into schools that were supposedly separate, but equal, and higher education was limited mostly to whites. Colleges and universities designed for African-Americans began to be created in the second half of the nineteenth century, however, mainly in the South. By 1940, there were more than 100 such schools. They focused on training teachers, who usually returned to their communities to teach in the segregated schools there (Guthrie, 1976).

Psychology, especially as it applied to education, was typically part of the curriculum in the black colleges, but few of these schools offered a concentration in psychology. A 1936 survey on psychology at black colleges by Herman Canady (1901–1970), psychology chair at West Virginia's black college (West Virginia State College at Institute, WV), found that only 14 of the 50 schools surveyed had psychology departments. Of those 14, only four offered majors in psychology (data from Guthrie, 1976, p. 105). Very few laboratory courses were offered and, aside from introductory psychology, the most popular courses were educational, child, social, and adolescent psychology. Thus, few black students had the background necessary to pursue graduate degrees in psychology. Those who did faced further obstacles. They were denied admission to graduate programs in the South and although a handful of graduate programs in the North welcomed them, few could afford to travel that far from home.[2] Consequently, only a handful of African-Americans received advanced degrees during a time when American psychology was growing by leaps and bounds. Between 1920 and 1950, only 31 blacks earned doctorates in psychology, and in the 10 most prestigious psychology departments between 1920 and 1966, only eight of the 3767 earned doctorates were granted to blacks (data from Guthrie, 1976, p. 124).

For the African-American who did manage to persevere and earn an advanced degree, the prospects for employment following graduate school were not bright. About the only opportunity for a black psychologist with an advanced degree was to return to a black college to teach, where conditions typically included a heavy teaching load (18 to 21

hours), minimal salary (often less then $2000 annually), no benefits, and poor research facilities, if any (Guthrie, 1976). Nonetheless, many bright young African-Americans took this path, significantly enhancing the educations of countless black college students. The best known of these pioneers was Francis Sumner.

Francis Sumner (1895–1954)

Sumner was born in Pine Bluff, Arkansas, but his family soon moved east, where he received his early education in New Jersey, Washington, D.C., and Virginia. During his high school years, he was taught at home by his father, who distrusted the quality of Virginia's segregated schools. In 1911, the 16-year-old Sumner was accepted "by examination" into Pennsylvania's Lincoln University, which had been founded in 1854 as the country's first black college. He earned a bachelor's degree in 1915, then a second bachelor's from Clark College, the undergraduate counterpart of G. Stanley Hall's Clark University (both located in the same building on the Worcester campus). He then returned to Lincoln to teach psychology and German, while also completing the requirements for a master's degree. Sumner returned to Clark in 1917 (see Figure 14.4) to study "race psychology" with Hall, financed by a university fellowship and strong moral support from Hall (Hicks & Ridley, 1979). After losing a year to military service in World War I, he earned his doctorate in 1920, the first African-American to complete a Ph.D. in psychology. His dissertation was a critical interpretation of Freudian and Adlerian psychoanalysis, which Hall praised by writing that Sumner had "shown unusual facility in mastering and even pointing out the limitations and defects of the great authorities in the field" (quoted in Guthrie, 1976, p. 182).

---

[2] Although G. Stanley Hall held typical stereotyped views about racial differences in intelligence, he welcomed "exceptionally talented" blacks at Clark University during his tenure there. Between 1915 and 1920, three African-American scholars earned master's degrees and two, Francis Sumner and Thomas Brown, earned doctorates (Guthrie, 1976).

Figure 14.4   Francis Sumner, as a graduate student at Clark University.

Like a handful of other black scholars, Sumner found his opportunities limited to teaching at black colleges, and he spent time at Wilberforce College in Ohio and West Virginia State College before finding his way to Howard University in Washington, DC, in 1928. Sumner remained at Howard as psychology department chair until his untimely death from a heart attack while shoveling snow in the winter of 1954. At Howard he established the country's leading psychology department at a black institution, offering both bachelor's and master's degrees in psychology. An indication of Howard's importance, and by extension Sumner's influence, is that of the 300 African-Americans who held doctorates in 1975, 60 had earned their bachelor's and/or master's degrees at Howard (Bayton, 1975). One of

these psychologists, Kenneth Clark, became the first African-American to be elected APA president (1971). Along with his wife, Mamie Phipps, another student of Sumner's, Clark conducted a series of renowned studies on the negative self-images of black schoolchildren, who were found to prefer white over black dolls (Clark & Clark, 1947). These studies were cited as evidence when the U.S. Supreme Court struck down the concept of separate but equal education and outlawed segregated schools in the landmark *Brown* v. *Board of Education* case of 1954.

As noted earlier, minorities are not well represented in psychology today. Nonetheless, the APA has made some organizational efforts over the years to create a climate of inclusiveness. In 1950, for example, the APA Council passed a resolution that it would only hold its annual meeting in cities free from overt discriminatory practices. The 1957 meeting, for instance, was moved from Miami to New York as a result of this policy (Smith, 1992). The APA also created the Board of Social and Ethical Responsibility during the presidency of Kenneth Clark; it in turn spawned today's Board of Ethnic Minority Affairs. The APA's Minority Fellows Program began awarding financial aid for graduate study in 1974, and in 1987, Division 45, the Society for the Psychological Study of Ethnic Minority Issues, was created.

TRENDS IN CONTEMPORARY PSYCHOLOGY

Chapter 1 included the argument that understanding psychology's present requires knowing something of its past, a point made eloquently by E. G. Boring in this chapter's opening quote. I hope that what you have learned from your history of psychology course and from this book has combined with the knowledge accumulated in other psychology courses to enhance your understanding of psychology's present. This next-to-last segment of the book sketches out three important developments in psychology over the last half century—the accelerated study of the relationship between the brain and behavior, the vigorous return of evolutionary models of behavior, and the increased professionalization of psychological practitioners. To these could be added a fourth, the advent of cognitive psychology, which was described in the previous chapter.

THE BRAIN AND BEHAVIOR

One of psychology's enduring mysteries concerns the relationship between stimulus events that produce physical changes in the body, especially in the nervous system, and the psychological experience of those events. Research psychologists long ago gave up on the idea of solving the mind-body problem through science—it is in essence a philosophical question. Thus, although researchers might be able to specify in extraordinary detail how the operation of certain combinations of neurons in the striate cortex is correlated with the perception of a line at a certain angle, they cannot answer the question: But how does the firing of these neurons actually result in the psychological experience of the tilted line? Recognizing this fundamental limitation, physiological psychologists have concentrated their attention on the search for relationships between physical and mental events by examining the functioning of the brain and nervous system and how the activity of these structures corresponds to experience and behavior.

Chapter 3 sketched the history of attempts to understand the brain, focusing on the past 200 years and ending with Karl Lashley. Lashley, you recall, investigated the localization of function question in the early years of the twentieth century, agreeing with Pierre Flourens, the great French neurologist of a century before, that the brain operates more like an integrated system than a set of structures with different functions. Ironically, Lashley's 1929 conclusions about mass action and equipotentiality had a dampening effect on brain research and encouraged behaviorists to think that the detailed study of conditioning could proceed without concern for the nervous system. Skinner (1938) reinforced the argument, explicitly rejecting the need for physiological explanations of behavior (Hilgard, 1987).

Donald O. Hebb (1904–1985)

Interest in the brain and behavior was rekindled by a student of Lashley's, Donald Hebb, the only Canadian psychologist ever elected to the presidency of the American Psychological Association (Hilgard, 1987). Hebb started slowly, barely graduating from college and being accepted into the graduate program at Montreal's McGill University because of personal connections. At McGill, he encountered two former students of Pavlov[3] and learned the Pavlovian conditioning techniques. Like Pavlov, Hebb wondered about the relationship between brain and behavior, but became skeptical of Pavlov's model of the cortex. After earning his master's degree in 1934, Hebb was encouraged to apply to Chicago and study with Lashley, who was at the height of his reputation. Lashley accepted the young Canadian, and when the mentor moved to Harvard the following year, he took Hebb with him. Hebb completed his doctorate there in 1938. Job prospects were bleak, however, a combination of the lingering effects of the Great Depression and the fact that "[p]hysiological psychology was in its long period of decline, between 1930 and 1950" (Hebb, 1980, p. 287).

Hebb was fortunate enough to land a job as research assistant to McGill's Wilder Penfield, who was looking for someone to study the behavioral effects of brain surgery. Penfield was just beginning his famous research on the surgi-

---

[3] One was Boris Babkin, whose 1949 biography of Pavlov included the description of Pavlov's laboratory that was featured in Chapter 10.

cal treatment of epilepsy, in which some patients reported what appeared to be intact memories during electrical stimulation of the temporal lobe (Penfield & Perot, 1963). This research was also consistent with Lashley's equipotentiality idea—patients' mental capacities did not seem to deteriorate even after the loss of substantial portions of their frontal lobes. Hebb was right in the center of this research and it had a profound effect on him—it "set the main course for all my subsequent work, and I would not have met it anywhere else" (Hebb, 1980, p. 290). From this experience and his earlier research, Hebb came to the general conclusion that human intelligence develops during early childhood and that "[i]njury to the infant brain interferes with that process, but the same injury at maturity does not reverse it" (p. 292). Thus, early childhood experiences were crucial for the kind of cortical development related to intelligence, Hebb believed.

Two fruitful years with Penfield were followed by three years of teaching at Ontario's Queen's University. In 1942, Hebb returned to Lashley, who had just been appointed director of the Yerkes Laboratory of Primate Biology in Florida, and studied primate behavior for five years. In 1947, his career came full circle when he was appointed to a professorship at McGill. Within a year, Hebb was named department chair, and he finished his distinguished career at McGill.

Hebb is best known for his 1949 book, *The Organization of Behavior*, which rekindled interest among American psychologists in the relationship between brain and behavior (Glickman, 1996). From the title, it is clear that the book is more than just a description of nervous system functioning. Rather, Hebb was aiming at a theory that would fully integrate physiology and psychology, not simply reduce the psychological to the physiological. As he later wrote, in criticism of such reductionist thinking, it was "not possible to substitute neurophysiological conceptions for psychological ones, either now or in the future, but it is pos-

sible to maintain liaison (translatability of terms) between the two universes of discourse" (Hebb, 1960, p. 744).

Hebb proposed that cortical organization occurs through the development of what he called "cell assemblies" and "phase sequences." A **cell assembly** is the basic unit, referring to a set of neurons that become associated with each other because they have been activated together by repeated sensory experiences. Hebb (1949) recognized the associationist roots of his construct, writing that the "general idea is an old one, that any two cells or systems of cells that are repeatedly active at the same time will tend to become 'associated,' so that activity in one facilitates activity in the other" (p. 70). Cell assemblies can be triggered by sensory events or by other cell assemblies. **Phase sequences** are higher levels of organization involving the incorporation of several cell assemblies, and for Hebb, they were the physiological equivalent of thinking. Taken together, cell assemblies and phase sequences accounted for the fact that stimuli do not simply produce responses, but are mediated by the brain. You will recognize this as similar to the "O" in the S-O-R formulation of Robert Woodworth (Chapter 7) and the neobehaviorists Tolman and Hull (Chapter 11), but more explicitly physiological.

To account for the effects of experience and hence to provide a physiological account of learning, Hebb proposed that cell assemblies and phase sequences are formed because the repeated stimulation of adjacent cells produces structural changes at the synaptic level. Thus, according to Hebb (1949), "[w]hen an axon of cell A is near enough to excite cell B and repeatedly...takes part in firing it, some growth process or metabolic change takes place in one or both cells such that A's efficiency, as one of the cells firing B, is increased" (p. 62). This idea has come to be called "Hebb's rule," and synapses that change as the result of experience are often called **Hebb synapses**.

Hebb applied his theory to topics ranging from attention to emotion to mental illness, and his small book, combined with such technological advances as the electroencephalograph (EEG) for measuring brain waves, triggered a renewal of interest in the relationship between brain and behavior. The story is much too complex to be described here, but some of the more important developments in the 1950s and 1960s included (a) discovery of reinforcement centers in the brain, by Hebb's students James Olds and Peter Milner (1954); (b) the use of EEG to identify stages of sleep and the discovery of REM sleep by Eugene Aserinsky and Nathaniel Kleitman (1953); (c) the development of the split brain operation as a way to control epilepsy and to examine left and right hemisphere functions by Roger Sperry (1961); and (d) the identification of cortical cells ("feature detectors") that respond to specific events in the visual field by David Hubel and Torsten Wiesel (1963). Sperry, Hubel, and Wiesel all earned Nobel Prizes for their efforts.

In more recent years, the study of the brain-behavior interface has become increasingly interdisciplinary. Thus, just as cognitive science combines several disciplines, "biopsychology," "behavioral neuroscience," "cognitive neuroscience," and "neuropsychology" all refer to evolving specialties that cross disciplinary boundaries and involve graduate training in psychology, biology, and computer science departments.

EVOLUTIONARY PSYCHOLOGY

Chapter 5 told the story of Darwin and his influence during psychology's formative years. One aspect of that influence was the tendency to explain some behaviors with reference to evolutionary mechanisms and, consequently, to take the nature side of the nature-nurture issue. Such explanations were commonplace in the early years of the twentieth century, in the form of "instinct theories" of human behavior (e.g., McDougall, 1908) and, as noted in Chapter 8, in the emphasis on the genetic basis for intelligence. Evolutionary explanations went out of vogue in American psychology during the hey-

day of behaviorism, which produced a shift to the nurture side of the debate. In recent years, however, the balance seems to be shifting again. Much attention is being given to **behavioral genetics**, the study of genetic influences on behavior, and **evolutionary psychology** is a label being heard more and more.

Even during the height of behaviorism's influence, Europeans interested in animal behavior, most notably Konrad Lorenz and Niko Tinbergen (Chapter 7), were studying species-specific behaviors and arguing that even human behavior was often under the control of instinctive forces. In American psychology in the 1950s and 1960s, a renewed awareness of biological influences on learning occurred when researchers realized that not all behaviors could be conditioned equally well—animals seemed best able to learn behaviors that they were biologically prepared to learn (Seligman, 1970). It is now generally recognized that "the behavior of any species cannot be adequately understood...without knowledge of its instinctive patterns, evolutionary history, and ecological niche" (Breland & Breland, 1961, p. 126). Presumably, this statement includes humans.

What is now coming to be called evolutionary psychology derives from the neo-Darwinian theories of naturalist Edmund O. Wilson, whose analysis of the evolutionary basis for social relations in nonhuman species led him to conclude that human societies were likewise strongly influenced by evolutionary forces. Wilson (1975) coined the term **sociobiology** to capture the idea that social behaviors had a biological basis and were the product of natural selection forces. As Wilson (1994) later explained in his autobiography, his basic argument was that humans:

> ...inherit a propensity to acquire behavior and social structures, a propensity that is shared by enough people to be called human nature. The defining traits include a division of labor between the sexes, bonding between parents and children,

heightened altruism toward closest kin, incest avoidance, other forms of ethical behavior, suspicion of strangers, tribalism, dominance orders within groups, male dominance overall, and territorial aggression over limited resources. (p. 332)

Although Wilson recognized that "people have free will and the choice to turn in many directions" (p. 332), he believed that "the channels of psychological development are...cut more deeply by the genes in certain directions than in others" (pp. 332–333). Thus, cultures might vary considerably, but they tend to converge in the direction of "human nature."

As just one example of a sociobiological analysis, consider the concept of **parental investment**, introduced in one of sociobiology's most famous papers, by Robert Trivers (1972). In different species, Trivers argued, males and females have different degrees of investment in the successful production and raising of the next generation. This is obviously important, because continuation of the species requires that offspring survive. In mammals, for example, which include primates and therefore humans, females have greater investment than males, according to Trivers. Offspring grow within the mother's body during gestation and feed from her for a period of time after birth. One consequence of the time constraints involved is that females produce relatively few children. To perpetuate the species, then, females must be careful in their selection of a mate. For male mammals, however, Trivers argued that there is less parental investment. All that is needed is copulation with available females, an act that takes little time for males. The optimal strategy for the male is therefore to mate with as many females as possible, in order to increase the chances that some of the copulations will be successful (i.e., produce offspring). The implications of the parental investment theory for humans are that females will tend to select mature, responsible males who will provide protection during pregnancy and contribute to the successful raising of children, whereas males will tend to select young (i.e., fertile) females; furthermore, males will be more likely to seek multiple partners than females. Trivers made it clear that these broad tendencies were much influenced by culture and that sexual behavior and parenting could not be understood without taking both genetics *and* culture (i.e., both nature and nurture) into account.

Edmund Wilson made the cover of *Time* magazine in 1977 and received the National Medal of Science from President Carter later in the same year, but his theory was also attacked as sexist and racist, and Wilson himself had a pitcher of water dumped on his head while trying to give a talk at a meeting of the American Association for the Advancement of Science in Washington, also in 1977 (Wilson, 1994). From the description of parental investment, it is easy to understand why the discussion became emotional. Feminist critics, for example, charged that sociobiology perpetuated the myth that females were inferior to males and were interested only in having children, excused male infidelity, and ignored evidence of female promiscuity. More generally, Wilson was condemned (unfairly) for ignoring culture and believing that all behavior was tightly controlled by genetic factors.

Sociobiology's intellectual descendant, evolutionary psychology, remains controversial today, for similar reasons, but its message is beginning to spread, even to the level of introductory psychology textbooks (e.g., Gray, 1994; Westen, 1996). Articles and books that reinterpret traditional psychological theory and research in evolutionary terms are also becoming more frequent. For example, a 1996 issue of the journal *Teaching of Psychology* included an article (Gray, 1996) that describes several ways in which evolutionary theory can be incorporated into the teaching of such topics as Piaget's model of cognitive development, Freud's concept of anxiety and defense, and Maslow's hierarchy of needs. And on the research front, evidence is accumulating from the behavioral genetics techniques of twin studies and adoption studies that heredity must be taken into account as an important factor, which influences traits ranging from intelligence (e.g., Bouchard & McGue, 1981) to shyness (e.g., Emde et al., 1992).

PROFESSIONAL PSYCHOLOGY

The APA's reorganization in 1945 expanded the group's purpose beyond the advancement of scientific psychology and into the realm of professional practice and service to society. Almost immediately, those interested in the practice of psychology gained in status and began to have an important influence on the direction taken by the new Association. Among the practitioners were industrial psychologists, school psychologists, counselors, and clinicians. The most visible were the clinical psychologists.

Chapter 12 documented the history of clinical psychology in America, from its origins in Witmer's laboratory-based clinic to the dramatic changes that occurred as a result of the need for mental health services following World War II. The new postwar model of the clinical psychologist, as both diagnostician and therapist, treating clients of all ages, and aspiring to equal status with psychiatrists, required some new thinking about training. The result was an APA committee on graduate training, followed by the Colorado Conference on Graduate Education in Clinical Psychology, held in August of 1949. The committee, chaired by noted clinical psychologist David Shakow, produced a plan that was elaborated and ratified at the Colorado meeting, yielding what came to be known as the "Boulder Model" for clinical training (Hilgard, 1987). It reflected the same theme of combining science and practice that just a few years before had produced the APA's postwar reorganization. Hence, the Boulder model is also referred to as the **scientist-practitioner model**; it required clinicians to have a Ph.D. from a university-affiliated graduate program accredited by the APA, a research-based doctoral dissertation, and a yearlong supervised internship, before being certified to practice.

An alternative to the Boulder model emerged in the 1960s, a training program that placed greater emphasis on professional practice than on research. Virtually identical to a proposal made by Carl Rogers in 1939, this approach emphasized training in diagnostic and therapeutic skills over research productivity, and was distinguished by the awarding of a Psy.D degree (Doctor of Psychology) instead of the traditional Ph.D (Doctor of Philosophy). The first such degree program was created at the University of Illinois in 1968, and the idea spread rapidly. Within a year, the California School of Professional Psychology was created, noteworthy because it was freestanding, unrelated to any university. The Psy.D. gained legitimacy in 1973 after another Colorado conference, this time at Vail, and by 1992 there were at least 40 Psy.D. programs located throughout the United States (Peterson, 1992). Today, although the APA officially considers both the Boulder and the Vail approaches to be appropriate training models for practitioners, and certifies both types of programs, considerable disagreement remains among psychologists over which is to be preferred. Perhaps reflecting psychology's historical identification with science, a 1992 survey of the directors of 138 Ph.D. programs in clinical psychology overwhelmingly endorsed the Boulder model (O'Sullivan & Quevillon, 1992).

Doctoral training programs and internships funded with federal funds quickly proliferated in the postwar years and by the early 1950s, clinical psychologists were becoming the leaders among mental health practitioners. One reason for their success was the creation of new forms of psychotherapy that went beyond traditional Freudian-based approaches. Two prime examples, both described in Chapter 12, were behavior therapy, an outgrowth of behaviorist learning theory, and client-centered therapy, which contributed to the development of humanistic psychology. Reflecting the growth of the movement described in the preceding chapter, cognitive-based therapies also developed, especially after 1960. An example was the "rational-emotive" therapy of Albert Ellis (1973), which is based on the idea that emotional distress results from the way we cognitively interpret the events in our lives. Failure to get a particular job, for example, leads some people to conclude that they are worthless, resulting in depression. The Ellis strategy is to train clients to reinterpret negative events in a more positive fashion.

A major part of the postwar story of clinical psychology has been its increased status in the community of mental health care providers. As you recall from Chapter 12, clinical psychologists prior to World War II had relatively low status among health care professionals and were often under the direct supervision of psychiatrists. Since the war, however, organized psychiatry's hegemony has gradually diminished. Over the past half century, sometimes after intense legal battles, clinical psychologists have gained the rights to (a) admit and release patients from mental hospitals, (b) serve as expert witnesses in court (e.g., in insanity cases), and (c) receive third-party payments from insurance companies. At present, organized psychology and psychiatry are skirmishing over prescription privileges, and there is every indication that before too long, psychiatrists will not be the only ones writing psychopharmacological prescriptions (Wiggins, 1994).

PSYCHOLOGY OR PSYCHOLOGIES?

Clearly, psychology has shown enormous growth and increased specialization during the last half of the twentieth century; it is worth considering whether the field can be said to be unified in any way. At the end of the twentieth century, is there a field of psychology or are there multiple psychologies?

First, the question implies that psychology was once unified, yet it is unclear if psychology has ever been a coherent discipline. It may have approached unity in its early years, when it was trying to forge an identity separate from physiology and philosophy, but it is evident that strong disagreements existed even then. The conflicts between Titchener and others over psychology's very definition illustrate the point, as do the long-standing squabbles within the APA between various constituencies. As was discussed in Chapter 12, applied psychologists were dissatisfied with the APA in the two decades prior to World War II, but the 1945 reorganization made the APA more attractive to them. The wartime spirit of cooperation that reshaped the APA soon dissipated, however, and conflicts developed between those who wanted the APA to retain its traditional role as the promoter of scientific psychology and those who thought of the organization as a promoter of the applied practice of psychology. Frustration among scientific psychologists produced several attempts to further reorganize the APA, including a major one in the mid-1980s. When it failed, many academician/scientists left the APA, believing that the organization was becoming dominated by issues related to the professional practice of psychology (e.g., prescription privileges). They formed a new organization in 1988, the American Psychological Society (APS), devoted to enhancing and promoting scientific research in psychology. By 1996, this vigorous new group could claim close to 16,000 members, a lively annual convention, and three journals. Organizationally, at least, psychology at the close of the twentieth century seems to be characterized more by disunity than unity.

As for modern psychology as an intellectual discipline, few commentators seem willing to consider it a unified field, other than in the institutional sense that most psychologists are trained in "departments of psychology" (Hilgard, 1987). When addressing the issue at an APA symposium celebrating the centennial of Wundt's laboratory in 1979, George Miller, trained in the traditional experimental psychology of E. G. Boring, "discovered several other psychologies, all claiming proprietary rights to the label, all competing for disciples, and each contemptuous of the others. In short, I discovered that psychology is an intellectual zoo" (Miller, 1992, p. 40). Some understanding of the range of species in this zoo can be achieved by examining the 49 divisions of the APA. Here is just a sample:

3 Experimental Psychology

7 Developmental Psychology

10 Industrial/Organizational Psychology

17 Counseling Psychology

19 Military Psychology

22 Rehabilitation Psychology

25 Experimental Analysis

26 History of Psychology

28 Psychopharmacology

30 Psychological Hypnosis

36 Psychology of Religion

38 Health Psychology

Many psychologists belong to more than one division, but it is clear that widely divergent interests are represented under the APA's broad umbrella. Also, some of the experimental psychology areas represented by the APS extend the range of specialties even further. It is difficult to imagine a neuropsychologist studying the effects of neurotransmitter X on memory, a developmental psychologist studying parallel play in children, an industrial psychologist developing a performance evaluation procedure, and a counselor in a rape crisis center having much in common.

Perhaps it is most reasonable to assume that psychology is not a single discipline but a collection of them. One of psychology's major theoreticians, Sigmund Koch, argued this point for years, recommending that the term "psychology" be replaced with the more pluralistic label of "psychological studies" (Koch, 1993). He viewed this as a historical process similar to that found in other sciences—biology, for instance, encompasses a wide range of "biological studies" (e.g., botany, zoology). Similarly, memory researcher and former APS president Gordon Bower, in an APA symposium on "The Fragmentation of Psychology," suggested that a more positive connotation results from labeling the phenomenon "specialization" rather than "fragmentation" (Bower, 1993). Although the term "psychology" has not been replaced with "psychological studies," most psychologists would agree with Koch's and Bower's general point that psychology today is really a plurality of subdisciplines, each a specialty in its own right. Bower used the metaphor of a growing tree to make his point, likening the growth and diversity of psychology to the growth process of a tree, with age producing increased branching. He compared the individual psychological scientist to a "small bug feeding on a succulent leaf at one end of a very tiny branch and perhaps talking to the other bugs feeding on the same leaf" (p. 905).

If there is any sense of a unifying force in modern psychology, other than the institutional one deriving from the academic category of "psychology department," one could argue that it derives from psychology's history. Regardless of one's modern specialty, there are common origins (to follow the tree metaphor, one trunk and one root system) and familiar themes, many of which have been discussed in the preceding pages. I hope that what you have read in those pages will entice you to learn more about what unites all psychologists and will deepen your understanding of psychology's rich heritage.

SUMMARY

The Growth and Diversity of Psychology

- Psychology has shown vigorous growth during its 100-plus years of existence as an independent discipline, and as it has grown, the interests of psychologists have become more specialized. Throughout most of its history, leading psychologists were white and male, a situation that is now changing, especially as more women enter the field. Although women were excluded from psychology's inner circles throughout most of the twentieth century, some made important contributions. Eleanor Gibson is a prime postwar example. She overcame negative stereotypes of "woman-as-scientist" and became a leading developmental psychologist, known for her research on depth perception (visual cliff research) and reading.

- Minority groups, including Jews and African-Americans, have also faced discrimination throughout psychology's history. Blacks in particular had to confront the prejudices deriving from the early twentieth-century belief in the inherited racial superiority of white males and the social policy of separate but (not really) equal schools. Black scholars found it virtually impossible to find adequate graduate training and if they did manage to complete a doctorate in psychology, their employment opportunities tended to be limited to teaching in black colleges.

- Francis Sumner was the first African-American to earn a doctorate in psychology; he studied with G. Stanley Hall at Clark University. As head of the psychology department at Howard, he helped turn the university into one of the country's most prominent institutions.

Trends in Contemporary Psychology

- During the second half of the twentieth century, there has been an acceleration of interest in studying the brain-behavior relationship. Interest was sparked by technological breakthroughs (e.g., EEG), but especially by the research and theoriz-

ing of Donald Hebb. Hebb's model of the brain centered on the cell assembly, an interrelated combination of associated neurons, and the phase sequence, an organization of cell assemblies and the neurological equivalent of thinking. Hebb synapses are synapses that have undergone structural change as a result of some learning process.

- A second trend has been an increase in the use of evolutionary thinking. This began as sociobiology, Edmund Wilson's theory about the evolutionary and biological basis for social behavior. Evolutionary psychology begins with the assumption that human behaviors reflect the outcome of natural selection processes; these behaviors can be studied by examining how they help the individual adapt to the environment.

- Third, the professional practice of psychology has grown considerably since the end of World War II. Clinical psychologists are trained primarily by the Boulder, or scientist-practitioner model, which emphasizes an integration of diagnostic, therapeutic, and research skills, and leads to a Ph.D. More recently, a Vail model has emerged, which emphasizes professional practice over research and leads to a Psy.D. degree. Practitioners and academician/scientists have often been at odds in psychology's institutional history, the most recent outcome being the creation of the American Psychological Society (APS) by the latter group.

Psychology or Psychologies?

- Psychology in the late twentieth century is not a unified discipline, and with its recurring debates over fundamental issues, it may never have been one. Modern psychology is marked by increased specialization, and it might be more appropriate to replace the idea of a single field of psychology with Koch's concept of there being a set of psychological studies. One unifying force in psychology lies in the discipline's history, however.

FOR FURTHER READING

GLICKMAN, S. E. (1996). Donald Olding Hebb: Returning the nervous system to psychology. In G. A. Kimble, C. A. Bonneau, & M. Wertheimer (Eds.) *Portraits of pioneers in psychology. Volume II* (pp. 227–244). Washington, DC: American Psychological Association.

An informative biographical chapter that portrays not just the events in Hebb's early career, but the character of the man as well; includes interesting narrative on Hebb's relationship with Lashley, who discouraged Hebb from writing his 1949 book, then apparently took credit for some of Hebb's ideas. (The book also includes chapters on Fechner, Dix, Dewey, Witmer, Yerkes, and Gilbreth, among others.)

GUTHRIE, R. V. (1976). *Even the rat was white: A historical view of psychology.* New York: Harper & Row.

A brief volume that documents the nineteenth- and early twentieth-century research on psychology and race, including chapters on early research comparing the performance of blacks and whites on numerous measuring scales and the effects of eugenic-based legislation; includes chapter-length biographical information on Sumner, and briefer sketches of the contributions of several other African-American psychologists (e.g., Herman Canady, the Clarks).

WILSON, E. O. (1994). *Naturalist.* New York: Warner Books.

An eloquent and candid scientific autobiography by sociobiology's founder; beautifully portrays Wilson's love of nature and his passion for science.

WINSTON, A. S. (1996). "As his name indicates": R. S. Woodworth's letters of reference and employment for Jewish psychologists in the 1930s. *Journal of the History of the Behavioral Sciences, 32,* 30–43.

A close analysis of Robert Woodworth's letters of recommendation on behalf of Jewish psychologists, set in the context of exclusionary hiring practices in academia and elsewhere, especially during the 1930s; avoids the simplistic presentism of condemning Woodworth for anti-Semitism, using the letters to illustrate what was taken for granted in non-Jewish society at the time.

▶ REFERENCES

ADAMS, G. (1934, January). The rise and fall of psychology. *The Atlantic Monthly*, 82–92.

ANASTASI, A. (1992). A century of psychological testing: Origins, problems, and progress. In T. K. Fagan & G. R. VandenBos (Eds.), *Exploring applied psychology: Origins and critical analyses* (pp. 13–36). Washington, DC: American Psychological Association.

ANDERSON, J. R. (1990). *Cognitive psychology and its implications* (3rd ed.). New York: Freeman.

ANGELL, J. R. (1904). *Psychology.* New York: Holt.

ANGELL, J. R. (1948). The province of functional psychology. In W. Dennis (Ed.), *Readings in the history of psychology* (pp. 439–456). New York: Appleton-Century-Crofts. (Original article published 1907)

APPLEBY, J., HUNT, L., & JACOB, M. (1994). *Telling the truth about history.* New York: W. W. Norton.

ASCH, S. E. (1968). Wolfgang Köhler: 1887–1967. *American Journal of Psychology, 81,* 110–119.

ASERINSKY, E., & KLEITMAN, N. (1953). Regularly occurring periods of eye motility and concomitant phenomena during sleep. *Science, 118,* 273–274.

ASH, M. G. (1985). Gestalt psychology: Origins in Germany and reception in the United States. In C. E. Buxton (Ed.), *Points of view in the modern history of psychology* (pp. 295–344). New York: Academic Press.

ASH, M. G. (1992). Cultural contexts and scientific change in psychology: Kurt Lewin in Iowa. *American Psychologist, 47,* 198–207.

ATKINSON, R. C., & SHIFFRIN, R. M. (1968). Human memory: A proposed system and its control processes. In K. W. Spence & J. T. Spence (Eds.), *The psychology of learning and motivation: Advances in research and theory* (pp. 89–195). New York: Academic Press.

AVERILL, L. A. (1982). Recollections of Clark's G. Stanley Hall. *Journal of the History of the Behavioral Sciences, 18,* 341–346.

BAARS, B. J. (1986). *The cognitive revolution in psychology.* New York: Guilford Press.

BABKIN, B. P. (1949). *Pavlov: A biography.* Chicago: University of Chicago Press.

BACHE, R. M. (1895). Reaction time with reference to race. *Psychological Review, 2,* 475–486.

BADDELEY, A. (1990). *Human memory: Theory and practice.* Boston: Allyn & Bacon.

BAHRICK, H. P. (1984). Semantic memory content in permastore: 50 years of memory for Spanish learned in school. *Journal of Experimental Psychology: General, 113,* 1–29.

BAKAN, D. (1966). The influence of phrenology on American psychology. *Journal of the History of the Behavioral Sciences, 2,* 200–220.

BAKER, D. B. (1988). The psychology of Lightner Witmer. *Professional School Psychology, 3,* 109–121.

BALANCE, W. D. G., & BRINGMANN, W. G. (1987). Fechner's mysterious malady. *History of Psychology Newsletter, 19* (1,2), 36–47.

BALDWIN, J. M. (1913). *History of psychology: A sketch and an interpretation.* New York: Putnam.

BANDURA, A. (1977). *Social learning theory.* Englewood Cliffs, NJ: Prentice-Hall.

BANDURA, A. (1986). *Social foundations of thought and action: A social cognitive theory.* Englewood Cliffs, NJ: Prentice-Hall.

BANDURA, A., ROSS, D., & ROSS, S. A. (1963). Imitation of film-mediated aggressive models. *Journal of Abnormal and Social Psychology, 66*, 3–11.

BARKER, R., DEMBO, T., & LEWIN, K. (1941). Frustration and regression: An experiment with young children. *University of Iowa Studies in Child Welfare, 18*, No. 1.

BARONE, D. F. (1996). John Dewey: Psychologist, philosopher, and reformer. In G. A. Kimble, C. A. Bonneau, and M. Wertheimer (Eds.), *Portraits of pioneers in psychology, Volume II* (pp. 47–61). Washington, DC: American Psychological Association.

BARTLETT, F. C. (1958). *Thinking: An experimental and social study.* London: Allen & Unwim.

BARTLETT, F. C. (1967). *Remembering: A study in experimental and social psychology.* Cambridge, UK: Cambridge University Press. (Original work published 1932)

BAYTON, J. A. (1975). Francis Sumner, Max Meenes, and the training of black psychologists. *American Psychologist, 30*, 185–186.

BECK, A. T. (1967). *Depression: Causes and treatment.* Philadelphia: University of Pennsylvania Press.

BECK, A. T. (1979). *Cognitive therapy and the emotional disorders.* Cleveland, OH: Meridian Press.

BEERS, C. W. (1908). *A mind that found itself.* New York: Longmans Green.

BELL, C. (1965). Bell on the specificity of sensory nerves, 1811. In R. J. Herrnstein & E. G. Boring (Eds.), *A sourcebook in the history of psychology* (pp. 23–26). Cambridge, MA: Harvard University Press. (Original work published 1811)

BELL, L. V. (1980). *Treating the mentally ill: From colonial times to the present.* New York: Praeger Publishers.

BENJAMIN, L. T., JR. (1993). *A history of psychology in letters.* Dubuque, IA: Brown & Benchmark.

BENJAMIN, L. T., JR. (1996). Harry Hollingworth: Portrait of a generalist. In G. A. Kimble, C. A. Bonneau, & M. Wertheimer (Eds.), *Portraits of pioneers in psychology. Vol. II* (pp. 119–135). Washington, DC: American Psychological Association.

BENJAMIN, L. T., JR., DURKIN, M., LINK, M., VESTAL, M., & ACCORD, J. (1992). Wundt's American doctoral students. *American Psychologist, 47*, 123–131.

BENJAMIN, L. T., JR., ROGERS, A. M., & ROSENBAUM, A. (1991). Coca-Cola, caffeine, and mental deficiency: Harry Hollingworth and the Chattanooga trial. *Journal of the History of the Behavioral Sciences, 27*, 42–55.

BERGIN, A. E. (1971). The evaluation of therapeutic outcomes. In A. E. Bergin & S. L. Garfield (Eds.), *Handbook of psychotherapy and behavior change: An empirical analysis.* New York: John Wiley & Sons.

BERKELEY, G. (1948). *An essay towards a new theory of vision.* In A. A. Luce & T. E. Jessup (Eds.), *The works of George Berkeley, Bishop of Cloyne. Vol. 1.* London: Thomas Nelson & Sons. (Original work published 1709)

BERKELEY, G. (1957). *Treatise concerning the principles of human knowledge.* Indianapolis: Bobbs-Merrill. (Original work published 1710)

BINET, A., & HENRI, V. (1965). Alfred Binet (1857–1911) and Victor Henri (1872–1940) on the psychology of individual differences. In R. J. Herrnstein & E. G. Boring (Eds.), *A sourcebook in the history of psychology* (pp. 428–433). Cambridge, MA: Harvard University Press. (Original work published 1895)

BINGHAM, W. V. (1952). Walter Van Dyke Bingham. In E. G. Boring, H. S. Langfeld, H. Werner, & R. M. Yerkes (Eds.), *A history of psychology in autobiography. Vol. 4* (pp. 1–26). Worcester, MA: Clark University Press.

BJORK, D. W. (1983). *The compromised scientist: William James in the development of American psychology.* New York: Columbia University Press.

BJORK, D. W. (1993). *B. F. Skinner: A life.* New York: Basic Books.

BLODGETT, H. C. (1929). The effect of the introduction of reward upon the maze performance of rats. *University of California Publications in Psychology, 4*, 113–134.

BLUMENTHAL, A. L. (1975). A reappraisal of Wilhelm Wundt. *American Psychologist, 30*, 1081–1088.

BLUMENTHAL, A. L. (1980). Wilhelm Wundt and early American psychology: A clash of cultures. In R. W. Reiber & K. Salzinger (Eds.), *Psychology: Theoretical-historical perspectives* (pp. 25–42). New York: Academic Press.

BOAKES, R. (1984). *From Darwin to behaviourism: Psychology and the minds of animals.* New York: Cambridge University Press.

BOORSTIN, D. J. (1971). *Democracy and its discontents: Reflections on everyday America.* New York: Random House.

BOORSTIN, D. J. (1983). *The discoverers.* New York: Vintage Books.

BORING, E. G. (1929). *A history of experimental psychology.* New York: Century.

BORING, E. G. (1942). *Sensation and perception in the history of experimental psychology.* New York: Appleton-Century-Crofts.

BORING, E. G. (1950). *A history of experimental psychology* (2nd ed.). Englewood Cliffs, NJ: Prentice-Hall.

BORING, E. G. (1950). The influence of evolutionary theory upon American psychological thought. In R. I. Watson & D. T. Campbell (Eds.), *History, psychology, and science: Selected papers by Edwin G. Boring, Harvard University* (pp. 159–184). New York: John Wiley.

BORING, E. G. (1961). *Psychologist at large: An autobiography and selected essays.* New York: Basic Books.

BORING, E. G. (1961). Edward Bradford Titchener, 1867–1927. In E. G. Boring (Ed.), *Psychologist at large: An autobiography and selected essays* (pp. 246–265). New York: Basic Books. (Original work published 1927)

BORING, E. G. (1963a). Eponym as placebo. In R. I. Watson & D. T. Campbell (Eds.), *History, psychology, and science: Selected papers by Edwin G. Boring, Harvard University* (pp. 5–25). New York: John Wiley.

BORING, E. G. (1963b). Fechner: Inadvertent founder of psychophysics. In R. I. Watson & D. T. Campbell (Eds.), *History, psychology, and science: Selected papers by Edwin G. Boring, Harvard University* (pp. 126–131). New York: John Wiley.

BORING, E. G. (1967). Titchener's Experimentalists. *Journal of the History of the Behavioral Sciences, 3*, 315–325.

BORING, E. G., LANGFELD, H. S., & WELD, H. P. (1939). *Introduction to psychology*. New York: John Wiley.

BOUCHARD, T. J. JR., & McGUE, M. (1981). Familial studies of intelligence. *Science, 212*, 1055–1059.

BOWER, G. H. (1993). The fragmentation of psychology? *American Psychologist, 48*, 905–907.

BRAINERD, C. J. (1996). Piaget: A centennial celebration. *Psychological Science, 7*, 191–195.

BREGMAN, E. O. (1934). An attempt to modify the emotional attitudes of infants by the conditioned response technique. *Journal of Genetic Psychology, 45*, 169–198.

BRELAND, K., & BRELAND, M. (1961). The misbehavior of organisms. *American Psychologist, 16*, 681–684.

BREUER, J., & FREUD, S. (1955). *Studies on hysteria*. New York: Basic Books. (Original work published 1895)

BRIDGMAN, P. W. (1927). *The logic of modern physics*. New York: Macmillan.

BRIGHAM, C. C. (1923). *A study of American intelligence*. Princeton, NJ: Princeton University Press.

BRINGMANN, W. G., BALANCE, W. D. G., & EVANS, R. B. (1975). Wilhelm Wundt 1832–1920: A brief biographical sketch. *Journal of the History of the Behavioral Sciences, 11*, 287–297.

BRINGMANN, W. G., BRINGMANN, N. J., & BALANCE, W. D. G. (1980). Wilhelm Maximilian Wundt 1832–1920: The formative years. In W. G. Bringmann & R. D. Tweney (Eds.), *Wundt studies: A centennial collection* (pp. 13–32). Toronto: C. J. Hogrefe.

BRINGMANN, W. G., BRINGMANN, N. J., & UNGERER, G. A. (1980). The establishment of Wundt's laboratory: An archival and documentary study. In W. G. Bringmann & R. D. Tweney (Eds.), *Wundt studies: A centennial collection* (pp. 123–157). Toronto: C. J. Hogrefe.

BROADBENT, D. E. (1980). Donald E. Broadbent. In G. Lindsey (Ed.), *A history of psychology in autobiography. Vol. 7* (pp. 39–73). San Francisco: Freeman.

BROADBENT, D. E. (1958). *Perception and communication.* London: Pergamon Press.

BROCA, P. (1965). Paul Broca (1824–1880) on the speech center, 1861. In R. J. Herrnstein & E. G. Boring (Eds.), *A sourcebook in the history of psychology* (pp. 223–229). Cambridge, MA: Harvard University Press. (Original work published 1861)

BROWN, R. (1973). *A first language: The early stages.* Cambridge, MA: Harvard University Press.

BROWN, R., & McNEILL, D. (1966). The tip of the tongue phenomenon. *Journal of Verbal Learning and Verbal Behavior, 5*, 325–327.

BROWNE, J. (1995). *Charles Darwin: A biography. Vol. 1. Voyaging.* New York: Knopf.

BROZEK, J., WATSON, R. I., & ROSS, B. (1970). A summer institute on the history of psychology: Part II. *Journal of the History of the Behavioral Sciences, 6*, 25–35.

BRUCE, D. B. (1986). Lashley's shift from bacteriology to neuropsychology, 1910–1917, and the influence of Jennings, Watson, and Franz. *Journal of the History of the Behavioral Sciences, 22*, 27–44.

BRUCE, D. B. (1991). Integrations of Lashley. In G. A. Kimble, M. Wertheimer, & C. L. White (Eds.), *Portraits of pioneers in psychology* (pp. 306–323). Washington, DC: American Psychological Association.

BRUCE, D. B. (1994). Lashley and the problem of serial order. *American Psychologist, 49*, 93–103.

BRUNER, J. S. (1988). Founding the Center for Cognitive Studies. In W. Hirst (Ed.), *The making of cognitive science: Essays in honor of George A. Miller* (pp. 90–99). New York: Cambridge University Press.

BRUNER, J. S., GOODNOW, J. J., & AUSTIN, G. A. (1956). *A study of thinking.* New York: John Wiley.

BUCKLEY, K. W. (1989). *Mechanical man: John Broadus Watson and the beginnings of behaviorism.* New York: Guilford Press.

BULATAO, E. Q., FULCHER, R., & EVANS, R. B. (1992). Appendix: Statistical data on the American Psychological Association. In R. B. Evans, V. S. Sexton, & T. C. Cadwallader (Eds.), *The American Psychological Association: A historical perspective* (pp. 391–394). Washington, DC: American Psychological Association.

BURNHAM, J. C. (1972). Thorndike's puzzle boxes. *Journal of the History of the Behavioral Sciences, 8*, 159–167.

CALKINS, M. C. (1894). Association I. *Psychological Review, 1*, 476–483.

CALKINS, M. C. (1896). Association II. *Psychological Review, 3*, 32–49.

CALKINS, M. W. (1906). A reconciliation between structural and functional psychology. *Psychological Review, 13*, 61–81.

CALKINS, M. W. (1907). *The persistent problems of philosophy.* New York: Macmillan.

CALKINS, M. W. (1913). Psychology and the behaviorist. *Psychological Bulletin, 10*, 288–291.

CALKINS, M. C. (1930). Mary Whiton Calkins. In C. Murchison (Ed.), *A history of psychology in autobiography, Vol. 1* (pp. 31–62). Worcester, MA: Clark University Press.

CAMFIELD, T. M. (1973). The professionalization of American psychology, 1870–1917. *Journal of the History of the Behavioral Sciences, 9*, 66–75.

CAPSHEW, J. H. (1996). Engineering behavior: Project Pigeon, World War II, and the conditioning of B. F. Skinner. In L. D. Smith & W. R. Woodward (Eds.), *B. F. Skinner and behaviorism in American culture* (pp. 128–150). Bethlehem, PA: Lehigh University Press.

CAPSHEW, J. H., & HEARST, E. (1980). Psychology at Indiana University: From Bryan to Skinner. *Psychological Record, 30*, 319–342.

CARMICHAEL, L. (1957). Robert Mearns Yerkes, 1876–1956. *Psychological Review, 64*, 1–7.

CARR, H. A. (1925). *Psychology: A study of mental activity.* New York: Longmans, Green.

CARR, H. A. (1935). *An introduction to space perception.* New York: Longmans, Green.

CARR, H. A., & WATSON, J. B. (1908). Orientation in the white rat. *Journal of Comparative Neurology and Psychology, 18*, 27–44.

CASHMAN, S. D. (1993). *America in the gilded age* (3rd ed.). New York: New York University Press.

CATTELL, J. M. (1885). The influence of the intensity of the stimulus on the length of the reaction time. *Brain, 8*, 512–515.

CATTELL, J. M. (1886). The time it takes to see and name objects. *Mind, 11*, 63–65.

CATTELL, J. M. (1895). Report of the Secretary and Treasurer for 1894. *Psychological Review, 2*, 149–152.

CATTELL, J. M. (1948). Mental tests and measurements. In W. Dennis (Ed.), *Readings in the history of psychology* (pp. 347–354). New York: Appleton-Century-Crofts. (Original work published 1890)

CHERRY, E. C. (1953). Some experiments on the recognition of speech with one and with two ears. *Journal of the Acoustical Society of America, 25*, 975–979.

CHOMSKY, N. (1959). Review of Skinner's *Verbal Behavior. Language, 35*, 26–58.

CHOMSKY, N. (1966). *Cartesian linguistics.* New York: Harper & Row.

CLARK, K., & CLARK, M. (1947). Racial identification and racial preferences in Negro children. In T. M. Newcomb & E. L. Hartley (Eds.), *Readings in social psychology* (pp. 169–178). New York: Holt.

COHEN, E. (1991, Fall). Psychology's attic. *Akron, 6*(1), 12–19.

COHEN, I. B. (1995). *Science and the founding fathers.* New York: W. W. Norton.

COLEMAN, S. R. (1996). Skinner's progress during the 1930s: Reflexes, operants, and apparatuses. In L. D. Smith & W. R. Woodward (Eds.), *B. F. Skinner and behaviorism in American culture* (pp. 109–127). Bethlehem, PA: Lehigh University Press.

COLLINS, A. (1977). Why cognitive science? *Cognitive Science, 1*, 1–2.

COLLINS, J. (1931). Lightner Witmer: A biographical sketch. In R. A. Brotemarkle (Ed.), *Clinical psychology: Studies in honor of Lightner Witmer* (pp. 3–9). Philadelphia, University of Pennsylvania Press.

COLP, R., JR. (1986). "Confessing a murder:" Darwin's first revelations about transmutation. *Isis, 77*, 9–32.

COON, D. J. (1992). Testing the limits of sense and science: American experimental psychologists combat spiritualism, 1880–1920. *American Psychologist, 47*, 143–151.

COON, D. J. (1994). "Not a creature of reason": The alleged impact of Watsonian behaviorism on advertising in the 1920s. In J. T. Todd & E. K. Morris (Eds.), *Modern perspectives on John B. Watson and classical behaviorism* (pp. 37–63). Westport, CT: Greenwood Press.

COSTALL, A. (1993). How Lloyd Morgan's Canon backfired. *Journal of the History of the Behavioral Sciences, 29*, 113–122.

COTTINGHAM, J. (1986). *Descartes.* New York: Basil Blackwell.

CRAVENS, H. (1992). A scientific project locked in time: The Terman genetic studies of genius, 1920s–1950s. *American Psychologist, 47*, 183–189.

CROCE, P. J. (1995). *Science and religion in the era of William James: Eclipse of certainty, 1820–1880.* Chapel Hill: University of North Carolina Press.

CRONBACH, L. J. (1957). The two disciplines of scientific psychology. *American Psychologist, 12*, 671–684.

CRONBACH, L. J., HASTORF, A. H., HILGARD, E. R., & MACCOBY, E. E. (1990). Robert R. Sears (1908–1989). *American Psychologist, 45*, 663–664.

CRUTCHFIELD, R. S. (1961). Edward Chace Tolman: 1886–1959. *American Journal of Psychology, 74*, 135–141.

DALLENBACH, K. M. (1913). The measurement of attention. *American Journal of Psychology, 24*, 465–507.

DANZIGER, K. (1980). The history of introspection reconsidered. *Journal of the History of the Behavioral Sciences, 16*, 241–262.

DARWIN, C. (1839). *Journal of researches into the geology and natural history of the various countries visited by the H.M.S. Beagle.* London: Henry Colburn.

DARWIN, C. (1871). *The descent of man, and selection in relation to sex*. London: Murray.

DARWIN, C. (1872). *The expression of the emotions in man and animals*. London: Murray.

DARWIN, C. (1877) A biographical sketch of an infant. *Mind, 2*, 285–294.

DARWIN, C. (1958). Autobiography. In F. Darwin (Ed.), *The autobiography of Charles Darwin and selected letters* (pp. 5–58). New York: Dover.

DARWIN, C. (1958). *On the origin of species by means of natural selection, or the preservation of favoured races in the struggle for life*. New York: Mentor Books. (Original work published 1859)

DAVIDSON, J. W., & LYTLE, M. H. (1982). *After the fact: The art of historical detection*. New York: Knopf.

DECKER, H. S. (1975). "The Interpretation of Dreams": Early reception by the educated German public. *Journal of the History of the Behavioral Sciences, 11*, 129–141.

DEGLER, C. N. (1991). *In search of human nature: The decline and revival of Darwinism in American social thought*. New York: Oxford University Press.

DENNETT, D. C. (1995). *Darwin's dangerous idea: Evolution and the meanings of life*. New York: Simon & Schuster.

DENNIS, P. M. (1984). The Edison questionnaire. *Journal of the History of the Behavioral Sciences, 20*, 23–37.

DENNIS, W. (Ed.). (1948). *Readings in the history of psychology*. New York: Appleton-Century-Crofts.

DENNY-BROWN, D. (1952). Charles Scott Sherrington: 1857–1952. *American Journal of Psychology, 65*, 474–477.

DESCARTES, R. (1960). *Discourse on method* (L. J. Lafleur, Trans.). Indianapolis: Bobbs-Merrill. (Original work published 1637)

DESCARTES, R. (1969). *Passions of the soul*. In E. S. Haldane & G. R. T. Ross (Trans.) *The philosophical works of Descartes, Volume I* (pp. 329–427). New York: Cambridge University Press. (Original work published 1649)

DESMOND, A., & MOORE, J. (1991). *Darwin: The life of a tormented evolutionist*. New York: W. W. Norton.

DEWEY, J. (1886). *Psychology*. New York: Harper.

DEWEY, J. (1899). *The school and society*. Chicago: University of Chicago Press.

DEWEY, J. (1900). Psychology and social practice. *Psychological Review, 7*, 105–124.

DEWEY, J. (1948). The reflex arc concept in psychology. In W. Dennis (Ed.), *Readings in the history of psychology* (pp. 355–365). New York: Appleton-Century-Crofts. (Original work published 1896)

DEWSBURY, D. A. (1984). *Comparative psychology in the twentieth century*. Stroudsburg, PA: Hutchinson Ross.

DEWSBURY, D. A. (1990). Early interactions between animal psychologists and animal activists and the founding of the APA committee on precautions in animal experimentation. *American Psychologist, 45*, 315–327.

DEWSBURY, D. A. (1990). Whither the introductory course in the history of psychology? *Journal of the History of the Behavioral Sciences, 26*, 371–377.

DEWSBURY, D. A. (1992). Triumph and tribulation in the history of comparative psychology. *Journal of Comparative Psychology, 106*, 3–19.

DEWSBURY, D. A. (1994). John B. Watson: Profile of a comparative psychologist and proto-ethologist. In J. T. Todd & E. K. Morris (Eds.), *Modern perspectives on John B. Watson and classical behaviorism* (pp. 141–144). Westport, CT: Greenwood Press.

DEWSBURY, D. A. (1996). Robert M. Yerkes: A psychobiologist with a plan. In G. A. Kimble, C. A. Bonneau, & M. Wertheimer (Eds.), *Portraits of pioneers in psychology. Vol. II* (pp. 87–105). Washington, DC: American Psychological Association.

DIAMOND, I. T. (1985). A history of the study of the cortex: Changes in the concept of the sensory pathway. In G. A. Kimble & K. Schlesinger (Eds.), *Topics in the history of psychology. Vol. 1* (pp. 305–387). Hillsdale, NJ: Lawrence Erlbaum Associates.

DIEHL, L. A. (1992). The discovering of Iva Lowther Peters: Transcending male bias in the history of psychology. In J. C. Christer & D. Howard (Eds.), *New directions in feminist psychology: Practice, theory, and research* (pp. 101–115). New York: Springer.

DENNETT, D. C. (1995). *Darwin's dangerous idea*. New York: Simon & Schuster.

DOLLARD, J., DOOB, L. W., MILLER, N. E., MOWRER, O. H., & SEARS, R. R. (1939). *Frustration and aggression*. New Haven: Yale University Press.

DONNELLY, M. E. (Ed.). (1992). *Reinterpreting the legacy of William James*. Washington, DC: The American Psychological Association.

DORN, H. (1972). Ernst Heinrich Weber. In C. C. Gillespie (Ed.), *Dictionary of scientific biography. Vol. XIV*. New York: Charles Scribner's Sons.

DUNCAN, C. P. (1980). A note on the 1929 International Congress of Psychology. *Journal of the History of the Behavioral Sciences, 16*, 1–5.

DUNCKER, K. (1945). On problem solving. *Psychological Monographs, 58*, Whole No. 270. (Original work published 1935)

EBBINGHAUS, H. (1908). *Psychology: An elementary textbook* (M. Meyer, Trans.). Boston: D. C. Heath.

EBBINGHAUS, H. (1964). *Memory: A contribution to experimental psychology* (H. A. Ruger & C. A. Bussenius, Trans.). New York: Dover. (Original work published 1885)

EBBINGHAUS, H. (1965). Hermann Ebbinghaus (1850–1909) on the completion test. In R. J. Herrnstein & E. G. Boring (Eds.), *A sourcebook in the history of psychology* (pp. 433–437). Cambridge, MA: Harvard University Press. (Original work published 1897)

EISELEY, L. (1958). *Darwin's century: Evolution and the men who discovered it.* New York: Doubleday.

ELLENBERGER, H. F. (1970). *The discovery of the unconsciousness.* New York: Basic Books.

ELLENBERGER, H. F. (1972). The story of "Anna O": A critical review with new data. *Journal of the History of the Behavioral Sciences, 8,* 267–279.

ELLIOTT, M. H. (1928). The effect of change of reward on the maze performance of rats. *University of California Publications in Psychology, 4,* 19–30.

ELLIS, A. (1973). *Humanistic psychotherapy: The rational-emotive approach.* New York: McGraw-Hill.

EMDE, R. N., PLOMIN, R., ROBINSON, J., CORLEY, R., DEFRIES, J., FULKER, D. W., RESNICK, J. S., CAMPOS, J., KAGAN, J., & ZAHN-WAXLER, C. (1992). Temperament, emotion, and cognition at fourteen months: The MacArthur longitudinal twin study. *Child Development, 63,* 1437–1455.

ENGLISH, H. B. (1929). Three cases of "conditioned fear response." *Journal of Abnormal and Social Psychology, 24,* 221–225.

ESTES, W. K. (1981). The bible is out. *Contemporary Psychology, 26,* 327–330.

EVANS, R. B. (1972). E. B. Titchener and his lost system. *Journal of the History of the Behavioral Sciences, 8,* 168–180.

EVANS, R. B. (1984). The origins of American academic psychology. In J. Brozek (Ed.), *Explorations in the history of psychology in the United States* (pp. 17–60). Lewisburg, PA: Bucknell University Press.

EVANS, R. B., & COHEN, J. B. (1987). "The American Journal of Psychology": A retrospective. *American Journal of Psychology, 100,* 321–362.

EVANS, R. B., SEXTON, V. S., & CADWALLADER, T. C. (1992). *The American Psychological Association: A historical perspective.* Washington, DC: American Psychological Association.

EYSENCK, H. J. (1952). The effects of psychotherapy: An evaluation. *Journal of Consulting Psychology, 16,* 319–324.

FANCHER, R. E. (1985). *The intelligence men: Makers of the IQ controversy.* New York: W. W. Norton.

FANCHER, R. E. (1990). *Pioneers of psychology* (2nd ed.). New York: W. W. Norton.

FARR, R. M. (1983). Wilhelm Wundt (1832–1920) and the origins of psychology as an experimental and social science. *British Journal of Social Psychology, 22,* 289–301.

FARSON, R. (1978). The technology of humanism. *Journal of Humanistic Psychology, 18,* 5–35.

FEARING, F. (1930). *Reflex action: A study in the history of physiological psychology.* New York: Hafner.

FERNBERGER, S. W. (1931). The history of the psychological clinic. In R. A. Brotemarkle (Ed.), *Clinical psychology: Studies in honor of Lightner Witmer* (pp. 10–36). Philadelphia: University of Pennsylvania Press.

FERNBERGER, S. W. (1932). The American Psychological Association: A historical summary, 1892–1930. *Psychological Bulletin, 29,* 1–89.

FERRIER, D. (1876). *The functions of the brain.* New York: Putnam.

FERSTER, C. B., & SKINNER, B. F. (1957). *Schedules of reinforcement.* New York: Appleton-Century-Crofts.

FESTINGER, L. (1957). *A theory of cognitive dissonance.* Evanston, IL: Row, Peterson.

FISKE, S. T., & TAYLOR, S. E. (1984). *Social cognition.* Reading, MA: Addison-Wesley.

FLAHERTY, F. C. (1985). *Animal learning and cognition.* New York: McGraw-Hill.

FLAVELL, J. H. (1963). *The developmental psychology of Jean Piaget.* Princeton, NJ: Van Nostrand Reinhold.

FLOURENS, P. (1978). *Phrenology examined* (C. D. Meigs, Trans.). In D. N. Robinson (Ed.), *Significant contributions to the history of psychology. Series E. Volume II.* Washington, DC: University Publications of America. (Original work published 1846)

FORREST, D. W. (1974). *Francis Galton: The life and work of a Victorian genius.* New York: Taplinger.

FRANK, J. D. (1978). Kurt Lewin in retrospect—A psychiatrist's view. *Journal of the History of the Behavioral Sciences, 14,* 223–227.

FREEMAN, F. N. (1922). The mental age of adults. *Journal of Educational Research, 6,* 441–444.

FREEMAN, F. S. (1977). The beginnings of Gestalt psychology in the United States. *Journal of the History of the Behavioral Sciences, 13,* 352–353.

FREUD, A. (1928). *Introduction to the technique of child analysis.* New York: Nervous and Mental Disease Publishing Co.

FREUD, A. (1937). *The ego and mechanisms of defense.* New York: International Universities Press.

FREUD, S. (1938). *The interpretation of dreams.* In A. A. Brill (Ed. & Trans.), The basic writings of Sigmund Freud (pp. 179–549). New York: Random House. (Original work published 1900)

FREUD, S. (1938). *The psychopathology of everyday life.* In A. A. Brill (Ed. & Trans.), The basic writings of Sigmund Freud (pp. 33–178). New York: Random House. (Original work published 1901)

FREUD, S. (1938). *Three contributions to the theory of sex.* In A.

A. Brill (Ed. & Trans.), The basic writings of Sigmund Freud (pp. 551–629). New York: Random House. (Original work published 1905)

FREUD, S. (1938). *Wit and its relation to the unconscious.* In A. A. Brill (Ed. & Trans.), The basic writings of Sigmund Freud (pp. 631–803). New York: Random House. (Original work published 1905)

FREUD, S. (1959). *Beyond the pleasure principle* (J. Strachey, Trans.). New York: Bantam Books. (Original work published 1920)

FREUD, S. (1959). *The ego and the id* (J. Strachey, Trans.). New York: Bantam Books. (Original work published 1923)

FREUD, S. (1977). *Five lectures on psycho-analysis* (J. Strachey, Trans.). New York: W. W. Norton. (Original work published 1909)

FRITSCH, G., & HITZIG, E. (1965). Gustav Fritsch (1838–1927) and Eduard Hitzig (1838–1907) on cerebral motor centers, 1870. In R. J. Herrnstein & E. G. Boring (Eds.), *A sourcebook in the history of psychology* (pp. 229–233). Cambridge, MA: Harvard University Press. (Original work published 1870)

FURUMOTO, L. (1979). Mary Whiton Calkins (1863–1930): Fourteenth president of the American Psychological Association. *Journal of the History of the Behavioral Sciences, 15,* 346–356.

FURUMOTO, L. (1988). Shared knowledge: The Experimentalists, 1904–1929. In J. G. Morawski (Ed.), *The rise of experimentation in American psychology* (pp. 94–113). New Haven, CT: Yale University Press.

FURUMOTO, L. (1989). The new history of psychology. In I. S. Cohen (Ed.), *The G. Stanley Hall lecture series* (Vol. 9, pp. 9–34). Washington, DC: American Psychological Association.

FURUMOTO, L. (1991). From "paired associates" to a psychology of self: The intellectual odyssey of Mary Whiton Calkins. In G. A. Kimble, M. Wertheimer, & C. L. White (Eds.), *Portraits of pioneers in psychology* (pp. 56–72). Washington, DC: American Psychological Association.

FURUMOTO, L. (1992). Joining separate spheres—Christine Ladd-Franklin, woman-scientist (1847–1930). *American Psychologist, 47,* 175–182.

GALL, F. J. (1965). Franz Joseph Gall (1758–1828) on phrenology, the localization of the functions of the brain, 1825. In R. J. Herrnstein & E. G. Boring (Eds.), *A sourcebook in the history of psychology* (pp. 211–220). Cambridge, MA: Harvard University Press. (Original work published 1825)

GALLISTEL, C. R. (1981). Bell, Magendie, and the proposals to restrict the use of animals in neurobehavioral research. *American Psychologist, 36,* 357–360.

GALTON, F. (1874). *English men of science: Their nature and nurture.* London: Macmillan.

GALTON, F. (1883). *An inquiry into human faculty and its development.* London: Macmillan.

GALTON, F. (1891). *Hereditary genius.* New York: D. Appleton. (Original work published 1869)

GALTON, F. (1965). Galton on mental capacity, 1883. In R. J. Herrnstein & E. G. Boring (Eds.), *A sourcebook in the history of psychology* (pp. 421–423). Cambridge, MA: Harvard University Press. (Original work published 1883)

GANTT, W. H. (1973). Reminiscences of Pavlov. *Journal of the Experimental Analysis of Behavior, 20,* 131–136.

GARDNER, H. (1985). *The mind's new science: A history of the cognitive revolution.* New York: Basic Books.

GARRETT, H. E. (1951). *Great experiments in psychology* (3rd ed.). New York: Appleton-Century-Crofts.

GAY, P. (1988). *Freud: A life for our time.* New York: W. W. Norton.

GIBSON, E. J. (1980). Eleanor Gibson. In G. Lindsey (Ed.), *A history of psychology in autobiography. Vol. 7* (pp. 239–271). San Francisco: Freeman and Company.

GIBSON, E. J. (1994). Has psychology a future? *Psychological Science, 5,* 69–76.

GIBSON, E. J., & WALK, R. D. (1960). The "visual cliff." *Scientific American, 202,* 64–71.

GILBREATH, F. B., & GILBREATH, L. M. (1916). *Fatigue study: The elimination of humanity's greatest unnecessary waste.* New York: Sturgis & Walton.

GILBREATH, F. B., & GILBREATH, L. M. (1917). *Applied motion study.* New York: Sturgis & Walton.

GILBRETH, F. B., JR., & CAREY, E. G. (1949). *Cheaper by the dozen.* New York: Bantam.

GILLIES, D. (1993). *Philosophy of science in the twentieth century: Four central themes.* Oxford, UK: Blackwell Press.

GLICKMAN, S. E. (1996). Donald Olding Hebb: Returning the nervous system to psychology. In G. A. Kimble, C. A. Bonneau, & M. Wertheimer (Eds.) *Portraits of pioneers in psychology. Vol. II* (pp. 227–244). Washington, DC: American Psychological Association.

GODDARD, H. H. (1910). Four hundred feeble-minded children classified by the Binet method. *Journal of Genetic Psychology, 17,* 387–397.

GODDARD, H. H. (1912). *The Kallikak family: A study in the heredity of feeble-mindedness.* New York: Macmillan.

GODDARD, H. H. (1913). The Binet tests in relation to immigration. *Journal of Psycho-Asthenics, 18,* 105–107.

GODDARD, H. H. (1917). Mental tests and the immigrant. *Journal of Delinquency, 2,* 243–277.

GODDARD, H. H. (1928). Feeblemindedness: A question of definition. *Journal of Psycho-Asthenics, 33,* 219–227.

GOLDSTEIN, E. B. (1996). *Sensation and perception* (4th edition). Pacific Grove, CA: Brooks/Cole.

GOODENOUGH, F. L. (1950). Edward Lee Thorndike: 1874–1949. *American Journal of Psychology, 63,* 291–301.

GOODWIN, C. J. (1985). On the origins of Titchener's Experimentalists. *Journal of the History of the Behavioral Sciences, 21*, 383–389.

GOODWIN, C. J. (1987). In Hall's shadow: Edmund Clark Sanford (1859–1924). *Journal of the History of the Behavioral Sciences, 23*, 153–168.

GOODWIN, C. J. (1991). Misportraying Pavlov's apparatus. *American Journal of Psychology, 104*, 135–141.

GOODWIN, C. J. (1991). Using psychologists' letters to teach about introspection. *Teaching of Psychology, 18*, 237–238.

GOODWIN, C. J. (1993, August). *Experimental psychology first-hand: The diaries of Walter Miles.* American Psychological Association, Toronto, Canada.

GOULD, S. J. (1981). *The mismeasure of man.* New York: W. W. Norton.

GRAVITZ, M. A. (1988). Early uses of hypnosis as surgical anesthesia. *American Journal of Clinical Hypnosis, 30*, 201–208.

GRAY, J. A. (1979). *Ivan Pavlov.* New York: Viking.

GRAY, P. (1994). *Psychology* (2nd ed.). New York: Worth.

GRAY, P. (1996). Incorporating evolutionary theory into the teaching of psychology. *Teaching of Psychology, 23*, 207–214.

GRAY, P. H. (1962). Douglas Alexander Spalding: The first experimental behaviorist. *Journal of General Psychology, 67*, 299–307.

GREEN, M., & RIEBER, R. W. (1980). The assimilation of psychoanalysis in America. In R. W. Rieber & K. Salzinger (Eds.), *Psychology: Theoretical-historical perspectives* (pp. 263–304). New York: Academic Press.

GRMEK, M. D. (1972). François Magendie. In C. C. Gillespie (Ed.), *Dictionary of scientific biography. Vol. IX.* New York: Scribner.

GROB, G. (1994). *The mad among us: A history of the care of America's mentally ill.* New York: Free Press.

GUNDLACH, H. U. K. (1986). Ebbinghaus, nonsense syllables, and three-letter words. *Contemporary Psychology, 31*, 469–470.

GUTHRIE, R. V. (1976). *Even the rat was white: A historical view of psychology.* New York: Harper & Row.

GUTHRIE, E. R. (1935). *The psychology of learning.* New York: Harper and Brothers.

GUTTMAN, N. (1977). On Skinner and Hull: A reminiscence and projection. *American Psychologist, 32*, 321–328.

HALDANE, J. B. S. (1954). Introducing Douglas Spalding. *British Journal of Animal Behavior, 2*, 1–11.

HALE, N. G., JR. (1971). *Freud and the Americans: The beginnings of psychoanalysis in the United States, 1876–1917.* New York: Oxford University Press.

HALL, C. S. (1954). *A primer of Freudian psychology.* New York: World Publishing Company.

HALL, C. S., & LINDZEY, G. (1970). *Theories of personality* (2nd ed.). New York: John Wiley & Sons.

HALL, G. S. (1887). Editorial. *American Journal of Psychology, 1*, 3–4.

HALL, G. S. (1890–1891). Review of "The Principles of Psychology." *American Journal of Psychology, 3*, 578–591.

HALL, G. S. (1904). *Adolescence.* New York: Appleton.

HALL, G. S. (1922). *Senescence: The last half of life.* New York: Appleton.

HALL, G. S. (1923). *Life and confessions of a psychologist.* New York: Appleton.

HALL, G. S. (1948). The contents of children's minds. In W. Dennis (Ed.), *Readings in the history of psychology* (pp. 255–276). New York: Appleton-Century-Crofts. (Original work published 1883)

HANNUSH, M. J. (1987). John B. Watson remembered: An interview with James B. Watson. *Journal of the History of the Behavioral Sciences, 23*, 137–152.

HARLOW, J. M. (1869). *Recovery from the passage of an iron bar through the head.* Boston: Clapp.

HARRIS, B. (1979). Whatever happened to Little Albert? *American Psychologist, 34*, 151–160.

HARROWER-ERICKSON, M. R. (1942). Kurt Koffka: 1886–1941. *American Journal of Psychology, 55*, 278–281.

HARTLEY, D. (1971). *Observations on man, his frame, his duty, and his expectations. Volume I.* New York: Garland. (Original work published 1749)

HAWKINS, H. (1960). *Pioneer: A history of the Johns Hopkins University, 1874–1899.* Ithaca, NY: Cornell University Press.

HEBB, D. O. (1949). *The organization of behavior.* New York: John Wiley.

HEBB, D. O. (1959). Karl Spencer Lashley (1890–1958). *American Journal of Psychology, 72*, 142–150.

HEBB, D. O. (1960). The American revolution. *American Psychologist, 15*, 735–745.

HEBB, D. O. (1980). D. O. Hebb. In G. Lindsey (Ed.), *A history of psychology in autobiography. Vol. 7* (pp. 273–303). San Francisco: Freeman and Company.

HEIDBREDER, E. (1933). *Seven psychologies.* New York: Appleton-Century-Crofts.

HEIMS, S. (1978). Kurt Lewin and social change. *Journal of the History of the Behavioral Sciences, 14*, 238–241.

HELMHOLTZ, H. (1965). Hermann Ludwig Ferdinand von Helmholtz (1821–1894) on the three-color theory of vision and visual specific nerve energies, 1860. In R. J. Herrnstein & E. G. Boring (Eds.), *A sourcebook in the history of psychology* (pp. 223–229). Cambridge, MA: Harvard University Press. (Original work published 1860)

HENLE, M. (1974). E. B. Titchener and the case of the missing element. *Journal of the History of the Behavioral Sciences, 10*, 227–237.

HENLE, M. (1980). The influence of Gestalt psychology in America. In R. W. Rieber & K. Salzinger (Eds.), *Psychology: Theoretical-historical perspectives* (pp. 177–190). New York: Academic Press.

HENLE, M. (1986). One man against the Nazis—Wolfgang Köhler. In M. Henle (Ed.), *1879 and all that: Essays in the theory and history of psychology* (pp. 225–237). New York: Columbia University Press.

HICKS, L. H., & RIDLEY, S. E. (1979). Black studies in psychology. *American Psychologist, 34*, 597–602.

HILGARD, E. R. (1948). *Theories of learning.* New York: Appleton-Century-Crofts.

HILGARD, E. R. (1957). Lewis Madison Terman: 1877–1956. *American Journal of Psychology, 70*, 472–479.

HILGARD, E. R. (1964). *Introduction to Dover Edition of "Memory: A contribution to experimental psychology."* New York: Dover.

HILGARD, E. R. (1967). Kenneth Wartinbee Spence: 1907–1967. *American Journal of Psychology, 80*, 314–318.

HILGARD, E. R. (1980). The trilogy of mind: Cognition, affection, and conation. *Journal of the History of the Behavioral Sciences, 16*, 107–117.

HILGARD, E. R. (1982). Robert I. Watson and the founding of Division 26 of the American Psychological Association. *Journal of the History of the Behavioral Sciences, 18*, 308–311.

HILGARD, E. R. (1987). *Psychology in America: A historical survey.* San Diego: Harcourt Brace Jovanovich.

HINDELAND, M. J. (1971). Edward Bradford Titchener: A pioneer in perception. *Journal of the History of the Behavioral Sciences, 7*, 23–28.

HOFFELD, D. R. (1980). Mesmer's failure: Sex, politics, personality, and the zeitgeist. *Journal of the History of the Behavioral Sciences, 16*, 377–386.

HOFSTADTER, R., & HARDY, C. D. (1952). *The development and scope of higher education in the United States.* New York: Columbia University Press.

HORNSTEIN, G. A. (1992). The return of the repressed: Psychology's problematic relations with psychoanalysis, 1909–1960. *American Psychologist, 47*, 254–263.

HOTHERSALL, D. (1995). *History of psychology* (3rd ed.). New York: McGraw-Hill.

HUBEL, D. H., & WIESEL, T. N. (1963). Receptive fields of cells in the striate cortex of very young, visually inexperienced kittens. *Journal of Neurophysiology, 26*, 994–1002.

HULL, C. L. (1920). Quantitative aspects of the evolution of concepts. *Psychological Monographs, 28*, No. 123.

HULL, C. L. (1928). *Aptitude testing.* Yonkers-on-Hudson, NY: Word Book.

HULL, C. L. (1933). *Hypnosis and suggestibility: An experimental approach.* New York: Appleton-Century.

HULL, C. L. (1943). *Principles of behavior.* New York: Appleton-Century-Crofts.

HULL, C. L. (1952a). *A behavior system.* New Haven, CT: Yale University Press.

HULL, C. L. (1952b). Clark L. Hull. In E. G. Boring, H. S. Langfeld, H. Werner, & R. M. Yerkes (Eds.), *A history of psychology in autobiography. Vol. 4* (143–162). Worcester, MA: Clark University Press.

HUME, D. (1969). *A treatise of human nature* (E. C. Mossner, Ed.). Baltimore: Penguin. (Original work published 1739–1740)

HUNTER, W. S. (1919). *General psychology.* Chicago: University of Chicago Press.

HUNTER, W. S. (1949). James Rowland Angell, 1869–1949. *American Journal of Psychology, 62*, 439–450.

IZARD, C. E. (1977). *Human emotions.* New York: Plenum.

JACOBSON, E. (1929). *Progressive relaxation.* Chicago: University of Chicago Press.

JAMES, W. (1891, December 20). *Letter to M. W. Calkins.* Calkins Papers, Wellesley College, Wellesley, MA.

JAMES, W. (1950). *Principles of psychology. Vol. 1.* New York: Dover. (Original work published 1890)

JAMES, W. (1950). *Principles of psychology. Vol. 2.* New York: Dover. (Original work published 1890)

JAMES, W. (1961). *Psychology: The briefer course.* New York: Harper & Row. (Original work published 1892)

JAYNES, J. (1969). Edwin Garrigues Boring: 1886–1968. *Journal of the History of the Behavioral Sciences, 5*, 99–112.

JEFFREYS, M. V. C. (1967). *John Locke: Prophet of common sense.* London: Methuen.

JENKINS, J. G. (1935). Review of *Remembering* by F. C. Bartlett. *American Journal of Psychology, 47*, 712–715.

JOHNSON, M. G., & HENLEY, T. B. (Eds.). (1990). *Reflections on "The Principles of Psychology."* Hillsdale, NJ: Lawrence Erlbaum.

JONÇICH, G. (1968). *The sane positivist: A biography of Edward L. Thorndike.* Middletown, CT: Wesleyan University Press.

JONES, E. (1953, 1955, 1957). *The life and work of Sigmund Freud* (Vols. 1–3). New York: Basic Books.

JONES, M. C. (1924a). The elimination of children's fear. *Journal of Experimental Psychology, 7*, 382–390.

JONES, M. C. (1924b). A laboratory study of fear: The case of Peter. *Pedagogical Seminary, 31*, 308–315.

JOYNT, R. J. (1973, October). Phrenology in New York State. *New York State Journal of Medicine*, 2382–2384.

JUNG, C. G. (1919). *Studies in word association.* New York: Moffat-Yard.

KAIL, R. V., JR., & HAGAN, J. W. (Eds.). (1977). *Perspectives on the development of memory and cognition.* Hillsdale, NJ: Lawrence Erlbaum Associates.

KANT, I. (1952). *Critique of judgment* (J. C. Meredith, Trans.). Oxford: Oxford University Press. (Original work published 1788)

KANT, I. (1959). *Critique of practical reason.* (T. K. Abbott, Trans.). New York: Longmans, Green. (Original work published 1790)

KANT, I. (1965). *Critique of pure reason.* (N. K. Smith, Trans.). New York: St. Martin's. (Original work published 1781)

KATONA, G. (1940). *Organizing and memorizing.* New York: Columbia University Press.

KAZDIN, A. E. (1978). *History of behavior modification: Experimental foundations of contemporary research.* Baltimore: University Park Press.

KELLEY, H. H. (1973). The process of causal attribution. *American Psychologist, 28,* 107–128.

KENT, D. (1992, September). E. Gibson, A. Newell receive National Medal of Science. *APS Observer, 5(1),* 14–15.

KESSEN, W. (1996). American psychology just before Piaget. *Psychological Science, 7,* 196–199.

KESSEN, W., & KUHLMAN, C. (Eds.). (1962). Thought in the young child: Report of a conference on intellective development with particular attention to the work of Jean Piaget. *Monographs of the Society for Research in Child Development, 27* (Serial No. 83).

KEVLES, D. J. (1968). Testing the Army's intelligence: Psychologists and the military in World War I. *Journal of American History, 55,* 565–581.

KIMBLE, G. A. (1991). Psychology from the standpoint of a mechanist: An appreciation of Clark L. Hull. In G. A. Kimble, M. Wertheimer, & C. L. White (Eds.), *Portraits of pioneers in psychology.* Washington, DC: American Psychological Association.

KING, D. B. (1992). Evolution and revision of the *Principles.* In M. E. Donnelly (Ed.), *Reinterpreting the legacy of William James* (pp. 67–75). Washington, DC: The American Psychological Association.

KINNAMAN, A. J. (1902). Mental life of two Macacus rhesus monkeys in captivity. II. *American Journal of Psychology, 13,* 173–218.

KINTSCH, W. (1985). Reflections on Ebbinghaus. *Journal of Experimental Psychology: Learning, Memory, and Cognition, 11,* 461–463.

KINTSCH, W., & CACIOPPO, J. T. (1994). Introduction to the 100th anniversary issue of the *Psychological Review. Psychological Review, 101,* 195–199.

KIRSCH, I. (1977). Psychology's first paradigm. *Journal of the History of the Behavioral Sciences, 13,* 317–325.

KLEIN, D. B. (1970). *A history of scientific psychology: Its origins and philosophical background.* New York: Basic Books.

KNAPP, T. J. (1985). Contributions to the history of psychology: XXXIX. T. V. Moore and his *Cognitive Psychology* of 1939. *Psychological Reports, 57,* 1311–1316.

KOCH, S. (1992). Postscript: The second century of psychology at age 12 and the American Psychological Association at age 100. In S. Koch & D. E. Leary (Eds.), *A century of psychology as science* (pp. 951–968). Washington, DC: American Psychological Association.

KOCH, S. (1993). "Psychology" or "the psychological studies"? *American Psychologist, 48,* 902–904.

KOFFKA, K. (1922). Perception: An introduction to Gestalt-theorie. *Psychological Bulletin, 19,* 531–585.

KOFFKA, K. (1924). *The growth of the mind: An introduction to child psychology* (R. M. Ogden, Trans.). New York: Harcourt, Brace. (Original work published 1921)

KOFFKA, K. (1935). *Principles of Gestalt psychology.* New York: Harcourt, Brace.

KÖHLER, W. (1926). *The mentality of apes* (E. Winter, Trans.). New York: Harcourt, Brace. (Original work published 1917)

KÖHLER, W. (1947). *Gestalt psychology.* New York: Liveright. (Original work published 1929)

KÖHLER, W. (1969). Gestalt psychology. In D. L. Krantz (Ed.), *Schools of psychology: A symposium* (pp. 69–85). New York: Appleton-Century-Crofts. (Original work published 1967)

KORN, J. H., DAVIS, R., & DAVIS, S. F. (1991). Historians' and chairpersons' judgments of eminence among psychologists. *American Psychologist, 46,* 789–792.

KRANTZ, D. L. (1969). The Baldwin-Titchener controversy. In D. L. Krantz (Ed.), *Schools of psychology: A symposium* (pp. 1–19). New York: Appleton-Century-Crofts.

KROLL, J. (1973). A reappraisal of psychiatry in the Middle Ages. *Archives of General Psychiatry, 29,* 276–283.

KUHN, T. S. (1962). *The structure of scientific revolutions.* Chicago: University of Chicago Press.

LAKIN, M. (1996). Carl Rogers and the culture of psychotherapy. *The General Psychologist, 32,* 62–68.

LANDY, F. J. (1992). Hugo Münsterberg: Victim or visionary? *Journal of Applied Psychology, 77,* 787–802.

LANDY, F. J. (1993). Early influences on the development of industrial/organizational psychology. In T. K. Fagan & G. R. VandenBos (Eds.), *Exploring applied psychology: Origins and critical analyses* (pp. 83–118). Washington, DC: American Psychological Association.

LARSON, C., & SULLIVAN, J. J. (1965). Watson's relation to Titchener. *Journal of the History of the Behavioral Sciences, 1,* 338–354.

LASHLEY, K. S. (1929). *Brain mechanisms and intelligence.* Chicago: University of Chicago Press.

LASHLEY, K. S. (1951). The problem of serial order in behavior. In L. A. Jeffress (Ed.), *Cerebral mechanisms in behavior: The Hixon symposium* (pp. 112–146). New York: John Wiley.

LEACOCK, S. (1924, March). A manual of the new mentality. *Harper's Monthly Magazine*, 471–480.

LEAHEY, T. H. (1979). Something old, something new: Attention in Wundt and modern cognitive psychology. *Journal of the History of the Behavioral Sciences, 15*, 242–252.

LEAHY, T. H. (1981). The mistaken mirror: On Wundt's and Titchener's psychologies. *Journal of the History of the Behavioral Sciences, 17*, 273–282.

LEAHEY, T. H. (1992). The mythical revolutions of American psychology. *American Psychologist, 47*, 308–318.

LEARY, D. E. (1992). William James and the art of human understanding. *American Psychologist, 47*, 152–160.

LEIBNITZ, G. W. (1982). *New essays on human understanding* (P. Remnant & J. Bennett, Trans.). New York: Cambridge University Press. (Original work published 1765)

LESCH, J. E. (1972). George John Romanes. In C. C. Gillespie (Ed.), *Dictionary of scientific biography. Vol. XI.* New York: Scribner.

LEWIN, K. (1931). Environmental forces in child behavior and development. In C. Murchison (Ed.), *Handbook of child psychology* (pp. 94–127). Worcester, MA: Clark University Press.

LEWIN, K. (1935). *A dynamic theory of personality* (D. K. Adams & K. E. Zener, Trans.). New York: McGraw-Hill.

LEWIN, K. (1936). *Principles of topological psychology* (F. Heider & G. M. Heider, Trans.). New York: McGraw-Hill.

LEWIN, K. (1937). Cark Stumpf. *Psychological Review, 44*, 189–194.

LEWIN, K., LIPPITT, R., & WHITE, R. (1939). Patterns of aggressive behavior in experimentally created "social climates." *Journal of Social Psychology, 10*, 271–299.

LEWIS, R. W. B. (1991). *The Jameses: A family narrative.* New York: Farrar, Straus, & Giroux.

LEY, R. (1990). *A whisper of espionage.* Garden Park, NY: Avery Publishing Group.

LEYS, R., & EVANS, R. B. (1990). *Defining American psychology: The correspondence between Adolf Meyer and Edward Bradford Titchener.* Baltimore, MD: The Johns Hopkins University Press.

LIPPIT, R., & WHITE, R. K. (1943). The "social climate" of children's groups. In R. G. Barker, J. S. Kounin, & H. F. Wright (Eds.), *Child behavior and development* (pp. 485–508). New York: McGraw-Hill.

LIPPMANN, W. (1922a). A future for tests. *New Republic, 33*, 9–10.

LIPPMANN, W. (1922b). The abuse of tests. *New Republic, 32*, 297–298.

LLOYD, M. A., & BREWER, C. B. (1992). National conferences on undergraduate education. In A. E. Puente, J. R. Matthews, & C. B. Brewer (Eds.), *Teaching psychology in America: A history* (pp. 263–284). Washington, DC: American Psychological Association.

LOCKE, J. (1960). *Two treatises on government.* New York: Cambridge University Press. (Original work published 1690)

LOCKE, J. (1963). *Some thoughts concerning education.* Germany: Scientia Verlag Aalen. (Original work published 1693)

LOCKE, J. (1963). *An essay concerning human understanding.* Germany: Scientia Verlag Aalen. (Original work published 1690)

LOFTUS, E. F. (1979). *Eyewitness testimony.* Cambridge, MA: Harvard University Press.

MACFARLANE, D. A. (1930). The role of kinesthesis in maze learning. *University of California Publications in Psychology, 4*, 277–305.

MACH, E. (1914). *Analysis of sensations.* La Salle, IL: Open Court. (Original work published 1886)

MACLEOD, C. M. (1992). The Stroop task: The "gold standard" of attention measures. *Journal of Experimental Psychology: General, 121*, 12–14.

MACMILLAN, M. B. (1986). A wonderful journey through skull and brain: The travels of Mr. Gage's tamping iron. *Brain and Cognition, 5*, 67–107.

MADIGAN, S., & O'HARA, R. (1992). Short-term memory at the turn of the century: Mary Whiton Calkins's memory research. *American Psychologist, 47*, 170–174.

MAGENDIE, F. (1965). François Magendie (1783–1855) on spinal nerve roots, 1822. In R. J. Herrnstein & E. G. Boring (Eds.), *A sourcebook in the history of psychology* (pp. 19–22). Cambridge, MA: Harvard University Press. (Original work published 1822)

MALONE, J. C. (1991). *Theories of learning: A historical approach.* Belmont, CA: Wadsworth.

MARROW, A. J. (1969). *The practical theorist: The life and work of Kurt Lewin.* New York: Basic Books.

MAYER, R. E. (1992). *Thinking, problem solving, cognition* (2nd ed.). New York: Freeman.

MAZLISH, B. (1975). *James and John Stuart Mill: Father and son in the nineteenth century.* New York: Basic Books.

MCCULLOUGH, D. (1992). *Brave companions: Portraits in history.* New York: Simon & Schuster.

MCDOUGALL, W. (1908). *Introduction to social psychology.* London: Methuen.

MCGINNIES, E. (1949). Emotionality and perceptual defense. *Psychological Review, 56*, 244–251.

MCGUIRE, W. (Ed.). (1974). *The Freud/Jung letters.* Princeton, NJ: Princeton University Press.

McReynolds, P. (1987). Lightner Witmer: Little-known founder of clinical psychology. *American Psychologist, 42,* 849–858.

McReynolds, P. (1996). Lightner Witmer: The father of clinical psychology. In G. A. Kimble, C. A. Bonneau, & M. Wertheimer (Eds.), *Portraits of pioneers in psychology. Vol. II* (pp. 63–71). Washington, DC: American Psychological Association.

Merton, R. K. (1961). Singletons and multiples in scientific discovery: A chapter in the sociology of science. *Proceedings of the American Philosophical Society, 105,* 470–486.

Micale, M. S. (1985). The Salpêtrière in the age of Charcot: An institutional perspective on medical history in the late nineteenth century. *Journal of Contemporary History, 20,* 703–731.

Miles, W. R. (1928, March 29). *Diary entry.* Walter Miles papers, Archives of the History of American Psychology, University of Akron, Akron, Ohio.

Miles, W. R. (1929). *Diary insertion* (Box 1165, Folder 4). From the Walter R. Miles papers, Archives of the History of American Psychology, Akron, Ohio.

Miles, W. R. (1930). On the history of research with rats and mazes: A collection of notes. *Journal of General Psychology, 3,* 324–337.

Miles, W. R. (1931, April 1). *Diary entry.* Walter Miles papers, Archives of the History of American Psychology, University of Akron, Akron, Ohio.

Mill, J. S. (1869). *The subjection of women.* London: Longmans, Green, Reader, and Dyer.

Mill, J. (1948). *Analysis of the phenomena of the human mind.* Excerpt in W. Dennis (Ed.), *Readings in the history of psychology* (pp. 140–154). New York: Appleton-Century-Crofts. (Original work published 1829)

Mill, J. S. (1987). *The logic of the moral sciences.* LaSalle, IL: Open Court Classics. (A reprinting of the sixth book of Mill's *A system of logic, ratiocinative and inductive, being a connected view of the principles of evidence, and the methods of scientific investigation;* Original work published 1843)

Mill, J. S. (1989). *Autobiography.* London: Penguin. (Original work published 1873)

Miller, G. A. (1951). *Language and communication.* New York: McGraw-Hill.

Miller, G. A. (1956). The magic number seven plus or minus two: Some limits on our capacity for processing information. *Psychological Review, 63,* 81–97.

Miller, G. A. (1992). The constitutive problem of psychology. In S. Koch & D. E. Leary (Eds.) *A century of psychology as science* (pp. 40–45). Washington, DC: American Psychological Association.

Miller, G. A. (1994). The magical number seven, plus or minus two: Some limits on our capacity for processing information. *Psychological Review, 63,* 81–97. (Original work published 1956)

Miller, G. A., & Frick, F. C. (1949). Statistical behavioristics and sequences of responses. *Psychological Review, 56,* 311–324.

Miller, G. A., Galanter, E., & Pribram, K. H. (1960). *Plans and the structure of behavior.* New York: Holt.

Miller, N. E., & Dollard, J. (1941). *Social learning and imitation.* New Haven, CT: Yale University Press.

Mills, W. (1899). The nature of animal intelligence and the methods of investigating it. *Psychological Review, 6,* 262–274.

Minton, H. L. (1987). Lewis M. Terman and mental testing: In search of the democratic ideal. In M. M. Sokal (Ed.), *Psychological testing and American society, 1890–1930* (pp. 95–112). New Brunswick, NJ: Rutgers University Press.

Minton, H. L. (1988). *Lewis M. Terman: Pioneer in psychological testing.* New York: New York University Press.

Mischel, W. (1979). On the interface of cognition and personality: Beyond the person-situation debate. *American Psychologist, 34,* 740–754.

Monastersky, R. (1997, March 1). The call of catastrophes. *Science News, 151,* S20.

Moore, T. V. (1939). *Cognitive psychology.* Philadelphia: Lippincott.

Moorehead, A. (1969). *Darwin and the Beagle.* New York: Harper & Row.

Morawski, J. G. (1986). Organizing knowledge and behavior at Yale's Institute of Human Relations. *Isis, 77,* 219–242.

Morgan, C. L. (1903). *An introduction to comparative psychology.* London: Walter Scott. (Original work published 1895)

Morgan, M. J. (1977). *Molyneux's question.* New York: Cambridge University Press.

Moskowitz, M. J. (1977). Hugo Münsterberg: A study in the history of applied psychology. *American Psychologist, 32,* 824–842.

Mowrer, O. H., & Mowrer, W. M. (1938). Enuresis—a method for its study and treatment. *American Journal of Orthopsychiatry, 8,* 436–459.

Münsterberg, H. (1908). *On the witness stand.* New York: The McClure Company.

Münsterberg, H. (1909). *Psychotherapy.* New York: Moffat, Yard.

Münsterberg, H. (1913). *Psychology and industrial efficiency.* New York: Houghton Mifflin.

Murchison, C. (Ed.). (1926). *Psychologies of 1925.* Worcester, MA: Clark University Press.

Murchison, C. (Ed.). (1930). *Psychologies of 1930.* Worcester, MA: Clark University Press.

Murphy, G., & Ballou, R. O. (Eds.). (1960). *William James on psychical research.* New York: Viking.

NAPOLI, D. S. (1981). *Architects of adjustment: The history of the psychological profession in the United States.* Port Washington, NY: Kennikat Press.

NEISSER, U. (1967). *Cognitive psychology.* New York: Appleton-Century-Crofts.

NEISSER, U. (1976). *Cognition and reality.* San Francisco: Freeman and Company.

NEISSER, U. (1988). Cognitive reflections. In W. Hirst (Ed.), *The making of cognitive science: Essays in honor of George A. Miller* (pp. 81–88). New York: Cambridge University Press.

NEUGEBAUER, R. (1978). Treatment of the mentally ill in medieval and early modern England: A reappraisal. *Journal of the History of the Behavioral Sciences, 14,* 158–169.

NEWELL, A., & SIMON, H. A. (1972). *Human problem solving.* Englewood Cliffs, NJ: Prentice-Hall.

NEWMAN, E. B. (1944). Max Wertheimer: 1880–1943. *American Journal of Psychology, 57,* 428–435.

NICOLAI, G. F. (1907). Die physiologische methodik zur erforschung der tierpsyche, ihre möglichkeit und ihre anwendung [The physiological method for research in animal psychology, its method and application]. *Journal für Psychologie und Neurologie, 10,* 1–27.

OGDEN, R. M. (1951). Oswald Külpe and the Würzburg school. *American Journal of Psychology, 64,* 4–19.

OLDFIELD, R. C. (1972). Frederick Charles Bartlett: 1886–1969. *American Journal of Psychology, 85,* 133–140.

OLDS, J., & MILNER, P. (1954). Positive reinforcement produced by electrical stimulation of septal area and other regions of rat brain. *Journal of Comparative and Physiological Psychology, 47,* 419–427.

OLTON, D. S. (1979). Mazes, maps, and memory. *American Psychologist, 34,* 583–596.

O'DONNELL, J. M. (1979). The crisis of experimentalism in the 1920s: E. G. Boring and his uses of history. *American Psychologist, 34,* 289–295.

O'DONNELL, J. M. (1979). The clinical psychology of Lightner Witmer: A case study of institutional innovation and intellectual change. *Journal of the History of the Behavioral Sciences, 15,* 3–17.

O'DONNELL, J. M. (1985). *The origins of behaviorism: American psychology, 1870–1920.* New York: New York University Press.

O'SULLIVAN, J. J., & QUEVILLON, R. P. (1992). 40 years later: Is the Boulder model still alive? *American Psychologist, 47,* 67–70.

PALERMO, D. (1971). Is a scientific revolution taking place in psychology? *Science Studies, 1,* 135–155.

PALMER, R. R. (1964). *A history of the modern world* (2nd ed.). New York: Alfred A. Knopf.

PASTORE, N. (1990). Espionage. *Journal of the History of the Behavioral Sciences, 26,* 366–371.

PAVLOV, I. P. (1906, November). The scientific investigation of the psychical faculties or processes in the higher animals. *Science, 24,* 613–619.

PAVLOV, I. P. (1928). *Lectures on conditioned reflexes* (W. H. Gantt, Trans.). New York: International Publications.

PAVLOV, I. P. (1960). *Conditioned reflexes: An investigation of the physiological activity of the cerebral cortex* (G. V. Anrep, Trans.). New York: Dover. (Original work published by Oxford University Press in 1927)

PENFIELD, W., & PEROT, P. (1963). The brain's record of auditory and visual experience. *Brain, 86,* 595–696.

PERIN, C. T. (1942). Behavior potentiality as a joint function of the amount of training and the degree of hunger at the time of extinction. *Journal of Experimental Psychology, 30,* 93–113.

PERLOFF, R., & NAMAN, J. L. (1996). Lillian Gilbreth: Tireless advocate for a general psychology. In G. A. Kimble, C. A. Bonneau, & M. Wertheimer (Eds.), *Portraits of pioneers in psychology. Vol. II* (pp. 107–116). Washington, DC: American Psychological Association.

PERVIN, E. J. (1991). *Introduction to personality* (5th ed.). New York: HarperCollins.

PETERSON, D. R. (1992). The doctor of psychology degree in professional psychology. In D. K. Freedheim (Ed.), *History of psychotherapy: A century of change* (pp. 829–849). Washington, DC: American Psychological Association.

PIAGET, J. (1952). Jean Piaget. In E. G. Boring, H. S. Langfeld, H. Werner, & R. M. Yerkes (Eds.), *A history of psychology in autobiography. Vol. 4* (pp. 237–256). New York: Russell & Russell.

PIAGET, J. (1959). *The language and thought of the child.* London: Routledge and Kegan Paul. (Original work published 1923)

PICK, H. L., JR. (1994). Eleanor J. Gibson: Learning to perceive and perceiving to learn. In R. D. Parke, P. A. Ornstein, J. J. Rieser, & C. Zahn-Waxler (Eds.), *A century of developmental psychology* (pp. 527–544). Washington, DC: American Psychological Association.

PILLSBURY, W. B. (1955). Harvey A. Carr: 1873–1954. *American Journal of Psychology, 67,* 149–151.

POFFENBERGER, A. T. (1957). Harry Levi Hollingworth: 1880–1956. *American Journal of Psychology, 70,* 136–140.

POFFENBERGER, A. T. (1962). Robert Sessions Woodworth: 1869–1962. *American Journal of Psychology, 75,* 677–689.

POPPLESTONE, J. A. (1975). Retrieval of primary sources. *Journal of the History of the Behavioral Sciences, 11,* 20–22.

POPPLESTONE, J. A. (1987). The legacy of memory in apparatus and methodology. In W. Traxel (Ed.), *Ebbinghaus-Studien 2* (pp. 203–215). Passau: Passavia Universitätsverlag.

POPPLESTONE, J. A., & MCPHERSON, M. W. (1984). Pioneer

psychology laboratories in clinical settings. In J. Brozek (Ed.) *Explorations in the history of psychology in the United States* (pp. 196–272). Lewisburg, PA: Bucknell University Press.

POPPLESTONE, J. A., & MCPHERSON, M. W. (1994). *An illustrated history of American psychology.* DuBuque, IA: Brown & Benchmark.

PORTER, J. P. (1904). A preliminary study of the psychology of the English sparrow, *American Journal of Psychology, 15,* 313–346.

PRENTICE, W. C. H. (1951). Edgar John Rubin: 1886–1951. *American Journal of Psychology, 64,* 608–609.

PRYTULA, R. E., OSTER, G. D., & DAVIS, S. F. (1977). The "rat rabbit" problem: What did John B. Watson really do? *Teaching of Psychology, 4,* 44–46.

RADBILL, S. X. (1972). Robert Whytt. In C. C. Gillespie (Ed.), *Dictionary of scientific biography. Vol. XIV.* New York: Scribner.

RAPHELSON, A. C. (1973). The pre-Chicago association of the early functionalists. *Journal of the History of the Behavioral Sciences, 9,* 115–122.

REED, J. (1987). Robert M. Yerkes and the mental testing movement. In M. M. Sokal (Ed.), *Psychological testing and American society, 1890–1930* (pp. 75–94). New Brunswick, NJ: Rutgers University Press.

RESTAK, R. (1984). *The brain.* Toronto: Bantam Books.

RESTLE, F. (1957). Discrimination of cues in mazes: A resolution of the "place-vs.-response" question. *Psychological Review, 64,* 217–228.

RICHARDS, R. J. (1983). Why Darwin delayed, or interesting problems and models in the history of science. *Journal of the History of the Behavioral Sciences, 19,* 45–53.

ROBINSON, J. K., & WOODWORTH, W. R. (1996). Experimental analysis of behavior at Harvard: From cumulative records to mathematical models. In L. D. Smith & W. R. Woodward (Eds.), *B. F. Skinner and behaviorism in American culture* (pp. 254–272). Bethlehem, PA: Lehigh University Press.

ROBINSON, D. N. (1981). *An intellectual history of psychology* (2nd ed.). New York: Macmillan.

ROEDIGER, H. L., III. (1985). Remembering Ebbinghaus. *Contemporary Psychology, 30,* 519–523.

ROGERS, C. R. (1942). *Counseling and psychotherapy.* Boston: Houghton-Mifflin Company.

ROGERS, C. R. (1954). Changes in the maturity of behavior as related to therapy. In C. R. Rogers & J. A. Precker (Eds.), *Psychotherapy and personality change* (pp. 215–237). Chicago: University of Chicago Press.

ROGERS, C. R. (1961). *On becoming a person.* Boston: Houghton-Mifflin Company.

ROHLES, F. H., JR. (1992). Orbital bar pressing: A historical note on Skinner and the chimpanzees in space. *American Psychologist, 47,* 1531–1533.

ROMANES, G. J. (1886). *Animal Intelligence.* New York: D. Appleton. (Original work published 1882)

ROSENZWEIG, S. (1992). *The historic expedition to America (1909): Freud, Jung, and Hall the king-maker.* St. Louis: Rana House.

ROSNOW, R. L., & ROSENTHAL, R. (1993). *Beginning behavioral research.* New York: Macmillan.

ROSS, D. (1969). The "zeitgeist" and American psychology. *Journal of the History of the Behavioral Sciences, 5,* 256–262.

ROSS, D. (1972). *G. Stanley Hall: The psychologist as prophet.* Chicago: University of Chicago Press.

ROTTER, J. B. (1966). Generalized expectations for internal versus external control of reinforcement. *Psychological Monographs, 80,* whole number 609.

RUBIN, E. (1958). Figure and ground. In D. C. Beardslee & M. Wertheimer (Eds.), *Readings in perception* (pp. 194–203). Princeton, NJ: Van Nostrand. (Original work published 1915)

RUSE, M. (1979). *The Darwinian revolution: Science red in tooth and claw.* Chicago: University of Chicago Press.

RUSSO, N. F. (1988). Women's participation in psychology: Reflecting and shaping the social context. In A. N. O'Connell & N. F. Russo (Eds.), *Models of achievement: Reflections of eminent women in psychology. Vol. 2* (pp. 9–27). Hillsdale, NJ: Lawrence Erlbaum.

RYALLS, J. (1984). Where does the term "aphasia" come from? *Brain and Language, 21,* 358–363.

RYAN, W. C. (1939). *Studies in early graduate education.* New York: Carnegie Foundation.

SAHAKIAN, W. S. (1975). *History and systems of psychology.* New York: John Wiley.

SAMELSON, F. (1981). Struggle for scientific authority: The reception of Watson's behaviorism in 1913. *Journal of the History of the Behavioral Sciences, 17,* 399–425.

SAMELSON, F. (1985). Organizing for the kingdom of behavior: Academic battles and organizational policies in the twenties. *Journal of the History of the Behavioral Sciences, 21,* 33–47.

SANFORD, E. C. (1910, August 8). *Letter to E. B. Titchener.* Titchener papers, Cornell University Archives, Ithaca, NY.

SATARIANO, W. A. (1979). Immigration and the popularization of social science, 1920 to 1930. *Journal of the History of the Behavioral Sciences, 15,* 310–320.

SCARBOROUGH, E., & FURUMOTO, L. (1987). *Untold lives: The first generation of American women psychologists.* New York: Columbia University Press.

SCHLERETH, T. J. (1991). *Victorian America: Transformations in everyday life.* New York: HarperCollins.

SCHULTZ, D. P. (1981). *A history of modern psychology* (3rd ed.). New York: Academic Press.

SCHULTZ, D. P., & SCHULTZ, S. E. (1987). *A history of modern psychology* (4th ed.). San Diego: Harcourt, Brace, Jovanovich.

SCOTT, W. D. (1903). *The theory and practice of advertising.* Boston: Small & Maynard.

SCOTT, W. D. (1910). *Human efficiency in business.* New York: Macmillan.

SCOTT-KAKURES, D., CASTAGNETTO, S., BENSON, H., TASCHEK, W., & HURLEY, P. (1993). *History of philosophy.* New York: HarperCollins.

SCRIPTURE, E. W. (1895). *Thinking, feeling, doing.* New York: Chautauqua-Century Press.

SEARLE, J. R. (1980). Minds, brains, and programs. *Behavioral and Brain Sciences, 3,* 417–424.

SECHENOV, I. M. (1965). Reflexes of the brain. Cambridge, MA: MIT Press. (Original work published 1863).

SEGAL, E. M., & LACHMAN, R. (1972). Complex behavior or higher mental processes: Is there a paradigm shift? *American Psychologist, 27,* 46–55.

SELIGMAN, M. E. P. (1970). On the generality of the laws of learning. *Psychological Review, 77,* 406–418.

SEX, RACE/ETHNICITY DATA AVAILABLE. (1995, Winter). *Trends in Education: APA Education Directorate News, 2(1),* 2–3.

SEXTON, V. S. (1965). Clinical psychology: An historical survey. *Genetic Psychology Monographs, 72,* 401–434.

SHAKOW, D. (1930). Hermann Ebbinghaus. *American Journal of Psychology, 42,* 505–518.

SHANNON, C. E., & WEAVER, W. (1949). *The mathematical theory of communication.* Urbana: University of Illinois Press.

SHERRINGTON, C. S. (1906). *The integrative action of the nervous system.* New Haven, CT: Yale University Press.

SIMONTON, D. K. (1994). *Greatness: Who makes history and why.* New York: Guilford Press.

SINGER, C. A. (1957). *A short history of anatomy and physiology from the Greeks to Harvey.* New York: Dover.

SKINNER, B. F. (1938). *The behavior of organisms: An experimental analysis.* New York: Appleton-Century-Crofts.

SKINNER, B. F. (1945). An operational analysis of psychological terms. *Psychological Review, 52,* 270–277.

SKINNER, B. F. (1948). *Walden Two.* New York: Macmillan.

SKINNER, B. F. (1953). *Science and human behavior.* New York: Macmillan.

SKINNER, B. F. (1956). A case history in scientific method. *American Psychologist, 12,* 221–223.

SKINNER, B. F. (1957). *Verbal Behavior.* New York: Appleton-Century-Crofts.

SKINNER, B. F. (1960). Pigeons in a pelican. *American Psychologist, 15,* 28–37.

SKINNER, B. F. (1979). *The shaping of a behaviorist.* New York: Knopf.

SKINNER, B. F. (1981). Pavlov's influence on psychology in America. *Journal of the History of the Behavioral Sciences, 17,* 242–245.

SKINNER, B. F. (1987). Whatever happened to psychology as the science of behavior? *American Psychologist, 42,* 780–786.

SKINNER, B. F. (1990). Can psychology be a science of the mind? *American Psychologist, 45,* 1206–1210.

SMALL, W. S. (1901). Experimental study of the mental processes of the rat. II. *American Journal of Psychology, 12,* 206–239.

SMITH, L. D. (1992). On prediction and control: B. F. Skinner and the technological ideal of science. *American Psychologist, 47,* 216–223.

SMITH, M. B. (1992). The American Psychological Association and social responsibility. In R. B. Evans, V. S. Sexton, & T. C. Cadwallader (Eds.), *The American Psychological Association: A historical perspective* (pp. 327–345). Washington, DC: American Psychological Association.

SOBEL, D. (1995). *Longitude: The true story of a lone genius who solved the greatest scientific problem of his time.* New York: Walker.

SOKAL, M. M. (1971). The unpublished autobiography of James McKeen Cattell. *American Psychologist, 26,* 626–635.

SOKAL, M. M. (1981a). The origins of the Psychological Corporation. *Journal of the History of the Behavioral Sciences, 17,* 54–67.

SOKAL, M. M. (Ed.). (1981b). *An education in psychology: James McKeen Cattell's journal and letters from Germany and England, 1880–1888.* Cambridge, MA: The MIT Press.

SOKAL, M. M. (1984). The Gestalt psychologists in behaviorist America. *American Historical Review, 89,* 1240–1263.

SOKAL, M. M. (1987). James McKeen Cattell and mental anthropometry: Nineteenth-century science and reform and the origins of psychological testing. In M. M. Sokal (Ed.), *Psychological testing and American society* (pp. 21–45). New Brunswick, NJ: Rutgers University Press.

SOKAL, M. M. (1992). Origins and early years of the American Psychological Association, 1890–1906. *American Psychologist, 47,* 111–122.

SOKOL, M. M., & RAFAIL, P. A. (1982). *A guide to manuscript collections in the history of psychology and selected areas.* Millwood, NY: Kraus International.

SOLSO, R. L. (Ed.). (1973). *Contemporary issues in cognitive psychology: The Loyola symposium.* Washington, DC: V. H. Winston.

SPALDING, D. A. (1873). Instinct, with original observations on young animals. *Macmillan's Magazine, 27,* 282–293.

SPENCE, K. W. (1952). Clark Leonard Hull: 1884–1952. *American Journal of Psychology, 65,* 639–646.

SPERRY, R. W. (1961). Cerebral organization and behavior. *Science, 133,* 1749–1757.

SPERRY, R. W. (1993). The impact and promise of the cognitive revolution. *American Psychologist, 48,* 878–885.

SPILLMAN, J., & SPILLMAN, L. (1993). The rise and fall of Hugo Münsterberg. *Journal of the History of the Behavioral Sciences, 29,* 322–338.

SPURZHEIM, J. G. (1978). *Outlines of phrenology.* In D. N. Robinson (Ed.), *Significant contributions to the history of psychology. Series E. Volume II.* Washington, DC: University Publications of America. (Original work published 1832)

A stash in the stacks. (1996, August/September). *Civilization, 3(4),* 15.

STERNS, C. Z. (1985). Victorian sexuality: Can historians do it better? *Journal of Social History, 18,* 625–634.

STETSON, G. R. (1897). Some memory tests of whites and blacks. *Psychological Review, 4,* 285–289.

STEUDEL, J. (1972). Johannes Peter Müller. In C. C. Gillespie (Ed.), *Dictionary of scientific biography. Vol. IX.* New York: Scribner.

STEVENS, S. S. (1935). The operational definition of concepts. *Psychological Review, 42,* 517–527.

STOCKING, G. W., JR. (1965). On the limits of "presentism" and "historicism" in the historiography of the behavioral sciences. *Journal of the History of the Behavioral Sciences, 1,* 211–217.

STROOP, J. R. (1992). Studies of interference in serial verbal reactions. *Journal of Experimental Psychology: General, 121,* 15–23. (Original work published 1935)

STRUNK, O., JR. (1972). The self-psychology of Mary Whiton Calkins. *Journal of the History of the Behavioral Sciences, 8,* 196–203.

SULLOWAY, F. J. (1979). *Freud: Biologist of the mind.* New York: Basic Books.

SULLOWAY, F. J. (1982). Darwin and his finches: The evolution of a legend. *Journal of the History of Biology, 15,* 1–53.

SWAZEY, J. P. (1972). Charles Scott Sherrington. In C. C. Gillespie (Ed.), *Dictionary of scientific biography. Vol. XII.* New York: Scribner.

TAYLOR, D. W. (1972). Santiago Ramón y Cajal. In C. C. Gillespie (Ed.), *Dictionary of scientific biography. Vol. XI.* New York: Scribner.

TEMKIN, O. (1947). Gall and the phrenological movement. *Bulletin of the History of Medicine, 21,* 275–321.

TERMAN, L. M. (1906). Genius and stupidity: A study of some of the intellectual processes of seven "bright" and seven "stupid" boys. *Pedagogical Seminary, 13,* 307–373.

TERMAN, L. M. (1924). The mental test as a psychological method. *Psychological Review, 31,* 93–117.

TERMAN, L. M. (1925). *Genetic studies of genius. Vol. 1. Mental and physical traits of a thousand gifted children.* Stanford, CA: Stanford University Press.

TERMAN, L. M. (1932). Trails to psychology. In C. Murchison (Ed.), *A history of psychology in autobiography. Vol. II* (pp. 297–332). Worcester, MA: Clark University Press.

TERMAN, L. M., & ODEN, M. H. (1947). *Genetic studies of genius. Vol. 4. The gifted child grows up: Twenty-five years' follow-up of a superior group.* Stanford, CA: Stanford University Press.

TERMAN, L. M., & ODEN, M. H. (1959). *Genetic studies of genius. Vol. 5. The gifted group at mid-life: Thirty-five years' follow-up of the superior child.* Stanford, CA: Stanford University Press.

THOMSON, K. S. (1975). HMS *Beagle,* 1820–1870. *American Scientist, 63,* 664–672.

THORNDIKE, E. L. (1899). A reply to "The nature of animal intelligence and the methods of investigating it." *Psychological Review, 6,* 412–420.

THORNDIKE, E. L. (1900). Comparative psychology. *Psychological Review, 7,* 424–426.

THORNDIKE, E. L. (1936). Edward Lee Thorndike. In C. Murchison (Ed.), *A history of psychology in autobiography. Vol. 3* (pp. 263–270). Worcester, MA: Clark University Press.

THORNDIKE, E. L. (1948). Animal intelligence. In W. Dennis (Ed.), *Readings in the history of psychology* (pp. 377–387). New York: Appleton-Century-Crofts. (Original work published 1898)

THORNDIKE, E. L., & WOODWORTH, R. S. (1901). The influence of improvement in one mental function upon the efficiency of other functions. I. *Psychological Review, 8,* 247–261.

THORNDIKE, R. L. (1991). Edward L. Thorndike: A professional and personal appreciation. In G. A. Kimble, M. Wertheimer, and C. L. White (Eds.), *Portraits of pioneers in psychology,* (pp. 139–151). Washington, DC: American Psychological Association.

TITCHENER, E. B. (1895). Note. *American Journal of Psychology, 7,* 448–449.

TITCHENER, E. B. (1898). Postulates of a structural psychology. *Psychological Review, 7,* 449–465.

TITCHENER, E. B. (1899). *An outline of psychology.* New York: Macmillan. (Original work published 1896)

TITCHENER, E. B. (1901). *Experimental psychology: A manual of laboratory practice. Vol. 1: Qualitative experiments. Part 1: Student's manual; part 2: Instructor's manual.* New York: Macmillan.

TITCHENER, E. B. (1905). *Experimental psychology: A manual of laboratory practice. Vol. 2: Quantitative experiments. Part 1: Student's manual; part 2: Instructor's manual.* New York: Macmillan.

TITCHENER, E. B. (1905). Review [of Thorndike's *Elements of Psychology*]. *Mind, 56,* 552–554.

TITCHENER, E. B. (1906, June 6). *Letter to L. N. Wilson.* Wilson Papers, Clark University, Worcester, MA.

TITCHENER, E. B. (1909). *A text-book of psychology.* New York: Macmillan.

TITCHENER, E. B. (1914). On "Psychology as the behaviorist views it." *Proceedings of the American Philosophical Society, 53,* 1–17.

TITCHENER, E. B. (1921). Wilhelm Wundt. *American Journal of Psychology, 32,* 161–178.

TODD, J. T. (1994). What psychology has to say about John B. Watson: Classical behaviorism in psychology textbooks, 1920–1989. In J. T. Todd & E. K. Morris (Eds.), *Modern perspectives on John B. Watson and classical behaviorism* (pp. 75–107). Westport, CT: Greenwood Press.

TODD, J. T., & MORRIS, E. K. (1986). The early research of John B. Watson: Before the behavioral revolution. *The Behavior Analyst, 9,* 71–88.

TODES, D. P. (1997). From the machine to the ghost within: Pavlov's transition from digestive physiology to conditional reflexes. *American Psychologist, 52,* 947–955.

TOLMAN, E. C. (1922). A new formula for behaviorism. *Psychological Review, 29,* 44–53.

TOLMAN, E. C. (1932). *Purposive behavior in animals and men.* New York: Appleton-Century-Crofts.

TOLMAN, E. C. (1938). The determiners of behavior at a choice point. *Psychological Review, 45,* 1–41.

TOLMAN, E. C. (1942). *Drives toward war.* New York: D. Appleton-Century Company.

TOLMAN, E. C. (1948). Cognitive maps in rats and men. *Psychological Review, 55,* 189–208.

TOLMAN, E. C. (1952). Edward Chace Tolman. In E. G. Boring, H. S. Langfeld, H. Werner, & R. M. Yerkes (Eds.), *A history of psychology in autobiography* (Vol. 4, pp. 323–339). Worcester, MA: Clark University Press.

TOLMAN, E. C. (1959). Principles of purposive behavior. In S. Koch (Ed.), *Psychology: A study of a science. Study 1. Volume 2* (pp. 92–157). New York: McGraw-Hill.

TOLMAN, E. C., & HONZIK, C. H. (1930). Introduction and removal of reward, and maze performance in rats. *University of California Publications in Psychology, 4,* 257–275.

TOLMAN, E. C., & NYSWANDER, D. B. (1927). The reliability and validity of maze-measures for rats. *Journal of Comparative Psychology, 7,* 425–460.

TOLMAN, E. C., RITCHIE, B. F., & KALISH, D. (1946a). Studies in spatial learning. II. Place learning versus response learning. *Journal of Experimental Psychology, 36,* 221229.

TOLMAN, E. C., RITCHIE, B. F., & KALISH, D. (1946b). Studies in spatial learning. I. Orientation and the short-cut. *Journal of Experimental Psychology, 36,* 13–24.

TOLMAN, E. C., TRYON, R. C., & JEFFRESS, L. A. (1929). A self-recording maze with an automatic delivery table. *University of California Publications in Psychology, 4,* 99–112.

TOLSTOY, L. (1942). *War and peace* (L. Maude and A. Maude, Trans.). New York: Simon and Schuster.

TRIPLETT, R. G. (1982). The relationship of Clark L. Hull's hypnosis research to his later learning theory: The continuity of a life's work. *Journal of the History of the Behavioral Sciences, 18,* 22–31.

TRIVERS, R. L. (1972). Parental investment and sexual selection. In B. Campbell (Ed.), *Sexual selection and the descent of man* (pp. 136–179). Chicago: Aldine Press.

TURING, A. M. (1950). Computing machinery and intelligence. *Mind, 59,* 433–460.

TURNER, R. S. (1972). Hermann von Helmholtz. In C. C. Gillespie (Ed.), *Dictionary of scientific biography. Vol. VI.* New York: Scribner.

TURNER, R. S. (1982). Helmholtz, sensory physiology, and the disciplinary development of German psychology. In W. R. Woodward & M. G. Ash (Eds.), *The problematic science: Psychology in nineteenth-century thought* (pp. 147–166). New York: Praeger.

TWITMYER, E. B. (1905). Knee-jerks without stimulation of the patellar tendon. *Psychological Bulletin, 2,* 43–44.

VALENTINE, C. W. (1930). The innate bases of fear. *Journal of Genetic Psychology, 37,* 394–420.

VEYSEY, L. R. (1965). *The emergence of the American university.* Chicago: University of Chicago Press.

VINEY, W. (1996). Dorothea Dix: An intellectual conscience for psychology. In G. A. Kimble, C. A. Bonneau, & M. Wertheimer (Eds.), *Portraits of pioneers in psychology. Vol. II* (pp. 15–31). Washington, DC: American Psychological Association.

VINEY, W., & ZORICH, S. (1982). Contributions to the history of psychology: XXIX. Dorothea Dix and the history of psychology. *Psychological Reports, 50,* 211–218.

VOYAT, G. (1981). Jean Piaget: 1896–1980. *American Journal of Psychology, 94,* 645–648.

VROOMAN, J. R. (1970). *René Descartes: A biography.* New York: Putnam.

WADE, N. J. (1994). Hermann von Helmholtz. *Perception, 23,* 981–989.

WALLIN, J. E. W. (1966). A red-letter day in APA history. *Journal of General Psychology, 75,* 107–114.

WARNER, L. H., & WARDEN, C. J. (1927). The development of a standardized animal maze. *Archives of Psychology, 15* (No. 92).

WARREN, R. M. (1984). Helmholtz and his continuing influence. *Music Perception, 1,* 253–275.

WASHBURN, M. F. (1908). *The animal mind.* New York: Macmillan.

WASHBURN, M. F. (1932). Margaret Floy Washburn. In C. Murchison (Ed.), *A history of psychology in autobiography. Vol. 2* (pp. 333–358). Worcester, MA: Clark University Press.

WATSON, J. B. (1903). *Animal education: An experimental study of the psychical development of the white rat, correlated with the growth of its nervous system.* Chicago: University of Chicago Press.

WATSON, J. B. (1907). Kinesthetic and organic sensations: Their role in the reactions of the white rat to the maze. *Psychological Review Monograph Supplements, 8* (#33).

WATSON, J. B. (1909). Some experiments bearing upon color vision in monkeys. *Journal of Comparative Neurology and Psychology, 19,* 1–28.

WATSON, J. B. (1910, February). The new science of animal behavior. *Harper's Monthly Magazine, 120,* 346–353.

WATSON, J. B. (1913). Psychology as the behaviorist views it. *Psychological Review, 20,* 158–177.

WATSON, J. B. (1914). *Behavior: An introduction to comparative psychology.* New York: Holt.

WATSON, J. B. (1916). The place of the conditioned reflex in psychology. *Psychological Review, 23,* 89–116.

WATSON, J. B. (1926, June). How we think: A behaviorist's view. *Harper's Monthly Magazine, 153,* 40–45.

WATSON, J. B. (1928). *Psychological care of infant and child.* New York: W. W. Norton.

WATSON, J. B. (1930). *Behaviorism* (2nd ed.). New York: W. W. Norton. (Original work published 1924)

WATSON, J. B. (1936). Autobiography. In C. Murchison (Ed.), *A history of psychology in autobiography. Vol. 3* (pp. 271–281). Worcester, MA: Clark University Press.

WATSON, J. B., & MORGAN, J. J. B. (1917). Emotional reactions and psychological experimentation. *American Journal of Psychology, 28,* 163–174.

WATSON, J. B., & RAYNER, R. (1920). Conditioned emotional reactions. *Journal of Experimental Psychology, 3,* 1–14.

WATSON, R. I. (1953). A brief history of clinical psychology. *Psychological Bulletin, 50,* 321–346.

WATSON, R. I. (1960). The history of psychology: A neglected area. *American Psychologist, 15,* 251–255.

WATSON, R. I., & EVANS, R. B. (1991). *The great psychologists: A history of psychological thought* (5th ed.). New York: HarperCollins.

WEAVER, K. A. (in press). Capturing the fervor of cognitive psychology's emergence. *Teaching of Psychology.*

WEBB, M. E. (1988). A new history of Hartley's "Observations on Man." *Journal of the History of the Behavioral Sciences, 24,* 202–211.

WEINER, J. (1994). *The beak of the finch.* New York: Vintage Books.

WERTHEIMER, M. (1967). Gestalt theory. In W. D. Ellis (Ed.), *A source book of Gestalt psychology* (pp. 1–11). London: Routledge and Kegan Paul. (Original talk delivered 1924)

WERTHEIMER, M. (1967). Laws of organization in perceptual forms. In W. D. Ellis (Ed.), *A source book of Gestalt psychology* (pp. 71–88). London: Routledge and Kegan Paul. (Original work published 1923)

WERTHEIMER, M. (1982). *Productive thinking.* Chicago: University of Chicago Press. (Original work published 1945)

WERTHEIMER, M. (1978). Humanistic psychology and the humane but tough-minded psychologist. *American Psychologist, 33,* 739–745.

WESTEN, D. (1996). *Psychology: Mind, brain, and culture.* New York: John Wiley.

WHITE, R. K. (1978). Has "field theory" been "tried and found wanting"? *Journal of the History of the Behavioral Sciences, 14,* 242–246.

WIGGINS, J. G. JR. (1994). Would you want your child to be a psychologist? *American Psychologist, 49,* 485–492.

WILLIAMS, D. H., BELLIS, E. C., & WELLINGTON, S. W. (1980). Deinstitutionalization and social policy: Historical perspectives and present dilemmas. *American Journal of Orthopsychiatry, 50,* 54–64.

WILLIAMS, S. B. (1938). Resistance to extinction as a function of the number of reinforcements. *Journal of Experimental Psychology, 23,* 506–521.

WILSON, E. O. (1975). *Sociobiology: The new synthesis.* Cambridge, MA: Harvard University Press.

WILSON, E. O. (1994). *Naturalist.* New York: Warner Books.

WINDHOLTZ, G. (1986). A comparative analysis of the conditional reflex discoveries of Pavlov and Twitmyer, and the birth of a paradigm. *Pavlovian Journal of Biological Science, 21,* 141–147.

WINDHOLTZ, G., & LAMAL, P. A. (1985). Köhler's insight revisited. *Teaching of Psychology, 12,* 165–167.

WINSTON, A. S. (1990). Robert Sessions Woodworth and the "Columbia Bible": How the psychological experiment was redefined. *American Journal of Psychology, 103,* 391–401.

WINSTON, A. S. (1996). "As his name indicates": R. S. Woodworth's letters of reference and employment for Jewish psychologists in the 1930s. *Journal of the History of the Behavioral Sciences, 32,* 30–43.

WINTERS, B. (1950). Franz Anton Mesmer: An inquiry into the antecedents of hypnosis. *Journal of General Psychology, 43,* 63–75.

WISSLER, C. (1965). Clark Wissler (1870–1947) on the inadequacy of mental tests. In R. J. Herrnstein & E. G. Boring (Eds.), *A sourcebook in the history of psychology* (pp. 442–445). Cambridge, MA: Harvard University Press. (Original work published 1901)

WITMER, L. (1893, July 14). *Letter to Hugo Münsterberg.* Münsterberg papers, Boston Public Library, Boston, MA.

WITMER, L. (1909). The study and treatment of retardation: A field of applied psychology. *Psychological Bulletin, 6,* 121–127.

WITMER, L. (1911). Criminals in the making. *The Psychological Clinic, 4,* 221–238.

WITMER, L. (1931). Clinical psychology. In R. A. Brotemarkle (Ed.), *Clinical psychology: Studies in honor of Lightner Witmer* (pp. 341–352). Philadelphia: University of Pennsylvania Press. (Original work published 1907)

WOLPE, J. (1958). *Psychotherapy by reciprocal inhibition.* Palo Alto, CA: Stanford University Press.

WOODWORTH, R. S. (1917). Some criticisms of the Freudian psychology. *American Journal of Psychology, 12,* 174–194.

WOODWORTH, R. S. (1918). *Dynamic psychology.* New York: Columbia University Press.

WOODWORTH, R. S. (1921). *Psychology.* New York: Holt.

WOODWORTH, R. S. (1931). *Contemporary schools of psychology.* New York: Ronald Press.

WOODWORTH, R. S. (1938). *Experimental psychology.* New York: Holt.

WOODWORTH, R. S. (1958). *Dynamics of behavior.* New York: Holt.

WOODWORTH, R. S., & SCHLOSBERG, H. (1954). *Experimental psychology* (2nd ed.) New York: Holt.

WRIGHT, R. (1994). *The moral animal. Why we are the way we are: The new science of evolutionary psychology.* New York: Vintage Books.

WUNDT, W. (1904). *Principles of physiological psychology* (5th ed.)(E. B. Titchener, Trans.). New York: Macmillan. (Original work published 1873–1874)

YERKES, R. M. (1911). *Introduction to psychology.* New York: Holt.

YERKES, R. M. (Ed.). (1921). Psychological examining in the United States Army. *Memoirs of the National Academy of Sciences, 15,* 1–890.

YERKES, R. M., & MORGULIS, S. (1909). The method of Pawlow in animal psychology. *Psychological Bulletin, 6,* 257–273.

YOAKUM, C. S., & YERKES, R. M. (1920). *Army mental tests.* New York: Holt.

YOUNG, R. M. (1972). Franz Joseph Gall. In C. C. Gillespie (Ed.), *Dictionary of scientific biography. Vol. V.* New York: Scribner.

ZAJONC, B. F. (1980). Feeling and thinking: Preferences need no inferences. *American Psychologist, 35,* 151–175.

ZEIGARNIK, B. (1967). On finished and unfinished tasks. In W. D. Ellis (Ed.), *A source book of Gestalt psychology* (pp. 300–314). London: Routledge and Kegan Paul. (Original work published 1927)

ZILBOORG, G. (1941). *A history of medical psychology.* New York: W. W. Norton.

Ablation Method of studying the brain, pioneered by Flourens, in which the function of some brain area is assessed after that portion of the brain has been destroyed.

Absolute Threshold Point on the continuum of a physical dimension where an increase in physical stimulation results in the initial perception of a stimulus.

Accommodation Visual phenomenon described by Berkeley; the tendency of the lens of the eye to change shape as objects move toward and away from the person.

Algorithm In math and computer science, a set of rules guaranteed to produce an eventual solution to a problem by exhaustively working through all possible solutions.

Analytical Psychology Jung's theory of psychology, which differed from Freud's in a number of ways, including a decreased emphasis on sex.

Anecdotal Method Research method in which evidence takes the form of an accumulation of examples supporting some principle or theory; associated with Romanes and the origins of comparative psychology; also used by phrenologists; heavy reliance on such evidence leads one to ignore counterinstances that might disprove a hypothesis.

Animal Magnetism Belief held by Mesmer and contemporaries that living organisms were influenced by magnetic forces and that cures for illness could result from the proper use of magnets.

Animal Spirits Hypothetical essence once believed (e.g., by Descartes) to inhabit the nervous system and to be the driving force behind muscle movement.

Anna O. Case Famous case of hysteria treated by Breuer and reported by Breuer and Freud in *Studies on Hysteria*; gave Freud the insight that hysterics suffer from their memories of traumatic events; details distorted over the years.

Anthropomorphism Tendency to attribute human characteristics to nonhuman entities; associated with Romanes and the origins of comparative psychology.

Apparent Motion Phenomenon studied by Wertheimer in which stationary stimuli appear to move under certain circumstances.

Apperception A high level of awareness, in which we focus our full attention on some object and apprehend it fully; associated with Leibnitz originally; central concept for Wundt's psychology.

Approach-Approach Conflict For Lewin, a situation in which a conflict exists within a person, resulting from having to make a choice between two goals with a positive valence.

Approach-Avoidance Conflict For Lewin, a situation in which a conflict exists within a person, occurring when a goal elicits both approach and avoidance tendencies.

Archive A repository of unpublished data of use to historians.

Argument From Design Explained the great complexity in nature by arguing that it required a superior being (i.e., God) to produce it; associated with Reverend Paley.

Army Alpha Group intelligence test developed by Yerkes for testing the abilities of literate soldiers in World War I.

Army Beta Group intelligence test developed by Yerkes for testing the abilities of illiterate soldiers in World War I.

Artificial Intelligence The study of whether machines can be said to act with some degree of intelligence.

Association For Locke, analogous to Newtonian gravity; a force that attracts ideas.

Associationism Philosophical school of thought, related to empiricism, which emphasizes the rules by which relationships between ideas and between experiences and ideas are formed.

Atomism Belief that nature can be understood best by reducing complexity to its smallest, most fundamental elements (opposed to holism).

Attributes In Titchener's system, these were the ways of classifying the various elements of conscious experience; for example, the element of sensation had the attributes of quality, intensity, duration, and clarity.

Attrition Methodological problem in longitudinal research, when participants drop out of the study; notably low in Terman's longitudinal study of giftedness.

Avoidance-Avoidance Conflict For Lewin, a situation in which a conflict exists within a person, resulting from having to make a choice between two goals with a negative valence.

Behavioral Environment For the gestaltists, this referred to the environment as perceived, as contrasted with the physical environment (the geographical environment).

Behavioral Genetics Study of the influence of genetics on behavior (e.g., twin studies of intelligence).

Behaviorist Manifesto Watson's 1913 paper that argued for a behaviorist approach to psychology.

Bell-Magendie Law A statement that the posterior roots of the spinal cord controlled sensation, while the anterior roots controlled motor movement; sometimes considered an example of a "multiple."

Binocular Vision Vision involving the use of two eyes; aids in depth perception.

Bit Abbreviation of "binary digit"; the amount of information that enables a choice between two alternatives.

Brass Instrument Psychology Term used (sarcastically) by William James to describe the German reaction time and psychophysics research, which relied heavily on apparatus made of brass.

Cartesian Dichotomy From Descartes, the distinction between humans (mind + body) and animals (only a mechanical body).

Catastrophism Theory in geology that geological change occurred infrequently and as a consequence of such catastrophic events as the Biblical flood.

Catharsis In Freudian psychoanalysis, an emotional release that occurs when one gains insight into the unconscious origins of some problem; key part of the Anna O. case.

Cause and Effect One of Hume's laws of association; Hume argued that we cannot be certain of the fundamental causes of events, only that events occur together regularly.

Cell Assembly For Hebb, a basic unit in the nervous system, a set of neurons that become associated with each other because they have been repeatedly activated together.

Chinese Room Problem Thought problem by Serle that illustrates a problem that would pass the Turing test but would still not support strong AI.

Chunk For Miller, a meaningful unit of information; short-term memory capacity said to be 7 ± 2 chunks of information.

Client-Centered Therapy Humanistic approach to psychotherapy created by Rogers; it assumed that responsibility for therapeutic change ultimately belonged to the client, while the therapist's responsibility was to create an atmosphere conducive to such change.

Clinical Method Method of studying the brain, pioneered by Broca, in which existing behavioral or cognitive deficits are correlated with brain damage upon autopsy.

Clinical Psychology Field of psychology concerned with the diagnosis and treatment of mental and behavioral disorders; named by Witmer.

Closure Gestalt organizing principle, a tendency to fill in missing gaps in our perception in order to perceive whole figures.

Cognitive Map For Tolman, a hypothetical spatial memory of a maze, acquired simply as a result of experiencing the maze (i.e., reinforcement not needed).

Cognitive Science An interdisciplinary field that includes cognitive psychology, linguistics, computer science, cultural anthropology, and epistemology.

Collective Unconscious Jung's concept that the unconscious included the collective experiences of our ancestors; reflected in the common themes that occur in the mythology of various cultures.

Comparative Psychology Study of the similarities and differences among species; originated from the implication of Darwin's theory of evolution that a continuity existed among species.

Completion Test Mental test designed by Ebbinghaus to measure mental fatigue in school children; because it focused on higher mental activity, it anticipated the approach later taken by Binet.

Complex Idea For Locke, ideas that were combinations of simple ideas.

Complication Experiment A nineteenth-century reaction time experiment, typically using the Donders subtractive method, in which reaction times for simple tasks were subtracted from reaction times for more "complicated" tasks.

Concomitant Variation From Mill's *Logic,* method that examines whether changes in event X are associated with changes in event Y.

Condensation In Freudian dream analysis, said to occur in dreams when two or more unconscious thoughts combine into one symbol.

Conditional Stimulus Any stimulus in Pavlovian conditioning that will be paired with an unconditioned stimulus to produce a conditioned response (e.g., tone).

Conditioned Reflex The outcome of Pavlovian conditioning; by pairing a conditioned (conditional) stimulus (e.g., tone) with an unconditioned stimulus (e.g., food), the conditioned stimulus eventually elicits a conditioned response or reflex.

Connectionism Thorndike's model of learning, emphasizing the development and strengthening of connections between stimulus situations and responses that became stronger with trial and error learning.

Conscious Attitudes In the Würzburg school, referred to such mental processes as hesitation and doubt; occurred during the imageless thought studies.

Consciousness Sense of awareness; how to study it became a contentious issue in the late nineteenth and early twentieth centuries.

Conservation of Energy Associated with Helmholtz and used by him to combat vitalism; proposed that the total energy within a system remains constant, even if changes occur within the system.

Conservative Focusing Concept identification strategy identified by Bruner, Goodnow, and Austin that emphasized the active nature of cognitive activities; involved arriving at a concept by testing one dimension at a time; less risky than focus gambling.

Contiguity One of Hume's laws of association and Hartley's fundamental law; events experienced together, either simultaneously (spatial contiguity) or successively (temporal contiguity), become associated with each other.

Convergence Visual phenomenon described by Berkeley; the tendency of the eye muscles to make the eyes move in the direction of "crossing" as objects move closer to the person.

Converging Operations Refers to a series of studies, each with different operational definitions of the main constructs, that nonetheless lead to the same general conclusion.

Correlation Statistical tool that assesses the degree of relationship between two variables; concept originated with Galton and his studies of intelligence.

Critical Period Certain instinctive behaviors (e.g., imprinting) must develop within a limited time frame, if they are to develop at all; associated with Lorenz and other European ethologists, but also proposed by Spalding.

Cybernetics Study of principles (e.g., feedback) involved in controlling and maintaining any living or nonliving system; feedback loop borrowed by Miller, Galanter, and Pribram for their TOTE unit.

Darwin's Finches Key data for his theory of evolution came from different species of finch on the Galápagos islands; birds on islands with different ecosystems evolved different adaptive mechanisms (e.g., beak shape).

Dedifferentiation For Lewin, a process that occurs under stress, in which a person reverses the normal differentiation process and reverts to an earlier, more primitive way of behaving; similar to Freudian regression.

Defense Mechanisms In Freudian theory, ways of behaving or thinking that serve to defend the ego against anxiety.

Dependent Variable Any variable in research that

is measured as an outcome of an experimental study; this usage introduced by Woodworth.

Derived Ideas For Descartes, ideas that result from one's experiences in the world.

Determinism Philosophical position that all events in the universe have prior causes.

Difference Threshold Point on the continuum of a physical dimension where a difference between two stimuli is first detected.

Differentiation For Lewin, a developmental process in which a child's life space becomes more complex; for Pavlov, refers to discrimination, the ability to distinguish between two stimuli.

Direct Action of the Nervous System Darwin's principle of emotional expression, stating that some expressions (e.g., blushing) are the side effects of the physiological arousal accompanying strongly felt emotions

Displacement In Freudian dream analysis, a minor part of the manifest content might be the major part of the latent content, and vice versa.

Dream Analysis A cornerstone of Freudian psychoanalysis; for Freud, dreams were the "royal road" to the unconscious; surface or manifest content of dreams needed to be analyzed for their deeper, or latent content.

Drill Courses Instructional courses in basic laboratory techniques, predominant in American universities in the late nineteenth century.

Drive Term referring to motivational processes (e.g., the hunger drive), introduced to psychology by Woodworth as an example of a factor that intervenes between stimulus and response; important intervening variable for Hull.

Drive Reduction Central to Hull's theory of learning; learning required reinforcers, which were any stimuli (e.g., food) that reduced a strong drive (e.g., hunger).

Dualist On the mind-body problem, someone (e.g., Descartes) who believes that mind and body are two separate and distinguishable essences.

Ecological Memory Study of memory as it occurs in everyday situations.

Ecological Validity In cognitive psychology, research that is relevant for understanding everyday cognitive activities is said to have ecological validity.

Ego In Freudian theory, the center of personality, the mediator between the demands of the id and superego, and the constraints of reality.

Empiricist Someone who believes that our knowledge of the world is constructed from our experiences in it; school of thought associated with such British philosophers as Locke, Berkeley, and Mill.

Enlightenment Historical period from mid-eighteenth century to late nineteenth century, characterized by a belief that true knowledge could be found through the use of science and reason and that progress was inevitable and good.

Epistemology Branch of philosophy concerned with studying the nature of and the origins of human knowledge.

Eponyms Historical periods or movements named with reference to some important historical person (e.g., Darwinian biology).

Equilibrium For Lewin, a steady state in which all needs have been satisfied for the moment.

Equipotentiality Principle associated with Lashley, proposing that if some portion of the brain is destroyed, other areas will be able to serve the same function (to a degree).

Ergonomics Study of how systems and equipment can be best designed to avoid human error; pioneered by Gilbreath.

Eros In Freudian theory, the name given to the life instinct and manifested in the sex drive.

Ethology The study of animal behavior in its natural surroundings; associated with Lorenz, but with roots in Spalding's work.

Eugenics Term created by Galton, referring to a variety of methods (e.g., selective breeding) for enhancing the quality of a species, especially humans.

Evolutionary Psychology Late twentieth century development in psychology, with roots in Darwinian thinking; proposes that virtually all human behavior, especially social behavior, must be understood in an evolutionary context, as the product of natural selection.

Experimental Neurosis In Pavlovian conditioning, an emotional response that occurs after training a discrimination between two stimuli, then making the stimuli too similar to be discriminated.

Explanatory Fictions For Skinner, hypothetical constructs proposed as mediators between stimuli and responses that erroneously become used as explanations for behavioral phenomena (e.g., recalling only a few words *because of* limited short-term memory).

External History A history that examines factors external to a discipline (e.g., social, political, institutional, economic) that influence the history of that discipline.

Extinction In Pavlovian conditioning, the gradual elimination of a conditioned response following the repeated presentation of a conditioned stimulus in the absence of an unconditioned stimulus.

Faculty Psychology Prevalent early and mid-nineteenth-century approach to psychology, derived from Scottish Realism; emphasized real existence of mind, which they believed held a number of innate attributes ("faculties"), such as intelligence and judgment.

Field Theory Associated with Lewin and Tolman; for Lewin, derived from his belief that to understand behavior requires knowing about all of the forces acting on a person at a particular time; for Tolman, reflected the extent to which his neobehaviorism was influenced by the gestaltists.

Figure-Ground Gestalt organizing principle stating that a fundamental perceptual tendency is to separate whole figures from their backgrounds.

Focus Gambling Concept identification strategy identified by Bruner, Goodnow, and Austin that emphasized the active nature of cognitive activities; involved arriving at a concept by testing more than one dimension at a time; riskier than conservative focusing.

Foreign Hull For Lewin, all events outside of the person's life space, and therefore having no effect on the individual at a given moment.

Forensic Psychology The application of psychology to the law, pioneered by Münsterberg.

Form-Quality As described by von Ehrenfels, the overall quality of some entity (e.g., a melody, a square) that exists over and above its individual components (e.g., notes, lines).

Fractionation Procedure developed in Külpe's laboratory in Würzburg, in which complicated events were broken down into sections ("fractionated"); then separate introspections were accomplished for each section.

Free Association In Freudian psychoanalysis, a procedure to probe the unconscious, in which patients describe whatever occurs to them without internal censorship.

Freudian Slip An apparent accident, error, or slip of the tongue that Freud considered a reflection of some unconscious motive.

Functional Fixedness Failure to solve a problem because of an inability to think of using some object in a manner different from its normal function.

Functionalism School of psychology favored by most early American psychologists; focused on the study of human conscious experience from an evolutionary perspective, concerned with studying the adaptive value of various mental and behavioral processes.

Generalization The tendency for a response learned to one stimulus to occur after the presentation of a second stimulus similar to the first.

Genetic Epistemology Piagetian psychology, which examined the manner in which knowledge developed within the individual.

Genetic Psychology Approach that emphasizes the evolution and development of the mind, including developmental psychology, comparative psychology, and abnormal psychology; associated with Hall.

Geocentric Ancient astronomical viewpoint that placed earth at the center of the known universe.

Geographical Environment For the gestaltists, this referred to the physical environment, as contrasted with the environment as perceived (the behavioral environment).

Gestalt Organizing Principles Perceptual principles described by the gestaltists that summarize the ways in which sensory phenomena become organized into a whole, meaningful figure.

Good Continuation Gestalt organizing principle, a tendency to organize perceptions in a smoothly flowing direction.

Grammar Set of rules allowing for (a) the production of all possible sentences in a language, and (b) the recognition and rejection of non-sentences.

Habit Strength For Hull, an intervening variable influencing behavior that was a direct function of the number of reinforced trials ($_sH_R$).

Hebb Synapses For Hebb, synapses that change their structure as a result of learning.

Heliocentric Astronomical viewpoint proposed by Copernicus and elaborated by Galileo that placed the sun at the center of the known universe.

Heuristic In math and computer science, a creative rule of thumb that, while not guaranteeing to produce a problem solution, is likely to produce one, and will be more efficient than an algorithm (e.g., means-ends analysis).

Historicist An interpretation of historical events

made from the vantage point of the knowledge and values in place at the time of the events.

Historiography The writing of history; historical methodology and theory.

Holism The philosophical assumption underlying gestalt psychology; argues that wholes (e.g., complex ideas) are more than the sum of their constituent elements (e.g., sensations, simple ideas); opposed to atomism.

Humanistic Psychology Movement pioneered by Rogers, Maslow, and others as a reaction to the deterministic assumptions of behaviorism and psychoanalysis; assumed that humans are characterized by free will, a search for meaning, and the potential for self-actualization.

Hypnotism State of heightened suggestibility, pioneered by Mesmer, Elliotson, and named by Braid.

Hypothetico-Deductive System General approach taken by Hull in which hypotheses for research are deduced from the formal postulates of the theory, and the outcomes of research support the theory or lead to its modification.

Hysteria Disorder in which a number of symptoms (e.g., paralysis) indicate neurological damage, but no such damage exists.

Id In Freudian theory, that part of personality that reflects the basic biological instincts of sex and aggression.

Ideas For Hume, ideas were "faint copies" of sensory impressions.

Imageless Thought Any thought process that could not be further reduced to mental images; considered nonexistent by Titchener, who believed that all thought included images.

Impressions For Hume, these were basic sensations, the raw data of experience.

Imprinting Instinctive tendency for newly hatched ducklings (and other related species) to follow the first moving object they encounter; associated with Lorenz, but also observed by Spalding and Watson.

Independent Variable Any variable in research that can be directly manipulated by an experimenter; this usage introduced by Woodworth.

Individual Differences Originally referring to the individual variation among members of a particular species, became for psychology the more general study of the characteristics that differentiated one person from another (e.g., intelligence).

Individual Psychology Label used by both Binet and Adler; for Binet, psychology should focus on ways of identifying and measuring individual differences (e.g., mental testing) rather than on general laws; for Adler, individual psychology was his version of psychoanalysis, which emphasized social factors in the development of the individual.

Inductive An approach to knowledge that emphasizes that general scientific principles are generalizations made after the collection of large amounts of data; associated with Sir Francis Bacon.

Inferiority Complex Concept associated with Adler, who believed that much of human behavior could be viewed as an attempt to compensate for feelings of inferiority.

Information Theory An influence external to psychology that helped develop cognitive psychology; concerns the manner in which information is structured (bits) and processed.

Inheritance of Acquired Characteristics Theory that characteristics developed as a result of experience during one's lifetime could be passed on biologically to offspring; associated with Lamarck.

Innate Idea Idea that exists or can be deduced in the absence of direct experience, through reasoning (the idea of a material object's "extension" in space was used by Descartes as an example).

Insight For the gestaltists, a sudden problem solution that occurred when the individual reorganized the elements of the problem situation into a new configuration.

Instinct Behavior is said to be instinctive when alternative explanations in terms of learning or experience can be ruled out; pioneering work done by early comparative psychologists, especially Spalding.

Intelligence Quotient Term invented by Stern and used by Terman in the Stanford-Binet tests; "IQ" equaled mental age divided by chronological age, the result multiplied by 100.

Interactionist A dualist who believes that body and mind directly influence each other.

Internal History A history of the ideas, theories, and findings of a discipline, without regard for the influence of external, contextual factors.

Internal Perception Wundt's version of introspection, in which "observers' would give brief verbal responses to controlled stimuli (e.g., in reaction time or psychophysics experiments).

Intervening Variables Used by Tolman and Hull; referred to hypothetical internal factors (e.g., cognitive map for Tolman; habit strength for Hull) that intervened between stimulus and response.

Introspection Method of experiencing some phenomenon, then giving a description of the conscious experience of the phenomenon.

Introspective Habit The result of extensive practice with introspection, this was a dissociative ability to make mental notes about an experience while the experience was occurring.

Isomorphism For the gestaltists, the idea that perceptual experience and underlying physiological events are functionally equivalent.

James-Lange Theory of Emotion Theory that held that the strong emotions were in essence the physiological reaction that followed the perception of some emotion-eliciting event.

jnd Or just noticeable difference; point where the difference (in weight, color, pitch, etc.) between two stimuli becomes just barely detectable.

Jost's Law If two associations have equal strength, additional practice strengthens the older of the associations more than the younger.

Latent Learning For Tolman, learning that occurred but was not reflected in an animal's performance.

Law of Effect Thorndike's principle that behaviors that were effective in problem solving would be strengthened (stamped in), while behaviors that were not effective would be weakened (stamped out).

Law of Exercise Thorndike's principle that learned connections between stimuli and responses were strengthened with additional practice.

Libido For Freud, psychic energy associated with the sex drive.

Life Space For Lewin, a field within which a person operates; includes all the factors that influence a person's behavior at a certain moment.

Linguistic Universals For Chomsky, common principles shared by all languages, the existence of which supports the notion that language is innate to the human species.

Lloyd Morgan's Canon Principle of parsimony, stating that the best explanation for some phenomenon was the one with the fewest assumptions; Morgan argued that there was no need to propose mental capabilities beyond the level needed for survival in a given species.

Localization of Function Concerns the issue of whether specific parts of the brain have specific functions.

Logical Positivism Philosophical movement associated with the Vienna Circle that extended positivist thinking; distinguished between theoretical and observable events and described ways of connecting the two through operational definitions.

Mass Action Principle associated with Lashley, proposing a limit on equipotentiality; the greater the amount of brain destroyed, the greater the difficulty for remaining areas of the brain to take over brain function.

Materialism Philosophical position that the only reality is physical reality and that living matter can be reduced to physical and chemical properties; held by most physiologists of the nineteenth century; opposed to vitalism.

Means-End Analysis Primary heuristic used in GPS (General Problem Solver), a computer simulation of logic by Newell and Simon; involves a feedback system of recognizing a difference between present state and goal state, then applying a series of operations to reduce the difference until it disappears.

Mechanist Someone who explains bodily actions in mechanical terms.

Memory Drum Device for presenting verbal stimuli in a memory experiment; invented by G. E. Müller.

Mental Age Mistranslation of Binet's mental level; indicated a child's level of mental ability, reported in terms of years.

Mental Chronometry Name given to nineteenth-century reaction time research, in which the goal was to measure the time taken for various mental events.

Mental Level Term used by Binet to indicate a child's level of mental functioning; those in need of remediation scored two levels below the norm for their chronological age.

Mental Set In the Würzburg laboratory, referred to the effect of giving observers some instructions that predispose them to think in certain ways; for the gestaltists, a fixed, habitual way of thinking.

Mental Test Any test designed to measure mental activity or ability; term introduced in 1890 by Cattell.

Meritocracy A model of society based on the idea that the most mentally competent should be the leaders; championed by most American mental testers, especially Terman.

Mesmerism Early version of hypnotism, associated with Mesmer; held that hysteria and other disorders could be cured through the use of magnets.

Metapsychology For Freud, a general theory about the causes of human behavior and mental processes.

Method of Adjustment Method of psychophysics, described by Fechner, in which the subject directly controls a physical stimulus, adjusting it until it is just barely detected.

Method of Agreement From Mill's *Logic*, a method in which a proposed cause is present whenever the effect is also present.

Method of Constant Stimuli Method of psychophysics, described by Fechner, in which stimuli of varying physical intensities are presented in random order.

Method of Difference From Mill's *Logic*, a method in which the absence of a proposed effect is always accompanied by the absence of a proposed cause.

Method of Limits Method of psychophysics, described by Fechner, which alternates ascending trials (stimulus is first below threshold, then increased until detected) and descending trials (stimulus is first well above threshold, then decreased until no longer detected).

Molar Behavior For Tolman, broad patterns of behavior that were goal-directed, in contrast with the molecular behavior that was the result of a reductionist model of behavior.

Monads For Leibnitz, the fundamental elements of both physical and mental reality.

Moral Anxiety In Freudian theory, feelings of guilt or shame that result from fear of violating one's moral code.

Moron Term invented by Goddard as a label for adolescents or adults scoring at a mental age of 8 through 12.

Motor Aphasia Found in Broca's patient Tan; speech apparatus normal, intelligence normal, but a serious inability to express ideas verbally.

Multiple The simultaneous or near simultaneous discovery of some phenomenon, used to support the importance of the zeitgeist and a naturalistic approach to history.

Nativism An extreme nationalist tendency, in which outsiders are considered inferior and dangerous; characterized United States in 1920s, contributing to restrictions placed on immigration.

Nativist Someone who argues for the existence of innate ideas or, more generally, believes that some knowledge, faculties, or abilities are innate.

Natural Selection Central idea in Darwin's theory of evolution; held that in the struggle for existence, those organisms with adaptive variations would be most likely to survive (i.e., be selected by nature) and pass their attributes on to the next generation.

Naturalistic An approach to history that emphasizes the importance of environmental and situational forces in shaping history.

Neobehaviorism Behaviorist movement that emerged in the 1930s, associated with Tolman, Hull, and others.

Neurotic Anxiety In Freudian theory, anxiety that results from a fear that id-based impulses will get out of control.

Neurypnology Term created by Braid to reflect his belief that hypnotism was related to the state of sleep.

Nonsense Syllables Consonant-vowel-consonant combinations, invented by Ebbinghaus as stimulus materials in his studies on the formation and retention of associations.

Normal Science In Kuhn's approach to the history of science, this is a period during which a paradigm is in control and a scientist's activities are shaped by the constraints of the paradigm.

Objective Anxiety In Freudian theory, the anxiety that results from a genuine threat from reality.

Observer Name used for someone participating in a psychological experiment in the late nineteenth and early twentieth centuries, so-called because the primary activity was observing one's mental activities through introspection.

Operant Conditioning Skinnerian conditioning in which a behavior occurs, and the immediate consequences of the behavior determine its future probability of occurrence.

Operational Definition A definition in terms of a specific, observable set of operations (e.g., hunger = 24 hours without food); more generally, defining scientific terms with precision.

Operationism Philosophical position that scientific concepts were to be defined in terms of a set of operations used to measure those concepts.

Ophthalmoscope Device for examining the retina, invented by Helmholtz.

Opponent Process Theory Theory of color vision

associated with Hering, which proposed that color-sensitive cells are arranged in opponent pairs (e.g., red-green, blue-yellow).

Orthogenics Witmer's term for his therapeutic strategy of helping those with school-related problems (e.g., learning disabilities) to recover.

Paired-Associate Learning Popular learning procedure in which pairs of stimuli are presented; after a study time, stimuli are presented and the associated response must be given; invented by Calkins.

Paradigm In Kuhn's approach to the history of science, an all-encompassing theory that determines which problems are to be solved and the methods used to solve them.

Parallelism Dualistic position on the mind-body problem, associated with Leibnitz and others; asserts that mind and body are separate and non-interacting, but in perfect harmony.

Parental Investment Sociobiological concept introduced by Trivers, referring to male-female differences in the process of perpetuating the species.

Personal Equation Calibrating the reaction of one astronomer against another astronomer; needed because different reaction times among astronomers yielded different astronomical measurements.

Personalistic An approach to history that emphasizes persons and their roles in shaping historical events.

Petites Perceptions For Leibnitz, perceptions below the level of awareness, but essential for higher levels of perception.

Phase Sequences For Hebb, a higher level of cortical organization than the cell assembly, in which combinations of assemblies are formed.

Phi Phenomenon Wertheimer's term for apparent motion, chosen to avoid the connotation that "apparent" motion was not really perceived, but was illusory.

Pineal Gland Portion of the brain selected by Descartes as the locus for mind-body interactions.

Positivism Philosophical position associated with Comte who argued that the only certain knowledge is obtained through objective, publicly observable events.

Pragmatic Philosophy Position taken by several late nineteenth-century American philosophers, most notably William James; judged the value of ideas by their usefulness in helping someone adapt to the environment.

Pragnänz Gestalt organizing principle of perception (translation—"good figure"), a tendency for our perceptions to mirror reality as closely as possible.

Presentist An interpretation of historical events made from the vantage point of present-day knowledge and values.

Primary Qualities For Locke, attributes of some object that are inherent to that object, that exist regardless of perception (e.g., extension in space).

Primary Reinforcers For Hull, unlearned reinforcers (e.g., food).

Principle of Antithesis Darwin's principle of emotional expression, stating that some emotions that were the opposite of each other were reflected in expressions that were likewise opposed.

Principle of Serviceable Associated Habits Darwin's belief that emotional expressions were the product of evolutionary forces; certain expressions (e.g., sneer) originally had some survival function.

Problem of Perception For Helmholtz, it was the dilemma posed by the fact that human perception is extraordinary, while the mechanisms (e.g., eye, ear) appeared to have design flaws.

Progressive Education Associated with Dewey, an approach to education that emphasized making the student an active learner (learning by doing).

Progressive Relaxation Technique of gradually and systematically relaxing major muscle groups; pioneered by Jacobson and used by Wolpe in systematic desensitization.

Projection A Freudian defense mechanism in which unwanted personal characteristics are attributed to others.

Proximity Gestalt organizing principle of perception, a tendency to perceive that objects in close proximity "belong" together.

Psychophysics Study of the relationship between physical stimuli and the perception of those stimuli; pioneered by Weber and (especially) Fechner.

Purposiveness For Tolman, this referred to goal-directedness and was believed by him to be a universal feature of learned behavior.

Rationalist Philosophical tradition emphasizing the use of reason and logic to arrive at truth; associated with Descartes.

Reaction Formation A Freudian defense mechanism in which unacceptable impulses are repressed and replaced with their opposites.

Reaction Potential For Hull, the probability that a

response will occur at a given time, depending on such factors as drive and habit strength (SER).

Recapitulation Hall's theory, taken from a similar idea in biology, that the development of the individual mirrors the evolution of that individual's species.

Recoding For Miller, a process of reorganizing information to increase the amount of information per chunk.

Reflex Arc Basic unit of behavior, reduced by physiologists into the stimulus producing sensation, the central processing producing an idea, and the motor response; analysis rejected by Dewey, who argued that the arc should be seen instead as a coordinated unit that adapted the individual to the environment.

Reliability The extent to which repeated measures yield the same outcome; some of Tolman's research on maze concerned the factors influencing the reliability of mazes.

Remote Associations Indirect associations between list items separated by more than a single item; studied by Ebbinghaus.

Repetition For Hartley and other British philosophers, the factor that most directly influences the strength of an association.

Replication Process of repeating an experiment to judge its validity and generality.

Repression A Freudian defense mechanism in which unwanted impulses or traumatic memories are forced out of awareness and into the unconscious.

Resemblance One of Hume's laws of association; objects similar to each other become associated with each other.

Resistance In Freudian psychoanalysis, occurs when a person is unable to free associate, and indicates (to a Freudian) the presence of repressed material.

Resonance Theory Theory of hearing associated with Helmholtz, which proposed that different frequencies of sound stimulated receptors located in different places along the basilar membrane of the cochlear (found in the inner ear).

Respondent Conditioning Term sometimes used in place of Pavlovian or what Skinner called Type S conditioning.

Retroactive Inhibition Interference from some activity that intervenes between the learning of a list of stimulus items and its recall.

S-O-R Model Proposed by Woodworth to recognize the importance of the organism intervening between stimulus and response.

Savings Method Measure of memory used by Ebbinghaus, based on the difference between the amount of time to learn a list of nonsense syllables during original learning and the amount of time to relearn the list some time later.

Schemas Term used both by Piaget and Bartlett to refer to hypothetical mental structures that represent knowledge.

Scholasticism Educational tradition combining the careful use of reason with the received wisdom of the Church and Aristotelian authority.

School Psychology Field of psychology concerned with the development of programs for treating children and adolescents with school-related problems (e.g., learning disabilities); pioneered by Witmer, although he did not use the term.

Scientist-Practitioner Model Training model for Ph.D. in clinical psychology that emphasizes a research dissertation; also called the Denver model.

Secondary Qualities For Locke, attributes of some object that depend on perception for their existence (e.g., color).

Secondary Reinforcers For Hull, reinforcers that are learned through association with primary reinforcers (e.g., money).

Seduction Hypothesis Freud's original belief that hysteria originated from actual childhood sexual abuse.

Selective Filter For Broadbent, a model of selective attention emphasizing our tendency to separate information on the basis of physical characteristics (e.g., pitch), then focus on one message, while filtering out other ones.

Self-Efficacy A general sense of our ability to solve problems effectively; from Bandura and social learning theory.

Self Psychology Theoretical approach to psychology taken by Calkins, influenced by James; held that all consciousness is ultimately self-consciousness.

Sensory Aphasia A disorder characterized by the inability to comprehend speech and while there is no difficulty producing speech, the speech product is incoherent and/or illogical.

Serial Learning Procedure used by Ebbinghaus that involved memorizing a list of verbal stimuli (e.g., nonsense syllables), then recalling them in the exact order of presentation.

Sign-Gestalt For Tolman, intervening variable referring to learned relationships between stimuli and an animal's expectation about the consequences of choosing path A over path B.

Similarity Gestalt organizing principle of perception, a tendency to perceive that objects resembling each other "belong" together.

Simple Ideas For Locke, ideas resulting from sensory experience or simple reflection

Social Contract Proposal that an implied contract exists between government, which provides for the common good, and the governed, which agrees to follow laws, pay taxes, etc.

Social Darwinism The belief that evolutionary forces were natural and inevitable and that any attempt to disrupt them (e.g., by creating programs for the poor) was misguided and doomed to failure; associated with Spencer.

Sociobiology Study of social behavior which holds that such behavior has biological roots; associated with Wilson.

Spatial Contiguity When experiencing two events simultaneously, they become associated, according to Hartley.

Spatial Summation Process described by Sherrington; individual stimuli fail to elicit a response, but several stimuli simultaneously in close spatial proximity to each other will produce one; supported Sherrington's proposal of the synapse.

Species Problem Problem of the origin of species, addressed by Enlightenment thinkers faced with increasing uncertainty over Biblical accounts.

Specific Energy of Nerves Doctrine proposed by Bell and Müller that different sensory nerves convey different qualities; pointed out that we perceive the world indirectly through the action of our nervous systems.

Spiritualism Popular nineteenth-century belief in the afterlife and in the ability to communicate with the dead; William James was a strong believer that spiritualist claims needed to be evaluated seriously.

Stimulus Error To be avoided for proper introspection, according to Titchener, this was a tendency to report the products of conscious experience instead of the conscious experience itself.

Strong AI Approach to artificial intelligence; argues that machine intelligence is ultimately the equivalent of human intelligence (see also Weak AI).

Structuralism School of psychology, associated with Titchener, that focused on identifying the structural elements of human conscious experience, primarily through basic laboratory and introspective methods.

Struggle for Existence Key idea in Darwin's theory; derived from Malthus, who argued that population growth would eventually surpass food supplies, creating competition for limited resources.

Subjective Idealism For Berkeley, the philosophical position that the reality of the material world cannot be determined with certainty; we can be certain of the reality of our own perceptions, however.

Sublimation For Freud, a process in which psychic energy associated with sex or aggression would be channeled into socially acceptable activities.

Subtractive Method Method of measuring the duration of mental events, pioneered by Donders; reaction times for simple tasks were subtracted from reaction times for more "complicated" tasks.

Subvocal Speech Watson's definition of thinking.

Suggestion The ability to uncritically accept an idea or command from another; underlies hypnosis and was central to the view of hypnosis held by Liebeault and Bernheim of the Nancy school.

Superego In Freudian theory, that part of personality that reflects the person's moral values.

Survey Method Research method that originated with Darwin's questionnaires on emotion and Galton's questionnaires on a variety of topics; Galton normally credited with their creation.

Synapse physical space between neurons, first proposed by Sherrington.

Systematic Desensitization Behavior therapy procedure in which fear response is replaced by an incompatible response (e.g., relaxation); pioneered by Jones and Wolpe, who named it.

Systematic Experimental Introspection Form of introspection associated with Külpe and Titchener, in which the experience of complex mental events was followed by detailed introspective descriptions; a more elaborate form of introspection than Wundt's.

Temporal Contiguity When experiencing two events in immediate succession, they become associated, according to Hartley.

Temporal Summation Process described by Sherrington; individual stimuli fail to elicit a response, but several stimuli in close temporal contiguity will produce one; supported Sherrington's proposal of the synapse.

Thanatos In Freudian theory, the name given to the death instinct and manifested in aggression.

Thresholds Points on a continuum of awareness where one passes from no conscious awareness to some awareness (absolute threshold) or from an awareness that one stimulus is noticeably different from another stimulus (difference threshold); associated with Leibnitz and begun as a topic in experimental psychology by Weber and Fechner.

Topology Mathematical field of nonquantitative spatial geometry, used by Lewin as a basis for his field theory.

TOTE Unit Feedback unit (Test-Operate-Test-Exit) to replace reflex arc; proposed by Miller, Galanter, and Pribram, and influenced by developments in cybernetics.

Transfer The effect of learning in one situation on learning in a second situation; could be positive or negative; pioneer studies by Woodworth and Thorndike.

Transference In Freudian psychoanalysis, occurs when the patient develops a strong emotional attachment to the therapist.

Trial and Error Learning Thorndike's explanation for the behavior of his cats in puzzle boxes— they escaped by trying various behaviors until hitting on one that worked; also used by Morgan to provide a parsimonious explanation for the behavior of dogs escaping from yards.

Trichromatic Theory The Young-Helmholtz theory of color vision, which proposed the existence of three different color-sensitive cells in the eye, one for each of the primary colors (red, green, blue); color vision believed to result from various combinations of firings of these cells.

Tropisms Forced movements, automatic responses to specific stimuli, as studied by Loeb.

Turing Test In artificial intelligence, a thought problem posed by Turing to distinguish humans from computers.

Twin Studies First suggested by Galton as a means of demonstrating the heritability of intelligence.

Two-Point Threshold Point where the perception of two points touching the skin changes from "one point perceived" to "two points perceived;" studied extensively by Weber.

Type R Conditioning Skinner's term for conditioning in which a behavior occurs and the immediate consequences of the behavior determine its future probability of occurrence; operant conditioning.

Type S Conditioning Skinner's term for Pavlovian conditioning

Unconditioned Reflex For Pavlov, any stimulus-response connection (e.g., food-salivate) that does not have to be learned.

Unconditioned Stimulus Any stimulus that will produce a specific reflex response (e.g., food elicits saliva).

Unconscious Inference For Helmholtz, a process, outside of our awareness, by which our perceptions are influenced by past experiences.

Uniformitarianism Theory in geology, championed by Lyell, that geological change occurred gradually, over a long period of time, and as a consequence of such regular phenomena as erosion.

Valence For Lewin, term used to describe whether an object is valued by the person (positive valence) or not valued (negative valence).

Vector For Lewin, refers to the direction of a desired goal

Vitalism Belief that a "life force" or vital force existed that went beyond the physical and chemical components of living organisms; opposed to materialism.

Voluntarism Wundt's system of psychology, so-called because of his emphasis on the idea that the mind actively organizes information.

Von Restorff Effect Increased recall of information that stands out in some manner from other to-be-learned information.

Weak AI Approach to artificial intelligence; argues that machine intelligence can provide unique insights into the nature of human intelligence, but does not argue that machine intelligence is ultimately the equivalent of human intelligence (see also Strong AI).

Weber's Law As stimulus A increases in intensity, it takes progressively larger differences between stimulus A and stimulus B for a person to detect a difference between the two; the jnd divided by the size of the standard stimulus is a constant.

Word Association Test Procedure associated with both Galton and Jung to investigate the nature of associations in the mind; involves responding to a stimulus word with the first response word that comes to mind.

Zeigarnik Effect Named for student of Lewin, refers to a tendency to be more likely to recall unfinished tasks than finished tasks.

Zeitgeist The overall intellectual, political, and cultural climate of a particular historical era.

▶ PHOTO, TEXT, AND ILLUSTRATION CREDITS

PHOTO CREDITS

Chapter 1 Figure 1.1: Courtesy of Harvard Alumni Bulletin. Figure 1.2: Rick Zaidan/Zaidan Photography.

Chapter 2 Figure 2.1: Courtesy The New York Public Library. Figure 2.3: The Granger Collection.

Chapter 3 Figure 3.2: The Granger Collection. Figure 3.3: From M. B. MacMillan, *Brain and Cognition*, 1986, pg. 85. Reproduced with permission of Academic Press.

Chapter 4 Figure 4.4: Courtesy Archives of the History of American Psychology, University of Akron. Figure 4.5: Courtesy Clark University Archives.

Chapter 5 Figure 5.1: The Granger Collection. Figure 5.2: Reproduced with permission of Syndics of Cambridge University Library. Figure 5.3: From Darwin, *The Expression of the Emotions in Man and Animals*, 1872. Murray Publishers, Ltd. Figure 5.5: Corbis.

Chapter 6 Figures 6.1 and 6.2: Courtesy The Houghton Library, Harvard University. Figure 6.3: Courtesy Archives of the History of American Psychology, University of Akron. Figure 6.4: Courtesy Clark University Archives. Figure 6.6: Photo by Partridge, Courtesy Wellesley College Archives.

Chapter 7 Figure 7.1: Courtesy Archives of the History of American Psychology, University of Akron. Figure 7.3: From Titchener, *Experimental Psychology*, Volume II, 1905. MacMillan Publishing. Figure 7.4: Courtesy Archives of the History of American Psychology, University of Akron. Figure 7.8: Courtesy University Press of New England.

Reproduced with permission. Figure 7.9: Courtesy Robert Mearns Yearkes Papers, Manuscripts and Archives, Yale University Library.

Chapter 8 Figures 8.1, 8.2 and 8.3: Courtesy Archives of the History of American Psychology, University of Akron. Figure 8.6: Courtesy National Research Council. Reprinted with permission of National Academy Press. Figure 8.7: UPI/Corbis-Bettmann.

Chapter 9 Figure 9.1: UPI/Corbis-Bettmann. Figure 9.2: Courtesy Archives of the History of American Psychology, University of Akron. Figure 9.3 and 9.7: From W. Kohler, *The Mentality of Apes*, 1926. Routeledge, Ltd. Reproduced with permission.

Chapter 10 Figure 10.2: Courtesy International Publishers, Co. Reproduced with permission. Figure 10.3a: ©1991 by the Board of Trustees of the University of Illinois. Reproduced with permission. Figure 10.3b: From G. F. Nicolai, *Die physiologische methodik zur erforschung der tierpsyche, ihre möglichkeit und ihre anwendung*, 1907. *Journal für Psychologie und Neurologie*, 10: 1–27. Figures 10.5 and 10.6: Courtesy Archives of the History of American Psychology, University of Akron.

Chapter 11 Figures 11.1 and 11.7: Courtesy Archives of the History of American Psychology, University of Akron. Figure 11.9: UPI/Corbis-Bettmann.

Chapter 12 Figures 12.1 and 12.3: Courtesy National Library of Medicine. Figure 12.2: Corbis. Figure 12.4: Courtesy Frank J. Sulloway. Figure 12.5: Mary Evans/Sigmund Freud Copyrights.

Chapter 13   Figure 13.1: Courtesy Archives of the History of American Psychology, University of Akron.   Figure 13.3: ©1998 J. T. Miller.   Figure 13.7: Courtesy Emory University.

Chapter 14   Figure 14.3: Courtesy George Bush Presidential Library & Museum.   Figure 14.4: Courtesy Clark University Archives.

TEXT AND ILLUSTRATION CREDITS

Chapter 1   Page 13: From "The 'zeitgeist' and American Psychology," by D. Ross, 1969, *Journal of the History of the Behavioral Sciences, 5*, p. 257. Copyright 1969. Reprinted by permission of John Wiley & Sons, Inc.

Chapter 2   Pages 30–33: "Passions of the Soul" from *The Philosophical Works of Descartes*, Vol. 1, by Rene Descartes, translated by Elizabeth S. Haldane and G. R. T. Ross, New York: Cambridge University Press. (Original work published 1649.) Copyright 1969. Reprinted with permission. Pages 46–48: From *Autobiography* by J. S. Mills, New York: Penguin Books Ltd. (Original work published 1873.) Copyright 1989.

Chapter 3   Page 64: From "Helmholtz and his continuing influence," by R. M. Warren, *Music Perception, 1*, p. 257. Copyright 1984. Reprinted by permission of University of California Press and Dr. Warren.   Pages 73–75: From Broca cited in *A Source Book in the History of Psychology*, by Herrnstein and Boring, 1965, Cambridge, MA: Harvard University Press. (Original publication 1861.)   Figure 3.4: From Fritsch & Hitzig cited in *A Source Book in the History of Psychology*, by Herrnstein and Boring, 1965, Cambridge, MA: Harvard University Press. (Original publication 1870.) Figure 3.5: From *A History of Experimental Psychology*, by E. G. Boring, 1950, Englewood Cliffs, NJ: Prentice Hall. Copyright 1950. Reprinted by permission of Frank Boring. Figures 3.6 and 3.7: From *Brain Mechanisms and Intelligence*, by K. S. Lashley, 1963, (Original work published 1929.) Copyright 1963. Reprinted by permission of Simon & Schuster.

Chapter 4   Figure 4.2 and 4.3: From *Sensation and Perception in the History of Experimental Psychology*, by E. G. Boring, 1942. Copyright 1942. Reprinted with permission of Frank Boring.   Pages 101–102: From *An education in Psychology: James McKeen Cattell's Journal and Letters from Germany and England*, by M. M. Sokal (Ed.), 1981, Cambridge, MA: MIT Press. Copyright 1981. Reprinted by permission of MIT Press.   Pages 106–112: From *Memory: A Contribution to experimental psychology*, by H. Ebbinghaus, 1964, New York: Dover Publications. (Original work published 1885.) Copyright 1964.   Page 114: From "Oswald Kulpe and the Wurzburg school," by R. M. Ogden, 1951,

American Journal of Psychology, 64, p. 9. Copyright 1951. Considered public domain by University of Illinois Press.

Chapter 5   Figure 5.4: From *From Darwin to Behaviorism*, by Robert Boakes, 1984, Cambridge, MA: Cambridge University Press. Copyright 1984.

Chapter 6 Pages 156–159: From *The Principles of Psychology, Vol. 1*, by W. James, 1950, New York: Dover Publications. (Original Publication 1890.) Copyright 1950.   Pages 159–162: From *Psychology: The Briefer Course*, by W. James, 1961, New York: Harper Collins. (Original Publication 1892.) Copyright 1961.   Page 165: From "letter of 6 June 1906 to L. N. Wilson" by E. B. Titchener. Reprinted from the Wilson papers found in the Clark University Archives. Page 168: From "Recollections of Clark's G. Stanley Hall" by L. A. Averill, 1982, *Journal of the History of the Behavioral Sciences, 18*, p. 342. Copyright 1982. Reprinted by Permission of John Wiley & Sons, Inc.   Page 170: From "On the history of research with rats and mazes," by R. W. Miles, 1930, *Journal of General Psychology, 3*, p. 331. Copyright 1930. Reprinted with Permission of The Helen Dwight Reid Educational Foundation. Published by Heldref Publications, Washington D.C.

Chapter 7   Page 183: From "Edward Bradford Titchener, 1867-1927" by E. G. Boring, 1927, *American Journal of Psychology, 38*, p. 489. Copyright 1927. Considered public domain by University of Illinois Press.   Pages 190–193, 195: From *A Textbook of Psychology*, by E. B. Titchener, 1909, New Jersey: MacMillan. Copyright 1909.   Pages 198 and 199: From "Psychology as the Behaviorist views it," by J. B. Watson, 1913, *Psychological Review, 20*, p. 164. Copyright 1913. In the public domain by the American Psychological Association.   Pages 194–195: From "letter of 8 August 1910 to E. B. Titchener" by E. C. Sanford. Reprinted from the Titchener papers by permission of the Division of Rare and Manuscript Collections, Cornell University Library. Pages 195: From "The letter of 14 July 1983 to Hugo Münsterberg" by Lightner Witmer. Reprinted from the Münsterberg papers by courtesy of the Trustees of the Boston Public Library.

Chapter 8   Figures 8.4 and 8.5: From *Army Mental Tests*, by Yoakum and Yerkes, 1920, New York: Henry Holt & Company. Copyright 1920.   Figure 8.6: From *The Mismeasure of Man* (p. 178) by J. S. Gould, 1981, New York: W. W. Norton. Copyright 1981. Pages 244–249: From *Psychology and Industrial Efficiency*, by H. Münsterberg, 1913, Boston, MA: Houghton Mifflin Co. Copyright 1913.

Chapter 9   Pages 266–270: From *The Mentality of Apes* by W. Kohler, 1926, UK: Routledge Ltd. Copyright 1926. Reprinted by permission of Routledge.   Figures 9.8 and 9.9: Four Figures as specified from *Productive Thinking* by

Max Wertheimer, 1982, New York: Harper Collins Publishers. (Original work published 1945.) Copyright 1959 by Valentin Wertheimer. Copyright Renewed 1987 by Michael Wertheimer. Reprinted by Permission of HarperCollins Publishers, Inc. Figure 9.13: From "On Problem Solving," by K. Duncker, 1945, *Psychological Monographs, Vol. 1*, p. 2. Copyright 1945. Page 224: From "Has 'field theory' been 'tried and found wanting'?" by R. K. White, 1978, *Journal of the History of the Behavioral Sciences, Vol. 14*, pp. 245–246. Copyright 1978. Reprinted by Permission of John Wiley & Sons, Inc. Table 9.1: From *Child Behavior and Development* by R. Lippit & R. K. White, (G. R. Barker, J. S. Kounin & H. F. Wright, Eds.), 1943, NY: McGraw Hill. Copyright 1943.

Chapter 10   Figures 10.1a and 10.1b: From *Lectures on Conditioned Reflexes* by I. P. Pavlov, (W. H. Gantt, Trans.), 1928, New York: International Publishers. Copyright 1928. Reprinted by Permission of International Publishers Co., Inc. Pages 296–297: From *Conditioned Reflexes: An Investigation of the Physiological Activity of the Cerebral Cortex* by I. P. Pavlov, (G. V. Anrep, Trans.), 1960. (Original work published 1927.) Copyright 1927. Reprinted by Permission of Oxford University Press. Page 299: From Miles Papers (clipping from diary), by W. R. Miles. Reprinted by Permission of the Archives of the History of American Psychology, University of Akron. Page 306: From "Psychology as the behaviorist views it," by J. B. Watson, 1913, *Psychological Review, 20*, pp. 158, 164, 163, 167. Copyright 1913. In Public Domain by the American Psychological Association. Page 309: From "Conditioned emotional reactions," by J. B. Watson & R. Rayner, 1920, *Journal of Experimental Psychology, 3*, pp. 1–13. Copyright 1920. In Public Domain by the American Psychological Association.

Chapter 11   Figures 11.2*a*, 11.2*b* and 11.3: From *Purposive Behavior in Animals and Men* by E. C. Tolman. Reprinted with permission of Irvington Publishers, Inc. Copyright 1932 by Appleton-Century-Crofts. Figure 11.4: From "Studies in spatial learning. II. Place learning versus response learning," by E. C. Tolman, B. F. Ritchie, and D. Kalish, 1946, *Journal of Experimental Psychology, 36*, p.

223. Copyright 1946. In Public Domain by the American Psychological Association. Page 334, Figure 11.5*a* and 11.5*b*, "Cognitive Maps in Rats and Men," by E. C. Tolman, 1948, *Psychological Review, 55*, p.208. Copyright 1948. In Public Domain by the American Psychological Association. Figures 11.8*a* and 11.8*b*: From *Principles of Behavior* by C. L. Hull, 1943. Copyright 1943 by Appleton-Century-Crofts. Reprinted by Permission of Ms. Ruth Hull Low and Dr. Richard Low. Pages 345–350, Figures 11.10 and 11.11: From "A case history in scientific method," by B. F. Skinner, 1956, *American Psychologist, 12*, pp. 221–227 and p. 232. Copyright 1996. In the Public Domain by the American Psychological Association.

Chapter 12   Pages 376–378: From *Five Lectures On Psycho-Analysis* by Sigmund Freud, translated by James Strachey, 1961, New York: W. W. Norton. Translation copyright 1961 by James Strachey. Reprinted by permission of W. W. Norton & Company, Inc.

Chapter 13   Figure 13.4: From *A Study of Thinking* by J. S. Bruner, J. J. Goodnow, and G. A. Austin, 1956, New York: John Wiley & Sons. Copyright 1956 by Dr. Jerome S. Bruner. Reprinted by permission of Dr. Jerome S. Bruner. Figure 13.5 and 13.6: From George A. Miller, Eugene Galanter, and Karl H. Pribram, *Plans and the Structure of Behavior*, 1960. Reprinted New York: Adams, Bannister, Cox, 1986, pp. 26 & 36. Pages 414–417: From *Cognitive Psychology* by U. Neisser, 1967, Englewood Cliffs, N.J.: Prentice Hall. Copyright 1967 by Appleton-Century-Crofts. Reprinted by permission of Dr. Ulric Neisser.

Chapter 14   Figures 14.1 and 14.2: From *The American Psychological Association: A Historical Perspective* by E. Q. Bulatao, R. Fulcher, R. B. Evans, (R. B. Evans, V. S. Sexton & T. C. Cadwallader, Eds.),1992, Washington, D.C.: The American Psychological Association. Copyright 1992 by the American Psychological Association. Reprinted by Permission of APA and Elizabeth Q. Bulatao. Page 428: From The Miles papers (entry from Miles diary of 1 April 1931) by W. R. Miles. Reprinted by permission of the Archives of the History of American Psychology, University of Akron.

▶ NAME INDEX

► SUBJECT INDEX

TIMELINE : 1900-1950

1950

Boulder model for clinical training
Lashley's Hixon paper on serial order

Gilbreath & Carey's *Cheaper by the Dozen*

Transistor invented at Bell Labs

Spock's *Baby and Child Care*
Wertheimer's *Productive Thinking* — **1945** — Atom bombs dropped on Japan, war ends

Hull's *Principles of Behavior*

Academy Award to *Casablanca*

Pearl Harbor attack, U.S. enters war

Hilgard & Marquis' *Conditioning and Learning* — **1940**

Germany invades Poland, W.W.II begins

Woodworth's "Columbia Bible"
AAAP formed by applied psychologists

Steinbeck's *Of Mice and Men*
Berlin Olympics, 4 golds for Jesse Owens
Koffka's *Principles of Gestalt Psychology* — **1935** — Gershwin's *Porgy and Bess* opera

Hitler appointed German Chancellor

Bartlett's *Remembering*

Al Capone arrested for tax evasion

Lewin introduces B = f(P, E) — **1930**
International Conference at Yale
Sumner begins tenure at Howard University

U.S. stock market crashes

Ruth hits 60 home runs

Köhler's *Mentality of Apes* — **1925** — Scopes "monkey trial"
21 day protest fast by Ghandi

Freud's *The Ego and the Id*

Watson & Rayner's Little Albert study — **1920** — Wharton's *The Age of Innocence*

Army Alpha/Army Beta

Rockne named Notre Dame coach

Terman's Stanford-Binet IQ test

1915 — Einstein proposes theory of relativity
W.W.I begins/Panama Canal opens

Watson's behaviorist manifesto
Wertheimer's apparent motion study

S.S. Titanic sunk by iceberg

1910 — DuBois founds NAACP

Freud's Clark lectures
Washburn's *The Animal Mind*

Foster's *A Room with a View*
Powell founds Boy Scouts

Calkins first female APA president

1905

Nobel Prize to Pavlov

Barrie's *Peter Pan*

Doyle's *Hound of the Baskervilles*

First of Titchener's *Manuals*
Small's maze learning study — **1900** — Planck formulates quantum theory